KNOW YOUR

HOME FURNISHINGS

KNOW YOUR

HOME FURNISHINGS

Virginia Hencken Elsasser

Centenary College

FAIRCHILD PUBLICATIONS, INC. ▪ NEW YORK

Executive Editor: Olga T. Kontzias
Assistant Acquisitions Editor: Carolyn Purcell
Development Editor: Sylvia L. Weber
Production Editor: Amy Zarkos
Art Director: Adam B. Bohannon
Director of Production: Priscilla Taguer
Editorial Assistant: Suzette Lam
Copy Editor: Words & Numbers
Interior Design: Carla Bolte
Cover Design: Adam B. Bohannon
Cover Illustrations: Julie Johnson

Library of Congress Catalog Card Number: 2002108015
ISBN: 1–56367–242–1
GST R 133004424
Printed in the United States of America

CONTENTS IN BRIEF

Preface ▪ *xix*
Acknowledgments ▪ *xxi*

PART ONE ▪ **INTRODUCTION TO THE HOME FURNISHINGS INDUSTRY**

Chapter 1. Home Furnishings and the Marketplace ▪ 3

PART TWO ▪ **MATERIALS IN HOME FURNISHINGS**

Chapter 2. Textiles ▪ 31

Chapter 3. Wood ▪ 67

Chapter 4. Glass ▪ 93

Chapter 5. Pottery ▪ 119

Chapter 6. Plastics ▪ 141

Chapter 7. Metals ▪ 162

Chapter 8. Other Materials ▪ 188

PART THREE ▪ **THE CATEGORIES OF HOME FURNISHINGS**

Chapter 9. Furniture ▪ 219

Chapter 10. Bedding ▪ 251

Chapter 11. Linens ▪ 279

Chapter 12. Carpets, Rugs, and Flooring ▪ 316

Chapter 13. Paints and Wallcoverings ▪ 348

Chapter 14. Lighting ▪ 374

Chapter 15. Tableware ▪ 400

Glossary ▪ 423

Index ▪ 446

EXTENDED CONTENTS

PREFACE ▪ XIX

ACKNOWLEDGMENTS ▪ XXI

Part One ▪ Introduction to the Home Furnishings Industry

CHAPTER 1. HOME FURNISHINGS AND THE MARKETPLACE ▪ 3

Marketing and Market Segmentation ▪ 4
    Market Research 5
    Market Segmentation 5
    Components of Marketing 8

Customer Purchase Behavior ▪ 17
    The Decision-Making Model 17
    Types of Purchase Decisions 17

Product Life Cycle ▪ 18

Variations of Product Life Cycles ▪ 19
    Classic 19
    Fad 19
    Seasonal Products 20
    Nostalgia or Revival Products 21

Wholesalers and Wholesale Markets ▪ 21

International Marketing ▪ 25

Summary ▪ 27

Part Two · Materials in Home Furnishings

CHAPTER 2. TEXTILES · 31

Major Components of Textile Products · 31
Fibers and Fiber Properties 33
Natural Fibers 33
Manufactured Fibers 42
Blends 47

Yarns · 47
Yarn Formation 47
Types of Yarns 48

Fabrics · 50
Woven Fabrics 50
Knitted Fabric 53
Nonwovens and Other Fabric Formations 54

Coloration · 56
Color Permanence 56
Dyes and Pigments 57
Dyeing 57
Printing 58

Finishes · 59
Preparatory Finishes 60
Aesthetic Finishes 60
Functional Finishes 61

Laws Affecting Textile Products · 62

Textiles and the Environment · 63

Summary · 65

CHAPTER 3. WOOD · 67

Trees · 69
Parts of a Tree Trunk 69
Classifications of Trees 70

Processing Wood ▪ 73

Lumber ▪ 73
   Sawing 75
   Seasoning 76
   Sizing and Surfacing 77
   Grading 77

Solid Wood ▪ 77

Veneer and Veneer Construction ▪ 78
   Veneer Construction 79
   Plywood 80
   Laminated Wood 81

Ornamenting and Finishing Wood ▪ 82
   Inlay 82
   Wood Finishes 83

Hardboard and Particleboard ▪ 84
   Hardboard 84
   Particleboard 85

Bamboo, Rattan, and Wicker ▪ 86
   Bamboo 86
   Rattan 86
   Wicker 87

Wood and the Environment ▪ 87
   Sustainable Forests 88
   Rain Forest Woods 89

Summary ▪ 91

CHAPTER 4. GLASS ▪ 93

A Brief History of Glass ▪ 94

General Properties of Glass ▪ 94

Types and End Uses of Glass ▪ 95
   Lime-Soda Glass 95
   Lead Glass 96
   Heat-Resistant Glass 98

Production of Glass ▪ 100
  Mixing and Firing 100
  Shaping the Glass 100
  Improving Durability 105
  Inspecting and Finishing the Glass 105

Decorating and Coloring Glassware ▪ 106
  Colorless Glass Decorations 106
  Adding Color to Glass 108

Glass Inspection ▪ 109

Other Uses of Glass in the Home ▪ 109
  Flat Glass 109
  Other Uses for Glass 115

Environmental Impact and Recycling ▪ 116

Summary ▪ 117

CHAPTER 5. POTTERY ▪ 119

A Brief History of Pottery ▪ 120

Types of Pottery ▪ 120
  Earthenware 120
  Stoneware 122
  China 123

Manufacture of Pottery ▪ 125
  Materials Used in Making Pottery 125
  Preparing and Mixing 126
  Shaping, Assembling, and Finishing Pottery 126
  Firing and Glazing 131
  Decorating Pottery 133
  Types of Pottery 137

Environmental Impact ▪ 138

Summary ▪ 138

CHAPTER 6. PLASTICS ▪ 141

A Brief History of Plastic ▪ 142

Materials Used in Plastics ▪ 143

    Resins 143

    Colorants 144

    Fillers 145

    Lubricants 145

    Plasticizers 146

    Solvents 146

    Stabilizers 146

Types of Plastics ▪ 147

    Thermoset Plastics 147

    Thermoplastics 150

Production of Plastic ▪ 153

    Shaping Plastics 153

    Finishing Plastics 159

Environmental Impact ▪ 159

    Plastics Recycling 159

    Flammability 159

Summary ▪ 159

CHAPTER 7. METALS ▪ 162

General Properties of Metals ▪ 162

A Brief History of Metals ▪ 163

Metallurgy ▪ 165

    Extractive Metallurgy 166

    Physical Metallurgy 167

Plating Metals ▪ 172

    Dipping 172

    Bonding 173

    Electroplating 173

Precious Metals ▪ 173

    Gold 174

    Silver 175

Ferrous Metals ▪ 176

    Iron 177

    Cast Iron 178

Steel *179*

Stainless Steel *179*

Nonferrous Metals and Alloys ▪ 180

Decorating Metals ▪ 180

Applied Borders *184*

Chasing *184*

Embossing *184*

Engraving *184*

Etching *184*

Hammering *184*

Piercing *184*

Polishing *185*

Repoussé *185*

Environmental Impact ▪ 185

Summary ▪ 186

CHAPTER 8. OTHER MATERIALS ▪ 188

Rubber ▪ 188

History of Rubber *188*

Production of Rubber *189*

Harvesting of Natural Rubber *189*

Characteristics and End Uses of Natural Rubber *190*

Production of Synthetic Rubber *190*

Important Synthetic Rubbers *191*

Processing Solid Rubber *191*

Processing Liquid Rubber *195*

Environmental Impact of Rubber *196*

Paper ▪ 196

Sources of Fibers for Papermaking *196*

Manufacture of Paper *198*

Production of Pulp *198*

Paper Manufacturing *199*

Paper Grades and Standardizations *200*

Paper Finishes *200*

Wallpaper *202*

Environmental Impact • 203

Leather and Suede • 203
    Skin Quality 203
    Skin Sizes 204
    Grain 205
    Preparation, Tanning, and Finishing 206
    Sources for Leather 209
    Environmental Impact of Leather and Suede 213

Summary • 214

Part Three • The Categories of Home Furnishings

CHAPTER 9. FURNITURE • 219

Furniture Design • 219
    Traditional Furniture 220
    Provincial Furniture 221
    Contemporary Furniture 221

Furniture Classifications • 222

Case Goods • 223
    Bedroom Furniture 225
    Dining Room Furniture 226
    Determining Quality in Case Goods 226
    Selection of Case Goods 231

Upholstered Furniture • 233
    Upholstered Chairs 233
    Sofas and Loveseats 235
    Sectionals 236
    Sofa Beds 236
    Determining Quality in Upholstered Furniture 236

Occasional Furniture • 241

Casual and Summer Furniture • 241
    Wicker, Rattan, and Bamboo 242
    Aluminum, Wrought Iron, and Steel 242

Redwood 242

Plastic and Fiberglass-Reinforced Plastic 243

Selecting Casual and Summer Furniture 243

Wall Systems ▪ 243

Ready-to-Assemble Furniture ▪ 243

Systems Furniture ▪ 244

Care of Furniture ▪ 246

Summary ▪ 249

CHAPTER 10. BEDDING ▪ 251

Mattresses ▪ 251

Innerspring Mattresses 253

Foam Mattresses 257

Other Mattress Formations 258

Mattress Support Systems ▪ 260

Box Springs 260

Low-Profile Foundations 261

Platform-Top Springs 261

Open-Coil Springs 261

Link Springs and Band Springs 262

Other Types of Foundations 262

Selection and Care of Mattresses and Foundations ▪ 262

General Selection Criteria 263

Care of Mattresses and Foundations 263

Mattress Pads and Covers ▪ 266

Styles 266

Construction 266

Alternatives to Traditional Mattress Pads and Covers 266

Bed Pillows ▪ 268

Fillings 268

Pillow Ticking 272

Specialized Pillows 272

Care of Pillows 273

Alternative Bedding ▪ 273

    Sofa Beds 274

    Space-Saving Bedding 276

Bedding Manufacturers ▪ 276

Summary ▪ 277

CHAPTER 11. LINENS ▪ 279

    Coordinated Linens 280

    Regulations of Household Linens 280

    Commercial Versus Residential Interior Textiles 280

Bed Linens ▪ 281

    Sheets and Pillowcases 281

    Blankets and Throws 286

    Comforters, Quilts, and Bedspreads 289

    Dust Ruffles, Canopies, and Decorative Pillows 293

Towels and Other Bathroom Textile Products ▪ 294

    Towels 294

    Shower Curtains 297

    Bathroom Rugs and Mats 298

Table Linens ▪ 299

    Tablecloths and Napkins 299

    Place Mats 304

Slipcovers ▪ 305

    Styles 305

    Construction 305

    Selection 307

    Care 307

Soft Window Treatments ▪ 307

    Styles 308

    Construction 312

    Selection 312

    Care 313

Summary ▪ 314

CHAPTER 12. CARPETS, RUGS, AND FLOORING MATERIALS ▪ 316

Soft Floor Coverings ▪ 316

Classifications of Soft Floor Coverings 316

Construction of Soft Floor Coverings 317

Handmade Rugs 320

Styles of Tufted Floor Coverings 324

Importance of Carpet Cushioning 326

Types of Cushioning 328

Installation of Carpeting 329

Selection of Soft Floor Coverings 329

Care of Soft Floor Coverings 332

Resilient Flooring ▪ 332

Vinyl 333

Cork 334

Linoleum 334

Rubber 335

Hard Flooring ▪ 335

Wood Flooring 336

Ceramic Tile 338

Selected Other Hard Floors 339

Selection of Resilient and Hard Flooring 341

Care of Resilient and Hard Flooring ▪ 342

Floor Coverings and the Environment ▪ 342

Off-Gassing 343

Recycling 343

Asbestos 343

Floor Coverings and Social Responsibility ▪ 344

Summary ▪ 344

CHAPTER 13. PAINTS AND WALL COVERINGS ▪ 348

Paint ▪ 348

Ingredients in Paint 349

Surface Preparation 354

Application 355

Decorative Painting Techniques 357

Other Types of Coatings 359

Selection of Paint 360

Care of Painted Surfaces 361

Wall Coverings ▪ 361

    Paper and Vinyl Wall Coverings 362

    Selection of Wall Coverings 364

    Installation of Wall Coverings 366

    Textiles as Wall Coverings 367

    Specialty Wall Coverings 368

    Care of Wall Coverings 370

Environmental Issues ▪ 371

Summary ▪ 371

CHAPTER 14. LIGHTING ▪ 374

Purposes of Lighting ▪ 374

    Ambient Lighting 375

    Task Lighting 376

    Decorative Lighting 376

    Lighting for Special Needs 378

    Controlling Glare 379

Categories of Light ▪ 380

    Natural Light 380

    Artificial Light 382

Luminaires ▪ 388

    Structural Luminaires 388

    Portable Luminaires 392

Selection of Lamps and Luminaires ▪ 392

    Lighting Recommendations for Specific Rooms 394

    Selection of Chandeliers 395

    Color-rendering Properties of Lamps 395

Care of Lamps and Luminaires ▪ 395

Environmental Issues ▪ 396

    Energy-Efficient Lighting 396

    Lighting Energy Conservation Practices 396

Summary ▪ 397

CHAPTER 15. TABLEWARE ▪ 400

Dinnerware ▪ 403

    Categories of Dinnerware 404

    Purchasing Dinnerware 405

    Raw Materials and Selection of Dinnerware 409

    Care of Dinnerware 410

Glassware ▪ 411

    Styles of Glassware 411

    Purchasing Glassware 413

    Raw Materials and Selection of Glassware 413

    Care of Glassware 414

    Storage of Glassware 414

Flatware and Hollowware ▪ 415

    Styles of Flatware 415

    Hollowware 418

    Raw Materials and Selection of Flatware and Hollowware 419

    Care and Storage of Flatware and Hollowware 420

Tableware and the Environment ▪ 421

Summary ▪ 422

GLOSSARY ▪ 423

INDEX ▪ 446

PREFACE

IN RECENT YEARS, RETAILERS AND CONSUMERS HAVE BECOME INCREASINGLY INTERESTED IN the home and its furnishings. The importance of home furnishings in the marketplace has expanded as new stores dedicated to home goods have opened and department stores have enlarged their home goods departments. Consumers are concerned about product service-ability, safety, and environmental issues. *Know Your Home Furnishings* presents information about the materials and products used in home furnishings.

TARGET READERS

Students preparing for careers in interior design, retailing, buying, and merchandising will find *Know Your Home Furnishings* a valuable textbook in a concise, easy-to-read format. Those already established in the industry will also find this book a useful resource. It provides college-level students a detailed study of the materials and products used in home furnishings. It is appropriate for students who have completed introductory-level courses. This includes second-year college students at community colleges or four-year institutions.

OBJECTIVES

The objectives of this book are:

- To present comprehensive coverage of the materials and products used in home furnishings
- To encourage students to be actively engaged in their learning
- To provide general information on the properties and characteristics of the materials used in home furnishings
- To provide selection criteria and care procedures for products used in home furnishings
- To increase awareness of the importance of recycling and environmental issues

COMPONENTS

The book is divided into three major parts:

Part One, Introduction to the Home Furnishings Industry (Chapter 1), presents an overview of the home furnishings and the marketplace. Consumer purchase behavior and product life cycles are emphasized. In Part Two, The Materials of Home Furnishings (Chapters 2–8), the focus is on the variety of materials used in the manufacture of home furnishings. These include textiles, wood, glass, pottery, plastics, metals, and other materials. Part Three, Categories of Home Furnishings (Chapters 9–15), provides a comprehensive study of the major products used in the home including furniture; bedding; linens; carpet, rugs, and flooring materials; paints and wall coverings; lighting; and tableware.

LEARNING FEATURES

To invite the reader to study each chapter, an opening quotation suggests the place the product or material holds in the home furnishings industry or in the lives and homes of consumers. Each chapter includes two boxed features: a Profile, which highlights a firm or individual important to the segment of the industry covered by the chapter, and one or more Industry Statements, which contain news about new products, materials, or marketing efforts within the industry segment. Numerous tables and illustrations summarize styles, qualities, uses, and other features of the products and materials. Key terms are highlighted and defined in the text and listed at the end of each chapter. End-of-chapter features also include a summary, study questions, and learning activities.

ACKNOWLEDGMENTS

THIS BOOK WOULD NOT HAVE BEEN POSSIBLE WITHOUT THE CONTRIBUTIONS OF MANY PEOPLE, several of whom deserve special thanks.

My family—Neil, Christian, and Meghan—deserve special thanks for their patience and love. My mother-in-law, Ruth Elsasser, provided much support and guidance. And, although they are not here to accept my appreciation for years of encouragement, I thank my parents, Robert and Jean Hencken, and my father-in-law Cornelius Elsasser, Jr.

My college students and colleagues, both former and present, have shaped my philosophy of teaching and learning. I would like to recognize the following people at Centenary College for their valuable contributions to the book: Nancy Madacsi, Director of the Taylor Memorial Learning Resource Center; the staff of Taylor Memorial Learning Resource Center; Terry Eason, Comprehensive designer, Professor, and Director of Graduate Studies at Centenary College; and the staff of Hackettstown Free Public Library. Reviewers, who provided many helpful suggestions and who were selected by the publisher, include Jan Cummings, Johnson County Community College; Elizabeth Davis, Florida Community College at Jacksonville; Kerri Keech, West Virginia University; Sarah Moore, Eastern Michigan University; Karen Schaeffer, University of Delaware; Susan Slotkis, Fashion Institute of Technology; Carolyn Trombly, Hesser College; and Robert Woods, Berkeley College. I hope this book will provide students with an enjoyable learning experience and instructors with an enjoyable teaching experience.

My sincere appreciation is extended to the Fairchild editors Olga Kontzias, Mary McGarry, Sylvia Weber, Amy Zarkos, and Suzette Lam for their help in developing the text and illustration program and to Adam Bohannon, art director, and Priscilla Taguer, production director. I am also grateful for the editorial support of Roberta Moore, and Jennifer Plum and Katherine Wenerick of Words & Numbers, who collaborated with the Fairchild staff.

—V.H.E.

PART ONE

INTRODUCTION TO THE HOME FURNISHINGS INDUSTRY

CHAPTER 1

HOME FURNISHINGS AND THE MARKETPLACE

Can there be that much of a disconnect with how people see themselves outside of their homes and what they want once safely ensconced? Can they really lead this kind of dual life? Can a nation that buys more trucks than cars still buy more woven jacquard floral bedspreads, formal china dinnerware, 18th-century French country bedroom sets and Oriental-style rugs than one can possibly imagine?

. . . Sure, people feel differently about their homes than their driveways . . . But is it possible that the American home furnishings industry is just totally miscalculating the needs and wants of its customers, forcing them to buy what's out there, not what they really want?

Maybe it's not that simple. But maybe it's not far off either. Look at the incredible success of an operation like IKEA, which most certainly is the home equivalent of the pickup truck. It's proven that a certain casual, easy-going design aesthetic, applied with sophisticated marketing and attractive pricing, can be enormously appealing to a broad swath of the consuming public.

"Trucking News," *HFN,* April 22, 2000

THE HOME FURNISHINGS INDUSTRY COVERS A WIDE VARIETY OF PRODUCTS, FROM TEACUPS TO tables, and carpeting to chandeliers. All of these products are designed to serve basic human needs for comfort, but beyond that function, home furnishings reflect the aesthetic tastes of the people who buy them. The changing and wide-ranging tastes of consumers make the home furnishings industry an exciting career destination for people with an interest in fashion and marketing, whether they want to work in the manufacturing or retailing sector. As you read this text, you will learn about the properties of materials used in home furnishings and the features of the various products that appeal to the ultimate consumers.

MARKETING AND MARKET SEGMENTATION

Marketing involves all of the activities required to direct the flow of goods to consumers. Figure 1.1 diagrams the distribution of consumer goods in the marketing channel. Marketing includes everything that takes place from the inception of a product design idea through the development, distribution, and sale of goods to the final consumer. Marketing may also include follow-up interactions with the consumer, such as postsale consumer satisfaction surveys.

See Figure 1.2 for a sample of an organization chart of the marketing department of a manufacturing company. Table 1.1 briefly summarizes the responsibilities of each office that answers to the director of marketing.

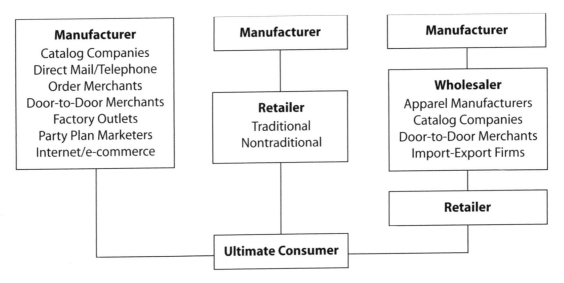

FIGURE 1.1
Distribution of consumer goods in the marketing channel.

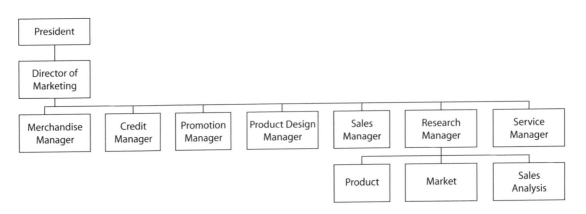

FIGURE 1.2
Organization chart of the marketing department of a manufacturing company.

TABLE 1.1

Responsibilities of Each Office That Answers to the Director of Marketing

Department Head	Responsibilities
Director of Marketing	Makes final decisions and is responsible for the coordination of the various activities of the department heads
Merchandise Manager *also called Product Manager*	Develops, executes, and delivers the product line; serves as the liaison between the sales and manufacturing departments
Credit Manager	Determines the value of the products and that customers will be able to pay for the merchandise received, follows up on payment
Promotion Manager	Plans and implements advertising, publicity, sales promotion campaigns and materials
Product Design Manager	Develops new products and/or redesigns existing products
Sales Manager	Sells the product and supervises the sales force
Research Manager	Conducts market surveys that support marketing, sales, and product development decisions
Service Manager	Provides assistance to the customer after a product has been purchased

The four components of marketing, often called the four P's, are product, price, promotion, and place. But before the components of marketing are presented, this chapter will discuss the ultimate consumer. Market research is conducted to gain information about the consumer.

Market Research

Market research is the systematic gathering of current information that can be used to make decisions about any component of marketing. Research related to the product includes information on the customer, what is already on the market, where it is selling, and the competition. Market research may be conducted internally or externally.

Internal market research includes accurately tracking sales by region and by store, conducting interviews with sales associates and department managers for feedback on consumer preferences, and conducting postpurchase surveys with customers. **External market research** includes collecting data on the competition, tracking overall sales in the industry, and following economic trends. Marketers collect and analyze all of these facts and figures to learn about their customers. Only by understanding their customers can marketers determine how to meet the customers' wants and needs while earning a profit.

Market Segmentation

Market segmentation allows a company to tailor all components of marketing to meet the expectations of its target market(s). The consumer market in the United Sates is very diverse with distinct segments, or groups of people, each having a set of unique characteristics. Successful companies usually use market segmentation to identify a specific segment, or segments, of the whole market as their target market. A **target market** is a group of consumers that a company wants to reach. **Niche marketing** is marketing to a very small market within a larger market segment. Larger companies may target more than one segment. Characteristics that define a profitable target market include fairly consistent preferences in style and color, fairly consistent responses to advertising and promotion, and a sufficient number of people with the purchasing power to buy the product.

A company must have a clear picture of its market(s) to produce or sell products that will appeal to that market(s). The company must fully understand its customer and the social trends that influence purchasing behavior. The two important ways to segment a market based on social trends are demographics and psychographics.

Demographics

Demographics are important statistics about the characteristics of a group of people. The statistics include information about the number of people, age distribution, ethnic mix, gender, marital status, education, geographic distribution, occupation, and income. These variables are constantly changing. For example, the education level of the average American is increasing. Education level often predicts a person's income, and people with higher levels of education typically have higher incomes.

Changes in demographics must be considered when developing or revising a marketing plan. Current demographic trends are presented in Table 1.2. One important demographic trend is the increase in ethnic diversity in America. For example, the Latino population is a market segment that has grown significantly. Marketers are developing products that target the growing Latino population (see Figure 1.3).

FIGURE 1.3
These candleholders reflect the influence of the Latino community.
Courtesy of Fairchild Publications, Inc.

TABLE 1.2

Important Demographic Trends

Demographic Trend	Description of Trend	Impact in the Marketplace
Economic Trends		
Income Growth	Imbalance in income growth resulting in an increasing gap between the rich and the poor.	Value-oriented shopping will increase, and up-scale shopping will also increase.
Savings	Rate of personal savings is going down.	Consumers are spending instead of saving. It is predicted that as baby boomers age and generation X matures, savings will increase, thus reducing consumer spending.
Working Women	Significant rise in the number of working women.	Increased family income but also increased spending on childcare. Convenience and service are important to the consumer. Catalog and Internet shopping will increase.
Geographic Trends		
Geographic Centers	In general, the population has been moving West and South for the past 200 years. Current percentages are: South—35 percent of the population West—22 percent of the population Midwest—24 percent of the population Northeast—20 percent of the population	Micromarketing (tailoring merchandise for each area to match the preferences of the consumer) strategies will become more important.
Urban Centers	Metropolitan statistical areas (MSA) are urban areas with populations of more than 50,000. More than 78 percent of the population lives in an urban center. California, Massachusetts, and New Jersey are more than 95 percent MSAs.	Sales in downtown areas have declined, while sales in suburban areas have increased. It is predicted that this trend will continue.
Mobility	On average Americans change their residences 12 times during a lifetime. Much of the mobility is accredited to the trend toward higher levels of education and the increasing divorce rate.	Chain stores and well-known national brands will have an advantage over local stores and brands.
Population Trends		
Ethnic Diversity	Black, Hispanic, Asian, and Native American segments of the population will grow at a faster rate than the white majority. It is estimated that legal immigration exceeds 700,000 people per year.	Increased opportunity for target and niche marketing. Manufacturers and retailers will need to cater to these different segments of the market.
Gray Market	One third of the population will be over the age of 50 by the year 2010. People who are over 50 years of age control 50 percent of the discretionary income and 77 percent of the financial assets in the United States.	Increased emphasis on quality and value for a more mature consumer. In general, as the population ages, much of the driving force in the economy slows down. The gray market is less acquisition oriented than the younger markets. Many in this age group are skeptical of product claims and not interested in shopping. Valet parking and lounges in malls, larger print in signage and advertisements, and brighter parking lots are important.

continued

TABLE I.2 *continued*
Important Demographic Trends

Demographic Trend	Description of Trend	Impact in the Marketplace
Population Trends (continued)		
Baby Boomers	Baby boomers are the age group born after World War II between 1946 and 1964. One half of the United States population is over 40 years of age and baby boomers represent 32 percent of the population.	Some analysts have suggested that women in this category are the most powerful consumer market. Quality, service, and comfort are very important to this market. Many are aggressively saving for retirement. Focus will be on financial security, comfort, families, good health, and home life. They tend to spend more on travel and medical services.
Generation X (also called Baby Busters or Millennium Generation)	Generation Xers were born between 1965 and 1978. This segment of the population is much smaller than the baby boomers.	Very family and career oriented. Some analysts have suggested that this age group is very skeptical of product claims. Manufacturers and retailers need to provide easily confirmed claims.
Generation Y (Echo Boom)	Generation Y was born between 1978 and 1994. They are racially diverse (one in three is not Caucasian). Many have traditional values and are conservative.	Oriented toward global issues, sports, entertainment, and computers. Does more catalog and Internet shopping than other groups.
Social Trends		
Education	The number of Americans with college degrees is increasing.	Consumers will become increasingly independent and discriminating. They are very aware of quality and advertising claims.
Marital Status	Marriage is occurring later in life, and more are electing not to marry at all. The divorce rate is increasing.	Smaller households for single and divorced people, increased expenditures on household goods.
Importance of Work	Work/career has become less important to people, while hobbies and acquisition of durable goods have become more important.	Sales of durable goods related to sports, hobbies, and leisure activities will increase.

Psychographics

Psychographics are descriptions about lifestyles that can be used to further analyze and segment a target market. Lifestyles are shaped by personal values and attitudes. Psychographics segment people into categories based on the way they live, how they spend their money, and what their personality characteristics are. Current psychographic trends that will continue to be important in the future are presented in Table 1.3. Industry Statement 1.1 relates the recent increase in sales of trucks to the desire for a more casual lifestyle.

Components of Marketing

Each of the four components of marketing has a role in connecting the marketer to the consumer. The *product* must meet the needs and/or desires of the consumer. The *price* must match

TABLE 1.3
Psychographic Trends

Psychographic Trends	Impact in the Marketplace
Cocooning—people value their privacy and isolate themselves from the world, stay home as much as possible.	Increased interest in home goods; increased catalog and Internet shopping.
Community and family—increased interest in the community and family life.	Increased spending on durable goods for the home and family and community-related activities.
Computers—increased use of computers.	Increased Internet shopping.
Desire for a more relaxed, simpler life—busy schedules have created a desire for more casual styles and to find the least time-consuming way to take care of necessities.	Overwhelmed consumers limit shopping to a few favorite stores, catalogs, or the Internet.
Time—people are placing greater value on the use of their time.	People are more willing to pay for time-saving products and to pay others to do tasks.
Leisure activities and travel—increased interest in nonwork activities.	Increased spending on goods related to hobbies, sports, and other leisure activities; increased travel will increase spending on luggage, wrinkle-free clothes, and travel accessories.
Environmental issues—there is an increased interest in the environment and energy conservation.	Increased spending on environmentally safe, biodegradable, and recyclable products, awareness of environmentally friendly companies.

the consumer's perception of the product's value. The *promotion* tells the customer about the product, and the *product* itself must be in a place where it is readily available to the customer. The marketer is responsible for ensuring that all four components are working together to create a profitable environment.

Product

Product development is the process of creating products that appeal to the consumer and conform to the image of the company. Decisions are based on extensive market research. For example, a very positive consumer response to ready-to-assemble furniture led companies to increase the selection of styles available. A team that includes the designer and the merchandise manager is responsible for product development. The designer, who creates a product that is within the production capabilities of the company, may be a freelancer or staff member. The merchandising manager is responsible for coordinating the phases of product development (refer back to Table 1.1). The product development process is summarized in Figure 1.4.

Price

The final price of a product is an important component in the product's overall success. It must match the consumer's perception of what the product is worth. For example, if a product is

---

INDUSTRY STATEMENT 1.1

Trucking News

An incredibly important thing for the home industry occurred last year that had absolutely nothing to do with the home industry.

Nothing . . . and yet quite a bit, if you think about it.

Last year, for the first time in history, Americans bought more trucks than they did cars. More pickup trucks, sport utility vehicles, and minivans than sedans, station wagons, and econoboxes. More Ford F150s, Honda Odysseys, Chevy Suburbans, and Dodge Caravans than Ford Tauruses, Honda Accords, Chevy Impalas, and Dodge Intrepids.

It's never happened before. And it is quite likely to happen again . . . and again . . . and again.

Now those of us who live in New York can't imagine this to be true. Most of us know a lot more pickup lines than we do people who own pickup trucks. We see plenty of minivans on the roads, sure, but not anywhere near as many as all the Civics and Camrys and Beemers we see.

All of which proves that someday New York should consider joining the United States of America. But for now, at least, we are most certainly a world unto ourselves.

For the rest of the country, trucks rule. More importantly, the lifestyles, the buying sensibilities, and the taste levels that trucks represent rule.

None of which is to be confused with most of the products the home furnishings industry produces and sells. It remains a sales and marketing conundrum of John Nashian proportions how a country that drives Jeeps, wears sweatpants and Gap shirts, and eats at Red Lobster and TGI Fridays then goes home and slips into its formal English/over-the-top Americana/early bordello decorated houses and is at all comfortable.

Can there be that much of a disconnect with how people see themselves outside of their homes and what they want once safely ensconced? Can they really lead this kind of dual life? Can a nation that buys more trucks than cars still buy more woven jacquard floral bedspreads, formal china dinnerware, 18th-century French country bedroom sets, and Oriental-style rugs than one can possibly imagine?

And don't get on that soapbox about it's the men buying the pickups, but the women decorating the home. I see more women behind the wheels of those Ford Explorers and Land Cruisers than anybody else. This is not a gender thing.

So is something else at play here? Sure, people feel differently about their homes than their driveways . . . or their appetites, for that matter. But is it possible that the American home furnishings industry is just totally miscalculating the needs and wants of its customers, forcing them to buy what's out there, not what they really want?

Maybe it's not that simple. But maybe it's not far off either. Look at the incredible success of an operation like IKEA, which most certainly is the home equivalent of the pickup truck. It's proven that a certain casual, easy-going design aesthetic, applied with sophisticated marketing and attractive pricing, can be enormously appealing to a broad swath of the consuming public.

It took decades—generations—for this switch to trucks to occur in the vehicle-buying habits of the American population. And there are factors—safety and practicality among them—present in the automotive market that don't come into play when it comes to home purchases.

But that's not enough. Consumers have changed, and so have their consumption characteristics. They are tattooed, pierced and jaded. They drive trucks.

And I think they're driving them right past your business.

Source: HFN, April 22, 2002, p. 18. Courtesy of Fairchild Publications, Inc.

---

priced too high, the consumer may feel it is not worth the price. The opposite is also true. If the price is too low, the customer may assume that the item is not well made. Inexpensive plastic food containers have become popular because they match the consumer perception of what a plastic food container should cost. Perception of value is also influenced by the level of customer service a company offers and the reputation, or image, of the brand or company. There are several pricing objectives that a company can choose to follow.

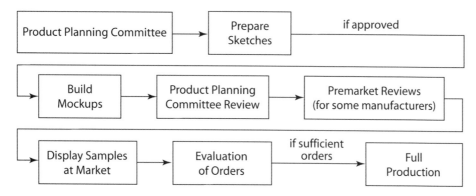

FIGURE I.4 *Product development process.*

Prestige pricing Prestige pricing is the policy of charging a higher price to suggest quality and distinction. If the product is priced too low, the consumer may feel the product is lacking in quality.

Target return pricing The company sets a price that meets its profit goal.

Follow-the-leader pricing The company sets prices that are consistent with other companies. This allows the company to use customer service, quality control, an assortment of products, rapid delivery time, and styling as selling features.

Penetration pricing The company offers its products at prices that are consistently lower than competitor prices.

Promotion

Promotion is the communication about a company and its products. The purpose is to create an atmosphere that is favorable for the sale of the company's products. Sometimes referred to as nonpersonal selling, promotion includes advertising and public relations. Personal selling usually occurs on a one-to-one basis. A company representative attempts to sell products to a wholesaler, buyer, or the ultimate consumer. Nonpersonal selling does not usually occur on a one-to-one basis, and is meant to reach larger groups of people.

Advertising **Advertising** is the vehicle a company uses to communicate information about itself and its products. Through print and broadcast media, advertising presents facts and benefits of a product to a group of potential consumers. Examples of advertising include direct mail, magazines, newspapers, radio, and television. Figure 1.5 illustrates the flow of a manufacturer's advertising. The objectives of advertising are to:

- Expand brand awareness
- Build a positive company image
- Counteract competition
- Provide product information, including features, benefits, and services

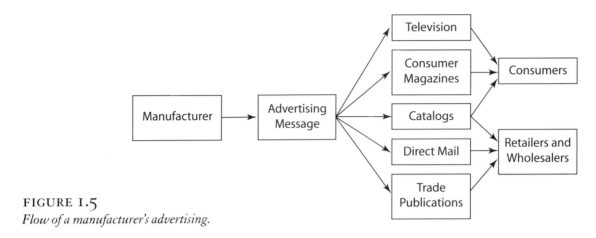

FIGURE I.5
Flow of a manufacturer's advertising.

Magazine advertising is especially effective for selling home furnishings. There are three categories of magazines that give coverage to home goods—bridal, shelter, and women's service. See Table 1.4 for a list of the magazines published in each category.

Public relations **Public relations** is the conscious effort to create a positive image for a company. Press releases and press kits are public relations tools that are used to create a favorable impression of the company. The company pays for the preparation of press releases and

TABLE I.4
Categories of Magazines for Home Furnishings Advertisements

Type	Title	Type	Title
Bridal	*Bridal Guide*	Women's Service	*Better Homes & Gardens*
	Bride's		*Family Circle*
	Modern Bride		*Good Housekeeping*
Shelter	*Architectural Digest*		*Ladies' Home Journal*
	Country Home		*Martha Stewart Living*
	Country Living		*O—The Oprah Magazine*
	Elle Décor		*Real Simple*
	Home		*Redbook*
	HomeStyle		*Women's Day*
	House & Garden		
	House Beautiful		
	Metropolitan Home		
	This Old House		
	Traditional Home		
	Veranda		
	Victoria		

Adapted from Closing the Book on 2001, *HFN*, February 11, 2002, p. 11.

press kits, but does not pay the media to use this information. To be profitable, it is important for a company to be perceived favorably by consumers, dealers, employees, government agencies, the media, and financial institutions.

The objectives of public relations are to create:

- Favorable publicity
- Favorable financial status at lending institutions
- Positive status as a "good citizen" in the community
- Support for education through donations, guest speakers, etc.
- An image as a provider of quality products

Companies use a variety of techniques to create positive public relations. Publicity or editorial news about a company includes press releases, speeches, interviews and other media appearances by executives, press conferences, and press kits that are distributed to wholesalers and retailers at trade shows. Some companies offer market showroom tours to give customers a firsthand look at production and processes. Many organizations host receptions and parties to increase visibility in the public.

Place

The place component of marketing is especially important for retailers. Retailers may be store based or nonstore based. Nonstore retailing is increasing in popularity with consumers. Figure 1.6 presents the variety of retail formats, and Industry Statement 1.2 discusses the impact of the Internet on retailing.

Selection of the Trading Area for Store-Based Retailing A store should be located in an area where there is a steady flow of customers. The **trading area** refers to the area from which a store attracts potential customers. Selection of the trading area and selection of the specific site within the trading area are important considerations that involve both demographics and psychographics. Stores have three main trading areas as shown in Figure 1.7. The **primary**

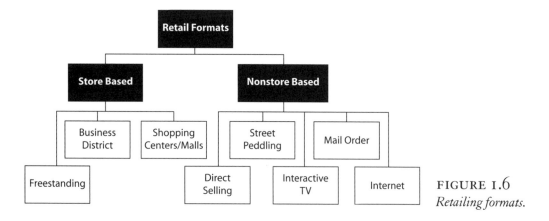

FIGURE 1.6
Retailing formats.

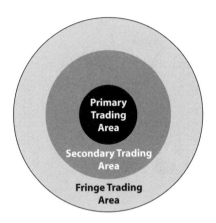

FIGURE I.7
Diagram of primary, secondary, and fringe trading areas.

trading area is the area closest to the store. Approximately 55 to 70 percent of a store's potential customers will come from the primary trading area. The **secondary trading area** is the area just outside the primary trading area. Approximately 15 to 25 percent of the store's potential customers will come from the secondary trading area. The **fringe trading area** encompasses all of the remaining potential customers for the store.

Selection of the Specific Site for Store-Based Retailing Once the trading area has been determined, it is necessary to select the site within the trading area. The factors to consider when selecting a specific site are:

- *Access and transportation* Customer and delivery vehicles must have access to the store. Most roads can accommodate customer vehicles, but large delivery vehicles may be limited to certain roads. Proximity to major roads and/or mass transit are important considerations.
- *Parking* Malls are popular sites because parking is plentiful. Downtown sites may have limited parking that is costly. Some mega-malls provide shuttle service from the parking areas to the stores. Appropriate lighting is important for safety in all parking areas.
- *Placement and visibility* Stores should be located where customers can find them. Corner locations are desirable because of their high visibility, but they are also more expensive.
- *Retail mix* Stores must be compatible with others in the competitive shopping area. A new store should blend in. Compatible stores will generate more sales as a group than if they were situated apart from each other.
- *Traffic* Both pedestrian and vehicular traffic must be considered in selecting the site. There should be sufficient potential customers that pass by the store on foot. Stores that are dependent on vehicular traffic must consider traffic patterns, road conditions, and traffic congestion.

A retailer can select from three basic locations: freestanding stores, central business districts, and shopping centers/malls.

INDUSTRY STATEMENT 1.2

Changing the Face of Retail

NEW YORK—The effect that Internet retail will eventually have on traditional retailers cannot be underestimated, said Tom Rubel, principal with Pricewaterhouse-Coopers.

Rubel, speaking at the global service organization's Inaugural E-Retail Conference, emphasized that e-tailers are changing what consumers expect from retailers.

"I've been in retail for 25 years," Rubel said. "I thought I'd seen it all, but I've never seen anything with the force and energy of the Internet. It's already rapidly changing the whole consumer marketing business."

Traditional retailers will eventually take on many characteristics of the trendsetting e-tailers, Rubel said. E-tailers will affect various aspects of traditional retail, including physical facilities, merchandising, pricing, promotion, customer service, and fulfillment.

Physical facilities: Web-savvy consumers, used to round-the-clock shopping, will increasingly count on retailers to meet their expectations about convenience. This may culminate with more brick-and-mortar stores staying open 24 hours a day, seven days a week, 365 days a year. Concurrently, there will be an increase of alliances between traditional stores and online shops, such as the recent pairing of Federated Department Stores and WeddingChannel.com.

Merchandising: The unlimited assortments available in the world of e-tail is already causing traditional retailers to expand their selections. Interactive kiosks are becoming commonplace among book retailers and may expand to other categories.

Internet retailers are also raising the bar in getting products to market faster. Apparel manufacturers such as Liz Claiborne are debuting collections on online showrooms, Rubel said.

Pricing: One facet of traditional retail that will be most affected by e-tail is pricing, Rubel said. "Traditionally, pricing in the retail industry is Byzantine and archaic," he said. "The Internet is facilitating modernized pricing processes that are demand-driven, dynamic and differential."

Brick-and-mortar stores must face the fact that some e-tailers such as Buy.com are giving away products and services to build relationships with consumers. Some computer retailers have teamed with Internet service providers to offer free goods in return for long-term service agreements.

Meanwhile, online auction sites allow customers to specify how much they're willing to spend on items. Also, e-tailers are using differential pricing on a customer-by-customer basis and offering various prices depending on the loyalty of the customer. CDNow.com e-mails its best customers a special Web site address that offers lower prices.

Customer Service: The Internet's ability to create communities is taking expectations of customer service to unprecedented heights, Rubel said. Sites such as iVillage.com, d'ELiA's gURL.com and Kasper A.S.L.'s kasper.com cater to groups of people with special interests.

E-tailers such as Furniture.com customize the high-tech, high-touch furniture buying experience with live expert "Design Consultant" assistance.

While Rubel is bullish on the Web, he does not think e-tail will replace traditional retailers. "We think stores and the 'Net are going to work together," he said. "The Internet, however, is changing the tools used as retail."

Source: HFN, November 15, 1999, p. 10. Courtesy of Fairchild Publications, Inc.

Freestanding stores are located on a highway or a smaller street away from the main commercial area. Discounters and other larger retailers such as furniture stores are often successful as freestanding stores. Advantages of freestanding stores include adequate parking and lower rent. One disadvantage of a freestanding store is that it may be difficult to draw customers because the store is harder to access.

Central business districts are usually located in downtown areas where there is a wide assortment of stores with a variety in prices, products, and services. San Francisco's Union Square is an example of a successful central business district. **String streets** are secondary shopping areas that are on the side streets of the central business district. Fisherman's Wharf, Castro, and Haight Asbury in San Francisco are examples of successful string streets.

Shopping centers and malls are centrally managed. They are surrounded with parking areas and have stores that complement one another. Frequently the terms *shopping center* and *mall* are interchangeable, but each has distinguishing characteristics. **Shopping centers,** which became popular in the 1950s, are planned groupings of stores usually found in suburban areas. They are not necessarily covered with a central roof. A **mall** is an enclosed structure with climate control. The major mall tenant is called an **anchor.** It typically is located on a corner or end of the mall. Types of shopping centers and malls are summarized in Table 1.5.

Nonstore Retailing Nonstore retailing includes interactive television such as the Home Shopping Network, mail order or catalog, street peddlers, Internet shopping, and direct selling. Examples of direct selling are Avon products and Tupperware Home Parties.

The growth in nonstore retailing is the result of changing consumer lifestyles and accelerated communication technology. Analysts predict that nonstore retailing will continue to expand and that the most successful store-based retailers will be those who reach their consumer through a variety of formats, such as traditional stores, catalogs, and an Internet Web site.

TABLE 1.5
Types of Shopping Centers and Malls

Type of shopping center or mall	Description
Neighborhood shopping center	Serves 7,000 to 40,000 people, usually has one large store with several small stores located next to each other. Attracts people from a radius of 3 to 5 miles.
Community shopping center	Serves 40,000–150,000 people with a larger trading radius than a neighborhood shopping center, usually has one large store with a variety of smaller stores.
Regional mall	Serves a minimum of 150,000 people, usually has at least two large stores and 80 to 150 small stores. Attracts people from a radius of 50 miles.
Super regional mall	Serves one million people, has 3 to 6 large stores and 200–350 smaller stores. Attracts people from a radius of 60–70 miles.
Mega-mall	Serves several states, contains 500 to 800 stores, service businesses, restaurants, and entertainment facilities. Examples of mega-malls are West Edmonton Mall in Canada and The Mall of America in Minnesota.
Specialized malls	
Festival marketplace	Provides entertainment as well as goods. Example: South Street Seaport in New York.
Theme mall	Shopping centers with a theatrical setting or a unifying theme, such as outlet malls. Example: The Crossings Outlet Mall in Tannersville, Pennsylvania.
Vertical mall	Shopping center located in a high-rise building. Example: Water Tower Place in Chicago is an early example of a vertical mall.

CUSTOMER PURCHASE BEHAVIOR

Customer purchase behavior is important to consider when planning marketing strategy. The decision-making model and three types of purchase decisions are central to customer purchase behavior.

The Decision-Making Model

The decision-making model suggests that there are five steps in the decision-making process as depicted in Figure 1.8.

1. *Stimulus* A stimulus is the signal to the consumer that a purchase should be made. The stimulus can be internal or external. An internal stimulus is an inner drive, or need, that directs behavior. For example, the desire to purchase a down comforter may be driven by the need to be warm. An external stimulus comes from outside motivation and can be a learned response. For example, a person may have the desire to purchase a new rug after seeing an advertisement.

2. *Information Search* The customer begins to search for information about the purchase. Sources for information include friends and family, magazines and newspapers, and sometimes a preliminary shopping trip to see what is available.

3. *Evaluation of Alternatives* The customer begins to narrow down the number of choices. Considerations may include price, service, delivery date, and friendliness of staff.

4. *Purchase* The customer makes the purchase.

5. *Postpurchase Evaluation* The customer experiences attitudes and actions as a result of the purchase. If the customer is satisfied, the original purchase decision is reinforced, thus resulting in repeat business. If the customer is dissatisfied, there may be complaints and negative word-of-mouth publicity.

Types of Purchase Decisions

Purchase decisions can be categorized into three types: extended, limited, and routine.

Extended Decisions

Extended decisions occur when the customer goes through all steps of the decision-making process. Major purchases, such as furniture, quality china, carpeting, wallpaper, and sterling silver, may require extended decisions because the products are usually expensive. The customer's

FIGURE 1.8 *Customer purchase behavior model.*

lifestyle and socioeconomic status are important in extended decisions because the purchase needs to accurately reflect the customer's values and status.

Limited Decisions

When making **limited decisions,** the customer goes through the five steps of the decision-making process very quickly. Postpurchase behavior affects limited decisions. For example, if a customer is pleased with a particular brand of sheets, he or she will continue to purchase the same brand.

Routine Decisions

Routine decisions occur when the consumer purchases the same products on a regular basis. For example, plastic food storage containers and paper plates are often routinely purchased. Brand recognition and advertising play a critical role in routine decisions.

PRODUCT LIFE CYCLE

Product life cycle describes the five stages of consumer acceptance: introduction, rise, maturity, decline, and obsolescence. Most consumer products pass through the five stages. Figure 1.9 illustrates the average lifecycle of consumer products.

1. *Introduction* This stage begins with aggressive market showings and promotion by the manufacturer. As the products appear in stores, sales gradually increase. The innovative consumer will be likely to purchase the product at this time.

2. *Rise* At this stage, sales increase dramatically as more people become aware of the product and are willing to try it. Emulation of the product is likely at this time. When other manufacturers see a favorable consumer response, they copy the product and introduce their version of it (see Figure 1.10).

3. *Maturity* At the maturity stage, sales level off. Competition has increased from other manufacturers producing similar products, and consumer interest and profits begin to decrease.

4. *Decline* Reduced sales, lack of consumer interest, and reduced profits mark the decline stage. At this time, the company should have new and exciting products to introduce to the consumer.

FIGURE 1.9
Product life cycle.

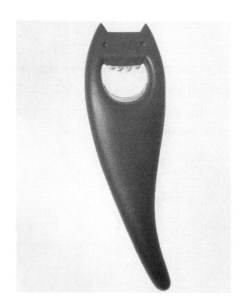

FIGURE 1.10
Biagio Cisotti by Alessi's red Diabolix bottle opener shown here costs $15 at the Terence Conran Shop, while a similar plastic opener sold at IKEA is 95 cents.

5. *Obsolescence* At this stage, the product is no longer being produced. Any products remaining in the stores are on clearance or markdown and can be purchased at severely reduced prices. Consumer-driven obsolescence occurs when the consumer no longer wants to purchase the product. Sometimes, obsolescence is driven by the manufacturer. To maintain a high level of interest and sales, manufacturers introduce new products that make existing products look dated or no longer fashionable.

VARIATIONS OF PRODUCT LIFE CYCLES

Products may go through the product life cycle at different rates of speed and attain different levels of consumer acceptance. Some styles never completely disappear, while others have a very short life cycle.

Classic

A **classic** is a product that never becomes completely obsolete. There is demand for the product for an extended period of time. For example, Queen Anne furniture and certain sterling silver flatware patterns such as those shown in Figure 1.11 are considered classics. Figure 1.12 charts the product life cycle of a product that becomes a classic.

Fad

A **fad** is in style for a relatively short period of time. Many fads come and go within a single season. A fad is often available at a low price and relatively simple and inexpensive to copy, so there are many imitations on the market. The consumer tires of fads very quickly (see Figure 1.13).

Seasonal Products

Seasonal products last for only one season and then are reintroduced the next year. For example, each spring new outdoor furniture is reintroduced into the marketplace. Sometimes the products are exactly the same as the previous years, and sometimes they undergo modifications, such as a change in color (see Figure 1.14). Figure 1.15 depicts the seasonal product life cycle.

FIGURE 1.11
Wallace Silversmiths based the design of this flatware on an original from a 19th-century hotel.
Courtesy of Fairchild Publications, Inc.

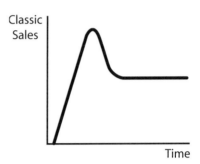

FIGURE 1.12
Variations in the product life cycle: Classic.

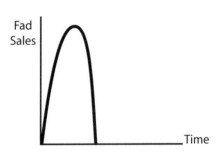

FIGURE 1.13
Variations in the product life cycle: Fad.

FIGURE 1.14
It can't be summer or the Fourth without the quintessential American grill, the Weber, now updated in blue. Photo courtesy of Weber-Stephen Products Co.

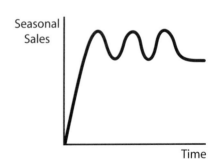

FIGURE 1.15
Variations in the product life cycle: Seasonal.

FIGURE 1.16
A retro look from Bloomingdale's. Courtesy of Fairchild Publications, Inc.

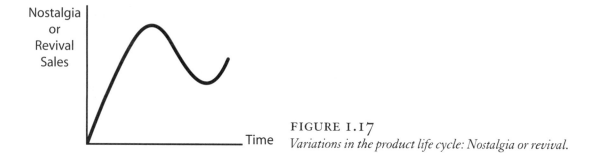

FIGURE 1.17
Variations in the product life cycle: Nostalgia or revival.

Nostalgia or Revival Products

Nostalgia or **revival products** are previously successful products that are brought back to the marketplace. Sometimes this variation is called a *recurring cycle.* The product is reinterpreted for a contemporary consumer. A nostalgia or revival product may copy the old design, but offer a modern look using new materials, colors, and details. A room with retro décor is an example of nostalgia products (see Figure 1.16). Figure 1.17 depicts the nostalgia product life cycle.

WHOLESALERS AND WHOLESALE MARKETS

Wholesalers serve as distribution liaisons between manufacturers and retailers. As the middlemen, they buy products that are to be resold. In general, wholesalers resell to small- and medium-sized retail stores, while large retailers purchase goods directly from the manufacturer.

Wholesale markets are regularly scheduled exhibits of products. Manufacturers use large showrooms to present many types of furniture and home furnishings to wholesalers and retailers. The showrooms are not open to the ultimate consumer. Markets are usually held twice a year in major cities (see Figure 1.18).

FIGURE 1.18
Jaclyn Smith and Oscar de la Renta at market.
Courtesy of Fairchild Publications, Inc.

All product development efforts are planned so that new products are ready for display at market. Retailers and wholesale distributors plan their merchandise assortments at market. Retail and wholesale buyers select products that are appropriate for their customers. The role of the buyer has gradually changed. Technological changes, corporate inventory management, and increased globalization have changed the function of the buyer (see Industry Statement 1.3).

Manufacturers use the orders generated at market to plan their production schedules. Many manufacturers also track buyers' comments to plan modifications to their product line. For example, a particular fabric may be dropped from a line of bedding if it is not popular with the buyers. Table 1.6 and Table 1.7 summarize the importance of the markets from the manufacturer, retailer, and wholesaler perspectives. During the weeks immediately following markets, the manufacturer's sales representatives maintain close contacts with their clients to track orders, encourage additional orders, and update those clients who were not able to attend market week.

TABLE 1.6

The Importance of the Markets from the Manufacturer's Perspective

Sales and production estimates	Generate sales and allow the company to plan for production
Information gathering	Learn from the buyers about the customer buying habits and preferences
Promote image of the company	Show products to their best advantage, generate excitement and interest in products
Share information about the company and its products	Distribute press kits, conduct showroom tours to representatives from magazines, trade press, and home fashion editors of major newspapers
Personal contact with others in industry	Enhance relationships with customer and other industry professionals
Educate others about new developments in the industry	Offer training on new sales features and merchandising approaches

TABLE 1.7

The Importance of the Markets from the Retailer's and Wholesaler's Perspectives

Plan merchandise assortment	Select products that will appeal to customers
Information gathering	Learn about new product lines
Personal contact with others in industry	Enhance relationships with suppliers and other industry professionals
Education/training	Learn about new developments in the industry and arrange for assistance in advertising, training, and display

INDUSTRY STATEMENT 1.3

Do Buyers *Really* Buy?

NEW YORK—Is it time to say "bye, bye" to the traditional title of buyer?

The role of the buyer in the retail industrial complex has gradually been changing and evolving over the past several decades. At the same time, technological advances may radically alter the way the retail arena does business by this time next year.

"You try to anticipate what the customer wants—that is the fundamental role of the buyer," said Kurt Barnard, president of Barnard's Retail Trend Report. "Other than that, everything is different. Buyers have become far more numbers-oriented today."

A century ago, merchandisers bought products based on intuition and gut feelings. Their role was largely creative, but of course they had to bring home the bacon.

Today, the creative hunches better be backed up by some hard numbers.

Technological advances in inventory and database management systems, along with an ever more demanding and fickle Wall Street investment community have over the past decade redefined the buyers' position within the retail hierarchy to a much heavier focus on numbers and data.

Whereas once they were just "creative types," today they also must wear the hat of numbers cruncher and analyst, and in many cases are also governed by the bean counters upstairs.

"We inspire our buyers to be creative within our framework," said William Podany, chairman, chief executive, and president at ShopKo. "Buyers have enormous ability to select goods that address the lifestyle changes in America."

But just how broad or limited a buyer's powers are in an organization depends on the company, how centralized and "efficient" it is.

"As to whether or not buyers buy, the answer depends on where they work," said a divisional merchandise manager of housewares at a regional discounter who preferred not to be named. "At our chain, the buyers are still buyers, which means they pick product, come up with merchandise ideas, and are buyers in the classic sense of what buyers have always been. But there are financial guidelines within which we have to work.

"The May Company and Federated corporate offices are driving a lot of the assortment centrally," he said. "If you are a buyer out of a medium-sized division, they are telling you what to buy."

Maybe J.C. Penney is the bellwether of what direction the buyer's role is moving in. J.C. Penney had buying power at the store level until this year. That structure was revamped into one centralized buying office, closely linked to the planning and logistics operations. The company declined comment for this article.

Though it may be easy to paint the chief financial officers and their need to court Wall Street as the bad guys, the villain in this case may be the unsuspecting American consumer, who places more pressure on retailers to reduce prices, boost quality, and offer the selection they want.

"Ultimately, the buyer's clout is diminished by the increasing influence of the consumer," said Roger Blackwell, a professor of marketing at Ohio State University. "That transforms the buyer into a sophisticated consumer researcher, and buyers who can't make the transition will have difficulty surviving as we move to the new millennium."

And though today the home furnishings buyer's duties in an organization vary from store to store, channel to channel, one thing is certain: The increasing power of the consumer and the Internet, more specifically online business-to-business solutions, will dramatically alter the role of the buyer of tomorrow.

"I've seen lots of changes happening over the past 30 years," said retail pundit Barnard. "And the latest change—and probably the most far-reaching—is electronic B2B access to vendors."

Barnard is specifically talking about a new B2B model emerging in the retail industry. He likes to call them "Buying cooperatives," more formally known as online, global supply exchanges.

"It's very exciting," Bardard said of the Co-ops. "It has taken the entire field of retailing to a new level."

"A benefit for buyers? Yes. But it also requires increased sophistication. With these international buying cooperatives, we have opened the field to global compeition."

So on top of mastering data mining, inventory management, and electronic data interface, buyers will have to learn to think and act on a global scale in concert with other retailers formerly viewed only as foes. They must also conquer emerging technologies and become auction house experts to boot.

"The globalization of the entire buying function will make things less cozy than they used to be and will also require buyers to think in global terms not only as far as expanding their store base, but [also] in terms of buying," Barnard said. "The buyer will have totally new doors open, and it depends on the buyers' expertise, savviness, and sophistication to exploit this new complex of opportunities."

Source: "Do Buyers Really Buy?", *HFN*, April 17, 2000, Page 1+. Courtesy of Fairchild Publications, Inc.

INTERNATIONAL MARKETING

As American products gain popularity overseas, and imported goods are prevalent in American stores, international marketing has become increasingly important. Many products sold in the United States are made overseas (see Figure 1.19). IKEA, a Swedish company, has become an important furnishings retailer in the United States (see Figure 1.20).

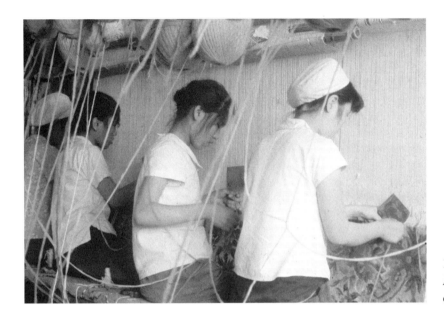

FIGURE 1.19
International workers.
Courtesy of Fairchild Publications, Inc.

FIGURE 1.20
IKEA Home Furnishings.
Used with the permission of Inter IKEA Systems B.V.

Ralph Lauren

Bronx Boy Creates Lifestyle Merchandising for the Masses

Determined to create an English country house without the English countryside or even the manor? How about creating a loft on Mercer Street without being in New York? Ralph Lauren has the product to create a complete environment wherever you happen to be.

Being a luxury label also lends itself to designing a product that others can't or wouldn't consider, such as the recent introduction of a $40,000 alligator highboy chest or the decadent White Label sheets that rival any European house.

Without a doubt, Ralph Lauren (born Lifshitz) has established himself as the master of lifestyle merchandising. The appeal of his thoroughly Anglo-American aesthetic transcends all levels of society—from Greenwich matrons to the B-Boys and Brooklyn's infamous 'Lo-Life gang. Such persuasive brand power could only be achieved by the strict attention to detail and commitment to a vision that the Ralph Lauren corporation is known for. Just ask its licensees.

From inauspicious beginnings to his rise to the top of the fashion and marketing worlds, the story of Ralph Lauren is the personification of the quintessential American dream. Born in the Bronx in 1939, he studied at the City College of New York and served in the Army from 1962–1964. In 1967, he started the Polo Label, and in 1968 became founder, designer, and chairman of Polo Fashions in New York.

Lauren's career was launched when he started selling ties to Bloomingdale's New York. He made a critical move in recognizing the value and importance of film in modern culture when he became costume designer for the movie version of F. Scott Fitzgerald's "The Great Gatsby." This important project is credited with launching Lauren into the world spotlight. His illustrious career has included many honors, including numerous Coty awards and the distinction of being the first fashion designer to open his own store.

"He stuck to his vision," said Brooke Stoddard, style editor of *House & Garden* magazine. "When you think about when he opened the store on 72nd Street and the lifestyle merchandising concept, he was really ahead of his time."

"His most significant accomplishment has been to convey a particular brand identity across an extraordinary number of product categories," noted Eric Wilson of *Women's Wear Daily.* "From home to ready-to-wear, everything has the stamp of Ralph Lauren." Wilson added that his mystique transcends price points—from Lauren to Couture.

Another part of the success that is Ralph Lauren is his ability to interpret extraordinary trends and embody them with a preppy American flavor.

Unlike many designers, Lauren's empire in home furnishings is successful across all product categories—from textiles to tabletop to furniture to all accessories in between. Recent additions have included rugs, lighting, and hardware.

Lauren's "Ayn Randesque" fidelity to his vision is consistently cited as the key to his success and longevity in the industry. "The details, fabrication, and coloration, along with never compromising the true design integrity of the vision, set him apart," said Jerry Balest, vice president and creative director for Federated Merchandising Group.

Source: Visionaries Supplement to *HFN,* November 27, 2000. Article by Michael D. Devine. Courtesy of Fairchild Publications, Inc.

Advantages of international marketing for the manufacturer and retailer can include the following:

- Opportunity for an increased customer base
- Lower production costs

- A more skilled labor pool
- Design ideas for product development
- Opportunity for the buyer to select from a wider assortment of merchandise

While there are many advantages to international marketing, there are also some disadvantages. There can be difficulties adapting to the culture(s) with which business is done, and differences in business practices and in the culture must be understood. Fluctuating economies can have an impact on successful marketing in foreign countries, and the cost of shipping may be very high.

SUMMARY

Marketing involves all the activities required to direct the flow of goods to consumers, and it includes everything that takes place from the inception of the design idea through the sale to the final consumer. Market research, conducted internally or externally, is the systematic gathering of current information that can be used to make decisions about any component of marketing.

The consumer market in the United States is very diverse with many segments or groups of people. Successful companies usually use market segmentation to identify a target market. A target market is a group of consumers that a company wants to reach. Target markets are identified by analyzing demographics and psychographics. Demographics are important statistics about the characteristics of groups of people. Psychographics are descriptions about lifestyles.

The four traditional components of marketing are product, price, promotion, and place. Product development is the process of creating products that are appealing to the consumer and conform to the image of the company. The final price for a product is an important component in the overall success of a product. Promotion is the communication about a company and its products. The place may be store based or nonstore based. Nonstore retailing is increasing in popularity with consumers.

Customer purchase behavior is important to consider when planning a marketing strategy. The decision-making model suggests that there are five steps in the decision-making process: stimulus, information search, evaluation of alternatives, purchase, and postpurchase evaluation. Purchase decisions can be categorized into three types: extended, limited, and routine.

Product life cycle describes the five stages of consumer acceptance: introduction, rise, maturity, decline, and obsolescence. Variations of the product life cycle include: classic, fad, seasonal, and nostalgia or revival.

Wholesalers serve as distribution liaisons between manufacturers and retailers. Wholesale markets are regularly scheduled exhibits. International marketing has become increasingly significant. American products have become very popular overseas, and imported goods are prevalent in American stores.

TERMS FOR REVIEW

advertising	mall	public relations
anchor	market research	routine decisions
central business districts	market segmentation	seasonal product
classic	marketing	secondary trading area
demographics	niche marketing	shopping center
extended decisions	nostalgia (revival) product	string streets
external market research	penetration pricing	target market
fad	prestige pricing	target return pricing
follow-the-leader pricing	primary trading area	trading area
freestanding stores	product development	wholesale markets
fringe trading area	product life cycle	wholesalers
internal market research	promotion	
limited decisions	psychographics	

REVIEW QUESTIONS

1. What is the difference between internal market research and external market research?
2. What are demographics and psychographics, and how do they relate to market segmentation?
3. What is the difference between advertising and public relations?
4. Why has nonstore retailing increased?
5. List the three types of decision making. Describe a purchase in each type.
6. Why are wholesale markets important in the home furnishings industry?

LEARNING ACTIVITIES

1. Contact a home furnishings company that interests you and request promotional literature.
2. Visit the home furnishings departments of a large department store. Read labels or ask a salesperson to help you determine what percentage of the merchandise is made overseas.

PART TWO

MATERIALS IN HOME FURNISHINGS

CHAPTER 2

TEXTILES

. . . Eighty percent of Americans have a more positive image of companies aligned with social issues. . . . My Sister's mission started even closer to home. Shari Bender founded the company last May after her sister Reenie, 38, was diagnosed with cancer. Beginning with luxury pillows and throws, the company has already expanded to top-of-the-bed and table linens, handloomed in the family's Los Angeles apparel factory. The silk velvet and rayon designs sell in the high-end specialty and furniture stores at prices ranging from $250 to $1000.

"Charity Begins in Home for Textile Supply and Retail," *HFN*, May 8, 2000

A VARIETY OF HOME FASHION PRODUCTS ARE MADE IN WHOLE OR IN PART FROM TEXTILES. Each product requires a set of features in its textile component to make it suitable for particular purposes. For example, bed linens must feel soft and comfortable against the skin. Bath towels must feel soft, too, but even more important, they must be absorbent. For carpeting and upholstery, durability is a crucial feature, and stain resistance is desirable in table linens. The business of producing textiles that meet these diverse needs is highly competitive.

Each phase of this profit-driven industry is focused on the production of products that will ultimately be accepted by the consumer. Figure 2.1 illustrates the steps in the production and distribution pipeline for consumer textiles. All steps are mutually dependent. For example, the carpet industry is dependent on both the retail outlets that distribute carpets to the consumer, and the fiber and yarn manufacturers that produce the raw materials necessary to create carpeting.

MAJOR COMPONENTS OF TEXTILE PRODUCTS

The major components of textile products are fiber, yarn, fabric, finish, and coloration. Most consumer textiles contain all of these components, but some do not. For example, fabric that is

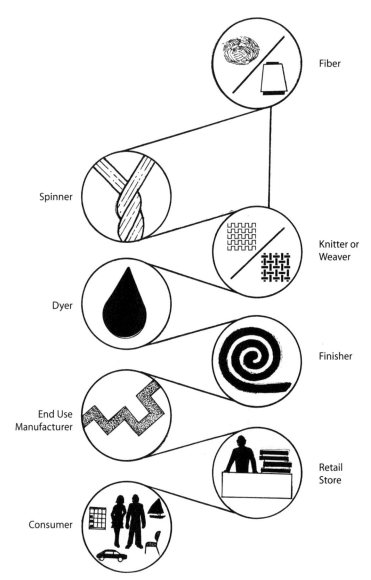

FIGURE 2.1
*Production and distribution
pipeline for consumer textiles.*

unfinished and naturally colored may be used in casual country-style curtains. This chapter begins by defining the major components of textile products and then presenting each product in depth.

Fibers are fine strands that resemble hair. They may be natural or manufactured. Cotton is a **natural fiber,** and nylon is a **manufactured fiber.** Fibers can be staple (short) or filament (long) (see Figure 2.2).

Yarns are assemblages of fibers into a continuous strand that can be used to make fabric. Both natural and manufactured fibers may be made into yarns.

Fabrics are cohesive structures made from yarns or directly from fibers. **Wovens** and **knits** are made from yarns. **Nonwovens** are made directly from fibers. Examples of products made from nonwoven fabrics include shower curtain liners and disposable tablecloths.

Finishes are processes that modify the properties of a textile product. Stain resistance and water repellency are examples of finishes. **Coloration** is the process of adding color to a textile product by using dyes or pigments.

When evaluating the suitability of a textile product, each component must be considered in relation to the larger combination of components. Each component of a textile product can affect or modify the overall performance of the final product. For example, cotton is a very absorbent fiber, but it can be modified through the finishing process to be water repellent.

Fibers and Fiber Properties

Textile fibers can be classified into two major categories—natural and manufactured.

Natural fibers come from plant, animal, and mineral resources. Cotton and linen are examples of **plant fibers.** Plant fibers are also known as **cellulosic fibers.** Natural rubber is a plant fiber, but the use of natural rubber is limited, and for most applications synthetic rubber is superior. Silk and wool are examples of **animal fibers.** Animal fibers are also known as **protein fibers.** Asbestos is a **mineral fiber,** but its carcinogenic (cancer-causing) properties limit its use.

Manufactured fibers are made from products that would not normally be used as textiles and can be engineered to have specific properties. Manufactured fibers are further divided into three main classifications: **regenerated, inorganic,** and **synthetic.** Table 2.1 summarizes the classification of major textile fibers.

The most suitable end use of a fiber is determined by its properties. Fiber properties and definitions are summarized in Table 2.2. The properties of major fibers are summarized in Table 2.3. Fiber properties often dictate the appropriate care procedures. Care labels should be followed very carefully because finishing procedures, pigments, and dyes applied to fibers, yarns, or fabrics may require special care. For example, linen is considered to be washable, but washing will frequently cause colors to fade.

Natural Fibers

Natural fibers are derived from both plants (cellulosic fibers) and animals (protein fibers). Important cellulosic fibers are cotton, flax, and ramie. Important protein fibers are silk, wool, animal hair fibers, and fur fibers.

Natural Cellulosic Fibers

Cellulosic fibers are derived from the seed, stem, or leaves of plants. Cotton is a *seed fiber.* **Bast fibers** such as flax and ramie are *stem fibers.* Sisal, piña, abaca, and henequen are *leaf fibers.* The properties of cotton are discussed first. Then other natural cellulosic fibers are compared to cotton.

Cotton Cotton is the major cellulosic fiber (see Figure 2.3). It makes up over 50 percent of all interior textiles. Examples include towels, sheets, curtains, and drapes. There are several varieties of cotton, and in general, longer fibers are more expensive than shorter fibers. Different varieties of cotton are presented in Table 2.4 (see Industry Statement 2.1).

TABLE 2.1

Classification of Major Textile Fibers

Natural Fibers

Cellulosic Fibers		Protein Fibers		Other Natural Fibers
Seed Fibers		**Silk (silkworm)**		**Mineral Fibers**
Cotton		**Wool (sheep)**		Asbestos
Kapok		**Specialty Hair Fibers**		**Natural Rubber**
Coir (coconut)		Alpaca (alpaca)	Mohair (angora goat)	
Bast Fibers		Cashmere (cashmere goat)	Qivuit (musk ox)	
Flax	Kenaf	Camel (Bactrian camel)	Vicuna (vicuna)	
Ramie (China grass)	Roselle	Guanaco (guanaco)	Cow and horse hair	
Jute	Sunn	Llama (llama)		
Hemp	Urena			
		Fur Fibers		
Leaf Fibers		Angora (angora rabbit)	Fox	
Abaca (manila fiber)	Piña (pineapple)	Beaver	Mink	
Henequen	Raffia	Chinchilla	Sable	
New Zealand Flax or New Zealand Hemp	Sisal			
Yucca		**Plumage (Feathers)**		

Manufactured Fibers

Manufactured Cellulosics	Major Synthetic Fibers	Special Application Synthetic Fibers	Inorganic Fibers
Regenerated Cellulosics	Acrylic	Fluorocarbon	Glass
Rayon	Aramid	Lastrile	Metallic
Lyocell	Modacrylic	Novoloid	
Derivative Cellulosics	Nylon	PBI	
Acetate	Olefin	Saran	
Triacetate	Polyester		
	Spandex		

Regenerated Protein Fibers

Azlon

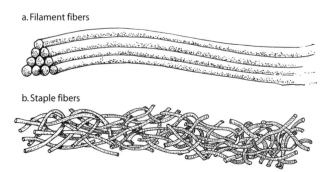

a. Filament fibers

b. Staple fibers

FIGURE 2.2

Comparison of filament and staple fibers.

TABLE 2.2

Fiber Properties and Definitions

Property	Definition and Description
Physical Properties	
Color	Manufactured fibers are usually white, while natural fibers vary in shade from white to brown, tan, and black.
Shape	Physical appearance—all fibers have length, cross section, surface contour, and diameter. Some fibers have crimp.
Length	Fibers may be staple (short) or filament (long). See Figure 2.2 for a comparison of filament and staple fibers. Staple fibers range in length from 3/4 inch to 18 inches. Filaments are very long and are measured in yards. All natural fibers, except silk, are staple. All manufactured fibers and silk are produced as filaments. The filaments may be cut into staple length.
Cross Section	The appearance of the fiber when viewed across its diameter. See Figure 2.4.
Surface Contour	Surface contour is sometimes referred to as longitudinal appearance. See Figure 2.4.
Diameter	The width of the cross section.
Crimp	The waves or bumps of a fiber.
Cover	The ability of a fabric to hide what is beneath it.
Hand	Texture, or how the fiber feels.
Luster	The amount of light that is reflected from a fiber.
Pilling Propensity	The likelihood that small balls of fiber will form on the surface of a fabric.
Mechanical Properties	
Abrasion Resistance	The ability to withstand the effects of rubbing or friction.
Dimensional Stability	The ability of a fiber to maintain its original shape, neither shrinking nor stretching.
Elastic Recovery	The ability of a fiber to return to its original length after being stretched.
Elongation	The lengthening or stretching of a fiber.
Flexibility	Fibers that bend or fold easily have good flexibility. **Drape** is the ability of a fabric to hang in graceful folds.
Resiliency or Wrinkle Recovery	The ability of a fiber to return to its original shape following bending or folding.
Specific Gravity or Density	Compares the fiber mass to an equal volume of water.
Tenacity	Fiber strength.
Chemical Properties	
Absorbency	Ability to take in moisture. **Hydrophilic fibers** can absorb moisture. **Hydrophobic fibers** do not readily absorb moisture.
Wicking	The ability of a fiber to carry moisture along its surface.
Electrical Conductivity	Fibers that do not conduct electrical charges create "static electricity." Hydrophobic fibers, because of their low absorbency, tend to have low electrical conductivity.
Chemical Reactivity	Fibers differ in their reaction to chemicals. Dyes, pigments, finishes, soaps, detergents, and bleaches are examples of chemical agents that are used on textiles.
Effect of Heat	Fibers react differently to heat. Most synthetic fibers are **thermoplastic.** They will melt or soften when exposed to heat.
Flammability	Fibers react differently to flame. Some will ignite; some will smolder, and some will not burn.
Environmental Properties	
Sensitivity to Microorganisms	Some fibers support the growth of microorganisms (mold and mildew); some do not.
Sensitivity to Insects	Some fibers are attacked by insects such as silverfish, carpet beetles, moths; some are not.

The properties of cotton are:

- Generally white or yellowish in color
- Twisted shape with a central canal called a lumen (see Fig. 2.4)
- Matte luster
- Soft, comfortable hand
- Relatively strong, and stronger wet than dry
- Poor resilience
- Poor elasticity
- Good dimensional stability
  (Cotton fabrics shrink in washing due to stretching during manufacturing.)
- Good moisture absorption
- Good static resistance
- Resistant to alkalis but damaged by acids
- Flammable
- Susceptible to attack by silverfish and mildew

TABLE 2.3
Properties of Major Textile Fibers

Fiber	Strength	Abrasion Resistance	Absorbency	Static Resistance	Resiliency	Resistance to Heat	Pilling Resistance	Resistance to Sunlight	Specific Gravity	Thermo-plastic
Cotton	Good	Good	Good	Good	Poor	Good	Good	Fair	1.54	No
Flax	Excellent	Fair	Good	Good	Poor	Good	Good	Good	1.52	No
Wool	Poor	Fair	Excellent	Fair	Good	Poor	Fair	Good	1.32	No
Silk	Good	Fair	Good	Fair	Fair	Poor	Good	Poor	1.30	No
Rayon-viscose	Fair	Fair	Excellent	Excellent	Poor	Good	Good	Fair	1.48–1.54	No
HWM rayon	Good	Good	Excellent	Excellent	Poor	Good	Good	Fair	1.51	No
Lyocell	Good	Good	Excellent	Excellent	Poor	Good	Good	Fair	1.56	No
Acetate	Poor	Poor	Fair	Fair	Fair	Poor	Good	Good	1.32	Yes
Triacetate	Poor	Poor	Fair	Fair	Good	Good	Good	Poor	1.30	Yes
Acrylic	Fair	Fair	Poor	Poor	Good	Poor	Fair	Excellent	1.14–1.19	Yes
Glass	Excellent	Poor	None	Excellent	Excellent	Excellent	Excellent	Excellent	2.54	Yes
Nylon	Excellent	Excellent	Fair	Poor	Good	Poor	Poor	Poor	1.14	Yes
Olefin—polypropelene	Excellent	Excellent	Poor	Good	Excellent	Poor	Good	Good	.91	Yes
Polyester	Excellent	Good	Poor	Poor	Excellent	Poor	Poor	Good	1.38	Yes
Spandex	Poor	Good	Poor	Excellent	Excellent	Poor	Excellent	Fair	1.21	Yes

FIGURE 2.3 *Cotton boll.*
Courtesy of Fairchild Publications, Inc.

TABLE 2.4
Varieties of Cotton

Variety	Length
Sea Island cotton	up to 2 1/2″
Egyptian cotton	up to 1 1/2″
Pima cotton	up to 1 5/8″
Upland cotton	about 13/16″

Nylon, Polyester
circular, uniform
in diameter

Flax
polygonal, lumen

Wool
oval to round,
overlapping scales

Cotton
flat, oval, lumen,
convolutions

Lima bean, smooth

Avril™ rayon
lima bean, serrated

Silk
triangular,
rounded edges

Antron™ nylon
Triobal

Acrylic
mushroom or multiform

Acrylic, Spandex
dog-bone

Acetate
flat, broad

Rayon
circular, serrated,
lengthwise striations

Acetate
lobular,
lengthwise striations

Y-shaped

Star or concertina

Collapsed tube,
hollow center

Anso IV™ nylon
square with voids

FIGURE 2.4 *Fiber cross sections and contour.*

INDUSTRY STATEMENT 2.1

Cotton, Cotton, Who's Got Which Cotton?

ATLANTA—A discussion of extra-log staple (ELS) cotton can be confusing. Even trade associations and textile dictionaries disagree about the exact length that can be so classified—but the minimum ranges from 1⅛ inches to 1⅜ inches. And quality in finished products depends on everything from growing season to finishing and processing. But until recently, the designation "Egyptian cotton" in and of itself created the perception that it was the longest-staple, finest cotton in the world—and the best fiber, first for apparel and then for home furnishings.

And, as any retailer knows, perception is everything. "Availability and promotion create cachet," said Bob Hamilton, vice president of advertising at Pillowtex Corp. "When the venue for Egyptian cotton was upscale shirts, upper-end vendors associated it with the finest quality."

"But now, Egyptian has been over-emphasized. It's a matter of exposure to the consumer," said Kathleen Cwirko Schorr, senior vice president of creative services at WestPoint Stevens. Part of Egyptian's image problem is that it has reached new lows at retail—$5.99 for towels at Wal-Mart, for instance. Another lack of image factor is that there is no Federal Trade Commission regulation on the cotton's quality. The only stipulation is that if any cotton product is designated as a certain type, it must be 100 percent of that type or list the percentage used.

Any cotton grown in Egypt is classified as Egyptian cotton, but 90 percent of that country's exported fiber is long staple, not ELS cotton, said Jesse Curlee, president of the Supima Association of America.

Most luxury home goods now in demand with American consumers require ELS cotton, said Curlee.

Pima, formerly known as American-Egyptian, is the generic term for ELS cotton grown in the United States—where it accounts for only 3 percent of annual cotton production—as well as in Peru, Israel, and Australia. Supima, the trademark licensed by the Supima Association to specific manufacturers and retailers, guarantees that a fiber is 100 percent American pima, as regulated by the association from seed selection to finishing and channels of distribution.

So, at retail, there is new emphasis on these designations to differentiate cotton products.

Kohl's has introduced pima towels; J.C. Penney is already closing out pima for Supima in its Masterpiece collection. Lands' End devoted the first 13 pages of its summer Coming Home catalog to Supima products.

Macy's West is among merchants that are training buyers and managers to understand the differences, said Julian Tomchin, senior vice president of special merchandising projects at the company. "The ability to speak to finer grades of cotton absolutely is meaningful to the consumer and very important to us," he said.

The changes, however, do not mean the death of Egyptian—only that there is more attention being paid, and more choices being offered, to the consumer: J.C. Penney still offers Martex's Grand Patrician Egyptian towel, for instance, and Coming Home continues to sell 100 percent ELS combed Egyptian cotton towels—in the same size and weight as its Supima towel. "Customers have preferences, and they should have choices," said Deborah Barney, vice president of the division.

Source: HFN, May 29, 2000, p. 21. Courtesy of Fairchild Publications, Inc.

Cotton may be machine washed with strong detergents and controlled bleach. It may be washed in hot water, but color can fade. Automatic drying is usually appropriate. Cotton may also be dry-cleaned. For furnishings, dry-cleaning is recommended if cotton fabric has not been preshrunk. Cotton drapes should be lined because the fiber is only moderately resistant to degradation from sunlight. Cotton is susceptible to mildew. Valuable cotton articles should be stored in acid-free boxes or tissue paper because the fiber is damaged by acids. Silverfish attack cotton.

Bast Fibers Flax and ramie are both bast fibers and have similar properties. Bast fibers come from the stem of the plant. The flax fiber is used to make **linen** fabric. The highest-quality flax comes from France, Belgium, the Netherlands, and Ireland. The properties of flax are similar to cotton, but it is stronger, more absorbent, longer, smoother, and more lustrous than cotton. It has very poor resilience and is subject to abrasion especially when folded. Linen fabric may be washed or dry-cleaned. Dry-cleaning is often recommended to improve color retention and minimize shrinkage. High automatic dryer and ironing temperatures will not harm the fiber. Linen is more resistant to sunlight than cotton. Dry-cleaning of home furnishings is recommended.

Ramie is also called *China grass*. The Philippines, China, and Brazil are the main producers of ramie. The properties of ramie are very similar to those of linen except that ramie is slightly heavier and less flexible. The care for ramie is the same as the care for linen. It is only moderately resistant to sunlight, so window treatments should be lined. Ramie is resistant to both insects and mildew.

Minor Cellulosic Fibers *Hemp* is yellowish-brown bast fiber that resembles flax but is coarser and harsher. *Jute* is a bast fiber that is coarse and brittle with good resistance to insects and microorganisms. It is inexpensive to produce and is used in interior furnishings, carpet backings, and cordage. *Burlap* is fabric made from jute. *Kenaf, roselle, sunn,* and *urena* are other minor bast fibers. They are used for the same purposes as jute.

Minor seed fibers include *coir* and *kapok*. Coir is obtained from the shell of the coconut. The fibers are extremely stiff and resistant to rot and abrasion. It is primarily used for floor mats. Kapok grows in the seedpod of the kapok tree. It is exceptionally resilient and buoyant but has a tendency to deteriorate. Foam has replaced kapok for most uses.

Leaf fibers are also called *hard fibers* and come from the leaves of tropical trees and plants. *Abaca* is obtained from the leaves of a member of the banana family. It is also called *manila fiber, manila hemp, sisal hemp,* or *sunn hemp* and is used primarily for matting and cordage. Other leaf fibers include:

- *New Zealand flax,* also called *New Zealand hemp,* is similar to abaca.
- *Henequen* is a leaf fiber used for twine.
- *Piña* is from the leaf of the pineapple plant; it is a fine fiber and is often used to make sheer lustrous fabrics.
- *Raffia* is a soft fiber that is used to make matting, chair seat, rugs, and window or wall coverings.
- *Sisal* is coarse and woody; it is used for matting, cordage, and bristles.
- *Yucca* is similar to sisal.
- *Agave* is the classification sometimes used to refer to sisal and henequen.

Natural Protein Fibers

The major protein fibers are silk, wool, specialty hair fibers, and fur fibers. Silk is the product of the silkworm. Wool, specialty hair, and fur fibers come from sheep, goats, rabbits, and other fur-bearing animals. These fibers have similar chemical structures and, thus, similar properties. The properties common to protein fibers are:

- Lighter in weight than cellulosics
- Good resiliency
- Good absorbency
- Damaged by dry heat, alkalis, and chlorine bleach
- Moderate abrasion resistance

Bird feathers, or **plumage,** are sometimes used to add interesting texture and color in home accessories such as wall hangings.

Silk A luxurious fiber, silk is the only natural fiber that occurs in filament form. The triangular shape of the fiber cross section contributes to its luster (refer back to Figure 2.3). The silkworm (actually a caterpillar) extrudes a continuous protein filament to make its cocoon. It is possible to unwind the cocoon and obtain long silk fibers. There are four types of silk: cultivated, wild, duoppioni, and waste.

Cultivated silk is characterized by long lustrous fibers and is considered to be higher-quality silk. It generally costs more than shorter silk fibers. The cocoon is unwound before the silk moth emerges.

Wild silk is coarser and less lustrous than cultivated silk. Wild silk is sometimes called *tussah silk.* The moth is allowed to emerge from the cocoon, so the resulting fibers are shorter.

Duoppioni silk results when two worms spin a cocoon together. The resulting silk has an uneven texture.

Waste silk is the short fibers from the broken cocoons and fibers from the outside of the cocoon. It is sometimes called *silk noil* and is of lower quality.

Silk has good dimensional stability but is only moderately resilient and has lower abrasion resistance. *Weighted silk* has been washed in metallic salts to improve hand and dyeability. It will break and disintegrate more quickly.

Silk fiber is washable in mild detergents. Dry-cleaning is frequently recommended when the silk fabric has been treated with special finishes and dyes because the fabric may discolor from contact with water. Insects, especially carpet beetles, attack silk. Sunlight will damage the fiber. Use of silk in interiors is limited to high-end applications. Upholstery will abrade quickly, and drapery must be lined.

Wool Sheep produce wool fiber. The highest quality wool comes from *Merino sheep* (see Figure 2.5). Australia is the major producer of wool. Wool is known for its excellent resilience, relatively high elasticity, inherent flame resistance, and inherent water repellency. Lower-quality wool has more luster than higher-quality wool. The wool fiber has natural crimp, which has

FIGURE 2.5 *Merino Sheep.* © Paul A. Souders/CORBIS

two distinct advantages: it is easier to spin into yarn, and when woven or knitted, the wool fiber forms air pockets that provide insulation. The microscopic scales (refer back to Figure 2.3) of the wool fiber allow the fibers to interlock, or felt, when subjected to entanglement. The dimensional stability of wool is poor, but it can be chemically treated to reduce felting and shrinkage.

Wool requires special care because it has a natural tendency to shrink and is very susceptible to moths and carpet beetles. Dry-cleaning is recommended unless the fabric has been treated to allow washing. All wool articles should be cleaned before storage. Special finishes provide mothproofing. Sunlight will deteriorate wool.

Specialty Hair Fibers The cost and beauty of most specialty hair fibers limits their use to high status products. These fibers are often blended with other fibers to reduce cost. Refer back to Table 2.1 for a listing of specialty hair fibers. Most come from animals in the goat or camel families. The properties and care of specialty hair fibers are similar to those of wool. Most, except alpaca and mohair, are very soft and have low abrasion resistance. Cow and horsehair have limited application. Cow hair is sometimes blended with wool to make low-end carpets, blankets, and felts. Horsehair is from the mane and tail of the horse. It has been replaced by synthetics as a stuffing for upholstered furniture.

Fur Fibers Occasionally fur fibers such as mink, fox, and rabbit are used to add interesting texture and feel to fabrics such as blankets and throws. They tend to be expensive.

Plumage—Feathers Plucked feathers are noted for their loft (volume) and resilience. They are used for pillows and in upholstery, but in many cases have been replaced by synthetics. *Down* refers to the undercoat of waterfowl. It is used primarily for pillows, quilts, and comforters. Goose down is more expensive than eider duck down. Additional discussion of down and feathers can be found in Chapter 11.

Manufactured Fibers

Manufactured fibers are separated into three major groups: **manufactured cellulosics,** synthetic, and inorganic (see Industry Statement 2.2). These fibers begin as chemical solutions that are extruded (forced) through a **spinneret** (see Figure 2.6). The fiber chemist controls the solutions and can modify the properties of the fiber and change the shape of the fiber by adjusting the size of the openings in the spinneret. Manufactured fibers are produced as filaments (very long fibers) but may be cut into staple (shorter lengths) (refer back to Figure 2.2).

Each manufactured fiber is identified by its **generic name.** These names have been established by the Federal Trade Commission (FTC). All fibers in a generic fiber type have very similar properties. Many manufactured fibers also have **trade names.** For example, nylon is a generic name. Antron® is a trade name for nylon made by DuPont; Acrilan® is a trade name for acrylic made by Solutia, Inc.; and Fortrel® is a trade name for polyester made by Wellman, Inc.

Manufactured Cellulosics

Manufactured cellulosics are further divided into two categories: **regenerated cellulosics** and **derivative cellulosics.** Both categories are created from cellulose, a substance for which wood

FIGURE 2.6
Spinneret.
Photo provided by American Fiber
Manufacturers Association.

INDUSTRY STATEMENT 2.2

Man–Made Fiber Set for Global Growth

Naturals expected to lose market share to manufactured materials

---

CLEVELAND—Worldwide consumption of manufactured fiber is expected to increase 5.4 percent per year to 37.8 million metric tons in 2003, according to *World Textile Fibers: Synthetic & Cellulosic,* a study from the Freedonia Group Inc., an industrial market research team based here.

Manufactured fibers are defined as: cellulosic—rayon, acetate, and triacetate derived from naturally occurring cellulose; and synthetic—nylon, polyester, olefins, and acrylic—made from petrochemical feedstock.

The report weighs a variety of market trends in reaching the conclusion that manufactured fibers will continue to grow at the expense of natural fibers.

Freedonia predicts that the synthetic fibers will offer the strongest gains. Olefins, especially polypropylene, will lead the synthetics as strong demand continues to grow for use as face fiber, as well as a primary and secondary backing material, for carpets and rugs. Nylon and polyester are also widely used in carpet and rug applications.

Synthetics are also forecast to increase in use in blends with cotton for household goods, including sheets, pillowcases, blankets, curtains, drapery, and upholstery, as well as in apparel.

While cellulosics are expected to continue to lose market share to synthetics, the extended decline is predicted to turn due to increased demand for rayon and acetate in apparel. Lyocel, a next-generation cellulosic, is forecast to see increased use in nonwoven and industrial applications.

Freedonia expects to see continued strength in China's and India's fiber markets, as well as recovery in much of the rest of Asia. Japan, however, is forecast to remain slow. North America will add to the global average as a slight decline in the United States is expected to be offset by rapid gains in Mexico. Eastern Europe is judged to be ready for a rebound, with lingering weakness in Russia expected to remain a negative in the region.

Source: HFN, May 1, 2000, p. 18. Courtesy of Fairchild Publications, Inc.

---

pulp is the main source. Regenerated cellulosics include *rayon* and *lyocell.* Derivative cellulosics include *acetate* and *triacetate.*

Regenerated Cellulosics Rayon was the first manufactured fiber to be developed, and many levels of quality are available to the consumer. There are several types of rayon including *viscose, cuprammonium,* and *high wet modulus (HWM).* Viscose and cuprammonium have very similar properties. Unfortunately, it is often impossible for the consumer to differentiate the various rayon fibers. The properties of rayon are:

- Good absorbency
- Ready dyeability
- Pleasant hand
- Beautiful drape
- Low strength, especially when wet
- Poor resilience
- Poor dimensional stability

High wet modulus (HWM) rayon is superior to both viscose rayon and cuprammonium rayon. It is stronger, more resilient, and more dimensionally stable.

Care labels should be followed closely. Dry-cleaning is recommended for viscose rayon and cuprammonium rayon. HWM rayon may be washed or dry-cleaned. Sunlight degrades rayon, which can also be attacked by silverfish and mildew.

Lyocell is the newest regenerated cellulosic fiber. It has all the positive characteristics of viscose rayon, but it is almost twice as strong, is washable and dry-cleanable, and has better resilience. However, it can develop pills (small balls of fiber attached to the fabric). The production of lyocell is less harmful to the environment than rayon, but it is more expensive.

Derivative Cellulosic Fibers *Acetate* and *triacetate* are derivative cellulosic fibers. During production the cellulose is chemically changed, so their properties are very different from those of rayon or lyocell. They are soft and lustrous but not as strong as regenerated cellulosics, and they are thermoplastic and have low abrasion resistance. Beautiful *moiré,* or grain-of-wood, patterns are often heat set into acetate. Pleats can be heat set into triacetate.

Acetate should usually be dry-cleaned. Acetate should not be exposed to nail polish remover, which will dissolve it. Sunlight degrades acetate, so drapery should be lined. Acetate is also susceptible to **fume fading.** This occurs when acetate is exposed to atmospheric gases in homes heated with gas. Blue and gray shades may turn pink or reddish, and greens turn brown.

Triacetate may be dry-cleaned or machine washed and dried. It has better wrinkle recovery than acetate. Nail polish remover will also damage triacetate.

Major Synthetic Fibers

Since the introduction of nylon in 1939, synthetic fibers have become well known for their superior performance characteristics. They are synthesized from complex chemical compounds and can be modified to meet consumer demands. The fibers presented in this section are *acrylic, aramid, modacrylic, nylon, olefin, polyester,* and *spandex.* The properties that are common to synthetic fibers are:

- Good to excellent abrasion resistance
- High pilling propensity
- Excellent resilience
- Lightweight
- Poor absorbency
- Good resistance to most chemicals
- Thermoplastic

In general, the care of synthetic fiber is easy. Most can be dry-cleaned, machine washed, and machine or line dried. Exposure to high heat in automatic dryers or in ironing can cause wrinkles, melting, or **glazing.** Glazing is undesirable shine caused by high heat. Most synthetic fibers are not subject to attack by moths, silverfish, or carpet beetles. Special finishes, coloring agents, or blending with other fibers may require special care, so it is important to consult the care label.

Acrylic Acrylic is not as durable as nylon, olefin, or polyester, and it has very high propensity to pill. The fiber has good resilience, cover, and insulating qualities, so it is frequently used as a substitute for wool. It also resists sunlight. There are several varieties of acrylic, so it is important to follow care label instructions. Dry-cleaning can cause stiffness. Steam may cause shrinkage, so steam cleaning of home furnishings is not recommended.

Aramid Aramid is primarily used in applications when strength and flame-resistance are necessary. It has exceptional strength and does not melt. Dyeing increases its flammability, and sunlight degrades it. Because of its high temperature and flame resistance, aramid is used for carpet and upholstery in aircrafts.

Modacrylic Modacrylic is a modified acrylic with properties that are similar to those of acrylic. It is sensitive to heat and shrinks at high temperatures, but it is difficult to ignite in open flame and self-extinguishes when the flame is removed. It has a fine hair-like structure that makes it useful for fleece and simulated-fur fabrics. Care labels must be read carefully because the fiber shrinks at high automatic dryer temperatures. Pile and fur-like products may require special care because brushing and pressing can cause damage. Steam cleaning can cause shrinkage.

Nylon Nylon, also called *polyamide,* is an extremely durable fiber, but it can pill. It has good elasticity. It is thermoplastic and accepts pleats and creases well. It does not conduct electricity, but it builds static electricity. Nylon is considered an easy-care fabric. Machine washing and drying at low temperatures is recommended. Chlorine bleach may cause yellowing. Nylon has a tendency to **scavenge colors** (to pick up colors from other fabrics in the wash). Sunlight degrades nylon, so unless it has been modified to resist sunlight, it should not be used for window treatments. Nylon is popular for carpeting because it is durable, easy to clean, and resilient.

Olefin There are two types of olefin—polyethylene and polypropylene. *Polyethylene* is used in insulation under the trade name of TYVEK®. *Polypropylene* has more textile applications. The fiber has very low absorbency, so it is difficult to dye unless color is added before production. Polypropylene has excellent resistance to stains, as well as good static resistance and resilience. It is very heat sensitive and should not be tumbled dry, but it can be washed by machine at low temperatures. Drapes should not be near radiators, and hot embers will melt carpet or upholstery. Olefin has poor resistance to sunlight.

Polyester Known for its good strength and resistance to abrasion, polyester has excellent resilience and can be permanently heat set. Polyester is known for its use as **fiberfill** in comforters and pillows. Fiberfill is staple polyester suitable for use as filling or stuffing. It also has excellent resistance to sun and is frequently used for curtains and drapes. Polyester is frequently used in blends. It has a tendency to pill. Usually it can be machine washed and dried, but all stains should be pretreated. Oil stains are especially difficult to remove.

Spandex Spandex can be stretched 500 to 600 percent and return to its original size. It is stronger than natural rubber, but is the weakest of the synthetic fibers. Spandex is used with other fibers. It can be machine washed and dried at moderate temperatures. Chlorine bleach will cause the fiber to yellow.

Selected Special-Application Synthetic Fibers

The following special-application fibers have been developed to meet specific needs:

- *Fluoropolymer* Fluorocarbon fibers are completely hydrophobic and resistant to abrasion, sun, aging, and mildew. The fiber can be formed into a thin membrane that provides water and stain resistance.
- *Lastrile* Lastrile is a type of rubber.
- *Novoloid* Novoloid is a weak fiber that is golden in color. It has excellent flame and chemical resistance and is often used in liners for aircraft seats and fire-protection curtains.
- *PBI (Polybenzimidazole)* PBI is strong and has good absorbency, but it is difficult to dye. It has excellent flame resistance and is used when furnishings must meet strict fire codes.
- *Saran* Saran is a stiff fiber that can be used in upholstery for summer furniture and on seats for public transportation. It is flame resistant. It has good strength and excellent abrasion resistance, elastic recovery, and resilience. It is nonabsorbent and is not attacked by insects or mildew. Sunlight resistance is very good, but long exposure can cause discoloration. It can be cleaned with soap and water.

Inorganic Fibers

Glass and metallic fibers are manufactured inorganic fibers.

Glass *Glass* fiber is strong, does not burn, is not attacked by insects or mildew, and is not harmed by extended exposure to sunlight. It has very low abrasion resistance, very poor elasticity, poor hand, poor drape, and is completely hydrophobic. It is also very heavy. It is excellent for drapes or curtains when strict fire codes must be met. It can also be used for lampshades, vertical blinds, and in electrical and thermal insulation. Window treatments should not be allowed to rub against sills, radiators, and the like, because of the low abrasion resistance. Glass drapes must also have extra supporting brackets because the fabric is very heavy. Glass fabric should not be dry-cleaned or machine washed because the agitation will cause the fibers to crack and break. It should be vacuumed instead.

Metallic *Metallic fibers* are used to add decorative effects to fabrics. Small amounts of superfine stainless steel and aluminum filaments are also used to reduce the static electricity build-up in industrial carpets. Users must read the care label because metallic fibers are combined with other fibers.

Blends

Blending, the use of more than one fiber in a textile product, is common in textile products. There are three benefits to blending. The first is reduced cost. A cheaper fiber can be blended with a more expensive fiber to reduce cost. For example, rayon can be blended with wool. The second benefit is aesthetic effect. A luxury fiber can be added to improve hand. For example, mohair can be blended with acrylic. The third benefit is improved function. A fiber can be added to provide additional benefits. For example, blends of polyester and cotton have the benefits of both fibers. Cotton provides soft hand and comfort, while polyester adds resilience and strength. Care procedures must be appropriate for both fibers.

YARNS

Yarns are used to make woven or knitted fabric. Nonwovens lack yarn structure and are made directly from fibers. Fibers are twisted together to create yarns. There are two main categories of yarns—**filament yarns** and **spun yarns.** Filament yarns are made from long, or filament, fibers. All manufactured yarns and silk are initially produced as filaments. Spun yarns are made from short or staple fibers. All natural fibers, except silk, are staple.

Yarn Formation

The process to create filament yarns is different than the process to create spun yarns. Table 2.5 summarizes the differences between conventional filament, textured filament, and spun yarns.

Filament Yarns

There are several subcategories of filament yarns: **monofilament, multifilament,** and **textured filament.** Monofilament yarns are simply one fiber. Multifilament yarns usually contain 20 to 140 filaments. Multifilament yarns have some twist to keep the fibers together in a strand. Textured filament yarns are made from manufactured fibers that have been treated to change the shape of the yarn by adding curl, crimp, or loop. The hand of textured filament yarns resembles the hand of staple yarns.

Spun Yarns

Staple fibers go through a series of steps to produce yarn.

1. The fibers are cleaned and fluffed.
2. The fibers are straightened to be somewhat parallel.
3. The fibers are pulled into a strand.
4. The strand is given twist to keep it together.

TABLE 2. 5

Summary of the Characteristics of Conventional Filament, Textured Filament, and Spun Yarns

Type of Yarn	
Conventional Filament Yarns	Fibers are parallel.
	Yarn does not pull apart when untwisted.
	Fibers are as long as the yarn.
	Yarn may be less tightly twisted.
	Yarn surface is smooth.
Textured Filament Yarn	Fibers are not parallel.
	Yarn does not pull apart when untwisted.
	Fibers are as long as the yarn.
	Yarn usually has low twist.
	Yarn surface is fuzzier.
Spun Yarns	Fibers are not completely parallel.
	Yarn pulls apart when untwisted.
	Fibers are shorter than the yarn.
	Yarns have higher twist.
	Yarn surface is fuzzier.

Combing is the process to remove short fibers and further parallel the fibers. This process is used on cotton and manufactured fibers that are similar to cotton. Combing creates a yarn that is smoother, more uniform, and finer. In general, these yarns are more expensive. Yarns that are not combed are called **carded yarns.** For example, *percale* sheets are made from combed yarns; while *muslin* sheets are made from carded yarns.

Wool and manufactured fibers that resemble wool may also be subjected to additional processing. **Worsted yarns** have had the short fibers removed, while woolen yarns have not. Worsted yarns are smoother, stronger, and more tightly twisted than **woolen yarns.**

Types of Yarns

Yarns are categorized as simple yarns or novelty yarns.

Simple Yarns

There are three types of simple yarns: single, ply, and cord (see Figure 2.7). A **single yarn** will separate into individual fibers when untwisted. A **ply yarn** has two or more single yarns twisted together. A two-ply yarn will have two singles, a three-ply yarn will have three singles, and so on. Ply yarns have more strength than single yarns. A **cord yarn** is created when two or more plies are twisted together.

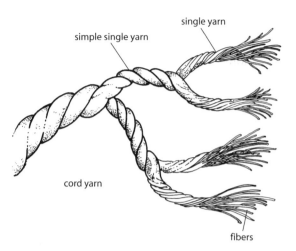

FIGURE 2.7
Single, ply, and cord yarns.

Novelty Yarns

In addition to simple yarns, there are many beautiful **novelty yarns** that add textural interest to fabrics. They are often used in blankets and drapery. See Figure 2.8 for examples of some novelty yarns. Novelty yarns are sometimes called *fancy yarns* because most have a fancy ply held to a base or core with a *binder yarn*. Most novelty yarns are not durable.

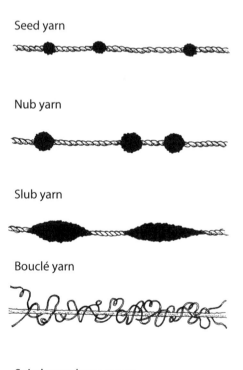

FIGURE 2.8
Novelty yarns.

FABRICS

There are three basic ways to make fabrics: from solutions, fibers, or yarns (see Table 2.6). The right side of the fabric is called the **face,** and the reverse side is called the **back.** Fabric that has no finish or color is referred to as **"greige fabric."**

Woven Fabrics

Weaving is the most common way to make fabric. Woven fabrics are created by interlacing yarns to form a cohesive structure. Warp yarns are placed on a loom, and filling yarns are interlaced across the width of the loom. **Warp yarns** are parallel to the **selvages,** or lengthwise edges, of the fabric. **Filling yarns** are perpendicular to the warp yarns. **Grain** refers to the relationship between the warp and filling yarns. In fabric that is **on-grain** the warp and filling yarns will be perpendicular to each other. Sometimes filling yarns are *skewed* or *bowed* (see Figure 2.9). If the fabric is not on-grain, it will not hang properly.

Basic Weaves

There are three basic weaves: plain, twill, and satin.

Plain Weave The **plain weave** is the most common. A filling yarn alternately goes over and under filling yarns across the width of the fabric. The next filling yarn will go under the warp yarns that had been on the bottom (see Figure 2.10). The smooth surface of the fabric is ideal for printed designs. When compared to other fabrics, plain weave fabrics wear well, ravel less, wrinkle more, and are less absorbent. Examples of plain weave fabrics include *muslin, percale, duck, batiste,* and *calico.*

Rib weave and *basket weave* fabrics are variations of plain weaves. Rib weaves are made by using larger yarns or by grouping warp or filling yarns to create a ridge in the fabric. *Cord* is a fabric with a lengthwise rib. *Broadcloth* and *taffeta* are rib weaves. Basket weaves have two or more warp yarns interlacing with two or more filling yarns. *Monk's cloth* is a basket weave.

Twill Weave The **twill weave** has diagonal lines, or **wales,** on the surface. The warp yarns go over as many as three yarns and then under one. Each subsequent warp yarn starts the sequence

TABLE 2.6
Basic Way to Create Fabric

Fabrics Made from Yarns	Fabrics Made from Fibers	Fabrics Made from Solutions
Wovens	Felt	Films
Knits	Nonwovens	Foams
Laces		
Stitch-Through Fabrics		

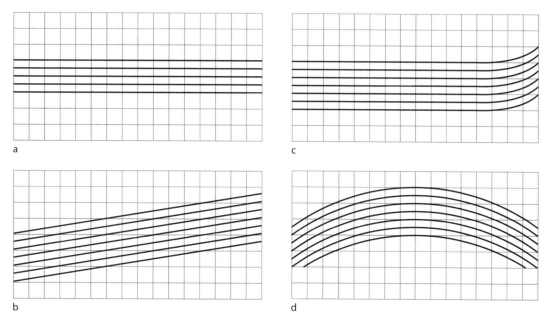

FIGURE 2.9 *Grain positions:* a. *on-grain,* b. *skewed,* c. *bowed,* d. *bowed.*

one warp yarn farther in (see Figure 2.11). The long strands of yarn on the surface of the fabric are called **floats.** Twill weaves usually have good abrasion resistance and drape well. *Denim* and *chino* are examples of twill weaves. *Herringbone* is a variation of the twill weave. The diagonal wale is continually reversed across the width of the fabric to create a zigzag effect.

Satin Weave Satin weave is created when warp yarns float over four or more filling yarns. The interlacings are regularly spaced, so the fabric appears to be smooth (see Figure 2.12). **Satins** are satin-weave fabrics made from filament yarns. **Sateens** are made from spun yarns. The fabric is subject to snagging and has poor abrasion resistance. Examples of satin weaves include antique satin and *peau-de-soie.*

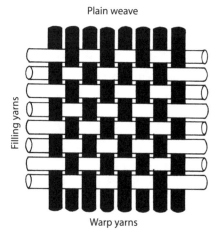

FIGURE 2.10 *Plain weave.*

FIGURE 2.11 *Twill weave.*

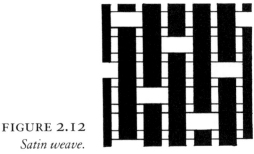

FIGURE 2.12
Satin weave.

Weave Variations

In addition to the basic weaves, there are many creative variations. Examples of these include *pile weaves, leno weaves, dobby weaves,* and *jacquard weaves.*

Pile Weaves Pile weaves have a base warp and filling with extra yarns to produce the pile. One example is corduroy, which has a cut pile. Traditional terry cloth has an uncut pile, while velvet terry cloth has a cut pile.

Leno Weaves Leno weaves have pairs of warp yarns twisted around filling yarns. *Marquiesette* is a sheer leno weave fabric used for curtains.

Dobby Weaves Dobby weaves are characterized by small geometric designs. *Piqué* is an example of a dobby weave.

Jacquard Weaves Jacquard weaves use long floats to create beautifully decorative fabric. Frequently they are not durable because the long floats are subject to abrasion and snagging. Examples of jacquard fabrics include *brocade, damask,* and *tapestry.*

Thread Count

Thread count is often used to determine fabric quality. It refers to the number of threads in one square inch of fabric. Higher thread counts indicate better quality because the fabric is stronger, and has better abrasion resistance and improved hand. A thread count of 100 × 80 would mean that there are 100 warp yarns per inch and 80 filling yarns per inch. A **balanced weave** has the same number of thread in the warp and the filling. A thread count of 90 square means that there are 90 warp yarns and 90 filling yarns in a square inch; 90 square can also be expressed as 180 thread count. Balanced fabrics wear more evenly than unbalanced fabrics. Percale and muslin sheets are balanced weaves that are commonly labeled with thread counts.

Fabric Weight

Fabric weight is another indicator of fabric quality. Higher weight indicates more fiber and therefore longer wearing products. Weight is especially important in towels and carpeting. Higher-weight towels have better drying ability because there is more fiber to absorb moisture; higher-weight carpet offers better wear because there is more fiber on the surface of the carpet.

Knitted Fabric

Knitting is the interlooping of yarns to create fabric. There are two major categories of knits—weft knits and warp knits. Weft knits are sometimes called **filling knits.**

Weft Knits

The face of a **weft knit** is a series of vertical columns of knit stitches. The columns are called **wales.** The back shows courses or horizontal rows of purl stitches. Figure 2.13 shows the arrangement of yarn in a weft knit. The rows are called **courses.** Jersey knits, *rib knits,* and *purl knits* are examples of weft knits.

Jersey Knits Jersey knits are sometimes called **single knits.** The face of a jersey knit is smooth, and it stretches crosswise and lengthwise. The fabric has a tendency to ladder or run (stitches unravel) if a stitch breaks, and the edges will curl when cut. Examples of jersey knits include T-shirts, sweaters, and knitted sheets. *Knitted-pile fabrics* are created by inserting additional fibers or yarns into the knitted base. Examples are fake-fur throws or bedspreads.

Rib Knits Variations of jersey knits in which wales and courses alternate across the fabric are called rib knits. A 3×3 rib knit would have three rows of wales alternating with three rows of courses going across the fabric. Rib knits have more crosswise stretch than jersey knits but do not curl when cut. They will ladder if a stitch is broken. Knit hats and socks are examples of rib knits. *Interlock knits* are specialized 1×1 rib knits that are similar to jersey knits but are more stable. They are used for underwear and blouses. *Double knits* are another special form of rib knits. They are very stable and usually thicker and heavier than jersey knits.

Purl Knits Purl knits have alternating rows of knit stitches and purl stitches. Purl knits have more texture than jersey knits, do not curl when cut, but do stretch out of shape more easily. They are used in children's wear and sweaters.

Warp Knits

Warp knits are characterized by yarns that zigzag along the length of the fabric. See Figure 2.14 for the arrangement of yarn in a warp knit. There are two types of warp knits—**tricot** and **raschel.**

FIGURE 2.13
Arrangement of yarn in a weft knit.

FIGURE 2.14
Arrangement of yarn in a warp knit.

Tricot Knits Tricot knits are similar to jersey knits on the face, but they have floats on the back. When compared to jersey knits, tricot knits are less resilient, lighter weight, more tightly knit, have less stretch, and ladder less easily. In lighter weights they are frequently used in women's apparel, while heavier weights are used for automobile upholstery. Some specialized tricot fabrics have open, or mesh-like, effects and may be used in apparel or window treatments.

Raschel Knits Raschel and tricot fabrics are often very similar, but raschel knits are usually more textured, have more open spaces, and are made from heavier yarns. Raschel knits are available in a wide variety of patterns and textures. They are frequently used in lacy window treatments, tablecloths, and doilies.

Nonwovens and Other Fabric Formations

Nonwoven and other fabric formations are used to make decorative and functional fabrics.

Nonwovens

Nonwoven fabrics are made directly from fibers. They are held together by entanglement or by chemical or heat bonding. Nonwovens:

- Are relatively inexpensive when compared to wovens and knits
- Have no grain
- Do not run
- Exhibit the properties of the fibers from which they are made

There are two categories of nonwovens—durable and nondurable. Durable nonwoven fabrics include carpet backing. Rayon, polyester, and olefin are frequently used for durable nonwovens. Disposable nonwovens are made from rayon and include disposable diapers and inexpensive tablecloths.

Other Fabric Formations

Other fabric formations include stitch-through fabrics, laces, embroidery, films and foams, and tufting.

Stitch-Through Fabrics Sometimes referred to as *mali fabrics,* **stitch-through fabrics** are a group of crosswise yarns laid over a group of lengthwise yarns and stitched together with thread. They are frequently used in tablecloths, curtains, and other window treatments such as casement drapery (see Figure 2.15).

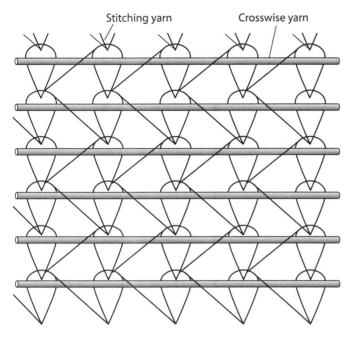

Stitching yarn   Crosswise yarn

FIGURE 2.15
Mali fabric.

Lace Beautiful lace is produced by machine or by hand. Handmade lace is very expensive and time-consuming to make. Many of the techniques used to make lace are also used to macramé and crochet. Lace can be thin narrow strips used for trimming, or lace can be fabric width. Lace is available at many price and quality levels.

Embroidery Embroidery is the process of adding decorative stitches to completed fabric. It can be done by machine or by hand. Machine embroidery is also known as *Schiffli embroidery,* named for the machine used to make it. Usually it is delicate and done on lightweight fabrics.

Films and Foams Films and foams are made directly from solutions that are similar to the solutions used to create synthetic fibers. Films may be very thin, such as disposable tablecloths, or thick, such as upholstery and table coverings.

Foams are created by incorporating air into rubber and are widely used in the carpeting industry as padding. They are also used for upholstery and bedding.

Tufting Tufting is the process used to create tufted fabrics such as carpeting. Yarns are stitched into the finished fabric to form a looped pile (see Figure 2.16). Various textures can be achieved by cutting the piles, shearing the pile to different lengths, or by selectively cutting some loops while leaving others uncut. Uses for tufted fabrics include upholstery, drapery, bedspreads, and blankets.

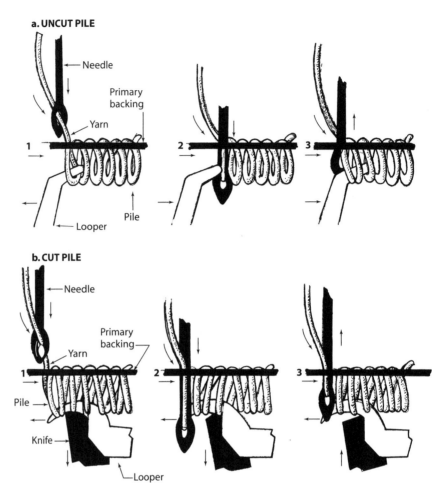

FIGURE 2.16
The tufting process:
a. *uncut pile,* b. *cut pile.*

COLORATION

The color of the fabric is a major consideration for the consumer when making a purchase decision.

Color Permanence

Most consumers want the original color to remain for the life of the product. Permanent colors are considered **colorfast.** They will remain permanent during care and use. Colors that are not permanent may:

- **Bleed**   Lose color in water and cause fading and staining
- **Crock**   Rub off
- **Fade**   Generally lose color, becoming lighter
- **Frost**   Lose color because of localized abrasion

Dyes and Pigments

Dyes and **pigments** are the coloring agents used to add color to textiles. Dyes are the most common. In most cases dyes chemically bond with the fiber, while pigments are not absorbed into the fiber. A *textile binder* must be used to adhere the pigment to the fabric. Table 2.7 compares the characteristics of dyes and pigments.

Dyeing

Color can be added to textiles at many stages in production. The advantages and disadvantages of the dyeing processes are summarized in Table 2.8. Some types of dyeing include:

- **Solution dyeing** Color is added before extrusion.
- **Stock** or **fiber dyeing** Color is added at the fiber stage.
- **Yarn dyeing** Color is added at the yarn stage.
- **Piece dyeing** Color is added at the fabric stage.
- **Product/garment dyeing** Color is added after the end product has been produced.

Color Consistency

Color consistency is important because all parts of a textile product should be the same shade. Long lengths of fabric must be free of streaks or blotches and must be the same color from end to end. It is also important that color is consistent from bolt to bolt of fabric.

TABLE 2.7
Characteristics of Dyes and Pigments

Colorant	Characteristics
Dyes	Chemically bond with the fiber.
	Generally more colorfast than pigments.
	Do not affect the texture of the fabric.
	Can be used on fibers, yarns, fabric, and garments.
	Washing and rinsing are required to remove chemicals and excess dye.
	Color is set with steam or heat.
Pigments	Cheaper and more efficient to apply than dyes.
	May stiffen the fabric.
	Color may rub off.
	Can be added to manufactured fibers before extrusion.
	Easier to match colors because the color is on the surface.
	Color is set with dry heat.

TABLE 2.8

Advantages and Disadvantages of the Dyeing Processes

Dyeing Process	Advantage	Disadvantage
Solution	Excellent colorfastness. Good for hard-to-dye fibers such as olefin.	Color decision is made very early in production. Appropriate only for manufactured fibers.
Stock	Excellent for coloring fibers for use in tweed or heather fabrics. Good dye penetration.	Relatively expensive. Early color decision.
Yarn	Excellent for use in woven or knitted stripes, plaids, ginghams, chambray. Excellent dye penetration.	More expensive than piece dyeing but less expensive than stock dyeing. Early color decision.
Piece	More cost effective than stock or yarn dyeing. Both knits and wovens can be piece dyed. Color decision is delayed.	Solid color fabric. Dye penetration not as good as stock or yarn dyeing.
Product	Cost effective because color decision is delayed as long as possible. Process can be used to overdye garments or other textile products from a previous season.	More costly than piece dyeing. All components must be compatible (fabric, thread, zippers, etc.). Sizing and shrinkage may be a problem. Penetration of color may be poor. Colorfastness may be poor.

Printing

There are two types of prints—wet prints and dry prints.

Wet Prints

Wet prints are fabrics that have been printed with dye. Wet prints must be **set** to make the color permanent with steam, and excess dye must be washed out. *Flat-bed screen printing, rotary-screen printing* and *roller printing* are methods of wet printing (see Figure 2.17). There are several variations of wet printing.

- *Blotch printing* The colors for the background and the design are applied during printing (as opposed to dyeing the background and then printing on the pattern). This method eliminates the dyeing step.
- *Burn-out printing* Chemicals are applied in a pattern to "burn out" or destroy areas of fabric.
- *Flock printing* The fabric is printed with an adhesive. Then short fibers are scattered over the surface and adhere in the pattern of the adhesive.
- *Jet printing* Small jets, or nozzles, are used to apply color.
- *Warp printing* The warp yarns are printed before the fabric is woven. The resulting fabric usually has subtle designs and is frequently used in home furnishings.

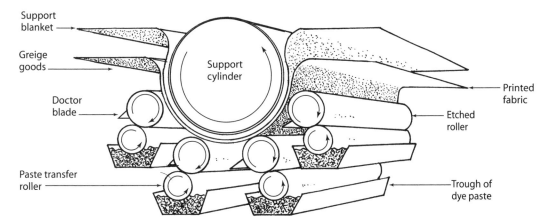

FIGURE 2.17 *Roller printing.*

Dry Prints

Dry prints are fabrics that have been printed with pigments. Dry prints are set with dry heat, and the dye does not need to be washed out. *Heat-transfer* or *paper printing* are examples of dry printing. First, the design is printed onto paper. To transfer the design to the fabric, the paper and fabric are put through hot rollers (see Figure 2.18). The advantages of dry printing are that it causes relatively little waste or environmental damage and is appropriate for knits (many knits are not stable enough for roller or screen printing). The disadvantages are that this method sometimes stiffens the hand of the fabric, and there is little color penetration into the fabric, so the background fabric may show through the print.

FINISHES

Finishes are processes that modify the properties of a textile product. Finishes may be applied at any stage in the production of fabric, but they are frequently applied after dyeing and printing. Finishes may be temporary, durable, or permanent. **Temporary finishes,** such as *calendering,* which is similar to ironing, are removed or considerably reduced during washing or dry-cleaning. **Durable finishes,** such as durable press, will usually last for the life of the product, but their

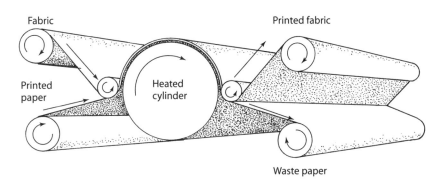

FIGURE 2.18
Heat-transfer printing.

effectiveness diminishes as the product ages. **Permanent finishes,** such as *mercerization,* last the full life of the product.

Finishes may also be either chemical or mechanical. **Chemical finishes** are also called *wet finishes* and frequently involve the application of **resins.** Resins are compounds often used for durable press finishes. **Mechanical finishes** are also called *dry finishes* and involve manipulation of the fabric. For example, napping, or the brushing up of surface fibers, is a mechanical finish. The many finishes that are applied to fabric can be classified into three categories: preparatory, aesthetic, and functional. Some finishes serve dual purposes. For example, a durable press finish may be considered functional because it eliminates or reduces the need for ironing. At the same time it may be considered aesthetic because it improves the appearance of the fabric during use.

Preparatory Finishes

Preparatory finishes prepare the fabric for additional treatment. Examples of preparatory finishes include:

- *Bleaching* Chlorine bleaches or oxygen bleaches are used to produce white fabric.
- *Tentering* Tentering straightens the grain.
- *Optical brightening* Fluorescent whiteners are added to intensify whiteness and brightness.
- *Mercerization* Sodium hydroxide is used to strengthen the fiber, increase absorbency, and improve the luster of cotton.
- *Singeing* The fabric is passed over a gas flame or heated copper plate to remove any protruding fiber ends; singeing helps prevent pill formation.

Aesthetic Finishes

Aesthetic finishes improve the appearance or hand of the fabric. Some examples of aesthetic finishes are:

Calendering Fabric is passed through heated rollers to remove wrinkles and/or create surface designs. There are several types of calendering. Examples include:

- *Simple calendering* Usually the temporary smoothing of fabric.
- *Embossing* Fabric passes through heated rollers that have been engraved with a design.
- *Glazing* Calendering that produces a highly polished surface.
- *Moiré* Specialized embossing using rollers that have been engraved with a "wood-grain" design (see Figure 2.19).
- *Schreinering* Special type of calendering that produces a soft hand and soft luster; one of the calendering rollers embosses the fabric with approximately 250 fine lines per inch; typically done on damasks.

Napping The brushing up of surface fibers is called napping.

FIGURE 2.19
Moiré.
Courtesy of Philip Jeffries.

Functional Finishes

Functional finishes improve the performance of the fabric. Examples of functional finishes are:

- *Shrinkage control treatments* Reduce shrinkage during washing or dry-cleaning.
- *Antimicrobial finishes* (also called *antibacterial finishes* or *antiseptic finishe*s) Inhibit the growth of bacteria and other germs.
- *Antirot finishes* and *antimildew finishes* Inhibit the growth of microorganisms.
- *Antistatic finishes* Increase absorbency, thus reducing the buildup of electrical charges.
- *Durable press (permanent press)* Reduces the need for ironing after cleaning and improves original appearance retention during use. The terms *permanent press* and *durable press* are used interchangeably. Most durable press finishes are effective for up to 50 cleanings.
- *Wrinkle-resistant (WR)* and *crease-resistant finishes (CRF)* Finishes that reduce wrinkles that occur during use.
- *Flame-resistant finishes* Halt or inhibit the combustion process. There are two types of flame-resistant treatments. Polymer flame-resistant treatments last up to 20 dry-cleanings but cause up to 5 percent shrinkage in the fabric and may result in color change and stiffness. Saline flame-resistant finishes are less expensive and less durable than polymer treatments. They may cause color change, and the salt solution corrodes metals such as upholstery tacks and staples. The fabric also becomes more absorbent, which affects the overall length of draperies as humidity levels change.
- *Moth-proofing finishes* Protect the fiber from moths and carpet beetles.
- *Soil-release finishes* Make the fabric easier to clean by increasing absorption.
- *Soil-* and *stain-resistant finishes* Prevent the fabric from getting dirty.
- *Water-resistant finishes* Prevent water from being absorbed into the fabric. (Note: water-resistant fabrics are not waterproof.)

- *Heat-reflectant finishes* Can be engineered to reflect heat away for cooling or direct heat inward to provide warmth.
- *Light-stabilizing finishes* Ultraviolet absorbers to protect fabric from sun damage.

LAWS AFFECTING TEXTILE PRODUCTS

Federal agencies oversee regulations and legislation that relate to the manufacture and consumption of textile products. Major legislation includes:

- Federal Trade Commission on the Weighting of Silk (1932)
  This law requires that all silk with more than 10 percent weighting with metallic salts be labeled as weighted silk. Black silk can have 15 percent weighting because it is less likely to be damaged by the weighting.
- Flammable Fabrics Act (1953, amended in 1967)
  This act prohibits the sale of highly flammable apparel and fabrics. The original act was amended in 1967 to include all interior furnishings used in homes, offices, and other public places. Paper, plastic, rubber, and synthetic foam were also included in the amendment.
- Fur Products Labeling Act (1951)
  All fur products must be labeled with the true English name of the animal from which the fur comes and the name of the country of origin.
- Permanent Care Labeling Ruling of the Federal Trade Commission (1972, amended in 1984)
  All apparel and bolts of fabric sold by the yard must have permanently affixed labels providing care instructions. Household textiles, items costing less than $3.00, footwear, and head and hand coverings are exempt.
- Textile Fiber Products Identification Act (1960 and later amendments)
  This law has six main requirements.

  1. The generic name of the fiber must be used.
  2. Fiber content must be listed vertically by percentage and in descending order. Any fiber composing less than five percent must be listed as "other" unless it has a specific function.
  3. The country in which the product was produced must be listed.
  4. The manufacturer's name or identification number must be listed.
  5. Misleading names are prohibited.
  6. Labels must be attached securely and conspicuously.

- Wool Products Labeling Act (1939, amended in 1980)
  This act requires that all recycled wool (any reclaimed wool fiber) must be labeled as recycled wool except when used in carpet, rugs, mats, and upholstery. The terms *wool, new wool,* and *virgin wool* refer to the unused fleece of sheep, lambs, and specialty hair fibers.

INDUSTRY STATEMENT 2.3

Fabric Vendors Are High on Hemp in Home Fashions

ATLANTA—Forget the jokes about smoking the drapes. Hemp is now a viable home furnishings fiber.

"Hemp is not such a novelty anymore. It's become mainstream as a fiber, and people are buying it for its merits," said Yitzac Goldstein, president of Hemp Tex, a division of Hemp Textiles International based in Bellingham, Wash. Hemp Tex's line of Cantiva hemp fabrics, introduced with a collection of 30 items just three years ago, now includes approximately 120 different weights, blends, and designs ranging from 2.5-ounce sheers to 10-ounce upholstery goods. The company is also expanding its line of private-label products ranging from table linens to shower curtains.

Hemp's major attractions in the market today are aesthetics, comfort, and performance, said Goldstein. "Its ecological, or 'green,' properties are selling points, but they are the fourth or fifth tier in supporting our market," he said.

While hemp's limited availability and costly processing make it relatively expensive, its price is competitive in an upscale market where bedding ensembles typically cost around $1,200 each.

Shari Bender, founder of For My Sister, based in Studio City, Calif., was first attracted to hemp because it is a natural fiber. But Bender, whose company makes hand-loomed velvet pillows, throws and table runners, also appreciated the durability and tactile appeal of the fiber. She blended hemp with silk for her new custom top-of-the-bed collection, shown in the Bausman & Co. furniture showroom at High Point market.

"People are surprised at its luxurious hand. They usually expect it to be coarser," said Bender, who plans to add to the current collection of four ensembles in three colorways coordinated with 590-count Egyptian cotton sheets.

Nicole Marshall, vice president of sales and marketing for The International Design Collection, based in Philadelphia, likes the way hemp takes to bright dyes. "You can get fantastic colors," she said. At High Point, IDC added hemp-lined trays and hand-painted and appliqued designs to her collection of brightly hued hemp decorative pillows.

Hemp's appeal as a fashion fabric only serves to enhance its attraction in the natural fiber market.

Designer Suzanne DeVall of Rancho Mirage, Calif., created her line of hemp bedding and fabrics as an integral part of the organic Indika collection of home textiles, which uses no chemicals or synthetic dyes, but includes intricate wood-block designs and textures. "It gives a choice to people who want to live naturally in their homes and be a part of the eco-friendly movement, but who still want color and design," said Devall. Other manufacturers of like mind include Earth Works of Tucson, Ariz., which makes hemp sheets and blankets and uses organic cotton in its duvets. Earth Weave Carpet Mills, in Dalton, Ga., which specializes in renewable-resource floor coverings, uses hemp in carpet and rugs.

Bean Products, a manufacturer and retailer in Chicago, makes a hemp and flax throw, along with bean bag chairs, cubes and ottomans, shower curtains, window treatments, and pillows. The company also makes knitted and woven fabrics, air-finished for softness. It just developed organic dyes using vegetables, flowers, and tree bark. And it's planning to add a collection of upholstered furniture that uses reclaimed hardwood in the frames.

Source: HFN, May 7, 2001, p. 23. Courtesy of Fairchild Publications, Inc.

TEXTILES AND THE ENVIRONMENT

The textile industry has made a commitment to address environmental and recycling issues. The American Textile Manufacturers Institute (ATMI) has encouraged over 50 textile companies to make a commitment to preserve the environment by joining its Environmental Excellence program. Companies are encouraged to recycle and to use environmentally efficient manufacturing.

❧

Charity Begins in Home for Textile Supply and Retail

Stores and Vendors Partner to Raise Money for Good Causes

Most companies have a mission statement—but some also have a mission. Louisville Bedding, for instance, has formed a corporate partnership with the Make-A-Wish Foundation, which grants wishes to critically ill children. It has developed Make-A-Wish pillows that have sold through Wal-Mart, Sears, Strouds, and BJ's Wholesale Club and donates a portion of sales to the foundation in those companies' names. Hang tags, packaging and point-of-sale materials show pictures of Make-A-Wish children with stories about their Wish experience, along with the foundation's mission statement and contact information.

BJ's also shows on the retail floor a video developed by Louisville and the Make-A-Wish Foundation. Some stores run specific back-to-school or holiday promotions, and others carry the line as part of their regular assortment, said Lisa Matusik Cook, director of merchandising for bed pillows at Louisville.

Although Cook could not give specific percentages—because they vary with each agreement—Christina Carmony, public relations manager of the Make-A-Wish Foundation, said the ongoing program has raised $39,000 in less than a year and a half.

"We're not doing this to sell more pillows," said Cook. "This makes us feel good, and it makes retailers feel good; they're giving something back to the community."

For My Sister's mission started even closer to home. Shari Bender founded the company last May after her sister Reenie, 38, was diagnosed with cancer. Beginning with luxury pillows and throws, the company has already expanded to top-of-the-bed and table linens, hand-loomed in the family's Los Angeles apparel factory. The silk velvet and rayon designs sell in high-end specialty and furniture stores at prices ranging from $250 to $1,000. Sales in the first quarter of 2000 were double 1999's entire seven months of sales. "But, apart from making an heirloom-quality product, our goal is to raise awareness," said Bender, who donates 5 percent of the company's net profits to the American Cancer Society. The society's 800 number appears on every hang tag, along with Reenie's story and a startling statistic: In the U.S. alone, half of all men and one-third of all women will get cancer in their lifetime.

Bender is not looking for mass distribution for her products—just a few good stores across the nation and around the world—and she's doing most of the marketing herself. "I'm knocking on doors," she said. "There's a story to be told, and either people get it right away, or they don't. I have been extremely moved in the short amount of time we've been in business by the response we've gotten from consumers and retailers that take a leap of faith with us."

The buying community is taking its own leap of faith—at the cash register. Eighty percent of Americans have a more positive image of companies aligned with social issues, according to the 1999 Cone/Roper Cause Related Trends Report, which surveys consumer attitudes toward cause marketing. The report also found that approximately 61 percent think cause marketing should be a standard business practice, and two-thirds, or approximately 130 million consumers, would not only switch to brands or retailers associated with a good cause if price and quality were equal, but would also pay more for the product.

"Consumers, more than ever, expect companies to stand for something, and companies are responding," said Alison DaSilva, director of cause-branding outreach for Cone Communications.

"As business people, it fits into who we are and what we do," said Harry Brown, executive vice president and general merchandise manager at Strouds, which has been with the Make-A-Wish program since its inception. "We think it is a win-win and can only be positive."

Source: *HFN*, May 8, 2000, p. 23 +. Courtesy of Fairchild Publications, Inc.

Companies are reclaiming scrap. Wellman, Inc., is the largest recycler of consumer plastics. It produces FORTREL ECOSPUN®, a heavy denier recycled staple polyester that is used for polyester carpet fiber, luggage, footwear, and apparel. Burlington Industries, in conjunction with North Carolina State University, has developed **reused denim.** This denim is 50 percent reclaimed cotton and 50 percent virgin cotton.

New developments are also being made in the finishing and coloring of textiles. Alternatives to traditional finishing detergents, cleaners, dyes, and other chemicals considered hazardous to the environment are being developed.

Companies are also using environmentally friendly products. Virgin hemp and kenaf are being sold as environmentally friendly fibers (see Industry Statement 2.3.) Sally Fox of Natural Cotton Colours, Inc. grows natural-colored cottons without using chemicals. Companies are also developing strains of cotton that can be grown without chemical insecticides or fertilizers. Cargill Dow has developed a corn-based resin that can be spun into fibers. It is biodegradable and fire resistant.

SUMMARY

The five components of textile products are fiber, yarn, fabric, coloration, and finish. Most, but not all, consumer textile products contain all five. Each component affects the performance of the textile product and, thus, affects end use suitability. Fibers are divided into two classifications—natural and manufactured. Natural fibers include cellulosic fibers, such as cotton and linen, and protein fibers such as silk and wool. Yarns may be classified as filament or spun. Yarns are also classified as single, ply, or cord. Novelty yarns add textural interest to textile products. Most fabrics are either woven or knit. Wovens are created by the interlacing of yarns and knits are created by the interlooping of yarns. Nonwovens lack a yarn structure. Dyes and pigments are used to add color to textiles. Dyes bond chemically with the fiber; pigments are not absorbed into the fiber. Finishes modify the properties of a textile product and are classified as preparatory, aesthetic, and functional.

TERMS FOR REVIEW

abrasion resistance	crimp	filament yarns
aesthetic finishes	crock	filling knits
animal fiber	cross section	filling yarns
back	derivative cellulosics	finish
balanced weave	diameter	flexibility
bast fibers	dimensional stability	floats
bleed	drape	frost
blending	dry prints	fume fading
carded yarns	durable finishes	functional finishes
cellulosic fibers	dyes	generic name
chemical finishes	elastic recovery	glazing
coloration	elongation	grain
colorfast	fabric	greige fabric
combing	face	hand
cord yarn	fade	hydrophilic fibers
courses	fiber	hydrophobic fibers
cover	fiberfill	inorganic fibers

TERMS FOR REVIEW *(continued)*

jersey knits	product/garment dyeing	synthetic fibers
knits	protein fibers	temporary finishes
knitting	raschel	tenacity (fiber strength)
linen	regenerated cellulosics	textured filament yarns
luster	regenerated fibers	thermoplastic
manufactured cellulosics	resiliency (wrinkle recovery)	thread count
manufactured fibers	resins	trade names
mechanical finishes	reused denim	tricot
mineral fiber	sateens	tufting
monofilament yarns	satins	twill weave
multifilament yarns	satin weave	wales
natural fiber	scavenge colors	warp knits
nonwovens	selvages	warp yarns
novelty yarn	set	weaving
on-grain	single knits	weft knits
permanent finishes	single yarn	wet prints
piece dyeing	solution dyeing	woolen yarns
pigments	specific gravity (density)	worsted yarns
plain weave	spinneret	wovens
plant fiber	spun yarns	yarn
plumage	stitch-through fabrics	yarn dyeing
ply yarn	stock (fiber) dyeing	
preparatory finishes	surface contour	

REVIEW QUESTIONS

1. List the five components of textile products.
2. List four natural fibers and four manufactured fibers.
3. What is the difference between filament yarns and spun yarns?
4. List the three basic weaves.
5. What are the two main categories of knits?
6. List two ways the textile industry has addressed environmental and recycling issues.

LEARNING ACTIVITIES

1. Visit a large fabric store. Select five different fabrics. List the following information for each: fabric, name of fabric, brief description of fabric (color, hand, weight, etc.), country of origin, fiber content, price, care instructions. Suggest two end uses for each fabric and justify your suggestions.
2. List two finishes that you would recommend for each of the following items. Justify your choices: wool carpeting, sheer white nylon curtains, cotton upholstery for a family room, formal linen tablecloth and matching napkins.

CHAPTER 3

&

WOOD

To use wood wisely, one wants to know how it grows, works, looks, feels, weathers, shrinks, swells, smells, and rots. Wood is alive and evocative, and we are connected to it in thousands of ways. When we are worried, we touch wood, and it touches us. It has always been a material at hand and a material of choice.

William McDonough, Learning to be Nature's Tool, *Interiors,* February 2000

Other materials are more durable, lighter, and cheaper, but wood trumps them all with its perpetual flicker of life. It breathes even under coats of paint or varnish, and its malleability, making it easy to bend, and carve, is like the limberness of trees them- selves. Woods are individual, both as a species and as specimens with unique patterns of grain and benign imperfections. Light embellishes their nicks and chinks and often seems to glow from within.

Julie Lasky, Pulp Psychology, *Interiors,* February 2000

WOOD PRODUCTS ARE USED EXTENSIVELY IN HOME FURNISHINGS. WOOD HAS BEEN USED FOR centuries to create furniture, flooring, cabinets, and paneling. Beautiful wallpapers, stationery, and packaging are other examples of end uses for wood. This chapter presents characteristics of selected types of wood and briefly discusses production methods used to create wood products.

Aesthetically, the grain, texture, and color of wood add warmth and beauty to the home. The natural beauty of wood can be enhanced by turning, carving, staining, and polishing. **Turning** is the process of making round pieces of wood to be used as bedposts, stair railings, and legs of fur- niture. Figure 3.1 is an example of turned bedposts.

Wood is the most frequently used building material for several reasons: it has excellent strength in relation to its weight; it retains its shape under pressure; and it resists breaking when subjected to bending and pulling forces. The tensile strength (resistance to pulling or tearing forces) of wood

FIGURE 3.1
Turned bed posts.
Courtesy of Fairchild Publications, Inc.

is very good parallel to the grain, but weaker perpendicular to the grain. The compression strength (resistance to compression) of wood is good parallel to the grain, but weaker perpendicular to the grain. Because wood is slightly resilient, it is ideal for flooring and furniture.

The main disadvantages of wood are that it burns, rots, decays, and can be attacked by insects. It also swells, shrinks, and warps as it absorbs and loses moisture, especially if it is not properly treated. **Warping** is the bending or twisting out of shape of a flat surface. Warping can cause floors to become uneven or doors to not close properly. There are four types of warping: bow, cup, crook, and twist. These are illustrated in Figure 3.2.

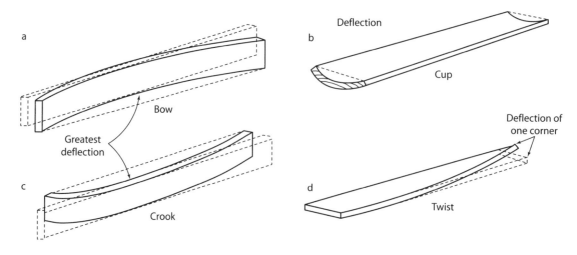

FIGURE 3.2 *Types of warp.*

Wood is also a major source for creating manufactured cellulosic fibers used in home furnishings. It is used to create fibers such as rayon, lyocell, acetate, and triacetate. These fibers are used in upholstery, slipcovers, drapes, and bedding.

TREES

Trees are an important natural resource. They grow slowly, and it can take as many as 35 to 50 years before a tree is large enough to be harvested. Some slow-growing varieties of hardwood trees can take as long as 75–125 years to reach economic maturity.

Parts of a Tree Trunk

The cross section of a tree trunk in Figure 3.3 shows the **annual ring**, which is the layer of wood produced by one year's growth. In addition, there are six basic parts:

1. **Bark**—the protective covering of the tree.
2. **Cambium layer**—a sticky substance found between the bark and the sapwood. It is composed of living cells and creates the new wood, usually late in summer.
3. **Sapwood**—newly formed outer wood that is lighter in color and contains more moisture than the heartwood.
4. **Heartwood**—the center of the tree. It is inactive and darker in color. It takes longer to season (cure), contains less water, and takes longer to absorb wood preservatives than sapwood. It is more durable than sapwood and is used for fine wood products.
5. **Pith**—core of the tree trunk.
6. **Medullary rays**—thin cellular lines that extend to the outside of the wood.

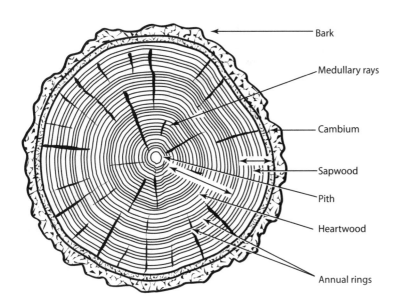

Bark

Medullary rays

Cambium

Sapwood

Pith

Heartwood

Annual rings

FIGURE 3.3
Cross section of a tree trunk.

Classifications of Trees

There are two main classifications of trees. Broadleaf trees are also called **hardwoods,** and conifers are sometimes referred to as **softwoods.** These terms refer to the botanical characteristics of the tree and not the hardness or softness of the wood.

Broadleaf Trees

Most **broadleaf trees** are **deciduous.** These trees, except the southern oak, shed their flat, broad leaves in the fall. (See Figure 3.4.) Because of their thicker cell walls, broadleaf trees are more durable and have a more pleasing grain than softwoods. They hold glue, nails, or screws more securely and are frequently used for furniture. They also take a polish better and do not burn as quickly as softwoods. The term *hardwood* is misleading, however, because some softwoods are actually harder than hardwoods. Table 3.1 summarizes the characteristics of common hardwood trees.

FIGURE 3.4 *Broadleaf trees.*

TABLE 3.I
Characteristics of Common Hardwoods

Hardwoods	Characteristics	End Uses	Where Grown
Alder	Uniform grain; lightweight, but not very strong; resists denting, abrasion; shrinks little; stains well	Chairs and other furniture	North Temperate Zone
Ash	Straight grain; good strength; hard; firm; intermediate in warping; good bending qualities; moderate weight; white in color	Cutting blocks, cabinet work, furniture frames, exposed parts of less expensive furniture	Europe, North America, Asia
Beech	Very strong, dense, hard; warps, shrinks, subject to dry rot; reddish brown in color; rag marks (small dark dashes); good for turning, polishes well	Cabinetmaking, furniture, flooring, woodware, handles and veneers (especially good for wooden food containers because it does not impart taste to the food)	North America and Europe
Birch (also known as yellow birch, silver birch, and sweet birch)	One of the strongest, hardest woods; little shrinking or warping; yellow to reddish brown in color; close-grained; durable; tends to warp; can be stained to imitate mahogany or walnut	Veneer for furniture and doors, flooring, upholstery frames, high-grade plywood, paneling, marquetry	North America, Europe, Asia
Ebony	Very dark brown (may have orange streaks); hard; heavy; very fine texture	Piano keys, ornaments, knife handles, parts of musical instruments, inlaid work, sometimes available as a veneer for repair of antiques	Japan, Philippines, India, Africa, Madagascar (North and South American ebony has little commercial value)
Fruitwoods (apple, cherry, olive, pear)	Fine, straight, close grain; cherry has natural luster; carves and polishes well; excellent for turning and carving	Ornaments, decorative veneers, furniture	Temperate Zone
Gumwood Red Gum	Medium strength, weight and shrinkage; rosy in color with a smooth grain pattern; easily split and dented; susceptible to decay; finishes well	A leading wood for unexposed parts of high-end furniture and exposed parts of low-end furniture	Sourthern Hemisphere
Black Gum (also called tupelo)	White-gray to gray-brown in color; heavier, harder, and has greater tendency to warp than red gum	Unexposed furniture parts	
Hickory	Strong; tough; good resilience; coarse texture	Handles for hammers, etc., sporting equipment	North America
Mahogany*	Light reddish brown in color; durable; strong; resists warping and shrinking; smooth surface; easy to work with; takes polish well	Paneling, ornaments, furniture	Latin America, Africa (see note)

continued

TABLE 3.1 *continued*

Characteristics of Common Hardwoods

Hardwoods	Characteristics	End Uses	Where Grown
Maple**			Northern Hemisphere
Hard Maple (also called rock, sugar, or northern maple)	Light in color; smooth surface; close grained; hard (does not dent easily); heavy; little shrinking or swelling if seasoned properly; hard to work; takes good polish; excellent for turning	Furniture, paneling, shoe lasts, croquet ball, bowling pins, flooring	
Soft Maple (also called soft or red maple)	Light in color; good for turning; less close grained than hard maple; not as strong or heavy as hard maple	Construction, flooring, furniture, paneling, decorative veneers	
Oak			Northern Hemisphere
White Oak	Durable	Flooring, furniture, wall panels, decorative veneers, parquet construction, (but not suitable for exterior use)	
Red Oak	Resilient; pale colored; coarse grained; hard; strong; splinters easily; carves well; (both white and red oak have similar characteristics except that red oak has a reddish tint)		
Rosewood	Dark reddish black in color; very durable; strong; takes high polish	Highest-quality furniture and cabinetmaking, parquet flooring, wood sculpture, carving, veneer, inlays	Brazil, Central America, Southern Asia, Madagascar
Teak	Durable, heavy; rich brown or golden brown in color; coarse textured; oily to the touch; carves well; takes oil finish well	Fine furniture, boat building, cabinetmaking	Southeast Asia
Walnut			Northern Hemisphere
Black Walnut (also called American walnut)	Dark brown to purple-black in color; resists warping; very durable; very strong; coarse texture; hard; heavy; takes finish well; good for turning and carving	High-quality furniture, cabinetmaking, decorative veneers, paneling	
White Walnut (also known as butternut)	Medium brown (not as dark as black walnut); softer than black walnut; coarse texture; carves well; resistant to shrinking and warping; takes polish well; good for carving	Substitute for black walnut in furniture and paneling, decorative veneer	

Note: In general, hardwoods are harder to work with than softwoods. They can dull cutting equipment and sometimes require boring before nailing.

*Most mahogany comes from Latin America or Africa. Mahogany from Africa should be labeled as African mahogany. Tanquile, or Philippine mahogany, is not a true mahogany. It is soft and lightweight with an open grain. It is considered to be poor quality wood.

**Bird's eye maple is a maple veneer with a distinctive grain pattern. Curly and wavy maple veneers are also available.

Coniferous Trees

Coniferous trees have needlelike leaves. With the exception of the cypress and the larch, they do not shed their leaves in the fall (see Figure 3.5). The cells of softwoods are thinner than those of hardwoods. Table 3.2 summarizes the characteristics of common softwoods. Softwoods are frequently used in construction, in paper production, and in the manufacture of inexpensive furniture. See Industry Statement 3.1 for discussion of a company using cedar for outdoor furniture.

PROCESSING WOOD

After a tree is felled, or cut down, the tree goes through a series of processes to make it into a product suitable for use in the building or furniture trade. The steps in the processing of wood are:

1. Cutting, or felling, the tree
2. Debarking
3. Sawing into lumber, timber, or veneer
4. Seasoning
5. Sizing and surfacing
6. Grading

LUMBER

After a tree is cut down, the bark is removed from the log and then cut into desired widths. **Lumber** is wood that has been sawn into boards.

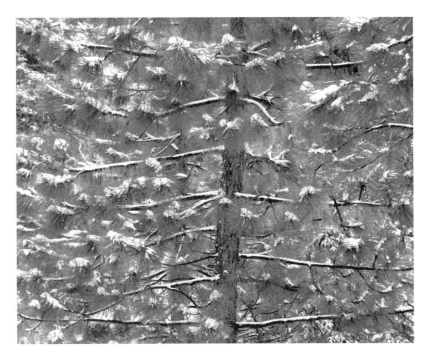

FIGURE 3.5
Coniferous trees.

TABLE 3.2
Characteristics of Common Softwoods

Softwoods	Characteristics	End Uses	Where Grown
Cedar			
Western Red Cedar	Soft; weak; lightweight; close-grained; decay resistant; pungent spicy odor; light brown in color; holds nails well; low stiffness; easy to work	Shingles and siding of houses; paneling; porch and trellis columns; cabinet work; interior paneling; some outdoor furniture	NOTE: True cedar trees grow in Africa and Asia. True cedars are the deodar tree (India), atlas cedar (North Africa), and cedar of Lebanon (Asia). The western red cedar and white cedar are actually juniper trees. They grow in North America.
Aromatic, or Eastern Red Cedar	Similar to western red cedar except that the wood contains an oil that kills moths	Especially useful in closets and chests to repel moths	North America
Cypress	Moderately strong; resists decay; lightweight	Doors, window sashes, siding, shingles, porch materials	North America, Europe, and Asia
Fir	Warp resistant; light color; lightweight; easy to work; moderate strength; knots may loosen; tends to check and split; does not sand or paint well	Plywood for exterior and interior walls, doors, cabinet work, trim, and interior finishing; flooring; low-cost furniture; top-quality fir for cabinets, bookcases	Cooler parts of the North Temperate Zone (North America, Europe, and Asia)
Pine			
Northern White Pine (also called western white pine and sugar pine)	Lightweight; soft; even-textured; relatively weak; easy to work; resistant to shrinkage, warping, and swelling; decays on contact with earth; pale color	Core for veneers; construction; unpainted furniture; interior trim	Subarctic zones to subtropic zones
Yellow Pine	Similar to northern pine, but somewhat harder; ideal for carving	Flooring, woodware, furniture, general carpentry	
Redwood	Moderately strong; fine grained; light red to mahogany in color; resistant to insects; resistant to decay; soft; splinters easily	Outdoor furniture; long-term construction, such as farm structures, towers	Northern California and Oregon
Spruce	Even textured; easy to use; creamy white in color; medium strength	Cabinetwork; scaffolding; fencing; papermaking	Northern Hemisphere

---

INDUSTRY STATEMENT 3.1

Whatever Floats Your Boat

It makes perfect sense: What better wood to use for making outdoor furniture than the same wood that's been used in boat-making for years? This was the idea of Peter Caporilli, founder and chief executive of Tidewater Workshop. Caporilli had the idea of building outdoor furniture that would bridge the gap between low-end resin furniture and pricey teak and metal offerings. He had to look no further than the cedar that his family had been using for generations in their custom skiff-building business.

"Cedar has the look and feel of teak, and it grows very fast, so it's an incredibly renewable resource," says Caporilli. But most important, it's used to make boats for a reason: it's durable, water-resistant, and weathers well.

Consumers who can't afford teak will like the prices of Tidewater's cedar furniture. "A set of our furniture retails for $400 to $700," says Caporilli. The company mainly sells via its Web site, www.tidewaterworkshop.com, its 20-page catalog, and its toll-free number. All the furniture has been designed to be shipped via United Parcel Service.

With its new 10,000-square-foot manufacturing facility and corporate headquarters, which opened last month in Egg Harbor City, N.J., the company is ready to expand its distribution.

"We're looking to sell to other retailers, like small garden centers and pool and patio stores," says Caporilli.

Caporilli launched the company in 1991 when he was only 29, and already it's expected to have revenues of $10 million this year. He was included in *Business News New Jersey's* "Young and Ambitious 40 Under 40" last year.

Source: Highpoints, June 2000, p. 5. Courtesy of Fairchild Publications, Inc.

Sawing

The two principal methods of making lumber from trees are **plain sawing** and **quarter sawing.** Each method creates a different **grain.** Grain is the pattern made by the annual rings in the sawed wood. The advantages of plain and quarter sawing are summarized in Table 3.3.

Plain sawing is illustrated in Figure 3.6. After each cut the log is rotated, so additional cuts can be made on each side of the log. The annual rings are at an angle to the surface of the lumber. This method makes efficient use of the log, and the resulting lumber has an arch-shaped grain pattern. Plain-sawn lumber is prone to warping.

TABLE 3.3

Comparison of Plain- and Quarter-Sawn Lumber

Plain-Sawn	Quarter-Sawn
More lumber obtained from the tree	Less twisting or winding
Easier to cut	Less warping
Less expensive to produce	Less shrinkage
Easier to season	More durable because the hard annual rings are exposed and protect the softer new growth
	Fewer blemishes after seasoning

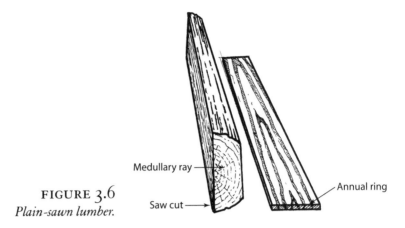

FIGURE 3.6
Plain-sawn lumber.

Quarter Sawing

Quarter sawing is illustrated in Figure 3.7. In this method the log is cut into lengthwise quarters called *flitches.* Each quarter is then sawed at right angles to the annual ring. The resulting lumber has a straight grain that may have designs, known as *flakes,* going across the face of the grain. Because this method yields less lumber, it is not used as frequently as plain sawing. Quarter-sawn lumber does not warp as readily as plain-sawn lumber, and it is more expensive than plain-sawn wood.

Seasoning

Seasoning, or **curing,** lumber is the process of removing moisture from the lumber. All lumber is subject to shrinkage and expansion across the grain as it absorbs or loses moisture. The shrinkage or expansion can result in warping, checking, or splitting of the wood. **Checking** is the formation of small checks on the surface of the wood.

There are two methods of seasoning lumber—**air-drying** and **kiln-drying.**

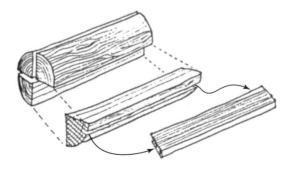

FIGURE 3.7
Quarter-sawn lumber.

Air-Drying

Air-dried wood is simply allowed to dry naturally in the open air. Months or years may be required to complete the drying process. Because the air-dried wood retains up to 18 to 20 percent of its moisture content, it is only suitable for products not affected by warping, checking, or splitting.

Kiln-Drying

When kiln-drying, the lumber is placed in large temperature- and humidity-controlled ovens for one to two days. Kiln-dried wood retains less moisture (four to eight percent) than air-dried wood and is preferred for use in furniture and in centrally heated buildings. Hardwoods must be kiln-dried for most furniture uses.

Sizing and Surfacing

Strips, boards, dimension, and **timbers** are the size classifications used for solid wood lumber. The classifications are summarized in Table 3.4. These sizes are commonly used in the building and furniture industries. Because lumber is finished by planing (smoothing) and sanding after cutting, the final dimensions of the piece will be 3/16 inch less in thickness and 3/8 inch less in width. Hardwoods are sold in their rough state. They are not planed or sanded.

Grading

High-grade lumber has fewer imperfections than lower-grade lumber. Knots, splits, spots, and discolorations reduce the value of lumber. The standard grades of lumber are listed in Table 3.5. Lumber for use in construction has different grade names for higher-quality materials.

SOLID WOOD

Solid wood offers the consumer beauty and function. It can be carved or turned, and the surface cannot loosen or peel off. Edges of furniture maintain the beauty of the wood, as opposed to veneered wood that can expose the layers of the veneer. (See the section on Veneer Construction).

TABLE 3.4
Size Classifications for Solid Wood Lumber

Classification	Dimensions
Strips	Less than 2″ thick and less than 6″ wide
Boards	Less than 2″ thick and 2+″ wide
Dimension	All lumber of any width with thickness from 2″ up to, but not including, 5″
Timbers	Any lumber measuring at least 5″ in the smallest dimension

TABLE 3.5
Standard Grades of Lumber

Hardwood Lumber	Softwood Lumber
Top Quality	Select
Firsts	Minor defects
Seconds	B
Second quality	C
Selects	D
No. 1 Common	Lower quality
Poorer quality	No. 1 Common
No. 2 Common	No. 2 Common
No. 3A Common	No. 3 Common
No. 3B Common	No. 4 Common

In case of damage, the surface can be refinished if the product is made of solid wood. The major disadvantages of solid wood are the high cost and the tendency to warp, shrink, or swell.

VENEER AND VENEER CONSTRUCTION

Veneer is wood that has been cut into very thin strips. Woods used for veneers are called **cabinet woods,** and they come from around the world. The most commonly used cabinet woods are ash, birch, maple, pecan, rosewood, walnut, and mahogany from the Philippines and Honduras (see Figure 3.8).

FIGURE 3.8 *Mahogany veneer.* Courtesy of Restoration Hardware.

Veneer Construction

Veneering is the method of gluing thin slices of wood over less expensive woods or other core products. Recent developments in adhesives have made the veneering process more satisfactory than in the past. Inappropriate use of adhesive can cause cracking, chipping, and loosening of the veneer. The thickness of the veneer strips can range from 3/16 inch to 1/200 inch. Veneers of 1/28 inch are commonly used in furniture. After the bark is removed, the logs are soaked or steamed, and then the thin strips of wood are rotary cut, half-round sliced, flat sliced, quarter sliced, or rift cut.

Rotary-cut veneers are sliced off a rolling log and create bold, variegated grain markings. The grain appears as a large cone called a *parabola*. Rotary-cut veneer is exceptionally wide and is used for plywood paneling, plywood packing boxes, and the hidden parts of furniture (see Figure 3.9a).

Half-round sliced veneers are cut from a log that has been cut in half and then revolved against the cutting blade. The resulting grain resembles rotary-cut veneer. Half-round sliced veneers are used for furniture surfaces and interiors (see Figure 3.9b).

Flat-sliced veneers are also made from logs that have been cut in half. The blade moves across the cut edge of the log. The resulting veneer has a center parabola with straight grain on either side (see Figure 3.9c).

Quarter-sliced veneers are cut from a log that has been cut into quarters. The log is sliced at right angles to the annual rings of the wood. The resulting grain is striped and may be straight or varied. Quarter-sliced veneer is the most costly and used for fine furniture and other wood products (see Figure 3.9d).

Rift-cut veneer is produced in oak. The comb grain effect is made by cutting perpendicular to the medullary rays (see Figure 3.9e).

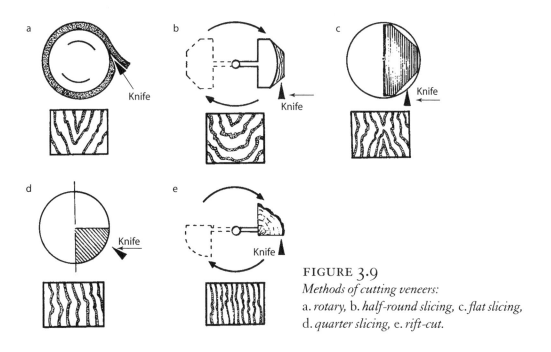

FIGURE 3.9
Methods of cutting veneers:
a. *rotary,* b. *half-round slicing,* c. *flat slicing,*
d. *quarter slicing,* e. *rift-cut.*

Specialized Veneer Patterns

Some special veneer patterns come from specific parts of a tree (see Figure 3.10). These include the **burl,** a small round or oval marking caused by unusual growths on a tree; the **crotch,** a V-shaped pattern caused by branches extending from a tree; and the **stump,** a swirled-grain pattern from the stump of the tree.

Other common veneer patterns include:

- **Bird's Eye** Tiny markings in the wood thought to be caused by undeveloped buds
- **Fiddleback** Fine wavy lines that run crosswise at right angles to the regular grain, seen in mahogany and maple
- **Mottle** Blurred figure created by the grain
- **Stripe** Straight-line effects in shadings of dark and light, seen in walnut and mahogany

Matching Veneer Patterns

Intricate patterns can be created when veneer patterns are matched. Sheets of veneer are carefully stacked after cutting so that adjacent pieces can be positioned edge-to-edge. Products with matched veneer patterns are very costly. Examples of matching effects are shown in Figure 3.11.

Plywood

Plywood is made using veneer construction. Thin layers of wood are bonded together, so the grains run at right angles to each other as shown in Figure 3.12. Fir and pine are used for common plywood. Plywood resists warping and cracking because the grains pull in opposing directions. Plywood comes in several thicknesses; it may be three, five, seven, or more layers (or plies) thick. Five-ply plywood is the most common. More plies indicate greater strength. Common plywood is used in interior and exterior construction and for flat, unexposed surfaces of lower-end furniture. It is measured by length, width, and thickness.

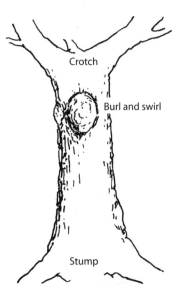

FIGURE 3.10
Location of veneer patterns on a tree.

DIFFERENT WAYS OF MATCHING VENEERS

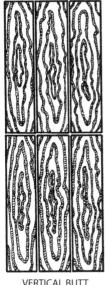

VERTICAL BUTT
AND HORIZONTAL
BOOKLEAF MATCH

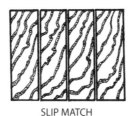

BOOK MATCH

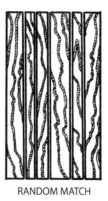

RANDOM MATCH

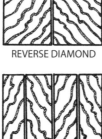

SLIP MATCH

SPECIAL MATCHING EFFECTS

DIAMOND   REVERSE DIAMOND

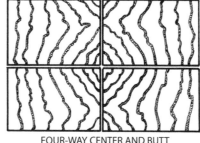

FOUR-WAY CENTER AND BUTT

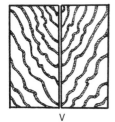

V   HERRINGBONE

FIGURE 3.11
Matching veneers.

Veneer plywood is available in six grades: N, A, B, C, C plugged, and D. The highest grade of veneer plywood is designated as N. It is all heartwood, free from defects, and must be special ordered. The highest-quality veneer that is available as a standard plywood is Grade A. The face of Grade A plywood can be joined or repaired. The lower grades have more imperfections.

Laminated Wood

Laminated wood is similar to plywood except that the grains of the laminated wood panels do not run at right angles to each other. Usually laminates are bonded with plastic resins and compressed to eliminate warping. See Figure 3.13 for an example of furniture made of laminated beech.

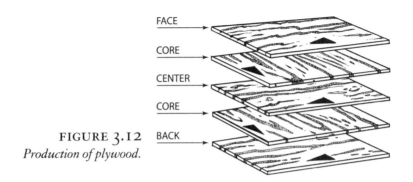

FIGURE 3.12
Production of plywood.

ORNAMENTING AND FINISHING WOOD

The natural grain of wood provides its own ornamentation. Roughly sawn wood has a very rustic appearance and is usually used for exteriors. Resawn wood is smoother but does not emphasize the grain. Smoothly finished wood reflects light, is smooth to the touch, and emphasizes the grain.

Wood can also be turned and carved. Refer back to Figure 3.1 for an example of turned wood. See Figure 3.14 for an example of carved wood.

Inlay

Inlay, intarsia, marquetry, and **parquetry** are additional ways to enhance the beauty of wood. The term *inlay* refers to all the techniques used to combine different woods, metals, ivory, and other materials, so the patterns are relatively smooth. Parquetry, marquetry, and intarsia are examples of inlay. Parquet is a mosaic of wood used for flooring. See Figure 3.15 for examples of

FIGURE 3.13 *Furniture made of laminated beech.* Courtesy of Fairchild Publications, Inc.

FIGURE 3.14
Carved detail.
Courtesy of Fairchild Publications, Inc.

common parquet patterns. Marquetry refers to inlaid design, especially in furniture. Colored woods are inlaid in veneers and then glued to a solid backing. Intarsia is a special technique in which the pieces are inlaid in solid wood. This technique was developed during the Renaissance period in Italy.

Wood Finishes

Finishes protect and beautify wood. They provide protection from dirt, stains, rot, decay, and insects. They also minimize the effect of moisture. Most woods benefit from the application of a finish, of which many are available. Some finishes enhance the grain; others provide a surface that is easy to clean. Table 3.6 lists some common finishes for wood. Wood can also be treated to make it resistant to the effects of weather. For example, pressure-treated wood resists rotting but is prone to twisting.

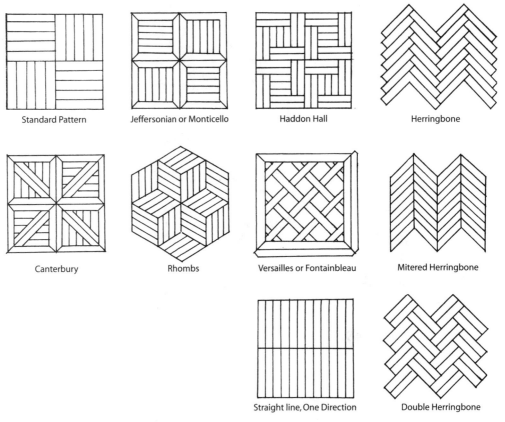

Standard Pattern   Jeffersonian or Monticello   Haddon Hall   Herringbone

Canterbury   Rhombs   Versailles or Fontainbleau   Mitered Herringbone

Straight line, One Direction   Double Herringbone

FIGURE 3.15 *Common parquet patterns.*

HARDBOARD AND PARTICLEBOARD

Hardboard and **particleboard** are low-end substitutes for wood. They are used in inexpensive furniture and other products traditionally made of wood. Both are created from wood fibers such as sawdust and wood chips.

Hardboard

Hardboard was originally made by William Mason in Mississippi in 1924. Masonite® is a common trade name for hardboard. The wood fibers are bonded with **lignin,** the natural bonding substance found in wood. Hardboard is available in standard widths, thicknesses, and lengths. The advantage of hardboard is that it has no grain, so it does not warp, chip, or peel. It is also free from defects, so there is no need for patching.

End uses for hardboard include low-end furniture, cores for veneers, and plastic laminates. Hardboard decorative panels are used for paneling, screens, and room dividers.

TABLE 3.6
Common Wood Finishes

Finish	Effect	Use
Bleach	Lightens wood, usually makes grain less conspicuous; wood loses some of its luster; may not be permanent	To make interior wood paneling and furniture pale, blond; give weathered look to outdoor furniture and siding
Enamel	Durable; hard; usually glossy, but may be dull; wide range of colors	Primarily used for furniture, cabinets, and walls that get hard use and washing; may be used on floors
Lacquer	Hard, durable coating; resistant to heat, acids; may be glossy, satiny, or dull	Transparent lacquer on furniture, cabinetry, and walls; opaque lacquer on furniture
Oil	Protective but not conspicuous; very durable finish with soft luster; darkens and yellows wood; must be renewed	For indoor and outdoor furniture and on siding
Paint	Opaque coating that hides the character of the wood; may be glossy to dull	Widely used on exterior and interior walls and furniture
Shellac	Very little change to character of wood; soft satiny finish to high gloss finish; wears poorly; affected by heat and moisture; retains water spots	Primarily a quick-drying undercoat
Stain	Changes color of wood without covering the grain; often emphasizes the grain; usually darkens wood	To alter color of furniture woods; used outdoors to compensate for weathering
Synthetics	Durable; long lasting; resistant to abrasion, chemicals, and water; may be clear or colored, and dull to glossy	Good when abrasion, moisture, or weathering is a problem; used on exterior and interior walls, floors, furniture
Varnish	Thin, durable brownish coating with little penetration; darkens the wood and emphasizes the grain; can be dull to high gloss	Usually used on furniture and interior walls and floors
Wax	Darkens, emphasizes the grain; soft to high luster; must be renewed often; may show water spots and make floors slippery; other finishes may not be used over wax	Generally an easily renewed finish over a more durable undercoat; durable wax finishes also available for use on walls, floors, furniture

Particleboard

Particleboard is made of wood chips bonded by adhesives. The wood chips may be of any size and from any type of wood. Particleboard is available in standard widths, thicknesses, and lengths, as well as many strengths and textures. It has the same advantages as hardboard, but it can also be painted, finished, and veneered. End uses for particleboard include cores for veneers, plastic laminates for countertops, and low-end furniture, paneling, and shelving.

BAMBOO, RATTAN, AND WICKER

While not traditionally included in discussion of wood, bamboo, rattan, and wicker have a place in the raw materials used for furniture and home accessories production.

Bamboo

Bamboo is a large tropical grass that resembles grass or cornstalks. There are 500 to 1000 varieties of bamboo, and most grow in tropical Asia. Some grow only a few feet in height, and some grow as tall as 120 feet with a width of 12 inches. The stems are smooth, hollow, and jointed, and most are straight and slender. It takes less than a year for a stalk to reach maturity.

Bamboo is very strong and has a density similar to that of hardwoods. Colors range from white to black, but most varieties are green while growing and turn golden when dry. Bamboo can be used for furniture, screens, lattices, and baskets. Indigenous Asian people saw it into sections for use as rafters and posts for houses.

Rattan

Rattan is made from a climbing plant found in Southeast Asia. It grows to lengths of 600 feet, and the diameter can range from 1/8 inch to 2 inches. There are several hundred varieties of rattan, some of which are used to make furniture (see Figure 3.16). Unlike bamboo, which

FIGURE 3.16 *Rattan lounge chair.* Courtesy of Fairchild Publications, Inc.

is hollow, rattan is solid. Cane is the stem of large rattans. It is naturally yellow, lightweight, and sturdy.

The term *reed* is sometimes used to refer to the cores of the rattan vine. More commonly it refers to items made by weaving swamp grasses. Early American wicker chairs are made from reed.

Wicker

The term *wicker* refers to a classification of furniture that is woven from a variety of materials, such as rattan, bamboo, reed, and willow (see Figure 3.17). Willow is grown in northern Europe and North America. It is light, durable, and because it retains its natural moisture, it is easy to weave. Wicker furniture is commonly made from rattan.

WOOD AND THE ENVIRONMENT

In the United States public concerns about ecology, recreational use of forests and conservation of resources have caused increased protection of timberlands and rain forest woods.

FIGURE 3.17 *Wicker chair.* Photo provided by Maine Cottage.

INDUSTRY STATEMENT 3.2

Learning to Be Nature's Tool

Start talking to any designer about wood and you will hear stories. Knowing enough about the qualities of various species of wood to speak of them intelligently is a rite of passage and a sign of experience. To use wood wisely, one wants to know how it grows, works, looks, feels, weathers, shrinks, swells, smells, and rots. Wood is alive and evocative, and we are connected to it in thousands of ways. When we are worried, we touch wood, and it touches us. It has always been a material at hand and a material of choice; you hold some wood in your hand at this very moment. But now that the world of images can bring us images of the world, we can see in an instant that it is time to reconsider the value of every tree.

What do you see when you see a tree? Commercial foresters see stumpage, while wood-turners see bowls. Ecologists, botanists, and biologists see complex habitats, while chemists see carbon dioxide transformed into carbohydrates and oxygen. Parents see delightful neighborhoods and a place for children to play as elders sit in the shade and talk. Mathematicians see fractal patterns, while landscape architects see color and shape. Interior designers see mahogany and lacewood, while environmentalists see clearcuts, soil erosion, global warming, and genocide. Oren Lyons, a friend and faithkeeper of the Onondaga tribe in New York State, once opened a lecture to my class at the University of Virginia with the words, "What you people call your natural resources, my people call our relatives." There's a lot to see in a tree, and everything is relative.

My grandfather was a lumberjack in the Olympic Peninsula in Washington State. At that time, loggers were still hunting the giant cedars because there were a few left. Although I lived in Hong Kong, I spent wonderful childhood summers playing in the Douglas firs around my grandparents' cabin. Every year I would single-handedly chop down the alder grove with my little hatchet like a miniature Paul Bunyan. Soon I would begin to grow into the world of human industry and forests: clearcuts, pulp plantations, selective harvesting and high-grading, paddy agriculture, burning forests for a few cattle for a few years. It was a utilitarian world; wood was there for humans to use, and trees were either wonderfully useful or simple weeds in the way of some other human desire. Couldn't this go on forever?

In 1980 I heard about the Menomonee tribe of forest people native to Wisconsin. They had persevered in keeping a quarter million acres of diverse forest healthy with the same mix of species for 140 years—all the while maintaining a commercial logging and mill operation. I found out how they did it: they made narrow harvest cuts through the forests, along the contour lines, thereby maintaining all the arboreal and terrestrial animal habitats. This also allowed the trees to fill in and replace themselves naturally without planting or the introduction of foreign species. In fact, after 140 years of logging, stumpage had been increased. This was a sustaining forestry, unlike everything we see in the world of conventional industrial forestry technique.

Sustainable Forests

Appropriate forest management in recent years has insured that annual growth of timber exceeds yearly consumption of wood for lumber. Several organizations, such as American Forest & Paper Association's Sustainable Forest Initiative (SFI), certify that forests are sustainably managed. Unfortunately, much of the supply of high-quality cabinet-grade woods has not been managed and is deteriorating. Because the use of trees for lumber increases as economic status rises, many developing areas of the world will need to assess their commitment to conservation and pollution control. See Industry Statement 3.2 for a discussion of how people relate to wood.

Use of **reclaimed wood** has increased. Particleboard and hardboard made from sawdust and wood chips are examples of reclaimed wood being processed into useable products. Manufactur-

INDUSTRY STATEMENT 3.2

Learning to Be Nature's Tool *(continued)*

We are now at a watershed moment in our use of wood. Modern culture is realizing that it has been timefully mindless about the fate of the forests. We have been in a hurry; we want our wood tomorrow, whatever the price, and we don't really care where it came from. But know this: mahogany does not, for all intents and purposes, ever come from sustainable sources. There was a film about mahogany shown a few years ago in the UK called "Your Furniture, Their Lives," equating tropical forestry with genocide. Monocultural plantations, on the other hand, do not encourage biodiversity. Even the famous mantra of the environmental movement, eco-efficiency, can't save us. It says to Mitsubishi, "Please make twice as many cardboard boxes out of the trees in Indonesia." It may slow down the destruction and increase profits in the short run, but the story hasn't changed; it's still "Good-bye Indonesia" or Oregon or British Columbia. Perhaps it's time to become timelessly mindful about the fate of the forests.

The ecological sciences are relatively young. We have only begun to factor the complex interactions and interdependencies of the natural world into the human utilitarian framework. As we move away from urgent daily concerns for basic survival, we can reflect on opportunities to use human intelligence instead of brute force and "raw" or "virgin" materials. We can reflect as well, on our spiritual connections with the inspiring cathedral of the forest, and even deepen our response to the world with the humble revelation of our love for a favorite tree.

About the current loss of rainforests in British Columbia (which enables us to read the Sunday *New York Times*), I paraphrase Margaret Atwood's devastating remark: "We inscribe our history on the skin of salmon with the blood of bears."

The challenge is here now. The tree is a model and metaphor for a new design protocol that honors nature's highly successful systems. We are trying to design buildings that act like trees. Imagine this design assignment: design something that makes oxygen, fixes nitrogen, sequesters carbon dioxide, accrues solar energy for food and fuel, makes complex sugars, distills water, provides habitat for thousands of species, changes with the seasons, builds soil, creates microclimates, and self-replicates. Where is a building as intelligent as a honey locust? There might be one at Oberlin College, in Oberlin, Ohio, thanks to David Orr, Nancy Dye, and Adam Lewis.

As we move from Le Corbusier's "the house is a machine for living in" toward biologist John Todd's idea of a "living machine," we must remember that our choice of tools and material flows sends messages about our intentions. The question, as chemist Michael Braungart notes, is not, "Should I use a steel machine or a natural machine to serve as a tool for human ends?" but may in fact be, "When can humans become tools of nature?" When do we become indigenous to this place?

Source: McDonough, W. *Interiors*, February 2000, p. 28.

---

ers and retailers at all price points have begun to promote specific products that are made from reclaimed or plantation-grown woods. Examples of these companies include Sundance, Crate and Barrel, and Home Decorators Collection.

Rain Forest Woods

Rain forest woods are important natural resources that have been challenged of late. Deforestation has jeopardized the future of these rare and beautiful woods. About 50 percent of the world's rain forests have already been destroyed. Slash-and-burn agriculture, the introduction of cattle ranching (especially in the Amazon basin), logging, and mining have all contributed to the destruction of rain forest woods. Teak, mahogany, and rosewood are examples of rain forest woods.

INDUSTRY PROFILE

Pulp Psychology

I am writing this essay on Sunday morning in the bedroom of my 19th-century apartment. The flooring is narrow planks of golden oak. The bedframe is maple. The late-'40s chifforobe with remnants of Deco in the carving has panels of burled elm, and next to it is a pine box that a carpenter once built to house my spare blankets. I am in the gritty precincts of the biggest city in the United States, but I am not out of the woods yet.

Other materials are more durable, lighter, and cheaper, but wood trumps them all with its perpetual flicker of life. It breathes even under coats of paint or varnish, and its malleability, making it easy to bend and carve, is like the limberness of trees themselves. Woods are individual, both as species and as specimens with unique patterns of grain and benign imperfections. Light embellishes their nicks and chinks and often seems to glow from within. Haunted houses are notoriously filled with dark wood carvings that become as restless and contorted as the walking dead.

Is it any wonder that architects and designers adore the stuff, and that clients go woozy over parquet floors, bentwood chairs, burled executive desks, and cherry moldings? Such treasures are not to everyone's taste—one might prefer the simplicity of Aalto to the florid stylings of Thonet—but high-maintenance, flammable wood will never go out of fashion. It is at once organic and crafted, contemporary and timeless, and we have long passed the days when the Eameses struggled to make the material conform to their designs for a mass market: even the most sinuous plywood shape is affordable thanks to modern technology, while veneers and laminates offer many of the benefits of solid wood furnishings and surfaces treatments, at a discount and with less threat to the environment.

Wood links the housebound and the office drone—which is to say, almost all of us—to nature. As recently reported in *Architecture* magazine, we spend on average 1,368 of 1,440 minutes each day indoors, but we don't seem to like it much. The results of a study for Herman Miller delivered at last autumn's IIDA research summit suggest that employees are more creative in office environments that evoke the natural world. (Miller's Resolve system, with its stemlike poles and leaflike canopies, is one answer the company proposes.) Meanwhile, designer Rosalyn Cama has conducted her own informal research by asking groups of peers to envision the place they would most like to be. Very few of these interior designers, she marvels, think of an interior.

And yet for all its evocations of nature, wood also expresses qualities that are frankly human. It has character, one might even say personality. And it has a virtue that defies social convention—it grows more beautiful with age. In his classic 1933 essay "In Praise of Shadows," the Japanese novelist Junichiro Tanizaki writes of his reluctance to sacrifice wood to the modern convenience of bathroom tile because of the loveliness it garners over time. Tanizaki, whose praise of shadows is a paean to the subtle play of light over surfaces, prizes most of all the spirit that is immanent in matter. He points out an appreciation more evident in Eastern than in Western aesthetics for beauty that grows under serene contemplation and changing conditions, as if inert materials possessed layers of skin. And while I would agree that Westerners are less likely to look beneath surfaces to anything but the bones of our built environment, surely there is something mutely appreciative of Tanizaki's deeper vision in our love of wood.

This issue presents the resource from several angles; it projects where wood is a dominant element: in new products that exploit its versatility; in an essay by the art historian Grace Jeffers on imitation wood; and in a discussion among manufacturers, regulators, and specifiers about the condition of our forests and designers' responsibilities in helping to preserve them. Setting the tone, architect William McDonough, a leader in the sustainable woods movement, offers a "Sight Line" essay in which he sets forth the tree as a model for productivity that is unlikely ever to be surpassed.

Source: Lasky, J. *Interiors,* February 2000, p. 8.

SUMMARY

Wood products are used extensively in home furnishings and as a building material. There are two main classifications of trees: broadleafs, or hardwoods, and conifers, or softwoods. Lumber is wood that has been sawn into boards. The two principal methods of making lumber from trees are plain sawing and quarter sawing. Each method creates a different grain. Seasoning, or curing, lumber is the process of removing moisture from the lumber. There are two methods of seasoning lumber—air-drying and kiln-drying. Solid wood offers the consumer beauty and function. It can be carved or turned, and the surface cannot loosen or peel off. Veneering is the method of gluing thin slices of wood over less expensive woods or other core products. Finishes protect and beautify wood. Hardboard and particleboard are low-end substitutes for wood. Bamboo, rattan, and wicker are also used for furniture and home accessories. Bamboo is very strong and has a density similar to that of hardwoods. Forest management in recent years has ensured that growth of timber exceeds consumption. Rain forest woods are important natural resources that have been challenged recently.

TERMS FOR REVIEW

air-drying	half-round sliced veneers	quarter-sliced veneers
annual ring	hardboard	rattan
bamboo	hardwoods	reclaimed wood
bark	heartwood	reed
bird's eye	inlay	rift-cut veneers
boards	intarsia	rotary-cut veneers
broadleaf trees	kiln-drying	sapwood
burl	laminated wood	seasoning
cabinet woods	lignin	softwoods
cambium layer	lumber	stripe
checking	marquetry	strips
coniferous trees	medullary rays	stump
crotch	mottle	timbers
curing	parquetry	turning
deciduous	particleboard	veneer
dimension	pith	veneering
fiddleback	plain sawing	warping
flat-sliced veneers	plywood	wicker
grain	quarter sawing	

REVIEW QUESTIONS

1. What are the two main classifications of trees?
2. What is the advantage of kiln-drying over air-drying?
3. What is veneering?
4. What is the difference between hardboard and particleboard?
5. Why are finishes applied to wood?
6. What are the major disadvantages of solid wood?

LEARNING ACTIVITIES

1. Search the Internet for sites about the rain forests, forest management, and other environmental issues. Compile your research and list five ways to reduce or eliminate the damage of wood harvesting.
2. Make a list of at least eight wood products in your home. Evaluate their serviceability, any special care they need, and the aesthetics of the products. List reasons for your general satisfaction or dissatisfaction with the products.

CHAPTER 4

GLASS

A five-block stretch of one of Manhattan's toniest shopping districts was recently designated as New York's official crystal district. Five high-end crystal manufacturers— Baccarat, Daum, Lalique, Steuben, and Swarovski—along with Cristyne L. Nicholas, head of New York City Tourism, and Robert Walsh, the city's commissioner of business services, christened the section of Madison Avenue between 58th and 63rd Streets as a crystal district.... The goal of the five members of the district is to work more closely together to help draw consumers to their stores and educate them about crystal. The idea for such a district was spearheaded by Steuben.

"New York Creates Crystal District", *HFN,* October 14, 2002

GLASS IS A HIGHLY VERSATILE MATERIAL THAT HAS MANY USES. GLASS IS A HARD, NONPOROUS, amorphous material that results from the fusing of silica from sand and alkalis at high temperatures. It can be delicate and fragile or very durable. It can be mass-produced and available at very reasonable cost, or it can be hand-crafted and very expensive. Glass is usually colorless, but it can be produced in a wide range of colors. In fact, the word *glass* comes from the Celtic word *glas,* which means blue-green and refers to the dye that comes from woad, a plant used to make blue dye. It is usually transparent but may be translucent or opaque.

There are four primary uses for glass:

- Container glass, including household uses such as bottles, drinking glasses, and baking and storage dishes
- Flat glass and architectural glass for uses in the home such as windows and glass blocks, mirrors, and tabletops

- Works of fine art such as vases, sculpture, and novelty items
- Other uses such as foamed glass for insulation, optical fibers used in telecommunications, optical uses such as lenses for telescopes and microscopes, and textile products.

The primary focus of this chapter is household glass. It also includes some discussion of architectural glass and glass as an art form.

A BRIEF HISTORY OF GLASS

The earliest glass was created by volcanic gasses and was called *obsidian*. It is usually black or brown in color. This sharp glass was used as tools by prehistoric people. Although there is controversy about the date when people started to make glass, many archaeologists think it was first made over 5,000 years ago. The earliest pieces were glass beads, probably from Mesopotamia. Later, decorative vessels were created and considered more valuable than gold. In about 1425 B.C. the Egyptians used decorative glass bottles. The early Romans also used glass for windows. Glass blowing was developed about 3,000 years ago and is still the technique for creating the most valuable glass products today. The United States, Japan, and Europe are important producers of glassware.

The United States is noted for its quality glassware. Illinois, Michigan, Missouri, New Jersey, Pennsylvania, Ohio, and West Virginia have rich deposits of silica sand that is good for the manufacture of many types of glass. Glassmakers prefer inland sand to seashore sand because the grains are more uniform and there are fewer impurities.

American glassmaking dates back to colonial times. The first glass made in the United States was produced in Jamestown, Virginia, in the early 1600s. In 1739 Casper Wistar established the first important glass house in Glassboro, New Jersey. Another noteworthy 18th-century producer was Henry William Stiegel of Manheim, Pennsylvania, who made high quality glassware from 1785 to 1794. The Boston and Sandwich Glass Company, founded in 1825 by Deming Jarves, produced inexpensive pressed ware that continues in popularity today. The Lenox Company, the first American manufacturer to produce fine crystal stemware, was founded in 1841. American Michael J. Owens began to produce containers with his automatic bottling machine in 1903.

GENERAL PROPERTIES OF GLASS

The main ingredients for glass are silica, which comes from sand, and alkali, which comes from soda ash, potash, or lime. Sometimes all three alkalis are used, as well as other ingredients to create different varieties of glass. Silica will frequently account for 50 to 75 percent of the mixture. Other ingredients are added to improve or change the characteristics of the glass. For example, boric oxide is added to improve resistance to heat. The ingredients are combined, heated until they are melted, shaped, and then cooled.

Pure silica can be melted at very high temperatures to make silica glass. This glass is used for very specialized end uses such as laboratory glass and telescope mirrors. It has a very high melting point and is not affected by temperature change.

There are many different varieties of glass with highly specialized characteristics, but all glass has the following general properties:

- It is either transparent, opaque, or translucent.
- It can be produced to refract light.
- It can be produced in a wide range of colors, shapes, and textures.
- It is impervious to water, most alkalis, and acids.
- It will not burn, but will melt at high temperatures (usually between 500 degrees Fahrenheit and 1,650 degrees Fahrenheit, depending on the composition of the glass).
- Tensile strength averages between 4,000 and 8,000 pounds per square inch. Specially treated glass can exceed 1,000,000 pounds per square inch. Tensile strength will depend on the composition of the glass.
- It has a specific gravity of two to eight.
- It has moderate resistance to scratching.
- It is tasteless and odorless (especially important when used to hold food or drinks).
- It will break upon impact and when exposed to sudden temperature changes, although it is possible to produce glasses that are break resistant.
- It is a poor conductor of heat and electricity, making it appropriate for use in thermal and electrical insulation.

TYPES AND END USES OF GLASS

The three basic types of glass are **lime-soda glass, lead glass,** and **heat-resistant glass.** Each has its own particular characteristics and end uses.

Lime-Soda Glass

Approximately 90 percent of the glass made is lime-soda glass, made from sand and alkali (soda ash, potash, and lime). It is the least expensive glass and is frequently colored. Figure 4.1. shows a dinnerware set made of lime-soda glass.

The characteristics of lime-soda glass are:

- Inexpensive
- Durable
- Brittle
- Dull tone when tapped
- May not take cut designs but may be shaped and/or decorated by pressing it into a mold

FIGURE 4.1
Lime-soda glass.
Courtesy of Fairchild Publications, Inc.

Lime-soda glass is used to make the following products:

- Drinking glasses
- Windowpanes
- Jars
- Bottles
- Mirrors
- Decorative articles such as ornaments
- Glass dishes
- Lamp bulbs

Lead Glass

Lead glass is also called **flint glass** or **lead crystal.** It contains silica, soda ash, potash, and high levels of litharge, or lead oxide, and is known for its brilliant luster and resonant ring when tapped. The lead oxide creates light refraction in the glass that contributes the lustrous sparkle and also increases the weight of the glass. A lead glass bowl will be heavier than a comparable bowl of lime-soda glass. This type of glass was developed in England during the 17th century by George Ravenscroft. It is much more expensive than lime-soda glass. Most lead crystal is not colored so the unique sparkle can be seen. See Industry Statement 4.1. for information about New York's crystal district. See Figure 4.2 for an example of lead glass.

International standards have set 24 percent lead as the minimum criteria for an item to be labeled as lead crystal. In the United Kingdom the British Standard for lead crystal is that it must contain 30 percent lead. Sometimes the term *full-lead crystal* is used. Some glass that contains a small amount of lead, 10 to 12 percent, is called **semi-lead crystal.** Glass that is at least 5 percent lead is called **leaded glass.** The term *crystal* is used to refer to fine glassware, which may or may not be lead crystal. **Potash crystal** is not lead crystal and is much less expensive.

INDUSTRY STATEMENT 4.1

New York Creates Crystal District

NEW YORK–A five-block stretch in one of Manhattan's toniest shopping districts was recently designated as New York's official crystal district.

Five high-end crystal manufacturers–Baccarat, Daum, Lalique, Steuben and Swarovski–along with Cristyne L. Nicholas, head of New York City Tourism, and Robert Walsh, the city's commissioner of business services, christened the section of Madison Avenue between 58th and 63rd Streets as a crystal district during a cocktail party that also featured several events which celebrated the history and manufacturing of crystal.

The goal of the five members of the district is to work more closely together to help draw consumers to their stores and educate them about crystal. The idea for such a district was spearheaded by Steuben.

After moving from Fifth to Madison Avenue two years ago, Marie McKee, chief executive officer of Steuben, began to see the potential of a group marketing effort, said Pat Marti, Steuben's director of public relations. "We realized we were among kindred spirits, and that very close to us were some of the best crystal companies."

The concept was discussed among the crystal companies and pitched to Matthew Bauer, president of the Madison Avenue Business Improvement District. "It's hard to get five highly visible crystal companies to agree," said Marti. "Matt deserves credit for getting everyone to the table."

"We were so happy to learn the boutiques wanted to work together," said Bauer. "They recognize that to serve clients better, they needed to know more about one another and work together to educate the public."

The formation of a specialized district helps everyone build their businesses and increase visibility of their brands, said Melissa Carden, public relations manager for Swarovski.

The goal of the crystal district members is to integrate their individual public exhibits and talks, and to heighten awareness of crystal in New York City. This new marketing initiative strengthened what existed already, according to Bauer. "It's one more jewel in the crown of New York City," he said.

Source: Zisko, A. (2000, Oct. 15). New York Creates Crystal District. *HFN*, p. 118.

Courtesy of Fairchild Publications, Inc.

FIGURE 4.2
Lead glass.

Courtesy of Fairchild Publications, Inc.

The characteristics of lead glass are:

- A resonant ring when tapped. The size, shape, and weight of the glassware may affect the tone.
- Brighter and more lustrous than other glasses.
- Heavier than other glasses.
- Softer surface than other glasses, so the glass scratches more easily but is appropriate for cutting by hand or machine.
- Usually colorless.
- Absorbs high-energy radiation.

The end uses of lead glass include the following:

- Fine art glassware
- Expensive glassware for the table
- Optical lenses
- Jewelry and imitation gemstones such as rhinestones
- Protective windows in nuclear installations
- Prisms

Heat-Resistant Glass

Three different types of heat-resistant glass have been developed. They are **borosilicate glass, glass-ceramic,** and **laminated glass.**

Borosilicate Glass

Borosilicate glass was created in 1910. Lime-soda and lead glass will break when exposed to temperature extremes due to the expansion and contraction of the glass. Boric oxide is added to the sand and soda ash mixture to help prevent this expansion and contraction. Trades names for borosilicate glass are Pyrex® and Glassbake®.

The characteristics of borosilicate glass are:

- Less clear than lime-soda glass
- Dull tone when tapped
- Withstands temperature extremes
- Usually thicker than lime-soda glass

The end uses for borosilicate glass are:

- Cookware
- Baking dishes
- Laboratory glassware
- Chemical processing equipment

Glass–Ceramic

Glass-ceramic was developed in the 1950s. It is a heat-resistant crystalline material that is a combination of glass and ceramic. This opaque white material, which resembles china, is durable and able to withstand temperature extremes. These characteristics make glass-ceramic appropriate for cook-and-serve dishes. It is even used for rocket nose cones and space shuttle tiles. Pyroceram® and Centura® are tradenames for glass-ceramic.

Laminated Glass

Laminated glass was developed in the 1970s. It is made of two glasses—a dense core glass covered with a thin coating of clear glass. Corelle® is the tradename for laminated glass.

Characteristics of laminated glass are:

- Resembles china
- Lightweight
- Withstands temperature extremes
- Durable

End uses for laminated glass include cook-and-serve ware and tableware. Figure 4.3 shows a Corelle serving bowl, mug, and dinner plate.

FIGURE 4.3
Corelle.
Photo courtesy of Corelle.

PRODUCTION OF GLASS

After the raw ingredients are combined and heated, the molten glass is shaped by hand-blowing, mold-blowing, or pressing.

Mixing and Firing

First the raw ingredients, including the coloring agents, are mixed together (see discussion of coloring glass later in this chapter). Table 4.1 summarizes the ingredients in lime-soda glass, lead glass, and borosilicate glass. At this stage the mixture is known as the **batch.** Old scrap glass, called **cullet,** is added to the batch. Cullet melts quickly, aids in melting the batch, and helps produce a more uniform product. Cullet must be the same type of glass as the batch. The batch and cullet are heated to 2,700 degrees Fahrenheit (1,482 degrees Celsius) in order to produce a molten liquid. After the liquid is cooled slightly, it is ready to be shaped. Container glass may be shaped by hand-blowing, mold-blowing, or pressing. It is also processed into flat glass, which is discussed later in this chapter.

Shaping the Glass

There are three basic processes used to shape glass. More expensive glass is shaped by hand-blowing. Less expensive glassware is produced by mold-blowing and pressing.

Hand-Blowing

Glassblowing was discovered in the early first century along the Phoenician coast. **Hand-blown glass** is also known as **free-blown glass.** This method requires teams of craftsmen with great skill. The team is called a *chair*. The head glassblower, or *gaffer*, sits in a specially designed glass-blower's chair that aids in the formation of the glass (see Figure 4.4). The arms of the chair slant to assist in the rotation of the **blowpipe.** The blowpipe, shown in Figure 4.5, is a hollow steel pipe four to six feet long. The chair also holds the glassblower's tools, shown in Figure 4.6.

TABLE 4.1

Basic Ingredients in Lime-Soda Glass, Lead Glass, and Borosilicate Glass

Type of Glass	Sand	Soda Ash	Potash	Lime	Lead Oxide	Boric Oxide
Lime-Soda Glass	X	X	X	X		
Lead Glass	X	X	X		X	
Borosilicate Glass	X	X				X

Note: Manganese is added to produce a clear colorless glass. It counteracts trace iron that will make the glass green or brown.

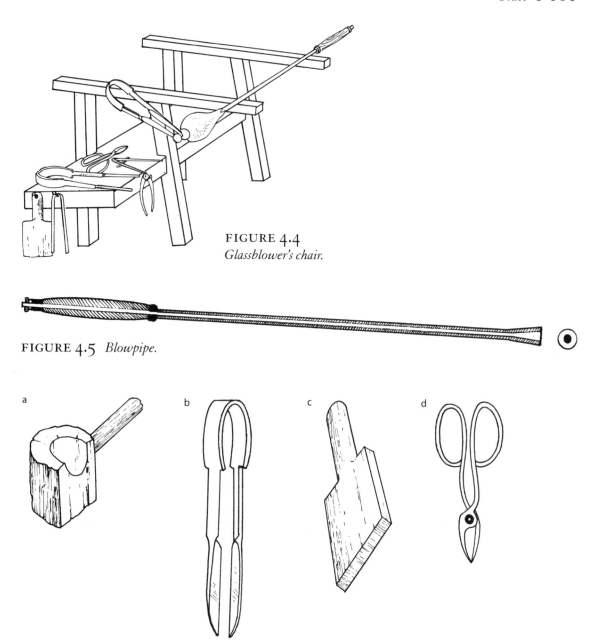

FIGURE 4.4
Glassblower's chair.

FIGURE 4.5 *Blowpipe.*

FIGURE 4.6 *Glassblower tools:* a. *block,* b. *tongs,* c. *paddles,* d. *shears.*

Famous designers of fine blown glass are René Lalique and Maurice Marinot in France, Sidney Waugh in the United States, and Edvard Hald in Sweden.

The basic steps in the process are as follows:

1. A small amount of molten glass, called a **gather**, is collected at the end of the blowpipe by the gaffer (see Figure 4.7).
2. The gather is rolled against a metal plate, called a **marver,** to cool and shape the exterior. This process is called marvering (see Figure 4.8).

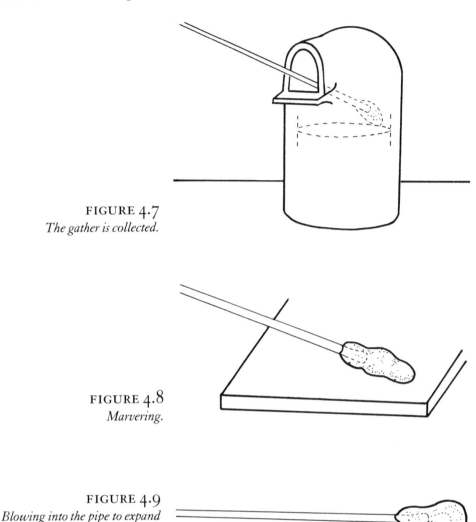

FIGURE 4.7
The gather is collected.

FIGURE 4.8
Marvering.

FIGURE 4.9
*Blowing into the pipe to expand
the gather and create a bubble.*

3. The glassblower blows into the pipe to expand the gather and create a bubble (see Figure 4.9).
4. The gather is turned in a wet block to achieve symmetry (see Figure 4.10). Constant rotation and skillful blowing create the desired shape. As the glass cools, it will harden. To continue the process, the glass must be softened by reheating it in a small furnace called a **glory hole.**
5. Hand tools, such as tongs, paddles, and shears, are used to refine the form of the glass (see Figure 4.6).
6. The base is flattened (see Figure 4.11).
7. The piece is transferred to a solid iron rod, called a **pontil** or **punty,** for finishing (see Figure 4.12).
8. The piece is whetted off the blowpipe. Whetting is accomplished by touching the glass with the wet ends of a tool. The hot glass will fracture and a slight tap will free the piece from the blowpipe (see Figure 4.13).

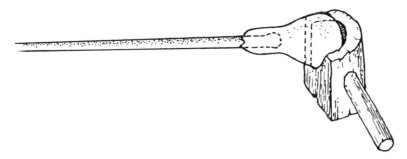

FIGURE 4.10 *The gather is turned in a wet block to achieve symmetry.*

9. The rim is shaped (see Figures 4.14a, b, and c).
10. If desired, handles may be added and shaped (see Figures 4.15a, b, c, and d).
11. The pontil is removed. This leaves a **pontil mark** that may be ground or polished away.
12. The edges are smoothed by grinding and polishing or by softening it again in the glory hole.

This method of producing glass is the most expensive and is used to produce high-quality lead crystal. Fine tableware and artistic pieces are hand-blown. Hand-blown glass is expensive because of the skill, specialized techniques, and care required for production.

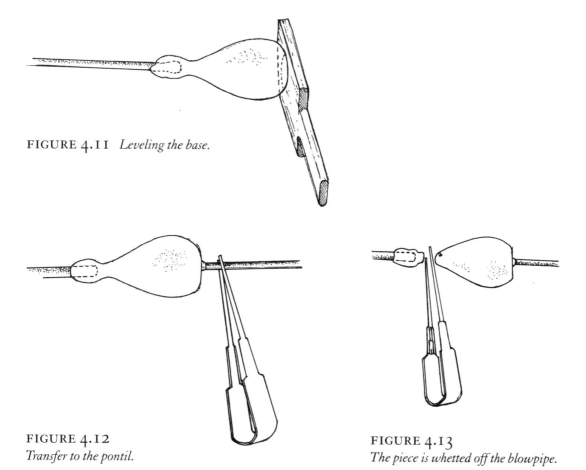

FIGURE 4.11 *Leveling the base.*

FIGURE 4.12
Transfer to the pontil.

FIGURE 4.13
The piece is whetted off the blowpipe.

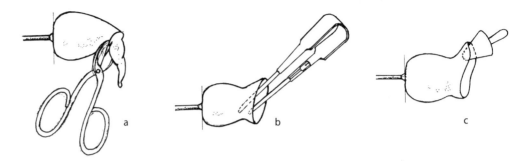

FIGURE 4.14   *The rim is shaped: a. glass is sheared at an angle, b. lip is formed, c. lip is shaped.*

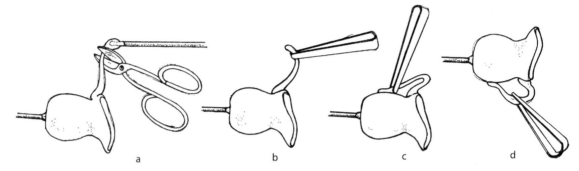

FIGURE 4.15   a–d *Adding and shaping the handle.*

Mold-Blowing

Mold-blowing is less expensive than hand-blowing. This process allows the glassmaker to create glassware that is exactly the same size. The molten glass is collected on the blowpipe. A bubble of air is blown into the glass. It is then placed in a cast iron mold. The glassmaker blows more air into the glass and forces the outside of the glass to take the shape of the mold. The air shapes the inside of the glassware. The mold can be shaped to create designs on the outside of the glass. Sometimes these designs resemble cut-glass patterns. (Glass cutting is discussed later in this chapter.) After the glass is formed, the mold opens, and the glass is removed. Lime-soda glass is frequently mold-blown.

In the early 1900s, Michael J. Owens created the automatic bottle-making machine. This machine made possible the mass production of uniform bottles and other glass containers. Mass production of uniform glass containers contributed to the development of mass packaging of food products, pharmaceuticals, beverages, and other products.

Pressing

Glass can be **pressed** by machine, by hand, or by a combination of both. Early Islamic craftsmen made pressed glass weights and seals. In the late 18th century, Europeans made pressed bases for stemmed tableware. In the early 1800s, Deming Jarves started the Boston and Sandwich Glass Company. Other manufacturers started to produce pressed glass, and soon the process was mechanized (see Figure 4.16).

FIGURE 4.16
*Diagram of a pressed glass plate
made during the 1800s.*

The majority of pressed glass is produced by machine. Pressing is appropriate for lime-soda and heat-resistant glasses but not lead glass. Lead glass does not cool rapidly enough to be shaped by this method.

The hot glass is cooled to 2,000 degrees Fahrenheit and then pressed into molds with a metal plunger. Both the mold and the plunger may imprint a design on the glass. After shaping, the glass is placed into the glory hole, which imparts the sparkle and luster traditionally found in pressed glass. The edges of pressed glass will be round and frequently the glass has symmetrical designs. The stems of glassware are pressed and then attached to the bases of mold- or hand-blown glass.

Improving Durability

After the piece is shaped, it must be annealed or *tempered*. **Annealing** improves durability by cooling the glass gradually. It allows the inner and outer layers of the glass to cool at the same time and prevents uneven internal and external strain in the glass. The glass is heated and then slowly moved through an annealing **lehr,** or tunnel-like oven, where the heat is gradually lowered to room temperature. The cooling time depends on the size and thickness of the piece. Smaller pieces may take several hours, while large thick pieces may take several days.

Inspecting and Finishing the Glass

During production products are periodically inspected for quality control. A polarscopic test shines polarized light through samples to determine if the pieces are free from strain and stress. If stress is found, the entire batch is retempered. Pressed glass may also be exposed to a thermal test. The glass is placed in alternating hot and cold water, or it is taken from a hot oven and placed in cold water. Better qualities of pressed glass will not crack under these conditions.

Hand-blown glass is finished by removing the **moil,** or excess glass, found around the tip of the glass where it was attached to the blowpipe. It is removed using a sharp diamond. After the moil is removed, the glass is placed in a glazing machine. Gas flames slightly melt the edge of the glass to make it smooth. Pressed glass, especially the bottoms of plates and bowls, may need grinding and/or polishing to achieve a smooth surface.

DECORATING AND COLORING GLASSWARE

Glassware is frequently decorated or colored to match or complement other tableware. The use of precious metals, expensive minerals, and labor-intensive techniques add to the cost of fine glassware.

Colorless Glass Decorations

There are several methods to add decoration to colorless glass: **copper-wheel engraving, cutting, decalcomania, embossing, etching,** and **frosting.**

Copper-Wheel Engraving

The glass is engraved using a small copper disk that is covered with oil and emery. The designs are delicate and can be quite intricate. The depth of the cut can vary and adds to the beauty of the design. The design is usually left frosted to provide contrast with the rest of the glass. This process is very time-consuming and expensive. Typically copper-wheel engraving is used for commissioned work.

Glass can also be engraved with a diamond wheel. These pieces are very expensive and one-of-a-kind works of art.

Cutting

There are two types of cutting used on glass: **glass cutting** and **intaglio cutting.** Both are time and labor intensive and are used on high-quality lead glass.

Glass Cutting Glass cutting was made possible after lead glass was discovered because lead glass is softer and more easily cut than lime-soda glass. First, a sketch of the design is drawn on the glass. Usually the design is a series of horizontal, vertical, and diagonal lines. The sketch is only a rough guide for the cutter. The more elaborate the designs that are cut into the glass, the more opportunity there is for the cutter to remove minor surface blemishes in the glass. Frequently, the more simply designed pieces are more expensive than the heavily cut ones because there is less opportunity to cut away blemishes.

There are three steps in the cutting process:

1. Roughing out—The glass is faceted by grinding on a carborundum wheel. The cutter holds the glass above the wheel and looks through the glass to cut it. Water continually runs over the glass to wash away dust and cool the surface.
2. Smoothing—A sandstone wheel is used to smooth the edges created by the carborundum wheel.
3. Polishing—After cutting, the glass is polished with pumice. Then it is dipped in a bath of sulphuric and hydrofluoric acids. The sulphuric acid cleans the glass, and the hydrofluoric acid attacks the surface of the glass. Some cut glass is polished by buffing with felt wheels. This method is slow and costly but results in a brilliant glossiness in the glass. Glass polished by this method is sold as "hand-polished glass."

Sometimes the cut glass is not polished but left rough or "in the gray" to create decorative contrast. This glass is sometimes referred to as "gray cutting."

Intaglio cutting is softer and uses more curves than glass cutting. The cutter uses a small sandstone wheel and holds the glass under the wheel. This process also gives the glass a frosted appearance. The frosting can be removed with polishing. Sometimes the glass is left frosted, and sometimes only specific areas are polished.

Decalcomania

This process is used for inexpensive glassware. A decal is stenciled on the glass, and then the glass is fired. This process imitates hand painting and is permanent.

Embossing

Designs can be pressed into the glass before it completely cools. This process is inexpensive.

Etching

Etching is the process of decorating glass by treating it with hydrofluoric acid. The areas not to be etched are protected with wax. The wax must harden for several hours before the glass is submerged in the acid bath. The acid decomposes the glass, leaving a grayed design. The glass stays in the bath about 6 minutes; then it is removed and rinsed carefully. A very hot bath is required to remove the wax. This process is permanent.

Frosting

A frosted effect can be achieved by three different methods: sandblasting, acid bath, and the use of powdered grains of glass.

Sandblasting is the process of directing a jet of sand onto the surface of a glass. A rubberized resist protects the glass that is not to be designed. The surface is pitted and has a frosted appearance. This surface is rougher than that of an etched surface. **Carved glass** is achieved when the design is deeply cut by the sand. The results are similar to engraving but take much less time.

Acid Bath The glass is placed in a hydrofluoric acid bath for a few minutes to achieve a frosted appearance.

Powdered Grains of Glass An adhesive is used to hold powdered grains of glass to the surface of the glass. The glass is then fired, so the grains of glass are permanently attached to the glass.

Adding Color to Glass

Color may be added to glass before it is formed, or it can be added to finished glass.

Coloring Glass

Colored glass is created by adding minerals to the glass before it is formed. The color is part of the glass and is permanent. Reds, blues, greens, and white are popular colors for glass. Table 4.2 indicates the color that specific minerals will produce.

Glass can also be colored by applying paint to glass that has already been formed. In enamel painting, color can be sprayed onto glass with ceramic enamels. The glass must be fired to be permanent. Another technique, cold painting, is the use of lacquer or oil paints on glass. The colors are not fired and are not permanent.

Case glass is very expensive decorative glassware. It has layers of colored glass superimposed over a layer of transparent or opal glass by dipping the glass into molten-colored glass. The colored glass is cut to reveal a bi- or multicolored effect.

Platinum, gold, and silver are also used to decorate glass. Because of the cost of these fine metals, they are usually applied to better qualities of glassware. There are three ways fine metals can be added to glassware: painting, encrusting, and electroplating.

1. **Painting** Platinum and gold are painted on to the surface of the glass. After painting, the glass is fired and then polished.
2. **Encrusting** Gold is applied over an etched surface. Then the glassware is fired and polished.

TABLE 4.2
Coloring Agents for Glass

Color	Mineral
Green	Chromium, copper, or aluminia
Blue	Cobalt oxide or copper oxide
Ruby	Copper or gold
Red	Copper
Yellow	Sulphur or selenium
Amber	Iron
Opaque White	Calcium antimony

3. **Electroplating** Electroplating is used to apply silver to glassware. This glassware is referred to as **silver depositware.** The design is painted or stenciled on the glass with a base metallic solution. The glass is fired, and the design becomes white. It is then suspended in the electroplating bath, and the silver adheres in the design pattern. Firing is not necessary, but to prevent tarnishing, the silver may be coated with another metal, such as rhodium. This is a costly process, and the metals can wear away.

GLASS INSPECTION

It is important that all fine glassware be inspected for flaws. Minor flaws do not affect function or beauty because much of fine glassware is handmade. But, glass with major flaws should be rejected. Criteria to evaluate include:

- **Cords** are almost invisible variations in the density of the glass that appear as streaks resulting from inadequate mixing of the ingredients. Overly prominent cords are unacceptable.
- **Bubbles,** also known as **seeds** or **blisters,** result from gases created during melting. Furnaces that provide accurate control of temperature reduce the occurrence of bubbles. Prominent bubbles are unacceptable.
- Speckles are caused by dirty tools that contaminate the molten glass and are unacceptable.
- Mold marks that result from the molding process are not considered a flaw unless they are overly prominent.
- Slight variations in diameter, height, weight, and overall dimension are acceptable in hand-crafted glassware.
- **Shear marks** are the slight puckering of the glass where the glassblower snipped off excess molten glass during shaping. Unless overly prominent they are not considered a flaw.
- **Sidens** (lopsided glassware) and **wob foot** (foot set at an angle) are unacceptable.
- Edges should be smooth. Details should be sharp and accurate.

OTHER USES OF GLASS IN THE HOME

Aside from tableware, most glass used in the home is flat glass. The most prevalent are mirrors and glass tabletops and two architectural glass products—windows and glass blocks.

Flat Glass

The first flat glass was made by the *cylinder method*. Hollow cylinders were blown, slit, and flattened into sheets. Later the *crown process* was developed. Crown glass was made by blowing a large flattened bubble of glass. The pontil was attached to the flat side, and the blowpipe was removed. The flattened bubble was spun until centrifugal force forced it into a large circular sheet. Then it was cut open and flattened.

Production of Flat Glass

Today there are three types of flat glass: sheet glass, plate glass, and float glass. All of these glasses are produced clear and can be tinted.

- **Sheet Glass** Sheet glass is produced by pulling the molten glass. It has optical distortions and is no longer made in the United States
- **Plate Glass** Also no longer made in the United States, plate glass is formed by using rows of rollers to flatten the molten glass. It has fewer distortions than sheet glass but does need grinding and polishing. This method is costly.
- **Float Glass** The most widely used method to make flat glass is float glass. It was introduced in Britain in the 1950s by Alistair Pilkington of the Pilkington Glass company. Molten glass (at about 1,800 degrees Fahrenheit) is layered over a bed of molten tin. The glass floats on the tin and forms a level surface that is virtually parallel. This method produces a sheet of clear, smooth glass.

Types of Flat Glass

There are four basic types of flat glass used in interiors: annealed, laminated, heat treated, and wired.

Annealed Glass The flat form of common lime-soda glass, also called clear window glass, is annealed glass.

Characteristics of annealed glass are:

- Usually produced clear but can be colored or tinted
- Easily broken—produces long shards
- Poor sound control
- Weak security
- Can be field cut (cut on site) and drilled

End uses for annealed glass include windows, mirrors, and glass shelves. Annealed glass should not be used in fire-rated situations.

Laminated Glass Made by laminating two or more layers of glass with transparent plastic between them. Use of vinyl as the inner layer makes the glass appropriate for energy conservation. The color of the inner layer (bronze, gray, green, blue silver, or gold) determines the transmission of light and reduces glare. Annealed, tempered, and wired glass can be laminated. For artistic effect decorative paper is laminated between sheets of glass (see Figure 4.17).

Characteristics of laminated glass are:

- Usually produced clear but can be colored or tinted
- May crack, but holds together because the pieces of glass adhere to the inner plastic layer

FIGURE 4.17
Diagram of laminated glass.

- Inner plastic layer can be modified to control heat, glare, light, and sound transmission
- Good sound control—effectiveness increases with additional layers
- Excellent security features
- Check with manufacturer for field cutting and drilling

End uses for laminated glass include:

- Safety glass in buildings and motor vehicles
- Acoustical glass
- Energy-conservation glass
- Bulletproof and theft-proof security glass
- Skylights
- Not for use in fire-rated situations

Heat-treated glass This glass uses heat processes to strengthen float glass. There are two types—**fully tempered glass** and **heat strengthened glass.**

Fully tempered glass is three to five times more resistant to breakage than annealed glass. The glass is heated almost to the softening point and then quickly cooled with air or in a liquid bath. The surface hardens quickly and creates surface tension that prevents breaking. Fully tempered glass cannot be field cut (cut on the job) because drilling or cutting the glass destroys the integrity of the surface. It must be made to size with the appropriate holes or cutouts. Fully tempered glass qualifies as safety glass, but heat-strengthened glass may not.

Heat-strengthened glass is only partially tempered. There is less surface tension because lower surface stresses are produced. It is about twice as resistant to breakage as annealed glass.

Glass can also be strengthened chemically. The composition of the glass surface is altered through an ion-exchange process. Using this process, glass strength can exceed 100,000 pounds per square foot.

Characteristics of fully tempered glass are:

- Usually produced clear but can be colored or tinted
- Difficult to break

- Shatters into small cubes
- Poor sound control
- Must be thickened for security
- Cannot be field cut or drilled

End uses for fully tempered glass include:

- Most common safety glass
- Entry doors
- Shower doors
- May be used as safety glass
- Not for use in fire-rated assemblies

Characteristics of heat-strengthened glass are:

- Usually produced clear but can be colored or tinted
- Twice as resistant to breakage as annealed glass
- Produces shards when broken
- Poor sound control
- Field cutting and drilling not recommended

End uses for heat-strengthened glass include:

- General usage
- Not for use as safety glass
- Not for use in fire-rated situations

Wired Glass **Wired glass** is plate glass reinforced with wire mesh that is rolled into the molten glass. This glass does not shatter when it breaks. Wired glass is the only type of glass that performs successfully in fire tests (see Figure 4.18).

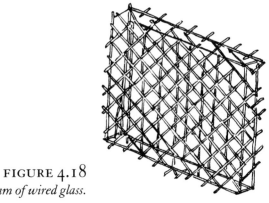

FIGURE 4.18
Diagram of wired glass.

Characteristics of wired glass are:

- Usually produced clear but can be colored or tinted.
- Breaks as easily as annealed, but the wire holds it together when subjected to impact, high temperatures, or air pressure.
- Poor sound control.
- Security better than annealed and tempered, but glass must be thickened.
- Can be field cut and drilled.

End uses of wired glass include:

- Common safety glass
- Appropriate for use in fire-rated situations

Variations of Flat Glass

Four variations of flat glass include: **insulating glass, reflective glass, beveled glass, and stained glass.**

Insulating Glass Two or three sheets of window glass are separated by an air space and hermetically sealed together at the edge. This is called double or triple glazed. A single layer of glass is called **single glazing.** The edges can be sealed with metal frames or welded glass. The air space between the sheets of glass provides insulation and reduces condensation. Double- and triple-glazed windows are excellent for energy conservation (see Figure 4.19).

Reflective Glass A thin film of transparent metal or metal oxides is bonded to the glass surface to reflect the rays of the sun.

Beveled Glass Beveled glass is made by grinding and polishing the edges of a piece of glass at an angle. Beveled glass is used for mirrors, doors, leaded glass windows, and other decorative applications. See Figure 4.20 for examples of different types of glass edges.

a   b   c

FIGURE 4.19
Diagram of insulating glass: a. *single glazing,* b. *double glazing,* c. *triple glazing.*

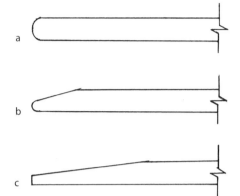

FIGURE 4.20
Examples of glass edges:
a. *polished edge,* b. *beveled and polished edge,* c. *clean cut edge.*

Stained Glass Glass that has been colored and set in lead or strips of copper foil is called stained glass. It is used for decorative purposes, such as windows, lampshades, and interior and exterior doors. Figure 4.21 is a Tiffany lamp made from stained glass. Louis C. Tiffany, an American artist in the late 1800s, designed and manufactured an iridescent glass that was used for various objects. Original Tiffany lamps are now very valuable.

The first known pictorial windows of colored glass are believed to have been made in 800 A.D. Many churches have beautiful stained-glass windows. Thirteenth and fourteenth century churches from France and England are famous for their stained-glass windows. Rose windows are common designs for stained glass. A **rose window** is a circular window with bars that radiate from the center (see Figure 4.22).

FIGURE 4.21
Tiffany-style lamp.
Courtesy of Fairchild Publications, Inc.

FIGURE 4.22
A rose window.
© Richard List/CORBIS

Other Uses for Glass

Other uses for glass include glass blocks, glass fibers, and foam glass.

Glass Blocks

Glass blocks are either solid or hollow. Solid glass blocks are used where strength or security is needed. In addition to their use as windows, they can also be used for shower enclosures, kitchen back splashes, and room dividers. The blocks are available in many shapes and sizes, and the sides of the blocks may have ribbed or patterned sides. The glass may be frosted or clear to allow for different levels of light transmission. They can be laid in mortar and can be used in both interior and exterior construction. Glass blocks can also be laid in with caulk.

Glass Fibers

Glass fibers are made by extruding strands of molten glass. Glass fibers are strong, chemically stable, and resistant to water and fire. These fibers are especially appropriate for use as drapes and curtains in areas that must meet strict fire codes. Glass fabric is very heavy, so drapery hardware must have additional support.

Glass fabric can be used for electrical insulation. It can also be combined with plastics to form a fiberglass composite that has the impact resistance of plastic and the strength of glass. Refer back to Chapter 2 for additional information about glass as a textile product.

Foam Glass

Foam glass is used to create thermal insulation batting. Foaming agents are added to ground glass. The mixture is heated until the foaming agent releases a gas that produces small bubbles and expands the mixture.

Swarovski Buffs Brand Image

Merges Jewelry, Giftware Divisions to Gain Cachet

CRANSTON, R.I.—Swarovski, known by some for its fashion jewelry collections and by others for its traditional crystal giftware, is reaching out to consumers with a new brand image and a restructured organization to back it up.

The company's goal, according to Daniel Cohen, president, is to make Swarovski, which generated roughly $300 million in crystal consumer products in the United States last year, "consistent, stable, dynamic, and interesting at retail for the customer." To that end, it has merged its consumer goods division with its crystal components unit to form one company: Swarovski North America Ltd.

Until about three years ago, the two divisions—jewelry and giftware—were marketed separately. Then the company began studying the synergies between them. It began to experiment with the two product categories to retail, placing them into each other's channels of distribution and reworking how they were presented to consumers. The response from retailers was great, said Cohen.

The Daniel Swarovski Paradise collection is an example of how Swarovski is blending fashion with tradition. The Paradise line of insect-shaped giftware combines the attributes of traditional Swarovski assortments, namely animal and nature motifs, with advanced glass technology and jewelry-making techniques to create subtle color gradations. The collection represents the first use of meaningful color for the company, according to Cohen.

Combining its fashion know-how with its knowledge of the collectibles business, Swarovski hopes to tell its brand story in a clearer way by presenting the two aspects of its business together. Consumers may soon find jewelry and giftware offered together at retail.

With this new approach to "fashionable gifts," Swarovski is examining its distribution channels, seeking out retailers—particularly high-end jewelry stores and department stores—that can translate its message of one coherent brand to consumers. The company is being "careful and selective" in choosing its retail partners and may trim its existing list, Cohen said.

Underlining its newly focused brand identity, Swarovski has refashioned its display cases, adjusted its product mix to better suit each channel, and restructured its field sales force to promote growth. The goal of this consumer-oriented sales force is to act as a consultant to retailers to make business more productive and ensure that consumer needs are being met, said Cohen.

So far, the plan is working. "We had a strong holiday season, despite what all of us heard about the economy," Cohen said. "We exceeded expectations last year" and hope to do the same this year, he added.

Swarovski operates 17 of its own retail stores and plans to open 10 to 13 more this year. These stores are marketed not as competition to its retail partners, Cohen said, but as unique Swarovski stores. "They're one of the best ways for us to tell our brand story," he continued.

Comparable-store sales were up double digits last year.

Source: Zisko, A. (2001, Feb. 12) Swarovski Buffs Brand Image. *HFN,* p. 34.
Courtesy of Fairchild Publications, Inc.

ENVIRONMENTAL IMPACT AND RECYCLING

The glass industry is working to improve the processes to melt, refine, fabricate, and form glass. There is an industry initiative to reduce energy consumption during production and to reduce pollutants, such as nitrogen oxide emissions and volatile organic compounds. Advance temperature sensors on furnaces are one way the industry is controlling energy costs. The industry is also researching new uses for glass.

Because of the health concerns regarding exposure to lead, glass products containing lead must be labeled as such. This includes lead crystal and stained-glass products. The solder used in stained glass contains lead. Glassmakers and polishers and stained-glass craftsmen are among the major occupational groups at risk for lead poisoning.

Glass is almost 100 percent recyclable. Cullet (old scrap glass) is an important component of each batch of glass. It speeds the melting process, while reducing consumption of raw materials and reducing waste going to landfills. There are also other uses for recycled glass. It can be ground and used as beach replenishment, landscaping, sandblast sand, fillers for fiberglass and concrete, and golf course sand traps.

SUMMARY

Glass is a very useful product that man has used for thousands of years. The many uses of glass can be divided into four categories: container glass, flat glass, glass as an artistic medium, and other uses, such as insulation, fibers, and scientific lenses. There are general characteristics that are common to glass, but because each type of glass also has very specific properties, it is important to select the appropriate glass for the intended end use.

There are three basic kinds of container glass used in household goods: lime-soda, lead, and heat resistant. Container glass can be shaped by hand-blowing, mold-blowing, or pressing. Container glass can be clear or colored; it may be transparent or opaque; it can be decorated by copper-wheel engraving, cutting, decalcomania, embossing, etching, and frosting.

Glass is also processed into flat glass for use as windows, mirrors, and tabletops. In the United States, flat glass is made by the float-glass method. There are three types of flat glass: laminated, heat-treated, and wired. Each type of glass has specific end uses.

The glass industry is meeting consumer demand by providing glass at many different prices and qualities that meet very specific needs. Currently, the industry is working to reduce the pollution associated with the manufacture of glass and also to increase the amount of glass that is recycled.

TERMS FOR REVIEW

annealing	crystal	foam glass
batch	cullet	frosting
beveled glass	cutting	full-lead crystal
blowpipe	decalcomania	fully tempered glass
borosilicate glass	electroplating	gather
bubbles (seeds, blisters)	embossing	glass
carved glass	encrusting	glass blocks
case glass	etching	glass cutting
copper-wheel engraving	flint glass (lead crystal)	glass fibers
cords	float glass	glass-ceramic

TERMS FOR REVIEW (*continued*)

glory hole	lime-soda glass	rose window
hand-blown (free-blown) glass	marver	sandblasting
	moil	semi-lead crystal
heat-resistant glass	mold-blowing	shear marks
heat-strengthened glass	painting	sheet glass
insulating glass	plate glass	sidens
intaglio cutting	pontil (punty)	silver depositware
laminated glass	pontil mark	single glazing
lead glass	potash crystal	stained glass
leaded glass	pressed	wired glass
lehr	reflective glass	wob foot

REVIEW QUESTIONS

1. Why is lime-soda glass the most common type of glass?
2. Why is lead crystal used in high-quality hand-blown glass stemware?
3. List two decorative techniques that might be used on lead crystal.
4. Define the following terms: full lead crystal, semi-lead crystal, leaded glass, crystal, and potash crystal.
5. What is case glass, and why is it expensive?
6. What are the three types of heat-resistant glass?

LEARNING ACTIVITIES

1. Compare and contrast the characteristics of the three major types of glass: lime-soda, lead, and heat resistant. List an appropriate end use for each one. Justify your suggestions.
2. Compare and contrast the characteristics of the four basic types of flat glass used in interiors: annealed, laminated, heat-treated, and wired. List an appropriate end use for each one. Justify your suggestions.

CHAPTER 5

POTTERY

A wonderful material, clay—probably the first to which [people] turned [their] hand when [they] felt the urge to make things, not for hunting or for war, but just for the pleasure of creating. Out of clay [they] contrived those first utensils for cooking and storing food which spelled the beginnings of civilization. Out of it also [they] made ornaments, representations of natural forms, objects of religious veneration, even books.

...It can be modeled, pressed, or stamped. It can be thrown on a wheel. It can be made into a liquid and cast in molds. It can be carved as a solid. It can be rolled, turned, scraped, incised, pulled, cut. When hardened by fire, it can be glazed with colors, brilliant or subdued, glossy or matte. It may be decorated with designs or given a variety of textures. Its range is almost limitless.

—John B. Kenny, *The Complete Book of Pottery Making,* April 1985

THE TERM *POTTERY* HAS TWO MEANINGS. IT CAN REFER TO ALL ARTICLES MADE FROM CLAY, including earthenware, stoneware, china, and bone china. It can also refer to a type of earthenware made from crude, porous clay. The term *ceramics* can also be used to describe articles made from clay. **Clay** is decomposed granite. It consists of aluminum oxide, silica dioxide, and water. Both terms, *ceramics* and *pottery,* indicate that heat has been used to remove water from clay.

Firing is the process of baking clay in a **kiln,** a specially designed oven that can be heated to very high temperatures, to make the clay more durable. Early potters fired their pottery in shallow pits using twigs as fuel (see Figure 5.1). Southwestern Native Americans continue to fire some of their ware in this manner. **Glazes** are finishes that are added to some pottery. The word *glaze* is derived from the word *glass.* It refers to the process of covering the ware with a glasslike coating after firing. Glazes may be aesthetic and/or functional. Firing and glazing are discussed more fully later in this chapter.

FIGURE 5.1
Primitive firing in a shallow pit.

A BRIEF HISTORY OF POTTERY

Many authorities believe that clay was first used to make pottery in the Neolithic period, about 6500 B.C., in the Near East. It is believed that early pottery was used to store grain, wine, oil, and other foodstuffs. Early peoples also used pottery to cook food and to make dishes for serving and eating food. In addition to the obvious functional uses of pottery, archaeologists have discovered that even the very earliest pottery was decorated. To this day pottery serves both a utilitarian and an aesthetic function.

TYPES OF POTTERY

There are three basic classifications of pottery: earthenware, stoneware, and china. Each classification has its own characteristics and end uses.

Earthenware

Earthenware is made from clay and other ingredients found in the ground. Earthenware is made in every country around the world (see Figure 5.2). There are two types of earthenware—**pottery** and **semi-vitreous ware.** Semi-vitreous ware is sometimes referred to as **fine earthenware.** The word *vitreous* means that the product has the qualities of glass. *Semi-vitreous* means that the ware is somewhat like glass.

Pottery

Pottery is frequently made by hand from very porous clay. The materials are not purified, and the ware is fired at a relatively low temperature, so it is not strong. The firing temperature for most pottery is about 1,000 degrees Centigrade (about 1,800 degrees Fahrenheit). It has very poor durability and chips very easily. For sanitary purposes, most pottery used to store or serve food has a transparent or opaque glaze or glass coating. If this glaze is chipped, the ware will absorb liquid and is considered unsanitary. **Terra-cotta** is unglazed earthenware. It is orange-brown in color. The word *terra-cotta* means "baked earth."

Pottery is characterized as:

- Heavy
- Thick
- Usually colorful with a primitive design
- Simply shaped
- Crude
- Not durable
- Unsanitary if the glaze is chipped
- Producing a dull tone when tapped

The clay is usually red or brown, but can be yellow, gray, bluish, or white. End uses of pottery include decorative pieces and informal dishes. Terracotta is typically used for decorations, statues, vases, and flower pots.

FIGURE 5.2
Earthenware pattern, Gourmet Garden, by Noritake. Photo courtesy of Noritake.

Semi-Vitreous Ware

Semi-vitreous ware, or fine earthenware, is fired at higher temperatures (about 1,150 degrees Centigrade) than pottery and is more durable. The clay underneath the glaze is less porous and therefore more sanitary, but it will absorb some moisture if chipped. **Ironstone** is an example of semi-vitreous ware. It is important not to confuse ironstone with stoneware, which is discussed in the next section. Ironstone is usually white. It is sometimes incorrectly called stone china.

Compared to earthenware pottery, semi-vitreous ware is:

- Similar in appearance, but not as crude
- More durable
- Less likely to chip
- More sanitary, but not completely sanitary if chipped
- Similar in producing a dull tone when tapped on the edge

End uses of semi-vitreous ware or fine earthenware include decorative pieces and informal dishes.

Stoneware

The Chinese were making stoneware in the 6th century A.D. It has been popular in Europe since the 16th century. Stoneware is also popular in the United States, especially since the 1960s.

Stoneware is sometimes called **high-fired ware** and is made from clay mixed with a fusible stone that has been vitrified (to become like glass) at a high temperature, usually 1,200 to 1,350 degrees Centigrade (about 2,190 to 1,350 degrees Fahrenheit).

Because stoneware is vitrified, it is impervious to liquids, and it will remain sanitary even if chipped. Glazing is not necessary. Some manufacturers of stoneware glaze only the inside of the ware. The glazed interior produces a smoother surface that makes cleaning easier. **Jasperware** is an example of stoneware that is left unglazed.

Stoneware is:

- Heavy
- Harder and stronger than earthenware
- More durable and less likely to chip than earthenware
- Usually colorful and casual in appearance
- Stone-like in texture if unglazed
- Dull in finish if not glazed
- Opaque
- Produces a ring similar to that of a stone when tapped
- Able to withstand temperature extremes well

- Can be used in the freezer, oven, and microwave oven. (Tall containers cannot be used in the freezer because they may crack when the contents expand upon freezing.)
- Dishwasher safe

End uses of stoneware include informal dishes, oven-to-table serving dishes, and decorative pieces.

China

China was first made in China about 1000 A.D., hence its name. It was made from fine, white clay called **kaolin** (silicate of alumina) and **china stone.** The main ingredient in china stone is **feldspar,** a crystalline mineral that melts at a rather low temperature. China is completely vitrified. It is fired between 1,250 and 1,400 degrees Centigrade (2,280 to 2,550 degrees Fahrenheit).

In the United States and England, the term *china* is still used. In Europe, it is more frequently called **porcelain.** Marco Polo is said to have first called it porcelain because it reminded him of the shell of a small crab, the porcellano, which is common to the Mediterranean. The major producers of china are European countries, Japan, and the United States (see Figure 5.3). Lenox is a well-known American china (see Industry Statement 5.1).

In the 1700s, alchemist Johann Friedrich Böttger and physicist Ehrenfried Walther von Tschirnhaus discovered deposits of china clay in Germany and began to produce both china and stoneware in Germany. Their factory later became famous as Meissen.

Most authorities agree that Josiah Spode perfected the process of making **bone china** in England in 1800. Originally oxen bone ashes were pulverized and added to the kaolin. Now the **bone ash** is made from cattle bones imported from South America. Bone china can be as much

FIGURE 5.3
Porcelain pattern, Fortessa's Opera Collection.
Courtesy of Fairchild Publications, Inc.

INDUSTRY STATEMENT 5.1

Lenox Moves Beyond Products with New Print Ad Campaign

LAWRENCEVILLE, N.J.–Three years ago, Lenox set out to establish itself in consumers' minds as a giftware company, as opposed to a tabletop company. Now it is taking its "Gifts That Celebrate Life" advertising campaign to the next level with ads that not only reflect the sentiment of the gift-giver, but, in a rare turn for a tabletop company, emphasize people over products.

"We felt the campaign needed to take a giant step forward," said Peter Cobuzzi, vice president of brand development. "We didn't have the best possible campaign we could have, and the Lenox brand deserved that.

"We know that in order to be a great gift company, you [must examine] the reason for giving gifts in the first place, the emotional attachment to gift-giving."

Lenox spent months reviewing ad agencies and concepts before assigning the job to Eisner Communications in Baltimore, which Cobuzzi described as "head and shoulders above anyone else."

The new ads connote Lenox as a premium, prestige gift brand, one appropriate for weddings, holidays and any other gift-giving occasion. Using candid, ivory-washed black-and-white photographs, the ads present people in joyous situations—a beaming wedding party, a child on Christmas morning—while the body copy relays the sentiments associated with the image shown. Lenox's signature color scheme of ivory and gold is carried through in the ads by a gold ribbon that "wraps" the ad as if it were a gift, and a Lenox gift card positioned in a corner of the ad that conveys the gift-giver's thoughts.

The bridal ads have begun to run in several bridal books, while holiday-themed ads will appear next month in 12 lifestyle publications, with Metropolitan Home, Bon Appetit, O: The Oprah Magazine and Victoria among them.

Future ads will focus on additional gift-giving moments, such as the birth of a baby and Mother's Day.

Source: HFN, October 28, 2002, p. 26.

---

as 50 percent calcined (oxidized by heating) bone ash. Bone china is prized for its whiteness and translucency. England continues to be the major producer of bone china. Some is produced in the United States and Japan.

There are two types of porcelain—soft-paste and hard-paste. The **soft-paste porcelain** is also known as *artificial porcelain*. It is made by mixing clay and glass frit. **Frit** is a fused mixture of glass and enamel that has been ground into a fine powder. Soft-paste porcelain is not as stable during firing and is not as durable as hard-paste porcelain. **Hard-paste porcelain** is similar to the original Chinese china. It is made from kaolin and feldspar.

China is used to make fine dinnerware, figurines, and other decorative objects. It is:

- Translucent (shadows can be seen through it when held to the light)
- Completely nonporous
- Durable
- Expensive
- Thin and delicate in appearance
- Produces a clear, bell-like tone when tapped on the edge (Cost and decoration may make oven, microwave, and dishwasher use inappropriate.)

MANUFACTURE OF POTTERY

In general, the manufacture of pottery traditionally involves the mixing, shaping, firing, glazing, and decorating of the raw materials. It can be quickly mass-produced or it can be time and labor intensive. It can be very decorative or very plain. Pottery is available at many prices and quality levels.

Differences in appearance, translucence, absorbency, and sound when tapped are determined by the kind of clay, other raw materials, processing methods, firing temperature, and decoration used in production.

Materials Used in Making Pottery

The main ingredient in pottery is clay. Various other materials are added to increase translucency, improve strength, or improve moldability. Metallic oxides can withstand the high temperatures of firing and are the only products used to color clay or apply colored designs to pottery. For example, cobalt is a silver-white metallic oxide used to make deep blue. Table 5.1 lists the common materials used to make pottery.

TABLE 5.1
Common Materials Used in Pottery

Material	Function
Types of clay	
Common clay Decomposed granite consists of aluminum oxide, silica dioxide, and water; it is pliable when wet; usually dark red or brown; hardens at low temperatures	Used for pottery
Ball clay or **blue clay** Sedimentary clay that has been carried in a stream and deposited on the bottom of a body of water; very fine in grain; nearly white	Used in semi-vitreous ware; adds moldability and strength
Fire clay Rough textured, refractory (resistant to high temperatures) clay	Used for cooking foods; also used for bricks
Kaolin Finest, whitest, purest, strongest clay found in some sections of the United States, China, England, Germany, France, and some other European countries; made primarily of kaolinite or aluminum silicate; essential for china and bone china; sometimes called china clay	Used to produce china and bone china
Other Materials	
Bone ash Animal bones calcined (oxidized by heating) and crushed into powder, usually cattle bones	Helps fuse clay particles together; adds whiteness and strength to bone china
Feldspar A crystalline mineral that melts at a rather low temperature; used in powder form; also called feldspathic stone	Helps hold the clay particles together; gives translucency to china; acts as a flux by lowering the melting point and helping the clay body to flow when it is heated
Flint A hard stone that is ground and mixed with the clay	Adds strength

Preparing and Mixing

The first step in making pottery is to prepare and mix the ingredients. For example, the ingredients for bone china are approximately 25 percent china clay, 25 percent feldspar, and 50 percent calcined (oxidized by heating) cattle bones. The ingredients are filtered and mixed well. Water is added to form **slip,** a liquid clay that has the texture of thick cream. The slip is passed through a fine sieve to further filter it. For fine china it is important to remove all iron particles because they may cause red or dark brown spots on the ware. To remove these particles, the slip is poured over a series of electromagnets.

Excess water is removed by passing the slip through filter cloths. The moist clay is aged for several weeks. Aging improves plasticity (moldability) and makes the clay easier to work. After aging, the clay is blended in a pug mill. **Pugging** is the process of shredding and kneading the clay mixture in a pug mill to create a smooth mixture with the correct amount of water. Air bubbles are also removed. At this stage the clay can be used to make plates, dishes, and cups using automatic machinery. It is also ready to be formed by hand. If it will be cast in a mold, water must be added to make it creamy and pourable. This liquid clay is also called slip. *Body* is the term that refers to the prepared ingredients that are used to make pottery. The steps in the preparation of the body can be summarized as follows:

1. Mixing ingredients—china clay, feldspar, and water (and bone if bone china)
2. Filtering and magnetizing to remove all impurities
3. Filter pressing to remove excess water
4. Aging to improve plasticity
5. Pugging—kneading the moldable clay to remove air bubbles

Shaping, Assembling, and Finishing Pottery

Once the clay body has been prepared, the following steps are followed to form pottery:

1. Shaping
   a. Moldable Clay—used for plates, shallow bowls, cups
      1) Throwing, coiling, or slab making
      2) Jollying
      3) Jiggering
      4) Molding or sprigging
   b. Casting—used for hollowware and figurines
2. Drying
3. Sticking up—joining of parts at the leather-hard or dry stage

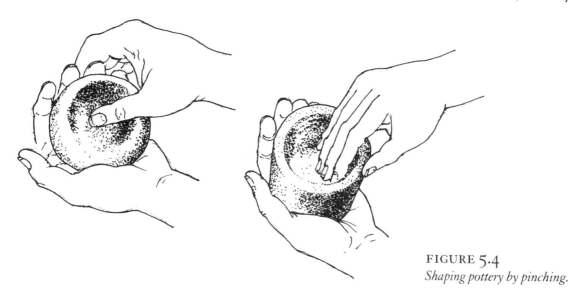

FIGURE 5.4
Shaping pottery by pinching.

4. Finishing
  a. Fettling
  b. Towing
  c. Sponging

Pottery can be made by hand or by machine. Commercially most pottery is made by machine. Forming clay by hand is reserved for the most expensive pieces.

Hand-Shaped Pottery

Archeologists have determined that the earliest pottery was made by simply shaping a lump of clay with the hands. This process is called **pinching** (see Figure 5.4). Later more sophisticated pieces were made by **coiling**. Coiling is the process of forming a flat disk and then coiling rolls of clay around the disk to build up the sides (see Figure 5.5).

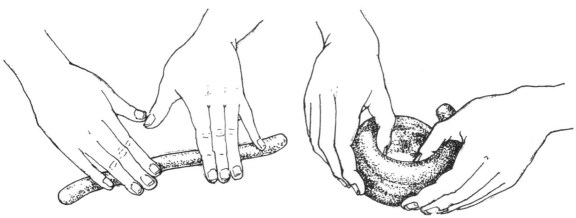

FIGURE 5.5
Shaping pottery by coiling.

Most authorities agree that the **potter's wheel** was used as early as the fourth millennium B.C. in the Middle East. It is a horizontal wheel on which the clay is shaped. The process of shaping a piece freehand on a potter's wheel is called **throwing** (see Figure 5.6). Power-driven wheels are used commercially. The person who operates the potter's wheel is called a **potter** (see Figure 5.7).

Studio craftsmen also hand make pottery by coiling and the **slab method.** Coiling is similar to the early method of coiling ropes of clay around a disk. To make a slab pot, slabs of clay are rolled out, cut into desired shapes, and assembled. Most slab pots are square or rectangular, rather than round (see Figure 5.8).

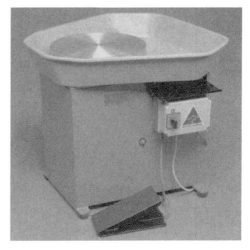

FIGURE 5.6
Manually driven potter's wheels.
Courtesy of Potterycrafts, Ltd, Campbell Road, Stoke on Trent ST4 4ET.

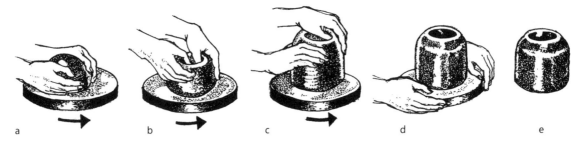

a   b   c   d   e

FIGURE 5.7
Steps in throwing a pot: a. *centering the clay,* b. *opening a depression at the top of the clay,*
c. *raising the cylinder,* d. *final shaping of the ware,* e. *the finished pot.*

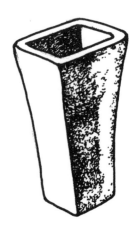

FIGURE 5.8
Diagram of a slab-built vase.

Commercial Shaping of Pottery

Jiggering, jollying, molding or sprigging, and slip casting are four production methods used to create ceramics.

Jiggering and Jollying Jiggering is the shaping of flat pieces of pottery, such as plates, saucer, and platters, using a jigger machine (see Figure 5.9). The lump of clay is placed on a mold and turned while a template is held against it. The base shapes the inside of the plate while the template shapes the outside. The jigger may be fully automated or semiautomatic. Cups can also be produced on a jigger.

Jollying is the shaping of hollowware, such as cups, bowls, teapots, and vases. A machine, called a jolly, molds the clay on the outside while the template forms the inside of the piece. The inside and outside are formed at the same time.

FIGURE 5.9
A jigger.
Courtesy of Potterycrafts Ltd, Campbell Road, Stoke on Trent ST4 4ET.

Jiggers and jollies have been replaced by roller machines in highly automated factories. A slice of clay is placed in a mold and then a heated die called a *bomb* spreads and shapes the clay in one operation. This method is especially suited to mass production of simple shapes.

Molding Molding is the process of pressing a lump of clay into a mold. When molding is used to create relief ornaments that are to be applied to a clay surface, it is called **sprigging.** Decorative additions to the ware and handles are created this way. The piece is removed carefully from the mold and attached to the body with slip as shown in Figure 5.10.

Slip Casting Slip casting requires the use of a mold. After the design has been developed, models are carved from clay. The model must be larger than the final piece will be to allow for shrinkage during the firing process. The model is then broken down into its component parts. For example, a teapot would have a body, handle, spout, and lid. The handle may be molded (as described above) while the body is slip cast. Plaster-of-paris molds are created for each part. Molds have a limited life and must be replaced frequently. Slip is poured into a plaster-of-paris mold. When set until the outer edges have set and the ware is the required thickness, the liquid center is poured out, leaving a hollow body. This method is appropriate for items such as teapots. Figure 5.11 summarizes the basic steps in slip casting.

Assembly and Finishing

Assembly After forming, the pieces of ware are allowed to dry. Drying takes place in large tunnel dryers. The ware may be allowed to dry completely or to a stage called **leather hardness** that is softer than the completely dry stage. Leather-hard ware has dried to a stage when most of the moisture is gone, but the ware can still be carved or joined. The joining of the parts is called **sticking up.** This can be accomplished at the leather hard or the completely dry stage. The parts are joined using thick slip.

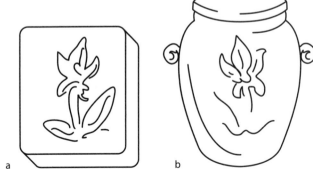

FIGURE 5.10
a. *Sprig mold,*
b. *sprig decoration applied to a piece.*

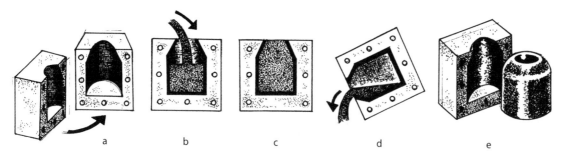

FIGURE 5.11 *Steps in slip casting: a. the mold, b. pouring slip into the mold, c. the wall is sufficiently established, d. excess slip is poured off, e. piece is removed after it is finally set.*

Finishing At this stage, metal tools are used to trim away excess clay from the form. Damp sponges are also used to remove any bumps that may mar the surface. Special attention is given to the areas where components have been joined, such as the handle of a teacup. The specific terms used for finishing processes are:

Fettling Using small scalpels called fettling tools to trim excess material, remove bumps from the surface, and smooth the joints of the ware. Fettling is done at the leather-hard stage or the dry stage.

Towing Using a small mop to take the seams off plates and to round off sharp edges.

Sponging Using damp sponges to smooth the surface of the pottery before firing.

Most of these processes have been adapted to semiautomatic or automatic machinery. All pieces are carefully inspected. When the ware is completely dry, it is ready to be fired.

Firing and Glazing

During firing the ware is subjected to intense heat. Most pottery is subjected to two firings—the bisque firing and the glost firing. Some decorations require additional low temperature firings. Table 5.2 summarizes the firing and glazing of pottery.

TABLE 5.2
Firing of Pottery

Firing	Purpose
First firing, bisque firing (also called biscuit-firing)	Makes the ware more durable
Glost firing	Fuses the glaze to the surface of the ware
Decorative firing(s)	Makes overglaze decorations more durable

Bisque Firing

The purpose of the initial firing, called the **bisque firing,** is to make the ware more durable and improve its appearance. This firing is sometimes called **biscuit-firing.** The higher the temperature, the less porous and the more durable the ware. The type of ware being produced determines the temperature of the kiln. (See the earlier discussion of firing temperatures.) Firing also shrinks the ware between 2 to 20 percent, depending on the nature of the ware.

Clay that has not been fired is called **greenware.** The greenware is stacked in racks and moved slowly through a tunnel-shaped oven called a bisque kiln. The bisque kiln is about 200 feet long. It takes from 70 to 90 hours for the bisque firing. At the beginning of the tunnel the temperature is about 300 degrees Fahrenheit. For earthenware it will gradually reach a temperature of 1,000 degrees Centigrade (180 degrees Fahrenheit) for pottery and 1,400 degrees Centigrade for china. Then the temperature will gradually cool until the ware is removed at the end of the kiln.

After firing, the ware is called bisque or biscuit ware. Typically it is dull with a rough texture. At this stage stoneware and porcelain bisque are completely vitrified and will not absorb liquids. The feldspar has melted to bind the infusible particles of clay together. Earthenware bisque is not vitrified and will absorb liquids.

Glost Firing

Glost firing occurs after glazing. It fuses the glaze to the surface of the body of the ware. Glost firing takes place in a glost oven, also called a glost furnace. The ware is in the glost oven for 5½ to 8 hours. Some earthenware is not bisque fired. It is fired only once, in the glost oven after the glaze is applied to the greenware. This produces inexpensive ware with surface blemishes.

Decorative Firings

Low-temperature firings increase the durability of decorations that are added after the glost firing. It is possible for the same piece of ware to go through several decorative firings.

Glazing

A **glaze** is a coating that adheres to earthenware and adds a glass-like finish. The earliest pottery was unglazed. It is believed that the earliest glazed pottery was made in Egypt about 4000 B.C. Materials used in glazing are summarized in Table 5.3. The three main ingredients in many glazes are silica, which is a glass forming substance; a flux to lower the temperature; and alumina that helps the silica and flux mixture adhere to the clay. The glazing on china fuses into it and is not a separate coating. The glazes for china are chemically similar to the body of the ware.

Glazing makes earthenware sanitary by preventing liquids from being absorbed. As long as the surface is intact, the earthenware is sanitary. Glazing also provides an attractive easy-to-clean surface for stoneware and china. The glaze may be shiny or dull. If it is dull, it is called a matte glaze. Glazes are liquid suspensions and can be applied by spraying, painting, or dipping. A low-firing vegetable dye is put into the glaze so it will be easy to see if the coating is uniform. The vegetable dye burns off during firing.

TABLE 5.3
Materials Used in Glazing

Material	Use
Beryllium	Used on Franciscan china to give it an extremely hard and brilliant surface
Tin	Used in English delftware, majolica ware, faience, and in other tin-enamel glaze coatings (see further discussion of these types of pottery later in chapter)
Silica	Glass-forming substance
Flux	Lowers the temperature needed for glazing
Alumina	Helps the silica and flux mixture adhere to the clay

During the glost firing it is important that pieces of ware not touch each other. The melting glazing would weld them together. It is also important that the ware not become welded to the rack on which it sits during firing. The glaze is wiped off the bottom of the piece or it sits on small clay triangles or pegs during firing. The marks left by the triangles are ground away after firing.

Decorating Pottery

The type and amount of decoration added to ceramic pieces can contribute significantly to the cost of the piece. Countless hours are spent drafting and evaluating designs. Handwork and costly materials are very expensive (see Figure 5.12).

FIGURE 5.12
Hand-decorated pottery. Courtesy of Potterycrafts Ltd, Campbell Road, Stoke on Trent ST4 4ET.

There are four types of decorations:

- **In-the-clay decorations** are added while the piece is still wet.
- **Underglaze decorations** are added before glazing.
- **In-the-glaze decorations** are colored glazes.
- **Overglaze decorations** are applied after glazing.

Table 5.4 summarizes the decoration of pottery. Decorations can be added to pottery while the piece is still wet, under the glaze, in the glaze, and after glazing.

In-the-Clay Decorations

In-the-clay decorations are made in the moist clay. These decorations are permanent and are integral to the body of the piece. There are several types of in-the-clay techniques:

- **Graffito** or **sgraffito** This is a technique of stacking two layers of differently colored clays and then scratching through the top layer to reveal the underlayer.
- **Pierced decoration** A lattice work or lace effect is created by cutting small holes in the clay (see Figure 5.13).
- **Relief decorations** There are two ways to create relief, or raised, designs:
  1. The original mold may have designs that are pressed into the ware.

TABLE 5.4
Decorating Pottery

In-the-clay decorations are added while the piece is still wet.	Graffito or sgraffito Pierced decoration Relief decorations Rice patterns Resist designs Slip decorations Colored clays
Underglaze decorations are added before glazing.	Hand painting Decalcomania Transfer printing or copperplate decoration Stamping
In-the-glaze decorations are applied over underglaze decorations.	Metallic oxides to add color Lusterware Crackle glaze Combination of matte and glossy surfaces Decorations are applied over the glaze, and the ware is refired
Overglaze decorations are applied after glazing.	Gilding Etching Encrusting Electrolytic process Onglaze colors

FIGURE 5.13
Candace Young carved and pierced stoneware Patio Lantern.
Photo by Norm Czuchra.

2. Separate clay designs may be molded and then attached to the piece with slip. These designs may be elaborate flowers or other embellishments. When the design is raised very slightly, it is called bas relief. Wedgwood® jasperware is an example of relief decoration.

- **Rice patterns** Rice pattern designs are created when small holes that have been cut in the clay are covered with glaze to form transparent spots.
- **Resist designs** Sizing is applied to the ware to protect certain areas from color or glazing.
- **Slip decorations** Raised decorations are painted on the clay with slip. Slip can also be thickened so it can be piped onto the ware. This process is similar to decorating a cake.
- Color can be added to pottery by using various colored clays.

Underglaze Decorations

Underglaze decorations are added after the first firing but before the final glaze. Colors and designs are permanent but must be able to withstand the intense heat of the glazing process.

Hand painting is a very time-consuming and expensive underglaze decoration. Sometimes the work is completely freehand, but it may also be outlined first with a series of dots as a guide for the painter. Painters grind their colors into a powder and mix them with oil and aniseed. Underglaze colors are usually mixtures of iron, chromium, copper, and cobalt.

Decalcomania is a less expensive alternative to hand painting. It is a widely used method of pottery decoration. The design is printed on tissue paper and then pressed into a sticky substance that has been applied to the piece. The tissue is rubbed to transfer the design. The tissue is washed away, and the piece is fired. Decalcomania is also referred to as **lithography.**

A new method called *slide off* has recently been developed. A transfer is made by printing the pattern on paper and then covering it with plastic. The transfer is soaked in water until the decorator can slide the pattern off the paper and onto the ware. The plastic burns away during firing.

Transfer printing, or **copperplate decoration,** involves a great deal of handwork and is very expensive. This technique was developed around 1750. The design is engraved into a copper plate, filled with the oil-based oxide color, and transferred to a piece of tissue paper. The tissue paper is placed on the dish and rubbed until the design is transferred to the place. Each color must be applied separately.

Stamping is a low-cost alternative to transfer printing. The design is cut into a rubber stamp. The stamp is dipped into the color and pressed against the ware.

Colored designs can also be added to pottery by silk screening. Designs are put on silk screens and then used to apply color to the ware. This is an inexpensive method of decorating pottery.

In-the-Glaze Decorations

Most glazes are transparent, but when they are colored, they are called in-the-glaze decorations. Again, the glazing process limits the use of coloring agents to those that can withstand intense heat. Metallic oxides are used to add color to ceramics. The firing temperature and atmospheric conditions will affect the color. For example, copper is green at low temperatures, but can become turquoise or red under certain conditions.

Lusterware is created by adding metallic powder to the glaze so the ware is covered with a thin layer that has a mirror-like sheen.

Centuries ago the Chinese developed **crackle glaze.** The ware is cooled very quickly after firing to create a fine web of lines on the surface. The cracks are often accentuated with coloring.

A combination of matte and glossy surfaces is another way to decorate pottery. The matte glaze is applied first, and the areas to remain matte are blocked off with wax. Then the glossy glaze is applied.

Another form of in-the-glaze decoration is when hand-painted or transfer decorations are applied over the glaze and the ware is refired. Gold and platinum can be applied in-the-glaze if the second firing is brief. In-the-glaze decoration has the advantage of being protected from wear.

Overglaze Decorations

Overglaze decorations are applied after the glazing process is completed. These decorations are not as durable as underglaze decorations and may rub off. All overglaze decorations are fired in decorating kilns, but the temperature in these kilns is much lower than the heat of the glost ovens. Onglaze colors are also applied after the glazing process. They are fired into the glaze at a lower temperature. Overglaze decorations may be identified because they will reflect light differently. They will be duller than the rest of the body.

Silver may be applied to pottery using an electrolytic process. It is then bonded to the ware by low-temperature firing. Gold and platinum are usually applied after glazing because the temperature of the glost oven destroys their beauty. (See previous discussion under In-the-Glaze Decorations.)

Gold is applied last because gold fires at the lowest temperature. Gold may be applied by **gilding.** The powdered gold is suspended in oil and painted on by hand with a brush. Depending on the quality of ware, either one or two coats of gold may be applied. One coat tends to appear brassy. Two coats produce a richer effect. After firing, the gold must be burnished (rubbed with agate) to make it bright and shiny.

Etching is another overglaze technique. An acid-resistant wax is applied to the ware, covering areas that will not be etched. The ware is dipped in an hydrofluoric acid bath to create a raised design, and the wax is washed off. After etching, gold or platinum can be applied to the raised area. This method of decoration is called **encrusting.**

Types of Pottery

A few selected styles of pottery are highlighted in Table 5.5.

TABLE 5.5
Selected Types of Pottery

Type	Description
Basalt	Hard black unglazed stoneware developed by Josiah Wedgwood in the 1700s
Delft	Dutch tin-glazed earthenware
Dresden china	May refer to Meissen porcelain, other ware made in the city of Meissen, or any figurine made in the Meissen style
Faience	Tin-glazed earthenware; originally made in Faenza, Italy; now a common French term for pottery
Famille	Chinese porcelain decorated with enamel Famille jaune – yellow decoration Famille rose – pink decoration Famille noire – black decoration Famille verte – green decoration
Imari	Type of Japanese pottery with blue and iron red enamel and gold; produced for export
Jasperware	Unglazed, intrinsically colored stoneware embellished with a slip decoration that was formed in a mold; originally made by Josiah Wedgwood
Kakiemon	Japanese or Japanese-style porcelain enameled in green, blue, red, and yellow; frequently with gold trim
Majolica (also spelled maiolica)	Tin-glazed earthenware
Parian ware	Unglazed china; resembles marble
Pâte-sur-pâte	Decorative technique perfected by Minton; carved slip design
Porcelaine noire	Black china (or porcelain) that results from metal oxides in the clay and firing in a special kiln
Raku	Low-fired, lead-glazed Japanese earthenware associated with the tea ceremony; frequently molded by hand
Salt-glazed pottery	Pottery that has been glazed by throwing salt into the glost oven; forms a glass-like skin over the ware
Willow pattern	Widely used decorative transfer-printed pattern for china in the 1800s; Chinese scene in cobalt blue ink

---

INDUSTRY PROFILE

Fiesta Ware Dinnerware

Fiesta Ware was a dinnerware pattern of the 1930s, but judging by the number of dedicated Web sites, books, conventions and other outlets for Fiesta fans, it is probably as popular today as it was then. The solid-color, Art Deco pattern designed by Frederick Hurton Rhead was a big hit with consumers in the 1950s, was phased out in the 1970s and enjoyed a rebirth in 1986, when it was relaunched in several new colors to mark the pattern's 50th anniversary. By 1997, manufacturer Homer Laughlin had churned out its 500 millionth piece of Fiesta Ware.

Fiesta Ware was one of the pioneers of the mix-and-match concept, for its many color options (there are now 11) enabled consumers to put together several different color statements on their tables. Thus it served as both a decorative and a conversation piece. By introducing contemporary colors, Homer Laughlin has managed to capture two markets: the original audience who never lost interest in the product as well as those drawn to retro design. It has also become a force in determining color trends for the entire housewares industry.

Source: HFN, May 27, 2002, p. 68.

ENVIRONMENTAL IMPACT

Lead poisoning is a possible effect of lead-glazed pottery, especially if the glaze is chipped, cracked, or improperly applied. It is important to store food in lead-free containers.

Acidic drinks like wine or juice, and acidic foods, such as tomatoes, can leach toxins out of leaded containers. The most common source of lead poisoning among adults is contact with glazed ceramics through the use of improperly glazed mugs for hot beverages, such as tea and coffee. Items that exhibit a dusty or chalky gray residue on the glaze after they're washed should not be used.

Additionally, lead poisoning has been reported in pottery workers and in those who practice the craft of pottery.

SUMMARY

Pottery refers to all articles made from clay including earthenware, stoneware, china, and bone china. It also refers to a type of earthenware made from crude porous clay. The term *ceramics* can also be used to describe articles made from clay. Clay is decomposed granite. Pottery is fired, or baked, in a kiln to make it more durable. Glazes are finishes that are added to some pottery.

There are three basic classifications of pottery: earthenware, stoneware, and china. There are two types of earthenware: pottery and semi-vitreous ware. Semi-vitreous ware is also called fine earthenware. The word *vitreous* means that the product has the qualities of glass. *Semi-vitreous* means that the ware is somewhat like glass. Stoneware is sometimes called high-fired ware and is made from clay mixed with a fusible stone that has been vitrified at a high temperature. China is completely vitrified. While it is frequently called porcelain in Europe, it is still known as china in the United States and England.

The main ingredient in pottery is clay. Various other materials are added to increase translucency, improve strength, or improve moldability. Metallic oxides can withstand the high temperatures of firing and are the only products used to color clay or apply colored designs to pottery.

The steps in the preparation of the clay body are mixing, filtering and magnetizing, pressing, aging, and pugging. The steps in forming the body are shaping, drying, sticking up, and finishing. The first firing is called the bisque or biscuit firing. The glost firing fuses the glaze to the body of the ware, and decorative firings make the overglaze decorations more durable. There are four basic ways to decorate pottery: in-the-clay decorations, underglaze decorations, in-the-glaze decorations, and overglaze decorations.

TERMS FOR REVIEW

ball clay (blue clay)
basalt
bisque firing (biscuit-firing)
body
bone ash
bone china
ceramics
china
china stone
clay
coiling
common clay
copperplate decoration
crackle glaze
decalcomania
delft
Dresden china
earthenware
encrusting
etching
Faience
Famille (Famille jaune, Famille noire, Famille rose, Famille verte)
feldspar
fettling
fine earthenware
fire clay
firing

flint
frit
gilding
glaze
glost firing
graffito (sgraffito)
greenware
hard-paste porcelain
high-fired ware
Imari
in-the-glaze decorations
in-the-clay decorations
ironstone
jasperware
jiggering
jollying
kaolin
Kakiemon
kiln
leather hardness
lithography
Lusterware
majolica (also spelled maiolica)
molding
overglaze decorations
Parian ware
pâte-sur-pâte
pierced decoration

pinching
porcelain
porcelaine noire
potter
potter's wheel
pottery
pugging
Raku
relief decorations
resist designs
rice patterns
salt-glazed pottery
semi-vitreous ware
slab method
slip
slip decorations
soft-paste porcelain
sponging
sprigging
stamping
sticking up
stoneware
terra-cotta
throwing
towing
transfer printing
underglaze decorations
vitreous
Willow pattern

REVIEW QUESTIONS

1. Compare the characteristics of the three major types of pottery: earthenware, stoneware, and china.
2. What is bone china?
3. What is the purpose of firing?
4. What is the purpose of glazing?
5. Why are gold and platinum applied after glazing?
6. List three decorative techniques that might be used on pottery.

LEARNING ACTIVITIES

1. Visit the china department of a large department store. Compare and contrast the presentation of the pottery, stoneware, and china. List at least 4 brands of dishware and describe two patterns sold by each company. Evaluate using the following criteria: colors used, type of design, and the look and feel of the dishes.
2. Search the Internet for articles on lead poisoning. Describe the legal issues related to lead poisoning.

CHAPTER 6

PLASTICS

Mr. McGuire (Walter Brooke) to Benjamin Braddock (Dustin Hoffman): I just want to say one word to you…just one word.
Ben: Yes, sir.
Mr. McGuire: Are you listening?
Ben: Yes, sir. I am.
Mr. McGuire: Plastics

—from the screenplay for *The Graduate*

WHY WOULD SUCH A SUCCESSFUL BUSINESSPERSON GIVE "PLASTICS" AS A WORD OF ADVICE TO A recent college graduate? When the film *The Graduate* appeared in 1967, plastics represented career opportunities in a variety of industries. Plastics continue to be all around us—in our apparel, in our homes and cars, and in all kinds of equipment and utensils we use every day. Plastics are widely used in industry for a vast array of products and equipment. Approximately 15,000 different plastic formulas are available throughout the world. Easy-care fabrics, stain-resistant finishes on home furnishings, and food packaging are all examples of products made from plastics.

Plastics are made from natural substances, such as air, coal, natural gas, petroleum, water, and wood. Most plastics are based on the carbon atom. Silicone is an exception, because it is based on the silicon atom. The word *plastic* refers to a synthetic material composed of long chains of atoms called polymers. **Polymers** are giant molecules that are comprised of many simple molecules. They are created through a chemical process called **polymerization.** Polymers have outstanding stability and a strong intermolecular force that prevents easy destruction.

Plastic is soft and moldable during production but will solidify into the final product. Usually heat and/or pressure are needed to solidify the material. A distinct advantage of plastics is that they can be mixed with other materials to change or improve characteristics.

Plastics are very versatile and can be formulated to meet specific requirements. They can be:

- Transparent or opaque
- Soft or hard
- Rigid or elastic
- Light or heavy weight
- Solid or filled with air
- Flame retardant or flammable

In addition, plastics are generally resistant to chemicals, corrosion, and moisture. They can be molded into complex shapes and are available in a wide range of colors.

At one time, items made of plastics were considered to be inferior substitutes for the genuine article, but now they are frequently preferred over the "real" product. For example, in many applications, polyethylene bottles are considered to be far superior to glass bottles.

A BRIEF HISTORY OF PLASTICS

Most authorities agree that Alexander Parkes developed the precursor to modern plastics. In 1862 Parkes exhibited a product he called Parkesine, which he made by treating cotton waste with a mixture of nitric and sulfuric acids and then combining it with castor oil. The product was very similar to plastic, but efforts to produce it commercially failed. In 1864 an American chemist, John Hyatt used camphor in place of the castor oil to produce a product he named celluloid. Celluloid had many uses, such as photographic film, dentures, knife handles, combs, dolls, and eyeglass frames. Unfortunately, it was very flammable.

In 1909 Leo Baekeland, a Belgian-born American, developed the first commercially profitable patent for Bakelite®, a trade name for a phenolic plastic (see Industry Statement 6.1). This was the first important man-made polymer. His process controlled the speed of the reaction between phenol and formaldehyde and allowed the material to be molded. Commercial production began in 1910. Figure 6.1 shows the chemical structure of Bakelite.

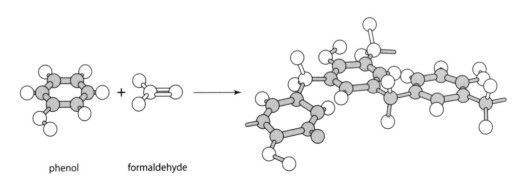

phenol   formaldehyde

FIGURE 6.1
Bakelite is created from phenol and formaldehyde.

INDUSTRY STATEMENT 6.1

1920s: Bakelite Is Born

Bakelite, one of modern plastic's most notable ancestors, brought fashion into the housewares industry.

This synthetic thermosetting resin was invented in the early 1900s by Leo H. Baekeland, a Belgian-born chemist who also invented Velox, a photographic paper.

After immigrating to the United States and settling on a large estate just north of New York City, Baekeland converted a barn into a lab and began work on a new material to be used as an electrical insulator. There, polyoxybenzylmethylenglycolanhydride, otherwise known as bakelite, was born.

Bakelite soon outgrew its industrial use, and by the 1930s, the material had found its way into almost everything from jewelry to radios to kitchen utensils.

General Bakelite Corp., founded by Baekeland to produce and license the manufacture of his new finding, advertised bakelite as "the material of a thousand uses."

Bakelite's ability to mold into any shape and take on a rainbow of hues brought fashion into housewares. Adding a bakelite handle in, say, key-lime green could turn the once-boring mixer into a chic gadget.

Oneida and GE are just a few of the companies that jumped on the bakelite bandwagon.

Source: HFN, May 27, 2002, p. 108.

Hermann Standinger, a German chemist, introduced the concept that plastics are long chain molecules created by polymerization in 1922. His theory led to the development of nylon fiber by DuPont de Nemours and Company in 1939. Also in 1939, British scientists discovered polyethylene, which became the basis for the development of epoxy resins, polycarbonates, polyethylene, terephthalates, and polyurethanes.

New machinery was developed to produce and process these new materials. Two important examples are the injection mold equipment that was invented in 1921 and the extrusion machines developed in 1937.

MATERIALS USED IN PLASTICS

The most important ingredient in a plastic product is resin. Other materials used in the production of plastic products are colorants, fillers, lubricants, plasticizers, solvents, and stabilizers. Not all plastics have additives. Many are left in their natural state. For example, polystyrene containers contain no additional materials.

Resins

A **resin** is an organic substance made by the polymerization of simple molecules. The resin, or polymer, will determine the characteristics of the plastic. The term *resin* is sometimes used in place of the word *plastic* (see Figure 6.2). The resin determines whether the plastic product will

FIGURE 6.2 *Woven resin furniture.* Courtesy of Brown Jordan International.

be thermoset or thermoplastic. These are the two main categories of plastics. **Thermoset plastics** are set into their permanent shape by heat. They cannot be remelted and reshaped. **Thermoplastics** become soft and pliable when exposed to heat and harden when the heat is removed. They may be shaped and reshaped numerous times.

Colorants

Plastics can be produced in a full spectrum of colors. This characteristic has contributed to the popularity of plastic for many products for the home, fashion accessories, and children's toys. Color can be added to plastics with dyes, pigments, and special-effect colorants. Dyes are seldom used in home fashions.

Pigments

Pigments are coloring substances that are mixed with the resin but do not chemically combine with the resin. Pigments may cause defects in the surface color and may stain.

Inorganic Pigments Inorganic pigments (pigments that do not contain carbon) do not produce colors as brilliant as dyes or organic compounds. They are primarily used for opaque, colored plastics, such as the handles and bases of toasters and irons. They are also used as the housings for radios, televisions, and telephones. See Table 6.1 for a listing of the inorganic pigments used to color plastics.

TABLE 6.1
Inorganic Pigments Used to Color Plastics

Pigment	Color
Carbon	Black
Iron oxide	Red
Cobalt oxide	Blue
Cadmium sulfide	Yellow
Lead sulfate	White

Organic Pigments Organic pigments (pigments that contain carbon) produce bright opaque colors. The translucent and transparent colors are not as brilliant as those produced with dyes, but they are superior to those produced with inorganic pigments.

Special-Effect Colorants

Special-effect colorants have improved consumer acceptance of plastics. They can provide both aesthetic and functional benefits to products. Table 6.2 summarizes some of the special effect colorants and their uses.

Fillers

Fillers are substances added to many plastics. They can contribute beneficial characteristics, such as increased strength, to the plastic. **Reinforcements** are fillers that increase the tensile strength (resistance to pulling forces) and impact strength (resistance to forceful blows) of the plastic. Glass fibers are the most widely used reinforcement, but mica flakes, boron, and graphite fibers are also used. Some fillers are **extenders** and are used to reduce costs. They are added to decrease the amount of resin used and increase the amount of the product. As the amount of filler increases, the plastic becomes less transparent. Common fillers include:

- *Wood flour* (granulated waste wood) Reduces brittleness, improves appearance
- *Silica* Used in paints for the home
- *Metals* Add strength or electrical conductivity
- *Wax, bran* Adds self-lubricating properties

Lubricants

Lubricants are added to plastics for three reasons:

- To reduce friction between the plastic mixture and the production machinery
- To aid in internal lubrication of the plastic so the compound combines more easily
- To add a nonadhering surface to the plastic product during and after production

TABLE 6.2

Selected Special-Effect Colorants and Their Uses

Special-Effect Colorant	Uses
Metallic flakes or powders of aluminum, brass, copper, or gold	Metallic sheen used, for example, on decorative items
Natural pearl essence from quanine crystals that are retrieved from the fatty skin of fish	Pearl luster on jewelry, toys, toilet seats
Synthetic pearl essence	Pearl luster on jewelry, toys, toilet seats
Luminescent materials	Hunting jackets, hard hats, gloves, raincoats, life preservers, hazard signs, paints

Excessive use of lubricants may inhibit polymerization and cause "lubrication bloom," a cloudy area on the surface of the product. Products used as lubricants include metallic soaps, waxes, and other plastics, such as polyamides, polyethylene, silicone, and polytetrafluoroethylene, which have nonstick characteristics.

Plasticizers

Plasticizers are important in the production of plastics. They make the plastic softer and more pliable at increased temperatures by reducing the intermolecular bonds that make some resins too viscous (thick) for use. Plasticizers also reduce the explosive reaction of plastics. Plasticizers make the final product more resilient, more flexible, and more impact resistant.

Over 500 plasticizers are available. They are selected for their compatibility with the resin and the specific properties they can bring to the plastic. They are especially important in the production of plastic coatings, films and sheets, molding, adhesives, and extrusions.

Solvents

In general, most resins are very thick, so **solvents** are used to dilute, dissolve, or liquefy resins. The solvents make the resins more manageable so they can be processed more efficiently. The solvent will evaporate during processing and leave only the resin.

Stabilizers

Stabilizers are chemical additives that give the plastic product protection from degradation by the environment. Many different stabilizers are available. The function of the stabilizer can be to reduce the effects of ultraviolet rays, protect the plastic from degradation during the high heat levels of production, increase the storage life of the plastic, or prevent degradation caused by weathering.

TYPES OF PLASTICS

As already mentioned, plastics are commonly divided into two categories—thermoset plastics and thermoplastics. The chemical nature of the resin determines the characteristics of the plastic. Thermoset plastics are permanently set into shape by heat. Thermoplastics can be reheated and reshaped many times.

Thermoset Plastics

The thermoset characteristic of these plastics is the result of the cross linkages that develop on the chainlike molecular structure during the initial application of heat. Bonds are created between the molecular chains. These cross linkages prevent the long chains from moving or slipping. The cross linkages remain during subsequent applications of heat and prevent the plastic from returning to a flow state. Most plastics in this classification are adversely affected by heat exceeding 350 degrees Fahrenheit. They will char when exposed to very high heat or open flame. Thermoset plastics are used extensively in industry and also have application for consumer goods. Plastics in this classification include epoxies, melamine formaldehydes, phenolics, polyesters, polyurethanes, silicones, and urea formaldehydes. Table 6.3 describes these plastics in more detail.

Epoxies

Epoxies are widely used and are especially good for bonding in difficult conditions. They have been in use for more than 100 years, but commercial use started in 1947 as a metal-to-metal adhesive. They are an important component in Corian®, a solid-surfacing material used for countertops.

Melamine Formaldehydes

Melamine formaldehydes were introduced in 1939 and are common forms of plastic that are used in consumer goods. They have unlimited color possibilities and an unusually durable surface when compared with many other plastics. Because melamine has no odor or taste, it is used extensively for dishes (see Figure 6.3).

Phenolics

As mentioned in the discussion about the history of plastics, **phenolics** are considered the first synthetic plastics. They were the forerunner of plastics production as the first plastics to be successfully produced and sold as consumer goods. Phenolic plastics are very versatile. They can be formulated for many uses by simply varying the ingredients with which the plastic is combined.

There are two main production methods for phenolic plastics—molding and casting. Both methods are discussed later in this chapter. The properties of cast and molded phenolics are slightly different.

TABLE 6.3
Thermoset Plastics

Plastic	Characteristics	End Uses	Cost
Epoxy	Outstanding adhesive qualities; resistance to abrasion, chemicals, weather; exceptional durability	Mobile homes, ceramics, floor protectors, appliance surfaces, adhesives, water-repellent fabric finishes, joint sealants	Expensive
Melamine formaldehyde	Available in an unlimited range of colors; very tough surface; resistance to scratching, heat, chemicals, detergents, stains; odorless; tasteless	Plastic dishes (trade name Melmac®), laminated countertop covering (trade name Formica®), switch gears for electrical current (especially for low frequency currency), refrigerator and range surface coatings, cabinetry, furniture	Moderate
Phenolic	Excellent strength, hardness, and rigidity; high resistance to grease and oil, water, detergents, and chemicals; low conductance of heat; great adhesive qualities; can be greatly foamed beyond their original volume; resistance to heat and electricity; clear and white phenolics have tendency to yellow with age	Molded furniture and frames; electrical supplies; handles on irons and cookware; handles and feet of heat-producing electrical equipment, such as irons and toasters; washing machine parts; camera cases; ashtrays	Low
Polyester	Resistance to scratching, denting, and weak acids; good strength	Surface coatings, such as enamels, paints, and lacquers; appliance cabinets; building panels; films; laminating resins; furniture; patio covers; skylights	Moderate
Polyurethane	Excellent resilience; good flexibility (unless formulated to be rigid); lightweight; compression strength; ability to adhere to metals; foaming ability; holds heat well; creamy tan in color; does not disintegrate when repeatedly exposed to air (as foam rubber does)	Cushioning materials for upholstered furniture, bedding, pillows; building and apparel insulation; sponges (it will hold up to 20 times its weight in water); padding under rugs and carpet	Moderate
Silicone	Chemical inertness; nonsticking, resistance to water; does not conduct electricity; antifoaming agent	Stain-resistant polish or spray, electrical coverings, scratch cover, foam (especially when produced at relatively low temperatures)	Very expensive
Urea formaldehyde	Odorless; hardness; durability; resistance to scratching; not affected by boiling water; lightweight; resistance to breakage but may crack if dropped	Bottle closures, buttons, toys, cutlery handles, cosmetic containers, lamp fixtures, housings for electrical products, textile and paper treatments; resin is used to bond plywood and other wood joints	Very low

FIGURE 6.3
Melamine dinnerware. Courtesy of Fairchild Publications, Inc.

Molded phenolics are exceptionally strong because filler materials are chosen to add strength. Usually, the filler is dark in color so the resulting plastic will be dark in tone—red, navy, dark brown, dark green, black, and dark purple. Black is the color most frequently used.

Cast phenolics are not as strong as molded phenolics. Because the dark filler is not used, the resulting plastic can be colored in lighter and brighter colors. They can also be transparent, translucent, or opaque.

Polyesters

In general, most **polyesters** are thermoset, but some are thermoplastic. Dacron®, a well-known textile fiber, is a thermoplastic polyester resin. **Alkyd resins** are a subcategory of polyester. They are thermoset and used extensively in paints.

Unlike most other plastics, polyester is not molded with pressure and heat. It cures (sets) at room temperature. Polyester is relatively inexpensive to produce and is often reinforced with glass to create fiberglass. Polyester is also used as a gel coating. For example, cultured marble countertops have a polyester gel coating.

Polyurethanes

Polyurethane foams were developed in the mid-1800s in Germany but were not used until World War II. They are so well known as a constituent of foam that the name *urethane foam* is commonly used to refer to all types of foam, even those made from other materials. There are many different varieties of polyurethane. Some polyurethanes are thermoplastic.

Polyurethanes release carbon dioxide that causes the foaming. The plastic will expand as much as 25 times its original size when poured into a mold. The polyurethane can be formulated to be very flexible or rigid. Rigid polyurethane is commonly used as building insulation.

Silicones

Research on **silicones** began in the 1870s, and they were commercially available in England in the early 1900s. Collaboration between General Electric and Corning Glass corporations brought commercial production of silicone to the United States. Silicone storage containers are a fairly popular end use for silicone plastic.

Silicones are often combined with rubber. Silicone makes the rubber nonflammable to combustibles, such as oil and grease. It also prevents the rubber from foaming.

Urea Formaldehydes

Urea Formaldehydes are very similar to melamine formaldehydes. The resin is mixed with cellulose to create a translucent plastic that will take any color.

Thermoplastics

Their ability to be heated and reformed numerous times is determined by the chemical structure of thermoplastics. Thermoplastics do not develop cross linkages during the first application of heat, so the chains can easily slip over each other when reheated. If thermoplastics are heated and cooled excessively, they may lose color or lose their thermoplastic nature.

The main thermoplastics are cellulosics, polyamides polycarbonates, polymethyl methacrylate, polyolefins, polystyrenes, polytetrafluoroethylene, and vinyls. Table 6.4 describes these plastics in more detail. The general characteristics and end uses are presented with the exceptions noted.

Cellulosics

Cellulosics use cellulose in the form of cotton or wood fibers as part of the resin. They are a chemical modification of the natural polymer present in cotton or wood. Their uses are limited because of their low melting temperature, which is about 160 degrees Fahrenheit. There are five cellulosic plastics: cellulose acetate, cellulose nitrate, cellulose acetate butyrate, ethyl cellulose, and cellulose proprionate.

Polyamides

Polyamides are more commonly known as nylons. They are well known for their uses in textile products. Since its introduction in 1939 by DuPont, nylon has become one of the industry's most widely used plastics.

TABLE 6.4
Thermoplastics

Plastic	Characteristics	End Uses	Cost
Cellulosic	Good durability and pliability; easily worked; moderate resistance to scratching; resistance to weathering; lightweight; cellulose nitrate is highly flammable, scratches easily, and is discolored by sunlight and heat; cellulose acetate is deformed by moisture.	Ingredient in lacquer, pens, and pencils. Uses with cellulose acetate: heels for women's shoes, display racks, toilet articles, outdoor advertising, textile fiber.	Expensive
Polyamide	Difficult to mold; very durable; great strength; lightweight; good resistance to chemicals; good flexibility.	Lubricant-free machinery parts, apparel, interior, and industrial fabrics, aerosol bottles, bristles for toothbrushes and paintbrushes, fishing line, rope, chair caster rollers, drawer glides.	Expensive
Polycarbonate	Very durable; good optics; high resistance to impact.	Moldings, electrical applications, glazing for shatterproof assembly, casual tableware.	Expensive
Polymethyl methacrylate	Excellent transparency, clarity, and sparkle; resistance to breakage and weather; ease of care; odorless; moderate resistance to scratching; lightweight; good chemical resistance.	Plastic furniture, decorative ornaments, safety glass and skylight glazing, toilet articles, food containers, control panels, dials, handles, jewelry, paints, waterproof garments, countertops (Corian®).	Moderate
Polyolefin Polyethylene (PE)	May be flexible or rigid; good strength; resistance to water, many chemicals, the effects of aging, and breaking; HDPE is difficult to heat-seal or bond with solvents; oils and greases tend to cling; waxy-like feel; can be stored for extended periods of time without loss of properties; allows gases to pass through it; good pliability.	Film applications, such as food packaging, household wraps, shrink wrap, shopping bags (LDPE). Uses with HDPE: blow-molded containers of up to 2-gallon capacity; extruded pipe and conduit; injection-molding applications, such as rigid furniture. Children's toys, ice cube trays, waterproof packaging.	Low
Polypropylene (PP)	Stronger than PE; resistance to heat up to approximately 300 degrees Fahrenheit; lightest weight plastic; may be rigid or flexible; may be transparent or opaque; resistance to chemicals, stains, the effects of aging, breaking, water; has a mar-resistant surface; good pliability.	Textile fiber for apparel and home furnishings, children's toys, ice cube trays, waterproof packaging.	Low
Polystyrene plastics	Ease of molding; available in a wide range of colors; rigid; resistance to chemicals; moderate resistance to scratching; sparkling clarity.	Children's toys, frozen food containers, fast food packaging, kitchenware, insulation, tile, light fixture diffusers, core materials for doors (in foamed or expanded form).	Low
Polystyrene alloys	Resistance to moisture and alkalis; ability to diffuse light; odorless; lightweight; clarity; buoyancy.	Appliance housings, paints, display cases, pipes for plumbing. Uses with ABS: vents, pipes for chemicals, outdoor furniture, drawer liners, chair shells.	Low
Polytetra-fluoroethylene	High heat tolerance; outstanding electrical insulator and resistance to chemicals; nonadhesiveness; almost no moisture absorption.	Wire insulation, transportation of hot adhesives, coating for nonstick cookware, stain-resistant coating on textiles.	Very expensive
Vinyl (PVC, PVB)	Lightweight; rigid or flexible; good elastic and adhesive qualities (PVB); transparent; good resistance to chemicals and impact; smooth but not slick; odorless; tasteless; resistance to warping, moisture, shrinkage, wear, tearing, and adherence of dirt.	Glues, safety glass production (PVB), hard surface floor coverings, rainwear, packaging, toys, fabrics (especially imitation leather), plumbing pipes, gutters, packaging films, wall coverings, moldings, window frames, window blinds, wall paneling, insulation (foamed or expanded vinyl).	Low

FIGURE 6.4
*Unbranched polymer chain
of high-density polyethylene.*

Polycarbonates

Polycarbonates are expensive thermoplastics that are used mainly as molding compounds. Recently they have become a popular substitute for acrylic in casual tableware.

Polymethyl Methacrylate

Polymethyl methacrylate is more commonly known as *acrylic.* Acrylic plastics are one of the most common plastics used in consumer goods. They were developed in the early 1930s and were first used for the production of safety glass. During World War II, acrylics were used for aircraft windows.

Polyethylene (PE) and Polypropylene (PP)

Polyethylene (PE) and **polypropylene (PP)** are the main forms of **polyolefins.** PE was first introduced in 1933 and is one of the simplest plastics. PE is available in both low- and high-density versions. High-density PE (HDPE) is rigid. Low-density PE (LDPE) is flexible and tough. *Density* refers to the organization of the long chain molecules. High-density polymers have straight chains with no branches (see Figure 6.4). Low-density polymers have side branches that prevent the chains from packing together (see Figure 6.5). PE is sometime referred to as polythene. PP was commercially introduced in 1957. It is one of the most used plastics. PE and PP have similar characteristics except that PP is stronger. The characteristics and end uses of PE and PP are addressed separately in Table 6.4.

Polystyrenes

Although **polystyrene** was developed in the early 1830s, it was not the 1930s that it was used commercially. Since then it has become one of the most used plastics. There are two basic groups of polystyrenes—general-purpose polystyrene and polystyrene alloys that are sometimes referred to as rubber blends. An important rubber blend is **acrylonitrile-butadiene-styrene (ABS).** (Refer to Chapter 8 for additional information about rubber.) Characteristics and end uses of polystyrene and polystyrene alloys are presented separately in Table 6.4.

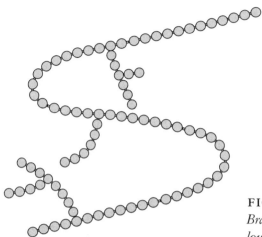

FIGURE 6.5
*Branched polymer chain of
low-density polyethylene.*

Polytetrafluoroethylene

Polytetrafluoroethylene (PTFE) plastic is more commonly known by the trade name Teflon®. It is processed like a metal instead of a plastic because it can withstand temperatures above 350 degrees Fahrenheit. It is still considered a thermoplastic despite its high-temperature tolerance. PTFE has become famous because of its use as a stain- and water-resistant coating for fabric and as a nonstick surface coating in cookware and bake ware. There are also many industrial uses for PTFE.

Vinyl

Vinyl was developed in 1925, but the resin is very hard and easily broken. The development of plasticizers (products that increase the pliability of the resin) enabled producers to process vinyl. Vinyl plastics are a very large group of plastics (see Figure 6.6). There are seven major groups. Two important ones, **polyvinyl chloride (PVC)** and **polyvinyl butyral (PVB)** are featured in Table 6.4.

PRODUCTION OF PLASTIC

Most companies that produce plastics ship the plastic material to manufacturers for final processing. The plastic can be shipped as a powder, pellet, or liquid. Sometimes the plastic will be shipped as "semifinished" tubing, films, or sheets.

Shaping Plastics

Plastics are very versatile and can be shaped by casting, coating, extrusion, laminating, molding, and thermoforming. Additionally, plastics can be produced in a wide range of weights and malleability, from soft and spongy to rigid and hard.

FIGURE 6.6
*Vinyl woven into a
high performance textile
for rugs and runners.*

Plynyl by Chilewich. Photo courtesy of Antoice Bootz.

Casting

Thermoset plastics and thermoplastics can be shaped by **casting**. This process is very similar to the procedure for making wax candles. If the polymer is a solid, it is heated until it liquefies. The liquid polymer is poured into lead-covered molds and baked in ovens until the plastic hardens as shown in Figure 6.7.

Casting is less expensive than compression or injection molding, which will be discussed later in this chapter, and the plastic products are less expensive. In general, cast plastics are not strong and cannot support heavy weight.

Plastics that are usually cast are polymethyl methacrylate (acrylic), epoxy, phenolic, polyester, and polystyrene. Cast phenolics are used to make imitation ivory and billiard balls. Marble dust is combined with polyester to make cultured marble that is used for bathroom sinks. Other uses for cast plastics include garment hangers, brush and mirror backs, jewelry stones, inexpensive buttons, and furniture trim. Plastic casting is also popular as a craft or fine art technique.

There are two variations of casting—rotational casting and dip casting. **Rotational casting** is used to create seamless, large, hollow objects, such as toy balls and one-piece modern chairs. The polymer is placed in hollow metal molds and rotated. The mold is heated, and the plastic melts on the wall of the mold. As the mold is rotated, the plastic flows over the entire surface of the mold. After cooling, the product is removed from the mold.

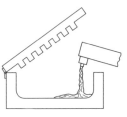

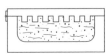

FIGURE 6.7
Casting.

Gloves and hot water bottles are made using **dip casting.** A heated mold is dipped into a liquid dispersion of the polymer. The plastic adheres to the hot mold. After curing (setting), the plastic is peeled off the mold.

Coating

A **coating** is a very thin protective layer applied to a material. It is not removable. Coatings are applied to paper, fabric, metals, and walls. There are several different ways to apply a coating. The product can be dipped or submerged in the plastic. Dish drainers, tool handles, bobby pins, and coated fabric gloves are coated in this manner. Paper and textiles can be coated by simply spreading the coating over the material and allowing it to dry. Electrostatic spray coating is another method that allows for even coverage of the coating. The product is heated and positively charged. It is then placed into negatively charged dry plastic powders. The powders melt and fuse onto the product. This method is used for parts for dishwashers, washing machines, and refrigerators.

Extrusion

The extrusion process is similar to that used to create textile fibers (see Chapter 2). Softened polymers are forced through a die (devices for cutting material in a press). Usually thermoplastics, such as cellulosics, polyamides, polymethyl methacrylate, polyolefins, polystyrenes, polytetrafluoroethylene, and vinyls, are shaped by extrusion. The shape of the die determines the resulting shape of the plastic. Rods, tubes, fibers, flat sheets, and moldings can be extruded. Polyethelyene bags are created by extruding a tube and sealing the ends.

Laminating

Laminating is the process of bonding two or more layers of any material together. The lamination process bonds layers of thermosetting resin-impregnated or resin-coated materials with high heat and pressure. The plastics most commonly laminated are phenolic, melamine, silicone, epoxy, and polyester. The reinforcing materials may be cotton fibers, paper, fibrous glass, textiles, or wood. The reinforcing materials are layered between two sheets of plastic that hold them together. The materials are impregnated with resin or alternated with plastic film. Then the layers are pressed between two highly polished steel plates and subjected to high heat. The plates press the layers together into a single sheet. The plates may be textured or patterned to create desired effects in the laminate. The surface may also be embossed to simulate fabric, stone, or wood.

Plastic laminates offer many advantages. Often their chemical, physical, and electrical properties are superior to other products. Laminates are very durable, and they are available in a wide variety or colors, textures, and patterns. They are easy to care for and are impervious to many chemicals. In the textile industry there are many uses for laminates. Layers of cloth, plastic film, and foam are bonded together to make tablecloths, imitation leather, raincoats, shower curtains, insulated fabric, and other specialized products.

Two types of laminates are used in interiors—low-pressure laminates and high-pressure laminates.

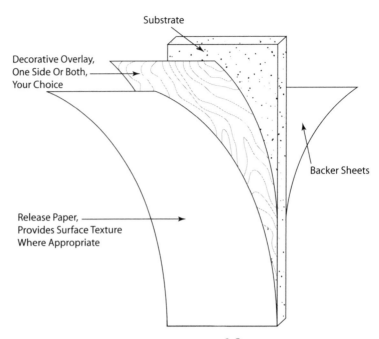

FIGURE 6.8 *Low-pressure laminate.*

Low-pressure laminates are sometimes called **thermoset laminates.** They are made by impregnating laminating paper with melamine or polyester resin and then applying it to a substrate under low heat and low pressure. The substrate is usually particleboard. These laminates are low cost and are usually used as interior panels and as shelves in casework. They are not as durable as high-pressure laminates (see Figure 6.8).

High-pressure laminates are created by layering a melamine-impregnated overlay and decorative surface papers over phenolic resin-impregnated papers. The layers are then compressed at temperatures exceeding 130 degrees Centigrade (265 degrees Fahrenheit) using high pressure. Formica® is the trade name of a well-known high-pressure laminate that is used for countertops and imitation veneers for furniture (see Figure 6.9).

Molding

Plastics can also be shaped by molding. There are several different ways to mold plastics: compression molding, injection molding, and blow molding. Thermoset plastics are shaped using compression molding. Thermoplastics have better flow and cooling properties, so they can be shaped by injection and blow molding.

In **compression molding** thermoset plastic pellets, powder, or preformed discs are preheated and poured into steel molds. The mold is closed, and heat and pressure are applied. The heat melts the plastic so it takes the shape of the mold. After cooling, the product is removed from the mold. Dinnerware, buttons, buckles, knobs, handles, appliance housings, and industrial parts are compression molded.

Injection molding is a fast and economical method of shaping solid plastic parts. Thermoplastic pellets of powder are melted and forced from a cylinder into a cool mold (see Figure 6.10).

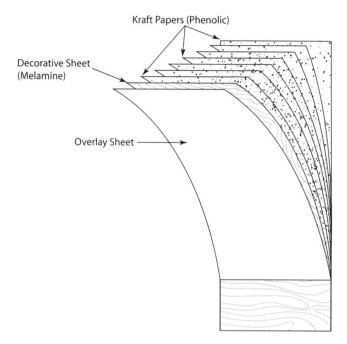

Kraft Papers (Phenolic)

Decorative Sheet
(Melamine)

Overlay Sheet

FIGURE 6.9
High-pressure laminate.

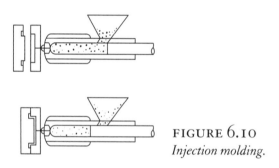

FIGURE 6.10
Injection molding.

The part is removed within seconds. Injection molding has the benefit of increased accuracy. Buttons, combs, bowls, and toys are injection molded.

The **blow-molding** technique was adapted from the glass industry. It was developed in the late 1950s. A hollow tube of molten thermoplastic is placed in a mold and forced against the walls of the mold with air pressure (see Figure 6.11). After cooling, the product is ejected from the mold. This method is fast and efficient and is especially appropriate for containers, although objects from tiny tubes to large barrels may be mold blown.

Foam Casting or Molding

Most plastics can be foamed, or expanded, before **foam casting** or **molding.** They are processed into a cellular form by the addition of foaming agents that generate a gas when the temperature is raised. Sometimes air is mechanically whipped into the resin just before polymerization. The foamed plastic can be cast or molded into its final shape. Foams can be rigid, semirigid, or flexible (see Figure 6.12).

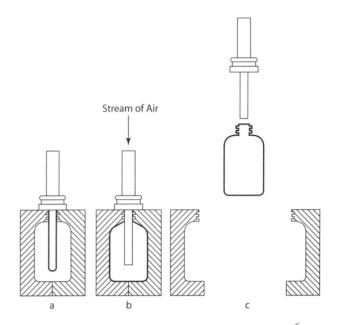

FIGURE 6.11

Blow molding: a. tube of molten plastic is placed in mold cavity, b. air pressure forces the plastic against the walls of the mold, c. the mold opens and ejects the product.

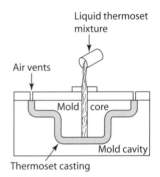

FIGURE 6.12
Foam molding.

Two common foams are polystyrene and polyurethane. Examples of foamed plastics include sponges, insulation, cushioning materials, imitation leather, plastic cups, and lightweight toys.

Thermoforming

Only thermoplastics can undergo **thermoforming.** Large sheets of plastic are softened and made to conform to a molded surface using air, mechanical, or vacuum pressure. This method is widely used because the tooling costs are low, and large pieces can be produced easily and quickly. Examples of thermoformed plastics include children's wading pools, blister packages, toys, and food packaging.

Finishing Plastics

After plastic products are formed, most of them need to be finished. The formed or molded parts are then fabricated into finished products. They can be assembled using mechanical fasteners, such as screws, nuts and bolts, spring clips, and hinges. They can also be joined using adhesives, heat, solvents, or ultrasonic methods.

Plastics can be sanded, buffed, tumbled, and polished for a smoother finish. They can also be painted, printed, stenciled, or metal plated for a decorative appearance.

ENVIRONMENTAL IMPACT

Despite the many advantages of plastic, there are environmental concerns about plastic products. Recycling and flammability are important issues affecting the use of plastic products.

Plastics Recycling

Plastics do not decompose like natural products, such as wood. The result is that waste plastic accumulates in landfills. Biodegradable plastics have been developed, but the shelf life of the products is reduced. Plastics are also hard to burn. They melt quickly and will clog an incinerator.

Many plastics are completely recyclable. Both pre- and postconsumer plastics can be reused in many products. Postconsumer recycled plastics are being used to manufacture new plastic bottles, carpet yarns, strapping tape, fiberfill insulation and stuffing, and drainage pipes. Plastic wood is a recycled product that has many benefits. It does not rot, so it is used as waterfront bulkheads and jetties and park benches. It can also be used in furniture and as man-made reefs.

Flammability

Most polymers are flammable. Neoprene (a synthetic rubber—see Chapter 8) and PVC are not flammable. Flame-retardant chemicals, such as antimony trioxide or compounds containing chlorine or bromine, are added to reduce the danger of fire.

SUMMARY

A plastic is a synthetic material that is composed of long chains of atoms called polymers. Thousands of formulas for plastics have been developed. Plastics have outstanding stability and strong intermolecular force that prevents easy destruction. This makes them appropriate for many consumer and industrial goods.

The most important ingredient in a plastic product is resin. A resin is an organic substance made by the polymerization of simple molecules. The resin, or polymer, will determine the characteristics of the plastic. Other materials used in the production of some plastic products are colorants, fillers, lubricants, plasticizers, solvents, and stabilizers.

There are two categories of plastics—thermoset plastics and thermoplastics. Thermoset plastics are set into their permanent shape by heat. They cannot be remelted and reshaped. Epoxies, melamine formaldehydes, phenolics, polyesters, polyurethanes silicones, and urea formaldehydes are thermoset plastics. Thermoplastics become soft and pliable when exposed to heat and harden when the heat is removed. Cellulosics, polyamides, polycarbonates, polymethyl methacrylate, polyolefins, polystyrenes, polytetrafluoroethylene, and vinyls are thermoplastics. Plastic can be shaped by casting, coating, extrusion, laminating, molding, and thermoforming.

Despite the many advantages of plastic, there are environmental concerns about plastic products. Recycling and flammability are important issues affecting the use of plastic products.

TERMS FOR REVIEW

acrylonitrile-butadiene-styrene (ABS)
alkyd resins
blow molding
casting
cellulosics
coating
compression molding
dip casting
epoxies
extenders
fillers
foam casting (molding)
high-pressure laminates
injection molding
laminating
low-pressure laminates
lubricants
melamine formaldehyde
phenolics
pigments
plastic
plasticizers
polyamides
polycarbonates
polyester
polyethylene (PE)
polymerization
polymers
polymethyl methacrylate
polyolefins
polypropylene (PP)
polystyrenes
polytetrafluoroethylene (PTFE)
polyurethanes
polyvinyl butyral (PVB)
polyvinyl chloride (PVC)
reinforcements
resin
rotational casting
silicones
solvents
stabilizers
thermoforming
thermoplastics
thermoset laminates
thermoset plastics
urea formaldehydes
urethane foam
vinyl

INDUSTRY PROFILE

Tupperware

In 1946, America was booming, fresh off World War II and heading into the baby boom. At the same time, Earl Tupper unveiled his eponymous line of plastic food storage.

Tupperware has grown with the times: From happy 1950s days to women entering the work force en masse. Today the company has sales of more than $1.1 billion worldwide.

In the early 1940s, Tupper—like most American manufacturers—devoted his plastics company to the war effort. But after the war, with the economy booming, he found new uses for plastic, especially as more consumers bought homes and refrigerators. The first products, the Wonderlier Bowl and the Bell Tumbler, offered homemakers lightweight and unbreakable food storage options. In 1947, Tupper introduced the legendary airtight seals, which he patterned after the inverted rim on a can of paint. Though the products didn't sell well at retail, Tupper soon discovered the untapped gold mine in home parties, launching the first party in 1948.

The company quickly gained ground as homemakers around the country hosted parties. The products were then removed from retailers altogether and for years Tupperware was sold only through direct sales. The products changed to meet consumers' evolving lifestyles, from the Tortilla Keeper of the 1960s—meeting consumers' ethnic food demands—to the MicroSteamer of the 1980s, in response to both the prevalence of the microwave and dual-income families with no time to cook.

Tupperware is still introducing new products to meet changing demands and has returned to traditional retail environments. The company has joined decidedly 21st-century retail: The products are available on the company's Web site. (Of course, there are still Tupperware home parties.)

Source: HFN, May 27, 2002, p. 96. Courtesy of Fairchild Publications, Inc.

REVIEW QUESTIONS

1. Define plastic and polymer.
2. Compare the reaction of thermoplastics and thermoset plastics to heat.
3. List three common end uses for melamine formaldehyde plastics.
4. List three common end uses for polyurethane plastics.
5. What are the advantages of Teflon®?
6. What is laminating?

LEARNING ACTIVITIES

1. Identify three products in your home made from plastic. Evaluate their aesthetic and functional suitability.
2. Make a list of the natural products that plastics have replaced. List the criteria you would use to determine whether the plastic or natural material was more appropriate (cost, aesthetics, ease of production, ease of care).

CHAPTER 7

METALS

A key to All-Clad's product performance and good looks is a patented metal-bonding process. The design features a pure aluminum core that provides the quick and even heat distribution so important to cooking. Each piece of cookware contains an 18/10 stainless steel cooking surface that won't react with food, a thick core of aluminum with three separate layers of aluminum for even heating....

Image Makers, 2000, pp. 50–51

METALS ARE THE BASE PRODUCT FOR MANY OF THE WORLD'S MOST IMPORTANT MANUFACTURING industries, including consumer goods, national defense, space exploration, and transportation. **Metals** are chemical elements that are usually found in ores. There are two major categories of metal ore—**ferrous** (iron bearing) and **nonferrous** (non-iron bearing.) Iron and its alloys (combinations of metals, or metals and other substances) are considered to be ferrous metals. All other metals are considered to be nonferrous.

GENERAL PROPERTIES OF METALS

Approximately two-thirds of the earth's natural elements are metals. Metals are inorganic materials that do not rot, decay, or support combustion; however, they will melt at high temperatures. Some metals rust or deteriorate if exposed to moisture or chemicals. Each metal has its own characteristics, but the following seven properties are common to all metals:

- *Conductivity* Metals are good conductors of heat and electricity.
- *Crystal structure* Metals are crystalline in nature. Figure 7.1 illustrates how the atoms in a metal are arranged in a regular geometric fashion.
- *Mechanical properties* Most metals are **malleable,** which means that the substance can be shaped by hammering or by pressure from rollers. Some metals are **ductile,** which means

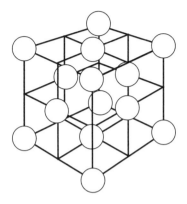

FIGURE 7.1
*Cubic arrangement of atoms in
aluminum and some other metals.*

that the substance can be hammered into thin sheets or that it can be drawn into thin strands or wires. The majority of metals are strong and, therefore, are appropriate for use in constructing buildings, automobiles, aircraft, and other structures, such as bridges.

- *Optical properties* Metals have luster, especially when polished, and they are opaque, so light cannot be seen through them.
- *Chemical properties* Metals can be combined with other metals and nonmetallic substances to form alloys. Metals have the capacity to lose electrons and form a positive ion.
- *Resistance to wear* Most metals are hard, durable substances. The metal mercury is a liquid at room temperature and is an exception to this generalization.
- *Magnetic properties* Iron and several other metals have natural magnetic properties. Some other metals and alloys can be magnetized.

A BRIEF HISTORY OF METALS

Metals have played an important role in the development of civilizations. Historically metals were used for weapons, cooking vessels, ornamentation, and currency. Because metals are durable, they have provided much information about early civilizations. Although not all authorities agree, there is evidence that copper, gold, and silver were the earliest metals used. Gold was used for plates, utensils, and ornaments as early as 3500 B.C. in the city of Ur in Mesopotamia. Silver was used by 2400 B.C. Because copper is found near the surface of the ground, it was used at a very early date. It is easy to shape. Copper has been found in prehistoric ruins in Egypt and was probably mined in Cyprus as early as 3000 B.C. Bronze, a mixture of copper and tin, was probably discovered at about the same time. Iron, and probably steel, were used by the Hittites of Asia Minor by 1600 B.C. Iron replaced bronze because of its superior strength.

Lead was probably the first metal separated from its ore by **smelting,** or melting the ore to remove impurities. Great advancements in the knowledge of metals and methods of using metals were made during the Middle Ages. At this time alchemists were trying to make gold from other materials.

Other important metal discoveries are listed in Table 7.1. Known supplies of iron, copper, lead, and zinc are diminishing, so modern-day scientists are searching for ways to substitute

Nambé Makes a Name for Itself in Metal

*A company 'dedicated to design' focuses on the clean,
simple shapes that remain true to its image*

You know Nambé the minute you see it—the clean, fluid lines, the simple, organic shapes, the promise of heft and weight when you pick it up.

The product's appeal has not changed much in the more than 50 years that Nambé has been making alternative metal giftware—some of the company's best-selling pieces this year are identical to the top sellers in the early 1960s.

From its original 1951 discovery of a metal alloy that contains no silver, lead or pewter yet retains the beauty of sterling and the durability of iron, Nambé has carefully crafted its image and remains, as its motto declares, "dedicated to design."

"From the beginning, our image has been that of a clean, elegant, simple product," said Bob Borden, vice president of sales and marketing. "The shapes have been the glue that kept our image and focus on design."

The company's origins in Santa Fe, N.M., originally gave Nambé a south-western connotation, and although the products are imbued with a certain spirituality, their appeal is not limited to a particular geographic region. Nambé has a large following among urban consumers.

"I think where we are today is in branding and marketing ourselves with a line that is simple and organic in shape, with an elegant feel," said Borden. "My goal is to maintain where we have come from, and not to let ourselves get too far off the path."

The company strayed from the path once before, about three and a half years ago, when it launched a col-

lection of stainless-steel desk accessories. The product was wrong for two reasons, according to Borden. First of all, Nambé is known for its alternative metal, not stainless steel, which has a different finish. "The look and feel of the product was not Nambé," he said.

Secondly, "It was a category—stationery—that we had no ownership in. It was the wrong category for us to pursue," Borden said.

TABLE 7.1

Metal Discoveries

Metal		Uses
Antimony	1604 A.D.	Alloys and use in medicine
Nickel	1751 A.D.	Alloys and use in the arts
Chromium	1797 A.D.	Making pigments in photography
Platinum	1803 A.D.	Jewelry, scientific apparatus, and as a catalyst
Cadmium	1817 A.D.	Plating, alloys
Aluminum	1845 A.D.	Alloys, making lightweight products

Nambé Makes a Name for Itself in Metal *(continued)*

"It really taught us that we need to be disciplined, in product development, what you're developing, what category you're developing product for. It's very easy to go into No-Man's Land looking for the golden egg, but it can take you on a road on which you should not be driving.

"We're very focused in what we're designing. Wishy-washy is not our discipline. And that's hard—you're always looking for the next home run, but you'll always hit it when you do what you do best."

Nambé's Butterfly bowls and Tricorner bowls have been a hit since they were introduced 30 years ago.

Other popular pieces include the kissing salt and pepper shakers (sinuously designed so that they fit together, like an embrace) and the Ellipsis vase. Nambé is known for its stable of hip designers, including Karim Rashid, Neil Cohen, the team of Lisa Smith and Linda Celentano, and, most recently, the 94-year-old Eva Zeisel.

Last year, the company launched a line of crystal that mirrors the shapes and lines of its alternative metal products. It's too early to predict which crystal pieces, if any, will have a lasting impact, although they have gotten favorable reviews from retailers.

"I think it's so important as a consumer, and more important as a company designing product, to understand that it takes a while for a product to reach maturity. Good design lives forever. It transcends all the trends."

In choosing designers, Borden goes with his gut. He chooses those whose design language and sensibility reflect Nambé's. With compatible sensibilities, the designers are free to explore Nambé's materials and develop their ideas using those materials.

"We need to gel," said Borden. He said he is personal friends with Nambé designers, which makes the working relationship stronger.

Borden also works closely with Nambé's graphic design team, which is responsible for the company's national advertising, its packaging and its art direction. Nambé takes its graphic design as seriously as it does product development, said Borden. "Dedicated to design" those three words make you work. It applies to everything. My job is to make sure everyone is doing their job in reaching that goal and maintaining that goal."

Nambé makes its work look deceptively easy, and its employees marvelously at ease. (Borden claims he never visits neighboring showrooms during trade shows because if he remains focused on his company's strengths, there is no need to look at anyone else.)

But the payback is great.

"Having a brand and a product identity in the consumer's mind is truly priceless. It's hard to quantify that, but if you don't, you're swimming in an ocean of ideas," Borden said.

"With a solid image, the employees are focused, the designers are focused, and the company runs smoothly because it's either right or it's not.

"When you are focused, it allows you to get your message clean and precise, rather than if you're changing your message weekly or monthly. It all comes back to discipline.

"As you grow and become more comfortable with your brand, it allows you to look at opportunities in the marketplace you might not have looked at," Borden said. "There's a little bit of peacefulness when you are focused."

Source: Image Makers, 2000, pp. 54–55.

---

aluminum, which is an abundant metal. Magnesium is another metal that is readily available. Examples of home furnishings made from metal are cookware and bake ware, stainless steel and silver flatware, and wrought iron furniture.

METALLURGY

Metallurgy is the science of extracting and processing metals. **Extractive metallurgy** deals with the taking of metals from their ores and refining them. **Physical metallurgy** is any process that converts a refined metal into a finished product.

Extractive Metallurgy

An **ore** is a metal-bearing rock that may contain one or more metallic minerals. Metals that are found in a naturally pure state are called native metals. Copper, gold, platinum, and silver are examples of native metals. The properties of the metal determine the process to remove the metal from the ore.

Extractive metallurgy includes the following:

- **Mineral dressing** Removal of waste materials from the ore, usually done by grinding the ore and washing away the waste.
- **Roasting** Heating the ore to remove impurities, such as sulfur.
- **Sintering** Roasting the ore at very high temperatures to partially melt fine particles of ore into coarse lumps.
- **Smelting** Melting the ore to remove impurities. For example, iron ore is placed in a blast furnace where it is subjected to intense heat (see Figure 7.2). The iron ore is put in the top of the furnace with coke and limestone. Blasts of air cause the coke to burn rapidly. The intense heat melts the limestone and the iron sinks to the bottom of the furnace. Impurities, or *slag*, are drained off. The resulting metal has been separated from the ore and is called **pig iron.** It still needs further refining.

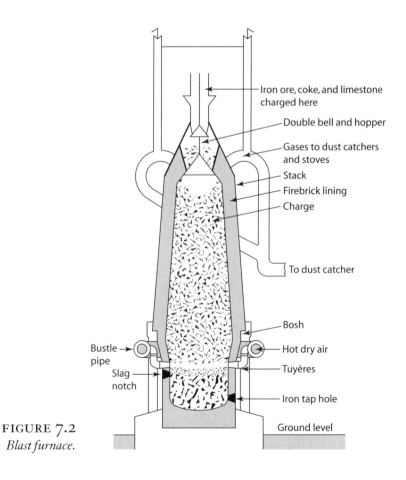

FIGURE 7.2
Blast furnace.

- **Leaching** Separating the metal from the ore by dissolving the metal in a chemical solvent. The metal is recovered by precipitation (using a reagent to separate out a solid form from a solution). For example, gold is separated from its ore by treating it with a dilute alkaline solution of sodium cyanide. After the gold is dissolved, it is placed in contact with metallic zinc. This causes the gold to precipitate from the solution and collect on the metallic zinc.

  1. **Electrolysis** The process of collecting metal from the leaching solution by placing it in an electrolytic cell where electric current flows from a positive pole through the solution to a negative pole. The metal has a positive charge and will collect on the negative pole. Copper, aluminum, and magnesium are recovered by electrolysis.
  2. **Amalgamation** The process of recovering metal by passing a solution of finely ground particles of ore over a plate covered with mercury. The mercury attracts the metal and forms an **amalgam,** or compound, with the metal. The amalgam is heated so the mercury passes off as gas leaving the metal. Gold and silver are recovered by amalgamation.

After the metal is extracted, it is formed into brick-like shapes called *ingots*. It is ready to be further processed into useful articles.

Physical Metallurgy

Most pure metals cannot be used alone. **Wrought iron** is an example of a metal that can be used alone. It is the purest form of iron and is used for some furniture and ornamental pieces. Some other pure metals are used for jewelry or decoration. The majority of metals undergo physical metallurgy processes that convert a refined metal into useful finished products. These processes include combining metals into alloys and amalgams, shaping metals, and joining metals.

Alloys and Amalgams

Metals are combined into alloys and amalgams. An **alloy** is a metallic substance that is formed by blending two or more elements, one of which must be a metal. Amalgams are alloys that contain mercury.

The benefits of combining metals are listed below:

- Characteristics can be modified. Alloys and amalgams can add strength, elasticity, hardness, and workability. Melting point can be changed to increase the usefulness of the alloy.
- Value can be increased. Addition of a small amount of costly metals can increase the value of the product; addition of less expensive metals can reduce the cost of the final product.
- Color can be changed. For example, alloys of gold may be pink, green, white, or the traditional gold color, depending on the metal that is alloyed with the gold.

More than 60 different alloys exist. They have the characteristics of a metal, but can be engineered to have specific properties. A *binary alloy* is an alloy that is composed of two major ingredients. A *ternary alloy* is composed of three major ingredients. Alloys are sometimes bonded with ceramics, graphite, and other substances to create composites.

Gold and silver are soft metals, so they are frequently alloyed with each other, or with other metals, to increase their hardness. Steel is an alloy of iron and carbon. Chromium is added to steel to make stainless steel. Brass is an alloy of copper and zinc. Bronze is an alloy of copper and tin.

Amalgams are widely used, especially in dentistry and in making mirrors. Silver, gold, and copper amalgams are used in dentistry. Tin amalgam is used to make mirrors.

Shaping Metals

The properties of the metal or alloy and the function of the final product determine how it will be shaped. The most common ways of shaping metals are casting, drawing, extrusion, forging, rolling, and stamping.

- **Casting** Cast metal is melted and poured into molds. Casting is often used for intricate shapes, such as handles, ornate decorations, and trophies (see Figures 7.3 and 7.4). Casting an inexpensive method of shaping metal. Products made by this method are not as durable or strong as products produced by other shaping methods.

- **Drawing** Wires and rods are made by drawing metal that is ductile. The metal is pulled through increasingly smaller and smaller holes in a die (or mold) until it reaches the required size (see Figure 7.5). **Annealing** is necessary to keep the metal from becoming brittle. Annealing is the process of heating a metal to just below its melting point, allowing it to stay at that temperature for a while, and then slowly cooling it.

- **Extrusion** Extrusion is used to create hollow tubes, rods, bars, strips, and pipes. Hot metal is forced through a die. The shape of the die determines the shape of the product (see Figure 7.6).

- **Forging** Forging is the hammering of heated metal into the desired thickness. The traditional hammer and anvil of the village blacksmith have been succeeded by the modern drop hammer. A steel block is mechanically lifted several feet above the anvil and allowed to fall onto the metal to be forged.

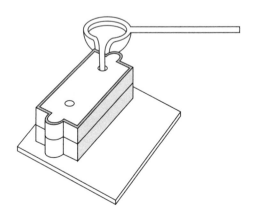

FIGURE 7.3
Pouring molten metal into a mold.

FIGURE 7.4
Cast aluminum cookware.
Courtesy of Regal Ware, Inc.

- **Rolling** Hot or cold metals may be rolled. Hot metals can be rolled more easily than cold metals, but the surface condition and accuracy are not as good. Generally, hot rolling is used for the initial shaping, and cold rolling is used for finishing the sheets of metal. The metal is passed between power-driven steel or cast iron rolls. Wrought metal shapes are made by cutting the shape out of a rolled sheet of metal (see Figure 7.7).
- **Stamping** Hollowware is commonly produced by stamping. Hollowware is any deep hollow item used to serve food, such as bowls, plates, creamers, and sugar bowls. Sheets of metal are stamped by steel dies that press and pound the metal until it is the desired shape.

Joining Metals

It is often necessary to join metal pieces together. Mechanical methods, **soldering,** and **welding** are the most common methods of joining. It is often more cost effective to assemble cheaply produced parts than it is to create a product in one piece.

Mechanical Methods **Riveting** is a mechanical method of joining metal. A **rivet** is a thick pin or bolt with a flat head at one end. A rivet may be solid or tubular and may be driven hot or cold, depending on the metal. It is passed through a hole in each of the metals that are to be joined. A second head is made by beating or pressing on the underside of the joined parts (see Figure 7.8). Other mechanical methods are bolting and screwing.

FIGURE 7.5
Wire drawing.

FIGURE 7.6
*Casual furniture constructed
of aluminum tubing.*
Photo provided by Telescope Casual.

Soldering **Solder** is an alloy that is used to join metallic components. It melts at a temperature slightly lower than that of the metal or alloy to be joined. The edges of the parts to be joined are thoroughly cleaned. The solder is heated and applied to the surfaces to be joined and the joints are fused together. When the alloy cools, the two pieces are united. The joint is weaker than the metal it joins. Tin and lead are the most commonly used solders because they melt at a low temperature (200 degrees to 250 degrees Centigrade). They are called soft solders and are used to solder metals that melt at low temperatures.

Brazing uses solder made of brass that is usually 60 percent zinc and 40 percent copper. It melts at about 850 degrees Centigrade and is referred to as hard solder. A hard-soldered joint is much stronger than a soft-soldered joint.

Welding Welding is the process of joining metal by heat, or hammering with or without heat. Welded sections are as strong as the rest of the piece. There are two types of welding—pressure and fusion. Pressure welding includes both forge welding and resistance welding. Fusion welding involves the use of molten metal to join two pieces of metal.

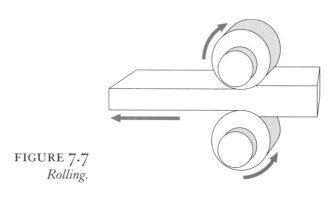

FIGURE 7.7
Rolling.

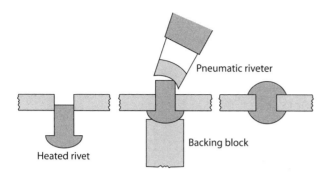

FIGURE 7.8
Riveting: a. *the rivet is inserted in the hole,*
b. *the pneumatic driver flattens the second head,*
c. *completed joining.*

Forge welding is the hammering of metal parts together. The metal may be heated before hammering. Some metals, such as gold, silver, and platinum, can be hammered cold until they are joined. Some metals, such as cast iron, cannot be forge welded because it is too brittle.

Resistance welding is also called *resistance butt welding.* It is a form of forge welding. Two metal parts are placed in separate current-carrying clamps and butted together while an electric current passes across the joint. The electric current causes the metals to heat up. When the welding temperature is reached, the metals are pressed together. Spot welding is a variation of resistance welding. It is used to join sheets of metal. The electric current is passed through the metals in intervals (see Figure 7.9).

Fusion welding occurs with heat. Two methods may be used—high temperature gas flames or metallic arc welding. During high temperature gas flames, the gas flame heats the metal parts to be joined and also a metal filler that runs between the parts. Upon cooling, the metal pieces are joined. In metallic arc welding, heat is developed when an electric current travels down the filler rod, creating an electric arc between the filler rod and the metals (see Figure 7.10).

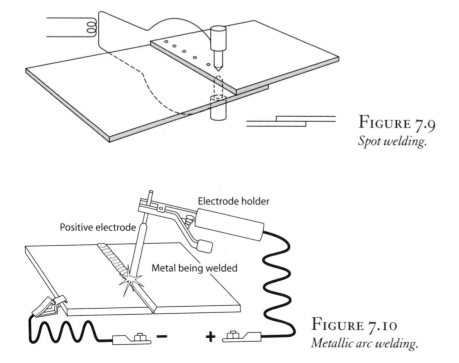

FIGURE 7.9
Spot welding.

FIGURE 7.10
Metallic arc welding.

PLATING METALS

Plating is coating of one metal over another metal. Plating can give an aesthetic or functional finish to the base metal. Expensive metals are frequently plated over inexpensive metals to provide low-cost alternatives for the consumer. For example, silver-plated flatware is a low cost alternative to sterling-silver flatware. The three main methods of plating are dipping, bonding, and electroplating.

Dipping

Dipping one metal into another melted metal is an effective way to provide a protective coating. An example of dipping is the process of coating with zinc. For example, a **galvanized steel** product is made by dipping sheets of steel into molten zinc (see Figure 7.11). The zinc coating protects the steel from rusting. Dipping is not as durable as electroplating or bonding.

FIGURE 7.11
Galvanized steel pitcher.
Courtesy of Fairchild Publications, Inc.

Bonding

Bonding is the process of using heat and pressure to join two or more layers of metal. Bonding is more durable than electroplating. The method of using heat and pressure to bond silver to copper, brass, or other metal was developed in Sheffield, England, in 1743. This silverware was known as Sheffield silver or Sheffield plate. It is no longer made, but a similar process is used to make gold-filled and rolled-gold-plate jewelry. Rolled gold is nine-karat gold bonded to brass or steel. Karat weight of gold is discussed in the next section on precious metals.

Electroplating

Electroplating is the decomposition of a chemical compound by an electric current. The plating metal is the *anode* (positive terminal) and the object to be plated is the *cathode* (negative terminal). Figure 7.12 illustrates the process. The anode and cathode are placed in a salt solution of the plating metal. The plating metal gradually dissolves and coats the object when an electric current is passed through the plating solution. The amount of metal coated on the item is determined by the length of time it is in the solution. A very thin coating is called a *wash* or *flash*.

Electroplating is the most frequently used method of plating, because it is relatively inexpensive and it securely binds the metals. It was first used to coat copper with silver in 1839 in France. Now it is used to plate chromium, gold, nickel, rhodium, and silver onto other metals.

Anodizing is a form of electroplating that is used on aluminum. The process works in reverse to deposit an oxide film on aluminum. The aluminum is placed at the anode. Anodized aluminum is resistant to wear, does not tarnish, and can be tinted with any color.

PRECIOUS METALS

The **precious metals** are platinum and rest of the platinum group, gold, and silver. Platinum, palladium, rhodium, osmium, iridium, and ruthenium are considered part of the platinum group of metals, which have similar properties and are prized for their beauty, rarity, and working properties. The primary uses for the platinum group of metals are jewelry.

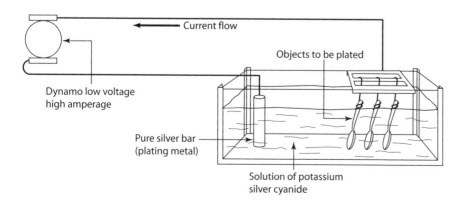

FIGURE 7.12
Electroplating.

Gold

Gold occurs in its natural state in many places in the world. It is too soft to be used alone, so it is typically alloyed with other metals, such as copper, silver, or zinc, to increase its strength and durability.

Pure gold is pale yellow, but when mixed with other metals, gold will take on different colors (see Table 7.2). Karat weight and plating are important indicators of the quality of gold products.

Karat Weight

The term **karat gold** is used to refer to gold that has been alloyed and indicates the proportion of pure gold in the metal. It is measured in 24ths. Solid gold, or 24-karat (24K) gold is 100 percent gold. It is generally used only for plating. The highest percentage gold used commercially is 22K. Other common karat weights are 18K, 14K, 12K, and 10K. Weights of less than 10K cannot be listed in karats on commercially sold products in the United States.

Gold Plating

Gold may be plated by bonding or electroplating. The two types of **gold bonding** are gold filled and rolled gold plating. During the process of creating a **gold-filled** product, a thin layer of gold is fused to a base metal. The base metal may be copper, brass, or nickel silver. The gold layer must weigh at least 1/20 of the weight of the entire piece in order for it to be called gold filled, while better quality gold-filled articles will be 1/10.

This process of **rolled gold plating** is very similar to gold filled, but the layer of gold is much thinner. It is only 1/30 to 1/40 of the total weight of the base metal. Rolled-gold-plated pieces are less expensive and less durable than gold filled.

Gold electroplating applies a thin layer of gold evenly over the surface of the article. The layer is thinner than gold filling or rolled gold. Quality depends on the thickness of the plating. Gold wash, or gold flash, is very thin electroplating of less than .0015 inch. Heavy gold plating is more durable with less chance of tarnishing. Gold that has been electroplated over sterling silver or silver plate is called **vermeil.**

TABLE 7.2
Color Effects of Common Gold Alloys

Alloying Metal	Color Effect
Copper	Pink
Silver	Green
Copper and silver	Shade of yellow
Nickel (alone or combined with copper or zinc)	White gold
Palladium	White gold

Characteristics of Gold

Gold is noted for the following characteristics:

- Most ductile and malleable metal
- Very soft
- Pale yellow in color
- Nontarnishing
- Not affected by acids
- Bright luster
- Able to take a high polish
- Easy to work (can be made into thin sheets for gold leaf)

End Uses of Gold

The end uses of gold include the following:

- Coinage
- Dental alloys
- Jewelry alloys
- Decorative coating on pottery and glass
- Fashion accessories
- Inlays on wood
- Decorative accessories for the home

Silver

Silver is the least expensive of the precious metals. Silver is the whitest and most lustrous metal; however, its major drawback is that it tarnishes. Cleaning and polishing will help to restore its appearance. Silver is also one of the easiest metals to work. It can be easily manipulated and is very versatile. Mexico is the major producer of silver.

Silver has become the standard for formal flatware. It has lustrous beauty and does not impart taste to the food. Thicker pieces are more durable than thinner pieces.

Characteristics of Silver

Silver is characterized as follows:

- Tendency to tarnish or blacken
- Most lustrous and whitest metal
- Ductile
- Reflectivity
- Excellent conductor of heat and electricity

End Uses of Silver

The characteristics of silver make it useful for practical and decorative purposes in home furnishings and other products including the following:

- Flatware
- Hollowware
- Decoration on pottery and glass
- Backing for mirrors
- Jewelry
- Bearings
- Dental amalgams
- Solders

Sterling Silver

Silver is usually alloyed with copper. The term *sterling* indicates the purity of the silver in the product. In order to be labeled sterling, the item must be 92.5 percent pure. It is weighed in troy ounces (31.103 grams).

Coin silver refers to the silver used to make American dimes, quarters, and half-dollars prior to 1965. It is an alloy of 90 percent silver and 10 percent copper. It is harder and less workable than sterling silver. Coin silver was a popular metal for use in Native American jewelry designs, but now silver is used.

Silver Plate

Silver is typically plated over copper, steel, or **nickel silver,** an alloy composed of nickel, zinc, and copper (see Figure 7.13). **Silver plate** is generally less expensive than sterling silver. The amount of plating on the product determines the quality of the piece and the durability of the silver. Levels of plating are:

A1	Single plated
I.	Double plated
XXX	Triple plated
XXXX	Quadruple plated

Sometimes additional silver is plated on areas that get the most wear. For example, the bottoms of the bowls of spoons and forks may have extra plating.

FERROUS METALS

Iron, cast iron, steel, and stainless steel are the ferrous metals. Cast iron, steel, and stainless steel are largely iron.

FIGURE 7.13
Silver-plated picture frame.
Courtesy of Fairchild Publications, Inc.

Iron

Iron is one of the most abundant and useful metals in the world. About five percent of the earth's crust is iron. Pure iron is soft and generally cannot be shaped. Pig iron is the crude iron produced from the blast furnace. It contains impurities, such as four percent carbon and small amounts of manganese, silicon, phosphorus, and sulfur. Wrought iron is refined pig iron. It was developed during the 14th century. It is almost pure iron but does contain about one percent impurities.

Iron is characterized by:

- One of the heaviest metals
- One of the strongest metals
- Good conductor of heat and electricity
- Will rust quickly in presence of moisture
- Malleable and ductile
- Easily cast or worked
- Attracted by a magnet and easily magnetized
- Silver-gray in color

The end uses of iron are:

- Ornamental work
- Railings

- Furniture
- Decorative grills
- Building hardware
- Cookware
- Fences
- Anchors

Cast Iron

Cast iron was developed in the early 1700s. It is iron that contains between five and ten percent other elements. Usually four to six percent will be carbon. The other elements may include silicon, manganese, phosphorus, and sulfur. It is hard, brittle, and somewhat resistant to corrosion. The characteristics of cast iron can vary according to the metals alloyed with it. In general it is less expensive, more rigid, and less affected by corrosion than iron (see Figure 7.14). A special category of cast iron is *nodular cast iron,* also called *ductile iron.* Cerium or magnesium and flakes of graphite are added to the iron.

The general characteristics of cast iron are:

- Good casting ability
- Moderate strength
- Hardness
- Somewhat brittle
- Usually less ductile

The characteristics of cast iron make it appropriate for these end uses:

- Machine parts
- Engine cylinder blocks
- Stoves
- Drainage pipes
- Cookware
- Ornamental railings

FIGURE 7.14
Cast iron skillet.
Courtesy of Fairchild Publications, Inc.

Steel

The steel-making process involves the removal of impurities, such as silicon, phosphorous, and sulfur. **Steel** is an alloy of iron with about 1.5 to 3 percent carbon. Other elements that are added to steel are manganese, nickel, chromium, molybdenum, and tungsten. Steel is the most important ferrous metal. It has a tendency to rust, but coating with oil, grease, paint, or porcelain, or plating with metals, such as zinc, tin, nickel, chromium, or cadmium will protect it from deterioration.

The amount of carbon in steel greatly affects its strength. For example, four percent carbon makes the steel twice as strong as pure iron; one percent carbon makes it three times as strong. **High-carbon steel** is about 1 to 1.5 percent carbon.

Alloys of steel are widely used. Stainless steel is an alloy of chromium and steel. It is discussed later in the chapter. Other important alloys of steel include aluminum steel, which is smooth and strong, and nickel steel, noted for its nonmagnetic and high strength.

Steel is more ductile than iron, stronger than iron, and less brittle than iron. However, steel deteriorates unless coated or plated or another alloy is added.

General end uses for steel include structural framing, concrete reinforcing, and ornamental work. High-carbon steel is used for dies and cutting tools, such as knives, and low- or medium-carbon steel is used for sheeting and structural framing.

Stainless Steel

Stainless steel was developed in 1915 and quickly became one of the most versatile and useful metals. Approximately 60 alloys of stainless steel are available (see Figure 7.15). A minimum of 11.5 percent chromium is added to the steel to make it corrosion resistant. It may contain up to 18 percent chromium. Nickel is sometimes added to stainless steel to make it finer and

FIGURE 7.15 *Stainless steel serving pieces.* Courtesy of Fairchild Publications, Inc.

whiter. Higher-quality stainless steels contain from 2 percent nickel and 12 percent chromium to 8 percent nickel with 18 percent chromium. This quality stainless is used for fine cutlery and hollowware products. Stainless steel has the same characteristics as steel except that it resists rusting and the effect of acids (see Figure 7.16 and Industry Statement 7.1).

End uses of stainless steel include decorative objects; household objects, such as cookware and flatware; sinks; countertops; and surgical equipment.

NONFERROUS METALS AND ALLOYS

The characteristics and end uses of some other metals and alloys that are used in home furnishings are presented in Table 7.3. Many are used for functional and decorative products.

DECORATING METALS

Many metal products, especially those for the home, are decorated. There are numerous ways to add design elements to the metal. Applied borders, **chasing,** embossing, engraving, etching, hammering, piercing, polishing, and **repoussé** are some of the methods used to decorate metals.

FIGURE 7.16
18/10 stainless steel flatware.
Courtesy of Fairchild Publications, Inc.

INDUSTRY STATEMENT 7.1

All-Clad Makes It Special

Just as golfers hanker after the nine-iron golfer Tiger Woods uses, so home cooks crave the frying pan of chef Daniel Boulud. And Boulud scrambles his oeufs in All-Clad.

While it took clever marketing to bring All-Clad cookware from the kitchens of New York's Restaurant Daniel to amateur cooks in East Podunk, it was product performance that turned the cookware pro in the first place.

"It was embraced by celebrity chefs," said All-Clad Metalcrafters chief operating officer Peter Cameron. "They used it because they liked it and were sophisticated enough to benefit from the unique attributes of the product. That set the tone."

In a category that has seen a huge leap in overall quality in the past 20 years, All-Clad continues to stand out as the object of the affluent consumer's desire and a benchmark for the competition. Retailers complain that supply can't keep up with demand. Prices for the cookware keep escalating. Undeterred, we keep buying.

While All-Clad used public relations and marketing to promote the line, ultimately the cookware's quality made its image, said Cameron.

"Had the product not been a superior product, it would not have been embraced as naturally by the culinary world," he added. "And you would not have gotten the rub-off effect that we have gotten from people who enjoy cooking as a hobby. They look, as they do with other hobbies, to see what the experts are using."

After years on the professional circuit, All-Clad slipped into the consumer market via independent gourmet stores. Sales were spurred on by cooking shows in which chefs made flambés seem effortless. Watching at home we thought, "We could do that without burning ourselves, if we had the right pan."

And All-Clad taught us that performance doesn't have to come at the expense of style.

Not long ago, pots and pans were heard, but not seen—stored in a dark closet after the day's work was done. That was before All-Clad captured our imaginations with its mirrored steel exteriors and metallurgically correct interiors.

Now, in many of the kitchens featured in glossy magazines, All-Clad pans are likely to be on display. The gleaming cookware is often pictured hanging from pot jacks like jewelry for the kitchen: as much a part of the design of the space as a tool for the cook.

A key to All-Clad's product performance and good looks is a patented metal-bonding process.

The design features a pure aluminum core that provides the quick and even heat distribution so important to cooking. Unlike many competitors who build pans with an aluminum disk on the bottom. All-Clad's aluminum core extends up the sides of the utensil, eliminating uneven heating.

Each piece of cookware contains an 18/10 stainless-steel cooking surface that won't react with food, a thick core of aluminum with three separate layers of aluminum for even heating, and one of four different exterior metals.

Other features that distinguish All-Clad cookware include handles that are ergonomically designed and well-balanced. The handles, which are securely attached with stainless-steel rivets, also stay cool to the touch, a feature much appreciated by home cooks.

"Professional cooks like the balance of the handle," said Cameron, who noted that the stay-cool feature is less important to the pros. "I think professional chefs have asbestos hands."

The product design extends to such details as having each piece of cookware machine-polished a number of times before it is hand-polished by master craftsmen.

All-Clad's image of quality has allowed the company to venture into new categories. All-Clad "All-Professional" tools, stainless-steel mixing bowls and new premium bakeware have been snapped up by consumers who collect All-Clad products as they would a set of fine china. Or as Cameron points out, a fine set of wheels.

"These products perform better than traditional cookware. If we were to relate that to automobiles, these are high-performance products," said Cameron. Think Jaguar, not Buick. "What has happened is that the people who most appreciate high performance have embraced the product."

Source: Image Makers, 2000, pp. 50–51.

TABLE 7.3

Characteristics and End Uses of Selected Metals and Alloys

Metal/Alloy	Characteristics	End Uses
Aluminum—the most plentiful metal (about 8% of the earth's crust)	Lightweight Ductile and malleable, corrosion resistant Thermal and electrical conductor Soft Strong (some aluminum alloys are stronger than structural steel) Silvery to soft gray in color May be anodized to give it color	Cooking utensils Building components Screens Hardware Furniture Electrical wiring Interior window frames Horizontal louver blind slats
Brass—alloy of copper and zinc; also called yellow brass, Dutch metal, and red brass	Hard Turns green in presence of moisture Will take high polish Easily shaped by casing, rolling, and stamping Yellow in color	Ornamental products Base for silver and gold plating Light fixtures Hardware Furniture
Britannia metal—alloy of copper, tin, and antimony (formerly an alloy of copper, tin, and lead); also called white metal	Soft, bends and dents easily Melts at low temperature Darkens when exposed to air (frequently plated with gold, silver, or chromium to prevent this) Pale silver in color	Ornamental tableware
Bronze—alloy usually made from copper and tin, usually 66–95 % copper, occasionally 1 or 2 % zinc is added, sometimes alloyed with silicone or aluminum	Fairly hard, durable Brittle, resonant Develops patina with age Russet in color	Coinage, church bells Medals, statuary Base material for plating Hardware, plaques
Chromium—usually used as an alloying element	Durable, does not tarnish readily Used in plating, bluish-white in color	Lighting fixtures, furniture Small appliances, plating metal
Copper	Resistant to corrosion, ductile and malleable Good conductor of electricity and heat Not affected by alkaline chemicals (often used where metal to masonry contact is required) Reddish orange in color Will oxidize to dull green	Electrical wiring Plumbing supply pipes and fittings Roof flashing Gutters, cookware Decorative accessories
German silver—alloy of 50% copper, 25% nickel, and 25% zinc	Resembles silver Does not oxidize when exposed to air Easily shaped, hard, durable	Ornamental objects

Continued

TABLE 7.3 *(continued)*
Characteristics and End Uses of Selected Metals and Alloys

Metal/Alloy	Characteristics	End Uses
Imitation gold—alloy of copper, aluminum, and nickel; trade name: Dirilyte		Substitute for gold
Lead	Resistant to corrosion Soft, very dense, low strength Hazardous to health, bluish-white in color	Waterproofing Radiation shields Stained glasswork
Magnesium	Resembles aluminum Easily worked, resists corrosion	Furniture, hardware
Monel metal—alloy of 50% copper and 50% nickel	Resembles steel Hard, stain resistant	Industrial uses Sinks, fountains
Nickel	Hard, malleable, ductile Resistant to corrosion Takes a bright polish Grayish-white in color	Primarily used as an alloy to improve hardness, corrosion resistance, and ductility
Nickel silver—an alloy of nickel and brass		
10% nickel	Soft and easily shaped Yellow tinge	Base for silver-plated hollowware products
18% nickel	Harder, more durable More silvery looking	Coins Silver- or gold-plated flatware
Pewter—an alloy of 90% tin with copper and small amounts of antimony and bismuth	Dull grey in color Soft Easily dented, easily shaped Melts at relatively low temperature Takes a high polish or rough finish Resists tarnish, warm gray in color	Hollowware Decorative ornaments for the home Lighting fixtures Tableware
Tin	Soft, nonrusting Tarnish resistant, easily worked Silver in color	Often used as an alloy Light fixtures, accessories Tin foil
Titanium	Easily worked	Often used as an alloy Furniture
Zinc	Easily worked Bluish-white in color	Often used as an alloy Plating metal for corrosion-resistant finishes

Applied Borders

Strips of metal are precast or prestamped and then soldered to the edge of metal articles. This method of decoration is often seen on the edges of silver tableware, such as serving bowls or teapots. The borders may be very simple or very elaborate designs.

Chasing

Chasing is the process of ornamenting metal with indented lines that outline a design into the surface of the metal. If done by hand, the artist uses small hammers to pound the silver and form the raised design. Machines are also used to stamp the designs into the metal. This process is done on sterling silver or the copper base of plated products.

Embossing

Embossing is frequently used to apply designs to flatware. The design is carved into steel dies. Great force is used to impress the design into the metal. Any metal may be embossed, but softer metals take more attractive and deeper impressions.

Engraving

Engraving is an expensive process. The surface of the metal is deeply scratched with the engraver's tools. Initials are commonly engraved on silver flatware. Thinly plated silver should not be engraved because the tool may cut through the silver coating.

Etching

During etching, the metal is coated with wax. The design is cut into the wax and the article is then immersed in a nitric acid bath where the acid eats into the exposed portions of the design. The acid is washed off and the wax is removed.

Hammering

A dented surface is created on the surface of a metal by hammering by hand or by machine. Silver-plated pitchers, sugar bowls, and creamers often have this textured surface.

Piercing

Piercing is the process of cutting small holes into the metal by hand or by machine. Handwork is done with small saws and files. When done by machine, cutting dies are used. This method of decoration is popular on sterling silver and silver plate.

Polishing

Polishing adds either a shiny or dull finish to the metal. Most metals used in the home are polished. There are two main categories of polishes—shiny and dull. For a bright mirror-like finish, metals are polished with brushes and buffing wheels. A dull finish is achieved by means of revolving brushes that scratch the surface. A dull finish on silver is called a **butler finish** or a gray finish. The traditional butler finish was originally achieved by hand rubbing. Most metals are available in a range of polished finishes, from very bright to low luster.

Stainless steel and other hard alloys will maintain their polish indefinitely. Silver is a soft metal, so a shiny finish will eventually show scratches. Metals can be coated in order to preserve the polish.

Repoussé

Repoussé is considered to be the most expensive method of decorating metal by hand. It is typically done on sterling silver. The design is worked from the inside of the piece. Small hammers and other tools are used to create a bas-relief (slightly raised) design on the surface of the silver. Repoussé is often combined with chasing and referred to as **repoussé chasing.**

ENVIRONMENTAL IMPACT

All phases of the metal industry have been challenged to ensure the safe production, use, and disposal of metals. Environmentally sound and socially conscious practices for the industry are national and international concerns. Organizations, such as the International Council on Metals and the Environment (ICME), work with other agencies, such as the United Nations and the Organization for Economic Co-operation and Development, to provide a direction for improvement.

The term *heavy metal* is used to refer to those metals that are potentially toxic. Cadmium, mercury, lead, and bismuth are most often referred to as heavy metals. Lead may be found in the home in the form of lead-based paint, leaching out of improperly fired pottery, and solder used in crafts. While lead-based paints are illegal, there are still many structures that contain old lead-based paints. The use of lead-based solder in the commercial decorative arts, such as stained-glass windows and Tiffany-style lighting has been challenged in court (see Industry Statement 7.2). Suppliers are now using 99.6 percent lead-free solder. The use of lead pipes in construction has been prohibited. The most severe health hazards for lead occurs with the spraying of molten lead and grinding or power sanding of lead.

Recycling of metals is an important environmental initiative. Ferrous metals and nonferrous metals, especially aluminum, are recycled in large quantities. Steel is one of the most important recycled metals. It can be recycled many times without loss of quality. It is magnetic, so it is easy to recover from construction debris, demolition sites, and old automobiles and appliances.

INDUSTRY STATEMENT 7.2

Lighting Vendors Settle in Lead Case

SAN FRANCISCO—A California environmental group has won a battle in what has become a war over the lead content in Tiffany-style lighting.

The Environmental Rights Foundation (ERF) sued nearly every supplier and retailer of Tiffany-style lighting and gifts in California for violating that state's Proposition 65, which requires the labeling of products containing lead and other carcinogens. The solder used to bind stained glass in the lamps contains lead.

In late November, three of the plaintiffs, Quoizel, Lamps Plus and Dale Tiffany, reached a settlement with ERF and entered a consent judgment into Superior Court here.

The settlement is far-reaching and complicated. It encourages the use of lead-free solder in new products and calls for the labeling of all lead-containing products already in the trade, as well as any new products that contain lead. It also calls for the payment of attorney's fees, assigns settlement amounts on the basis of company sales volume and includes a provision for manufacturers to pay a premium to protect the retailers to which they sold lead-containing goods. There is a clause that allows other defendants to opt in under the same terms but prevents them from settling on more favorable terms.

Dale Tiffany and Quoizel have already begun to use lead-free solder; Lamps Plus has been labeling the stained-glass products in its stores since October.

"Some people are battling it, but we decided to settle," said Ken Kallett, vice president of sales and marketing for Dale Tiffany, citing the cost of a legal battle. In any case, "retailers are forcing manufacturers to go lead-free," he said.

"For us, it's more expeditious to settle it and move on," said Clark Linstone, chief financial officer of Lamps Plus.

The issue is far from resolved, however. The rest of the industry, including Catalina Lighting, Cheyenne Lamps, Robert Abbey, Hunter Lighting Group, Target Corp., Home Depot, HomeBase, Kmart and others, are affected.

Attorneys for nonsettling defendants said they oppose the settlement on many grounds. They said the labeling provisions are unreasonable for mass retailers; monetary payments are unfairly based on gross sales volume of all products, not just Tiffany-style products; and compliance within the settlement's timing would be impossible for large retailers.

Attorneys for nonsettling plaintiffs have entered a motion with the court to consolidate their cases. A hearing has been set for Dec. 13 in San Francisco.

"We always consider settling any case if the economics are right," said Alan Long, president of Cheyenne. "We will continue to work through our attorneys to reach some kind of agreement. We are switching to 99.6 percent lead-free beginning with January 2001 shipments. There is no 100 percent lead-free solder that we are aware of," Long said.

Source: HFN, December 11, 2000, p. 3. Courtesy of Fairchild Publications, Inc.

SUMMARY

Metals are chemical elements that are usually found in ores. There are two major categories of metals—ferrous (iron bearing) and nonferrous (non-iron bearing.) Iron and its alloys are ferrous metals; all other metals are nonferrous.

Metallurgy is the science of extracting and processing metals. Extractive metallurgy deals with extracting metals from their ores and refining them. Physical metallurgy is any process that converts a refined metal into a finished product. Most pure metals cannot be used alone. They are combined into alloys and amalgams. An alloy is a metallic substance that is formed by blending two or more elements, one of which must be a metal. Amalgams are alloys that contain mercury.

The properties of the metal or alloy and the function of the final product determine how it will be processed. The most common ways of shaping metals are casting, drawing, extrusion, forging, rolling, and stamping. Mechanical methods, soldering, and welding are used to join metals. The coating of one metal over another metal is known as plating. Dipping, bonding, and electroplating are coating methods.

Important classifications of metals include precious metals (platinum, gold, and silver), ferrous metals (iron, cast iron, steel, and stainless steel), and nonferrous metals (aluminum and copper).

There are numerous ways to add design elements to metal products. These include applied borders, chasing, embossing, engraving, etching, hammering, piercing, polishing, and repoussé.

TERMS FOR REVIEW

alloy	fusion welding	resistance welding
amalgam	galvanized steel	rivet
amalgamation	gold bonding	riveting
annealing	gold filled	roasting
anodizing	high-carbon steel	rolled gold plating
brazing	karat gold	rolling
butler finish	leaching	silver plate
cast iron	malleable	sintering
casting	metallurgy	smelting
chasing	metals	solder
coin silver	mineral dressing	soldering
drawing	nickel silver	stainless steel
ductile	nonferrous metal	stamping
electrolysis	ore	steel
electroplating	physical metallurgy	sterling
extractive metallurgy	pig iron	vermeil
extrusion	plating	welding
ferrous metal	precious metals	wrought iron
forge welding	repoussé	
forging	repoussé chasing	

REVIEW QUESTIONS

1. List seven properties of metals.
2. What is an alloy?
3. List the three precious metals.
4. Compare gold-filled and rolled-gold-plated articles.
5. Compare sterling silver and silver-plate articles.
6. How does stainless steel differ from steel?

LEARNING ACTIVITIES

1. Select three magazine advertisements for cookware (pots and pans) items made from three different metals (example: stainless steel, aluminum, cast iron). List one advantage and one disadvantage of each metal.
2. Compare and contrast the characteristics of silver plate and sterling silver. Visit a large department store to evaluate styling and cost of silver plate and sterling silver. Discuss the characteristics of each with a salesperson.

CHAPTER 8

OTHER MATERIALS

The chair that launched a thousand imitations was first designed for Academy Award winning film director Billy Wilder. Charles Eames wanted to give his friend a fitting birthday gift – literally. Eames intended for the glovelike chair to have "the warm receptive look of a well-used first baseman's mitt." . . . It was first produced in 1956 and was one of the many Eames designs manufactured and distributed by the Herman Miller Co. . . . In the original interpretation, rosewood veneer shells were shaped and then topped with 6-inch-thick urethane foam cushions and leather covers.

HFN, Eames lounge chair and ottoman, May 27, 2002, p. 66

THIS CHAPTER PRESENTS INFORMATION ABOUT RUBBER, PAPER, AND LEATHER, WHICH ARE important industrial materials used in commercial and consumer products. Carpet backing, wall coverings, and upholstery are examples of products made from these three products.

RUBBER

Rubber is used for flooring and coatings for fabric and paper. In many of its consumer applications it is combined with other products, such as textiles and plastics. These combinations into Europe from the New World, he brought samples of natural rubber. The natural qualities of untreated rubber make if difficult to use. It is very sensitive to temperature. It is stiff and hard in cold weather and soft and sticky in hot weather. In 1839 Charles Goodyear, an American inventor, was credited with the development of a method to cure rubber that overcame the negative qualities of natural rubber. He mixed it with sulfur and heated it. The process became known as **vulcanization.**

Research into the development of synthetic rubber began in the early 1800s. The demand for rubber greatly increased during World War I and World War II and shortages spurred the research and development of synthetic rubber. Today synthetic rubber is considered superior to natural rubber for many applications.

Production of Rubber

Natural rubber is harvested from rubber trees, while synthetic rubber is produced via chemical processes.

Harvesting of Natural Rubber

Natural rubber is harvested from the *Hevea brasiliensis* (rubber) tree as **latex,** a white liquid that is collected from the bark of the tree. Rubber trees require a warm, moist climate. Most rubber is grown on plantations in Southeast Asia. A rubber tree will grow 30 to 60 feet in height and 30 inches in diameter. It will produce approximately 6 to 10 pounds of rubber each year for more than 25 years (see Figure 8.1). The plantation worker makes diagonal slashes that allow the liquid latex to flow from the tree.

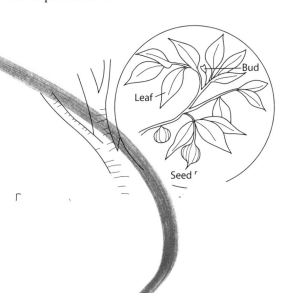

After the latex is collected, it is formed into curdled or coagulated rubber. The latex is curdled with acetic acid. It is coagulated with formic acid. Sometimes it is reserved in its liquid state by treatment with ammonia. The rubber is then processed into *crude rubber*. The two methods of preserving rubber are described below.

Air-dried method Sodium bisulfite is added to prevent mold. This rubber is pale in color and used for final products that are light in color. Air-dried rubber is called *pale crepe*.
Smoking method Moisture is pressed out and the rubber is hung over a smoking fire to dry. The rubber will be reddish brown in color. It is known as a *smoke sheet*.

Crude natural rubber is sold in liquid form, in solid form as pale crepe or smoke sheet, or crumbled into granules. Production of natural rubber is summarized in Figure 8.2.

Characteristics and End Uses of Natural Rubber

Natural rubber offers the positive qualities of being elastic and resistant to moisture and electricity. However, exposure to sunlight and heat causes hardening, and repeated bending may cause cracking. Oil may cause softening. Natural rubber can be used for a wide variety of applications, including automobile tires, textiles, imitation leather, paper, and building construction.

Production of Synthetic Rubber

Production of synthetic rubber is a complex chemical process that was developed through years of research. There are about 20 chemical formulas for synthetic rubber. Within each type there are many grades. Production methods and chemical composition affect the final characteristics and applications of the rubber. Production of synthetic rubber is summarized in Figure 8.3.

In general, synthetic rubber is more uniform, of higher quality, and more adaptable to various end uses than natural rubber. It is, therefore, preferred for most end uses.

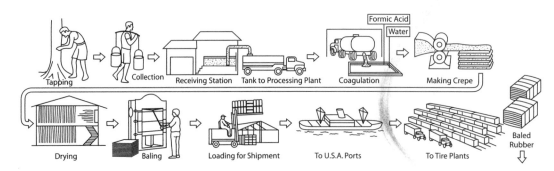

FIGURE 8.2
Production of natural rubber.

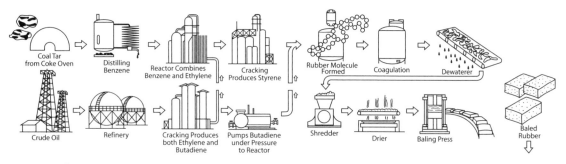

FIGURE 8.3
Production of synthetic rubber.

Important Synthetic Rubbers

Each type of synthetic rubber has its own characteristics and end uses. Some of the more important types, distinguishing characteristics, and selected end uses are presented in Table 8.1. **Styrene-butadiene rubber** is presented first because it is one of the most common types of rubber the consumer encounters. The other types are listed in alphabetical order.

Processing Solid Rubber

Conversion of natural or synthetic rubber into useful products is costly and complicated. It requires a great deal of energy and expensive equipment and involves complicated procedures. After the rubber, natural or synthetic, is delivered to the processing plant, the steps can be summarized into four basic processes: masticating, mixing, shaping, and vulcanizing.

Masticating

Solid rubber must be broken up by a machine called a *plasticator*. The rubber is shredded and chewed until it becomes soft and malleable. The large molecules are reduced in size. Synthetic rubber generally has shorter molecules than natural rubber and needs less masticating. Masticating is also called *plasticizing*.

At this stage the rubber is known as **unvulcanized rubber.** It will become soft and sticky under warm conditions and stiff and rigid under cold conditions. Applications for unvulcanized rubber include adhesive tape, rubber cement, and electrical insulation tape.

Mixing

At this stage sulfur and other chemicals are added to the rubber. The sulfur is essential to vulcanization. The other chemicals add properties essential for the end use, such as durability, hardness, and color. A single batch of rubber may be mixed with more than 20 ingredients. There are thousands of ingredients from which to choose. See Table 8.2 for a listing of some common products mixed with rubber.

TABLE 8.1

Characteristics and End Uses of Synthetic Rubber

Type of Rubber	Characteristics	End Uses
Styrene-Butadiene Rubber (SBR)	Similar to natural rubber, better abrasion resistance than natural rubber, less resilient than natural rubber	Tires, heels and soles of footwear, flooring, conveyor belting, adhesives, carpet backing, paper coating, latex foam for carpet backing and upholstery
Acrylate Rubber (ACM)	Good resistance to hot oil and lubricants	O-rings, oil seals, gaskets for vehicles, textile coating, leather finishing, paper making
Butyl Rubber (IIR)	Outstanding low permeability to air and other gases; low resilience; very good resistance to sunlight, ozone, and aging; relatively high resistance to temperatures	Inner tubes, linings for tubeless tires, steam hoses, roofing membranes, reservoir sheeting, anticorrosion linings
Chloroprene Rubber (CR)	Better resistance to oils and solvents than natural rubber or SBR; resistance to sunlight, oxidation, and aging; good resistance to abrasion and heat; good strength; flameproof; good adhesive qualities; less resilient than natural rubber or SBR	Seals; oil hoses; glazing strips; roofing sheeting in construction; linings and coatings for chemical products; waterproofing for tents, tarpaulins, life rafts; adhesives; paint additive
Chlorosulphonated Polyethylene Rubber (CSM)	Very high resistance to oxidation	Linings for hoses for acids, elastic coating for outdoor applications, anticorrosive applications
Ethylene-Vinyl Acetate Rubber (EVAC)	Highly resistant to weather, oxygen, ozone, and heat	Heat-resistant cables, cable coverings, and oil seals; waterproofing
Ethylene-Propylene Rubber (EPM and EPDM)	High resistance to ozone, sunlight, weather, and aging	Automobile components, acid hoses, roller coverings, reservoir linings, roofing sheets, general building applications, electric cable insulation
Fluororubber (CFM)	Good resistance to hot lubricants and hydraulic fluids (200 degrees Celsius)	Aerospace industry

Continued

TABLE 8.1 *(continued)*

Characteristics and End Uses of Synthetic Rubber

Type of Rubber	Characteristics	End Uses
Isoprene Rubber (IR) NOTE: Isoprene has the same chemical composition as natural rubber.	Similar to natural rubber, more pure than natural rubber	Tires, footwear, sponge rubber, sheeting, adhesive, extruded thread, dipped products
Nitrile Rubber (NBR)	More resistant to oil and heat than chloroprene rubber, poor resistance to sunlight, good oil and heat resistance	Hoses for oil, gasoline and solvents; oil seals and gaskets; brake linings; industrial adhesives; blended with polyvinyl chloride for use as heavy-duty cable coverings and soles of industrial footwear; blended with other plastics to use in paper making and coating, nonwoven textiles, artificial leather, and as a finish and waterproof coating for real leather
Polybutadiene Rubber (BR)	Better resilience than natural rubber, outstanding abrasion resistance, excellent low-temperature flexibility, poor tearing strength	Tires, additive for polystyrene to make it less brittle
Polysulphide Rubber (TM)	Excellent resistance to oils and solvents	Roller coverings, hoses for paints and agricultural sprays, sealant for fuel tanks
Polyurethane Rubber (Ue)	Great strength (in solid form), great resistance to abrasion (in solid form), good resistance to oil and all forms of oxidation	Solid tires; roller coverings; fabric coatings; synthetic leathers; elastic thread; foam—flexible polyurethane rubber foams are used for upholstery in vehicles and furniture; semirigid polyurethane rubber foams are used for safety padding in vehicles; rigid polyurethane rubber foams are used as insulation
Silicone Rubber (SI)	Retained strength and elasticity over a wider range of temperatures than organic rubbers; good electrical properties; good resistance to aging, ozone, and weathering; excellent color consistency; excellent nonstick properties	Aerospace industry, food processing and confectionery industries, surgical applications
Thermoplastic Rubber (TR)	Good resistance to heat, oil, gasoline, and flame	Automobile engines, the building industry

TABLE 8.2

Common Ingredients Used in Production of Rubber

Ingredient	Purpose
Carbon black	Increase the strength of the rubber
Barites, chalk, clay, lithopone talc, whiting	Reduce cost, increase hardness
Antioxidants	Reduce deterioration from age and exposure to sunlight
Antiozonants	Reduce deterioration from exposure to ozone
Peptizers, such as ammonia, organic sulfur compounds, mineral oils	Soften the rubber
Blowing agents	Produce cellular (foam) rubber
Pigments	Color
Reclaimed rubber	Filler

Foam rubber is made by mechanically incorporating air into the rubber mixture. Foam rubber is a lightweight material that is used for seat cushioning, mattresses, pillows, and underlays.

Reclaimed rubber is an important filler that is added to some rubber mixtures. It aids in the processing and manufacturing of some rubber products, but it may reduce the wear life if excessive quantities are used. Rubber apparel, tires, and shoe soles are examples of products made from reclaimed rubber.

Shaping

The rubber is shaped by extrusion, calendering, or molding.

Extrusion The rubber is forced through a shaped metal die to produce flat strips, rounded cords, cable coverings, and tubing. Elaborate gaskets, such as those used on refrigerator doors and automobile windows, can also be produced.

Calendering Flat sheets of rubber are formed on calendering machines. The rubber is passed through rollers that may be heated. Rubber may be pressed into fabric to create rubberized textile products. Steel-wire-reinforced belting and plies of tires are laminated by calendering.

Molding Rubber may be shaped by forcing it into molds under heat and pressure. Examples of molded rubber products include water bottles, footwear, tires, and rubber ball halves.

Vulcanizing

The basic process of vulcanization (or curing) rubber is the same as the one developed by Charles Goodyear in 1839. The rubber is mixed with sulfur, then it is molded and heated. The amount of sulfur added varies from 3 percent to 32 percent. **Soft rubber** will be 1 to 3 percent sulfur; **hard rubber** will be 32 percent sulfur. The rubber is subjected to heat of 245–300 degrees Fahrenheit.

The benefits of vulcanization are:

- added strength
- increased resistance to wear
- greater ability to return to original shape after stretching
- improved resistance to temperature extremes
- improved ability to absorb shock or vibration
- nonconductor of electricity and gases
- improved resistance to water
- not soluble in ordinary solvents such as gasoline and chloroform

Processing Liquid Rubber

Products can be made directly from liquid natural or synthetic rubber. There are two methods of forming the product—dipping and electrodeposition.

Dipping A mold is dipped in the liquid latex. A thin layer of rubber adheres to the mold. This method is used to make rubber gloves and balloons.

Electrodeposition An electric current is run through a bath of latex, and the negatively charged rubber particles adhere to metal molds. Rubber gloves and bathing slippers are made by this process.

Liquid latex is also used as a nonskid coating on the back of carpeting and rugs like the example shown in Figure 8.4. It can also be applied to fabric or paper to create imitation-leather products.

FIGURE 8.4
Latex-backed rugs.
Courtesy of Fairchild Publications, Inc.

Environmental Impact of Rubber

An important issue to be aware of when selecting rubber products is that some people are extremely sensitive to latex and must avoid contact with latex or products containing latex. It can cause mild to severe skin rashes.

Rubber is a recyclable product. Tires are the predominant end use for rubber, and the majority of used tires are recycled into a wide variety of applications. They are used as fuels, additives for asphalt and cement, floor mats, and molded-rubber products. Some recycled old tires are used in construction as insulation or stabilizers. Scientists are also conducting research into reversing the vulcanization process to extend the usability of recycled rubber.

PAPER

Papermaking developed in China in about 105 A.D. The original sources for the fibers used in papermaking were ground mulberry trees, bamboo stems, hemp, and silk rags. Paper is both aesthetic and functional, as well as important in the lives of many people. Beautiful wall coverings, lampshades, and works of art are often made from paper (see Figure 8.5). Paper also provides inexpensive, sanitary products for food storage, preparation, and serving. Packaging, such as wrapping paper, boxes, and shipping cartons, is another important use for paper.

Sources of Fibers for Papermaking

Today wood pulp is the major source of cellulosic fiber for making paper. Cellulosic wood fibers are readily available, relatively inexpensive, and durable. They also maintain their strength when wet. Other sources include rags, grasses and plants, manufactured fibers, and waste paper.

Trees

Trees are the primary source for cellulosic (plant) fibers for papermaking. Both *deciduous trees* (broad-leaves) and *coniferous trees* (softwoods) are used in the paper industry. The cellulosic fibers from hardwoods are shorter than those of softwoods, so the resulting paper is more opaque with a smooth surface.

Rags

Cotton and linen rags are another important source of cellulose for papermaking. Textile and garment mill scraps, **cotton linters** (the short fibers that remain on the cotton seed after ginning), flax, and clean rags are collected to be processed into paper. Rag fibers are longer and finer than most wood fibers. Because the fibers are longer, they contribute durability, strength, and improved texture to the paper. Rag papers are used when texture, strength, and appearance are critical. Examples include legal documents, security certificates, bond paper and letterhead, and high-grade stationery.

Grasses and Plants

Papers made from the cellulose of grasses and plants tend to be stiff with low opacity and low tearing strength. Examples of nonwood cellulosic sources for paper include:

- **bagasse** (the residue after sugar cane has been crushed)
- bamboo
- cereal straw
- **esparto** (a desert grass found in northern Africa and southern Spain)
- hemp, jute, and knaf

Manufactured Fibers

Many fibers from the manufactured-fiber industry are used in making specialized papers. Examples include rayon, nylon, polyester, acrylic, and glass. These fibers are much more expensive than wood pulp but provide exceptional strength, softness, and uniformity. Synthetic fibers are also used to create papers that are resistant to acids for use in industrial filtration. Glass fiber paper is resistant to both chemicals and heat.

Manufacture of Paper

Paper is manufactured from pulp, which is further processed to manufacture papers with different qualities.

Production of Pulp

The manufacture of paper begins with the production of pulp. **Pulp** is a moist, cohesive mass of fibers. Wood, recycled paper, and rags are the primary sources for pulp.

Chemical and Mechanical Wood Pulp

Production of pulp from wood is complex, involving a variety of processes to produce chemical and mechanical wood pulp. Pulp is also made from rags and recycled paper.

There are three processes to make **chemical wood pulp**—kraft, soda, and sulphite. Each process involves the cooking of wood chips in a chemical solution for one or more hours. This stage is called digesting and takes place in a large tower called a digester, diagramed in Figure 8.6. After processing, the pulp is washed to remove chemicals and impurities.

The Kraft Process The kraft process, also called the **sulfate process,** adds a water solution of sodium hydroxide and sodium sulfide to the cooking solution. The resulting pulp is brown in color and may be bleached to the desired whiteness. Brown kraft paper is commonly used for bags. The kraft process dominates the industry.

The Soda Process The soda process uses sodium hydroxide to cook hardwood chips under pressure. This method is seldom used because the resulting pulp, unless it is combined with a stronger fiber, creates a weak paper.

Chipper

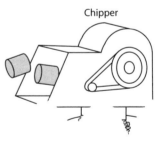

The Sulfite Process In the sulfite process the chips are soaked in a solution of bisulfite and sulfuric acid or its normal salt. This pulp is lighter than kraft pulp and bleaches easily.

Mechanical, or **groundwood, pulp** is created by grinding wood into very fine fibers. Paper made from groundwood pulp is speckled and grayish in color and will become brittle and yellow with age. Examples of end uses include newspapers and tissue papers.

Rag Pulp

To make **rag pulp,** cotton and linen rags are cut into small pieces and then boiled in a solution of lime and sodium hydroxide. Then the chemicals are washed out, and the rags are chopped to shorten the fibers and then bleached to produce a white pulp. Rag-content paper is made by adding a percentage of wood pulp. For example, a 25 percent rag-content paper would be 25 percent rag pulp and 75 percent wood pulp.

Recycled Paper Pulp

Waste paper is an important source for pulp because it is environmentally responsible. The waste paper is reshredded and de-inked before it is reprocessed into pulp.

Paper Manufacturing

After beating and refining the pulp, which is about 99 percent water, the pulp is formed into paper on a Fourdrinier or Verti-Forma papermaking machine. The Fourdrinier paper machine, shown in Figure 8.7, uses filtration through a fine mesh screen to make paper of desired weight. The pulp is given a final mixing, and then it passes onto the mesh screen, which vibrates to entangle the fibers and remove most of the water. Suction boxes remove additional water. The paper is formed horizontally so the textures of the bottom and the top of the sheet are different.

As the paper is removed from the papermaking machine, it is rolled to the desired thinness, completely dried, polished with calenders, and wound into large rolls. The Verti-Forma operates faster than the Fourdrinier and makes the paper in a vertical position so both sides have identical textures. The process of making paper can be summarized in the following steps:

1. Preparing Wood Pulp
   A. Mechanical or groundwood
   B. Chemical—kraft, soda, sulfite
   C. Rag/recycled
2. Washing the pulp to remove chemicals and impurities
3. Beating and refining—further separating the fibers
4. Forming paper on the Fourdrinier or Verti-Forma machine by entangling the fibers and removing most of the water
5. Drying—complete drying of the paper
6. Calendering and winding

Paper Grades and Standardizations

Many different grades and qualities of paper are available. Grades of paper are summarized in Table 8.3. To be usable, the paper is typically cut into standardized sizes and is sold in standardized quantities (see Table 8.4 and Table 8.5).

The final consumer usually buys paper by the **ream,** a package of 500 sheets. Paper is also categorized by weight. The term ***ream weight*** refers to the weight of one ream of writing paper, $17'' \times 22''$. A ream of $17'' \times 22''$ paper that weighs 24 pounds is still labeled as 24-pound paper after it has been cut into $8^{1}/2'' \times 11''$ sheets.

Paper Finishes

Special finishes are given to paper to achieve textural and decorative interest and to increase its functional application. Decorative finishes include embossing and watermarking. Functional finishes include carbon paper, sandpaper, and waxed paper.

Decorative Finishes

TABLE 8.3
Grades of Paper

Paper Grade	Characteristics	End Uses
Bond Paper		
Rag content (25% to 100%)	Stiff, durable, bright color	Announcements, currency, deeds, letterhead
Chemical wood pulp	Stiff, durable, bright color	Announcements, currency, deeds, letterhead
Book Paper		
Uncoated eggshell finish	Rough surface	Stationery, parchment
Machine finish	Medium smooth surface	Utility book paper, catalogues, circulars
English finish (EF)	Smoother, higher quality than machine finish	Books, brochures, magazines
Supercalendered	Smoothest paper available without a coating	Books, brochures, magazines
Coated	Used especially when uniformity, high gloss, and folding without cracking are needed	High-end brochures, books, magazines
Bible paper	Lightweight, strong, and opaque	Bibles, dictionaries, encyclopedias
Kraft wrapping paper	Unbleached paper with high strength	Paper bags
Bristol	Heavy, stiff	Folders
Groundwood	Opaque, off-white in color, yellows with age	Newspapers, books, catalogues
Paperboard	0.012 inch or more in thickness	Paper plates, paper boxes, shipping cartons
Sanitary paper	Absorbent, soft, bulky	Tissues, paper towels, paper napkins

TABLE 8.5
Standard Paper Quantities

Long ream	500 sheets (commonly called a ream)
Short ream	480 sheets
Quire	24 sheets (sometimes 25 sheets)

- *Edging* Decorative borders are created by embossing the edges of paper. Edges may be beveled or sloped. A rough or uneven edge is called a **deckle edge.**
- *Coating* Coating creates a very shiny paper. The paper is treated with substances such as aluminum sulfate, casein, or clay and then calendered.

Functional Finishes

Among functional finishes are the following:

- *Carbon* and *carbonless paper* These papers are used to create copies. Carbon paper is tissue paper with carbon on one side. Carbonless paper contains chemicals that create a blue image when pressed with a pen, pencil, or typewriter key.
- *Grease-resistant paper* Paper is treated with sulfuric acid, washed, and then dried. This paper, which is also known as vegetable parchment, is translucent. It is used to wrap food.
- *Sandpaper* This paper has sand or other abrasive glued to one side.
- *Waxed paper* This paper is coated with wax. It is used to wrap food.

Decorative and Functional Finishes

Metallic and plastic finishes serve both decorative and functional purposes. For metallic finishes, thin sheets of metal, most commonly aluminum, are glued to paper. Aluminum paper is used for decoration and food wrapping. Plastics, such as vinyl resins and silicones, are used to coat paper to make it more durable, or waterproof, or to add interesting texture. End uses of paper with plastic finishes include coffee cups, place mats, and playing cards.

Wallpaper

Wallpaper has been popular in the home for hundreds of years. Rice paper was used on the wall in China in 200 B.C. Wallpaper was also used in England and France in the early 1500s. Wallpaper from the 1700s was painted or block printed on sheets of paper rather than on a roll.

Usually wallpaper is used in residential applications (see Figure 8.8). It wears easily and is too fragile for use in commercial applications. Wallpaper is often coated with a protective vinyl finish that provides protection from dirt and is washable. Wallpapers are sold in rolls that contain 28 square feet. Double and triple rolls are also available.

FIGURE 8.8
Wallpaper.
Courtesy of Fairchild Publications, Inc.

ENVIRONMENTAL IMPACT

Energy consumption, pollution, solid waste, and cutting of trees can be reduced by recycling paper and by using less paper. Currently, about half of the paper used is not recycled.

Paper sludge, or paper mill waste, has been used experimentally as fertilizer and can be spread on dirt roads. Some conservationists question its use because it may contain toxic substances, such as sulphur and dioxins, that are used to process the paper.

LEATHER AND SUEDE

Leather is the treated hides and skins of certain animals. Early man discovered that the skin of animals could be preserved. Ancient Egyptians, Hebrews, Babylonians, and Native Americans all processed animal skins into leather. **Tanning** is the conversion of a **rawhide,** the untanned animal skin or hide, into leather. Skins and hides are obtained primarily from domesticated animals, with cattle being the most predominant. Other important sources are the skins of calves, sheep coats, and swine. Snakes, reptiles, sharks, and ostrich skins can also be used for leather products. Leather is available in varying sizes and thicknesses. It can be dyed, embossed, and otherwise treated to achieve many surface effects. **Suede** is a napped (raised surface) effect on leather.

Skin Quality

The highest quality leather usually comes from the center back section of the animal called the **bend.** Figure 8.9 illustrates the sections of a cow from which leather of different qualities is made. Bend leather is the most durable and firmest. The shank and belly yield the poorest quality leather. This leather does not wear as well or resist moisture as well as bend leather. Leather made from the head and shoulder is of moderate quality.

Skin Sizes

Skin sizes determine the weight of the skin. There are three sizes—skin, kip, and hide. There is a waste factor of 10 to 15 percent when calculating the yield from a skin, kip, or hide. The term ***skin*** has two meanings. It can refer to the outer covering of an animal. It can also refer to a skin of a young animal that weighs 15 pounds or less when it is shipped to the tannery. Examples of skins that weigh 15 pounds or less include calves, goats, deer, sheep, and alligators. A skin averages 2.3 to 3.2 square meters or 25 to 35 square feet (see Figure 8.10).

A **kip** is a skin that weighs between 15 and 25 pounds. These usually come from oversized calves. A kip will be approximately 3.2 to 4.6 square meters or 35 to 50 square feet.

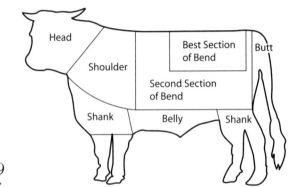

FIGURE 8.9
Qualities of cowhide.

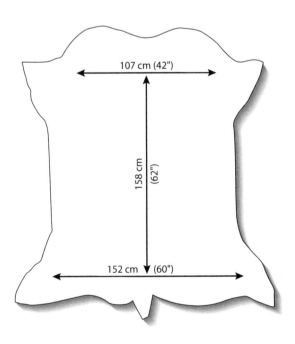

FIGURE 8.10
Approximate size of a calf skin.

A **hide** is a skin that weighs more than 25 pounds. A cowhide comes from a fully grown cow. Other examples of animals with skins that weigh 25 pounds or more are oxen, buffalo, walruses, and horses. A hide will range in size from 4.6 to 5.5 square meters or 50 to 60 square feet (see Figure 8.11).

Grain

Grain refers to the natural markings that are used to identify the type of animal skin. Animals with coarse hair, such as a pig, will have a very noticeable grain. The feathers of an ostrich also leave a very noticeable grain. Calfskin has a very small grain. Alligators, snakes, and lizards have scales that form the grain for these animal skins.

The hair or scale side of the leather is known as the **grain side** and is superior to the other side, which is called the **flesh side.** It is more attractive, smoother, more durable, and firmer than the flesh side. The grain does not show on the flesh side of the skin. Figure 8.12 illustrates the three layers of a raw hide. They are:

1. Epidermis—top layer with the grain markings
2. Corium—middle layer of interlaced bundles of fibers made from collagen
3. Flesh tissue—bottom layer of the hide

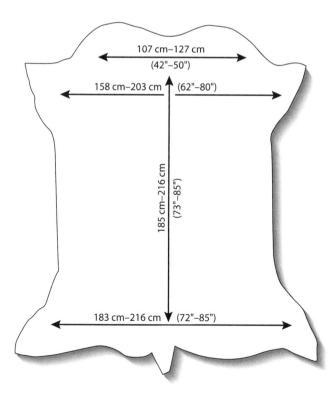

FIGURE 8.11

Approximate size of a cowhide.

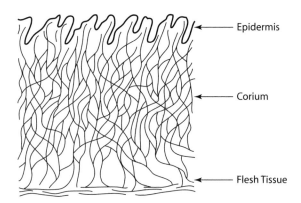

FIGURE 8.12
The three layers of a rawhide a. *epidermis,*
b. *corium,* c. *flesh tissue.*

Preparation, Tanning, and Finishing

There are three steps in the process of transforming a skin into a piece of leather—preparation, tanning, and finishing.

Preparation

Prior to arrival at the tannery, the skins are cured to prevent rotting. The skins must be soaked to soften them and remove chemicals used in curing. After soaking, the skins are subjected to fleshing, unhairing, and bating. During **fleshing,** the flesh is removed from the inner side of the skin to leave a clean surface. **Unhairing** is when the hair is removed chemically by soaking it in a lime solution for several days. When the skin is removed from this solution, the hair is easily rubbed off by machinery. **Bating** removes the lime from the skins by washing it with cold water and a lime-neutralizing agent. Bating softens the skin and gives it a silky feel.

Tanning

During tanning a chemical change occurs to convert the hides, skins, and kips into leather. The five types of tanning are summarized in Table 8.6. Chrome tanning is the most commonly used process. It is less expensive and takes less time than the other methods.

To achieve a specific combination of characteristics, leather may be tanned by two processes. For example, formaldehyde and alum tanning make good glove leather, and chrome and vegetable tanning produce leather that is especially good for heavy-duty work shoes.

Finishing

After tanning, the leather is wrinkled, dull, and unattractive. The finishing processes make the skin pliable and beautiful. The natural grain of the leather can be enhanced, removed, or changed, and color or other characteristics can be added to the leather using processes described below.

TABLE 8.6
Tanning Methods

Tanning Method	Characteristics	End Uses
Oil Tanning An oil solution, frequently cod oil, is worked into the skins	Washable, porous, supple, creamy yellow in color	Chamois skins for gloves and cleaning purposes, doe and buckskins may be oil tanned
Vegetable Tanning Tannin, a tanning acid from bark extracts, is used on the skins	Firm, durable, attractive, porous, water resistant	Shoe soles, upholstery, luggage, belts
Formaldehyde Tanning Formaldehyde gas and water are used to convert the skin to leather	Soft and pliable, white in color	Superior quality for gloves, shoe uppers (all parts other than the sole)
Mineral Tanning Alum Tanning Alum mineral salts are used to turn the skins into leather	Soft and flexible, must be dry cleaned, white in color	Gloves
Mineral Tanning Chrome Tanning Chrome salts are used to convert the skins into leather	More durable and less water resistant than vegetable-tanned leather, somewhat slippery when wet, may be damp sponged to clean, bluish gray in color	Gloves, handbags, shoe uppers

Splitting

Skins may be split into as many as five layers, depending on the thickness of the skin. The top layer is called **full-grain leather** or **full top-grain leather** if the surface has not been embossed or altered. It is the strongest, most beautiful, and most expensive of the layers. **Top-grain leather** is the top layer, but the original surface pattern, including scars, is removed by abrasion. This surface is embossed with a pattern, usually similar to the grain of the skin that was removed.

The other layers are called **splits.** Split leather is not as durable, has a coarser appearance, and is less expensive than top grain. Splits may be napped or have artificial grains embossed on them. Only full-grain leather and top-grain leather may be labeled and sold as **genuine leather** (see Figure 8.13).

Boarding Boarding creates a creased, bumpy texture on the surface of the leather. The leather is folded over itself, and the two surfaces are rubbed together. Examples include boarded calf and cow, and morocco and pin seal leather.

Coloring Opaque pigment dyes and transparent aniline dyes are used to color leather. Opaque dyes cover blemishes and partially obscure the grain. Aniline dyes permit the grain to

FIGURE 8.13
Top grain and splits of a skin.

show and darken with age. They are used on top-grain leather. Semianiline dyes contain some pigments. They are used to insure uniform color among many hides.

There are three methods of dyeing leather.

- *Brush dyeing* Dye is applied to the surface. Rubbing may remove the color.
- *Dip dyeing* The leather is immersed in dye so color retention is good and all sides are colored. This is the most expensive method.
- *Spray dyeing* Air sprayers are used to spray dye on one side of the leather.

Embossing

An imitation grain is placed on leather by pressing it with a steel plate that has the design etched on it. Split leather and scarred-grain side leathers are commonly embossed. Less expensive leathers are often embossed with a full-grain look.

Fat liquoring

Fat liquoring is the process that replaces the natural oil that the tanning process has removed from the leather. Animal, mineral, or vegetable oils are rubbed into the surface of the leather. Without oil, leather will dry out and crack.

Metallic Finishes

Thin sheets of gold or aluminum are bonded to leather under high pressure. The aluminum gives the appearance of silver.

Napping

The leather fibers are raised by a revolving buffing wheel. This process is called napping. If it is done on the flesh side, the leather is called suede. The leather has a soft, velvety surface. Doeskin, finished lambskin, and mocha leathers have been napped on the grain side.

Patent Finish

A plastic urethane coating gives smooth leather a shiny finish. Patent leather is usually made of calfskin, cowhide, coltskin, or kidskin. It is less porous and less elastic than other leathers.

INDUSTRY STATEMENT 8.1

Eames Lounge Chair and Ottoman

The chair that launched a thousand imitations was first designed for Academy Award-winning film director Billy Wilder.

Charles Eames wanted to give his friend a fitting birthday gift—literally. Eames intended for the glovelike chair to have "the warm receptive look of a well-used first baseman's mitt." The chair became synonymous with the lean and modern design philosophy that Eames and his wife and partner, Ray Eames, were known for.

It was first produced in 1956 and was one of many Eames designs manufactured and distributed by the Herman Miller Co. The chair had its public debut on NBC's "Today Show" in the same year. It has been in continuous production since then.

The Eames were fond of molding plywood shapes for their furniture designs. In the original interpretation, rosewood veneer shells were shaped and then topped with 6-inch-thick urethane foam cushions and leather covers. A swivel mechanism and diecast aluminum legs were added for functionality and clean lines. In 1989,

©2003 Lucia Eames dba Eames Office (www.eamesoffice.com)

non-sustainable forestry practices forced the shift to cherry and walnut veneers. The ubiquitous symbol of privileged leisure is still seen in homes, offices and public facilities, and also occupies space in the permanent collection of New York's Museum of Modern Art.

Source: HFN, May 27, 2002, p. 66. Courtesy of Fairchild Publications, Inc.

Waterproofing

Silicone is applied to the surface of the leather to make it resistant to water.

Sources for Leather

There are five main sources for leather—cowhides and calf skins, sheep skins and lamb skins, pigskins, deer and elk skins, and other resources.

Cowhides and Calf Skins

Most of the leather used in the United States comes from cows and calves. This leather is produced as a by-product of the meat-processing industry. Leather made from the skins of young calves is smoothly surfaced, finely grained, and firm. It is durable, scuff and scratch resistant, stretches moderately, takes a lustrous polish, and cleans easily. It is used for fine footwear and handbags, patent leathers, and suede. The leather from cowhides has a more distinct grain and is thicker, heavier, and larger. Cowhide leather is used for durable footwear, leather briefcases, luggage, and upholstery. Table 8.7 lists variations of calf skin and cowhide leathers.

TABLE 8.7

Variations of Calf Skin and Cowhide Leathers

Name	Description
Reversed calf	Coarse calfskin suede
Elk side	Cowhide that has been finished to look like elk hide
Rawhide	Cowhide that has been oil treated but not tanned
Retanned cowhide	Cowhide tanned by the chrome and vegetable process and then saturated with grease to make it moisture resistant
Saddle leather	Vegetable-tanned calfskin or cowhide used to make footwear and handbags
Scotch grain	Rough, embossed leather used for heavy walking and sport footwear
Side leather	Another name for leather made from cowhide
Vellum	Cowhide and calfskin processed to be used like parchment (paper)

Sheepskins and Lambskins

Leather from domestic and imported sheep and lambs is the second most common leather in the United States. It is generally less expensive and less durable than most other leathers. It stretches and abrades easily. See Table 8.8 for variations of leathers from sheep and lambskins.

Goatskins and Kidskins

Goatskins are imported from Africa, Asia, Europe, and South America. Kid leather is made from the skins of young goats. The term *kid leather* usually refers to animals that are milk fed. After the animals have been put out to pasture, they are no longer kids.

Generally the leather is chrome tanned to make it pliable, soft, and attractive. It is a fine leather with a close grain, and it is strong, durable for its weight, and has good elasticity. It scratches and peels easily and also wrinkles easily, but it can be finished to hide wrinkles. Table 8.9 describes some variations of goat and kid leather.

Pigskins

The primary sources for pigskins are **peccary,** a wild hog from South America and Mexico; **carpincho,** a water rodent from South and Central America; and domesticated pigs. The best quality pigskin comes from the peccary. The skin of the carpincho is heavier. The appearance of all three skins is similar—a coarse pebbled grain with visible bristle holes in groups of three. The holes go through the skin and offer the benefit of ventilation. Pigskin is frequently scarred, but unless the scarring is excessive, it does not affect the durability or aesthetic appeal of the leather. Excessively scarred pigskin is sometimes embossed and called **pig-grained pig.** Pigskin is used for small leather articles.

TABLE 8.8

Variations of Leathers from Sheep and Lambskins

Name	Description
Capeskin	Closely grained, sturdy, pliable leather from the skin of a South American haired sheep. It is more durable than ordinary sheepskin used for formal gloves.
Cabretta	Made from the skin of a South American hair sheep; similar to capeskin.
Chamois skin	Split layer of oil-tanned sheepskin that has been napped; used for cleaning.
Doeskin	Originally from a female deer, now commonly made from lambskin that is tanned in formaldehyde. The grain side is removed and a napped finish is applied. It takes color readily.
Electrified sheepskin	Sheepskin that is tanned with the wool left on. The wool pile is straightened chemically for a finely textured pile.
Flesher	Coarse flesh split of lamb or sheepskin that is alum tanned, dip dyed, and napped; used for inexpensive gloves.
Mocha leather	African or Asian hair sheepskins that have been alum tanned, then chrome tanned, so they are washable.
Parchment	Alum-tanned sheepskin with a smooth finish; used for diplomas, documents, and lampshades.
Shearling leather, also called sheepskin	Sheepskin that is tanned with the wool left on; used as a lining in caps, coats, gloves and footwear.
Skiver	Top-grain sheepskin that is thin; used for small leather goods.

TABLE 8.9

Variations of Goat and Kid Leather

Name	Description
Morocco leather	Goatskin that has been vegetable tanned and boarded for a pebbled surface
Bronze, silver, and gold kid	Kid leather that is coated with metallic powder
Crushed kid	Kid leather that has been creased in different directions to create a rough texture that does not show scratches or wrinkles
Glacé kid	Kid leather with a polished shiny finish

Deer and Elk Skins

Deer and elk skins have similar qualities. They are durable, flexible, porous, and smooth textured, and have excellent stretch. Because they are wild animals, their skins are frequently scarred. The grain side can be napped to hide the scarring. Cowhides and calfskins are sometimes finished to resemble elk.

Real doeskin is made from the skin of a female deer. It is lightweight, porous, absorbent, and washable. It is tanned in formaldehyde, napped, and takes dye well. Buckskin usually has the grain removed and is napped. If the skin is scarred, the flesh side is napped.

Other Sources

Other natural sources of leather are summarized in Table 8.10.

TABLE 8.10
Other Natural Sources of Leather

Name	Description	Source
Alligator and Crocodile Skins	The belly sections are the most valuable and have square-like markings. The back section has tiny oval or round horny markings.	Tropical waters
Buffalo Hides	Coarser and more durable than cowhides; frequently embossed to hide scarring.	Asia and Eastern Europe
Horse Hides	Nonporous, strong, and durable leather that resist scuffing; usually chrome tanned. Cordovan leather comes from the hindquarters of the animal.	Various
Kangaroo Skins	Similar to kidskins but stronger and does not scuff as easily; may be glazed or napped.	Australia
Lizard Skins	Very durable leather. Some species resemble alligator skins; some have a grain that looks like grains of uncooked rice.	Tropics and warmer areas of the temperate zone, especially in deserts
Ostrich Skins	Expensive leather with unique spiral markings called rosettes.	Africa
Seal Skins	Smooth soft leather that is frequently boarded. Pin seal is the highest-quality leather from the skin of young seals.	Northern Pacific coast
Shark Skins	Scuff-resistant leather with a diamond-shaped grain.	Various
Snake Skins	Decorative leather that is very thin, usually backed with fabric. Cobra, diamondback, and water snakes are the most common.	Various
Walrus Hides	Thick, durable hide; frequently embossed.	Arctic seas

Imitation Leathers

There are two main categories of imitation leathers—**bonded leathers** and **synthetic leathers.**

Bonded Leathers

Bonded leathers are also called **reconstituted leathers.** Waste leather fibers are mixed with a plastic binder and then formed into sheets. The sheets are embossed with patterns that resemble leather.

Synthetic Leathers

Vinyl is the most common plastic used to imitate leather (see Figure 8.14). It is frequently referred to as "pleather." Expanded vinyl (vinyl with internal air bubbles) is used to make imitation leather that is crushable and soft. Nonexpanded vinyl looks like calf, kid, or patent leather. Grain-like designs are frequently embossed into vinyl. Polyurethane is another plastic that is used to make imitation leather.

Environmental Impact of Leather and Suede

The leather industry has been challenged by animal rights activists. It is important to note that the leather industry primarily uses by-products of the meat industry as sources for its hides and skins.

Reduction of landfill waste and conservation of water are other important issues in the leather industry. Wastewater treatment plants have been developed that allow the tanneries to reuse wastewater. The solids from treatment plants can be composted and processed into fertilizer. Scrap leather can also be processed into fertilizer and animal feed.

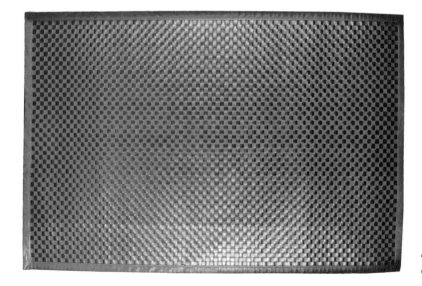

FIGURE 8.14
Synthetic leather rug.
Courtesy of Fairchild Publications, Inc.

SUMMARY

There are two types of rubber—natural and synthetic. A synthetic rubber is a synthetic polymer that has properties similar to those of natural rubber. Natural rubber is harvested from a *Hevea brasiliensis* (rubber) tree. Production of synthetic rubber is a complex chemical process. There are about 20 chemical formulas for synthetic rubber.

The steps for processing natural or synthetic rubber are—masticating, mixing, shaping, and vulcanizing. In 1839 Charles Goodyear developed vulcanization (or curing) of rubber. The rubber is mixed with sulfur, molded, and heated.

Synthetic rubber is more uniform, of higher quality, and more adaptable to various end uses than natural rubber, so synthetic rubber is usually preferred.

Papermaking developed in China in about 105 A.D. Today, wood pulp is the major source of cellulosic fiber for papermaking. Cellulosic wood fibers are readily available, relatively inexpensive, and durable, and maintain their strength when wet. Other sources include rags, grasses and plants, manufactured fibers, and waste paper.

The manufacture of paper begins with the production of pulp, a moist cohesive mass of fibers. Wood, recycled paper, and rags are the primary sources of pulp. There are two kinds of wood pulp—chemical and mechanical. The three processes to make chemical wood pulp are—kraft, soda, and sulphite. Mechanical, or groundwood, pulp is created by grinding wood into very fine fibers. Rag pulp is made from cotton and linen rags that are cut into small pieces and then boiled in a solution of lime and caustic soda. Then the chemicals are washed out, and the rags are chopped to shorten the fibers.

Many different grades and qualities of paper are available. Paper is typically cut into standardized sizes and is sold in standardized quantities. Special finishes achieve textural and decorative interest and increase the functional applications of paper. Textural finishes include watermarking and embossing; functional finishes include carbon paper, sandpaper, and waxed paper and vinyl finishes on wallpaper.

Leather is the treated hides and skins of animals. Tanning is the conversion of a rawhide into leather. The highest-quality leather usually comes from the bend, the center back section of the animal. Skin sizes are determined by the weight of the skin. There are three sizes—skin, kip, and hide.

Grain refers to the natural markings that are used to identify the animal from which the leather came. There are three steps in the tanning process—preparation, tanning, and finishing. Finishes used on leather include splitting, boarding, coloring, embossing, fat liquoring, metallic finishes, napping, patent finish, and waterproofing. Skins may be split into as many as five layers. Only full-grain leather and top-grain leather may be labeled and sold as genuine leather.

There are two main categories of imitation leathers—bonded leathers and synthetic leathers.

INDUSTRY PROFILE

Natuzzi: Leader of The Leather Revolution

From Gucci handbags to Armani jackets, Italian leather holds a certain mystique.

Pasquale Natuzzi had that Italian mystique on his side when he ventured into the U.S. market in the early 1980s, selling handmade leather sofas to Macy's.

Besides the Italian leather label and the unheard-of price of $999 retail, the Natuzzi product had another thing going for it: good design.

When Natuzzi began making and selling sofas in Italy in 1959, one of his primary goals was to make good design affordable for the masses.

A native of impoverished southern Italy, Natuzzi perhaps has more affection for the masses than most. He has shown this in his dogged determination to bring economic prosperity to the region by maintaining and expanding his operations there despite the lack of trained workforce or well-maintained infrastructure.

The company trains its own work force and keeps close tabs on productivity.

Natuzzi keeps costs down by controlling every aspect of the manufacturing process, from the tannery to the poly-urethane foam to the shipping materials. Furniture designs, too, must incorporate cost savings in materials and labor.

It is said that Natuzzi's designers start with a price and design a sofa to accommodate it.

Natuzzi entered the American market at a time when leather furniture meant contemporary design. But, not one to be pigeonholed, the company has increased its selections to cover a wide range of styles.

At Natuzzi Americas' High Point, N.C., showroom, dealers can find clean, simple European silhouettes or more generously proportioned, U.S.-friendly pieces.

In fact, a growing segment of Natuzzi's business today is traditional silhouettes with detailing such as exposed wood and nailhead trim.

Although affordable, high-quality, beautifully styled leather furniture is available from domestic producers, an Italian pedigree still carries a certain cache. And when consumers think "Italian leather sofa," they probably have a Natuzzi design in mind, even if they don't know the name.

Source: HFN Image Makers, May 29, 2000, p. 48. Courtesy of Fairchild Publications, Inc.

TERMS FOR REVIEW

bagasse
bating
bend
boarding
bonded (reconstituted) leather
carpincho
chemical wood pulp
cotton linters
deckle edge
dipping
electrodeposition
esparto
fat liquoring
flesh side

fleshing
foam rubber
full-grain leather
full top-grain leather
genuine leather
grain
grain side
hard rubber
Hevea brasiliensis
hide
kip
kraft (sulfate) process
laid paper
latex

leather
mechanical (groundwood) pulp
natural rubber
peccary
pig-grained pig
pulp
rag pulp
rawhide
ream
ream weight
skin
soda process
soft rubber

TERMS FOR REVIEW *(continued)*

splits	synthetic leather	unhairing
styrene-butadiene rubber	synthetic rubber	unvulcanized rubber
suede	tanning	vulcanization
sulfite process	top-grain leather	watermarking

REVIEW QUESTIONS

1. Why is synthetic rubber considered superior to natural rubber for most applications?
2. What is styrene butadiene? Why is it important?
3. What is the major source of cellulosic fibers for paper?
4. Why is rag content paper of higher quality than chemical pulp paper or mechanical wood pulp paper?
5. What is genuine leather?
6. List three sources for leather.

LEARNING ACTIVITIES

1. Visit a stationery store to examine various grades of paper. Record your observations. Why would a company choose to use recycled paper for letterhead?
2. Visit a furniture store selling chairs with both leather and vinyl upholstery. Describe your impressions of each. What is the price difference? Which would you recommend to a customer? Justify your decision.

PART THREE

THE CATEGORIES OF HOME FURNISHINGS

CHAPTER 9

FURNITURE

Nathan "Nat" Ancell (1908–1999) pioneered concepts that are taken for granted today in the furniture industry. Vertical integration, gallery settings, room vignettes — all are results of Ancell's vision. He started a lot of what we see in furniture retail today, bringing all the parts of a home together into one display. He was into vertical marketing in its truest sense, from the forest to the consumer.

—*HFN,* Nov. 27, 2000, p. 26. Courtesy of Fairchild Publications, Inc.

THE FURNITURE INDUSTRY PRODUCES GOODS THAT CONSUMERS CAN SELECT ON THE BASIS OF function and aesthetics at a full range of quality and price levels. As noted in Industry Statement 9.1, consumers have been price conscious, but furniture brands and aesthetics are becoming more important factors in furniture purchases.

The major functions of furniture are to provide comfort, utility, and a place for social interaction. Furniture can be made from a wide variety of materials, such as wood, plastic, glass, and metal. Wood is the most common material used to make furniture. Simulated wood products, such as plastic laminates, are also used. Wicker, rattan, and cane are frequently used in more casual furniture.

The two main categories of furniture are residential and contract. **Residential furniture** is purchased by the individual consumer for use in a home. **Contract furniture** is designed to be used by institutions or businesses, or in public buildings.

FURNITURE DESIGN

Furniture is designed with both function and aesthetics in mind. Functionally, furniture provides seating, storage space, conversation areas, and workspace. Aesthetically, furniture is an important feature in the décor in public places, work environments, and the home.

INDUSTRY STATEMENT 9.1

The Suite Life

The furniture industry is seen largely as a price-driven business, even by insiders. But in recent years, while the low end of the business has collapsed in retail failures, furniture's luxury market has quietly flourished.

Generally considered brand-deficient, furniture has some of its strongest brands at the upper end. Names such as Lexington, Drexel Heritage, Henredon, Thomasville and Century mean something to consumers, and they're willing to pay for the quality they represent.

The retailers that carry high-end furniture have also fared well—stores such as Robb & Stucky, Gabberts and The Home Co. The luxury producers are carrying their names to retail as well, with Thomasville and Drexel Heritage rolling out dedicated stores. And of course there's Ethan Allen, which has transformed its well-known but stodgy brand into an upper-end furniture nameplate.

"With all the new stores and remodelings, there's been a real boom in upper-end retail activity over the past 10 years," said Alan Cole, chief executive officer of Lifestyle Furnishings International. "In the '80s, the upper-end segment wasn't nearly as robust."

Lifestyle companies include Drexel Heritage, Lexington and Henredon.

"The reinvestment in stores, the aggressiveness, the advertising—all of that has just mushroomed," Cole said. "Today there's a very strong network of upper-end retailers in this country."

Housing trends have had a major impact on the luxury furniture business. Larger, more open rooms and higher ceilings beg for larger, more dramatic—and more expensive—furniture.

"Over the last several years, there's been an extreme amount of activity in design overstatement," Cole said. "We've found in all of our upper-end divisions that design has been embraced enthusiastically by the upper-end marketplace. The furniture is about drama, to make the home a dramatic environment."

Despite the success of the luxury market, the furniture industry still has much work to do if it is to shed its pervasive promotional mentality and enhance its image with consumers, Cole said.

"We have a wonderful opportunity in this business, because of the advent of the economies of import furniture, to invest more money in the branding of our industry to the consumers," he said.

"Even though we're focused on cost reduction, one of the areas we're actually increasing our expenditures in is in marketing to consumers," Cole said. "If we don't do more of that in this industry, it will become a commodity industry where price reigns.

"I can remember, years ago, when margins were much better at retail and manufacturing," he continued. "But somewhere along the way, when we built bigger factories, we convinced ourselves that the best avenue for success was lowering the price and selling more.

"We are largely an unbranded industry," said Cole. "But look at the companies that have invested in those brands. Those are the bright signs that I see. This industry doesn't have to be just a product at a price."

Source: HFN, May 14, 2001, p. 30. Courtesy of Fairchild Publications, Inc.

Furniture is frequently categorized by its **style** or particular set of design characteristics. There are three basic styles of furniture design—traditional, provincial, and contemporary. The traditional and provincial styles are typically named by the historical period or reigning monarch during the time in which they developed, or by the area of the world where they developed.

Traditional Furniture

Traditional furniture designs are adapted from those of cabinetmakers and artisans of the 17th, 18th, and 19th centuries. Craftsmen from England, France, and the United States produced the original furniture that is still being copied today. Important traditional furniture styles include

Queen Anne, Chippendale, Victorian, Louis XVI, Hepplewhite, and Duncan Phyfe (see Figure 9.1). The term *traditional furniture* may be used to refer to original pieces or to reproductions that resemble the original. Original pieces are in the category of antiques—furniture that is more than one hundred years old. There are official reproductions that exactly copy the early styles, and they are more expensive than furniture that uses just the design elements. See Industry Statement 9.2 which details the genesis of a new line of traditional furniture copied from an antique collection.

Provincial Furniture

Provincial furniture is sometimes called **country furniture.** It was first made during the 16th to 18th centuries in France. Craftsmen made furniture that reflected the lives of people who lived in the more rural areas of the country. This style is a simplified version of traditional furniture that is less formal and more durable than traditional. Usually it is solid wood, practical, and more rustic in design with less ornamentation. Examples of provincial furniture include Italian Provincial, French Provincial, English Country, and Early American, or colonial, furniture.

Contemporary Furniture

Contemporary furniture originated in the late 19th century. It was the result of advances in technology and is made with a variety of materials, such as wood, plastic, glass, chrome, and steel. Although sometimes the terms *modern* and *contemporary* are used synonymously, *modern* usually refers to pieces produced during the late 1800s to early 1900s. Charles Rennie Mackintosh, Ludwig Mies van der Rohe, and Michael Thonet are well-known modern designers. Contemporary furniture design is simple, graceful, versatile, and easy to maintain (see Figure 9.2).

FIGURE 9.1
Duncan Phyfe reproductions by Showcase Furniture.

FIGURE 9.2 *20th-century furniture.*
Courtesy of Fairchild Publications, Inc.

INDUSTRY STATEMENT 9.2

McClintock: From Dresses to Dressers

GREENSBORO, N.C.—Fashion designer Jessica McClintock is known for her romantic formalwear, and now the designer is extending that look with a home furnishings collection. American Drew, the case goods producer based here, is designing the furniture collection based on pieces from McClintock's Pacific Heights home in San Francisco.

The collection includes bedroom, dining room and occasional furniture and will officially debut with 50 pieces at the High Point market next month as Jessica McClintock Home—The Romance Collection.

"Most women associate the name Jessica McClintock with a special occasion in their life," said Jeffrey Scheffer, president of American Drew. "It's both a great name and a great brand, but what we really like is that she brings us a very fresh and timely design perspective—that being the romantic style."

McClintock is best known for her special-occasion dresses, which she's been designing for 30 years. She also has designed fragrances and fabrics, and has her own retail stores.

McClintock has decorated her 110-year-old Victorian home, which was once owned by Francis Ford Coppola, in a style that reflects her interest in romance and heirlooms. She's collected antiques from all over the world.

"The inspiration for [American Drew] was to take my romantic inspiration from the house and do the best they could at copying the armoires, chairs, tables and consoles," said McClintock. "There's definitely the feeling of romance and a feminine touch throughout the collection."

Clay, Metal & Stone, based in Fort Lauderdale, Fla., has signed on to do the decorative accessory program for Jessica McClintock Home—The Romance Collection. That line, which also debuts in October, includes decorative boxes, candleholders, finials, vases, trays and urns. The initial line of 35 pieces is designed to coordinate with American Drew's furniture collection. Like the furniture, the line is derived from McClintock's antiques, as well as from wall finishes and architectural details in her home.

McClintock is also designing a tabletop collection for PTS and will be adding a new bedding line, as well as other home furnishings categories.

American Drew is no stranger to the fashion world. The manufacturer introduced the Bob Mackie collection in the fall of 1998.

The Jessica McClintock Home collection will be comparable in price range to the Bob Mackie furniture, but Scheffer sees the McClintock name enabling American Drew to extend its retail reach.

"I think it will open some new doors for us with retailers, possibly department stores and some better-end [furniture] stores around the country," said Scheffer.

Source: HFN, September 11, 2000, p. 39. Courtesy of Fairchild Publications, Inc.

FURNITURE CLASSIFICATIONS

Furniture manufacturers divide furniture into four major classifications—case goods, upholstered, occasional, and bedding. Summer furniture, indoor/outdoor furniture, wall systems, and ready-to-assemble furniture are special furniture classifications. This chapter covers case goods, upholstered, occasional furniture, and selected special furniture classifications. (See Chapter 11 for discussion of bedding.)

Within each classification of furniture, manufacturers create groupings that denote how pieces of furniture are designed to be used. The three groupings are:

- **Correlated groupings** Pieces designed to go together to create living environments for the living room, dining room, and bedroom. The term *suite* is also used to refer to a grouping of furniture pieces for use in a specific room.

- **Modular groupings** Pieces designed to be used either separately or together in a variety of ways (see Figure 9.3). Ethan Allen offers modular office furniture that can be purchased and used separately or together, depending on the customer's wishes.
- **Wrap groupings** Pieces designed to be used beside each other or on top of each other. For example pieces may "wrap" around a wall as in modular seating, or stack on top of each other to create a wall unit.

CASE GOODS

Originally the term *case goods* meant box-like furniture, such as desks, chests of drawers, buffets, bookcases, and china closets. Because chairs, tables, and beds are commonly sold with these case goods, the term now refers to dining room and bedroom furniture as a whole. The parts of typical case goods are shown in Figure 9.4. It is important to use the correct terminology when referring to the parts of furniture.

The term *casework* is usually used to refer to cabinets, cases, storage units, and other fixtures that are built-in or attached to walls and closets. They can be prefabricated or custom built. Prefabricated casework is called *modular casework* and custom-built casework is called *architectural cabinetry*. Casework is commonly used in residential kitchens. It is also used extensively in commercial interiors.

FIGURE 9.3 *Modular home office furniture.* Courtesy of Fairchild Publications, Inc.

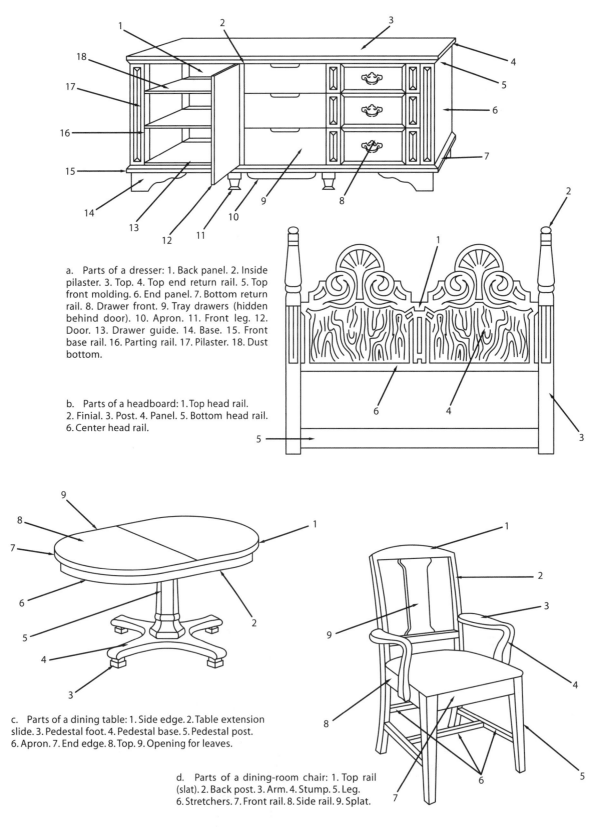

a. Parts of a dresser: 1. Back panel. 2. Inside pilaster. 3. Top. 4. Top end return rail. 5. Top front molding. 6. End panel. 7. Bottom return rail. 8. Drawer front. 9. Tray drawers (hidden behind door). 10. Apron. 11. Front leg. 12. Door. 13. Drawer guide. 14. Base. 15. Front base rail. 16. Parting rail. 17. Pilaster. 18. Dust bottom.

b. Parts of a headboard: 1. Top head rail. 2. Finial. 3. Post. 4. Panel. 5. Bottom head rail. 6. Center head rail.

c. Parts of a dining table: 1. Side edge. 2. Table extension slide. 3. Pedestal foot. 4. Pedestal base. 5. Pedestal post. 6. Apron. 7. End edge. 8. Top. 9. Opening for leaves.

d. Parts of a dining-room chair: 1. Top rail (slat). 2. Back post. 3. Arm. 4. Stump. 5. Leg. 6. Stretchers. 7. Front rail. 8. Side rail. 9. Splat.

FIGURE 9.4

a. *Parts of a dresser,* b. *parts of a headboard,* c. *parts of a table,* d. *parts of a chair.*

TABLE 9.1

Approximate Sizes of Selected Bedroom Furniture Pieces

Piece	Approximate Dimensions
Single dresser	42″ × 19″ × 35″ H
Double dresser	50″ × 19″ × 35″ H
Triple dresser	66″ × 20″ × 35″ H
Chest	35″ × 19″ × 47″ H
Chest-on-chest	36″ × 19″ × 51″ H
Night table	22″ × 18″ × 26″ H
Armoire	40″ × 20″ × 64″ H

Note: See Chapter 10 for discussion of beds.

Bedroom Furniture

A grouping of furniture pieces for use in the bedroom is called a bedroom suite. The basic bedroom suite includes a headboard (and sometimes a footboard), chest of drawers, dresser, and mirror. Additional pieces may include nightstands or bedside tables, bookcases, lingerie drawers, desks, and chairs. An *armoire*, a tall case piece with doors covering an inner compartment for hanging clothes, and a *bachelor's chest*, a small three drawer chest, may also be part of a bedroom suite. Basic pieces of bedroom furniture are available in a variety of sizes. For example, beds are made in twin, double, queen, king, and California king sizes, and dressers may be single, double, or triple. Approximate sizes of selected bedroom furniture pieces are shown in Table 9.1. A variety of mirror shapes are available as separate pieces or as part of the dresser (see Figure 9.5).

Landscape mirror

Twin vertical mirrors

Wing, or triplex, mirror

FIGURE 9.5 *Basic types of mirrors.*

Dining Room Furniture

Dining room suites are made in three sizes with a varying number of pieces. Approximate sizes of selected dining room furniture pieces are shown in Table 9.2. The three sizes of dining room suites are:

- *Full-size dining room suites* typically include a table, four side chairs (chairs without arms), and a china cabinet (hutch and base). The table will extend to accommodate additional guests. Most consumers purchase at least six chairs, usually including one or two matching armchairs. Frequently a buffet, or server, is available.
- *Junior dining room suites* are designed for smaller dining rooms, such as those found in apartments or condominiums. The suite usually includes a table, four side chairs, and a china cabinet. The china cabinet will be smaller than that in a full-size suite. The table may not extend, or if it does, it will not extend as far as a full-size table.
- *Dinettes* are informal dining room furniture, also known as party sets. These sets are typically used in kitchens and might be made of various materials. Tables may be made of wood, wrought iron, glass, vinyl, chrome, or plastic laminates. Chairs may be made of wood, wrought iron, chrome, or aluminum. Often materials are combined, such as wrought iron with glass. Recently there has been a trend toward more expensive, higher-quality furniture in this category.

Determining Quality in Case Goods

The workmanship and quality of materials—the type of wood, external construction, types of joints, construction details, decoration, and finish—determine the overall quality of case goods. Because furniture is a fashion product, the desirability of the pieces is determined to some extent by its style as well as overall quality.

TABLE 9.2

Approximate Sizes of Selected Dining Room Furniture Pieces

Piece	Approximate Size Ranges
Square tables	$30'' \times 30''$ to $60'' \times 60''$
Round tables	$30''$ diameter to $76''$ diameter
Rectangular tables	$36'' \times 60''$ to $48'' \times 96''$
Side chairs	$16'' \times 16''$ to $20'' \times 20''$
Arm chairs	$22'' \times 22''$ to $24'' \times 24''$
Buffet	$20'' \times 36''$ to $24'' \times 72''$
China cabinet	$18'' \times 36''$ to $20'' \times 48''$ (to be placed on a buffet)
Serving table	$18'' \times 36''$ to $24'' \times 48''$

Type of Wood

Most case goods are made from wood or materials that simulate wood. The type of wood used in case goods is an indicator of quality. Hardwoods, such as walnut, oak, and cherry, are more expensive than softwoods, such as pine. Likewise, hardwood veneers are also considered to be high quality. As styles change, the popularity of certain wood changes. (See Chapter 3 for additional discussion of the types of woods and veneers.)

External Construction

The construction of the outside of a piece is important to its overall quality. Sometimes the surface is painted or covered with laminates of different colors or designs.

In higher-quality furniture made from a combination of solid wood and veneer, the solid wood is used for pilasters, drawer fronts, parting rails, and other external structural pieces. The veneer is used for flat surfaces. Usually the core, or center ply, of the veneer is thicker than the other plies. It provides strength and should be one-half inch thick. In the best-quality furniture, the core of the veneer is solid wood. Lower-quality furniture has a core made of wood composition materials, such as particleboard.

Particleboard can be printed to resemble solid woods or veneers. The process is called engraving and is used on less expensive furniture. Large rollers apply ink to particleboard panels that are very smooth. The printed wood is used on the sides, back panels, and other areas that are less visible. Sometimes dressers or chests of drawers have laminated tops.

The least expensive simulated-wood furniture is made from particleboard that has been covered with a thin layer of vinyl printed to resemble wood grain. The vinyl is simply glued to the surface of the particleboard. In some less expensive furniture, vinyl coated particleboard is combined with printed particleboard.

Joining

Joining is the process of attaching one piece of wood to another. The manner in which the wood is joined is an indicator of quality. Nails and staples are used in lower-quality furniture. Screws are used in higher-quality furniture. Screws give more support and hold the pieces of wood together more securely than nails. Glue is used in most joints. There are nine basic types of joints used in furniture.

Dado joint A piece of wood fits into a groove that has been cut into another piece of wood (see Figure 9.6a). This joint is particularly suitable for drawer fronts, to hold shelves and drawer bottoms to the sides of drawers, and to secure the sides of furniture to front and back panels.

Dovetail joint The ends of the wood are cut so the pieces will interlock (see Figure 9.6b). Dovetail joints are considered to be one of the strongest joints in woodworking. The wood cannot warp out of shape or come apart. This joint is frequently used to assemble drawers.

Dowel joint Holes are drilled into the pieces of wood that are to be joined. Pegs of kiln-dried hardwood are fitted into the holes with glue (see Figure 9.6c). Dowel joints are commonly used

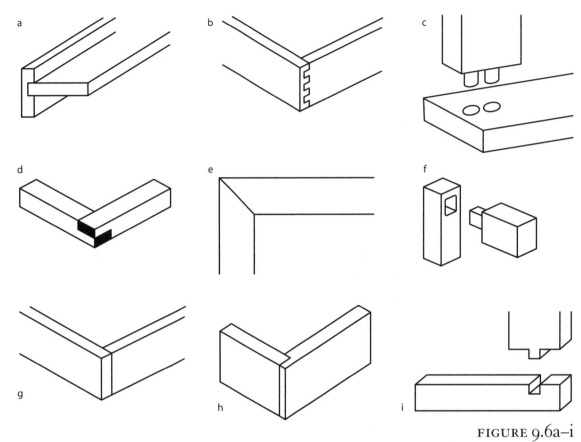

FIGURE 9.6a–i

Basic types of joints: a. *dado joint,* b. *dovetail joint,* c. *dowel joint,* d. *lap joint,* e. *miter joint,* f. *mortise-and-tenon joint,* g. *plain butt joint,* h. *rabbet joint,* i. *tongue-and-groove joint.*

to join parts of chairs, sofas, desks, and tables. Often double-dowel construction is used. Dowels that have spiral or vertical grooves are better because they hold the glue and make a better bond.

Lap joints Equal amounts are cut away from two pieces of wood so they can be fit together (see Figure 9.6d). Lap joints are often used in chairs, couches, and beds.

Miter joint A miter joint is a relatively weak joint that is commonly used in picture frames. Two pieces of wood are joined together at the ends to hide the ends (see Figure 9.6e). This joint is frequently reinforced with decorative hardware or **splines,** thin strips of metal or wood.

Mortise-and-tenon joint One piece of wood has a projection (tenon) that is inserted into a rectangular hole (mortise) in another piece of wood (see Figure 9.6f). This joint is frequently used for bracing, rails, and framing. It is especially important where the side rails and leg stretchers of a chair join the back post.

Plain butt joint One piece of wood is attached to another piece of wood using glue, nails, or screws. It is a poor quality joint (see Figure 9.6g).

Rabbet joint The end of a piece of wood is trimmed to accept the width of another piece of wood. Splines may be inserted in both pieces for reinforcement (see Figure 9.6h).

Tongue-and-groove joint A piece of wood has a projection that fits into a groove in another piece of wood (see Figure 9.6i).

Reinforcing Joints

The joints in higher-quality furniture are reinforced with braces or blocks made of wood or metal. They prevent the loosening of the joints and are usually used in furniture with legs. Three methods to reinforce joints are wood corner blocks, wood corner braces with a hanger bolt, and metal corner braces with a hanger bolt (see Figure 9.7).

Construction Details

Construction details are important in the overall quality of case goods. The care in matching and assembling furniture parts also affects the quality. Some important construction details that indicate higher quality include:

- **Floating construction** High-quality solid wood furniture is built by placing the screws that hold the sides and top together in slotted screw holes so the furniture can expand and contract without damage.
- **Dust bottoms** Better-quality furniture will have wooden dust bottoms separating drawers to prevent dust from settling on the contents of the lower drawer.
- *Piano-type hinges* Long doors will be hung with piano-type hinges (hinges that runs the full length of a door and its frame) for additional stability and easy access.
- *Drawers*
  1. *Guides* Center drawer guides are usually found in more-expensive furniture. Side drawer guides are found in less-expensive furniture. Drawers should slide easily.
  2. *Corner blocks* Small blocks are glued underneath the drawer for support and strength.
  3. *Dovetail joints* Used to join the drawer fronts to the sides.
  4. *Smooth Surfaces* Drawer interiors should be sanded smooth.
- *Back* The back of the piece is finished to match the front and sides in better furniture.
- *Color* There should be no unevenness of color and no rough spots.
- *Doors and drawers* Doors and drawers should fit tightly without sticking.

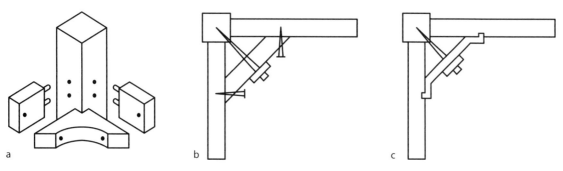

FIGURE 9.7 a–c *Methods to reinforce joints:* a. *wood corner block,* b. *wood corner brace with a hanger bolt,* c. *metal corner brace with a hanger bolt.*

Decorating

Furniture is often decorated in ways that take advantage of the natural beauty of the wood. Less attractive pieces of wood can be painted (see Figure 9.8). Some of the many methods to decorate furniture are discussed below.

- Carving of solid wood pieces can done by hand or by machine. More expensive pieces are carved by hand. Often machine-carved pieces are touched up by hand after they have been turned on a lathe. Fluting and reeding are variations of carving.
- **Fluting** is a special type of carving in which perpendicular groves are carved into posts or legs. They may be parallel or funnel shaped.
- **Reeding** is the opposite of fluting. Raised lines with rounded edges are used to decorate posts or legs.
- Moldings are applied to the surface of the wood. They may be made from wood or synthetic materials. Wood moldings are fitted into grooves on the surface of the piece. Synthetic moldings are simply glued on to the piece. They are used on low-end furniture.
- Inlay is a method of inserting strips of wood or other materials, such as metal or marble, into grooves that have been cut into the surface of the piece. Marquetry and intarsia are variations of inlay (see Chapter 3 for additional discussion of inlay).
- Applique or overlay resembles inlay except that it creates a raised design glued to the surface of the wood.
- Decalcomania is an inexpensive imitation of hand painting. Transfer designs are applied to the wood surface before or after varnishing.
- Printing can be put on wood that has little or no natural grain so that there is a pattern on the wood. The textural effects of a natural grain can be embossed over the printed pattern.

FIGURE 9.8
Hand painted headboard and footboard.
Courtesy of Fairchild Publications, Inc.

Finishing

Most wood furniture is finished. Finishes coat or treat wood surfaces to protect and/or decorate them. There are four purposes for finishing:

- To improve the appearance of the wood by enhancing its natural color and grain
- To keep moisture out of the wood and prevent warping
- To protect the wood from minor scratches
- To provide a smooth nonporous surface that is easy to clean

An inexpensive wood can be finished to appear like better-quality wood. Federal regulations require that a wood that has been finished to look like another wood must be labeled with the word *finish* in the name. For example, "mahogany-finished gumwood" indicates that the gumwood has been finished to look like mahogany. Common finishes for wood are summarized in Chapter 3.

Selection of Case Goods

Interior designers, decorators, and retail sales associates who assist consumers in selecting furniture need to know about design features, functional features, styles, quality, and construction details in order to satisfy their customers' needs and tastes. Furniture is a major investment, so consumers also benefit from learning how to select items for their own use.

Chairs

Selection of chairs is very important because most people spend many of their waking hours sitting. Proper support is essential for comfort. The size and dimensions of the chair should provide appropriate height and back support and should be based on actual body shape and size.

Specific criteria for the selection of chairs include:

- The height of the seat should be slightly less than the length of the lower leg so the feet can rest on the floor.
- The depth of the seat should be slightly less than the length of the upper leg so there is no pressure point under the knee.
- The width of the seat should allow room for some movement.
- The seat should be shaped, or somewhat resilient, so pressure is not concentrated on the weight-bearing edge of the pelvis.
- Both the seat and the back should be tilted slightly back to buttress the weight.
- The chair back should support the small of the back.

Additional information on the selection of chairs is included in the discussion of upholstered furniture.

Dining Tables

Rectangular tables are well suited to the shape of rectangular dining rooms. Round or oval tables offer more intimacy. Most dining room tables are made with **leaves** (matching panels that can be attached to the table so the table can be easily expanded). Drop leaves are hinged to the tabletop and hang vertically when not in use (see Figure 9.9). Kitchen tables are often used for food preparation in addition to dining, so they are usually made of materials that are stronger, more durable, and easier to clean than dining room tables.

Criteria for the selection of dining tables include:

- The top should allow for two feet of space for each diner.
- There should be adequate legroom between the chair and the tabletop.
- Supports should be out of the way of diners.
- The top should be expandable in size.

Box-Like Furniture

Box-like furniture includes desks, chests of drawers, buffets, bookcases, and china closets. Because these units are typically used for storage, they should be evaluated in relation to the items they are intended to store. The height and depth of shelves in bookcases and china closets; the length, width, and depth of drawers; and the appropriateness of a desk for a computer are all important considerations in the selection of these pieces.

More expensive pieces provide:

- Adjustable shelves
- Lighted shelves, especially in a china closet
- A set of several shallow drawers with flexible dividers instead of a single large drawer
- Doors with piano-style hinges for easy access

FIGURE 9.9 *Drop-leaf table.*

UPHOLSTERED FURNITURE

The classification of upholstered furniture includes pieces that are made with filling materials and covered with a surface material. Items included in this category are sofas, chairs, loveseats, sectionals, and sofa beds. Approximate sizes of selected upholstered pieces are presented in Table 9.3. Upholstered furniture is considered the most fashionable classification. Basic shapes of the pieces do not change, but the surface materials are constantly changing with current fashion trends. The surface material can be fabric, leather, or plastic, and popular colors and designs are continually evolving.

Upholstered Chairs

Upholstered chairs are commonly used in living rooms and family rooms and sometimes in bedrooms. Upholstered chairs are often sold as part of a living room suite or with matching, or complementary, sofas or love seats.

Several distinct chair shapes have developed, as shown in Figure 9.10. Each shape is made with many variations in design details, such as surface fabric, finish of the exposed wood, and skirt. An ottoman is often available as a companion piece to a chair. An **ottoman** is an upholstered stool that is placed in front of an upholstered chair to be used as a footrest.

Motion Chairs

Motion chairs are a subcategory of upholstered chairs. Included in this category are recliners, upholstered rockers, and swivel chairs. These chairs are sold individually and are not manufactured to match other pieces of upholstered furniture.

TABLE 9.3
Approximate Sizes of Selected Pieces of Upholstered Furniture

Piece	Approximate Size Range
Sofa	28″ × 72″ to 36″ × 108″
Love seat	28″ × 48″ to 36″ × 60″
Chair	28″ × 28″ to 40″ × 39″
Rectangular ottoman	17″ × 22″ to 25″ × 30″
Square ottoman	24″ × 24″ to 35″ × 35″
Chaise longue	24″ × 48″ to 28″ × 66″

FIGURE 9.10
Common upholstered chair shapes.

Recliners have adjustable backs and built-in foot rests that allow a person to recline at a number of different levels. The original recliner was the Morris chair designed by William Morris in the late 1800s. This chair had no footrest. Traditionally recliners are bulky and require a large amount of space to operate. Advances in the reclining mechanism have allowed manufacturers to produce smaller chairs that take up much less room. Figure 9.11 shows a large traditional-style recliner.

Rocking chairs are classified as conventional or platform. The conventional rocker rests on wooden rockers. The platform rocker rests on a stationary base with a spring mechanism attached to the base to allow for rocking.

FIGURE 9.11
Traditional wingback recliner.
Courtesy of Fairchild Publications, Inc.

Swivel rockers are very popular. The swivel base is stationary on the floor but is constructed to allow the chair to both rock and swivel. They are often fully upholstered.

Sofas and Loveseats

Sofas and loveseats are available in a wide variety of shapes and sizes. A sofa has seating for three or more people; a loveseat, which is also called a settee, has seating for two people. The sofa is usually the dominant piece of furniture in a living room or family room. As with chairs, several shapes of sofas have emerged as traditionally popular (see Figure 9.12). Upholstered sofas, loveseats, and chairs are often manufactured as groupings and sold as sets for living rooms and family rooms.

Camel back   French settee   Lawson

Tuxedo   Charles of London   Chesterfield

FIGURE 9.12 *Common sofa shapes.*

Sectionals

Sectionals offer the advantage of flexibility. These modular units are available in right-arm pieces, left-arm pieces, and armless pieces. They can be arranged to meet the needs of the customer. Some sectionals have pieces that act as recliners, and ottomans are also available.

Sofa Beds

Several different types of sofas, loveseats, and chairs that transform into beds are available. A sofa bed has a concealed spring mechanism and a mattress that pulls out to form a queen or full size bed. Loveseats and chairs form smaller beds. A studio couch has a second set of springs under the regular sofa-spring unit. The jackknife bed has a mechanism that allows the back of the sofa to fall back so it is level with the seat to form a bed.

Large ottomans that transform into beds are also available. Some manufacturers are producing upholstered blocks of foam that can be hinged together as a chair or unhinged to form a bed. Additional information about sofa beds is in Chapter 10.

Determining Quality in Upholstered Furniture

The four inner-construction components that need to be considered in upholstered furniture are the frame, webbing, springs, and cushioning. The outer-construction component, or cover, is also important in the quality of the piece.

Inner Construction

The inner construction of upholstered furniture, while not visible to the eye, is very important to the comfort and durability of the piece and is a major factor in the price and quality of the piece. Figure 9.13 shows the various parts of upholstered furniture.

Frame The frame of the best-quality upholstered furniture is made from kiln-dried hardwood, such as ash, birch, maple, or oak. Gumwood, yellow poplar, and pine are not acceptable. The frame should be put together with double-dowel or mortise-and-tenon joints. The joints should be well glued and reinforced for additional stability and strength. Exposed parts of the frame should be high-quality woods.

Webbing Webbing is placed on the bottom of the frame and sometimes on the back and along the sides of the arms. Webbing is made from jute, cotton, or rubber. In higher-quality furniture, the webbing is closely interlaced and securely nailed to the frame. In place of the webbing panels of heavy cotton, fabric may be stretched across the chair bottom, sides, and back, and held tightly in place with springs. Steel or wood slats are sometimes used in place of

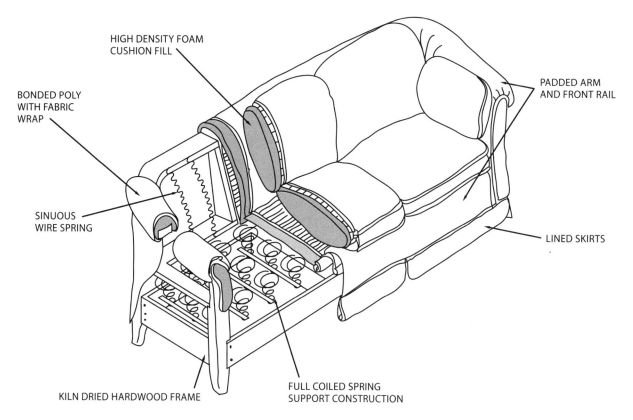

HIGH DENSITY FOAM
CUSHION FILL

BONDED POLY
WITH FABRIC
WRAP

PADDED ARM
AND FRONT RAIL

SINUOUS
WIRE SPRING

LINED SKIRTS

KILN DRIED HARDWOOD FRAME

FULL COILED SPRING
SUPPORT CONSTRUCTION

FIGURE 9.13 *Inner construction of upholstered furniture.*

webbing or fabric. These are strong but may lack the elasticity necessary for comfort. In some furniture styles, the cushions are placed directly on the webbing system.

Springs Springs are attached to the webbing or to slats. Springs provide greater resilience and longer wear. There are several different types of springs.

- *Coil or cone springs* The highest-quality furniture is made with eight-way, hand-tied, high-tempered steel, double-cone spring construction. These springs are the most labor intensive, expensive, and durable. The springs are tied together so that all springs work in union and do not cause lumps in the furniture. The size and number of springs vary with the size and section of the furniture. Larger springs are used in the seat and back, while smaller ones are used in the arms. The number of springs is an indicator of quality. Twelve springs per seat section are used in better furniture; nine are typical in medium quality; and six are used in poor-quality furniture. In some less expensive furniture, the springs are tied four ways instead of eight. The springs can also be manufactured as a prefabricated unit that is tied with steel wire and simply attached to the frame. This method is less costly but has many of the advantages of hand-tied springs. See Figure 9.14a for a diagram of a side view of a coil, or cone, spring.

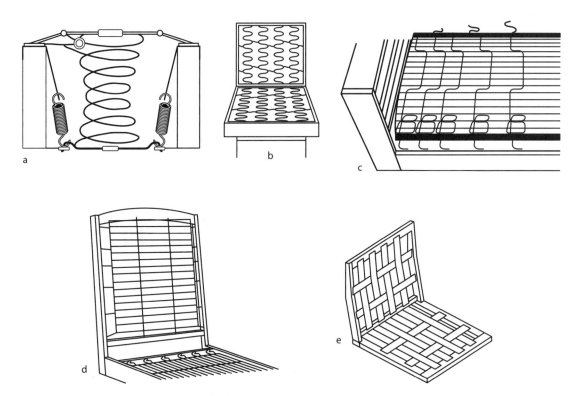

FIGURE 9.14a–e
Types of spring construction: a. *coil or cone,* b. *sinuous wire,* c. *formed wire,*
d. *grid suspension system,* e. *rubber webbing or flat bands of steel.*

- *Sinuous wire spring* The sinuous wire spring, or no-sag spring, is manufactured in a zigzag shape. Both ends of the spring are fastened to the frame. The springs are fastened parallel to each other at regular intervals with small helical, or spiral, springs. This type of spring system requires less vertical space, so it is appropriate for thin-profile furniture (see Figure 9.14b).
- *Formed wire spring* The formed wire spring is similar to the sinuous wire spring except that the wire is shaped into long rectangular bends instead of zigzags. Formed wire springs are also appropriate for low profile furniture (see Figure 9.14c).
- *Grid suspension system* In this system a wire grid is fastened directly to the frame on one side. The other side is attached to the frame with helical springs that provide the spring action (see Figure 9.14d).
- *Rubber webbing or flat bands of steel* These are sometimes used in place of springs to provide flexibility and comfort (see Figure 9.14e).

Cushioning There are two types of cushioning in upholstered furniture—padding and seat cushions. Padding is a soft layer of batting that covers the springs and frame and gives shape to the piece. It should be smooth, and there should be enough padding so the hard lines of the frame cannot be felt. A layer of fabric separates the springs from the cushioning and prevents the padding from working into the springs. A muslin casing holds the padding in place.

Most upholstered furniture has loose cushions that can be removed from the furniture. Loose cushions are usually reversible and extend the life of the piece. Some upholstered furniture has tight seat construction, which means that there are no separate cushions.

Polyurethane foam is the most common type of filling for a cushion. There are three grades priced to match furniture price ranges. Manufacturers of more-expensive furniture use polyurethane foam covered with a wrapping of polyester batting and sewn into a muslin cover. Polyurethane foam is available in several densities. It is resilient, nonallergenic, and is impervious to moisture. The polyester batting provides added softness, resilience, and comfort to the cushions. Moderate-priced furniture has polyurethane cushions with polyester batting bonded or glued to each side. The cushion is then inserted into the decorative cushion cover without the muslin cover. Lower-quality furniture has polyurethane foam cushions that do not have the polyester batting. They may be solid foam or laminated foam. Laminated foam cushions have thinner, less dense layers of foam around a firmer core. They have some of the feel of the more expensive polyester-wrapped cushions.

Other types of fillings include spring down and down. In spring-down fillings, small wrapped coil springs are placed inside a polyurethane core that is wrapped with a mixture of polyurethane and down. The unit is then covered with muslin and placed inside the decorative cover. These cushions are quite expensive. Down cushions are very expensive. They are very soft but lack resiliency. These cushions require frequent plumping. A combination of 75 percent down and 25 percent feathers provides improved body (see Chapter 10 for additional discussion of down).

Outer Construction—Surface Cover

The cover of an upholstered piece of furniture has a major impact on both aesthetics and function. It is the visual focus as well as an integral part of the furniture. The three most popular materials used for coverings are fabric, leather and vinyl (see Chapter 2 for discussion of textiles, Chapter 8 for discussion of leather, and Chapter 6 for discussion of vinyl).

In many cases the consumer special-orders upholstered furniture and specifies the covering. Coverings are usually available in a variety of grades, or qualities, affecting the overall price of the piece. The quality of the covering is dependent on the material as well as on the workmanship. The covering is usually purchased as part of the overall price of the piece, or it may be **COM** (customer's own material). COM means that the customer supplies the fabric to be installed on the piece. The estimated yardage of fabric is purchased from a fabric supplier or retail store.

Cover materials may have soil-resistant finishes to minimize soiling and staining. Finishes are highly recommended for upholstery fabrics, especially on pieces used in family rooms or dens.

Showroom pieces should be evaluated carefully. Criteria to be considered include:

- The hand of the cover should feel pleasant.
- Plaids and patterns should be carefully matched. Fabric may be railroaded or run vertically (see Figure 9.15). The direction of the pile (nap) should be consistent. Large designs should be centered on chair backs and seats. If the back of the sofa or chair will be seen, the pattern should be consistent with the front.

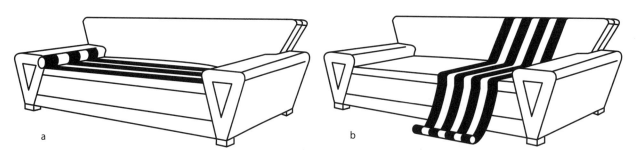

FIGURE 9.15   a. *Railroaded upholstery fabric,* b. *vertical upholstery fabric.*

- Seams should be smooth and straight. Welts (covered cords used in seam lines) should be tight and neatly finished.
- Loose threads should be removed.
- Quilting stitches should be evenly spaced and neat.
- The buttons on tufted pieces should be tight. See Figure 9.16 for an example of a tufted chair.

Selection of Upholstered Furniture

Selection of upholstered furniture includes evaluation of the frame, webbing, springs, filling, and cover. Characteristics of higher-quality pieces include:

- Joints that are glued and screwed and have corner blocks
- Securely attached webbing
- Eight-way hand-tied springs (for superior quality)
- Filling that is smooth and thick enough to soften the hard edges of the frame
- Comfortable cushions (better cushions will be polyurethane-foam wrapped in layers of polyester batting)
- Tightly fitting loose cushions
- Perfectly matched high-quality fabric

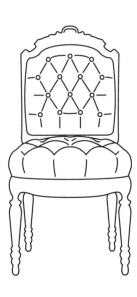

FIGURE 9.16
A tufted chair.

The overall appearance of the piece should exhibit care and attention to detail in manufacturing. All aspects of the piece should blend together.

OCCASIONAL FURNITURE

Occasional furniture includes a wide variety of small pieces that can be considered as furniture accessories. They add interest and charm to a room and are often selected to provide a center of attention for a room. Pieces in this classification include occasional tables, magazine racks, lamp tables, étagères, and small desks and chairs. An **étagère** is a cabinet used to display items. Sizes of selected pieces of occasional furniture are presented in Table 9.4.

Occasional tables are coffee tables, end tables, and library tables. Coffee tables are also called cocktail tables. They are low tables usually found in front of a sofa. End tables are usually at either end of a sofa. They hold lamps, books, etc. An enclosed end table that is square, round, hexagonal, or octagonal and has doors that open is sometimes called a **commode.** A **library table** is a long narrow table. If a library table is used behind a sofa, it is called a **sofa table.**

Occasional furniture may be selected to match, complement, or accent other furniture in the room. It is often made from wood or simulated-wood products, as well as a wide variety of different materials, such as glass, chrome, and iron.

Wood and simulated-wood occasional pieces are constructed in the same manner as case goods. Evaluation of quality and selection criteria is also the same. Expensive pieces will be solid wood or wood veneers. Less-expensive pieces may be molded plastic or vinyl-coated particleboard. Occasional furniture is often sold as ready-to-assemble furniture. (See a more complete discussion of ready-to-assemble furniture later in this chapter.)

CASUAL AND SUMMER FURNITURE

This classification includes furniture that is used in casual settings inside the home, and furniture that is used primarily outside. Manufacturers classify this furniture according to the materials from which it is constructed. These materials include wicker, rattan, and bamboo;

TABLE 9.4
Sizes of Selected Pieces of Occasional Furniture

Round coffee table	24″ diameter to 48″ diameter
Square coffee table	24″ × 24″ to 48″ × 48″
Rectangular coffee table	18″ × 36″ to 36″ × 60″
End table	18″ × 10″ to 36″ × 20″
Bookcase	10″ to 12″ deep, comes in a variety of widths and heights

aluminum, wrought iron and steel; redwood; plastic and fiberglass-reinforced plastic. Generally casual and summer furniture is perceived as being less expensive than traditional furniture, although some pieces and sets can be very expensive.

Wicker, Rattan, and Bamboo

Wicker, rattan, and bamboo are very popular in warm climates and may be used throughout the house. In cooler climates they are usually used on porches or in sunrooms. They are often used as exposed frames for casual upholstered furniture. Informal étagères, dining room tables, and occasional tables are also made from these materials.

Most of the wicker, rattan, and bamboo used in the United States is imported from the Far East. Frequently the handwork is done overseas with final finishing done in the United States.

Aluminum, Wrought Iron, and Steel

Metals are used for outdoor furniture and some casual indoor pieces. Aluminum, wrought iron, and steel are the most commonly used metals.

Aluminum

Aluminum is widely used for the frames of outdoor furniture. It is sturdy, lightweight, and does not rust. However, it will become dull from oxidation when exposed to normal weather conditions. Tubular aluminum is the standard frame material for folding outdoor furniture. It is also used as poles for umbrellas. Cast aluminum is also used for frames, but it is much heavier. Plastic straps, webbing, and vinyl-coated fabrics are used for the seats and backs of aluminum furniture.

Wrought Iron

Wrought iron furniture is used inside and outside the home. It is well known for its beautiful curvilinear designs. It is typically combined with glass tops for tables. It is heavy and extremely durable.

Steel

Steel is the heaviest metal used for casual furniture. It is extremely durable and is used both indoors and outdoors. Usually it is protected with a baked-enamel finish. It is frequently combined with woven fabric or vinyl cushions.

Redwood

The highest-quality redwood furniture is made from the heart of the redwood tree. To prevent cracking and splitting, the wood is dried to reduce the moisture content. It is strong, durable, and resistant to decay and insects. It is popular for outdoor sofas, chairs, chaise lounges, and picnic tables. Redwood seating often has cushions covered in vinyl or woven fabrics. Pine, or other less-expensive wood, is sometimes stained to resemble redwood. This furniture is less costly and much less durable.

Plastic and Fiberglass–Reinforced Plastic

Molded plastic, or resin, casual furniture is very popular for use on porches and patios. It is lightweight and durable, but it scratches easily and may be degraded by sunlight. It is available in a limited number of colors. The chairs can be stacked for easy storage. Tables, plant stands, lounges, bookcases, and many other pieces are available. Vinyl fabric is used for many umbrellas.

Selecting Casual and Summer Furniture

All components of furniture for outside use should be fade resistant, able to withstand temperature extremes, waterproof or dry very quickly, and resistant to degradation from ultraviolet rays. Furniture to be used indoors is not subject to these conditions, and a wider variety of fabrications may be used.

WALL SYSTEMS

A **wall system** offers space-saving storage. It is composed of a number of wall units placed together. These units can be arranged to meet the needs of the customer. The wall units may be étagères, bookcases, desks, or bars. They frequently have enclosed compartments with doors. Sometimes smaller wall units are designed to be stacked on top of each other.

Wall systems are ideal for in-home entertainment equipment. The shelves are frequently deeper than the traditional bookcase or display case. This allows them to hold large televisions and other electronic equipment.

Wall systems can be used very effectively in small rooms, as well as in large spaces. They are used in living rooms, dining rooms, family rooms, and living rooms. A wide variety of styles is available. They are usually wood or simulated wood and may be finished to match the other case goods in the room. Criteria for determination of quality and selection of wall systems are similar to those for case goods.

READY-TO-ASSEMBLE FURNITURE

Casual lifestyles and the growth of mass merchandisers that stock a wide variety of styles at low cost have led to the increased importance of **ready-to-assemble (RTA) furniture** in the marketplace. RTA furniture is designed to be assembled by the consumer. It is also called **flat-package**

furniture or **knock-down furniture**. Higher-priced RTA furniture is also sold through specialty stores that cater to the RTA furniture market. As this market has matured, there has been increased emphasis on fashion, so more upholstered styles are available. Style options include modern European looks, traditional, contemporary, country, and casual.

RTA furniture is manufactured for use in both the home and the office. Youth and adult bedroom, kitchen, and living room pieces are available. Manufacturers are working with electronics companies to create audio/visual entertainment units that are appropriate for oversized TVs and accessories (see Figure 9.17).

RTA furniture is available in a variety of fabrications—solid wood, medium-density fiberboard (MDF) and particleboard, tempered glass, and metal. Companies are also experimenting with other fabrications, such as lightweight medium-density fiberboard that has hollowed out sections and straw and polyurethane composites. The advantage of these newer materials is that they are lighter in weight; however, consumers tend to equate weight and thickness of wood with quality and durability.

SYSTEMS FURNITURE

Systems furniture is widely used in nonresidential applications. It provides flexible use of space through modular pieces that can be arranged in different configurations. Vertical panels, work surfaces, and storage units are combined to create what are commonly called workstations. As the function of the space changes, the pieces can be adapted to the new requirements. See Figure 9.18 for examples of configurations of systems furniture. Very durable surfaces and construction methods are typically used in systems furniture.

FIGURE 9.17
O'Sullivan entertainment center.
Courtesy of Fairchild Publications, Inc.

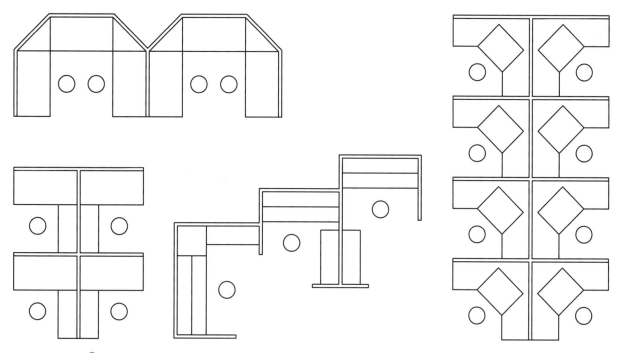

FIGURE 9.18
Possible configurations of systems furniture.

The size and configuration of systems furniture is determined by the functional needs of the user. Standardized classifications that many systems-furniture manufacturers use are clerical, secretarial, supervisory, word processing, middle management, and executive. See Figure 9.19 for the configurations of these classifications.

The space for systems furniture may be private, semiprivate, or open. Full or partial-height dividers or panels may be used to divide the spaces. Panels are available in three heights—low (30 inches to 48 inches), medium (about 60 inches), and high (about 80 inches). Panels are generally sound absorbing. All wiring for telephone and computer hook-up, electricity, and lighting is included in the system. Laboratory furniture systems have flexible plumbing connections. Freestanding furniture can be integrated into the system.

There are two types of systems furniture—panel supported and freestanding. **Panel-supported systems** are workstations, desks, filing cabinets, bookcases, computer stations, etc., that are attached to dividers or panels. The panel-supported system is more popular than the freestanding. **Freestanding systems** are independent of wall or panels. They function much like a freestanding desk. They may be surrounded by panels or traditional walls. Sometimes furniture components, such as privacy screens, are attached to the work surface.

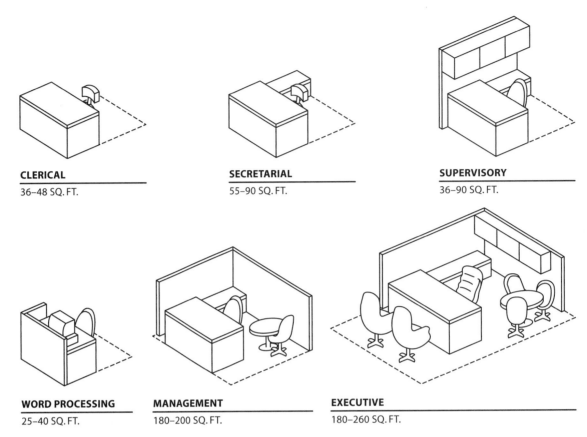

CLERICAL
36–48 SQ. FT.

SECRETARIAL
55–90 SQ. FT.

SUPERVISORY
36–90 SQ. FT.

WORD PROCESSING
25–40 SQ. FT.

MANAGEMENT
180–200 SQ. FT.

EXECUTIVE
180–260 SQ. FT.

FIGURE 9.19
Classifications of work stations.

CARE OF FURNITURE

The wide variety of both materials and finishes used on furniture makes it essential to read and follow manufacturer's care instructions. Selected brand names of furniture are listed in Table 9.5. Waterproof finishes on wood or wood-substitute products, and soil-release and stain-resistant finishes on upholstery fabrics, are highly recommended to lengthen the wear life of pieces.

The following general care procedures can extend the life and preserve the appearance for wood and simulated-wood furniture:

- Dust furniture frequently with a soft, lint-free cloth.
- Fingerprints on wood, metal, or plastic can be removed by rubbing with a soft cloth that has been dipped in a mild detergent mixed with water and wrung out. The piece should be rubbed dry with a clean dry cloth.

TABLE 9.5
Selected Brand Names of Furniture

Price Range	Brands
Upper End	American Drew
	Baker
	Bernhardt
	Century
	Drexel Heritage
	Ethan Allen
	Flexsteel
	Harden
	Henredon
	Hickory Chair
	Kincaid
	Lexington
	Marge Carson
	Natuzzi
	Pennsylvania House
	Thomasville
	Sherrill
Moderate	Bassett
	Berkline
	Broyhill
	Lane
	La-Z-Boy
	Rowe Furniture
	Stanley Furniture
Lower End	IKEA
	Seaman's
Ready-To-Assemble	Bush
	O'Sullivan Furniture
	Sauder

- Water left on wood may cause water spots. Spots may sometimes be removed by rubbing with furniture wax or polish. Pieces that have been damaged with water spots may need to be refinished.
- Wood may be polished with wax. Rub wax into the grain. Excess wax or polish should be removed because it attracts dust.
- Use a humidifier to prevent checking (tiny lines on the surface) and cracking in a dry environment.
- Professional refinishing may be required for dents, deep gouges, deep scratches, and to repair damage from cigarette burns.

INDUSTRY PROFILE

Nat Ancell: A Maestro of Merchandising

An industry leader who revolutionized the way furniture is sold

Ethan Allen is arguably the most forward-thinking company in home furnishings history, and co-founder Nat Ancell was the heart and the brains behind this revolutionary company.

Nathan "Nat" Ancell (1908–1999) pioneered concepts that are taken for granted today in the furniture industry. Vertical integration, gallery settings, room vignettes—all are the result of Ancell's vision.

Ethan Allen, now a 300-store furnishings superpower, began as a producer of Colonial-style furniture and, under Ancell's leadership, eventually started selling its own merchandise in its own stores and in gallery settings in department stores.

"He revolutionized the furniture industry," said Pat Norton, chief executive officer of La-Z-Boy. "It changed forever as a result of what he did with the stores. No question. There were few people that believed in what he was about, but that didn't bother him a whole lot. He just fought that much harder."

The company, originally named Baumritter & Co., was started in 1932 by Ancell, who was a lawyer, and his brother-in-law, Theodore Baumritter, a housewares vendor. In 1936, they bought a 150,000-square-foot factory in Beecher Falls, Vt., and began making Colonial-style furniture, naming it after the Revolutionary War hero. They gradually established a continent-wide network of manufacturing and distribution facilities.

In 1939, the brothers-in-law introduced a 28-piece collection of Ethan Allen furniture at the annual Housewares Show in Chicago, limiting its distribution to a select group of dealers, the first step toward an exclusive Ethan Allen dealership network. By the mid-'50s, Ethan Allen was promoting itself as the "one complete source for all your furniture needs in modern or traditional styling" and finding itself in a who's who of retail stores.

Norton, who worked for Ancell from 1961 until 1981, joined the Ethan Allen team during the time that Ancell started turning the retail furniture industry on its head by displaying his home furnishings in real-life room settings, kindling the imaginations of consumers.

Norton was involved in opening the first freestanding store in Raleigh, N.C. Locations in Nashville, New York and Columbus, Ohio, quickly followed.

In 1964, the first Ethan Allen storefront design, styled along Colonial architectural lines, with its white columns, was opened. The style became a landmark for Ethan Allen customers everywhere.

"I dealt with several Nats over the years," Norton said. "He was a very brilliant man and an energetic man. He was a true visionary, and he persevered awfully hard. What he believed in, he believed in strongly. Many times he was not a nice guy to work for, but most of the time, in the end, he was fair. He was an egomaniac, but a brilliant egomaniac.

"He had a good creative sense," Norton continued. "He envisioned what he thought would happen, and then he had such great communication skills that he would try to sell that vision, whether it was right or not. He really was a powerful, powerful communicator. He could move people with the spoken word."

Designer Joe Ruggiero worked for Ancell from 1973 until 1988.

"He started a lot of what we see in furniture retail today, bringing all the parts of a home together into one display," Ruggiero said. "In those days, they had sofas lined up and never put all the accoutrements together. He was into vertical marketing in its truest sense, from the forest to the consumer."

From a designer standpoint, Ruggiero was impressed by Ancell's ability to present traditional furniture designs to various geographic areas, such as Florida, that had not previously embraced that style. Ancell also opened the retail doors to a Japanese market hungry for Western-style furniture.

"I'm forever indebted to him," Norton said. "To sit at his right arm for as long as I did was a hell of a lot better than an M.B.A. He was a great mentor. But you paid a price for it. He was not an easy guy to deal with."

Source: HFN, Nov. 27, 2000, p. 26. Courtesy of Fairchild Publications, Inc.

General care procedures for upholstered furniture include the following:

- Vacuum sofas and chairs (using specially designed attachments) on a regular basis to remove surface dirt. Down-filled cushions should not be vacuumed because the down may be pulled through the cover. These pieces should be brushed on a regular basis.
- Spot-clean soiled areas of upholstered furniture promptly, using specialized cleaning agents. All fabrics should be tested for colorfastness prior to cleaning, by applying the cleaning solution to a portion of the fabric that is hidden from view. Upholstered pieces that are heavily soiled can be cleaned professionally.
- Vinyl and leather upholstery can be wiped with a damp cloth.
- Professional care may be needed for repair of cigarette burns, tears in upholstery, and scratches and gouges in leather or vinyl.

Plastic furniture can be washed with a damp cloth. Take care not to scratch plastic furniture or expose it to high heat or an open flame, which will cause melting.

SUMMARY

The major functions of furniture are to provide comfort, utility, and a place for social interaction. Furniture can be made from a wide variety of materials, such as wood, plastic, glass, and metal. Wood is the most common material used to make furniture. Simulated-wood products, wicker, rattan, and cane are also used. There are three general styles of furniture design—traditional, provincial and contemporary.

Furniture manufacturers frequently divide furniture into four major classifications—case goods, upholstered, occasional, and bedding. Summer furniture, indoor/outdoor furniture, wall systems, and ready-to-assemble furniture are special furniture classifications. Within each classification of furniture, manufacturers create correlated, modular, or wrap groupings.

The type of wood, external construction, types of joints used, construction details, decoration, and the finish determine the quality of case goods. Proper support is essential for comfort. Occasional furniture includes a wide variety of small pieces that are considered furniture accessories.

The classification of upholstered furniture includes pieces that are made with filling materials and covered with a surface material. Upholstered furniture is considered the most fashionable classification. The components that need to be considered in upholstered furniture are the frame, webbing, springs, cushion, and cover.

A wall system offers space saving storage. It is composed of a number of wall units placed together. Ready-to-assemble (RTA) furniture is gaining in popularity in the marketplace. Systems furniture is widely used in nonresidential applications. It provides flexible use of space with modular pieces that can be arranged in different configurations.

The wide variety of both materials and finishes used on furniture makes it essential to read and follow manufacturer's care instructions. Waterproof finishes on wood or wood-substitute products, and soil-release and stain-resistant finishes on upholstery fabrics, are highly recommended to lengthen the wear life of pieces.

TERMS FOR REVIEW

case goods

casework

COM (customer's own
    material)

commode

contemporary furniture

contract furniture

correlated groupings

country furniture

dado joint

dovetail joint

dowel joint

dust bottom

étagère

flat-package furniture

floating construction

fluting

freestanding systems

joining

knock-down furniture

lap joints

leaves

library table

miter joint

modular groupings

mortise-and-tenon joint

occasional furniture

ottoman

panel-supported systems

plain butt joint

provincial furniture

rabbet joint

ready-to-assemble (RTA)
    furniture

reeding

residential furniture

sofa table

splines

style

suite

systems furniture

tongue-and-groove joint

traditional furniture

wall system

wrap groupings

STUDY QUESTIONS

1. What is the difference between traditional furniture and provincial furniture?
2. What is a suite?
3. Why are screws used in higher-quality furniture?
4. Describe the characteristics of the frame in higher-quality upholstered furniture.
5. What are coil or cone springs?
6. List criteria to consider when selecting casual or summer furniture.

LEARNING ACTIVITIES

1. Examine several pieces of upholstered furniture in your home. Evaluate each piece for appearance and serviceability. What are the characteristics of the pieces that have given good service? What are the characteristics of those that have given poor service?
2. Visit a local furniture store. Ask a sales representative to show you the inner construction of case goods and upholstered goods. Summarize the main points in your own words. In your estimation, does the store you visited carry low-, moderate-, or high-quality merchandise? Justify your answer.

CHAPTER 10

BEDDING

*Goldilocks was very sleepy after eating the porridge, so she went into the three bears'
bedroom. She lay down on Papa Bear's bed, but it was too hard. Then she tried Mama
Bear's bed. It was too soft. Finally, she tried Baby Bear's bed, and it was just right.
Goldilocks fell fast asleep.*

—from *Goldilocks and The Three Bears,* a traditional fairy tale

A BED IS THE MOST BASIC PIECE OF BEDROOM FURNITURE, AND A COMFORTABLE BED IS AN
essential item in a well-furnished home. **Bedding** usually refers to furniture that is used to sleep
on at night, but some bedding is used for sitting during the day. Bedding includes traditional
mattresses and foundation sets, sofa beds, daybeds, cribs, and waterbeds. Bedding is available in
a wide variety of price ranges and quality levels. Mattress covers, mattress pads, and pillows are
also part of the bedding industry. Industry Statement 10.1 gives a brief history of bedding.

MATTRESSES

Bed frames and mattresses are sized to accommodate either one or two people. Within the basic
size groups is a range of sizes, so consumers who want the luxury of a roomy bed or those who
need to fit their beds into a small space can find sizes to meet their requirements.

Size and thickness of typical mattress and box spring combinations are presented in Tables
10.1 and 10.2. Figure 10.1 compares the relative sizes of mattresses. Simmons introduced
queen- and king-size mattresses in the 1950s. Sales of the queen-size mattress have increased in
recent years. Some bedding companies have recently introduced larger queen-size mattresses
that are 66 inches wide. There has also been a trend toward thicker mattresses.

INDUSTRY STATEMENT 10.1

A Brief History of Bedding

Anyone who thinks sleep isn't important should try going without it for a day. Beds of some kind have always been part of the equation for recharging one's body and getting out of the maelstrom for a few hours, whether they be the stacked hides of animals or the water-filled goatskins used by Persian nomads 3,000 years ago.

Over the centuries, mattresses have evolved as the preferred sleeping surface, made with the best cushioning materials on hand. Throughout the ages, bedding has been made of feathers moss, straw, corn husks, wheat hulls, cotton, horsehair, or wool.

North Americans began their love affair with coiled springs around the 1860s and metal coil innerspring mattresses around the turn of the century, when machinery was developed that could produce the spring systems cheaply enough for the average family.

Foam rubber, developed during World War II research projects, was used to make mattresses in the 1950s. By the 1960s, plastic foam was more prevalent in bedding. Today, most mattresses are crafted from a combination of materials.

Source: InFurniture, November, 2000, p. 36. Courtesy of Fairchild Publications, Inc.

The two basic types of mattresses are innerspring and foam mattresses. The process for making innerspring mattresses is similar to that used to make upholstered furniture. Foam mattresses are also called nonspring mattresses or solid mattresses. Other mattress formations are also available.

Mattresses must conform to the requirements of the 1967 amendment to the Flammable Fabrics Act, which prohibits the sale and use of highly flammable mattresses. The Consumer Product Safety Commission sets the standards.

TABLE 10.1

Mattress Sizes

Name	Length	Width
Single	75″	30″–34″
Twin (regular)	75″	39″
Twin (king or extra long)	80″–84″	39″
Full (regular)	75″	54″
Full (king or extra long)	80″–84″	54″
Queen (regular)	75″	60″
Queen (plus)	75″	66″
Queen (king or extra long)	80″–84″	60″
King (regular)	75″	76″
King (king or extra long)	80″–84″	76″
King (Eastern)	80″	78″
King (California)	84″	72″

TABLE 10.2

Mattress Heights (measurements are approximate)

Name	Height
Pillow top	14″
Standard mattress	8″–12″

Innerspring Mattresses

Innerspring mattresses are the most popular style of mattress. There are four components to an **innerspring mattress**—springs, padding, edge guards, and ticking. Figure 10.2 presents the overall configuration of an innerspring mattress.

Spring Systems

Mattress springs are made from tempered steel wire. The gauge, resilience, and grade of the wire determine the firmness and comfort of the mattress. The thickness of the coil wire, the number of coil convolutions, and the way the coils work together to support the body determine the quality of the mattress. Thicker wire with more convolutions will produce firmer support. High-quality mattresses are usually made from lower-gauge wire with six convolutions. Medium- and lower-priced products will have higher-gauge wire and fewer convolutions.

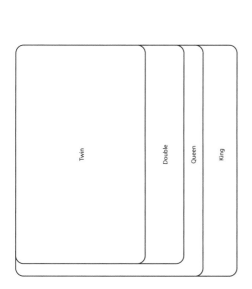

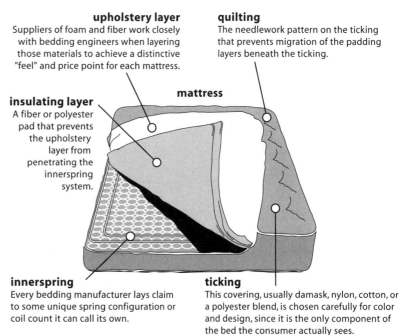

upholstery layer
Suppliers of foam and fiber work closely with bedding engineers when layering those materials to achieve a distinctive "feel" and price point for each mattress.

quilting
The needlework pattern on the ticking that prevents migration of the padding layers beneath the ticking.

insulating layer
A fiber or polyester pad that prevents the upholstery layer from penetrating the innerspring system.

mattress

innerspring
Every bedding manufacturer lays claim to some unique spring configuration or coil count it can call its own.

ticking
This covering, usually damask, nylon, cotton, or a polyester blend, is chosen carefully for color and design, since it is the only component of the bed the consumer actually sees.

FIGURE 10.1
Comparison of mattress sizes.

FIGURE 10.2
Part of an innerspring mattress.

The number of springs in a double-bed mattress can vary from 180 to 360 heavy-gauge springs to 500 to 850 thinner ones. There are two main types of innerspring coil assemblies—the Marshall-type and the Bonnell-type. A third type of spring is continuous springing.

Marshall-type innersprings are used in more expensive mattresses. They are also called **pocket-coil mattresses** or **pocket-spring mattresses.** Springs may be barrel shaped or cylindrical. Each spring is individually sewn into a pocket of muslin. The barrel-shaped springs are held together at the waist by twine. The cylindrical springs are held together at the top and bottom by metal clips or twine. This allows the springs to function independently even though they are connected to neighboring springs. They provide greater comfort and support by conforming to the shape of the body more easily. The amount of firmness in the mattress is controlled by the gauge of the wire in the spring and the number of coils (see Figure 10.3). **Coil-on-coil** is a variation of traditional innersprings. The spring has a smaller, finer coil that rests on top of the innerspring to provide more cushion.

Bonnell-type innerspring mattresses are the most common and are less expensive than Marshall-type innersprings. Bonnell-type innerspring mattresses are also called **open-coil mattresses** or **traditionally sprung mattresses.** Rows of hourglass-shaped coil springs are joined together by a continuous small spiral spring (see Figure 10.4). Helical springs are used to combine the rows together into a flat surface.

In **continuous springing** mattresses, supple steel wire is used to make an interwoven spring web that is similar to an old iron frame bed.

In many mattresses a protective screen is placed on the bottom and top of the coils to provide a more solid surface. The screen is typically made from plastic webbing, a nonwoven fabric, or a metal grid.

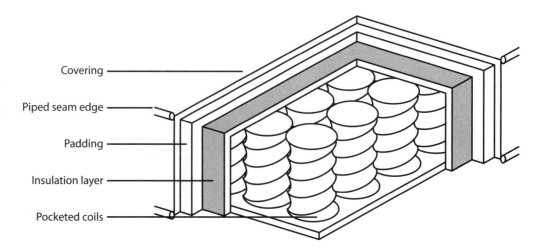

Covering

Piped seam edge

Padding

Insulation layer

Pocketed coils

FIGURE 10.3 *Marshall-type innerspring mattress or pocketed-coil mattress.*

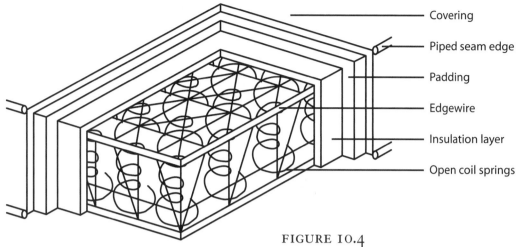

Covering
Piped seam edge
Padding
Edgewire
Insulation layer
Open coil springs

FIGURE 10.4
Bonnell-type innerspring mattress or open-coil mattress.

Padding

Padding, or filling material, is placed over the protective screen. Padding provides comfort, and generous cushioning indicates higher quality. Most mattresses will have the same padding on the top and bottom so the mattress can be flipped for longer wear. There are two primary layers of padding—an upholstery layer and insulation padding.

The upholstery layer consists of the top padding and middle padding. The top layer of padding is usually polyurethane foam. Sometimes a layer of polyester batting is added. The middle padding may be convoluted foam, slab foam, or garnetted cotton. Garnetted cotton will compress quickly. The convoluted foam distributes weight over a wider surface than the slab foam or garnetted cotton. The term *garnetted* refers to used material that has been torn apart back to the fiber stage.

Insulation padding lies on the springs or the protective screen. It is commonly made of coco (or coir) pad or shoddy pad. Coco pad is made from the fibrous matter of a coconut. Shoddy pad is made from pieces of fabric that are matted or glued together. Coco pad produces a stiffer mattress.

Mattresses are now available with an extra layer of padding (see Figure 10.5). This layer is sometimes referred to as a **pillow top.** The pillow top provides an especially soft layer of padding. Pillow-top mattresses are typically the highest priced and highest quality in a line. They require deep-pocket contour sheets to accommodate their extra thickness. Traditional sheets are not large enough.

Conventional innerspring mattresses are designed to be flipped and rotated regularly to minimize wear. Because many consumers do not bother to flip and rotate their mattresses, some manufacturers have developed *no-flip mattresses.* Some pillow-top mattresses have the pillow top on only one side.

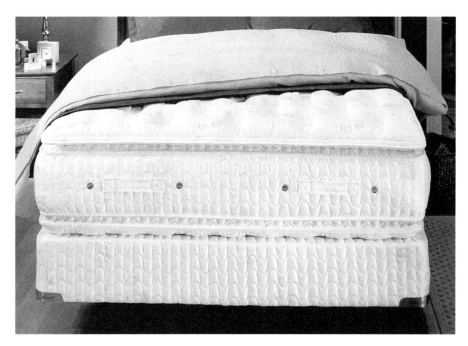

FIGURE IO.5 *Pillow-top mattress.*

Courtesy of Fairchild Publications, Inc.

Edge Guards

Edge guards are prebuilt borders along the edges of the mattress. These borders are important because they prevent the edges of the mattress from sagging. They add durability and shape retention to the mattress. Edge support also provides stability to the edge of the mattress, so sleepers will not feel as though they are going to roll off the mattress.

Ticking

Any fabric used to cover pillows, mattresses, or box springs is called **ticking.** In general, ticking should be made from firmly woven fabrics of strong smooth yarns. Cotton and cotton-polyester blends are commonly used as ticking. For satisfactory durability, the fabric weight should be about eight ounces. Less expensive fabrics will be made of coarser yarns and have lower thread counts. Many manufacturers are now offering ticking that has been treated with an antimicrobial finish what will retard the growth of germs.

Blue-striped or black-striped twill-weave cotton ticking is traditional, but sateens and damasks are more aesthetically pleasing. Lower-end mattresses may have vinyl ticking. The vinyl is likely to stretch and sag out of shape. The outer material should be quilted to prevent the filling materials from shifting. All stitching should be even, and seams should be straight.

Mattresses may have air vents in the sides for ventilation as well as handles to assist in flipping and rotating the mattress. There are three types of handles—those that go through the sides of the mattress and are attached to the springs, those that are attached to the tape edging of the mattress, and those that are inserted trough the fabric and clipped to plastic or metal strips inside the mattress. The handles that are attached to the springs are longer lasting.

Foam Mattresses

Foam mattresses are available in latex foam, polyurethane foam, or a combination of both. (See Chapters 6 and 8 for discussions about Plastics and Other Materials.) The foam has a honeycomb structure with thousands of air bubbles. A foam mattress should be at least 4 1/2 inches thick. Latex foam is heavier and more expensive than polyurethane. It provides more cushion and is very durable. Latex foam is made from synthetic rubber that has been molded while it is in the liquid state. Then it is allowed to harden into a dense foam core. High-quality latex foam has high density, so it is heavy.

The majority of foam mattresses are made of polyurethane. The polyurethane is manufactured in large slabs and then cut to size. High-resilience polyurethane, or polyurethane that has been embedded with thermoplastic beads, provides the best support and performance. Polyurethane foam mattresses are less expensive and less resilient, but may be as durable as latex foam mattresses. The major drawback is that they are lightweight and may slide off the foundation (the framework that supports the mattress). (See later discussion of foundations.)

Foam mattresses are also covered with ticking. See Figure 10.6 for a diagram of foam mattress construction.

Both latex and polyurethane can be produced in a variety of soft, firm, and extra firm levels. Frequently, foam mattresses have several layers of different density foam to provide additional comfort. One advantage of foam mattresses is that they distribute weight evenly.

Latex foam mattresses are graded for firmness. Compression is measured in pounds. A soft mattress measures 10 to 20 pounds; a medium-firmness mattress measures 20–30 pounds; and a hard-firmness mattress measures 30–40 pounds. Foam mattresses:

- Are lighter in weight than innerspring mattresses
- Provide less support for the body than innerspring mattresses
- Do not develop lumps or lose shape as innerspring mattresses sometimes do

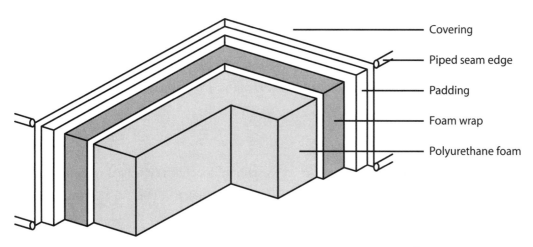

FIGURE 10.6 *Foam mattress construction.*

- Are free of dust and lint
- Are nonallergenic
- Are resistant to mildew and insects
- Have a tendency to hold moisture and odors

Other Mattress Formations

Other types of mattresses include water- and air-filled.

Water-Filled Mattresses

Water-filled mattresses are sometimes referred to as *waterbeds*. This type of mattress reached its peak of popularity in the 1970s, but that popularity has gradually dissipated. Waterbeds support the body more uniformly than a traditional mattress. There is evidence that waterbeds aid in the prevention of bedsores, but they are difficult for some people, especially those with arthritis, to get into and out of.

Unless no air is left in the mattress after filling, it is likely to make "gurgling" noises. Waterbeds can contain 150 gallons of water and can weigh as much as one thousand pounds. It is important to use a waterbed heater to provide comfort and to prevent condensation. There are two basic types of water-filled mattresses—a simple bladder type and a more complex hybrid flotation system.

Bladder-Type Water-Filled Mattress The simple bladder-type water-filled mattress is designed to be inserted into a decorative frame that rests on a pedestal base. This type of mattress is very heavy because of the weight of the water and prone to exhibit "waves" when moved.

The Hybrid Flotation System There are several styles of **hybrid flotation systems,** but the most common has an internal water-filled bladder that is surrounded by a foam shell. The foam shell is covered by a heavy quilted ticking and resembles a traditional innerspring mattress. The matching foundation is designed to accommodate the weight of the water. Hybrid water flotation systems are not as heavy as the simple bladder-type water-filled mattress because they are not as deep, and they use less water.

The hybrid flotation system is "waveless" because it has built in baffles to control the flow of the water. The baffles may be cone-, coil-, or cylinder-shaped and restrict the up-and-down and side-to-side motion of the water. Sometimes a chemical is added to the water to solidify it. This also reduces the wave motion.

Air-Filled Mattresses

The core of an **air-filled mattress** is a heavy-duty vinyl bladder that is encased in a foam shell. It is covered with a cushioned zip-on ticking that is very similar to the type used on a hybrid waterbed. The air-filled mattress is based on the same principle as the air mattresses used in swimming pools and on camping trips.

The firmness of an air mattress is determined by the amount of air in the mattress. Depending on the style, the mattress can be filled with air using a vacuum cleaner, hair dryer, or a compressor. Some larger mattresses have a dual-air chamber system so couples can select different levels of firmness.

Adjustable Beds

Adjustable beds have specially designed frames that allow the head and foot of the bed to be raised and lowered, much like a hospital bed (see Figure 10.7). The electronic controls can also provide heat and massage features. Usually these frames and mattresses are high quality and high cost because of the construction of the flexing mechanism.

Orthopedic Beds

Many doctors have recommended that people sleep on firmer beds. **Orthopedic beds** may have extra-firm mattresses or mattresses that have a slot for a **bed board,** a hard panel. Sometimes the mattress is placed on a bed board instead of a traditional support system. The bed board will have holes in it to allow for ventilation.

Crib Mattresses

Crib mattresses may have either foam or innerspring constructions. The majority are innerspring. The foam is lighter in weight and usually less expensive than innerspring crib mattresses, which keep their shape longer. A very dense foam mattress will also keep its shape well. Most safety experts recommended that crib mattresses be very firm.

A waterproof cover protects the mattress from wetness. Less expensive crib mattresses are covered with a single layer of vinyl. More expensive ones have multiple layers made of quilted vinyl or several layers of vinyl laminated together and reinforced with nylon. The side of the ticking may be fabric or vinyl. One advantage of fabric is that it makes the mattress more flexible. Side vent holes in the ticking allow ventilation. Other indicators of quality in crib mattresses include the use of wire rods and coir fibers. Wire rods are used along the edges of the mattress to prevent sagging. Thicker rods are more effective. Coir fiber used as insulation padding is exceptionally durable and strong.

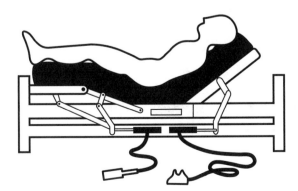

FIGURE 10.7
Mechanism of an adjustable bed.

MATTRESS SUPPORT SYSTEMS

The framework that supports the mattress is called the **foundation.** The foundation is usually sold with the mattress and is designed to support the mattress properly. There are several types of foundations—box springs, low-profile foundations, platform-top springs, open-coil springs, link springs, band springs, and a few other types of mattress support systems.

Box Springs

A box-spring foundation is made of resilient tempered steel springs attached to a wooden base or steel slats. The process for making a **box spring** is similar to that used to make upholstered furniture. The box spring is usually covered in the same fabric as the mattress and is typically about seven inches high. The wooden base should be made of kiln-dried wood. The more springs that are used makes a higher-quality box spring. The gauge of the wire used in the spring is as important as the number of springs in the box spring. The general configuration of a box spring is presented in Figure 10.8.

It is important that the springs move together to provide support for the body. The springs are hand tied in more expensive box springs. In less expensive sets, helicals (small tightly wound springs) are clipped from spring to spring.

The springs are covered with an insulating layer of padding to prevent them from ripping the mattress. The pad may be made from cotton batting, rubberized felt, polyurethane foam, or

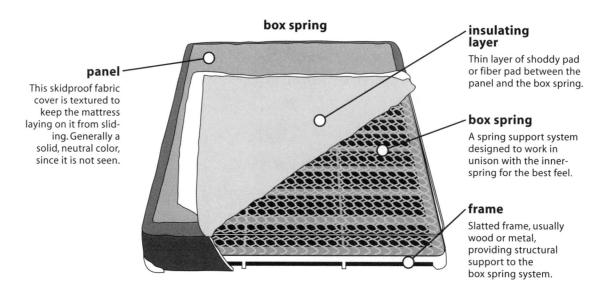

box spring

panel
This skidproof fabric cover is textured to keep the mattress laying on it from sliding. Generally a solid, neutral color, since it is not seen.

insulating layer
Thin layer of shoddy pad or fiber pad between the panel and the box spring.

box spring
A spring support system designed to work in unison with the inner-spring for the best feel.

frame
Slatted frame, usually wood or metal, providing structural support to the box spring system.

FIGURE 10.8 *Configuration of a box spring.*

rubberized felt. The pad and sides of the springs are covered with fabric to match the mattress. In some box springs, the top is covered with a skidproof cover that prevents the mattress from sliding. The bottom of the box spring is covered with thin muslin. Corner guards on the bottom of the box spring are important. They prevent the fabric from rubbing on the bed frame to increase the wear life of the box spring.

Low-Profile Foundations

Most innerspring mattresses are placed on either a traditional box spring or a low-profile foundation. A **low-profile foundation** is about 4 1/2 inches high. Instead of springs, low-profile foundations contain metal grids or torsion bars bent in a square zigzag-shaped bar design using steel leaf springs. Corner guards, padding, and fabric cover are also important on low-profile foundations.

Platform-Top Springs

Platform-top springs are not covered with fabric, and they do not have a pad. The top of the spring is covered with a crossed bar of flat metal that aids in supporting the mattress and prevents the spring from penetrating the mattress (see Figure 10.9).

Open-Coil Springs

Open-coil springs are springs that are not covered with the insulating layer of padding found in box springs. There is less support, but the springs are more resilient and are notable for their good recovery. With open-coil springs, the mattress is more likely to be damaged than a mattress with springs protected by a pad or platform. Open-coil springs are less expensive than platform springs.

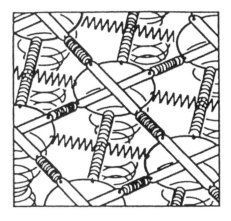

FIGURE 10.9 *Platform-top coil.*

Link Springs and Band Springs

Link springs have interlacing wires in a checkerboard pattern. **Band springs** are flat strips of metal that run lengthwise and are held on the ends by helical-coil springs. These springs do not have the resilience of the other types of springs, so mattresses may sag after limited use. They are used in less expensive bedding, such as children's beds, cots, and lower-quality sofa beds. A distinct advantage of link and band springs is that they take up less space than traditional springs.

Other Types of Foundations

Following are some less commonly used mattress foundations:

- **Slatted wood** A slatted-wood foundation does not have any springs. It is made entirely of wood. All joints should be mortise and tenon (see Chapter 9 for a description) to provide stability as the wood settles.
- **Solid (or pallet) base** This foundation is made of wood; some have a thin layer of foam on the wooden base. Solid-base foundations are often sold as the base for an "orthopedic" mattress.
- **Sprung bed** This traditional foundation is seldom made now. A sprung bed was an iron frame with a dense web of wires that were stretched over the springs.
- **Foam** Foam and wood are combined to create a foundation. The foam layer should be several inches thick for resilient support.

SELECTION AND CARE OF MATTRESSES AND FOUNDATIONS

Comfort is primary in the selection of a mattress and foundation. During sleep, the muscles of the body relax, so the mattress needs to support the body properly. In order for the mattress to be comfortable, the spine needs to be supported in its anatomically normal position, and the set should support all parts of the body.

A mattress that is too hard will not give even support to all parts of the body. It will support only the body's heaviest parts, such as the shoulders and hips. The increased pressure on these points reduces blood circulation. A mattress that is too soft will not keep the spine in proper alignment, so the heavier parts of the body will sink below the rest. This causes tension and fatigue because the muscles are working to straighten the spine (see Figure 10.10).

In general, a hard bed provides better postural support than a soft one. Most experts recommend that people purchase the firmest bed that still feels comfortable. People with arthritis or back problems should discuss the purchase of mattresses and foundations with their physicians. Bedding manufacturers often use medical endorsements as part of their marketing plan (see the example in Figure 10. 11).

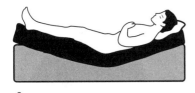 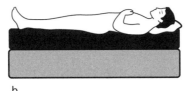

FIGURE 10.10
a. *Poor body support,*
b. *good body support.*

Mattresses are categorized in several levels of firmness—soft, medium, firm, and extra firm. Each manufacturer has its own definitions of firmness. The mattress should provide firm support with enough surface resilience to provide comfort. When purchasing bedding it is essential to lie down on the mattress to evaluate its comfort. Some manufacturers have single beds and mattresses that zip together or slot together for couples who have different needs.

General Selection Criteria

Consumers selecting a mattress and sales associates assisting them should keep the following considerations in mind.

- The mattress and foundation should be approximately six inches longer than the tallest person sleeping in it.
- The mattress and foundation should be resilient.
- The mattress and foundation should be durable.
- Consumers should always measure their beds before ordering mattresses and foundations, and they should know the dimensions of their mattresses before purchasing sheets, comforters, blankets, or bedspreads.
- The more weight put on a mattress, the firmer it should be.
- A new mattress should never be put on an old foundation. The proper foundation extends the wear life of the mattress. Most innerspring mattresses can be combined with either low-profile foundations or standard box springs.
- The mattress edge is an indicator of quality. Reinforced edges will prevent sagging. The edge will give a little when someone sits on it, but it should spring back quickly when the person stands up.
- All seams and stitching should be straight and even.
- For a waterbed system, it is important that there is a vinyl safety liner to hold the water should there be a puncture.

Care of Mattresses and Foundations

The following will help to extend the life and serviceability of mattresses and foundations.

- Upon delivery, all outer wrappings on the mattress must be removed to avoid condensation and subsequent mildew.
- For even wear, spring mattresses should be rotated and flipped twice a month for the first three months of use and then once every two months. It is important to follow the

FIGURE 10.11 *Bedding manufacturers often use medical endorsements as part of their marketing plan. (See inset photo.)*

Sealy: The Fine Art of Selling Sleep

Ask any consumer to rattle off the names of the first mattress companies they can think of and inevitably the name of Sealy will be on that list—and probably first. That's no coincidence.

Sealy, the largest bedding producer in North America, has long been a powerful promoter, cultivating an image for itself by providing good products to the mainstream middle class and pushing those products with aggressive and memorable advertising.

The company is famous for its affordable Posturepedic line and more recently for its step-up Crown Jewel line from Posturepedic.

As far back as the 1960s, Sealy commissioned a research study to define the profile of the Posturepedic consumer. In 1967, Sealy Posturepedic commercials aired on network television during prime time—an industry first.

Last year, Sealy celebrated the 50th anniversary of the Posturepedic with a huge promotion and a special Golden Anniversary collection of mattresses.

To cultivate new generations of consumers, Sealy has been promoting a line of crib mattresses and introduced its My First Posturepedic line of juvenile mattresses a year ago.

Sealy's famous blue butterfly logo on a newspaper advertisement says more about the store and its products than any text could. Just ask Larry Schneiderman. Chairman of Schneiderman's Furniture near Minneapolis, Schneiderman gets great mileage from the logo and from Sealy's marketing support.

"Sealy, along with La-Z-Boy, are the two brands that actually do have the power to bring customers to our store," Schneiderman said.

"We are faced with not being able to match the promotional efforts of some of our competitors in the bedding business, and we need all the help we can get as far as getting the most for our money in advertising in this market. The Sealy name and the Posturepedic name are meaningful to a large segment of our bedding customers."

"The Sealy logo is an icon. The consumer recognizes it and trusts it," said Gary Gevurtz, president of Somnia, a Philadelphia furniture store.

Long Haymes Carr, a Winston-Salem, N.C., advertising company, has been steering—and redirecting—Sealy's consumer exposure efforts since being hired as agency-of-record last fall.

The new campaign, "Sealy—We support you day and night," launched in February, emphasizes the importance of good sleep.

One television commercial features a woman who must juggle her roles as wife, mother, professional, and family diplomat, realizing that getting a good sleep will help her function better.

"We believe our mission with Sealy goes beyond reinforcing the awareness of the brand to building brand conviction among consumers—that is, helping consumers find a way to think differently about bedding and their mattresses," said Pete Woods, executive vice president and chief client officer with Long Haymes Carr.

Sealy's image extends beyond product promotion. The company, under the leadership of chief executive Ron Jones, has been a leader in its support of community projects in its own backyard—an effort not lost on its own employees or the public.

Since moving its corporate headquarters last year from Cleveland to the High Point, NC, area, Sealy has aided victims of Hurricane Floyd by donating 500 mattresses to people along the Carolina coast.

Source: HFN Supplement, Image Makers 2000, May 29, 2000, p. 32. Courtesy of Fairchild Publications, Inc.

manufacturer's directions carefully. Some foam mattresses are not intended to be flipped. Some pillow-top mattresses cannot be flipped because the pillow top is only on one side. These mattresses may not last as long as those that can be flipped.

■ Mattresses should be covered with mattress covers or mattress pads to protect them from dead skin cells and dirt.

■ It is essential that bedding receive proper ventilation. Placing a mattress directly on the floor for an extended period of time will cause the mattress to mildew. The body releases up to half a pint of liquid in the form of vapor each night. If this liquid cannot escape mildew will form.

MATTRESS PADS AND COVERS

Mattress pads and **mattress covers** protect mattresses from dust, dead skin cells, and dirt. They also protect the bottom sheet from undue wear from rubbing against the mattress. Covers are one-layer structures that simply cover the mattress. Mattress pads cover the mattress but also provide a layer of padding. Many pads and covers are available with antiallergenic and antimicrobial finishes. Mattress pads must conform to the requirements of the Flammable Fabrics Act Standard for the Flammability of Mattresses.

Styles

Mattress pads and covers come in sizes to fit all standard beds. It is important to purchase a mattress cover or pad that is appropriate for the height of the bed. Some pads and covers are designed with very wide elasticized sides that will accommodate any mattress height. Some do not have sides, but are held in place by elasticized corner straps that slip under the mattress to hold it in place. Both pads and covers that fully encase the mattress are available. Vinyl covers are available for occasions when maximum protection from moisture is necessary.

Construction

Mattress covers are single-layer structures. The process for creating a mattress pad is similar to that of a machine-stitched or pinsonically melded (electronically bonded to resemble stitching) quilt or comforter. See additional discussion of pinsonic melding in Chapter 11. Some pads are very thick and require sheets with deeper sides. These thick pads can provide the feel of a pillow-top mattress (see Figure 10.12).

There are several options for the top and back fabric of a mattress pad. Both may be tightly woven cotton or polyester/cotton blend plain-weave fabric. The top may be the plain-weave fabric and the back the nonwoven fabric, or both the top and the back may be nonwoven fabric. The quilting may be done by machine or by pinsonic melding if all components are at least 50 percent thermoplastic fibers. All stitching should be firm and even.

Mattress pads and covers are available with special finishes. Antimicrobial finishes are excellent for products used in institutions and hotels. These finishes prevent the growth of bacteria and fungi. Treatments that reduce exposure to allergens are also available. See Industry Statement 10.2 for a profile of a company that specializes in mattress covers.

Alternatives to Traditional Mattress Pads and Covers

There are several alternatives to the traditional mattress pad or cover. The filling of the traditional pad is usually a polyester fiberfill, but feather, wool, and foam are also available. Natural fills for mattress pads are described in Industry Statement 10.3.

FIGURE 10.12
Thicker mattress pads provide a pillow-top effect.
Photo provided by Louisville Bedding, Inc.

Wool Underblanket

A wool mattress pad is sometimes called a **wool underblanket.** It resembles fleece and is created by inserting wool fibers into a polyester-knit base fabric. Its advantages are that it is soft, warm, and absorbent.

Feather Bed

A **feather bed** is a thick mattress pad filled with feathers.

Latex- or Polyurethane-Foam Mattress Pads

Latex- or polyurethane-foam mattress pads are sometimes classified as comfort sleep products. They cover only the top of the mattress and are available in a variety of textures—basic convoluted covers, multizone convoluted covers, and carved covers. The multizone varieties are designed for even weight distribution while sleeping.

Latex- or urethane-mattress covers are open-celled foamed plastics, either latex or urethane. Sometimes these are referred to as **egg-crate-foam mattress pads.** These foam pads permit the body to rest on a series of raised ridges. They allow better circulation in the body than the pressure of a flat mattress. They also may keep the sleeper cooler because air is able to move through the raised ridges.

INDUSTRY STATEMENT 10.2

American Textile Manages to Refine Its Niche

PITTSBURGH–American Textile Co. is never satisfied. Even after 75 years in business, after finally finding its niche, it keeps on tweaking–through product innovation, strategic expansion and aggressive marketing.

"This is our business. We want to do what we do best," said Reid Ruttenberg, chairman of the company and the son of one of its founders.

During its first half-century, the company produced coverings for everything from ironing boards to appliances, but in the 1970s it decided to become very focused. Since becoming the exclusive manufacturer and distributor of allergen-barrier AllerEase mattress and pillow protectors made of 3M Propore Fabric, American has added 100 percent cotton covers to the collection. It expanded the category to include comforter covers and fashion colors. At this month's New York Home Textiles market, it will offer a full line of feather bedcovers and new dobby and jacquard weaves.

"We're providing not only a new look, but also an allergen-based comfort level," said Ruttenberg.

But beyond creating products, the company also manages the category for its retailers, which span channels of distribution from The Bon Marche to Wal-Mart.

"When we decided to stay with our core competency, we knew that most retailers that buy our product don't have a lot of time to buy it," said Ruttenberg. "So we decided to show them how to be successful." After American Textile consolidated and managed one retailer's program, he said, sales went from $100,000 to $2.5 million in two years.

The company recently introduced lifestyle packaging–a unique approach in this niche–after its research showed that consumers look for a package that provides information, while buyers look for presentation and appearance.

"We never lose sight of the fact that we're manufacturing a nonglamorous product," said Ruttenberg. "We must package it properly and inform the buyers so that consumers can buy accordingly."

Looking to extend its European distribution, American Textile, which already has a distribution center in Belgium, is about to sign a distribution agreement in the United Kingdom, said Ruttenberg. Even though the company has moved most of its manufacturing offshore to Central America and China, it has maintained its original Pittsburgh base and plans to expand its facility here by the end of 2001.

Source: HFN, September 4, 2000, p. 19. Courtesy of Fairchild Publications, Inc.

BED PILLOWS

Bed pillows support the head so that the neck and back stay in alignment. Many varieties of pillows are available in a range of qualities and prices. Bed pillows are usually 21 to 22 inches wide. They are available in lengths that correspond to the size of the bed (see Table 10.3).

Fillings

The most common fillings in pillows are down, feathers, feather blends, polyester fiberfill, synthetic/down blends, and foam latex.

TABLE 10.3
Pillow Sizes

Name	Length
Standard	26″ to 27″
Queen-size pillows	30″ to 31″
King-size pillows	37″ to 38″

INDUSTRY STATEMENT 10.3

Natural Fills Going Mainstream in Retail Basic Bedding Lines

ATLANTA—The basic bedding category is getting back to nature.

Natural fills are growing in importance, with demand being driven by several types of consumers, including those with allergies to synthetic and down fills, those with sleep problems and those who simply want all-natural products as part of a holistic approach to living.

While specialty stores and catalogs remain the major channels of distribution for these materials, traditional retailers are adding natural fill products to their assortment. And consumers don't blink at prices ranging from $25 for an organic cotton pillow to $325 for a merino wool and cashmere mattress pad.

"A few years ago, natural fills were unique, but they are becoming much more mainstream. They appeal to customers both as a luxury and a natural product," said Edythe Jacobs, chief operating officer of DownTown Co., which makes cotton, wool and silk mattress pads.

"People continue to look for a natural story in a variety of ways," said Eric Moen, chief financial officer of Pacific Coast Feather, which is building its cotton program, especially in mattress pads. "In addition," he said, "natural products are a way for retailers to keep things fresh on the shelf."

Hudson Industries, which developed Nature's Own—a pillow with all-natural unbleached, undyed fill, ticking and thread—for a specialty catalog, has since found a market for the pillows in traditional channels, said Lonnie Scheps, the company's vice president of sales and marketing.

"I think the category grows a little more every year because there is more product knowledge," said Catherine Stemmler, sales manager at SDH Enterprises, which carries wool pillows and pads under its Purist line.

In American homes, which are often closed and heated or air conditioned all year, breathable fibers are essential to getting a good night's sleep, according to research from The Natural Bedroom, which makes organic wool, cotton and hemp mattress pads, toppers and pillows, as well as mattresses.

Natural fibers offer a range of benefits that appeal to consumers. Wool, for instance, has increased absorbency and wicking ability; it keeps sleepers warm in winter and cool in summer. Wool and cotton are naturally antimicrobial and anti-bacterial. Silk is the least allergenic natural fiber. Wool is also flame-resistant, as is hemp, which is also inherently mold- and mildew-resistant.

Canadian manufacturer Natura offers wool and organic cotton pads and pillows. Imported Products for Healthy Living makes a wool and cashmere pad. Hollander Home Fashions is introducing a wool mattress pad to complement its Wooly Bully comforter program. Louisville Bedding offers a cotton mattress pad. Ogallala Down offers pillows, mattress pads and mattress enhancers in wool and Hypodown, a mixture of down and Syriaca, the fluffy cellulosic fiber inside milkweed pods.

Other unique fills include buckwheat seeds, a new addition to the buckwheat- and millet-hull pillows offered by Bucky Products. The company is developing a Bucky Sleep Systems line with more choices in fill, size and shape. It has added a line of Hotties, a neck wrap, body wrap and hot water bottle filled with buckwheat seeds, that can be heated or cooled for on-the-spot comfort. The grains offer ventilation as well as flexible support.

Source: HFN, July 23, 2001, p. 16. Courtesy of Fairchild Publications, Inc.

Down

Down is the undercoat of waterfowl. It is considered to be the finest and most expensive filling for a pillow. It is very soft and lightweight. Down has fine-barbed filaments growing from a quill point (see Figure 10.13). Down does not have the quill shaft or vanes of feathers so it is softer. Goose down is the most expensive and considered to be the best. Eider down, which comes from the eider duck, is less expensive. Terminology used in the labeling of down is listed in Table 10.4. The term *down* is used to describe products that contain down, plumules, and down fiber. A product labeled "100 percent down," "pure down," or "all down" must contain only down.

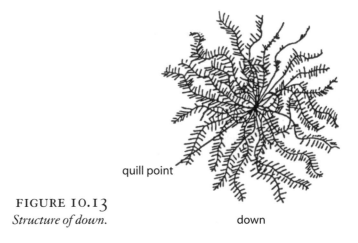

quill point

FIGURE 10.13
Structure of down.

down

Down pillows are evaluated by bulk. A goose-down pillow should weigh about 1 1/2 pounds for a standard 21 inches by 27 inches size. Duck down weighs about twice as much as goose down. The finest down comes from Poland; down of lower quality comes from Asia.

A down pillow is soft but not resilient. For adequate support, a feather or foam under-pillow may be used.

Feathers

Feathers are the plumage of fowl. Feathers from ducks, geese, turkeys, and chickens are used for pillows. Goose feathers are the softest, but duck feathers are also soft. Both have natural curl and remain resilient much longer than chicken or turkey feathers. Chicken and turkey feathers are artificially curled to make them resilient. They are the least expensive but are not usually desirable because they are stiff, hard, and heavy. Figure 10.14 shows the structure of a feather. Terminology used in the labeling of feather products is presented in Table 10.5.

Down/Feather Blends

Down is often blended with feathers to reduce the cost. A pillow made from better-quality down and feathers will have good resiliency. Characteristics of pillows made with various percentages are shown in Table 10. 6.

TABLE 10.4
Down Terminology

Name	Description
Down	Undercoat of waterfowl, filaments with no quill shaft
Plumules	Down with underdeveloped quills
Down fiber	Detached barbs from down and plumules

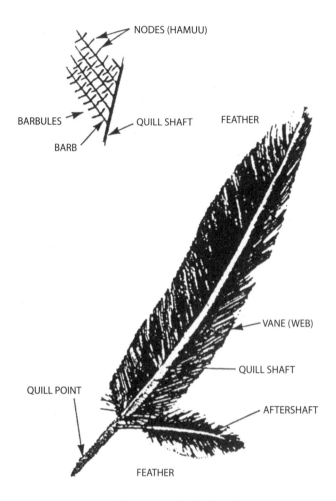

FIGURE 10.14 *Structure of a feather.*

Polyester Fiberfills

Polyester fiberfills, such as Dacron®, are comfortable, soft, resilient, lightweight, mothproof, mildew proof, and nonallergenic. They should be compactly filled and have no lumps.

Synthetic/Down Blends

These blends are relatively new in the marketplace. Polyester fiberfill, down, and goose feathers are combined to produce a pillow that is comfortable and easy to care for.

Foam

Foam pillows are made from polyurethane or latex foam. Solid molded foam is more comfortable and wears longer than shredded foam. Foam pillows are available in soft, medium, and firm grades. Foam is resilient, mothproof, mildew resistant, buoyant, odorless, and nonallergenic. Sometimes the foam is padded with polyester fiberfill. These pillows keep their shape well.

TABLE 10.5
Feather Terminology

Name	Description
Feathers	Plumage from fowl, whole and not processed
Waterfowl feathers	Plumage from ducks and geese
Nonwaterfowl feathers or land fowl feathers	Feathers from turkeys, chickens, and other land fowl
Quill feathers	Feathers that are more than four inches long
Feather fiber	Detached barbs of feathers

TABLE 10.6
Characteristics of Down/Feather Pillows

Percentages	Characteristics
20% down/80% feathers	Firm, compact pillow
40% down/60% feathers	Medium soft pillow
50% down/50% feathers	Semiluxurious pillow

Pillow Ticking

The **pillow ticking,** or interior casing, covers the filling of the pillow. It frequently is not removable. When the filling is down, the ticking should be very closely woven. A thread count of 220 is recommended to prevent the down from escaping.

Specialized Pillows

Gusseted Pillows

Gusseted pillows have a more structured shape than traditional pillows (see the example in Figure 10.15). The side-wall construction of the gusset keeps the pillow's filling from shifting. If it has a synthetic filling, the pillow will be denser and more uniform. With a natural filling the pillow will be rounder and puffier. Some gusseted pillows have a pocketed-coil structure similar to an innerspring mattress. The coils are wrapped with foam and then with polyfill.

Other Specialized Pillows

Specialized pillows are often developed to assist people with arthritis or other painful conditions. See Industry Statement 10.4 for discussion of three types of pillows developed for people

FIGURE 10.15
Gusseted pillows.
Courtesy of Fairchild Publications, Inc.

who suffer from chronic muscle pain syndrome, headaches, and stress. Other types of specialized pillows include:

- **Cervical-roll foam pillow** Filled-collar pillow designed to prevent neck pain caused by arthritis or muscle spasms.
- **Contoured pillows** Foam pillows that are lower in the middle and higher on the sides to support the neck. They are recommended for arthritis or neck pain.
- **Full-body pillows** Pillows that are usually about five feet long and often filled with down or feathers. They contour to the body and provide support in any sleeping position.

Care of Pillows

All pillows should have two covers—one that contains the filling, one that can be zipped off and washed. The pillowcase goes over both covers.

Down and feather pillows should be shaken daily and aired occasionally. Directions on care labels should be followed carefully. Down and feather pillows can usually be professionally dry-cleaned or home laundered.

ALTERNATIVE BEDDING

The bedding described in this category can also be classified as sofa beds or space-saving bedding. **Sofa beds,** such as sleeper sofas and futons, can be used for sitting during the day and for sleeping when needed. Bunk, fold-up, loft, and wall beds provide space-saving bedding. They are ideal in smaller homes or apartments that have limited space.

Innovative Pillows Are Prescription for Pain

Suppliers Target Special Needs with New Shapes and Sizes

ATLANTA—If necessity is the mother of invention, in the case of pillows, pain is often the source of inspiration.

More than 80 million adults in the United States and Canada suffer from neck pain and associated headaches in a given year, according to statistics from Johns Hopkins University in Baltimore.

Jean Kelly, a registered nurse in Oshkosh, Wis., suffered for years from fibromyalgia, or chronic muscle pain syndrome, which causes intense pain at 16 pressure points in the body's fibrous connective tissues. Sleeping was extremely uncomfortable.

What Kelly needed, and created, was a body pillow: a five-foot-long, u-shaped, virtual cocoon that cushions the back, legs, shoulders, and head.

Through a serendipitous turn of events, Kelly's Comfort-U pillow was licensed to the Denver-based Feel Good For Life catalog for manufacturing, marketing and distributing. The company is selling the pillow in its own and Hammeracher-Schlemmer catalogs, and on its feelgoodfast.com Web site. It is also currently negotiating with several specialty and chain retailers. The large size retails for $129.99, with a smaller one available soon at $79.99.

When Maurice Bard could not find a pillow that effectively alleviated his headaches after a car wreck, he invented a waterbase pillow and started his own company, Mediflow Inc., in Ontario, Canada.

The pillow consists of a four-inch layer of polyester fiber positioned at the top. The Mediflow has a specially engineered thin water pouch at the base, with a thermal insulating layer developed at NASA for the space program. Firmness is regulated by the amount of water poured into the pouch through a leakproof valve.

The patented design, which is manufactured in the United States, allows the pillow to conform to the sleeper's head and neck, reducing pain in both.

The Mediflow pillow is available at Linens 'n Things, chiropractic clinics and specialty health-care stores for approximately $39.95.

Savitri Ermini, president of Boxi Pillows in Albuquerque, N.M., said she never slept comfortably: her neck and shoulders tense from stress and holding her head back to read through bifocals. Realizing that an oval pillow—basically the same shape as the head—was not supporting her neck properly, she designed a rectangular pillow that conforms to the head.

The double-chamber Rejuvenation pillow contains buckwheat hulls in the bottom and wool batting that keeps the hulls from shifting and provides a resilient loft to the pillow.

The pillow retails for $29, and is available on the Web at www.boxi.com and SelfCare, a personal-care products site. It is also in catalogs, including Harmony, Inner Dimensions, and Total Body and Image; as well as small specialty and futon stores.

Source: HFN, November 15, 1999. Courtesy of Fairchild Publications, Inc.

Sofa Beds

Comfort and durability of sofa beds are dependent on the same factors as traditional bedding. A variety of mattress configurations, such as air-chamber mattresses with easily adjustable firmness levels, are available. Because many of these pieces are upholstered, information about upholstered furniture should be reviewed in Chapter 9. There are several styles of sofas that can be converted into a bed—daybeds, studio couches, sleeper sofas, and futons.

Daybed

A **daybed** is simply a twin- or single-sized mattress on a frame. It is usually placed against a wall to provide support for bolsters or wedges. The bolsters or wedges are removed, and the bed can be made up for sleeping.

Studio Couch

A **studio couch** has two sets of springs. One set is under the regular sofa-spring unit. The bottom set is pulled out, and detachable seat cushions are placed on it to form a double bed.

Sleeper Sofa

A **sleeper sofa** looks much like a traditional sofa. It has a concealed-spring mechanism and mattress that pulls out to form a bed. Sleepers are available in double- and queen-size beds. Loveseats and chairs that have the same mechanism are also available.

Futons

Futons are especially popular in situations where there is limited space or where people need to use the bedroom as a living area during the day (see Figure 10.16). A traditional Japanese futon is a thin mattress stuffed with a natural fiber. In Japanese homes, the futon is placed on flooring called a *tatami* for sleeping. It is rolled up when not in use. The Western adaptation includes a solid wood or a slatted frame that can be adjusted to be flat for sleeping or to form a sofa seat and back. The futon can be draped over the frame to serve as cushioning. A futon should not be placed directly on the floor because air cannot circulate, and the futon can become mildewed.

The frame for a futon can be made from a variety of materials, but predominantly wood and metal are used. Futons may be decorative or plain and are available in many different styles. The mattresses are also made from a variety of materials, such as solid garnetted acrylic, latex and down combinations, all foam, foam and cotton, and latex wrapped in wool. Futon covers are easily changed when soiled or old, and they are easy to replace.

FIGURE 10.16
Futon.
Courtesy of Fairchild Publications, Inc.

Space-Saving Bedding

Foam Blocks

Recently some companies have developed reasonably priced upholstered chairs and loveseats that are hinged blocks of foam. When the hinges are released, the blocks of foam open out to form a bed.

Bunk Beds and Trundle Beds

When one bed is stacked on top of another it is called a **bunk bed** (see Figure 10.17). They are ideal for children's rooms. A **trundle bed** has storage space underneath the mattress. This space can be used for storage or to hold an extra bed (see Figure 10.18).

Fold-Up and Wall Beds

Fold-up and wall beds allow for full use of living space during the day but are available for sleeping at night. Fold-up beds fold in half so they can be stored in a closet. Wall beds are stored in the wall and pull down for sleeping. They take excellent advantage of seldom-used space.

BEDDING MANUFACTURERS

The three major manufacturers of mattresses and box springs are Sealy, Simmons, and Serta. Each of these manufacturers produces two lines of bedding—a line that retails under its own nationally advertised name and a separate line that is store specific. Store-specific lines are private-label brands that are sold by a specific retailer. Table 10.7 lists the top 10 bedding producers. Important specialty bedding manufacturers are listed in Table 10.8.

FIGURE 10.17
Bunk beds.

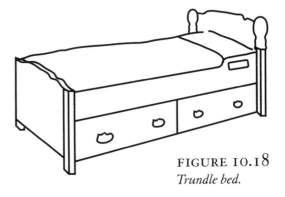

FIGURE 10.18
Trundle bed.

TABLE 10.7

Top 10 Bedding Producers

1. Sealy	6. King Koil
2. Serta	7. Ther-A-Pedic
3. Simmons	8. Restonic
4. Stearns & Foster	9. Englander
5. Spring Air	10. Kingsdown

Source: HFN, September 10, 2001, p. 16. Courtesy of Fairchild Publications, Inc.

TABLE 10.8

Specialty Bedding Manufacturers

Producer	Products
Select Comfort	Air beds
Natura World, Inc.	Latex beds
	Wool and latex combinations
Land & Sky	Air and foam combinations
	Waterbeds
	Foam beds
	Air beds
Comfortaire	Air and foam combinations
Classic Sleep Products, Inc.	Foam beds

SUMMARY

Bedding refers to furniture that is used for sleeping on at night, although it may also be used for sitting during the day. Bedding is available in a wide variety of price ranges and quality levels. Mattress covers and pads and pillows are also included in the bedding category.

There are two basic types of mattresses—spring and solid, or nonspring mattresses. Innerspring mattresses are the most popular style of mattress. The two main types of innerspring coil assemblies are the Marshall-type and the Bonnell-type. Pillow top mattresses with an extra layer of padding are popular now. Other types of mattresses are made from foam, water, or air. Adjustable beds have specially designed frames that allow the head and foot of the bed to be raised and lowered, much like a hospital bed.

The framework that supports the mattress is called the foundation. The foundation is usually sold with the mattress and is designed to support the mattress properly.

Mattress pads and covers protect mattresses from dust, dead skin cells, and dirt. They also protect the bottom sheet from undue wear from rubbing against the mattress. Covers are one-layer structures that simply cover the mattress. Mattress pads cover the mattress but also provide a layer of padding.

Bed pillows support the head so that the neck and back stay in alignment. They may be filled with synthetic fibers, down, feathers, or foam. Down is considered the finest and most expensive filling for a pillow. Down and feathers are blended to reduce the cost of pillows. Gusseted pillows have a more structured shape than a traditional pillow.

Sofa beds and space-saving bedding are alternatives to traditional bedding. Included in this category are daybeds, studio couches, sleeper sofas, bunk beds, trundle beds, and wall beds.

The three major manufacturers of mattresses and box springs are Sealy, Simmons, and Serta. Each of these manufacturers produces two lines of bedding—a line that retails under its own nationally advertised name and a separate line that is store specific.

TERMS FOR REVIEW

adjustable beds	feather bed	pillow ticking
air-filled mattress	feathers	pillow top
band springs	foundation	platform-top springs
bed board	full-body pillows	pocket-coil mattresses
bedding	futons	pocket-spring mattresses
Bonnell-type innerspring	gusseted pillow	slatted wood
box spring	hybrid flotation systems	sleeper sofa
bunk bed	innerspring mattresses	sofa beds
cervical-roll foam pillow	link springs	solid (or pallet) base
coil-on-coil	low-profile foundation	sprung bed
continuous springing	Marshall-type innerspring	studio couch
contoured pillows	mattress cover	ticking
daybed	mattress pads	traditionally sprung mattresses
down	open-coil mattresses	trundle bed
edge guards	open-coil springs	water-filled mattresses
egg-crate-foam mattress pads	orthopedic bed	wool underblanket

REVIEW QUESTIONS

1. Why are Marshall-type innersprings used in higher-quality mattresses?
2. What is one advantage of foam mattresses?
3. What is the purpose of the foundation?
4. What are advantages of egg-crate-foam mattress pads over traditional mattress pads?
5. Which pillow filling is recommended for someone with allergies?
6. What is a futon? Under what circumstances is a futon a good choice for a bed?

LEARNING ACTIVITIES

1. Visit the Web sites of Sealy, Simmons, and Serta. Describe their advertisements. Would you want to purchase their products? Why?
2. Interview a nurse or a doctor who deals with people with chronic back pain. Ask them for their suggestions about the proper bedding for people with chronic back pain.

CHAPTER II

LINENS

"When Royal Sateen sheets were introduced in 1990, they set a standard for luxury linen in the United States. Retailers discovered that luxury can be offered in numerous ways, and Royal Sateen's way is through sheen and hand, not just thread counts.... Sateen these days is a common phrase often used as vendors attempt to differentiate themselves in their solid-color, print and jacquard offerings."

HFN, May 27, 2002, p. 86

LINENS INCLUDE BED SHEETS AND COVERS, TOWELS AND OTHER BATHROOM TEXTILE PRODUCTS, tablecloths, furniture slipcovers, and curtains and drapes. The term *linen* reflects the historical importance of linen fabric in these goods. Today, much of the linen originally used in these products has been replaced by other natural and manufactured fibers that offer greater ease of care. Linens are also sold as domestics, home textiles, and interior textiles. They are sold in large department stores, discount store chains, and specialty stores, as well as through catalogs and on the Internet.

Traditionally, department stores classify **home textiles** as either **domestics** or **linens.** Domestics include the following textile products for use on beds:

- Sheets and pillowcases
- Blankets
- Comforters and quilts
- Bedspreads
- Mattress covers and pads
- Pillows

Linens include the following textile products for bathroom and tabletop use:

- Towels
- Shower curtains
- Bathroom rugs and mats
- Tablecloths, place mats, runners, and napkins.

Some stores still use these classifications; some simply have a home textiles department. This chapter includes all of these products and selected others that are sold in the linen section of large department stores, with the exception of mattress covers, pads, and pillows, which are discussed in Chapter 10 "Bedding."

Coordinated Linens

Linens are available to the consumer in a wide variety of prices and qualities and an almost unbelievable range of colors and designs. The consumer may wish to match or coordinate linens with upholstery and slipcover fabrics and also with paint, wallpaper, and borders. Retailers and designer/manufacturers collaborate to create room vignettes, in-store displays, and display shelves that demonstrate to consumers how linens can be used to coordinate a room. For example, Ralph Lauren sheets can be coordinated with Ralph Lauren paints. Fieldcrest offers coordinating products for the bed, bath, and table. In recent years both men's and women's apparel designers, such as Calvin Klein, have expanded their lines to include fashions for the home. Refer to Table 11.1 for a listing of selected brands.

Regulation of Household Linens

All of the products categorized as linens must be labeled in accordance with the laws that relate to the consumption of textile products. The Textile Fiber Products Identification Act (TFPIA) requires that generic fiber names and fiber content be listed on the label. Flammability standards for mattress pads, floor mats, and small rugs are set by federal agencies. Refer to Chapter 2 for more discussion of federal regulations affecting labeling and flammability standards.

Commercial Versus Residential Interior Textiles

The selection criteria for residential interior textiles are different from those for commercial interior textiles. Function and aesthetics are important in both residential and commercial settings, but the extreme wear and the need to meet federal regulatory codes in a commercial setting limits the selection for commercial use to items that meet specific performance standards. Contractors may set their own standards in addition to federal regulations.

TABLE 11.1

Selected Brands of Textiles for the Bath, Bed, and Table

Type of Linens	Popular Brands	Type of Linens	Popular Brands
Bed	Alexander Julian	Bath	Avanti
	Bay Linens		Calvin Klein Home
	Burlington		Croscill Fieldcrest
	Calvin Klein Home		Martha Stewart
	Cannon		Martex
	Collier Campbell		Ralph Lauren
	Croscill		
	Crowncrafts	Table	Burlington
	Dan River		Fieldcrest
	Fieldcrest		Joseph Abboud
	Hollander Laura Ashley		Pfaltzgraff
	Martex		Pimpernel
	Martha Stewart		Ralph Lauren
	Ralph Lauren		Villeroy & Boch
	Sheftex		Waterford
	Sheridan		Waverly
	The Source		
	Thomasville		
	Tommy Hilfiger		
	Utica		
	Wamsutta		

BED LINENS

Bed linens include:

- Sheets and pillowcases
- Blankets and throws
- Bedspreads, comforters, and quilts
- Dust ruffles, canopies, and decorative pillows

Sheets and Pillowcases

Sheets and pillowcases are sold separately or in sets in beautiful colors, exciting prints, and traditional white (see Figure 11.1). They are also available as component parts of a product called **bed-in-a-bag,** an entire ensemble for the bed that can include top and bottom sheets, two pillowcases, and a matching comforter. Sometimes a bed skirt is included. Consumers look for linens that can be matched or coordinated with other decorative elements in the bedroom. Some consumers purchase the sheets to make window curtains or shower curtains.

FIGURE II.I
Newport bed ensemble.
A product by Springmaid,
a brand of Spring Industries.
Photo: Mayo Studios.

Styles

A set of sheets consists of a **flat sheet** made to function as the top sheet and a **fitted,** or **contour sheet,** to be used as a bottom sheet. Elastic banding or elasticized corners provide the shaping needed to make the fitted sheet mold to the mattress.

Table 11.2 lists standard sheet sizes. Mattresses are made in two basic thicknesses—standard (8–12 inches) and pillow top (14 inches). It is important to ensure that fitted bottom sheets will accommodate mattress height. Many sheet manufacturers design fitted bottom sheets with deeper pockets (longer sides) and more elastic to allow for different heights.

Sheets and pillowcases are sized and sold in matched sets or separately. Pillowcases are sold as pairs. A twin set includes one bottom sheet, one top sheet, and one pillowcase. Full, queen,

TABLE II.2
Sheet Sizes

Type of Bed	Flat Sheet (width × length)	Fitted Sheet (width × length)
Crib	45″ × 68″	29″ × 54″
Twin	66″ × 104″	39″ × 75″
Extra long twin	66″ × 114″	39″ × 85″
Full or double	81″ × 104″	54″ × 75″
Queen	90″ × 110″	60″ × 80″
King	108″ × 110″	78″ × 80″
California King	108″ × 119″	72″ × 84″

Note: These measurements are approximate and based on measurements taken before hemming. Each manufacturer sizes differently.

INDUSTRY PROFILE

Eugene Kalkin Linens 'n Things

A Master of Merchandising Creates a Category Killer

Eugene Kalkin likes to modestly claim that his ideas for founding Linens 'n Things were not particularly revolutionary, his merchandising not particularly inspired, his vision not particularly clear. But spend a few minutes talking to him, and you quickly realize the foundation for what has become one of retailing's giants was exactly that: revolutionary and inspired, with a clarity of purpose.

Despite the fact that Kalkin says his career in retail was rather a fluke, adding that the only reason he entered the field in the first place was because he was "fired from his first job after three days," he took to retailing immediately. He excelled in his first position as an assistant floor coverings buyer at Stern's and moved up the ranks quickly; when he was still in his 20s, Kalkin was promoted to divisional merchandise manager.

"I loved it," said Kalkin. "I was single, I was able to work to my heart's content, and I saw I had an affinity for it." His tenure at Stern's provided him with his merchandising knowledge base, which served him well when he started out on his own in 1958 to establish Great Eastern Linens in partnership with Great Eastern Mills. Then, in 1975, Kalkin lost everything when Daylin Inc., Great Eastern's parent company, filed for bankruptcy.

Kalkin describes the day Daylin filed for Chapter 11 as "the worst day in my life," but his unflagging commitment and enthusiasm for retailing remained. Kalkin said he "never considered working for anyone else, and I didn't know anything else [but retailing]."

Kalkin decided to buy back seven units of Great Eastern Linens from the bankruptcy court for $300,000, and thus began Linens 'n Things. "It was the most excruciating experience of my life," said Kalkin. "It was like buying my own baby back."

Undaunted, Kalkin went on to achieve something truly remarkable: He took a seven-unit regional chain with annual sales of $2 million and in just eight years turned it into a 50-store chain with $80 million in annual sales before eventually selling it.

While Kalkin claims he had no idea that Linens 'n Things would become hugely successful, he admits that he was "mature enough to recognize what was happening [in retail in the mid-1970s] and run with it." Linens 'n Things was the first true home textiles chain, and Kalkin was the first to hit on a formula of selling quality merchandise at a discount. "We had available to us merchandise that we previously couldn't sell," said Kalkin of the first-quality, branded merchandise he carried. "Before 1975, department stores had a lock on it, and [vendors] wouldn't sell to an off-price store."

Kalkin knew that in order to be successful selling off-price goods, he had to find a way to lower costs. After attending a lecture given by a marketing professor and hearing about merchandising techniques being employed by European food chains, he decided the same approach could be used to sell linens.

"Something had to happen structurally to bring costs down," said Kalkin. "I had the insight of using the cube and stacking merchandise up 10 feet in the air, which allowed me to fit a 12,000-square-foot store into a 7,000-square-foot space. That cut the rent, the lights, the taxes—everything—in half, but I still had the sales volume of a 12,000 foot store."

"I just hoped I was going to make a living, I really had no idea it would turn into what it did," said Kalkin, with no false modesty, of his innovations. "But as I saw how it was moving, I just took my little feet and ran as fast as I could go."

Other industry members attribute much of Kalkin's success not only to his business acumen, but to his ability to inspire and involve his employees. Kurt Hamburger, president and managing director of Lintex/Cobra Group, described the twice-yearly buying meetings that Kalkin held for all store managers and vendors. "He gave managers the feeling that they were part of the buying operation. He developed a real esprit de corps, and they really felt they had something invested in the merchandise, in the company's success," he said. "He created a kind of energy and camaraderie that's absolutely lacking today."

Hamburger also praised Kalkin's unfailing devotion to his work. "He was unique in his dedication, his knowledge, his vision."

Kalkin himself recognized the role his dedication played in the success of Linens 'n Things. "Being smart and insightful is not enough; you really have to devote yourself, even at the expense of your family," he said. "You have to have an indomitable will to achieve success."

Source: HFN, November 27, 2000, p. 40. Courtesy of Fairchild Publications, Inc.

and king sets include one bottom sheet, one top sheet, and two pillowcases. See Table 11.3 for the sizes of pillowcases. Waterbed sheets are also available and are sized according to standard waterbed dimensions.

Construction

Cotton and polyester/cotton sheets dominate the market. Cotton provides absorbency and soft hand, while polyester adds durability and wrinkle resistance. Most sheets are made with spun yarns. Polyester-filament yarns tend to pill (the formation of little balls of fiber). **Muslin** or **percale** fabrics are the most common. Muslin sheets are made with carded yarns, and percale sheets are made with combed yarns.

Other varieties of sheets include the following:

- *Sateen,* an increasingly popular weave for sheets, is very smooth and soft but is not as durable as plain weave and is subject to snagging.
- *Satin sheets,* made from filament yarns, are very slippery. They are not durable and are subject to snagging.
- *Flannel,* which is usually a plain-weave cotton, is popular for use in cool climates, but it is not as durable as plain-weave sheets.
- *Knitted jersey* or *tricot* sheets are available. The inherent stretch of knit fabrics makes these sheets fit well, but they are not durable and are subject to "running" and snagging. One hundred percent cotton jersey sheets do not have good elastic recovery.

Finishes are used for different purposes. Many one hundred percent cotton sheets are treated with durable-press finishes, which improves their resiliency but reduces durability. Soil-release finishes allow for easy removal of oil-based stains from sheets that are polyester/cotton blends or have a durable-press finish. Antibacterial finishes are especially important for sheets used in the hotel business.

The hems of sheets may be very plain or quite decorative. The lower edge of the top sheet is typically finished with a plain one-inch hem. The hem of the top edge may be three to four inches in width and may be plain or have embroidery, lace, eyelet, monogramming, or other embellishment. See Figure 11.2 for a diagram of simple embroidery stitches.

TABLE 11.3
Pillowcase Sizes

Type of Pillowcase	Size (width × length)
Standard	21″ × 35″
Queen	21″ × 39″
King	21″ × 44″

Note: These measurements are approximate. Each manufacturer sizes differently. Some manufacturers offer a Standard/Queen pillowcase.

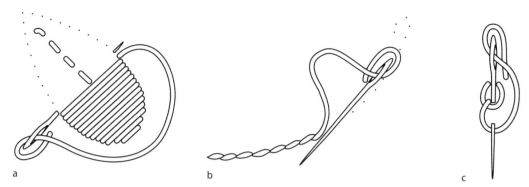

FIGURE 11.2
Embroidery stitches: a. *satin stitch,* b. *outline stitch,* c. *chain stitch.*

Selection

Thread count, the number of filling (crosswise) and warp (lengthwise) yarns in an inch, is the traditional indicator of quality in sheets. The more yarns per inch, the higher the quality. The thread count of muslin sheets is from 112 to 140, and 128 is common. Muslin sheets are considered to be lower quality than percale sheets. Percale sheets are made with combed yarns and the thread counts start at 168 and go as high as 340. Moderately priced sheets commonly have a thread count of 200. More expensive lines have higher thread counts. **Pinpoint percale** sheets are basket- or rib weave fabrics with a thread count of 220 to 250. The thread count of sateen sheets usually varies from 230 to 300, but may be much higher.

In addition to thread count, it is important to consider balance. Balanced fabrics have approximately the same number of threads in the warp and filling directions. They are more durable than unbalanced fabrics.

Sheets should be examined to ensure that stitching is even. The fabric should be free of flaws and uniformly woven. Preshrinking of sheets by the manufacturer is important to ensure appropriate fit and eliminate puckering (see Figure 11.3).

Care

Sheets should be machine washed and dried according to the manufacturer's instructions. Bleach should not be used on colors or prints. Overuse of bleach on white sheets will cause them

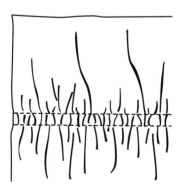

FIGURE 11.3
Puckered seam in pillowcase.

to wear out more quickly. Dark colors should be washed before use and subsequently washed separately from whites or light colors. All colored sheets, regardless of price, tend to fade over time. Thus, components, especially for prints and dark colors, should be washed together so the color continues to match.

Sheets will last longer if they are rotated in use to avoid using one set continuously. Mattress pads or covers protect sheets from exposure to the mattress top and extend the life of bottom sheets.

Blankets and Throws

Blankets and throws are available in beautiful colors and patterns and a wide variety of textures. They can coordinate or contrast with sheets, bedspreads, quilts, comforters, window treatments, or wall treatments.

Styles

Blankets and blanket-like throws have no filling or stuffing. They offer both aesthetics and function in the bedroom. They can be lightweight for the summer or very heavy for extra warmth in the winter. Electric blankets and throws provide warmth with little weight. Most blankets are woven, but some are knit and some are nonwoven.

Blankets are available in the same size categories as sheets. They should be long enough to tuck in at the foot of the bed and also on the sides if desired. Most blankets are 84 inches long and should be approximately 20 inches wider than the mattress. Blankets are intended to be used above the top sheet and underneath the bedspread, quilt, or other cover.

Throws are usually smaller than blankets and may be folded and placed at the end of the bed during the day. Throws are also popular in family rooms during cool weather. They frequently are very decorative and are selected to coordinate with the room décor. The styles, construction, selection, and care of throws are similar to those of blankets.

Construction

Woven and knit blankets are primarily made with spun yarns of cotton or synthetic fibers. Some wool and specialty hair fibers are also used. Wool provides the greatest warmth, but it can be damaged by moths and/or shrink in laundering. Acrylic is popular because it is easy to care for, lightweight, and does not attract moths. Most summer blankets are cotton or polyester/cotton blends.

Woven Blankets Most woven blankets are plain, twill, or leno weave. The weave should be balanced for durability. The warp yarns are tightly spun for durability. The filling yarns are loosely spun so the fabric can be napped during finishing. To provide more durability the core of the filling yarn can be tightly spun, and then additional fibers are loosely spun around the core. The napped surface helps trap air for insulation. Leno-weave blankets are usually loosely woven, provide less insulation, and are appropriate for summer-weight blankets. Figure 11.4 illustrates a leno weave. There are several other variations of woven blankets—tufted, double-faced, and electric.

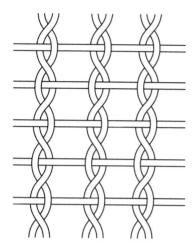

FIGURE 11.4 *Leno weave.*

Tufted blankets typically do not provide satisfactory service because the tufts pull out easily. After tufting, both sides are napped, which serves to stabilize the tufts and also provide insulation for warmth. See Chapter 2 for discussion of the tufting process. The resulting finish is soft and luxurious but mats (flattens) quickly.

Double-faced, or reversible, blankets are created with two sets of filling yarns and one set of warp yarns. One set of filling yarns is on the face of the fabric, and the other set is on the back of the fabric. Double-faced blankets offer interesting decorating options because they are one color on one side and another color on the other side.

Electric blankets are popular for cold seasons. The fabric for an electric blanket is frequently a double-cloth fabric with two warp yarns and two filling yarns. The electric wires are inserted before the edges are finished, and interlacings between the face and back create channels that keep them in place. A control unit is used to adjust the temperature. Larger blankets should be equipped with dual controls so that each side can be set to personal preference if desired. Electric throws are also available. All electric blankets must be Underwriters Laboratories, Inc. (UL) approved for safety. The UL label certifies that the blanket has passed flammability and electrical test requirements.

Knit Blankets Knitted blankets are usually raschel knits. They are popularly known as **thermal blankets.** They are characterized by a distinctive waffle-like effect. This three-dimensional surface provides excellent insulation and these blankets are known for providing lightweight warmth if covered by another fabric. Uncovered they are suitable for use in the summer. Raschel-knit thermal blankets are usually cotton. Some thermal blankets are made of woven acrylic.

Beautiful intricately hand-knit blankets called **afghans** are used as blankets or throws. These pieces are often heirloom quality. Similar blankets are sometimes hand crocheted.

Nonwoven Blankets There are two main categories of nonwoven blankets—needlepunched blankets and flocked blankets.

Needle-punched blankets are created by forcing numerous barbed needles through a thick web of 12 to 18 layers of fibers. The Chatham Manufacturing Company developed this technique under the name of Fiberwoven Process® (see Figure 11.5). The needle board entangles the fibers as it punches through the formed web. There are about 2000 needle holes in a square inch of fabric. The final fabric is about 1/4 inch thick and is finished with slight napping. These blankets are low cost because of the speed of production. They are commonly used in hotels and hospitals.

Flocked blankets are popular for their soft, luxurious velvet-like hand. Vellux®, a well-known brand of flocked blanket, is made by Westpoint Stevens. Nylon fibers are electrostatically bonded to an inner core of polyurethane foam (see Figure 11.6). The resulting blanket is soft, warm, and lightweight.

Selection

Blankets should provide warmth without weight. Most consumers prefer lightweight blankets in which the thickness of the fabric and nap provide the insulation needed for warmth. The fabric construction should be even for durability and firm. Woven blankets should be cut on-grain. Holding the fabric up to light can provide a quick visual assessment of its thickness, the grain, and the evenness of the weave.

There should be no loose fibers on the surface. Loose fibers indicate that the fabric may pill. The buyer can check to see if the nap is securely attached to the base by gently lifting the blanket by the nap.

The top and bottom of the blanket should be bound with satin or taffeta **nylon blanket binding** in a color that matches or complements the body of the blanket. Blanket binding is approximately two inches wide. The binding should be stitched on with two parallel rows of stitching or a zigzag stitch. The sides of the blanket may be the fabric selvages, or they may be bound with a machine stitch.

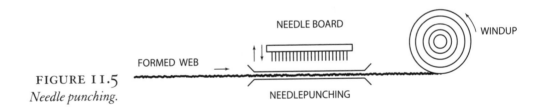

FIGURE 11.5
Needle punching.

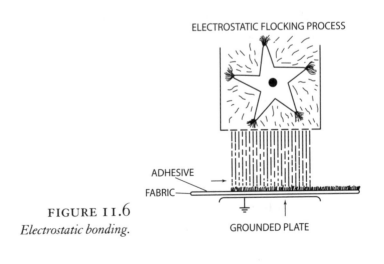

FIGURE 11.6
Electrostatic bonding.

Care

Most blankets can be machine washed and dried at home according to the manufacturer's directions, but their size, bulk, and weight may necessitate professional cleaning. Wool blankets, unless the manufacturer's care label indicates differently, should be dry-cleaned.

Comforters, Quilts, and Bedspreads

Comforters, quilts, and bedspreads are used as the top layer of bedding. They are frequently the focal point of a bedroom and may be used purely for decorative purposes and removed for sleeping. Designers create coordinated bedroom ensembles that include bedding, wallpaper, paint, slipcovers, and window treatments. Comforters, quilts, and bedspreads are sold in the same size categories as sheets: twin, full or double, queen, king, California king, and specialized sizes.

Comforters and Quilts

Comforters and **quilts** are not fitted to the top of the mattress. Typically a quilt or comforter will cover the top of the bed and go partially down the sides of the bed but not completely to the floor. A quilt usually has less filling and is thinner than a comforter but both are composed of three layers—a backing fabric, filling, and top fabric. Some are reversible, with the back in a solid color and the top a pattern. Various methods are used to stitch the three layers together— traditional hand stitching; machine stitching, either hand-guided or automatic; and **pinsonic melding,** sometimes called *electronic welding.* This process involves the use of heat and sound waves to meld the three layers together. It is used only for products of at least 50 percent thermoplastic fibers. It simulates the appearance of stitching but is not as durable.

Stitching may follow simple lines in rows or channels, geometric patterns, or outline a design (see Figure 11.7). In addition to the textural and visual beauty of the quilting, the stitches also prevent the filling from shifting. Most comforters are channel quilted. Quilts and comforters are frequently sold with matching pillow covers called **shams.** A sham frequently has piping and/or ruffles.

Hand quilting is a time-consuming and painstaking craft, and handcrafted quilts are beautiful and costly. The tops of some handcrafted quilts are patchwork, or pieced together from smaller pieces of fabric. There are many traditional patterns, such as the crazy quilt, which has randomly cut pieces of fabric and is usually heavily embellished. Other tops are appliquéd before quilting with shaped pieces of fabric almost invisibly stitched to the top. Sometimes embroidery is added. Some quilts are used as wall hangings (see Figure 11.8).

Bedspreads

A **bedspread** is used to cover the top of the bed and is usually placed so that it extends to the floor on three sides. Bedspreads can be designed with extra length at the top to cover the pillow(s), or they can be sold with matching pillow shams. Bedspreads may be constructed from quilted fabrics or single-layer fabrics.

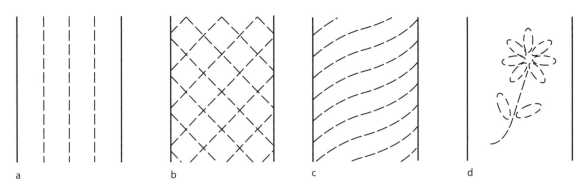

a b c d

FIGURE 11.7
Quilting patterns: a. *channel,* b. *simple geometric pattern,*
c. *more intricate pattern,* d. *outline of a design printed on the fabric.*

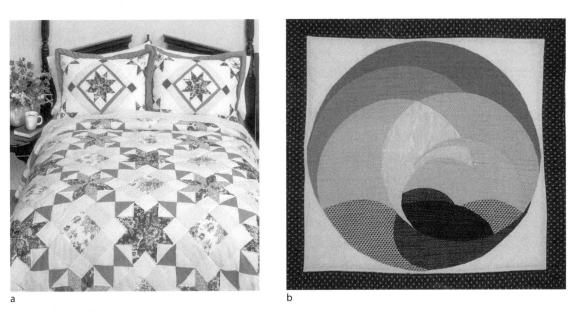

a b

FIGURE 11.8 a. *Traditional Flying Geese quilt.* Courtesy of Fairchild Publications, Inc.
b. *Handcrafted quilt made by Nancy Madacsi, based on a pattern by Jean Johnson.*

Bedspreads can be fitted or unfitted. A fitted bedspread is seamed to fit the top of the bed. The length of fabric that falls to the floor is called the **drop.** It may be plain or shirred (gathered). The corners of a bedspread with a plain drop may have pleats at the foot of the bed (see Figure 11.9). If the bed has a footboard, then the bottom corners of the bedspread must have slits to allow the fabric to fall to the floor (see Figure 11.10). It is important that the weight and texture of the fabric be considered so the drop will hang properly. For example, a stiff fabric might not gather well.

An unfitted bedspread, sometimes called a **throw-style bedspread,** simply hangs to the floor. At the foot of the bed the bottom corners may be rounded, as shown in Figure 11.11, or left square. Throw-type bedspreads may not be appropriate for beds that have footboards because the footboard prevents the fabric from falling to the floor.

Construction

A wide variety of fibers is used in comforters, quilts, and bedspreads. These include both filament and spun yarns. Filament yarns provide a luxurious hand but are slippery. Many different fabrics are used, and selection will depend on final use. For example, sturdy corduroy is appropriate for a boy's bedspread, while quilted chintz is appropriate for a master bedroom. In quilts and comforters it is important that the fabric be woven tightly to avoid **fill leakage,** the penetration of the filling through the fabric. Sometimes a separate liner is used to prevent fill leakage. Backing and face fabric should be preshrunk to avoid excessive puckers.

There are several choices for the filling of comforters and quilts:

- Cotton batting is the traditional filling of choice for many handcrafted quilts. It is fairly thin and does not provide much warmth. It is available in a range of thicknesses, but has a tendency to mat and lump. Small, even, closely spaced quilting stitches will control lumping. Quilts with cotton filling can be washed with extreme care.
- Polyester fiberfill is the most common filling for comforters and quilts. It is nonallergenic, lightweight, provides warmth, and may be machine washed and dried. It is available in many thicknesses, from very thin to very thick. Thicker fiberfill provides more warmth. Quilting stitches do not need to be as closely spaced as with cotton batting. Sometimes the polyester fibers are bonded together to prevent lumping.

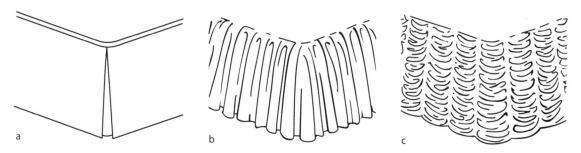

FIGURE II.9 *Bedspread drop:* a. *plain drop with corner pleat,* b. *gathered,* c. *shirred.*

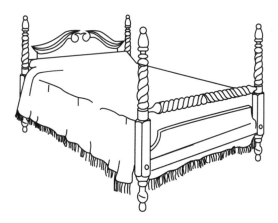

FIGURE II.10 *Plain drop with slit at bottom corners to accommodate footboard.*

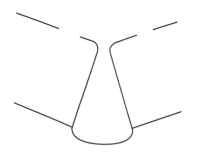

FIGURE II.11
Throw-style bedspread.

- Polyurethane is not as common as fiberfill. Polyurethane batting is usually thin and light-weight but is somewhat stiff and inflexible.
- Wool is occasionally used in comforters. It is costly and should be dry-cleaned.
- Down is the premier filling for comforters. Products containing down must conform to the labeling requirements of the Federal Trade Commission Guide for the Feather and Down Products Industry. Down is the undercoating of waterfowl, consisting of clusters of fluffy filaments. There are no quills (the tubes of feathers) in down. It is seldom used in quilts because quilts traditionally are thin, and down is very light and fluffy. The most expensive down is from the goose. It is the softest, most resilient, and lightest. Some down comforters have a removable cover. A down comforter is also called a **puff** (New England), **duvet** (France), or **federbett** (Germany). Additional information about down is presented in Chapter 10 "Bedding."

Selection

Consumers have a wide range of options when purchasing comforters, quilts, and bedspreads. Personal preference is very important in the final selection, but there are several factors to consider. Slippery fabrics are not advisable because they tend to slip from the bed. Very stiff fabrics do not drape well.

The fabric should have a close, even construction. All stitching should be close and even, and bindings should be securely attached. The seams of an expensive fitted bedspread should have welt cording. If quilted, there should be enough stitches to keep the filling in place. Hand quilting is the most expensive, followed by hand-guided machine quilting. Simple automatic machine quilting is less expensive. Low-cost quilts and comforters may be electronically stitched.

Down is expensive and requires special care, but it is very warm. One hundred percent down is considered the best. The higher the percentage of plumules (down with underdeveloped quills), down fiber (detached bars from down and plumules), and feathers (plumage of fowl, whole and not processed), the lower the quality will be. Cotton and wool are costly, while polyester and polyurethane are relatively low cost. Polyester fiberfill is usually preferred over cotton because cotton tends to form lumps. Soil-release finishes make cleaning easier and soil-resistant finishes will help keep the fabric clean. Both finishes are recommended.

Care

Generally consumers prefer products suitable for home washing and drying. But, even if they can be cleaned at home, the extreme size and bulk of some spreads and comforters makes professional cleaning a necessity. Antique or handcrafted quilts need very specialized care.

To minimize the clumping and shifting of down, many manufacturers suggest dry cleaning. Sometimes home laundering and automatic drying are suggested for down. Duvets should be encased in envelope-style covers to minimize the need for cleaning. These covers are called **duvet covers** or **sheet casings.** They may be closed with zippers, buttons, snaps, or ties.

Dust Ruffles, Canopies, and Decorative Pillows

Dust ruffles, canopies, and decorative pillows are aesthetic, not functional, additions to the bed. They usually match or complement the bedspread, comforter, or quilt.

Dust Ruffles

Dust ruffles are used with comforters and quilts to hide the space between the edge of the quilt or comforter and the floor. Styles of dust ruffles vary with the style of the comforter or quilt. They may be gathered (see Figure 11.12), pleated, or plain. Some are especially decorative with lace, embroidery, or eyelet. Most bedspreads fall completely to the floor and do not need a dust ruffle.

The construction of dust ruffles is similar to that of bedspreads. Similar fibers, yarns, and fabrics can be used. Because the fabric needs to be quite flexible, it is usually not heavy or stiff. The drop fabric is stitched to a lightweight basic fabric that lies between the mattress and the box spring. All stitching should be firm and even.

Dust ruffles are coordinated with comforters and quilts, and frequently they are sold together or included as components in a bed-in-a-bag ensemble.

Dust ruffles that can be machine washed and dried are preferable. The consumer should read and follow the manufacturer's care label.

Canopies

A **canopy** is a frame that is attached to a four-poster bed and to the fabric that is draped over the frame. Frames may be flat or arched with six to seven foot posts as shown in Figure 11.13. Modern canopies are adaptations of the heavy drapes that were traditionally used for warmth. Canopy-like structures are also used in the tropics to support mosquito netting. The fabric for canopies is selected to match or complement the other decorative elements in the room. Lace and eyelet canopies are popular. The construction, selection, and care criteria are the same as for dust ruffles.

Decorative Pillows

Decorative pillows, also called **throw pillows,** are frequently used to add more beauty to the bed. They are usually placed at the head of the bed near the bed (or sleeping) pillows.

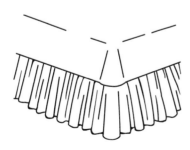

FIGURE 11.12 *Dust ruffle.*

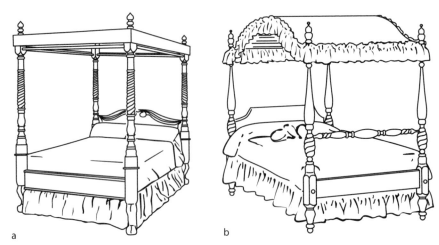

FIGURE 11.13
a. *Flat canopy without fabric,*
b. *arched canopy.*

Styles Decorative pillows are available in a wide variety of shapes and sizes. They may be round, square, or cylindrical. Table 11.4 summarizes the shapes and sizes of selected decorative pillows.

A unique pillow that does not fit into any category is the **bed rest,** sometimes called a "husband." This pillow has a back and arms. This pillow was introduced in the 1980s and is still popular. It is available in many colors and fabrics. The bed rest reflects a trend toward functional decorative pillows (see Industry Statement 11.1).

Decorative pillows may be made of nearly any fiber, yarn or fabric. They are frequently trimmed with lace, eyelet, or embroidery, and they may be painted, quilted, ruffled, smocked, or otherwise embellished. Because of their decorative nature and the manufacturer's assumption that they are not used regularly, they can be quite fragile. They are often selected solely for their aesthetics, and this fact is reflected in the construction. Nevertheless, all stitching should be neat, even, and sturdy. Decorative pillows may be filled with any of the materials used in traditional bed pillows (see Chapter 10 "Bedding"). Care is frequently not an issue because pillows may be strictly aesthetic, but those that are going to be used should have specific care labels. Pillows that are machine washable and dryable are recommended.

TOWELS AND OTHER BATHROOM TEXTILE PRODUCTS

As with textile products used in the bedroom, consumers have a range of choices for beautiful and functional textile products in the bathroom. Towels, shower curtains, and bath mats are both attractive and serviceable. Complete bathroom ensembles are sold together and sometimes coordinate with the bedroom décor.

Towels

The primary function of towels is to absorb moisture. They also provide beautiful accents in the bathroom.

INDUSTRY STATEMENT 11.1

In Decorative Pillows, Function's in Fashion

ATLANTA–Decorative pillows are bigger and bolder than ever. New shapes, sizes and constructions are going beyond fashion to broaden the category's functionality and flexibility. Certainly funky forms are fun.

But an infinite assortment of wedges, rolls, balls and cubes also provide more specific support for the neck, back, feet and knees than the standard decorative pillow does.

Unique constructions are also expanding marketing opportunities by filling niches in the marketplace, crossing distribution channels, attracting new consumers and raising price points.

Casual lifestyles and younger consumers have turned pillows-as-furniture into a growth category. Sure Fit, the leading U.S. manufacturer of slipcovers, has introduced Slouch Furniture, a collection of cubes, rounds and a kid's chair designed from a group of pillows. Hudson Industries, a manufacturer of foam basic bedding and also the largest maker of bean-bag chairs in the country, has introduced a collection of hassocks filled with expanded polystyrene beads.

Louisville Bedding also combined its decorative and basic bedding capacities last market, adding a decorative foam cube into its Back to Campus basics line. And Ex-Cell Home Fashions continues to build its Stackables collection of floor cushions, neckrolls, cubes and bedrests with more fabric choices and price points.

Biederlack of America is expanding its newly launched TimLin Hill pillow collection with sizes and constructions customized for specific retailers, and adding bean bags, body pillows and bed rests to match the most popular Nick and Nora bedding lines.

The new styles often command double or triple the price of standard decorative pillows, and offer opportunities to expand into new retail channels.

Hollander Home Fashions' juvenile line, including Todd Parr's Silly City characters and mascot pillows shaped like T-shirts and caps, can be merchandised as toys, sports team souvenirs and travel pillows.

C&F Enterprises' game board pillows appeal to antique dealers and collectors. Brentwood's new travel cushion with a handle is a natural for catalogs and specialty stores. Newport has expanded both its floor cushion category and potential furniture store sales with a box-shaped, buttoned style that looks like upholstery.

Even the "husband," that chunky bedrest with arms introduced about 20 years ago by Brentwood, has been reinvented. Brentwood's own contemporary version has flat seams, a handle and optional pocket on the arm. It comes in fashionable master bedroom fabrics and in a child's size.

Ex-Cell's sporty nylon version in neon colors includes zippered and mesh pockets, with a definite focus on Gen X and Y.

Source: HFN, October 23, 2000, p. 34. Courtesy of Fairchild Publications, Inc.

TABLE 11.4

Selected Decorative Pillow Shapes and Sizes

Shape	Size
Square	
Common	10″ square and 12″ square
European	26″ square
Turkish (has gathered corners)	16″ square
Round	
Common	12″
Cylindrical	
Bolster	40″ to 50″ long
Neckroll	6″ by 14″, sometimes larger
Boudoir (also called breakfast pillow)	12″ × 16″

Styles

Towels are available in an assortment of sizes that are designated for different uses. See Table 11.5 for a summary of the names and sizes of towels. They are typically made from terry cloth and may be called **terry towels** or **Turkish towels. Velour towels** are also popular.

Construction

The predominant fiber in towels is cotton because it is soft and absorbent. The spun yarns used for the base, or ground fabric, are usually tightly twisted for durability. The yarns for the pile are less tightly twisted for absorption.

Terry cloth is created on slack-tension looms. Some warp yarns are held at regular tension, while others are held at slack-tension (very loosely) on the loom. During weaving the loosely held yarns create the pile. The regular-tension yarns create the base, or ground, fabric (see Figure 11.14). After weaving, the loops may be cut or sheared, to create velour towels.

The sides and ends of towels may be finished with narrow machine-stitched hems, or sometimes they are serged (overlocked). The ends may also be fringed. Towels may be embellished with woven-in borders, decorative embroidery, or sewn-on bands of trim or appliqués. Some are monogrammed.

Selection

The primary factors to consider when selecting towels are absorbency and durability. Cotton fibers are very absorbent and carry moisture away. Tightly twisted yarns in the ground fabric provide strength, and softly twisted yarns in the pile contribute to good absorbency. Tightly twisted yarns do not absorb as well as softly twisted ones, but tightly twisted yarns are stronger.

TABLE 11.5

Summary of the Names and Sizes of Towels

Style	Size
Bath sheet	36″ × 68″
Bath towel	22″ × 42″
Hand towel or face towel	16″ × 26″
Fingertip or guest towel	11″ × 18″
Washcloth or face cloth	12″ × 12″
Baby bath towel	36″ × 36″, usually a knit terry cloth
Beach towels	46″ by 64″

These measurements are approximate. Each manufacturer sizes differently. Some manufacturers offer products that are significantly larger or smaller.

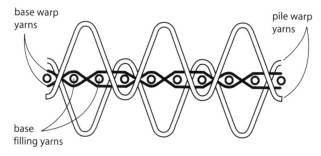

base warp yarns

pile warp yarns

base filling yarns

FIGURE 11.14
Slack-tension weaving.

A denser pile (more loops per inch) and a more compact ground increase resistance to wear. A balanced weave is more durable than an unbalanced weave. Velour towels are not as absorbent as terry towels but are soft with luxurious hand. Hems should be narrow and stitched with small, even stitches. If there are selvages, they should be even and firm. Towels should be examined to make sure they are cut and sewn on-grain.

Care

Towels should be machine washed and dried according to the manufacturers' care instructions. Tumble drying increases absorbency and softness. Usually warm water is recommended for washing. Only minimal bleaching of white towels is recommended because it damages the fiber. Dark-colored towels should be washed separately to avoid bleeding and staining. New towels should be washed alone during the first few cleanings because they may produce excess lint. Overuse of laundry fabric softeners can cause build-up and reduce absorbency. Care should be taken that towels are not exposed to rough surfaces that may snag the pile or cause premature wear.

Shower Curtains

In the early 1950s consumers were introduced to the use of colors and patterns in the bathroom. Since that time shower curtains that match or coordinate with towels and other bathroom accessories have been popular with consumers.

Styles and Construction

Polymer film, vinyl, and fabrics are used to make shower curtains. Sizes range from 68 inches by 68 inches to 72 inches square. Polymer-film curtains are available in several gauges, or thicknesses, and can range from completely clear to opaque. Almost any fabric, except one that is very stiff or heavy, can be used for a shower curtain. If the fabric is not waterproof, a vinyl liner is placed behind the curtain to protect it. The curtain is hung from the shower rod with decorative hooks.

Selection and Care

Fabric shower curtains should be on-grain and have even hems. The stitching should be tight and even. The design should match if the fabric is pieced. Better-quality polymer-film shower curtains are thicker. The grommets (metal eyelets) used to hang the curtain from the hooks should be securely attached and rustproof. Fabric shower curtains should be machine washable and dryable.

Bathroom Rugs and Mats

Bathroom rugs and mats are lightweight soft floor coverings used on bathroom floors. They are available in beautiful colors and patterns (see Figure 11.15). Because rugs and mats are floor coverings, they are subject to federal flammability regulations for small carpets and rugs.

Styles

Bath mats are small and absorbent. They are used primarily to absorb moisture from sinks, tubs, and showers. Bath rugs are larger and are not necessarily designed to absorb moisture. Both mats and rugs provide insulation from bare floors and may have slip-resistant backings.

Construction

Bathroom rugs can be made from nylon, acrylic, or other synthetic fibers. They are usually cut from a length of tufted fabric or pile knit. (The tufting process is described in Chapter 2). The edges are bound, hemmed, or otherwise finished. The pile of a bathroom rug is much less dense than that of a tufted rug used elsewhere in the home. The pile is usually 1/2 inch to 3 inches long. An embossed slip-resistant backing holds the tufts in place. Bath mats are usually made from cotton because of its absorbency. They are usually warp-pile weave fabrics, and can be woven to size and hemmed or otherwise finished at the ends. Sometimes they are cut from a larger piece of fabric, and all the edges are hemmed or otherwise finished.

Selection

Mats that are woven to size are generally more expensive than those that are hemmed on all sides. Both mats and rugs are designed for machine laundering at home. They are relatively lightweight with a pile that is less dense than carpeting or rugs used elsewhere in the home.

Care

Bath mats and rugs should be washed separately the first time to avoid getting lint on other fabrics. Dark colors should always be washed separately. Machine drying is usually acceptable, but all manufacturers' instructions should be followed carefully.

FIGURE 11.15
Bathroom rugs and mats.
Courtesy of Fairchild Publications, Inc.

TABLE LINENS

Whether it's a casual Saturday night supper or a formal holiday dinner, tablecloths, place mats, table runners, and napkins make the dining experience more enjoyable. Other items included in the category of table linens include:

- **Mats** or **pads** Used to protect table surfaces from heat. May be any size or shape but frequently are approximately 12 inches by 12 inches.
- **Scarves** Used on the top of dressers and cabinets; may be any shape and are frequently sized to fit.
- **Coaster** Small squares used under glasses to protect tabletops from moisture.
- **Doilies** Small decorative covering, frequently lace.

These items are available at all prices and qualities and in a wide selection of colors and patterns. Tablecloths and napkins are emphasized in the discussion here, but the content applies to all table linens.

Tablecloths and Napkins

Napery is an industry term sometimes used to refer to tablecloths and napkins. Tablecloths come in different styles, fabrics, and colors. They can be woven fabrics with prints and plaids, have metallic threads, or other decorations. **Damask** is the traditional fabric for a formal tablecloth.

Beautiful lace and lace-trimmed cloths are also appropriate for formal occasions. Plastic and paper tablecloths are used for very casual events. Napkins, both paper and fabric, are available to match or coordinate with tablecloths.

Fabric tablecloths must conform to the trade regulation rule relating to the Deceptive Advertising and Labeling as to Size of Tablecloths and Related Products. This rule requires that all tablecloths be conspicuously labeled with the **cut size.** Cut size refers to the dimensions of the product after hemming and/or trimming.

Styles

Tablecloths and table runners are available in a variety of sizes and styles to suit the table and the occasion. Sizes of common tablecloths and runners are summarized in Table 11.6. The drop, or distance the cloth hangs down, is generally 10 to 12 inches. Longer drops are reserved for more formal occasions.

It is customary to use a table pad or a **silencer** between the tablecloth and the tabletop. The table pad provides protection from hot dishes, spills, and dampness as well as softens the impact and dulls the sound of tableware. A silencer is a thick flannel-like heavily napped fabric. The silencer will also soften the impact and dull the sound of tableware but does not protect the surface from moisture. Flannel-backed vinyl is sometimes used as a temporary table pad. This inexpensive alternative is often quilted.

TABLE 11.6
Summary of Tablecloth and Runner Sizes

Table Size	Tablecloth Size
Rectangular	
32″ × 47″	52″ × 67″
40″ × 60″	60″ × 80″
47″ × 70″	67″ × 104″
47″ × 84″	67″ × 104″
47″ × 104″	67″ × 124″
Oval	
40″ × 60″	60″ × 80″
47″ × 70″	67″ × 90″
47″ × 84″	67″ × 104″
47″ × 104″	67″ × 124″
Round	
44″ (diameter)	67″ (diameter)
Table runner	usually 12″ wide with a drop of 5″ to 10″

Note: These measurements are approximate. Sizes may vary.

Types and sizes of napkins are summarized in Table 11.7. Napkin fabrics are similar to tablecloths, and for formal occasions, napkins generally match the tablecloth.

Construction

Fibers The predominant fibers used in tablecloths are cotton, rayon, and polyester. The high cost of linen makes it appropriate for expensive tablecloth and napkin sets. Rayon and polyester blends are frequently used to create linen-like cloths that are serviceable and beautiful. Most yarns for table linens are spun.

Fabrics Damask may be made from a variety of fibers including linen, cotton, rayon, and synthetic fibers (see Figure 11.16). It is an intricate weave with a filling satin ground and a warp satin pattern. Long floats (yarns that "float" over four or more yarns) create the pattern. A float may be as long as 20 threads. The twill weave is sometimes used for the design, and the ground is a satin weave. Another option is that the background may be plain or twill weave with a satin-weave design. Damask tablecloths are beautiful but may not be durable. The long floats create a lustrous design but are subject to wear and snagging. **Utility damasks** that have shorter floats, up to four threads, are less lustrous but more durable. Utility damasks are sometimes called **single damasks.**

Most lace tablecloths are made from cotton or cotton/polyester blends, and are raschel knits or machine-made Nottingham lace. **Nottingham lace** usually has a large design and fairly rough texture. Venetian lace and Battenberg lace are also popular. **Venetian lace** is needlepoint lace. The pattern is embroidered over base threads. **Battenberg lace** has a design outlined with tape. Linen-lace tablecloths are also available; they are very expensive.

Other fabric structures for tablecloths include the following:

- Hand-crocheted tablecloths are heirlooms (see Figure 11.17). This traditional craft is also used to make table runners, doilies, and place mats.
- **Momie weave** tablecloths are frequently used in institutional settings. Momie weaves are a special class of weaves that have a grainy surface.
- Stitch-bonded fabrics are a low-cost alternative to traditional wovens. See Chapter 2 for more discussion of stitch-bonded fabrics.

TABLE 11.7
Summary of Napkin Sizes

Name of Napkin	Size
Cocktail napkins	5″ to 7″ square
Dinner napkins	18″ to 22″ square

Note: These measurements are approximate. Sizes may vary.

FIGURE 11.16
Damask.

FIGURE 11.17
Hand-crocheted tablecloth.

- Polymer film tablecloths are commonly called plastic tablecloths and are especially appropriate for casual events. They may be embossed or printed with a design. Polymer films that are supported by wovens or knits are more durable; they are commonly called flannel-backed tablecloths.
- Spun-bonded nonwovens are used as very low-cost disposable tablecloths; they are frequently printed with a design.
- Paper is the traditional low-cost disposable alternative to fabric. Paper tablecloths that are lined with lightweight polymer films provide protection from spills. They are frequently embossed or printed with a design.

Finishes Finishes commonly used on fabric tablecloths include durable press, soil release, and soil resistant.

- Durable-press resins result in a cloth that requires little or no ironing. The appearance is acceptable after machine washing and drying.
- Soil-release finishes make it easier to clean the tablecloth after use. These finishes are especially important on fabrics treated with durable-press resins and also on 100 percent polyester or polyester-blend cloths. Soil-release finishes make the fabric more absorbent

and improve the cleaning action of the water and detergent. Durable-press finishes make the fabric less absorbent. Polyester has a tendency to hold oil-based stains. **Visa®** is a well-known soil-release finish.

■ Soil-resistant finishes prevent soil from being absorbed by the fabric.

Edges and Embellishments The edges of fabric tablecloths and napkins can be finished in a variety of ways:

■ *Traditional hem* Edges should be even; stitching should be close and even.
■ *Overcast or overlocked with matching or contrasting thread* Too narrow an overlocked edge may pull out.
■ *Fringe* A self-fringe edge should be reinforced with zigzag stitching.
■ *Binding* Bias binding is durable but must be neatly done.
■ *Decorative trim* Trim should be securely attached.

Some tablecloths are embroidered or appliquéd with designs. **Hardanger,** a drawn-thread technique, is a traditional handicraft in which threads are removed from the fabric (see Figure 11.18).

Selection

The selection of tablecloth and napkins should match the circumstances of use. A paper tablecloth and napkins are very appropriate for a casual outdoor buffet. A formal sit-down dinner would require a damask tablecloth and matching napkins.

Paper and nonwoven tablecloths and napkins should be evenly and neatly cut. Patterns should be straight and, when necessary, the patterns should match.

The qualities to look for in fabric tablecloths and napkins are:

■ Smooth, even yarns.
■ Balanced weave.

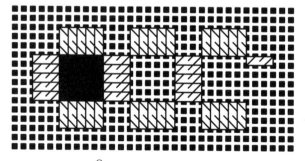

FIGURE 11.18 *Simple hardanger.*

- Closeness of weave or thread count (Better-quality tablecloths will have a thread count of 80 yarns per square inch, moderate quality 64 yarns per square inch, and low grades 55 yarns per square inch. Damask should be very tightly woven. Damask tablecloths should have a thread count around 180 yarns per square inch. Utility damasks will be lower.)
- Even hems with tight, even stitching.
- Tight, even stitching on decorative trims and appliqués.
- Soil-release, soil-resistant finishes, and durable-press finishes. (Synthetic fibers do not need a durable-press finish. Soil-release finishes are especially important for polyester because polyester holds oily stains.)

Care

Care for paper, most nonwoven, and polymer-film (plastic) tablecloths is not an issue since they are considered disposable. Film and supported-film (flannel-backed plastic) tablecloths may be wiped with a damp cloth for easy cleaning. They should be fully dry before storing.

Manufacturers' care instructions should be followed for all fabric tablecloths. Durable-press, soil-release, and soil-resistant finishes will make most tablecloths and napkins easy care. Oil-based stains (gravy, salad dressings, etc.) should be pretreated before washing.

Tablecloths made from stiff fibers, such as linen or ramie, should not be folded for storage because they have a tendency to wear where they are bent. They should be rolled or stored flat. If folding is necessary, they should be refolded occasionally so crease positions are shifted.

Heirloom-quality linen tablecloths should be carefully washed. They may need professional pressing to remove wrinkles. Handcrafted, crocheted, embroidered, and appliquéd tablecloths require very delicate home or professional care.

Place Mats

For many occasions, especially casual dining, place mats are preferred over tablecloths (see Figure 11.19).

Styles

Place mats are typically rectangular, round, or oval. Sometimes they are whimsical shapes, such as seashells, or other fanciful shapes especially for children. Rectangular place mats are typically 12 inches by 18 inches.

Construction

Place mats are available in the same materials as tablecloths. Other common materials are laminated polymer films and minor cellulosic fibers, such as raffia and sisal. Raffia and sisal are rather stiff fibers that are woven into rich textures and interesting patterns for place mats and hot pads (used to protect the table from heat.)

FIGURE 11.19 *Place mats are used for informal table settings.*

Selection and Care

The selection and care of place mats is the same as for tablecloths. Laminated polymer films, raffia, and sisal are simply wiped with a damp cloth. They must be completely dry before storing.

SLIPCOVERS

Slipcovers are temporary fabric covers for upholstered furniture. They may be used to protect, or sometimes hide, the upholstery already on the furniture or to create a new atmosphere for the room.

Styles

There are two basic styles of slipcovers—custom-made and ready-made. Custom-made slipcovers are available in a wide variety of fabrics to suit any décor. They are labor intensive and costly. Often the cost is prohibitive, making reupholstering or purchase of new furniture reasonable alternatives. Ready-made slipcovers are usually reasonably priced. Innovations in ready-made slipcovers, such as easy-to-fit styles, one-piece elasticized construction, and innovative fabrics, are discussed in Industry Statement 11.2. Very low-cost knit readymade slipcovers are available, but they may not fit well, and the knit structure is not durable.

Construction

The construction of custom-made slipcovers is very similar to that of upholstery except that all components can be removed from the piece of furniture (see Chapter 9 for discussion of

---

INDUSTRY STATEMENT 11.2

Sure Fit Updates Slipcovers

Manufacturer Promotes a New Fashionable Coverup

ALLENTOWN, PA.—Slipcovers need a new image—and they're getting one from Sure Fit Inc., the largest U.S. manufacturer of ready-made furniture covers, which accounts for 85 percent of the category's market share. "Our vice president of sales calls us the Rodney Dangerfield of home furnishings," said Bert Shlensky, the company's president. "Most people still think of the old plastic variety of slipcovers. But we've dramatically changed the product and the fabrication."

Dramatic change has been the mantra of Sure Fit, which began manufacturing slipcovers, apparel and other home products in 1914. After a leveraged buyout in 1990, Shlensky came on board and turned the company around. He discontinued all products except slipcovers; developed a patented, easy-to-fit style; and introduced high-fashion fabrics to the category. He also upgraded the manufacturing facility to state-of-the-art production equipment and instituted an aggressive vendor-management strategy, partnering with vendors to merchandise its product.

Along the way, a look called "shabby chic" appeared in home decor, the slipcover market exploded, and about 20 other manufacturers got into—and then out of—the business. Sure Fit was bought out in 1995 by Fieldcrest Cannon Corp. In 1998, after Pillowtex Corp. bought Fieldcrest Cannon, Sure Fit bought itself back, with money secured by 16 of its managers.

Today, there are only a handful of competitors in the category. While the slipcover market has been growing at a rate of 20 percent annually since 1991—and Sure Fit's own sales increased 40 percent last year—Shlensky sees major untapped potential. The company's research shows that about 30 percent of America's 100 million households redecorate each year, but only 20 percent are even slightly aware of slipcovers, and only 1.5 percent purchased the product in 1999.

"The market right now is about $220 [million] to $250 million at retail, and we sell about one and a half percent of households," said Shlensky. "We're confident we can sell 4 to 5 percent of households and raise the market to $800 million to $1 billion."

In order to change the public's perception of slipcovers, Sure Fit is budgeting approximately $8 million this year on marketing, including $5 million on an aggressive consumer awareness and advertising program that will be seen in home decorating magazines and HGTV programs.

The company is focusing on slipcovers as fashion and appealing to the category's buyer profile: 25- to 54-year-old buyers who are as often single as married and have an income over $50,000. It also caters to Gen-Xers, who want frequent and instant change at a reasonable price.

Products include a one-piece elasticized construction in covers for sofas, wing-back chairs and ottomans. There are also dining room chair covers, table rounds and squares—even a chair cover that includes a pocket for the TV remote control. Prices range from $25 for a dining room chair cover to $200 for a sofa cover.

The use of innovative fabrics, including denim, khaki and matelasse, is a key factor in the resurgence of slipcovers, said Joel Mintz, vice president of merchandising at Domestications, which has seen double-digit growth in the category over the past several years.

Marketed under Fieldcrest, Cannon, a private label and its own brand, Sure Fit slipcovers sell in approximately 5,000 stores across all retail channels. Sales are almost evenly distributed, with 33 percent at specialty and department stores, 34 percent at mass retailers, and the remainder through catalogs, the Internet, and QVC and HSN home shopping channels. The roster includes Strouds, Bed Bath & Beyond, Linens 'n Things, Homeplace, Stern's, the May Co., Bradlees, Ames, Wal-Mart, Target, Domestications and Linen Source.

Sure Fit's vendor management strategy is a partnership effort. A sales and marketing staff of 23 people includes a product team that develops product and works with buyers on individual assortments, an account management team that forecasts and plans retailers' needs, and a marketing team that handles advertising and in-store promotions. Six merchandisers go to stores and work with retailers on fixturing, signage and promotions.

A prime example of Sure Fit's innovative retail cooperation is its focus on special events, such as one in partnership with *People* magazine at Bed Bath & Beyond in New York on June 17. Sure Fit will launch its largest in-store slipcover boutique—a 52-square-foot space that will include major signage, slipcovered mini-chairs and floor-to-ceiling slipcovers. "It's the ultimate display," said Sarah Falcinelli, marketing and merchandising manager at the company.

Source: HFN, May 15, 2000, p. 35. Courtesy of Fairchild Publications, Inc.

upholstery). Usually slipcover fabric is lighter in weight than upholstery fabric. Woven ready-made slipcovers are available in approximate sizes. Elasticized seams provide for flexible fitting, and the customer does final fitting at home. Knit slipcovers are made in a raschel knit. The stretch of the knit provides flexible fitting, but wrinkles and stretching of the fabric may be apparent.

Selection

The selection of fabrics for slipcovers in most instances parallels that of upholstery. Woven slipcovers are more durable than knit slipcovers. Aesthetics plays a major role because the customer wants to match or coordinate the slipcover with the rest of the room. Frequently, slipcovers are selected to coordinate with the seasons of the year. Because most customers will want to clean slipcovers at home, it is advisable to select machine washable and dryable fabrics. Soil-resistant and soil-release finishes are also important.

Care

Manufacturers' care instructions should be followed when cleaning slipcovers. Because of their size and bulk, it may be necessary to have them cleaned professionally even if they are washable.

SOFT WINDOW TREATMENTS

Soft window treatments include curtains and draperies. **Curtains** are lightweight window coverings that do not have linings. **Drapes** are heavy opaque window coverings that are usually lined. **Casements** are medium-weight fabrics made from novelty yarns. They have some transparency. They may be lined and hung as drapes or left unlined and hung as curtains. Soft window treatments are made from fabrics and are both functional and decorative.

Functionally, curtains and drapes aid in temperature control and provide privacy, sound absorption, and protection from light and glare. For example:

- Drapes can be lined with thermal insulators that block the cold to keep the room warm. Heavy opaque coverings provide the best insulation. Window treatments with metallic or light-colored backings can block the sun to help keep the room cool.
- Lined drapes provide the most privacy. During the day translucent coverings provide privacy, but at night opaque coverings that can be fully closed are required.
- For maximum sound absorption, window coverings should be made from a closely woven fabric.
- Window coverings can reduce glare while allowing natural light to filter through.

Aesthetically, soft window treatments focus attention indoors and complement other furnishings. Curtains and drapes may be short or long. They will usually be one of four lengths:

■ To the windowsill
■ To the bottom of the apron
■ To the floor
■ Puddled several inches on the floor

Styles

A wide variety of curtains and drapes is available to meet individual preferences and tastes. Specific hardware is required for the installation of soft window treatments. Table 11.8 summarizes selected hardware for soft window treatments.

The **heading** of draperies or curtains is how the fabric is arranged at the top of the fabric, which determines how the fabric will fall. Types of headings include gathering, shirring, scallops, loops, and pleats (see Figure 11.20).

Valances are decorative treatments used with drapes or curtains at the top of a window. They may be flat, shirred, pleated, ballooned, or otherwise decorated (see Figure 11.21).

TABLE 11.8

Selected Hardware for Soft Window Treatments

Curtain rods, sometimes called stationary rods	Plain, smooth wooden or metal rods used for stationary curtains or draperies.
Café rods	Decorative curtain rods.
Spring-tension rods	Hollow curtain rods with springs inside so the length can be adjusted to fit inside the window casing.
Carriers	Plastic or metal eyelets in a traverse track to hold the drapery hooks.
Hooks	Metal devices that attach draperies to the carriers.
Traverse rods	Rods with pulley mechanisms so the curtain or drape can be opened and closed. Carriers that hold the hooks slide along a traverse track.
Brackets	Devices attached to the window casing or the wall to support the rods.
Weights	Thin, flat pieces of metal inserted into curtains or draperies to provide weight so the fabric hangs well.
Finials	Decorative end pieces.

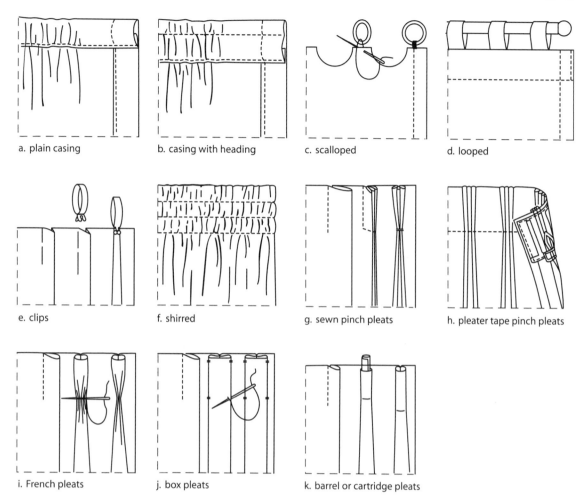

a. plain casing   b. casing with heading   c. scalloped   d. looped

e. clips   f. shirred   g. sewn pinch pleats   h. pleater tape pinch pleats

i. French pleats   j. box pleats   k. barrel or cartridge pleats

FIGURE 11.20
Headings for curtains and draperies.

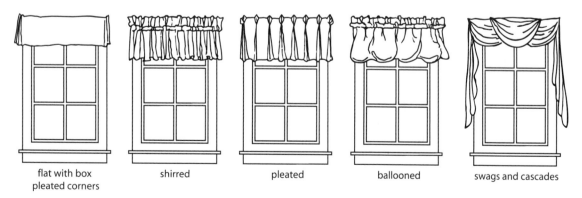

flat with box pleated corners   shirred   pleated   ballooned   swags and cascades

FIGURE 11.21 *Styles of valances.*

Curtain Styles

Curtains may be hung with stationary rods or traverse rods. Some curtains have **tiebacks**—fabric or other items (chain, ring, ribbon, tape, sash) used to hold the curtains back on the sides. Common styles of curtains are illustrated in Figure 11.22. Popular styles include:

- **Café curtains** Double- or triple-tiered, usually windowsill length.
- **Draw curtains** Sheer or opaque, hung on traverse rods.
- **Poufed curtain** Fabric gathered horizontally to create puffs that are held in place with cords, tiebacks, or stitching; also called **bishop's sleeve treatments.**
- **Ruffled curtains** Ruffles on the hem, sides, and sometimes the middle of the curtains. Usually they have a ruffled valance and are tied back, sometimes called **ruffled tiebacks.**
- **Sheers** Curtains made of very lightweight fabric.
- **Shirred curtains** The fabric is gathered directly on rods and hangs straight down; they are not put on traverse rods.
- **Stationary curtains** Sheer curtains used under draperies, also called **under curtains** or **glass curtains.**
- **Stretched curtains** The top and bottom of the curtain are gathered on rods and stretched from top to bottom; used on French doors and windows; also called **sash curtains.**

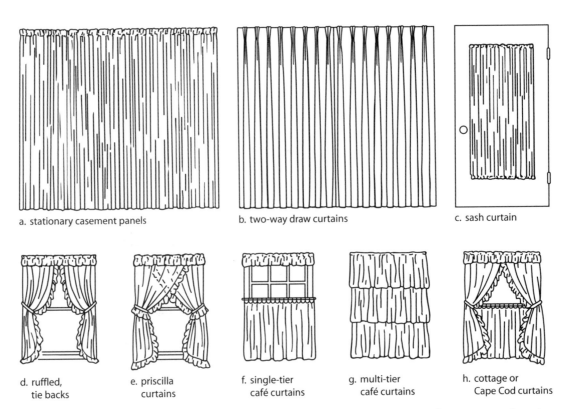

a. stationary casement panels

b. two-way draw curtains

c. sash curtain

d. ruffled, tie backs

e. priscilla curtains

f. single-tier café curtains

g. multi-tier café curtains

h. cottage or Cape Cod curtains

FIGURE 11.22 *Common curtain styles.*

Drapery Styles

Draperies are more complex than curtains. A drape that is combined with a sheer curtain is called an **over drape.** The sheer curtain beneath the over drape is called a glass curtain or an under curtain. Some common styles of drapery are listed below (see Figure 11.23).

- **Decorative drapes** Drapes that do not move. They are hung so they open in the center and are held back on the sides with tiebacks or hardware.
- **Draw draperies** Draperies that can be open and closed. There are two basic styles—two-way draw that opens at the center and pulls back to both sides, and one-way draw that opens on one side only.
- **Cascades** Falls of fabric that hang in graduated lengths on either side of the window.
- **Pavilions** Draperies that are tied back, much like the flaps of a tent.
- **Jabots** Pleated falls of fabric that hang on either side of the window.
- **Swags** Lengths of fabric that are draped at the sides of windows.

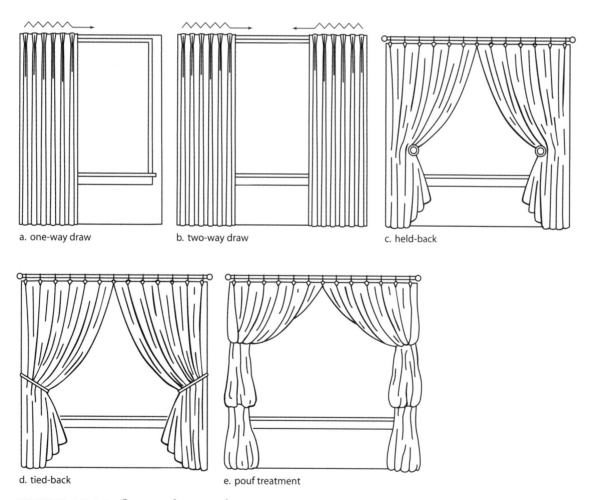

a. one-way draw   b. two-way draw   c. held-back

d. tied-back   e. pouf treatment

FIGURE 11.23 *Common drapery styles.*

Construction

A wide variety of fabrics is used for soft window treatments. Thin fabrics are usually used for curtains, while more opaque ones are usually used for drapes.

Both natural and manufactured fibers are used for curtains. Polyester has the distinct advantage of being durable, resilient, and easy-care. Nylon is also excellent but must be finished with a light-resistant finish to prevent degradation by the sun. Fabrics are created by weaving, knitting, and stitch-through methods. Common fabrics for curtains include ninon (sheer plain weave fabric with every third warp yarn omitted), marquisette (transparent leno-weave fabric), and batiste (translucent, balanced plain-weave fabric). A curtain should have at least a four-inch hem to help it hang evenly.

Drapes are considered more formal than curtains. Popular fabrics for drapes are cretonne, chintz, brocade, velvet, antique satin, damask, and satin. They are made from both natural and manufactured fibers. Silk is very luxurious, while synthetics, such as polyester are easy care and less expensive. Glass fibers are popular choices when adherence to flammability standards is important. Glass fibers are much heavier than other fibers, so additional supports for rods will be needed. Drapery lining is usually plain and less expensive than the face fabric. The lining looks better from the exterior of the house and provides insulation.

Drapes are generally pleated and hung on a rod. The rod may be installed at the ceiling or just above the top of the window frame. All fabric should be cut on-grain to prevent distortion when hanging. Stitching should be straight and even, and all trimmings should be firmly attached.

Selection

Individual preference determines selection of curtains or drapes. Both are available in a wide variety of textures and weights. Curtains are often chosen for kitchens and bathrooms. Drapes are often used in living and dining rooms.

Curtains and drapes may be purchased ready-made, made-to-measure, or custom-made. The necessary measurements are illustrated in Figure 11.24.

- Ready-made curtains and drapes can be purchased in standardized lengths (36, 45, 63, 72, 81, 84, and 90 inches). The customer is responsible for the installation.
- Made-to-measure curtains and drapes are produced based on measurements supplied by the customer. The customer is responsible for the installation.
- Custom-made curtains and drapes are made individually by professionals who also measure and install them.

The width of a curtain or drape is very important. It should be wide enough to fit the window at the top and fall into folds. The weight of the fabric is also important because the ability of a fabric to hang in folds is dependent on its weight. The general guidelines for determining the appropriate width of a curtain are as follows:

- *Lightweight fabrics* Approximately three times the width of the space to be covered
- *Medium-weight fabrics* Two and one half times the width of the space to be covered
- *Heavy-weight fabrics* Two times the width of the space to be covered

After size and aesthetic factors have been addressed, there are two important factors in the selection of soft window treatments. Fabrics that are not colorfast to the sun should be lined to prevent fading. Soft window treatments should be treated to resist soil.

Care

As with any textile product, it is essential to follow manufacturer's care instructions. Most synthetics, cotton, and polyester and cotton blends can be machine washed and dried, although special finishes or decorative effects may require dry cleaning. Most rayon, acetate, damask, satin, velvet, velveteen, and tapestry should be dry-cleaned. Fiberglass can be cleaned by vacuuming. The size and/or weight of some curtains and drapes will necessitate professional cleaning even if they are machine washable and dryable.

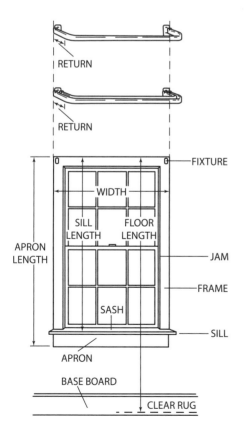

FIGURE 11.24
Measurements for determining sizes of curtains and drapes.

SUMMARY

Bed linens, towels, and other bathroom textile products, table linens, and slipcovers can be purchased in the linen departments of large department stores, discount store chains, and specialty stores as well as catalogs and on the Internet. As a group, they are generally referred to as linens, but they also may be called domestics, home textiles, and interior textiles. Sometimes they are categorized as domestics (sheets, pillowcases, blankets, comforters, quilts, bedspreads, mattress covers and pads) and linens (towels, shower curtains, bathroom rugs and mats, tablecloths, place mats, runners, napkins.) These products are available to the consumer in a variety of prices, qualities, colors, and designs. Consumers match or coordinate linens with upholstery and slipcover fabrics and also with paint, wallpapers, and borders. In recent years apparel designers have expanded their lines to include interior textiles.

Linens that have balanced weaves with higher thread counts are more durable than those with unbalanced weaves and low thread counts. Manufacturers' care labels should be followed carefully. It is usually recommended that linens be machine washable and dryable for easy care.

Soft window treatments include curtains and draperies. They are made from fabrics and are both functional and decorative. Thin fabrics are usually used for curtains, while more opaque ones are usually used for drapes.

Functionally curtains and drapes aid in temperature control and provide privacy, sound absorption, and protection from light and glare. Specific hardware is required for the installation of soft window treatments. Curtains and drapes may be purchased ready-made, made-to-measure, or custom-made. Two important factors in the selection of soft window treatments are colorfastness to sunlight and soil resistance. As with any textile product, it is essential to follow manufacturer's care instructions for soft window treatments.

TERMS FOR REVIEW

afghans	damasks	flat sheet
Battenberg lace	decorative drapes	glass curtains
bed-in-a-bag	doilies	hardanger
bed rest	domestics	heading
bedspread	drapes	home textiles
bishop's sleeve treatments	draw curtains	jabots
café curtains	draw draperies	linens
canopy	drop	momie weave
cascades	dust ruffles	muslin
casements	duvet	napery
coasters	duvet covers	Nottingham lace
comforters	federbett	nylon blanket binding
curtains	fill leakage	over drape
cut size	fitted (contour) sheet	pavilions

percale

pinpoint percale

pinsonic melding

poufed curtains

puff

quilts

ruffled curtains

ruffled tiebacks

sash curtains

scarves

shams

sheers

sheet casings

shirred curtains

silencer

single damasks

slipcovers

stationary curtains

stretched curtains

swags

terry towels

thermal blankets

throw pillows

throws

throw-style bedspread

tiebacks

Turkish towels

under curtains

utility damasks

velour towels

Venetian lace

Visa®

REVIEW QUESTIONS

1. What is a bed-in-a-bag?

2. Why are percale sheets more expensive than muslin sheets?

3. Why is acrylic a popular fiber for blankets?

4. Why is cotton the predominant fiber for towels?

5. List two finishes that are recommended for slipcovers.

6. Describe the difference between curtains and drapes.

LEARNING ACTIVITIES

1. Lay out a terrycloth towel and a velour towel on a waterproof surface. Pour 1/4 cup of water on each. Describe what happens to the water. Which towel is more absorbent? Why are most velour towels terrycloth on the reverse side?

2. Poll class members to determine the style of mattress pad or cover each person uses. Ask class members to describe why they like their choices and make a graph that represents the information gathered. Summarize the data and draw conclusions about the important characteristics in mattress pads.

CHAPTER 12

CARPETS, RUGS, AND FLOORING MATERIALS

At night the princess said good-bye to her father, and set out on the carpet for Aladdin's palace, with his mother at her side, and followed by the hundred slaves. She was charmed at the sight of Aladdin, who ran to receive her.
—from *The Arabian Nights,* Chapter 28, Aladdin and the Wonderful Lamp Lang Edition

IN FAIRY TALES MAGIC CARPETS TAKE CHARACTERS TO EXOTIC PLACES, BUT THE MAGIC OF carpeting and other flooring in the real world lies in their functional and aesthetic properties.

Flooring Materials are divided into three major categories:

- soft floor coverings, such as carpet and rugs
- resilient floors, such as vinyl, cork, and rubber
- hard floors, such as wood, stone, and ceramic

Floor materials are carefully selected for their aesthetics, functional attributes, and maintenance requirements.

SOFT FLOOR COVERINGS

Soft floor coverings are textile products. They are aesthetically pleasing and add textural interest and beauty to a room. They also provide sound and thermal insulation.

Classifications of Soft Floor Coverings

Soft floor coverings are available in four classifications—broadloom, carpet, carpet modules, and rug. The terms *broadloom, carpet,* and *rugs* should not be used interchangeably.

Broadloom

Broadloom is seamless carpeting that is constructed on a wide loom. It is usually used for wall-to-wall carpeting and is generally available in widths up to 18 feet. Broadloom carpet can be cut into rugs. Major brands of broadloom are Bigelow, Karastan, LEES for Living, Mohawk, and Shaw.

Carpet

Carpet is a soft floor covering that is sold by the square yard. It is usually installed as **wall-to-wall carpet** that completely covers the floor. It is secured to the floor with stripping that attaches the underside of the carpet to the floor. It can also be cut and finished to the customer's specification.

Carpet Modules

Carpet modules are also called **carpet squares** or **carpet tiles.** They are usually 12, 18, or 36 inches square. Properly installed carpet modules resemble wall-to-wall carpeting. Some modules have a permanent or releasable adhesive backing that adheres to the floor. Some are heavy and stiff enough to lie smoothly without adhesive.

Rug

A **rug** is a soft floor covering that has finished edges. The edges may be finished with serging or bound with tape. Often a decorative fringe is added to the edge of a rug. Usually a rug covers only a portion of the floor and is not attached to the floor. Rugs may be round, oval, square, rectangular, or irregularly shaped and are usually produced in standard sizes. Larger rugs, called room-sized rugs, are available in the following sizes: $9' \times 12'$, $12' \times 12'$, $12' \times 15'$, $12' \times 18'$ and $12' \times 21'$.

Smaller rugs are available in the following sizes: $5\ 1/2' \times 8\ 1/2'$, $4' \times 6'$, $27'' \times 45''$. Smaller rugs are also called area rugs, scatter rugs, or accent rugs. A runner is an elongated small rug that is frequently used in hallways or on stairs. Runners are normally 27 inches wide and can be cut to specification. Scatter rugs are used for decoration or in heavy traffic areas where soiling is a problem.

Well-known brands of rugs are Beaulieu of America, Burlington, Claire Murray, Couristan, Karastan, Milliken, Mohawk, Oriental Weavers, Shaw Rugs, and Sphinx.

Construction of Soft Floor Coverings

The two main ways to construct soft floor coverings are tufting and weaving. Other machine methods include braiding, flocking, fusion bonding, and needlepunching. Traditional hand-made carpets are also available.

Tufting

Tufted fabrics are commonly used for carpeting because they can be produced quickly and efficiently. Approximately 90 percent of soft floor coverings are produced by tufting. The **pile,** or fibers that project from a backing and act as a wear surface, is created by stitching yarns into a primary backing fabric. Once the pile is stitched into the backing, it can be cut or left as a loop. The dominant fiber for primary backings is olefin. An adhesive coating is applied to the underside of the backing fabric. Synthetic latex is commonly used as the adhesive layer. The secondary backing, or scrim, is rolled onto the adhesive coating. Jute and olefin are commonly used for the secondary backing (see Figure 12.1). Sometimes a foam rubber cushion is applied as a secondary backing. It eliminates the need for a separate cushion. Cushioning is discussed later in this chapter.

Weaving

Woven floor coverings are more expensive than tufted floor coverings. Less than five percent of soft floor coverings are produced by weaving. Most woven carpet is heavy, dimensionally stable (does stretch or shrink), and strong. It does not require a secondary backing as do tufted carpets. There are five main types of woven floor coverings—Axminster, Brussels, chenille, velvet, and Wilton.

- **Axminster** Carpet woven on an Axminster loom. The carpet has a single-level cut pile and is identified by heavy ridges across the back of the carpet. Each tuft is inserted individually (see Figure 12.2a).
- **Brussels** Uncut pile carpet made on a jacquard loom with three sets of warp yarns.
- **Chenille** Chenille yarns used as filling yarns.
- **Velvet** A cut-pile weave created with extra warp or filling yarns to produce the pile (see Figure 12.2b).
- **Wilton** Cut-pile carpet made on a modified Jacquard loom with three sets of warp yarns. Most Wilton carpets are plain with a smooth velvety surface (see Figure 12.2c).

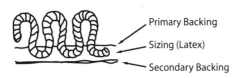

FIGURE 12.1 *Simple carpet construction.*

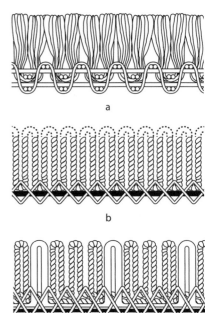

FIGURE 12.2
a. *Axminster construction,*
b. *velvet construction,*
c. *Wilton construction.*

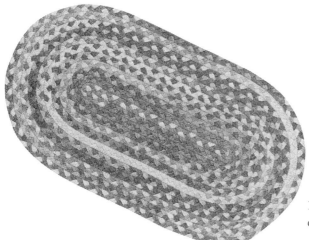

FIGURE I2.3 *Braided rug.*
Courtesy of Fairchild Publications, Inc.

Other Machine Methods

In addition to tufted and woven carpets there are other soft floor coverings. They include:

- **Braided rugs** Three groups of yarns are braided; the braided strands are then assembled side by side in a round or oval shape and stitched together (see Figure 12.3).
- **Flocked carpet** Large quantities of straight nontextured high-denier fibers of uniform length are embedded in an adhesive coating on a substrate. The substrate is frequently heavy-gauge vinyl sheeting.
- **Fusion-bonded carpet** A vinyl-adhesive compound is spread on a backing; the pile yarns are imbedded in the adhesive.
- **Knitted carpet** Pile and backing yarns are integrated in one operation. Needles interlace yarns in a series of connecting loops. Stretching is a problem with knitted carpets.
- **Needlepunched carpet** Barbed needles are repeatedly inserted into a fiber web to tangle the fibers; a scrim may be added for strength and stability. Needlepunched floor coverings are commonly used as indoor-outdoor carpeting (see Figure 12.4).

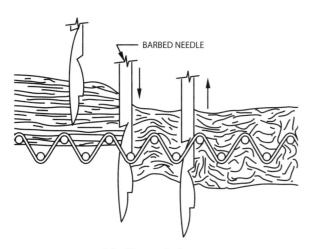

BARBED NEEDLE

FIGURE I2.4 *Needlepunched carpet.*

Handmade Rugs

Handmade rugs are made by weaving, but they are also made by braiding, hooking, and felting (see Figure 12.5). Frequently, these rugs, because of their cost and beauty, are used as wall hangings. Folk artisans, such as those from Kyrgyzstan, create rugs specifically for the American market (see Industry Statement 12.1). The two main categories of handmade rugs are woven-pile rugs and flat rugs.

Hand Woven Pile Rugs

There are three types of hand woven pile rugs—Flokati rugs, Oriental rugs, and rya rugs.

Flokati Rugs Authentic **Flokati** (or **Floccati**) **rugs** are thick shaggy rugs that are hand-woven in Greece. They are made of wool and have a very long pile. After weaving, the rug is immersed in swirling water, causing it to felt. Because these rugs require a lot of wool and labor, they are expensive (see Industry Statement 12.2).

Oriental Rug **Oriental rugs** are characterized by traditional designs that reflect the culture and history of the original weavers. Warp pile tufts are tied in as the base fabric of an Oriental rug is woven. Usually the base yarns are cotton or linen, and the pile yarns are silk or wool. Each pile tuft is hand knotted using either the **Sehna (Senna), or Persian knot,** or the **Ghiordes, or Turkish knot.** The Sehna knot is made by wrapping the tufting yarn around one warp yarn and under the adjacent warp yarn. The tufting yarn in the Ghiordes knot wraps around adjoining warp yarns and extends from between them (see Figure 12.6). The number of knots per square inch determines the quality of an Oriental rug; more knots indicate higher quality. Modern Oriental rugs usually have 100 to 225 knots per square inch, but they may contain over 300.

FIGURE 12.5 *Weaving on a ground loom.*
©Margaret Courtney-Clarke/CORBIS

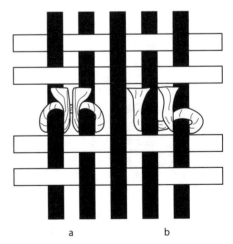

a   b

FIGURE 12.6 *Knots used in hand-woven Oriental rugs:* a. *Ghiordes or Turkish knot,* b. *Sehna (Senna) or Persian knot.*

INDUSTRY STATEMENT 12.1

For Tradition's Sake

Group Helps Artisans Sustain Livelihood by
Showing Them How to Make Their Rugs More Salable

NEW YORK–When a design consultant shows pink and orange color swatches to artisans in Kyrgyzstan, where felt rugs with traditional brown backgrounds have been created for centuries, the artisans laugh, "You Americans are so crazy!"

But after the laughter subsides, the artists in Kyrgyzstan, one of the former Soviet republics, get to work, adapting their products to make them more salable for U.S. and European markets with the help of a non-profit organization called Aid to Artisans.

"The best way to sustain folk art is to sustain folk artisans," said Keith Recker, executive director. "And if that means introducing pink and orange, then we do it. You'd be surprised—they don't mind. It does not diminish the emphasis on traditional products or what they make for themselves. They don't want pink or orange for themselves."

But buyers want these fashion-forward colors, and that is what it's all about. Felt rugs from Kyrgyzstan, called shyrdaks, and for the first time, woven palm mats from Malaysia, known as pandanuf, will be shown at the New York International Gift Fair through Aug. 23 in booths 5012-5024.

Recker, who is a former vice president of merchandising at Gump's by Mail and was the director of home furnishings at Saks, expects buyers from small trendy stores to larger chains like Pier 1 Imports to return to place their orders for floor coverings or other categories the organization promotes.

For 25 years, the non-profit has assisted artisans by sending product designers to give indigenous artists valuable design and marketing advice, provide training to help them create their own business and price the products accordingly. Small grants are also given to help artisans purchase equipment or materials. The organization markets the products by bringing them to international arenas such as the gift show and works with rug importers like AMS Imports to give the artisans greater visibility.

Recker said the artisans appreciate the group's input. "They get it. Most artisans are very up front; they want to sell more product. We make a big emphasis on product development and on linkages. We want to get their product in front of the right buyers."

The felt rugs are made of many layers of pounded felt, with an abstract vine pattern worked into the top layer.

The gift show will feature rugs in trendy color combinations like pink and orange or blue and purple. Consultants had suggested adding a finished edge to give it more value. A 5-by-10 will retail for $750, a 5-by-8 will be listed at $600, a 3-by-4 will be marked $264 and a 2-by-3 will go for $144.

"We're emphasizing consistency, especially in our dye recipe, so we can turn out many rugs that look the same to fill catalog orders," said Recker. The organization has partnered with catalogs like Garnet Hill and Orvis to sell other products in the past.

Filling catalog orders is probably not something the artisans dreamed about. Of the 4.5 million residents of Kyrgyzstan, most are far too poor to buy crafts; the per capita income is $330 a year.

But with the fall of the Soviet Union and the subsequent closing of Soviet-run factories, indigenous crafts are proving to be an alternate source of income and are experiencing what could be called a rebirth. Aid to Artisans organizes workshops to reteach traditional folk arts as a source of economic support.

The situation in Malaysia is strikingly different. In 2000, Malaysia's exports to the world totaled $98.24 billion, an increase of 16 percent as compared with 1999. Higher exports compared to imports resulted in Malaysia enjoying a trade surplus of $16.04 billion.

But residents of the rural areas live far more simply, evident in their production of a woven mat made from cutting strips of palm leaves and weaving them together. The material takes dye well, soaking up color to produce a luminous finish.

As in Kyrgyzstan, design consultants also introduced the weavers to colors fashionable in the United States. The mats being shown at the gift show will feature a plaid-like pattern in three-color combinations, blue-green, pink-red and natural brown. A 3-by-5 will retail for $64 and a 5-by-7 will retail for $134.

The benefit of helping artisans is multifold, said Recker. "They make very disciplined use of the money," he said. In addition to investing in their craft, "they are able to send more of their children to school, [and] obtain medicine, bicycles for transportation and housing materials."

"They do admirable things with the money," he said.

Source: HFN, August 20, 2001, p. 42. Courtesy of Fairchild Publications, Inc.

INDUSTRY STATEMENT 12.2

Don't Get Shagged by Faux Flokatis

According to Webster's Ninth New Collegiate Dictionary, a flokati is a hand-woven Greek woolen rug with a thick shaggy pile.

In Greece, a rug must meet certain specifications, established in 1966 and still enforced to be exported as flokatis:

■ The flokati rug must be handwoven.
■ It must be made in Greece. If it's made elsewhere, it's not a flokati.

■ A true flokati is 100 percent wool, including the warp, weft and pile.
■ Its total weight must be at least 1,800 grams of wool per square meter.
■ The flokati must be subjected to the water friction process for the pile to unravel and fluff out.

Flokatis that don't make the cut are called "Flocos." Flocos weigh less than flokatis and may have a polypropylene warp and weft.

Source: HFN, January 1, 2001, p. 28. Courtesy of Fairchild Publications, Inc.

Antique Oriental rugs are over 100 years old and prized for their beauty and scarcity. They were dyed with natural dyes and usually have more knots per square inch than modern Oriental rugs. A semiantique Oriental rug is over 50 years old.

There are six major styles of Oriental rugs—Caucasian, Chinese, Indian, Persian, Turkish, and Turkoman. The names reflect the city or area where they were first produced.

Caucasian rugs Caucasian Oriental rugs were originally made in central Asia. The patterns are crowded with strong geometric designs. They are usually combinations of red, blue, and yellow. These rugs are usually smaller in size than Turkish rugs. Examples of Caucasian rugs include Shirvan, Kazak, Kabistan, and Karaja.

Chinese rugs Most Chinese Oriental rugs have motifs, such as trees, animals, dragons, and clouds. The colors are usually soft and muted. Frequently they have tan or blue designs and circles that contain dragons or flowers. Chinese rugs are often sculpted. The pile is carved or cut back to give dimension to the motifs.

Indian rugs Rugs made in India are usually of Persian design. They frequently have floral, vine-like designs, or "tree of life" designs. High-quality rugs in the style of Aubusson and Savonnerie are also produced in India. Aubusson rugs have a fine loop pile. Savonnerie rugs have classic designs and muted pastel colors. Both styles frequently have carved piles.

Persian rugs There are many different types of Persian rugs, including Hamadan, Heriz, Isfahan, Kashan, Kirman, Kurdistan, Sarabend, Sarouk (Saruks), and Tabriz (see Figure 12.7). The names reflect the towns where they were originally produced. Persian rugs are famous for elegant all-over designs, soft colors, and high density of knots. Frequently the designs are floral patterns or may have animal or human figures represented.

Turkish rugs Turkish rugs have designs that are similar to Caucasian and Turkoman rugs. Usually Turkish rugs have a longer pile and a coarser construction. Geometric designs are common. Brilliantly colored Turkish prayer rugs are famous. Examples of Turkish rugs include Koula, Ladik, Bergoma, Milas, and Ghiordes.

Turkoman rugs Turkoman (or Turkmen) rugs are made in central Asia. They are usually red or red/brown with green and white and have bold geometric designs or medallion-like designs. Examples of Turkoman rugs include the Afghan, Beshir, Bokhara, Kirman, Sarouk, and Samarkand (see Figure 12.7).

Machine-made Oriental design rugs are woven on Axminster looms. Sometimes machine-made Oriental rugs are called **American Oriental rugs.** They are usually high quality, but they must be labeled as "Oriental-design" or "Oriental-style." The back of a handmade Oriental rug is rougher than that of a machine-made rug. The fringe of a handmade Oriental formed by the warp yarns will be an integral part of the rug itself. The fringe of machine-made rugs is added after the rug is woven. Handmade Oriental rugs should only be purchased from a reputable dealer.

Rya Rugs Originally **rya rugs** were made by hand in Scandinavian countries. Weavers use the Ghiordes knot to create a pile that is one to three inches long. The pile yarns are usually wool. The traditional designs for a rya rug are gently curving patterns of related colors.

  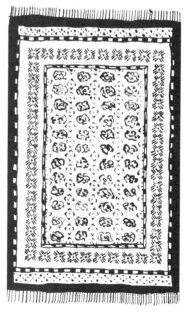

a   b   c

FIGURE 12.7   a. *Kirman rug,* b. *Sarouk rug,* c. *Bokhara rug.*

Hand Woven Flat Rugs

Most hand woven flat rugs are plain, twill, or jacquard weaves. The designs reflect the culture and history of the weavers. Examples of hand-woven flat rugs include Dhurrie rugs, Kelim rugs, and rugs made by Native Americans.

Dhurrie Rugs **Dhurrie (durrie, dhurry, durry) rugs** are handmade in India. They usually have striped designs and are made entirely from cotton. The filling yarns are hand spun. Older dhurries have bold geometric designs in bold colors. Modern dhurries are available in pastel colors.

Kelim Rugs **Kelim (khilim or kilim)** rugs are tapestry-woven rugs made in eastern European countries. Because one color is woven in at a time, slits may occur where the colors change (see Figure 12.8). Sometimes the slits are sewn closed. All the ends of the filling yarns are woven in so kelims are reversible. There are two types of kelims—Kurdish and Afghan. The Kurdish kelim is brightly colored; frequently embroidery is added. Afghan kelim rugs are generally thicker with less pattern than the Kurdish kelim. Colors tend to be less intense with more rust magenta, yellow, brown, and blue.

Native American Rugs Most **Native American rugs** are made by the Navajo, Cheyenne, or Hopi tribes. Sometimes they are referred to as **Navajo rugs.** These tapestry-woven rugs are primarily made in Arizona and New Mexico. The ends of the filling yarns are woven in so the rugs are reversible. To avoid slits, the weavers dovetail or interlock the filling yarns when the colors change (see Figure 12.9). The designs are usually bold graphic symbols that represent tribal life (see Figure 12.10). Authentic Native American rugs should display the Certificate of Genuineness issued by the Indian Arts and Crafts Board of the U.S. Department of the Interior.

Styles of Tufted Floor Coverings

Diagrams of common tufted carpet styles are presented in Figure 12.11, and Industry Statement 12.3 describes current popular styles. The relative density, height, and amount of twist are summarized in Table 12.1.

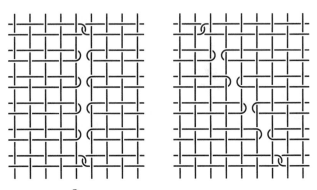

FIGURE 12.8 *Slits formed by color changes in Kelim rugs.*

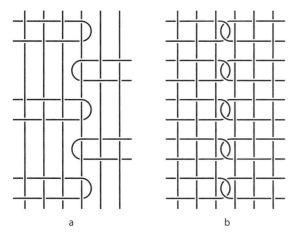

FIGURE 12.9
a. *Dovetailing filling yarns,* b. *interlocking filling yarns.*

FIGURE 12.10 *Navajo rugs.* Courtesy of Fairchild Publications, Inc.

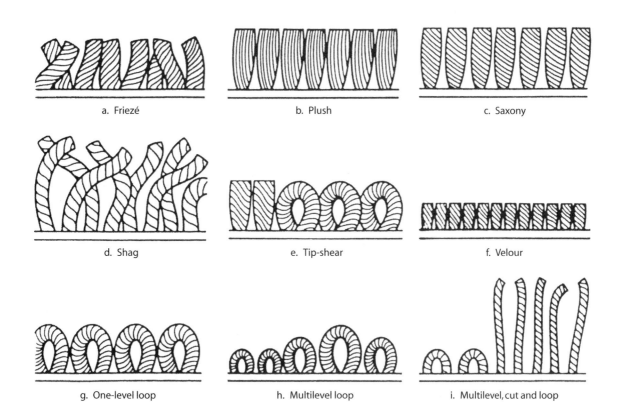

a. Friezé

b. Plush

c. Saxony

d. Shag

e. Tip-shear

f. Velour

g. One-level loop

h. Multilevel loop

i. Multilevel, cut and loop

FIGURE 12.11 *Common tufted carpet styles.*

Styling in Residential Carpets Is Becoming More Sophisticated

NEW YORK–The U.S. carpet industry is vastly dominated by tufted products, according to the Residential Carpet Analysis compiled by RBI International Carpet Consultants. The 1990s saw some distinct styling changes, including more use of multicolor effects and more sophisticated tufting techniques.

RBI, based in Dalton, Ga., solicits information from U.S. manufacturers each year. In spring 2000, a total 4,334 residential styles were reported. Of those, 94 percent were tufted and the remainder were woven, needle-punched or bonded.

Construction

Among the tufted residential styles, only 169 (4 percent) were graphics-tufted constructions. There has been an 8 percent growth in the number of loop-pile residential carpet styles, although cut pile still dominates with 66 percent. Textured saxony styles, which use a more tightly twisted yard, represented 59 percent of cut-pile styles, an increase of 37 percent since 1990, when straight-set saxonies held the dominant share with 61 percent of residential constructions. Straight-set saxonies now make up 34 percent of cut-pile styles.

There has also been a significant increase in multilevel loop-pile styles and a decrease in level-loop residential styles. Multilevel loop constructions can be used to create textural patterns without using additional colors in a carpet.

In cut/loop products, multilevel constructions have increased slightly since 1990, from 73 to 76 percent of those styles, while level cut/loop styles have declined slightly from 27 to 22 percent.

Fiber Makeup

Nylon continues to be the market leader in residential carpet composition, although the use of nylon BCF continues to grow as the use of nylon staple has declined.

The most popular blend in use on the U.S. residential market is polypropylene/nylon with 69 percent of blended constructions, followed by nylon/polyester with 23 percent. All other blends make up 8 percent. Nylon BCF is used in all types of constructions, while nylon staple is used only in cut-pile styles. Polypropylene is used more in loop-pile constructions, while polyester is used mostly in cut-pile constructions.

Coloration

Residential carpet is still dominated by solid-color styles, although there are more choices available than ever. Overall, 64 percent of residential carpets are solid color and 26 percent are of a berber coloration. Berber is a term that has evolved to mean a flecked/tweed-like combination of shades. Originally, berber referred to carpets made by Berber tribes of natural wool yarns, which had a multicolor appearance due to variances in the wool from white to brown and flecks of black. Berbers are now offered in all sorts of colorations—from muted natural combinations to primaries and pastels.

Face Weights

Americans like their residential carpets to feel luxurious. While constructions are made in face weights from 21 ounces to 80 ounces, the largest number of styles is in the 36- to 40-ounce category.

Source: HFN, June 18, 2001, p. 20. Courtesy of Fairchild Publications, Inc.

Importance of Carpet Cushioning

There are many names for the structure that is placed between the floor and the rug or carpet. Most industry professionals use the term *cushion* or *carpet cushion.* Alternate terms include *foundation, lining, padding,* and *underlayment.* Usually cushions are priced according to the weight per square yard. In most residences a 40-ounce cushion is appropriate. A 48-ounce cushion is recommended for heavy traffic areas.

TABLE 12.1

Characteristics of Common Carpet Styles

Carpet Style/Texture	Characteristics		
	Density	Height	Amount of Twist
Cut Pile			
Friezé—high stability, long wear-life, very resilient, grainy appearance, hides dirt well (see Figure 12.15a)	Medium	Medium	Very tightly twisted heat-set yarns
Plush—(also called velvet or velvet plush) a very smooth luxurious surface that may show footprints and shading (see Figure 12.15b)	Very dense	Low (.625 to .75 inch)	Relatively low
Splush (or semishag)	Medium	Shorter than shag	Relatively low
Saxony—similar to plush but with higher twist, uneven surface with textured appearance, may show footprints and shading (see Figure 12.15c)	Medium	Low (.625 to .75 inch)	Medium to high (higher than plush, usually made with heat-set yarns)
Shag—may mat down, informal appearance (see Figure 12.15d)	Lower than plush or Saxony	Over 1 inch	Low
Tip-shear—good for hiding dirt (see Figure 12.15e)	Medium to very dense	Usually low	Medium
Velour—good wear resistance (see Figure 12.15f)	Very dense	Low (.25 inch)	Tightly twisted
Loop Pile			
One-level loop—durable, wear resistant, pebbled surface that hides footprints; a Berber rug is an example of a one-level loop pile rug (see Figure 12.15g)	Medium	Low	Medium
Multilevel loop—usually durable, depending on density (see Figure 12.15h)	Medium	Variable	Medium
Combination—multilevel cut and loop styles (see 12.15i)	Medium	Variable	Medium
Sculptured—three-dimensional appearance, usually higher loops are cut and lower loops are uncut, usually formal in appearance	Medium	Variable	Medium
High-low—similar to sculpture but informal in appearance	Medium	Variable	Medium
Random Sheer—multiple levels of pile and cut yarns produce tonal contrast	Medium	Variable	Medium

The purpose of the carpet cushion is to:

- Provide a softer walking surface
- Protect the carpet from the indentations of footsteps and furniture
- Increase durability and improve appearance
- Reduce noise
- Protect the backing fibers
- Provide insulation for cold floors
- Prevent the carpet from slipping

Types of Cushioning

Five types of cushions are available—felt, foam rubber, sponge rubber, urethane foam, and gas-filled polyester fibers bonded into a cushion (see Industry Statement 12.4).

- *Felt* Felt may be made of 100 percent animal hair, or it may be a combination of hair and other fibers. The 100 percent hair is very expensive and provides excellent service and excellent insulation. The 100 percent fiber felt is inexpensive and does not wear well. It is less resilient than other types of cushioning. It should not be installed over radiant-heat floors. Hair may cause allergic reactions in sensitive people. Because hair is subject to mold and mildew, antimicrobial finishes are suggested. Combinations of hair and other fibers may be rubberized to prevent shedding and slipping. Felt padding is excellent for Oriental rugs because too much resilience causes damages to the back of the rug.
- *Foam rubber* Foam rubber padding is made of natural or synthetic rubbers. It is suitable for medium traffic. It is nonallergenic and resists mildew. It is available in thicknesses ranging from 1/16" to 7/16." Increased thickness provides better wear. It absorbs sound well and conducts heat well. It is available in two finishes—flat and waffle. The waffle feels softer but does not wear as well as the flat.
- *Sponge rubber* Combinations of natural and synthetic rubber and fillers are formed in a flat or waffle cushion. It is more porous than foam rubber and makes a softer, springier cushion but is less buoyant than foam rubber. It is not recommended for outdoor use. Sponge cushioning is suitable for light to medium traffic; it tends to mat down with heavy traffic.
- *Urethane Foam* Made from synthetic polymers, urethane foam is available in many grades of firmness and quality. It should be at least 3/8" thick. It is especially good for below-grade installations because it resists mildew and insects.
- *Gas-filled polyester fibers bonded into a cushion* This pneumatic cellular pad is made of small, gas-filled polyester fibers. It provides excellent insulation and should not be used over radiant-heated floors.

A **self-cushioned carpet** has a layer of latex cushion bonded to the underside. It is usually less resilient than other cushions because it is thinner and less dense than a separate cushion.

INDUSTRY STATEMENT 12.4

Anti-Microbial Carpet Cushion Inhibits Bacterial Odors, Stains

LINWOOD, Pa.—At a time when American consumers are increasingly conscious of bacteria and molds, cushion manufacturer Foamex International Inc. has developed a carpet cushion that inhibits the odors, stains and destructive actions of these organisms.

Performance™ incorporates Ultra-Fresh, an Environmental Protection Agency-registered anti-microbial agent developed by Thomson Research. This prevents the growth of mold, mildew and odor-causing bacteria in the cushion. Because the anti-microbial function is built in to the polymer structure of the material rather than sprayed on post-manufacture, it prevents destructive microbial growth throughout the entire carpet cushion, keeping the carpet looking newer longer and protecting the customer's new carpet investment.

"Consumers are concerned about bacteria," said Terry Kall, president of the Foamex Carpet Cushion Group. "They demand that products purchased for their homes provide the very best in value and comfort. Our Performance™ line of products provides a first line of defense against destructive microbial growth. Instead of reacting to the problems of stains, odors and premature wear caused by bacteria and mold, customers can now feel more comfortable knowing that Performance™ Cushioning with Ultra-Fresh protects against those conditions."

Foamex's Performance™ collection will eventually also include sponge rubber, prime urethane and felt carpet cushion underlayment.

Source: HFN, Jan. 7, 2002, p. 38. Courtesy of Fairchild Publications, Inc.

Installation of Carpeting

The way carpeting is installed affects its appearance. The following list of factors helps ensure quality carpet installations. Tufted fabrics are frequently one-way fabrics. Care must be taken to make sure that all pieces of wall-to-wall carpet are installed so that the nap goes in the same direction.

- Seams should be parallel to the pile and should not be placed perpendicular to a doorway or in the center of a hallway.
- The nap should run in the longer direction and down on stairs.
- Proper stretching and tacking will eliminate stretching and wrinkling of the carpet.

Selection of Soft Floor Coverings

It is important to note that the useful life of a carpet or rug is based on both durability and appearance factors. Modern manufactured fibers are so durable that they seldom wear out before the general appearance of the carpet is no longer acceptable. Staining and matting are issues related to unacceptable appearance.

The characteristics of the components of the soft floor covering affect appearance and performance and influence selection. The components to consider are fiber, yarn, pile, and backing. The carpet cushion is also an important consideration.

Fibers

Manufactured fibers dominate the soft floor-covering industry. Nylon, polyester and olefin are the primary fibers used for face fibers. **Face fibers** are used in the surface, or pile, of the carpet, rug, or broadloom. Bulk continuous filament (BCF) nylon is the dominant carpet fiber. BCF olefin is also important. Wool was once considered the "best" pile fiber, but manufactured fibers are lower cost with superior performance. Face fibers should be evaluated for durability, soil resistance, abrasion resistance, resilience, and care requirements. Table 12.2 summarizes the characteristics of the major soft floor-covering fibers. See Chapter 2 for additional discussion of fiber properties.

Sisal and coir are also used for carpeting or rugs. They are rough, coarse fibers. Sisal is fairly inexpensive and long wearing. Its appearance is informal. Coir is especially useful as walk-off mats (floor coverings used to protect entrance areas) because the fibers are very stiff. They effectively remove dirt from the soles of shoes.

Yarns

The characteristics of yarns affect both the appearance and performance of the pile. Higher-denier (thicker) yarns and multiple-ply yarns are indications of quality. BCF yarns account for the majority of pile yarns. Some staple yarns are still used. The number of plies in a spun yarn and the amount of twist are important. Most spun carpet yarns are two-ply or three-ply yarns made from staple fibers that are four to eight inches long. Sometimes one-ply and four-ply yarns are used. Heavier yarns are more durable than lightweight yarns.

Tightly twisted yarns are more durable than loosely twisted yarns. Tightly twisted yarns are more compact. Loosely twisted yarns that are cut tend to flare at the tip (see Figure 12.12).

Pile

The pile determines surface texture. The characteristics of the pile include sweep, density, height, and whether the pile is cut or loop. **Pile sweep** is also called *directional pile lay* or *nap*. It is the angle at which the pile yarns are oriented, and it determines the quantity of light that is reflected from the rug or carpet. It is important that all the nap go in the same direction when carpet is installed.

The density of the pile is determined by the closeness of the yarns. Density is an important factor in durability. Dense piles have closely spaced yarns, and sparse piles have widely spaced

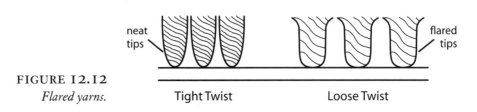

FIGURE 12.12
Flared yarns.

neat tips   flared tips

Tight Twist   Loose Twist

TABLE I2.2

Characteristics of the Major Soft Floor-Covering Fibers

Fiber		Characteristics
Acrylic	Durability	Good
	Soil resistance	Good
	Abrasion resistance	Good
	Resilience	Good
	Care requirements	Easy care
	Additional Comments	Available in a wide range of colors; nonallergenic; resistant to mildew, moths, and insects; resists degradation from sunlight; may pill
Nylon	Durability	Very good
	Soil resistance	Very good
	Abrasion resistance	Very good
	Resilience	Very good
	Care requirements	Easy care, hides dirt well
	Additional Comments	Available in a wide range of colors; good color retention; resistant to mildew, moths, and insects; nonallergenic; may cause static
Polyester	Durability	Good
	Soil resistance	Fair unless soil-resistant finish is added
	Abrasion resistance	Good
	Resilience	Good
	Care requirements	Easy care; resists most soil, but oil-based stains may be difficult to remove
	Additional Comments	Available in a wide range of colors; good color retention; resists moths, mildew, and insects; nonallergenic
Olefin	Durability	Good
	Soil resistance	Excellent
	Abrasion resistance	Excellent
	Resilience	Average, may flatten and crush
	Care requirements	Very easy care, stain resistant, resists almost all acids and chemicals
	Additional Comments	Nonabsorbent, can withstand weather and moisture
Wool	Durability	Very good
	Soil resistance	Very good
	Abrasion resistance	Very good
	Resilience	Very good
	Care requirements	Resists soil well but cannot be cleaned as easily as synthetic fibers, may be damaged by alkaline detergents
	Additional Comments	Very expensive, flame resistant, attracts moths
Cotton	Durability	Fair
	Soil resistance	Fair unless soil-resistant finish is added
	Abrasion resistance	Poor
	Resilience	Poor
	Care requirements	Easy care, small rugs can be washed and dried at home
	Additional Comments	Not appropriate for high traffic areas
Rayon	Durability	Poor
	Soil resistance	Good
	Abrasion resistance	Poor
	Resilience	Poor
	Care requirements	Easy care
	Additional Comments	Not appropriate for high traffic areas

yarns. High-density piles are more durable and retain their attractiveness longer than low-density piles. They are also more resistant to soil and stains. Low-density piles will crush and flatten with use. The **face weight** (also called **pile weight** or **yarn weight**) is the weight of the fabric on the face of the carpet. It reflects the density of the fiber in the pile. Closely packed pile that is firmly secured to the backing is an indicator of long-wearing carpet.

The height of the pile is the length of the yarn above the base fabric. Pile height usually ranges from 0.187 to 1.250 inches. Lower-pile height and higher-pile density provide the best durability.

Looped piles are more durable and retain their appearance longer than cut piles. Cut piles tend to mat down more quickly than cut piles. Tightly twisted uncut loops wear well.

Reputable carpet manufacturers label their carpets with a grade of A, B, C, etc., and provide data on performance ratings. Other considerations are that light colors show soil and dark colors show lint. Multilevel and multicolor carpets show less soil than plain, smooth, one-color carpets.

Care of Soft Floor Coverings

It is important to follow the manufacturer's instructions for carpet care. General care recommendations for soft floor coverings are as follows:

■ Vacuum frequently to remove soil and restore the pile. Vacuuming a new rug or carpet will remover the fuzz or fibers left when the pile was sheared. Frequent vacuuming will eliminate "shedding," or fibers that have worked loose.
■ Use mats and runners in heavy-wear areas.
■ Rotate rugs to extend wear life.
■ Remove stains immediately.
■ Shampoo a carpet every one to three years. Wall-to-wall carpet must be cleaned in place. Rugs may be sent out for professional cleaning.
■ Cut pulled loops, or "sprouts," level with the pile.
■ "Walk-off mats" should be placed at entrances to collect dirt before it reaches the carpet.
■ Use a humidifier or antistatic spray to reduce static electricity.

RESILIENT FLOORING

Resilient flooring provides the comfort and sound control of carpeting or rugs but does not allow penetration of dirt or moisture. The major resilient flooring used today is vinyl. Both vinyl tile and sheet flooring are very popular. Vinyl is easy to clean, absorbs sound, and is comfortable to walk on. Other resilient flooring materials are cork, linoleum, and rubber. Cork and linoleum are increasing in popularity because they are biodegradable and produced from sustainable resources. Rubber is used primarily in flooring for commercial interiors but is gaining appeal in residential applications.

Vinyl

Vinyl is made in two forms—sheeting and tiles. The sheeting is made in widths of 6, 9, or 12 feet. Tiles are usually 9 inches square or 12 inches square. Both sheeting and tiles are available in a wide range of patterns, textures, and colors. Vinyl flooring is categorized as inlaid vinyl sheeting, rotogravure vinyl sheeting, and vinyl laminate.

Inlaid vinyl sheeting The pattern runs through the entire thickness of the sheet and it will not wear away. It is more expensive than rotogravure vinyl sheeting, but it is very durable (see Figure 12.13).

Rotogravure vinyl sheeting (rotovinyls) The pattern and/or color is printed or embossed on the surface of the sheet and protected with a coating of vinyl resin or urethane. The surface will wear, and the pattern will fade (see Figure 12.14).

Vinyl laminate Vinyl laminate is used for custom work and is expensive. Any fabric or wallpaper can be laminated and made into flooring.

The advantages of vinyl flooring are that it is waterproof, resistant to oils and most residential chemicals, and resistant to denting and chipping. It can be installed over radiant-floor heating up to 80 degrees Fahrenheit. Textured vinyl is slip resistant and does not show marks easily. Many vinyl floors have a no-wax finish, but this finish may wear off, especially under high traffic conditions. Higher qualities of vinyl flooring usually have a cushioned backing that make it resilient, quiet, and warm.

Disadvantages of vinyl flooring are that it can be damaged by intense heat, lighted cigarettes, and rubber or foam-backed mats or rugs. Unbacked vinyl has poor noise absorption, and it is hard and cold.

For all of these varieties of vinyl floor coverings, it is important to follow the manufacturer's suggested care procedures.

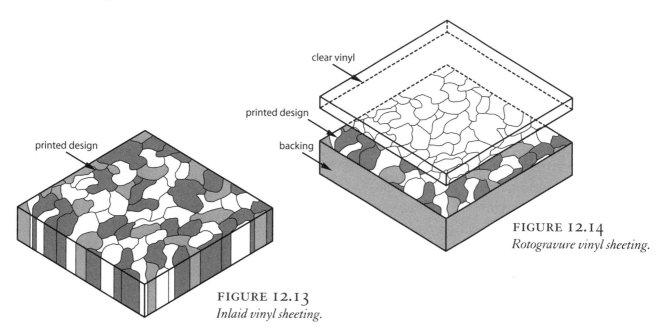

clear vinyl

printed design

backing

FIGURE 12.14
Rotogravure vinyl sheeting.

printed design

FIGURE 12.13
Inlaid vinyl sheeting.

Vinyl Tiles

The advantages of **vinyl tiles** over sheeting are that installation is easier and interesting patterns and effects can be created using different tiles. Disadvantages of vinyl tiles are that the seams are very visible and can collect dirt. Also, the edges can curl if not installed properly or if the edges become saturated with water.

Vinyl Composition Tiles

Vinyl composition tiles (VCT) are made of vinyl, resins, plasticizers, fillers, and coloring agents. These materials are formed into sheets and then cut into tiles. Vinyl composition tiles are inexpensive and easy to maintain. The disadvantages are that they have low-impact resistance, poor noise absorption, and are semiporous.

Solid Vinyl Tiles

Solid vinyl tiles are made of polyvinyl chloride with a small amount of additive. The color is consistent throughout the depth of the tiles. These tiles are available in a limited range of solid colors and natural patterns, such as wood, marble, and brick. They are coated with clear vinyl or urethane; urethane lasts longer. Solid vinyl tiles are more expensive than vinyl composition tiles and are easy to maintain. They have low-impact resistance and poor noise absorption.

Cork

Cork tiles are made from granules of cork and natural or synthetic binders that are compressed and baked (see Figure 12.15). They are available in beige to dark brown colors. Cork has good insulation qualities and is warm, resilient, and quiet. It should not be installed over floors with radiant heating. For longer wear, it should be sealed or polished immediately after installation to prevent damage. Cork tiles are also available with a laminated top layer of vinyl, which makes them more durable as well as nonporous. Otherwise, cork chips at the edges, dents easily, and fades in strong sunlight. Rubber-backed mats or rugs may cause discoloration. Furniture guards should be used. Cork tiles can be cleaned by damp mopping. Water degrades cork, so the floor should not be soaked.

Linoleum

Linoleum is an all-natural product produced from sustainable crops. It is also biodegradable. Linoleum is made from ground cork, wood flour, linseed oil, and resins. The mixture is pressed onto a jute or burlap backing. Linoleum is available in a variety of plain colors and patterns, but colors tend to be more muted than in vinyl.

There are many qualities of linoleum. Better qualities of linoleum are very long wearing, resilient, warm, and have excellent noise absorption. Linoleum does have a tendency to rise, peel, and rot if water gets underneath. Linoleum is sensitive to alkalis and cannot be installed directly over concrete. It should not be sealed, but it can be waxed. It is slippery when wet. Although

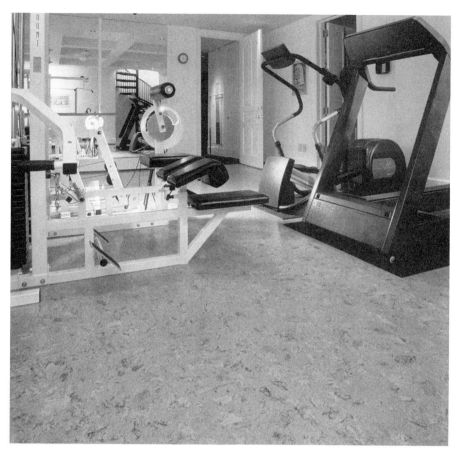

FIGURE 12.15
Cork flooring. Photo courtesy of corkdirect.com © 2000.

linoleum is no longer produced in the United States, a limited quantity can be imported from Scotland and Holland.

Rubber

Rubber flooring is sold in sheets or as tiles. It is made of a combination of natural and synthetic materials. The colors are usually brighter and clearer than the colors in vinyl. Rubber is long-wearing, very resilient, quiet, and stain resistant. All stains should be wiped up immediately because moisture degrades rubber. It is also affected by strong detergents, cleaning fluids, sunlight, oil, grease, and acids. It can be damp-mopped with mild detergents, but it should never be saturated. It is very slippery when wet.

HARD FLOORING

The two most common hard floors are wood and ceramic. Other hard floors include marble, granite, and cement. When compared to soft floors and resilient floors, hard floors tend to be noisier and colder and more slippery, but they are also more durable.

Wood Flooring

When purchasing wood floors, consumers can choose from many types of woods, styles or patterns, and finishes.

Types of Woods

Most wood floors are oak, but improvements in manufacturing and refinements of laminates have made it possible to use such woods as birch, beech, and pecan. Maple and cherry are also used as flooring, and pine is sometimes used in very casual country-style rooms. When selecting wood flooring, it is important to understand the grading of wood (see Chapter 3).

Styles of Wood Floors

The three styles of wood floors are strip, plank, and parquet (see Figure 12.16).

Strip flooring The strips, or boards, are usually 2 1/2 inches wide and 25/32 inches thick, although other widths and thicknesses are available. They may be as narrow as 1 1/2 inches. They have **tongue-and-groove** edges on both sides to provide interlocking joints. See Figure 12.17 for a close-up view of tongue-and-groove flooring.

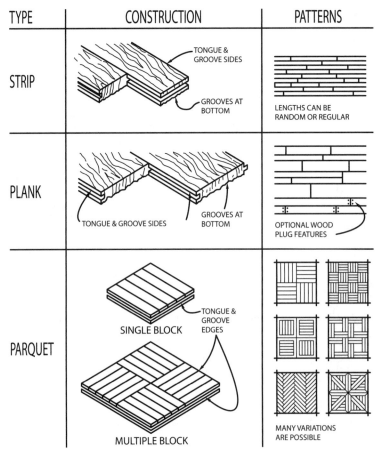

FIGURE 12.16
Types of wood flooring: a. *strip,*
b. *plank,* c. *parquet.*

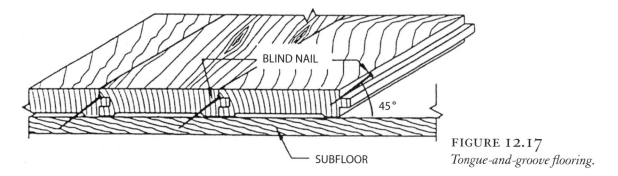

FIGURE 12.17
Tongue-and-groove flooring.

Plank Flooring Planks are wider than strips, ranging in widths from three to eight inches. Flooring may have regular-width planks with all the same width, or random-width planks with varying widths. Planks also interlock with tongue-and-groove edges.

Parquet Flooring Parquet floors are made of small pieces of wood laid in a pattern. (See Chapter 3 for diagrams of common parquet patterns.) Parquet patterns are available in 12-inch squares for easy installation. The thickness varies from 3/8 inches to 3/4 inches. See Figure 12.18 for a diagram of a pattern for a parquet floor.

Prefinished and Unfinished Wood Flooring

The two types of finishes used on prefinished wood flooring are urethane and acrylic. Urethane finishes are either matte or glossy. Durability and appearance are dependent on the number of coats. The average product has about seven coats. For an acrylic finish the wood is impregnated with acrylic and then subjected to irradiation, causing the liquid acrylic to harden. This product is exceptionally durable and is more expensive than urethane-finished products.

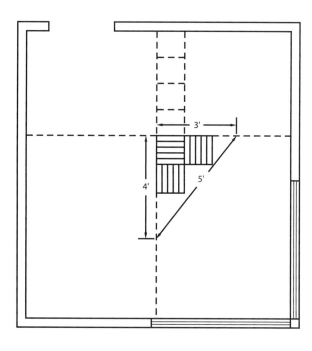

FIGURE 12.18
Diagram of parquet floor installation.

Prefinished wood can also be stained to the desired color before finishing. The advantages of prefinished wood floors are that the customer knows the exact color of the floor before installation, and there are no sanding marks near the walls. This is not true of unfinished wood flooring.

Unfinished wood flooring can be finished with wax, matte urethane, or glossy urethane. The main advantage of unfinished wood flooring is that the color can be customized.

Laminate Flooring

Laminate flooring is composed of three layers. The surface, a high-pressure melamine laminate, is bonded to a moisture-resistant wood-based core. The surface is durable and resistant to wear and water. A balancing layer is the stabilizing base, glued to the wood-based core. Laminate flooring has tongue-and-groove construction. It has the look of wood with the durability and ease of care of laminated countertops. Most of the patterns available in laminate flooring are wood-like, but others, such as marble and stone, are also available. Most manufacturers guarantee that the product will not stain, wear, dent, scratch, or fade for ten years.

A major disadvantage of laminate flooring is that it has a tendency to sound hollow. The tongue-and-groove construction and the laminate itself cause the "hollow sound." A foam acoustical barrier can be added to the subfloor to reduce the hollow sound. Laminate flooring is not recommended for use in bathrooms or other wet areas because the wood base will warp.

Ceramic Tile

Ceramic tiles are most commonly made from natural clay. They are also made from porcelain or mixtures of clay and ceramic materials. Floor tiles are thicker and heavier than wall tiles, and they should be textured for nonslipping. Floor tiles should be labeled as floor tiles (see Figure 12.19).

Tiles are available in several sizes; 8 inches square, 12 inches square, and 16 inches square are common. Many finishes are available, ranging from very shiny to dull matte. There is also an unglazed impervious tile. These finishes make the tiles easy to clean. Tile floors are noisy, cold to the touch, and may be slippery, especially if glazed. Some tiles chip, crack, and fade easily. Hand-painted tiles are likely to show wear and fade. Tile floors should be swept and washed but should not be polished. The four types of ceramic tiles used in flooring are ceramic mosaic, paver, quarry, and Mexican.

Ceramic Mosaic Tiles

Ceramic mosaic tiles can be made from porcelain or natural clay. They are small (no larger than six square inches) and can be glazed or unglazed. The most common sizes are one or two inches square by 1/4 inch to 3/8 inch thick.

Pavers

Pavers are unglazed porcelain or natural clay tiles, six square inches or more in size. They are frequently made with a textured surface or raised-surface patterns for slip resistance.

FIGURE 12.19
Ceramic floor tiles. Courtesy of Fairchild Publications, Inc.

Quarry Tiles

Quarry tiles are made from shale and fine clays. They are very heavy and may not be suitable for some installations. They are usually square or rectangular in various sizes and are available in buff, yellow, various reds, browns, dark blue, and black. Some quarry tiles are very porous and need a wax or sealer finish to be less porous.

Mexican Tile

Mexican tiles are made by hand, dried in open fields, and fired in ovens. They are about one inch thick and uneven. These tiles must be sealed after installation. Mexican tile can be swept, vacuumed, and damp mopped. Commercially made Mexican tiles are available. They are more uniform, stronger, and less porous, and can be prestained.

Selected Other Hard Floors

Table 12.3 summarizes the advantages, disadvantages, and care of other selected hard floors.

TABLE 12.3
Selected Hard Floors

Hard Floor	Advantages	Disadvantages	Care
Brick—usually available in shades of buff, purple, blue, and a variety of browns; thickness ranges from 1/4 inch to 1 1/2 inches	Can be used inside and out, very hard surface, suitable for radiant heating, can be very rough or very smooth, presealed bricks are available for indoor use	Hard, cold, poor noise absorption	Sweep and wash, must be sealed to prevent absorption of spills
Concrete and Cement Floors— (generally used in commercial interiors or residential basements and garages)	Durable, low-cost, can be painted or sealed	Cracks and chips, difficult to repair, hard, cold, poor noise absorption, limited colors but can be waxed with colored wax	Sweep and wash with detergent, must be sealed to prevent absorption of spills
Cement Tiles—can be customized with colors, shapes, or patterns	Durable, less expensive alternative to stone, clay, or marble tiles	Cracks and chips, difficult to repair, hard, cold, poor noise absorption	Sweep and wash, must be sealed to prevent absorption of spills
Flagstone—thin slabs of stone; generally fine-grained sandstone, bluestone quartzite, or slate; irregularly shaped (1 to 4 square feet, 1/2 inch to 4 inches thick)	Durable	Uneven surface unsuitable for tables and chairs, hard, cold, poor noise absorption	Sweep and wash, sealing necessary to make flagstone impervious to staining and wear
Glass Block—especially good for use as covers for lighting that is recessed in floors	Excellent light transmission, good visibility	Hard, cold, slippery, but available in nonslip finishes	Sponge or mop
Granite—an igneous rock having crystal grains of visible size; light to dark shades of white, grey, buff, beige, pink, red, blue, green, and black	Durable, may be polished	Hard, cold, poor noise absorption	Similar to marble
Marble—true marble is a metamorphic rock derived from limestone; all rocks that are capable of taking a polish are considered to be marble; dolomitic limestone (hard limestone) is known commercially as marble; it is available in a wide variety of colors; most marble today is 3/8 inch thick and backed with fiberglass, epoxy resins, or Styrofoam	Very long wearing natural material	Cold, very hard, very heavy, porous, scratches, very slippery when wet, very expensive	Must be sealed to prevent staining; can be swept and washed; do not use harsh abrasives or acid cleaners; worn marble can be sealed with a water-based sealer

(continued)

TABLE 12.3 *(continued)*
Selected Hard Floors

Hard Floor	Advantages	Disadvantages	Care
Cast Marble—polyester product containing ground marble; also refers to agglomerated marble combined with 5 to 10 percent resins	Very long wearing	Cold, very hard, very heavy, porous, scratches, very slippery when wet	Must be sealed to prevent staining; can be swept and washed; do not use harsh abrasives or acid cleaners; worn marble can be sealed with a water-based sealer
Serpentine—(stone classified as marble)	Very long wearing	Cold, very hard, very heavy, porous, scratches, very slippery when wet	Must be sealed to prevent staining; can be swept and washed; do not use harsh abrasives or acid cleaners; worn marble can be sealed with a water-based sealer
Travertine—(stone classified as marble) porous limestone, pores are filled with an epoxy resin	Very long wearing	Cold, very hard, very heavy, porous, scratches, very slippery when wet	Must be sealed to prevent staining; can be swept and washed; do not use harsh abrasives or acid cleaners; worn marble can be sealed with a water-based sealer
Slate—a dense fine-grained metamorphic rock; nonporous; available in blues, grey-green, purple-red, charcoal, and heather colors	Beautiful, easy to care for, exceptionally long wearing	Very expensive, poor noise absorption, cold, hard, very heavy, can be slippery when wet	Sweep and wash; may be waxed but turns the stone a darker shade
Stone—sandstone, York stone, Portland stone, granite, and limestone slabs	Extremely long wearing	Very expensive, very hard, very heavy, cold, may chip and crack, poor noise absorption	Sweep and wash, some are polished or sealed
Terrazzo—there are two types of terrazzo 1. marble chips set in cement 2. marble chips set in a polyester resin	Fairly hard wearing and maintenance free, good in bathrooms; terrazzo made with polyester resin is less hard	Poor noise absorption and sometimes slippery; if set in cement the floor must be sealed	Sweep and wash but do not polish; do not use acid or alkaline cleaners

Selection of Resilient and Hard Flooring

The advantages and disadvantages of each type of resilient and hard flooring must be carefully evaluated. Aesthetics and performance are both important in the final decision. Other essential ingredients in the selection process are the services of a reputable dealer and skilled installer.

The characteristics of the installation site are very important. Grade level (see Figure 12.20) affects the amount of moisture the floor will be exposed to. For example wood, is very sensitive to moisture. Wood can be installed **above grade** when moisture is not a problem. **On grade**

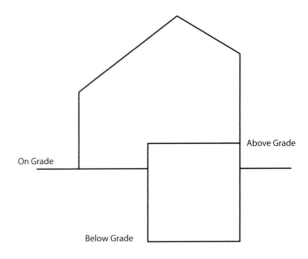

FIGURE 12.20
Grade levels.

means that the concrete is in contact with the ground, and moisture may be present. **Below grade** has a greater potential for the presence of moisture. Only laminated wood floors may be installed below grade.

Stone, marble, and brick are very heavy, and the **subflooring,** the floor to which the finished floor is attached, must be strong enough to support it.

The subfloor must also be free from oil, grease, wax, old floor finishes, paint, dust, dirt, and other coatings that might affect the flooring or the adhesive. Vinyl cannot be laid over an old floor covering that contains asbestos. The asbestos will degrade the vinyl. Flooring that contains asbestos should be removed by a trained asbestos-abatement contractor. Frequently the subfloor is concrete or plywood. If it contains cracks, an underlayment is used to cover them and level the floor. The underlayment may be exterior-grade plywood or particleboard.

CARE OF RESILIENT AND HARD FLOORING

The individual characteristics of each material and the variety of finishes used on resilient and hard flooring require that the consumer follow the manufacturer's directions carefully.

To prevent denting resilient vinyl flooring, it is important that furniture be equipped with the proper load-bearing devices shown in Figure 12.21. It is also essential that refrigerators and other heavy equipment be "walked" across the floor on a piece of wood. This will prevent gouging of a resilient floor and scratching of a hard floor.

FLOOR COVERINGS AND THE ENVIRONMENT

Off-gassing, recycling, and asbestos removal are environmental issues related to floor coverings.

TYPE OF LOAD	KENTILE FLOORS INC. RECOMMENDS	KENTILE FLOORS INC. DOES NOT RECOMMEND	TYPE
HEAVY FURNITURE, more or less permanently located, should have composition furniture cups under the legs to prevent them from cutting the floor.	Right 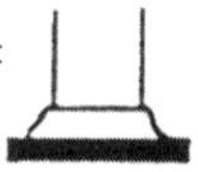 Wide Bearing Surfaces Save Floors	Wrong  Small Bearing Surfaces Dent Floors	Composition Furniture Cups 
FREQUENTLY MOVED FURNITURE requires casters. Desk chairs are a good example. Casters should be 2" in diameter with soft rubber threads at least ¾" wide and with easy swiveling ball-bearing action. For heavier items that must be moved frequently, consult the caster manufacturers as to the suitable size of equipment that should be used.	Right 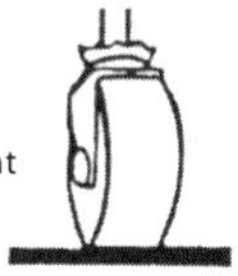 Rubber Rollers Save Floors	Wrong 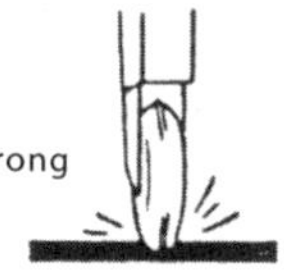 Hard Rollers Mark Floors	Rubber Wheel Casters 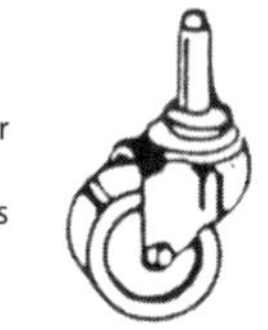
LIGHT FURNITURE should be equipped with glides having a smooth, flat base with rounded edges and a flexible pin to maintain flat contact with the floor. They should be from 1¼" to 1½" dia., depending upon weight of load they must carry. For furniture with slanted legs apply glides parallel to the floor rather than slanted ends of legs.	Right 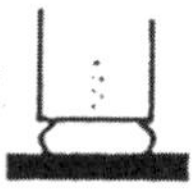 Use Flat Bearing Surfaces	Wrong  Remove Small Metal Domes	Flat Glides With Flexible Shank 

FIGURE 12.21
Static load for furniture.

Off-Gassing

Off-gassing, or the dissipation of toxic fumes from floor textiles, is unpleasant and potentially harmful. The finishes applied to the textiles and the adhesive being used contribute to off-gassing. It is a major contributor to **sick building syndrome (SBS).** SBS is caused by poor indoor air quality that impairs worker well-being, comfort, and productivity. Adverse effects of off-gassing can be reduced by ventilating the carpet for 48 hours before installation.

Recycling

Discarded carpeting contributes to the landfill problem. New technology allows nylon-carpet fiber to be recycled into carpet fiber with no discernible difference in characteristics. PET (polyethylene terephthalate) polyester fiber is made from recycled soft drink bottles and can be used for carpet. Ground tire scraps can be recycled for use in producing carpet cushions.

Asbestos

Asbestos is an ingredient used in vinyl and vinyl-composition floor coverings produced prior to the mid-1980s. It is not considered harmful in that state. When the floor covering is removed, it may not be sanded, sawed, or treated in any manner that reduces it to a dust or powder.

FLOOR COVERINGS AND SOCIAL RESPONSIBILITY

Illegal and unethical child labor and sweatshop labor practices exist in some parts of the world. Conscientious importers and retailers deal only with producers who hire adults and provide safe working conditions. The RUGMARK organization is an example of efforts to eliminate child labor. The also provide educational opportunities for children in India, Nepal, and Pakistan. The RUGMARK label assures consumers that child labor was not used to produce the rug.

SUMMARY

Flooring materials are divided into three major categories—soft floor coverings, such as carpet and rugs; resilient floor such as vinyl, cork, and rubber; and hard floors, such as wood, stone, and ceramic. Floor materials are carefully selected for their aesthetics, functional attributes, and maintenance requirements.

Soft floor coverings are available in four classifications—broadloom, carpet, carpet modules, and rug. The two main ways to construct soft floor coverings are tufting and weaving, with approximately 90 percent produced by tufting. Handmade rugs are made by weaving, braiding, hooking, and felting. Frequently these rugs, due to their cost and beauty, are used as wall hangings. There are three types of hand-woven pile rugs —Flokati rugs, Oriental rugs, and rya rugs. Machine-made Oriental design rugs are woven on an Axminster loom and are sometimes called American Oriental rugs.

The characteristics of soft floor coverings affect appearance and performance and influence selection. The components to consider are fiber, yarn, pile, and backing. Bulk continuous-filament (BCF) nylon is the dominant carpet fiber. Carpet cushions will improve the durability and appearance of soft floor coverings. Modern manufactured fibers are so durable that they seldom wear out before the general appearance of the carpet is no longer acceptable.

The major resilient flooring used today is vinyl. Tile and sheeting are easy to clean, quiet, and comfortable to walk on. Cork and linoleum are increasing in popularity because they are biodegradable and produced from sustainable resources. Rubber is used primarily in contract and industry but is gaining appeal for residential use.

The two most common hard floors are wood and ceramic; other hard floors include marble, granite, and cement. When compared to soft and resilient floors, hard floors tend to be noisier, colder, and more slippery; they are also more durable. The four styles of wood floors are strip, plank, block, and parquet. Ceramic tiles are commonly made from natural clay. Aesthetics and performance of the floor coverings are important in the selection. A reputable dealer and skilled mechanic are essential in the selection process. The individual characteristics of flooring materials, and the variety of finishes used on resilient and hard flooring, require that the consumer follow the manufacturer's directions carefully.

Off-gassing, recycling, asbestos removal, and child and sweatshop labor are environmental and social issues related to floor coverings.

INDUSTRY PROFILE

Exclusive Areas

What is considered "luxury" in the area rug business varies according to category and retail channel. Each broad segment—machine-made, handmade, hand-knotted—has entry-level and high-end products. Most retailers pride themselves on having a range of goods to satisfy most consumers.

ABC Carpet & Home has become the standard by which carpet and rug stores are measured. Established as a carpet and rug store at 881 Broadway here in 1961, ABC overflowed that building and, in 1980, began renting space across the street. A year later, ABC purchased the entire building—888 Broadway.

While Jerome "Jerry" Weinrib, founder and chairman, turned over much of the space at 888 to his daughter, Paulette Weinrib Cole, and her husband, Evan Cole, he reserved the sixth floor of 888 and the entire building across the street for carpets and rugs. The sixth floor is dedicated to one-of-a-kind rugs, antique and new. Many of the rugs are made exclusively for ABC and are hand-picked by the buying staff to assure that the selection at ABC is second to none.

The assortment at 881 is made up of broadloom, rugs and related accessories. The rugs are generally programmed lines from a variety of suppliers, and include handmade and machine-made products. All told, consumers have about 80,000 rugs to choose from and, while not all are strictly luxury rugs, most sales in a 6-by-9 size ring up at $500 to $3,000, according to Graham Head, managing director for ABC.

"In the past 15 years, there [have been] more great decorative rugs available—in quality and price—than ever before," Head stated. "There are more countries making rugs and the styling is now to American tastes."

ABC's success in high-end rugs is built on its vast assortment, the amount of prime retail space it dedicates to rugs and respect for its customers, Head explained, adding, "Luxury implies indulgence and rugs really aren't necessities—so they're all luxury in a sense—but at ABC, we can trade a customer up or down."

"Many retailers underestimate the consumer. But the customer is smart, especially here in New York," Weinrib stressed. The final ingredient at ABC is a professional sales staff of some 40 individuals who know rugs and how to present the category. "The biggest difference between ABC and other rug stores is that ABC is a merchant, not just a retailer," Weinrib said.

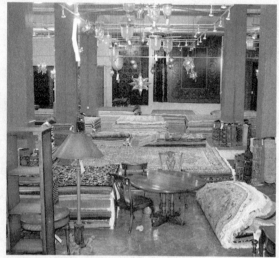

The inside of ABC Carpet & Home flagship store.
Courtesy of Fairchild Publications, Inc.

The reputation that ABC has built as the consummate rug merchant is similar to the name that Karastan owns as a luxury brand for its machine-made rugs that retail in an approximate 5-by-8 at $499 to $1,500. While there are many handmade rugs with higher price tags, Karastan has a cachet that's hard to beat. Because handmade rugs are somewhat mysterious to the average consumer, many are intimidated by the range of choices in a specialty rug store. But when a rug comes with a name like Karastan, the customer feels more confident in making a purchase, according to Phil Haney, senior vice president of marketing.

Ten years ago, if a consumer wanted a luxury rug, she'd go to her favorite high-end department or furniture store, or, if she was daring, a specialty rug store. Now she's just as likely to see high-end rugs in catalogs, big-box home furnishings stores and even home centers.

The emergence of retail venues such as Expo Design Center and The Great Indoors are bringing luxury goods to more consumers. "Expo is raising the bar," said Haney.

Expo Design Centers has added Heirlooms for Tomorrow areas in many of its locations, according to Pat Shaw, global product manager for rugs. The concept, which has worked very well, is to have a separate area where a consumer can sit down and have products shown to her in a comfortable, quiet environment, according to Shaw. The rugs in the Heirloom area are one-of-a-kind styles and the best programmed rugs, priced from $5,000. Most are hand-knotted in wool and silk or all silk.

(continued)

INDUSTRY PROFILE

Exclusive Areas *(continued)*

Shaw noted that he deliberately created an environment with some "snob appeal," where some of the rugs are folded and tied, so that they are "unwrapped" for presentation, while others are shown on wall racks and still others shown in stacks.

For suppliers, the luxury segment of the handmade rug business is a good place to be during a softening economy, according to Nasser Rahmanan, president of Masterlooms, a high-end supplier of fashion-forward handmade rugs. "The fluctuations in the luxury segment are not as severe as in the medium range," Rahmanan said. "There is an effect but not as much."

Ed Vairo, director of creative marketing for Nourison, said one change in the luxury business for handmade rugs is the growth of higher-end programmed goods, which means that consumers can find luxury in running lines rather than having to shop one-of-a-kind merchandise.

Having the inventory to back up samples of programmed merchandise is one of the toughest parts of being in the luxury business for suppliers and retailers. "To have backup inventory with all the SKUs and all the various sizes is a huge expense," said Amir Loloi, president of Feizy Import & Export.

Feizy offers a wide range of products—from machine-made rugs of polypropylene to fine hand-knotted—in order to be a one-stop shop for its customers. The Chaillot Collection is its top-of-the-line product, retailing in a 9-by-12 at $8,500.

For retailers, presenting fine rugs on a consignment basis used to be an answer to the high cost of buying high-end rugs outright. Rugs would be placed on a retail floor but were not paid for until the item sells. While still done occasionally, this method is not as common as it once was.

Tufenkian Tibetan Rugs does not place rugs on consignment, according to Mark DaSilva, director of marketing. "We do allow dealers to exchange the rugs out within six months for another piece or pieces of equal value," he said. Tufenkian's rugs open at about $2,250 and range upwards to more than $9,000 in a 6-by-9. The line is sold mostly through interior designer showrooms, independent rug dealers and a few select furniture stores. "In New York, it's the opposite of the rest of the country because here we sell through ABC Carpet & Home and Bloomingdale's, too," DaSilva explained.

Business has remained strong despite the current soft economy, and demand for larger rugs is growing, according to DaSilva. Consumers are buying more large rugs for larger homes but sometimes the design is so powerful in a bigger size that the fashion statement sells the rug, he explained.

Noonoo Rug Co.'s strength is in hand-knotted rugs that retail for $7,500 to $8,000 in a 9-by-12, according to Gene Newman, president.

"The most dramatic change in the business over the past five years is that there are better designs, colors, new constructions, new finishing techniques from all the major rug-making countries—China, India, Pakistan and Nepal," said Newman. "It's coming from U.S. importers giving more time, energy and attention to fashion. There's more and better product available."

The re-emergence of Iran as a legal source of hand-knotted rugs has also added excitement to the business, Newman said. Noonoo has formed an alliance with Ramezani Oriental Carpets, which has given it access to a steady stream of Iranian handmade Persian rugs without having to rebuild sources and connections in Iran.

"Iran is still weaving what they want, when they want," Newman said, "but we are beginning to be able to develop product that is more specifically for the U.S. market. And right now, the currency exchange is such that it's an excellent time for the U.S. to buy Iranian rugs." Noonoo's primary distribution is through the traditional specialty store, some department and furniture stores, and some designer showrooms.

"The specialty rug dealers have become more sophisticated and offer more kinds of product than in the past—other kinds of flooring and other home furnishings products," Newman said. "Noonoo had a good year in 2000 and [we] have met expectation so far in 2001. We expect the second half to come back as consumer confidence improves."

Source: HFN, May 14, 2001, p. 36. Courtesy of Fairchild Publications, Inc.

TERMS FOR REVIEW

above grade

American Oriental rugs

Axminster

below grade

braided rugs

broadloom

Brussels

carpet cushion (cushion, foundation, lining, padding, underlayment)

carpet modules (carpet squares, carpet tiles)

carpet

Caucasian rugs

ceramic mosaic tiles

ceramic tiles

chenille

Chinese rugs

dhurrie (durrie, dhurry, durry) rugs

face fibers

face weight (pile weight, yarn weight)

flocked carpet

Flokati (Floccati) rugs

fusion-bonded carpet

Ghiordes (Turkish) knot

Indian rugs

inlaid vinyl sheeting

kelim (khilim or kilim) rugs

knitted carpet

laminate flooring

linoleum

machine-made Oriental design rugs

Mexican tiles

Native American (Navajo) rugs

needlepunched carpet

off-gassing

on grade

Oriental rugs

parquet flooring

pavers

Persian rugs

pile

pile sweep (directional pile lay or nap)

plank flooring

quarry tiles

rotogravure vinyl sheeting (rotovinyl)

rug

rya rugs

Sehna/Senna (Persian) knot

self-cushioned carpet

sick building syndrome (SBS)

solid vinyl tiles

strip flooring

subflooring

tongue-and-groove

tufted fabric

Turkish rugs

Turkoman (Turkmen) rugs

velvet

vinyl composition tiles (VCT)

vinyl laminate

vinyl tiles

wall-to-wall carpet

Wilton

REVIEW QUESTIONS

1. Explain the differences between an authentic Oriental rug and an American Oriental rug.
2. Describe the differences between a Native American rug and a kelim rug.
3. Why is most carpeting in the United States produced by tufting?
4. Why are cork and linoleum increasing in popularity?
5. Why has vinyl become the most popular choice for resilient floor coverings?
6. Why is the popularity of laminated flooring increasing?

LEARNING ACTIVITIES

1. Visit a store(s) that sells soft, resilient, and hard flooring. Speak with a salesperson to learn more about the types of flooring available. Compare and contrast the advantages and disadvantages of each type of flooring.
2. Research the significance of the symbols and colors used in Native American rugs.

CHAPTER 13

PAINTS AND WALL COVERINGS

Decorating a room is an age-old problem. Some love it, others dread it — how to decorate this room? Should it be Country French or English Country? For generations, Waverly Fabrics has consistently come to the rescue and guided homeowners through the perilous world of home decorating with a sure and confident hand.

HFN Imagemakers, May 29, 2000

ORIGINALLY, PAINTS AND WALL COVERINGS WERE USED PRIMARILY TO DECORATE A ROOM. They are still usually selected for their aesthetic qualities. But modern technology has created paints that protect as well as beautify surroundings. Wall coverings may be used to create exceptionally durable surfaces. When compared to other components of a room, such as furniture and flooring, paints and most wall coverings are fairly easy and relatively inexpensive to change. They set the stage for the furniture and home accessories within a room.

PAINT

Paint is a thin, protective, liquid film that dries to a hard finish when applied to a surface. It is made in a full range of colors, but it can also be colorless. It is the most commonly used finish for walls and the most economical method of changing the environment. Paint is inexpensive and relatively easy to apply. Use of different colors and textures can perceptually alter the sizes and shapes of rooms. Paint can add visual excitement to a room or serve as a quiet background for the furnishings.

The first prepared paints were sold in 1867 in the United States. Since that time, products have been developed that make application easier and make the paint more durable. The variety of paints has been increased to include luminous paints and metallic paints. Consumers can do their own painting or can hire contractors to paint. Paint can be purchased at home-improvement stores, local hardware stores, and even in discount stores. It can be custom mixed to create the exact color the customer wants. Table 13.1 presents selected brands of paints.

Ingredients in Paint

The three basic ingredients in paint are pigments, thinner, and resin. Additives are used to provide desirable characteristics to the paint. The pigments are solids, and the thinner and resin are liquids.

Pigment

Pigment gives the paint color, opacity, and sheen. It is frequently the most expensive ingredient in the paint. Several pigments are usually combined to achieve the desired color. **Opacity** is the covering power of the paint. Titanium dioxide is the best white pigment for opacity. Other pigments are listed in Table 13.2. White lead was used as a pigment in paint, until it was found to cause lead poisoning in small children who had ingested it from chipped paint. Interior house paints containing more than one percent lead have been banned by the United States Department of Health and Human Services.

Extender, or inert, pigments are added for a shiny finish. The quantity of pigment in the paint determines the finish, or sheen, of the paint. **Pigment volume concentration** (PVC) indicates the volume of pigment relative to the volume of resin in a paint. Higher amounts of pigment produce a more textured, flatter appearance. Figure 13.1 shows the relative amounts of thinner, pigment, and resin that produce different finishes.

There are five basic finishes available in paints—flat or matte, satin or eggshell, semigloss, high gloss or gloss enamel, and flat enamel or eggshell enamel. Glossy finishes are generally harder and reflect more light. Matte finishes produce a soft glow of surrounding light. The finish affects the perception of the color as well. Table 13.3 lists and describes the characteristics of paint finishes. (Industry terminology for the amount of sheen is not standardized.)

TABLE 13.1
Selected Brands of Paints

Behr
Benjamin Moore
Dutch Boy
Glidden
Martha Stewart (Kmart)
McCloskey
Pittsburgh
Pratt & Lambert
Sherwin-Williams

TABLE 13.2
Paint Pigments

Color	Pigment
White	Titanium dioxide, zinc oxide
Reds	Iron oxides
Yellow	Siennas (oxides of iron and manganese) and ochres
Brown	Manganese
Green	Chromic oxide
Blue	Iron, cobalt, and coal-tar derivatives
Black	Burned animal bones or carbon

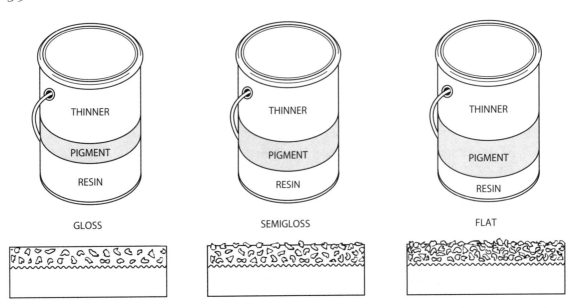

FIGURE 13.1 *Pigment volume concentrations.*

Additives

Manufacturers add products to improve the performance of the paint. Additives that are commonly added to paint are presented in Table 13.4.

Resin

Resin is also called the binder or film former. It binds the pigments together to form the cured paint and provides abrasion resistance, stain resistance, hardness, and strength. The resin determines the type of paint. There are two basic types—those that are dissolved in solvent-based solution and those that are dispersed in a water-based solution.

TABLE 13.3
Characteristics of Paint Finishes

Finish	Characteristics	Application
Flat (also called *matte*)	Very little sheen; least washable of the finishes	Appropriate for walls and ceilings when a soft velvet-like texture is desired
Satin (also called *eggshell*)	Small amount of light reflecting quality; hides fingerprints better and is more washable than flat	Appropriate for walls and ceilings when a slightly more durable finish is desired
Semigloss	Has some sheen that hides marks; more washable than satin	Areas requiring wear resistance and washability
Gloss enamel (also called *high-gloss*)	Highly reflective; the shiniest paint luster; most durable and scrubbable	Areas requiring maximum wear resistance and washability; surface must be smooth and properly prepared since imperfections are more likely to show
Flat (or eggshell) *enamel*	Matte finish with good durability	Areas requiring a matte surface and maximum wear resistance and washability

TABLE 13.4
Common Paint Additives

Additive	Purpose
Antiskinning	Prevents skin from forming in can prior to use
Biocides	Prevents spoilage resulting from bacterial growth
Coalescent	Aids in formation of continuous film in latex paint
Defoamer	Eliminates air from paint or reduces bubbling upon application
Driers	Accelerates conversion of solvent paints from liquid to solid state
Freeze-Thaw Stabilizers	Lowers latex paint freezing point
Mildewcide	Resists growth of mildew
Surfactant	Stabilizes mixtures of resins or pigments in solvents or water
Thickeners	Increases consistency of paint and prevents separation of pigment in oil-and water-based paints

Solvent-Based Paints There are two common types of solvent-based paints—oil-based and alkyds. Solvent-based paints have better adhesion, a smoother appearance, and dry harder than water-based paints.

Solvent-based paints dry and harden through the process of oxidation. While the paint is drying, **volatile organic compounds (VOCs)** are released into the air. VOCs can have adverse effects on health and the environment. States and communities have established regulations regarding VOC levels. Disposal of old oil-based paints is an environmental concern.

Oil-based paints need long drying times, have a very strong odor, and require solvent or paint thinner cleanup. The common paint thinner used for oil-based paints is mineral spirits. Oil-based paints are produced in limited quantities. Water-based and alkyd paints have largely replaced them.

Alkyd paints are oil-modified polyesters. They were introduced in the 1930s, and today they are moderately priced and popular. Alkyds:

- dry quickly and evenly
- have a harder finish with outstanding washability and resistance to scrubbing
- are easy to apply
- have very good coverage
- are available in a wide range of colors
- have less odor than oil-based paints, but fumes are toxic
- have poor resistance to alkaline surfaces such as masonry
- must be cleaned up with solvents or paint thinners
- have lower gloss than water-based paints
- tend to yellow over time, especially exterior paints
- are flammable until the surface has dried

Water-Based Paints

Water-based paints were introduced in the 1940s. They dry and harden through evaporation and they are the least expensive. Water-based paints are frequently referred to as latex paints, but they do not contain latex. Because they are water based, they are inherently lower in VOCs. Industry Statement 13.1 has more information about VOC levels and fumes.

There are many brands of water-based paints, and quality and durability varies. Water-based paints are:

- fairly durable, but not as durable or scrubbable as alkyd paints
- blister and peel resistant because they are somewhat porous and allow moisture to escape
- available in a wide range of colors
- easy to apply
- able to be cleaned up with soap and water
- quick drying
- nearly odorless
- the least fire hazard

Other Types of Paints

Epoxy paints, also known as high-performance paints, are used to paint metals and objects that hold water, such as tubs and swimming pools. Catalyzed epoxies are specialized paints that are polyesters, polyamides, or urethanes. The catalyst and the resin must be mixed just before application. Polyester epoxies are noted for their tough glossy surface; polyamides have a flexible but durable surface. Urethanes are the most versatile of the epoxy paints.

Epoxy coatings are:

- impermeable
- chemically resistant
- abrasion resistant with superior durability
- relatively expensive
- solvent based

Epoxy coatings require extensive surface preparation before application, and ventilation must be provided during and after application.

Fire-retardant coatings are often required in public buildings, especially hotels and offices. They are more expensive and less durable than other types of paint. They retard the rate of combustion, and some are **intumescent.** This means that when they are exposed to very high heat, they create a foam-like material that protects the substrate (base) from the fire as shown in Figure 13.2. Intumescent paints may be solvent based or water based. The proper application of these paints is critical because the effectiveness of the finish is based upon the number of coats

---

INDUSTRY STATEMENT 13.1

Good Paint Without the Odor

Most people aren't affected by latex paint fumes. But if you're particularly sensitive to the smell of wet paint or the chemicals in it, you can use one of the growing number of products that claim to be low odor or to contain low levels of volatile organic compounds. VOCs like ethylene glycol and aliphatic petroleum distillates can cause headaches, nausea, and dizziness in some people. Propylene glycol is less toxic. Low-odor paints are formulated to give off less fresh-paint smell.

All the low-VOC or low-odor paints we tested performed very well overall. Their prices are in line with those of regular interior latex paint: $15 to $25 a gallon for the products we tested. Low-VOC paints can dry much faster, however, forcing you to work fast. Otherwise, you may see marks where brush strokes overlap. You'll also need to clean brushes and rollers as soon as you're done so the paint doesn't dry in them.

If you're especially sensitive but aren't using a low-odor or low-VOC product, you can follow a few simple steps to keep the paint fumes down to a minimal level:

- Try to paint on a warm day when the paint will dry fast, even though that makes painting harder. Keep the windows open.

Low odor, low VOC

Product	Claim
Ace Royal Touch	Uses propylene glycol
Behr Premium Plus Satin	Uses propylene glycol
Benjamin Moore Pristine Eco Spec Eggshell	Low odor and low VOCs
Coronado Air-Care Eggshell	No VOCs
Dutch Boy Kid's Room Satin	Low odor
ICI Lifemaster 2000 Eggshell	No odor and no VOCs
Sherwin-Williams HealthSpec Eg-Shel	Low odor and low VOCs

- If possible, use a window fan to exhaust fumes from the room once you've finished painting.
- Avoid sleeping in the room or staying in it for extended periods during the first day.

Source: Consumer Reports, May 2000, p. 35.

---

and thickness of the coating. Other fire-retardant paints give off a gas that excludes air from the surface, thus extinguishing the fire.

Fire-resistant coatings are also available. They do not contribute to a fire, but they are not as effective as fire-retardant coatings at reducing the spread of flames.

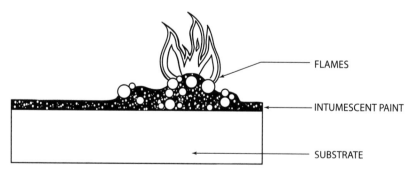

FLAMES

INTUMESCENT PAINT

SUBSTRATE

FIGURE 13.2
Intumescent paint forms a charred layer of foam when exposed to high heat.

Other paints are:

- **Texture paint** A water-based paint with a silica sand additive that creates a stucco-like texture on the wall.
- **Primers** Liquid **sealers** that are applied to the substrate, or the surface to be painted, prior to painting. Primers may be solvent based or water based. They make the surface smoother and the paint more durable. Some primers also function as sealers on porous surfaces, such as gypsum board and some woods. **Gypsum board** (dry wall) is made up of thin pieces of plaster covered with heavy-weight paper. Sealers effectively seal the paper so it will not absorb paint. Sealers are also important under wall coverings. They reduce the damage when the wall covering is removed.
- **Acrylic paint** A synthetic resin water-based paint. It is odorless, quick drying, easy to use, moderately priced, and cleans up with soap and water.
- **Luminous paints** Paints created by adding chemicals to other types of paint. **Fluorescent paints** glow under ultraviolet light; **phosphorescent paints** glow in the dark.
- **Metallic paints** Paints containing tiny flakes of aluminum, copper, or other metal as the pigment. They are very durable.
- **Mildew-proof paints** Paints with a mildew-resistant additive. They are used in bathrooms or other moist environments. Wm. Zinsser & Company, Inc., makes a mildew-proof paint with a five-year guarantee. It is blister- and peel-proof and scrubbable.

Thinner

Thinner provides the *viscosity* (fluidity) necessary to apply the paint to the surface. It enables the paint to flow onto the wall and then level itself. The thinner is the least expensive ingredient in paint. Inferior-quality paint will frequently contain more thinner than higher-quality paint. Coverage will be inferior or will require several more coats to achieve the same results as higher-quality paint. The thinner for water-based paints is water. The most common thinner for solvent-based paints is mineral spirits.

Surface Preparation

Before paint is applied, the surface must be prepared to ensure smoothness and adhesion. One of the most common reasons for paint-adhesion failure is mildew growth. *Mildew* is a fungus that grows in damp, warm environments. It must be removed before painting. A mixture of bleach and water or the use of other commercial products will effectively kill mildew. These products are potentially hazardous and should be used very carefully.

The surfaces that paint is commonly applied to are gypsum board, masonry, metals, plaster, and wood.

Gypsum Board

New gypsum board must be carefully prepared with all seams taped and nail and screw holes filled with spackling compound. It should be sanded smooth. The paper should not be sanded excessively because the abraded area may be visible after painting. All dust particles should be brushed off before the primer is applied.

Masonry

Masonry (items made with cement) may require an alkaline-resistant primer to prevent efflorescence, a white powder caused by an alkaline chemical reaction with water. Because masonry usually has a very porous surface, masonry paint contains calcium carbonate that acts as a filler to give a smooth topcoat. A gallon of masonry paint covers a smaller area than other paints because of the block filler.

Metals

Before priming, metals must be cleaned of loose rust, loose paint, and mill scale. *Mill scale* is a fine coating of oxide that forms when iron is heated. Sandblasting is effective for large areas; hand sanding is appropriate for small areas. The primer should inhibit rust and be formulated for the specific type of metal.

Plaster

Plaster must be smooth and free of all cracks before painting. The surface must be sanded and the dust removed. Plaster is very porous, so a primer/sealer must be applied before the paint.

Wood

All cracks and nail holes in wood must be filled in with wood putty or filler. Knots can bleed through the paint, so knot sealer must be used prior to painting. Moisture in the wood may affect the paint. Wood has approximately five to ten percent moisture content.

Application

The optimum temperature for the application of paint is 70 degrees Fahrenheit. It is essential that ventilation be provided when paint is being applied and when it is drying. The four methods of applying paint are—spray, brush, pad, and roller. These methods produce smooth surfaces.

Spraying

There are two types of spraying guns—airless and air compression. Airless spraying uses fluid pressure and undiluted paint. This spraying gun uses more paint, but it does provide better coverage. Air-compression spray guns use diluted paint, and coverage is less complete.

Spraying covers large areas quickly and economically. A roller should be used on the walls after spraying to even out the paint. Spraying is especially good for coating uneven or irregular surfaces. Another advantage is that the paint will dry quickly. All surrounding areas must be carefully covered to avoid overspray, the clean up of which can be time consuming.

Paint is also available in aerosol spray cans. A metal ball in the can acts as an agitator to mix the paint when the can is shaken. Aerosol paints are ideal for hard-to-reach areas or hard-to-paint items. They are easy to use and dry quickly. However, they are expensive, and overspraying can be a problem.

Brush

Paintbrush bristles may be natural hair or synthetic. Natural bristles are recommended for alkyd paints, and synthetic bristles are recommended for water-based paints. Hog bristles from China or Siberia are considered the best, and those from India and Korea are also good. High-quality nylon bristles are less expensive than high-quality natural bristles. Nylon bristles can be used with any type of paint and are especially good for use with water-based paints because they do not swell when they come in contact with water. Nylon bristles last longer and are easier to clean than natural bristles.

All brushes should have **flagged bristles,** which have split ends. They help the brush hold more paint and allow the paint to flow more smoothly. Brushes are used for uneven surfaces and detail work, such as moldings and window grids. Figure 13.3 shows the different sizes of paintbrushes.

Brushes made from polyurethane foam can be used with oil-based, alkyd, and water-based paints. They are inexpensive and can be cleaned or disposed of after use.

Pads and Rollers

Pads are made from foam or a carpet-like material that is attached to handles. They apply paint easily and evenly without splatter (see the example of a pad in Figure 13.4). Rollers have a tendency to splatter paint. Figure 13.5 shows a roller and pan.

Rollers are made from a synthetic material that resembles lamb's wool. The nap length varies from 1/16 to 1 1/2 inches. The length of the nap required is determined by the texture of the surface to be painted and the type of paint. See Table 13.5 for guidelines on length of nap as related to wall texture. Rougher surfaces require longer naps, while smooth surfaces require shorter naps.

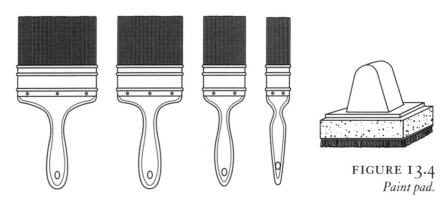

FIGURE 13.3
*Paintbrushes are available
in various widths.*

FIGURE 13.4
Paint pad.

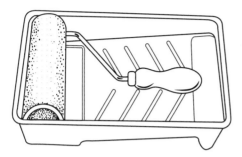

FIGURE 13.5 *Paint roller and tray.*

TABLE 13.5
Guidelines on Length of Nap As Related to Wall Texture

Nap Length	Surface
1/8″ to 3/8″	Very smooth
3/8″-1/2″	Somewhat smooth
1/2″ to 3/4″	Somewhat rough
3/4″ to 1 1/4″	Very rough

The higher the paint sheen, the shorter nap needed. For example, a 3/8-inch nap is appropriate for eggshell paint.

Decorative Painting Techniques

Decorative painting techniques are easy ways to add interest to a room. Paint-texturizing techniques are sometimes called **faux finishes.** Some visual texturing techniques make the surface look old and imitate the patina found on antiques. Other techniques create the look of marble or granite.

Bagging This technique creates a marbled effect by using a plastic bag to remove wet glaze and reveal a base color. The bag can be empty or half-filled with rags and securely tied (see Figure 13.6).

Color washing A coat of thinned or translucent paint is applied over a white or colored background. If the surface is rough, the effect is a rugged texture. If the surface is smooth, the effect is shimmering translucence.

Combing A hard comb-like tool is dragged over a wet glaze to reveal a base coat. Combing produces fine lines and may be used in wood graining. Cross-hatching can produce a fabric-like texture.

Dragging Subtle stripes are created by dragging a dry brush over a wet glaze to reveal a base color. Dragging can imitate fabric (see Figure 13.7).

Glazing Transparent colors are overlayed in sequence to produce gradations of color.

Graining Graining is brushing on a glaze and drawing wood grains and lines with an artist's brush.

Marbling This technique imitates polished marble.

Porphyry *Porphyry* is a term that describes a family of rock types that are found in many different colors. The painting technique produces a granite-like texture by crisscross brushing, then stippling, spattering, and finally cissing (dropping mineral spirits on the spatters to dilute and make shadows of the spatters).

Ragging or **rag rolling** Wet paint or glaze is partially removed by dabbing with a rag or rolling the paint off with a rolled rag. It usually works best with light neutrals or pastels over white (see Figure 13.8).

Shading Blending color values from light to dark across a wall or ceiling is called shading. It usually works best with lighter colors.

Smooshing To create a slightly marbled effect, a thin piece of plastic is applied to a wall of wet paint, rubbed with the hands, and then peeled off.

Spattering Uneven spots or spatters are achieved by filling a brush with paint and flipping the paint onto the base color. Spattering can vary from tiny irregular dots to large globs of paint. Spacing can be very close or sparse.

Sponging Painting with sponges creates a broken, splotchy effect. Large-pore sponges produce a coarser-looking texture than finer sponges. Oil-based paints look crisper, while water-based paints look softer (see Figure 13.9).

Stenciling In stenciling, a cutout pattern is used to reproduce a painted design. It is frequently seen around windows and doorways (see Figure 13.10).

Stippling A stipple brush, or other brush, is used to dab on a colored glaze or paint, creating a mottled, orange-peel texture (see Figure 13.11).

Washing A sponge dipped in glaze is washed over the wall in a circular motion.

FIGURE 13.6 *Bagging.*

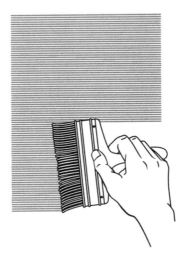

FIGURE 13.7 *Dragging.*

FIGURE 13.8 *Rag Rolling.*

FIGURE 13.9 *Sponging.*

FIGURE 13.10 *Stenciling.*

Courtesy of LA Stencilworks.

FIGURE 13.11 *Stippling.*

Other Types of Coatings

Other liquid products are applied to surfaces as films. These include stains, varnishes, shellac, lacquer, and Danish oil.

Stains

Stains are pigments that are applied to bare or sealed wood. They may be transparent or opaque. Light to medium stains will enhance the wood surface. Five types of stains are—water based, oil based, alcohol based, nongrain raising, and stain waxes.

- *Water-based stains* These penetrate the surface of the wood rapidly but not evenly. Water raises the grain of the wood, so sanding is necessary.
- *Oil-based stains* The most commonly used stain for interiors is oil-based stain. The oil penetrates the wood well and gives a more durable colored base. High-use areas, such as cabinets, doors, and windowsills, should be coated with a urethane varnish for a protective, durable finish.
- *Alcohol-based stains* Alcohol-based stains dry very quickly. They are usually applied by spraying and used under lacquer, mostly in industrial applications.
- *Nongrain raising (NGR) stains* These stains do not penetrate the wood well but do stay on the surface. They do not require sanding before application of the final coat. Like alcohol-based stains, they are primarily used in industry.
- *Stain waxes* These provide color and a protective wax finish in a one-step process.

Varnishes

Varnishes are transparent films that are applied to stained or unstained wood. They are available in different levels of sheen—gloss or high gloss; satin, semigloss, or medium-rubbed-effect; and dull or flat.

There are several different types of varnishes:

- *Spar varnish* This varnish is used when a hard, glossy finish that is impervious to moisture is needed; it can be used both indoors and outdoors.
- *Alkyd varnish* Slightly longer lasting than spar varnish, but alkyd varnish can only be used where moisture is not present.
- *Polyurethane varnish* Resistant to water and alcohol, polyurethane varnish is especially good as a finish on wood floors and tabletops. It does not yellow or change color as much as other varnishes. Manufacturer's application instructions must be followed carefully. Proper humidity levels are essential during application.
- *Pigmented varnish stains* These inexpensive stains impart only a superficially colored protective finish to wood. If the surface of the finish is scratched, the natural wood color will show through.

Shellac

Shellac is inexpensive and seldom used. It was the original glossy, transparent finish for furniture, but it has been replaced by urethane and oil varnishes because they are not affected as much by heat and water. Shellac will turn white when exposed to water and/or heat.

Lacquer

Lacquer is used commercially to finish wood furniture and cabinets. It may be clear or colored and is applied using a spray gun. Many layers of lacquer will produce a fine, durable finish.

Danish Oil

Danish oil is primarily tung oil and boiled linseed oil. It gives wood a rich, penetrating oil surface and seals the pores of the wood. There are two types of Danish oil—clear and stain.

Selection of Paint

Selection of paint is usually based on the desired amount of sheen and the durability of the finish. Alkyds are more durable than water-based paints, and glossier paints are more durable than flat paints. Matte paints hide wall imperfections better than glossy paints. Table 13.6 recommends specific finishes for painting rooms and other items in the home. If an important consideration in the selection of the paint is the residual smell, use low-VOC and no-VOC paints.

Paints generally dry lighter than they appear in the can; the intensity of the color increases from the cumulative reflection of four walls. Pale colors will appear much lighter over a large area, and bright colors will appear much bolder or darker over a large area.

The calculation of the amount of paint needed for a project is determined by the area to be covered and the **spreading rate,** or **coverage rate,** of the paint. The spreading rate is the number of square feet of a specific surface that can be covered by a specific quantity of paint (rough surfaces require more paint). To determine the square footage to be covered, multiply the length of each wall by its height and add those figures. If there are very large windows or doorways, their areas can be deducted from the overall square footage. To compute the square footage of the ceiling, simply multiply the width of the room by its length. Divide the surface area by the spreading rate of the paint, which can be found on the paint label.

Proper preparation of the surface to be painted is important. The surface must be clean, dry, smooth, and free of any blemishes. All cracks and holes should be filled with plaster or spackling compound, sanded, and painted with primer. The primer, sealer, and topcoat must be compatible with the substrate, or base. Improper preparation or incompatible coatings may result in peeling, blistering, cracking, or flaking. Semigloss or high-gloss surfaces must be primed or sanded before repainting. Shiny surfaces do not have the texture necessary for good adhesion of the new coats of paint.

TABLE 13.6

Recommendations of Specific Finishes for Painting Projects

	High-Gloss Enamel	Semigloss	Satin/Eggshell	Flat	Flat, or Eggshell, Enamel
Trim and Accessories					
Cabinets	X	X			
Doors	X	X			
Furniture	X	X			
Moldings	X	X			
Shutters	X	X			
Windows	X	X			
Walls					
Bath	X	X	X		X
Bedroom—master			X	X	
Bedroom—children			X		X
Dining room			X	X	
Family room		X	X		X
Hallway		X	X		X
Kitchen	X	X	X		
Living room			X	X	

* Ceiling paint can be used for ceilings in all rooms.

Care of Painted Surfaces

The paint manufacturers provide guidance on appropriate care methods for their products. In general, the more durable paints may be scrubbed, but flat paint may develop shiny spots from scrubbing. Extra paint should be saved for touch-ups, but because most paint will fade with age and exposure to sun, it may be necessary to repaint the entire wall.

WALL COVERINGS

Wall coverings are available in a wide range of colors, textures, and patterns. They can be used to visually alter the dimensions of a room and to create atmosphere (see Figure 13.12). They can imitate many other materials, be coordinated with fabrics, and reflect historical periods. The original material for wall coverings was paper, but now many materials are used. The Chinese used rice paper on their walls as early as 200 B.C. Prior to the Industrial Revolution, only the wealthy could afford wallpaper. William Morris, a famous designer who created many beautiful patterns, was responsible for the popularity of wallpaper in the late 19th and early 20th centuries. Wall coverings may be all paper, paper backed with fabric, vinyl face with paper or fabric backing, or fabric with a paper backing.

FIGURE 13.12
Phillip Jeffries wall coverings.
Courtesy of Philip Jeffries Ltd.

Customers select wall coverings because they contribute to the aesthetics of a room. Wall coverings are also selected for their durable surfaces, easy cleaning, and their ability to cover damaged walls. Industry Statement 13.2 provides techniques for using color schemes in the home.

Traditional paper, vinyl, and fabric are the most common wall coverings. Cork, tile, and mirrors are also used. Sometimes, instead of covering the entire wall, a border is applied to painted walls or on top of another wall covering. Table 13.7 lists selected brands of wall coverings.

Paper and Vinyl Wall Coverings

A wide variety of patterns and colors is available, and usually the wall coverings are pretrimmed. **Pretrimmed wall coverings** have had the selvages cut off. **Untrimmed wall coverings** must have the selvages cut off. **Semitrimmed wall coverings** have only one side of the selvage trimmed off. The other side must be left on as an overlap, or it is trimmed off at the site. Paper and vinyl wall coverings are usually purchased by the roll and adhered to the wall with an adhesive.

Traditional Paper Wall Coverings

Traditional wallpaper is more fragile and difficult to hang than vinyl wall covering. It also has a tendency to stretch and can shrink or distort after drying. There are three types of traditional paper wall coverings—machine printed, hand printed, and plastic coated.

- Machine-printed paper wall coverings are the least expensive. They are printed with rollers and are usually only suitable for low-use areas.
- Hand-printed paper wall coverings are more expensive than machine printed. They may be hand screen printed or block printed. The cost will depend on the design and background material. They are not usually pretrimmed, are very fragile, and should be hung by a professional. They may need to be special ordered.
- Plastic-coated paper wall coverings have a vinyl coating that can be wiped off with a damp cloth. These wall coverings are sometimes labeled as washable, which means that the wall covering can be cleaned gently with a little soap and water, but abrasives and detergents may damage them.

INDUSTRY STATEMENT 13.2

Waverly—How to Choose a Color Scheme

---

1. Think first about practical aspects of the room such as

   ▪ Function: How is the room used? Warm colors work well for active rooms, cool colors for relaxation areas.
   ▪ People: Who will use the room? Consider their color preferences when selecting your color scheme.
   ▪ Location: What is the exposure to sunlight? Northern and eastern exposures benefit from warm color schemes; western and southern exposures from cool schemes.
   ▪ Size: Do you want to increase or decrease the apparent size? Warm colors advance, making the room seem smaller; cool colors recede, making the room appear larger.

2. Choose a print you love. This will be your "signature print" that will set the color scheme for the room. Signature prints usually contain several colors and large scale pattern that is suitable for window treatments, bedcoverings, wallcoverings, and upholstery.
3. Let one color from your signature print dominate. Use this color in as much as 2/3 of the available area.
4. Pull 2–3 other colors from your signature print to act as support or accent colors. Use them in smaller areas and in accessories.
5. Carry your color scheme throughout the entire house to create a strong visual continuity. Varying the dominant color and patterns you use in each room— while remaining faithful to your basic color scheme— will keep your home interesting, yet unified.

Vinyl Wall Coverings

Vinyl wall coverings should always be hung with a fungicidal adhesive to prevent the growth of mold and mildew. Vinyl wall coverings are usually backed with drill, osnaburg (a heavy fabric), or scrim for dimensional stability. Varieties of vinyl wall coverings include vinyl-impregnated fabric-backed, polyvinyl-chloride, and cushion-backed wall coverings.

Vinyl-impregnated fabric-backed and polyvinyl chloride wall coverings are similar to traditional wallpaper in style and application. Vinyl is stronger and more durable than most wallpapers, and scrubbable. Grease and smoke stains will come off without damage to the surface. These wall coverings are labeled as scrubbable and can be scrubbed repeatedly with strong detergents. Vinyl wall coverings can be very heavy and difficult to hang because of their weight. They are sometimes patterned to imitate wood, leather, tile, marble, or other hard materials.

TABLE 13.7
Selected Brands of Wall Coverings

Albert Van Luit and Co.	Katzenbach & Warren
Bradbury & Bradbury Art Wallpapers	Richard E. Thibaut, Inc.
Brunschwig & Fils	Scalamandré
Imperial	Schumacher
JM Lynne Co., Inc.	Waverly

Cushion-backed wall coverings are heavily backed for installation over rough subsurfaces, such as severely cracked walls. They can also be installed over concrete or cinder block walls. They have a cushion and woven glass-fiber backing that prevents the wall covering from conforming to the irregularities of the wall.

Other Options with Wall Coverings

Consumers can also select from a variety of other types of wall coverings.

- **Prepasted wall coverings** The covering has an adhesive coating. The paper is soaked in water or wet with a damp sponge before hanging. Most of the more expensive papers are not prepasted.
- **Peelable wall covering** The top layer of the wall covering will peel off and leave a substrate material that can be papered over.
- **Strippable wall coverings** These wall coverings can be pulled off the wall in strips without scraping or the use of a steamer. Ease of removal is a definite advantage. Many, but not all, fabric-backed vinyl wall coverings are strippable.
- **Blank stock** Also called **lining paper,** black stock is the material used as a base under wallpaper to provide a smooth or slightly textured surface so that the wall will look smooth and even. It is available in several weights. A heavier blank stock is used to cover cracks, unevenness, and other flaws. Blank stock should be hung horizontally.
- **Flocked wall covering** This decorative effect imitates velvet. Tiny fibers are glued, usually in a pattern, to the surface of the base.
- **Moiré** This wall covering is embossed to took like watered silk.
- **Foil/Mylar® wall coverings** Highly reflective, these wall coverings may be patterned or flocked.
- **Ceiling paper** Used specifically on ceilings where blank stock is too thin to hide the defects, ceiling paper sometimes has a bubbly texture that is almost unnoticeable, but it hides surface damage well.
- **Borders** This band of wall covering is used as a trim and/or accent on ceiling lines, chair rails, doors, windows, and other architectural features. It may be glued over wallpaper or over painted walls. Borders are generally packaged in spools of 15 feet. The width of borders varies.

Selection of Wall Coverings

Wall coverings should be selected for both their aesthetics and the functional requirements of the room. Amount of use, noise and thermal insulation, and the condition of the walls are all factors that will help determine the correct wall covering. Paper wall coverings and most fabric wall coverings should be used where there is light traffic and little chance that they will become soiled.

Vinyl wall coverings are appropriate for kitchens and baths. They can be scrubbed repeatedly without damage.

Wall coverings are usually sold in single, double, and triple roll packages. Widths usually range from 18 to 28 inches. Some heavy vinyl wall coverings are 54 inches wide.

A **single roll** of wall covering made in the United States is usually 27 inches wide and 28 feet long. It contains between 30 and 36 square feet and will cover approximately 25 to 30 square feet after allowances for matching and trimming. European wall coverings are sold in shorter lengths and will usually cover about 25 square feet per single roll. Most wall coverings are priced as single rolls and can usually be purchased as single rolls. An American **double roll,** called a **double-roll bolt,** is twice as long as a single roll and contains about 72 square feet. A **triple roll,** or **triple-roll bolt,** contains about 108 square feet. It is the most economical use of the covering. Always order an extra roll of wall covering, especially if it is a do-it-yourself project. Commercial wall coverings are usually packaged in 30-yard bolts that are 52 to 55 inches wide.

It can be difficult to estimate how many rolls of wall covering will be needed for a project. The size of the design repeat, the number of doors, windows, height of the ceiling, and architectural details are important considerations. See Table 13.8 for some general guidelines for determining the number of rolls needed.

To ensure color matching, all rolls should come from the same dye lot. Each roll should be inspected for defects before it is cut. Coordinated or companion fabrics for drapes or bedding are often available for use with paper or vinyl wall coverings. The wall covering should be hung first so the drapes can be adjusted to match the pattern with the wall covering.

A precise color match between wall covering and fabric is frequently not possible. Dyes are absorbed differently and the fabric and covering reflect light differently. For a perfect match, the fabric can be backed for use as a wall covering.

The repeat pattern affects the amount of paper needed and, therefore, the total cost of the wall covering. The **repeat pattern** is an identical shape or image that occurs in a set sequence. The **vertical pattern** is the distance between one point and the next repeat of the same point. A

TABLE 13.8
Roll Estimator for American Wall Coverings

Area in Square Feet	Number of Double Rolls Needed
150	3
200	4
250	5
300	6
350	7
400	8
450	9

large repeat pattern is wasteful because a complete pattern repeat must begin at the top of each length. Extra allowance must be made for patterns with large repeats. A **random match,** or **free match,** pattern has designs that are not split at the seam. See Figure 13.13 for an example of matching.

In a horizontal pattern, a **straight match** means that the pattern on the left side of the strip will match with the right side of the previous strip. If the second strip has to be lowered to match, it is called a **drop match** (see Figure 13.14). When the strips are hung, they must be aligned very carefully in order to produce good results.

Installation of Wall Coverings

With the wide variety of wall coverings available, it is essential to follow the manufacturer's recommendations on adhesives and hanging instructions.

Wall preparation is essential for successful installation of paper and vinyl wall coverings. Some general guidelines are:

- Wash walls to remove all grease.
- New wall coverings can be hung over old paper covering if the old is still tight at the seams and there is no overlapping. Old vinyl wall coverings must be removed before hanging new.
- A freshly painted wall should be a month old before applying a wall covering.
- Old semigloss or gloss paints should be roughened with coarse sandpaper to make a good surface for the adhesive.
- Unpainted walls should be at least a month old, and a priming coat of glue sizing should be applied. Sizing is a thin liquid that is painted onto the wall to seal the surface so alkali cannot penetrate into the wallpaper and to reduce the amount of paste absorbed. It also gives the surface "tooth," or enough roughness to allow the paper to stick well.
- Wallboard and other paper-faced surfaces should be sealed with primer. The primer should dry for 24 hours.
- Repair all cracks and holes in the walls.

FIGURE 13.13
Matching a simple design.

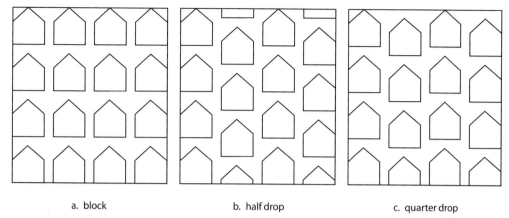

a. block   b. half drop   c. quarter drop

FIGURE 13.14 *Repeat patterns.*

Textiles as Wall Coverings

Almost every kind of textile can be used as a wall covering. Sometimes naturally colored or dyed yarns or fibers are used. Simple or complex yarns are placed on a backing fabric.

Tightly woven fabrics usually work best for use as wall coverings because the edges are less likely to fray. Woven-pile weaves, such as velvet and corduroy, create interesting surface textures. Tricot or interlock knits are also suitable for use as wall coverings. Carpeting adds textural interest and softness to a room. It also deadens sound. Fabrics tend to soil, but they can be treated with a soil repellent. In addition to installating fabrics as a flat layer, they can also be folded, padded, pleated, shirred, draped, or stitched into interesting surface treatments. Fireproofing is required for commercial installations.

Most wallpaper manufacturers sell prebacked fabrics for use as wall coverings. Fabrics can also be laminated. The backing of textiles can be acrylic foam, vinyl spray, paper gypsum, or a spunbonded or spunlaced nonwoven fabric. The backing prevents the adhesive from staining the front of the fabric.

Because fabrics may spot or discolor when they are spot cleaned, textile wall coverings can be laminated with a vinyl film to protect the surface and make it washable. This film may turn yellow with age. Fabric wall coverings are more fragile than vinyl or vinyl-coated wallpaper, so they should not be hung in heavy traffic areas.

Latex-Coated Fabric

Latex-coated fabrics have been stretched on a frame while a latex compound is applied. The textile will retain some of its flexibility. It is not dimensionally stable and can shrink during processing and stretch during handling. Sometimes the grain slips during processing, so it is difficult to match the pattern horizontally. Latex backing will improve ravel resistance and seam slippage. The process of hanging latex-coated fabric is labor intensive and requires a higher level of skill than traditional wall coverings.

Paper-Backed fabric

For **paper-backed fabric,** paper is laminated to the back of the fabric. The paper stiffens the fabric and makes it easier to hang. The fabric will have properties similar to that of traditional wall coverings and can be hung using the traditional wallpapering method.

Wall Upholstery

Wall upholstery is very expensive. The fabric is backed with foam or polyester padding. Each piece is sewn together prior to hanging and then stapled to the wall. Welting is then added. Sometimes the foam or batting is applied to the wall, the fabric is stapled over the padding, and trim is added to hide the staples. Both methods have the added benefits of sound control and thermal insulation.

Other Methods of Installing Wall Fabric

Other methods of installing wall fabric include:

- *Covered frame method* Fabric is stretched tightly over a lath frame (strips of wood). The frame is then hung on nails protruding from the wall.
- *Direct paste-up* Fabric is dipped in liquid laundry starch and applied to the wall, or the starch is sponged on the wall. The fabric will adhere to the wall until it is remoistened and peeled off.
- *Hook-and-loop tape* One half of the hook-and-loop tape is adhered to the wall; the other half is adhered to the fabric. This method is especially useful when the fabric may need to be taken down frequently for cleaning. A well-known brand of hook-and-loop tape is Velcro®.
- *Lath method* Wood lath strips are nailed to the wall; the fabric is then stapled, glued, or fastened to the wood with hook and loop tape.
- *Panel-track method* Ready-made metal track systems are usually used in nonresidential sites, such as office systems furniture where fabrics can be changed as necessary.
- *Shirring* Casings are stitched on the top and bottom edges of the fabric; conventional curtain rods are slipped through the casings and positioned on the walls.
- *Stapling* The fabric is simply stapled to the wall. The staples are usually covered with trim. This is a fast, easy method.

Specialty Wall Coverings

Other specialty wall coverings are paneling, planks, tiles, cork, mirrors, and leather. Specialty wall coverings provide interesting alternatives to paint and vinyl or paper wall coverings. They can also cover defective walls, absorb sounds, and create extremely durable surfaces.

Panels

Most paneling comes in sheets that are 4 feet by 8 feet. Wood paneling needs to be finished for durability. Paneling may be prefinished at the factory or finished on-site before or after it is hung. Five types of paneling are available:

- *Plywood paneling* Veneers are available for rustic to elegant interiors.
- *Hardwood panels* Hardwood panels can be simulated to look like wood, brick, or a variety of other surfaces. They are much cheaper than plywood paneling.
- *Plastic laminated paneling* Resin-impregnated paper bonded together by heat and pressure creates a fairly rigid sheet of material. It is a durable, easy care, water-resistant surface that comes in a variety of colors and patterns.
- *Peg-Board*® Peg-Board is the perforated hardboard that is usually seen in workrooms.
- *Flexwood*® Flexwood is a two-ply construction of veneer and cloth that can be applied to flat or curved surfaces. It can be used where fire or building codes do not permit the use of wood paneling.

Planks

Wooden planks can be attached to walls horizontally, vertically, and diagonally. They can be stained and finished if desired. Wooden strips can also be used to create interesting patterns on walls.

Tiles

Many of the tiles described in Chapter 13 can also be used on the wall. Ceramic tiles are especially good for kitchens and bathrooms. A wide selection of colors, designs, shapes, and sizes is available. It is important to use the right adhesive. Tile is cold and noisy, but it cleans easily and is very durable.

Cork

Cork is especially useful to cover damaged walls. It is cut into thin layers and has a paper backing. Its natural color is warm and earthy, but it is available in other colors. It has the advantages of providing good heat and sound insulation. Cork is also available as 12-inch square tiles that are 1/8 to 5/8 inch thick or thicker. Cork's natural porous nature allows nails, pins, and tacks to be imbedded. It usually needs to be sealed with polyurethane or wax polish.

Mirrors

Mirrors increase light and can make a room look larger or expand a view. They are available in a variety of styles—beveled, unbeveled, clear, smoked, bronze, black, and peach or other tints. Two-way mirrors are available for use in apartment doors, children's observation areas, department stores, banks, and prison security areas. Quality mirrors are made of float glass. Mirror sheeting is heavy, so it must be screwed into place. Mirror tiles are less expensive and are attached with an adhesive.

Lifestyles Drives Waverly

It's more than just pretty fabric

Decorating a room is an age-old problem.

Some love it, others dread it—how to decorate this room? Should it be Country French or English Country? For generations, Waverly Fabrics has consistently come to the rescue and guided homeowners through the perilous world of home decorating with a sure and confident hand.

"I am really impressed with their approach to the customer: They want to help them decorate and [say] 'By the way, we sell this product that can help you,'" said Don Morgan, managing partner from WestWane Inc., a consulting firm based in Georgia. "People have ideas and want their ideas confirmed, and that's what Waverly does."

Waverly knows its customers and what they want. They are 25- to 54-year-old females who are "passionate about decorating," according to Daniel L. Bonini, vice president of marketing for Waverly. For the most part, these consumers are homeowners who are married with children and are looking for decorating with an individual point of view.

Today, the company enjoys an unparalleled success as being "the most recognized brand in home decorating," Bonini said. He attributes the success, in part, to the 1998 shift in the focus of the company's advertising to an "overall lifestyle approach that creates a recognizable identity for the consumer." Models are shown in the advertisements to reflect the target customers, thus reinforcing the message.

The company's advertising constantly works to expand its brand awareness. Until 1998, the advertising had been done strictly in shelter publications. However, the latest phase has seen the introduction of Waverly advertising in non-shelter publications, including *People* and *InStyle*. The goal of this move, according to Bonini, "is to expand our reach beyond the baby boomers into generations X and Y. We want to continue to nurture our current customers while at the same time introducing younger customers to our product," he said.

Waverly is also reaping the benefits of a strong economy where second homes are becoming more common.

"Waverly's prints are perfect for the second home because [many of them] are done in brights," explained Morgan.

The scope of the Waverly product line goes well beyond fabrics and wallpapers. The company has licensed product for furniture, rugs, window treatments, dinnerware, personal care and books, among others.

"That they are in so many rooms is great," Morgan stressed. "They have done a good job in continuing to reinforce the style of the brand."

Bonini noted, "After we run a collection in an ad, the sales of that collection increase 30 percent to 40 percent." In addition to sales, the advertising generates approximately 7,000 phone referrals and e-mails a year and 2.8 million hits on its Web site.

The site provides a store locator and home-decorating project ideas, as well as product information. The average visit to the company's Web site lasts approximately 33 minutes.

Waverly's newest line extension is a recently launched furniture collection in collaboration with Lexington Furniture. The co-venture was described as "a brilliant move" by Morgan.

Source: HFN Imagemakers, May 29, 2000.

Leather

Leather is cut into design blocks much like tiles. Because of the nature of leather there are distinctive color variations.

Care of Wall Coverings

Labels and manufacturer's care instructions should be followed carefully. Paper wall coverings are usually best cleaned with putty-like cleaners especially made for this purpose. Sometimes small marks can be cleaned with a gum eraser. Wall coverings labeled as washable can be gently washed with soap and water. Those marked *scrubbable* can be scrubbed repeatedly with strong detergents. Textile wall coverings can be very fragile and must be handled with care. Grass cloth, suede, sisal, and carpeting should be vacuumed to remove dust. Specialty wall coverings each have their own care requirements, and the manufacturer's guidelines should be followed.

ENVIRONMENTAL ISSUES

The important environmental issues related to paint involve storage and disposal, VOCs, and the removal of old lead paint. Paint can be stored in its original container for many years if it is properly sealed. The opening of the can should be covered with plastic wrap and the lid replaced tightly. The can should be stored upside down. An empty paint can should be allowed to dry out, and then the can should be recycled. Disposal of solvent-based paints should conform to local hazardous waste guidelines. The local waste-management office can provide details.

Lead-based paints were used in many homes built prior to 1978. Lead can cause serious health problems in adults but especially in children who eat paint chips containing lead. Lead paint that is in good condition is not usually hazardous. Sanding, scraping, or use of a propane torch or heat gun on lead-based paint will create large amounts of lead dust and fumes. Certified, professionally trained contractors can permanently remove lead hazards.

VOCs are released into the air as solvent-based paints dry and can have adverse effects on health and the environment. Providing adequate ventilation can minimize the impact on health. States and communities have established regulations regarding VOC levels. Installation of wall coverings in a home does not have the environmental impact that painting does.

SUMMARY

Paints and wall coverings are used to create beautiful interiors and also to impart very durable protective surfaces to walls. Paint is a thin, protective, liquid film that, when applied to a surface, dries to a hard finish. It is the most commonly used finish for walls.

The three basic ingredients in paint are pigments, thinner, and resin. The pigments give the paint color, opacity, and sheen. There are five basic finishes available in paints—flat, satin, gloss, semigloss, and eggshell. Glossy finishes are harder and reflect more light. Matte finishes produce a soft glow of surrounding light. There are two basic types of resins—those that are dispersed in a water-based solution and those that are dissolved in solvent-based solution. Latex paint is water based. Oil paint and alkyd paints are solvent based. Alkyds are oil-modified polyesters. They are popular and moderately priced.

The four methods of applying paint are spray, brush, pad, and roller. These methods produce smooth surfaces. Decorative painting techniques are easy ways to add interest to a room. Paint-texturizing techniques are also called *faux finishes.*

Selection of paint is usually based on the desired amount of sheen and durability of the finish. Alkyds are more durable than latex paints, and glossier paints are more durable than flat paints. Matte paints hide wall imperfections better than glossy paints.

Paint manufacturers provide guidance on appropriate care methods for their products. The more durable paints may be scrubbed.

Wall coverings may be all paper, paper backed with fabric, vinyl face with paper or fabric backing, or fabric with a paper backing. Wall coverings are frequently selected because they contribute to the aesthetics of a room and for their durable surfaces and easy cleaning. Some are used to cover damaged walls. Specialty wall coverings include cork, tile, and mirrors.

Tightly woven fabrics usually work best for use as textile wall coverings, and pile weaves, such as velvet and corduroy, create interesting surface textures. Fabrics are very fragile and tend to soil, but they can be treated with a soil repellent or laminated with a vinyl film.

Wall upholstery is very expensive. Fabric and foam or polyester padding are fastened to the wall.

Wall coverings should be selected for both their aesthetics and the functional requirements of the room. Labels and manufacturer's care instructions should be followed carefully.

TERMS FOR REVIEW

acrylic paint
bagging
blank stock (lining paper)
border
ceiling paper
color washing
combing
double roll (double-roll bolt)
dragging
drop match
efflorescence
faux finishes
flagged bristles
flocked wall covering
fluorescent paints
foil/Mylar® wall coverings
glazing
graining
gypsum board
intumescent
latex-coated fabric

luminous paints
marbling
metallic paints
mildew-proof paints
moiré
opacity
paint
paper-backed fabric
peelable wall covering
phosphorescent paints
pigment volume
   concentration (PVC)
porphyry
prepasted wall covering
pretrimmed wall covering
primers
ragging (rag rolling)
random match (free match)
repeat pattern
sealers
semitrimmed wall covering

shading
single roll
smooshing
spattering
sponging
spreading rate (coverage rate)
stains
stenciling
stippling
straight match
strippable wall covering
texture paint
triple roll (triple-roll bolt)
untrimmed wall covering
vertical pattern
volatile organic compounds
   (VOCs)
wall upholstery
washing

REVIEW QUESTIONS

1. What are the 2 basic types of paint?
2. List the 4 main ways to apply paint.
3. What factors need to be taken into consideration when estimating the amount of wall paper needed for a room?
4. What are the advantages of vinyl wall covering?
5. List three specialty wall coverings.
6. Why are lead-based paints dangerous?

LEARNING ACTIVITIES

1. Visit a home-improvement store to find out the variety of paints available and the services offered to do-it-yourselfers.
2. Measure the wall space of your bedroom (length × width × height minus doors and windows). Go to a store that sells wall coverings and select a paper that you like. Calculate the number of rolls needed to cover your walls.

CHAPTER 14

LIGHTING

Everything we see…most of what we do…and much of what we feel is touched by light. Managing the effects of light is what great lighting is all about.

www.lightolier.com

Lighting is an essential aspect of home furnishings that also makes interiors more pleasant and allows for tasks and activities to be completed much more easily. Careful selection, placement, and control of lighting create an internal environment that is both functional and aesthetically pleasing.

Lighting energy and therefore, consumer cost, is a necessary consideration. Energy-efficient lamps and luminaires help reduce the cost of lighting. *Lamp* is the technical term for what is commonly called a light bulb. A *luminaire* is the technical term for what is commonly called a lamp or a **fixture,** which is a complete lighting unit. It includes the lamp holder, power connection, and any internal devices such as reflectors.

PURPOSES OF LIGHTING

The purposes of residential lighting are threefold:

- **Ambient lighting** Needed to perform routine activities
- **Task lighting** Needed to perform specific tasks, such as reading
- **Decorative lighting** Needed to create an aesthetically pleasing environment

All three types of lighting are frequently combined in a space, and their purposes may overlap as required by the time of day or the uses of the room. For example, ambient light may be needed on a cloudy day but not on a sunny day.

Ambient Lighting

Ambient lighting is also referred to as **general lighting.** It provides uniform light for general use but does not usually provide enough light for specific tasks. Ambient lighting can be direct or indirect. Some utilitarian ambient lighting, such as that found in workrooms and kitchens, does provide enough light for specific tasks.

Direct–Ambient Lighting

When **direct light** is used, nearly all (90 to 100 percent) of the light is directed toward the surface to be lit. Direct-ambient lighting shines directly from the luminaire downward. **Downlights** are fixtures that are installed on the ceiling or wall to cast pools of light below. Downlights that are directed toward the wall are called **wall washers** because they bathe the wall in light. Recessed, ceiling-mounted, or suspended luminaires are usually used for direct general lighting like that in Figure 14.1.

Indirect–Ambient Lighting

When **indirect light** is used, 90 to 100 percent of the light is redirected toward the surface to be lit. Sometimes indirect light is called *reflected light.* Indirect-ambient lighting shines against a surface and is reflected into the space indirectly. It generally produces a softer effect than direct lighting. It may be an **uplight** that casts light onto the ceiling, where it is reflected back into the room (see Figure 14.2a). Another method used to create indirect-ambient light is the placement of luminaires that are recessed into the ceiling around the perimeter of a room. The light is directed toward the walls and "washes" them with light (see Figure 14.2.b).

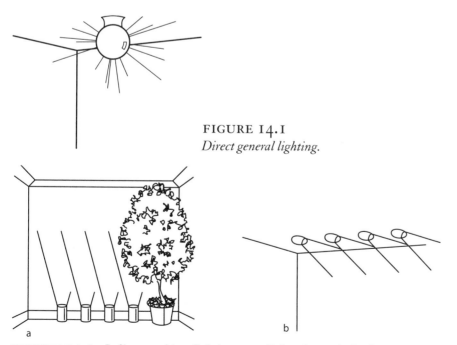

FIGURE 14.1
Direct general lighting.

FIGURE 14.2 *Indirect ambient lighting:* a. *uplighter,* b. *spotlights "wash" the wall.*

Task Lighting

Good task lighting improves visual clarity and helps prevent fatigue. It directs a pool of light where it is needed for activities, such as hobbies, reading, writing, word processing, preparing food, eating, and grooming.

Task lighting must be carefully planned to avoid both glare and shadows. Task lighting should be mounted with opaque reflectors that eliminate glare. The source of the light should not be seen. Shadows can be avoided by combining task lighting with ambient lighting. Eyestrain can occur if the pool of light ends and the rest of the room is in the shadows.

Task lighting may be portable or mounted. Examples of portable task lighting are table lamps and floor lamps (see Figure 14.3a). Examples of mounted task lighting are track lights, spotlights, or strips of lights (see Figure 14.3b).

Decorative Lighting

There are two types of decorative lighting—accent and mood.

Accent Lighting

Accent lighting, sometimes called **special emphasis lighting,** highlights an area of a space, such as a piece of art or an accessory, and gives it greater importance in the room. Track lighting is an example of accent lighting when placed above a painting as in Figure 14.4. Small lights, such as candles on a table or multiple small lamps, create dramatic shadows and interest in a room. Accent lighting is usually used in dining rooms and living rooms.

a

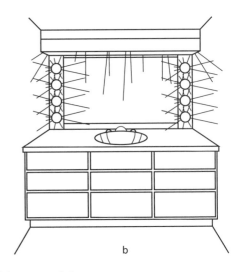

b

FIGURE 14.3   a. *Task lighting for reading, writing, or studying.*   Courtesy of Fairchild Publications, Inc.
b. *strips of lights around a mirror for personal grooming.*

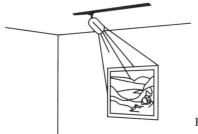

FIGURE 14.4
Accent lighting.

Mood Lighting

Mood lighting creates not only visual interest but also an air of comfort. It is usually soft and mellow. Low lighting from a table lamp or flickering light from a fireplace are both good examples of mood lighting (see Figure 14.5).

Mood lighting can affect a person's sense of well-being positively or negatively. Some of the feelings and effects that lighting can create are:

- *Low lighting* Intimacy and intrigue, relaxation and privacy, sense of security, and diminished eyestrain; can also cause feelings of depression and fear.
- *Colored lighting* Warm white and soft warm-colored lights—welcoming and uplifting; intensely colored light—possible eyestrain; cool white light and cool-colored lights—more restful, but can become depressing.

FIGURE 14.5
Mood lighting.

Courtesy of Fairchild
Publications, Inc.

- *Large areas of bright light* Produce a surge of energy, but may cause fatigue after long exposure; can also create boredom.
- *Moderately bright light* Generates an overall feeling of well-being.

Lighting as an Art Form

The light source and the luminaire can be creatively developed into art forms that are used as decorative lighting in the home. The light source can become artistic in several different ways:

- Etched acrylic sheets can be lit to create patterns of light.
- Light pipes can conduct light—colored light can be inserted into the pipe, which can be formed into many different shapes.
- Common articles, such as wine bottles, can be used to hold candles or can be made into fixtures.

Two examples of lighting as an art form are shown in Figure 14.6.

Lighting for Special Needs

People with poor vision have special lighting needs that require careful attention to ensure a safe environment. Specific visual limitations of the elderly may include perception of color, depth perception, visual acuity, and size of visual field. Studies have shown that a person 60 years of age needs approximately twice the light to do the same task as a 30-year-old. Because the population is aging, manufacturers are creating more special-needs lighting like the lamp in Figure 14.7. Dimmers are useful devices to help individuals adjust the level of light to their personal needs. A

FIGURE 14.6
Existing products reinvented as art forms in lighting by comprehensive designer Professor Terry Eason.

FIGURE 14.7
Verilux reading lamp simulates daylight, thus relieving eyestrain.
Courtesy of Fairchild Publications, Inc.

dimmer is a switch that is pushed to turn a light on and rotated to increase or decrease the light's brightness. Industry Statement 14.1 describes some other innovative lighting technology. Other techniques that can help people with limited vision are accent lighting to highlight switches, electrical outlets, and keyholes, as well as lights at steps, pathways, and doorsills.

Controlling Glare

Glare is excessive light that causes irritation or fatigue. Three common types of glare are direct glare, reflecting glare, and veiling glare.

Direct glare occurs when a bright light or inadequately shielded light is in the field of view. An accent light or a light in the center of the room can produce direct glare. It can also be caused by strong sunlight.

Reflecting glare is when something shiny is reflected in the area of a task, such as a light reflecting in a television screen or a computer monitor screen.

Veiling glare is caused by light that reflects off a surface and causes a blind spot. It prevents clear vision of a task. The reflected images are seen instead of the task. It is caused by incorrect placement of the lighting source or an inadequate baffle on the fixture. A **baffle** is a device used to screen light.

Both natural light and artificial light can cause glare. Glare from natural light can be controlled with window treatments. Glare from artificial light can be controlled by adjusting the direction of the light source, reducing the wattage, switching to a cool-beam lamp (see later discussion of lamps), or using baffles to divert the light. Suggested baffles include:

- **Bracket** Length of board or other opaque screen, placed in front of the light (see later discussion of brackets).

❧

INDUSTRY STATEMENT 14.1

Salton Putting Technology to Work in Lighting Line

CHICAGO—Salton has invested heavily in new technology for its lighting business, which includes the Stiffel brand, and previewed a variety of innovations to top retail executives at recent trade shows.

The company incorporated soft-touch switches, dimmers, timer controls, and other design and technology strengths from its small-electrics businesses into new lamp designs.

"We intend to be the brand in lighting and Salton is giving us the muscle," said Rick Spicer, vice president of sales for Salton at Home, the home decor unit. "We're putting a lot of opportunities here in front of top retail executives and getting their reaction."

In its booth at the International Housewares Show in Chicago, Salton showed a good-better-best line of Intelligent Lighting, featuring touch pads with on/off, dimmer and timer controls that slide out from under the base of the lamp. These allow consumers to program their lights as they do their clocks, electronics and appliances.

Salton also showed several Multi-Lights combining a decorative table lamp with a hidden, convertible reading spotlight, and ambient and task lights.

Spicer said Salton got "tremendous reaction" from top retail executives to its new concepts, and was deciding which products to offer under the Stiffel brand, which to offer under a yet-to-be decided Salton home decor brand and which to offer as private label, Spicer said.

"We're being overly protective of the Stiffel brand and we are not going to sell to anybody and everybody," Spicer said. "We're being very careful and cautious."

Before a brand relaunch takes place, upper management has to be convinced that the consumer understands what the brand means at every level, Spicer said. "We don't want to take Stiffel to a discounter where the consumer won't understand it. It has to fit."

Source: HFN, February 12, 2001, p. 30. Courtesy of Fairchild Publications, Inc.

- Grooves or louvers on or inside a luminaire.
- Metal or wood grids to distribute the light more evenly.
- Textured or coated lenses or glass coverings to distribute the light more evenly.

CATEGORIES OF LIGHT

There are two main categories of light—natural and artificial.

Natural Light

Natural light has two main forms—sunlight and combustion light.

Sunlight

The primary source of natural light is the sun, and sunlight provides health benefits. It is the main source of vitamin D, and many people enjoy the warmth and psychological benefits of natural sunlight.

The disadvantages of relying on sunlight as a source of illumination include the following:

- There is frequently excessive glare associated with natural sunlight.
- Excessive heat from sunlight can make a room uncomfortably warm.

- Direct sunlight can cause fabrics to fade and deteriorate.
- Long-term exposure to sunlight is associated with skin damage and certain types of skin cancer.
- Sunlight does not provide sufficient illumination in rooms with limited exposure, or, of course, in any interior during evening hours.

Quality and quantity of sunlight are determined by the latitude, the season, and location relative to the compass. The length of days and intensity of the sun are determined by the distance from the equator. The sun is more intense closer to the equator. In northern latitudes, days are longer, and the sun is higher in the sky in the summer than in the winter. The sun rises in the southeast and sets in the southwest during the winter. In the summer it rises in the northeast and sets in the northwest. Eastern light is strong and bright in the morning, and western light is the strongest in the later afternoon. Northern light is generally consistent and does not cast many shadows. Southern light is consistent with pleasant brightness, and during the summer it can be extremely intense.

Window treatments can be used to control sunlight. The following types of placement of windows can also control sunlight:

- *Clerestory windows* allow deep penetration of light into the room (see Figure 14.8a).
- *Horizontal windows* allow the most even distribution of light in a room (see Figure 14.8b).
- *Vertical windows* allow good penetration of light but can create dark areas between the windows (see Figure 14.8c).
- *Skylights* allow illumination throughout the room (see Figure 14.8d).

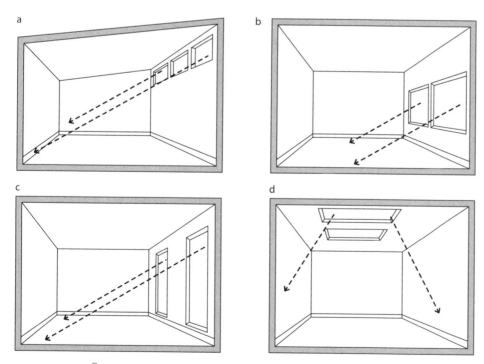

FIGURE 14.8 *How windows control natural light:* a. *clerestory windows,* b. *horizontal windows,* c. *vertical windows,* d. *skylights.*

Wall color can also control sunlight. White matte-finish ceilings will reflect the light and distribute it more evenly in the room.

Combustion Light

The second source of natural light is combustion light. Gas lights, fireplaces, and candles are all sources of combustion light. These are usually used for decoration. Gas lamps are seldom used, but gas fireplaces are becoming more common. Candles and fireplaces provide low levels of light and create atmosphere.

Artificial Light

The use of artificial light began with Thomas Edison's invention of the electric light bulb in 1880. Artificial lights can be used to create moods and emphasis and to focus attention. Although artificial light is generally considered to be a stable source of light, it does lose brightness over the life of the lamp.

Artificial lights are designed for many different purposes and are available in a very wide range of sizes, shapes, and colors. The selection of a lamp suitable for its purpose is crucial. The general factors to be considered are summarized in Table 14.1.

Lighting is an important factor when selecting colors for interiors. Samples of fabrics, floor coverings, paints, and wall coverings should be observed on site under both artificial and natural light settings and at different times during the day and the evening. It is important to avoid **metameric shift,** the changing of a color's appearance under different lighting conditions. For example, two blue fabrics may appear to match under artificial light but not under natural light.

Two primary kinds of artificial indoor lighting are incandescent lamps and electric or gaseous-discharge lamps. Incandescent lamps are commonly used in the home. Fluorescent lamps are examples of gaseous-discharge lamps, commonly used outdoors and in nonresidential settings. Their use in homes is limited.

TABLE 14.1

General Factors to Consider in the Selection of Lamps

Factor	Effect
Color	Lighting can affect the appearance of a color.
Decorative effects	Lighting can be used to create decorative effects.
Energy consumption	The type of lighting chosen affects energy consumption.
Length of life or hours expected	The type of lighting chosen affects the frequency of bulb replacement.
Psychological effects	Lighting can be used to create psychological effects.
Quantity of light	The lighting should be adequate for the specific purposes of the space to be illuminated.

Incandescent Lamps

Heating a metal with an electric current until it glows produces **incandescent light.** The metal is usually a tungsten filament sealed in a glass bulb (see Figure 14.9). Incandescent light is warm, mellow, and flattering. It is similar to natural sunlight, but it has more red and yellow and less blue and green. It is commonly used for ceiling lights and portable fixtures, such as table lamps, in the home. Controlling the quality and quantity of light is easy with incandescent lamps. They are available in a wide variety of shapes and wattage (see Figure 14.10). Dimmers can also be installed.

Wattage is the unit for measuring electricity consumed by a lamp. It serves as a guide to operating cost. Lamps, or light bulbs, are categorized by their wattage. Higher-wattage bulbs consume more electricity. **Lumens** are a measure of the amount of light produced by a lamp or light source. The efficiency of a lamp is rated as the number of lumens produced per watt of electricity consumed. Lamp packaging is frequently labeled with both lumens and watts.

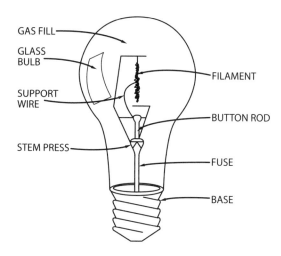

FIGURE 14.9 *Diagram of an incandescent lamp.*

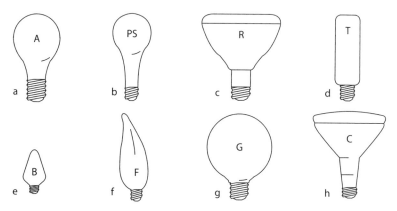

FIGURE 14.10 *Selected incandescent lamp shapes:* a. *A lamp (arbitrary-shaped lamp),* b. *PS lamp (pear-shaped lamp),* c. *R lamp (reflector lamp),* d. *T-lamp (tubular lamp),* e. *B lamp (candelabra lamp),* f. *F lamp (flame lamp),* g. *G lamp (globe-shaped lamp),* h. *C lamp (cone-shaped lamp).*

Incandescent lamps are a point light or near-point light. They tend to form bright highlights and cast sharp shadows. They are not frequently placed in nonresidential settings because they use a lot of energy. They are used to highlight displays in retail stores and to light restaurants because the light is flattering.

The disadvantages of incandescent lighting are that it is costly and produces heat. Lamps wear out quickly and are discarded. The average life span of an ordinary lamp is 750 to 2500 hours. A long-life bulb will last 2500 to 3500 hours but will deliver less light than standard lamps for the same amount of electricity. Generally, low-wattage bulbs last longer than higher-wattage bulbs.

The finish of the lamp glass determines the brightness and appearance of the light. Lamps may be clear or frosted. The filament is visible in a clear lamp, and the light is intense and bright. The light of a frosted bulb is soft and diffuse. The inside of a frosted lamp is coated with a silica powder that diffuses the light so it does not come from one direction. A frosted lamp gives off about 1 percent less light than a clear bulb.

Incandescent lamps are either standard or tungsten halogen. Standard incandescent lamps operate on 120 volts and have argon or nitrogen gas around the filament. Table 14.2 summarizes the characteristics of some standard incandescent lamps.

TABLE 14.2
Characteristics of Selected Standard Incandescent Lamps

Type of Lamp	Wattage	Characteristics
A lamp—arbitrary-shaped (see Figure 14.10a)	15 to 1500	The most common lamp shape, used for general service; available in clear or frosted bulbs
PS lamp—pear-shaped (see Figure 14.10b)	15 to 1500	Same as A lamp
R lamp—reflector (see Figure 14.10c)	15 to 750	Cone shaped with built in bright reflectors; available as wide beams (flood lights) or spotlights
ER—elliptic-shaped reflector	15 to 750	Reflector lamp that focuses the light beam two inches in front of the lamp; more efficient than R lamps
PAR lamp—parabolic aluminized reflector	15 to 750	Reflector lamp that has heavy protective glass; suitable for use indoors and outdoors; available as wide beam or spotlight; costs three to four times as much as A or PS lamps
T lamp—tubular lamp (see Figure 14.10d)	6 to 750	Long and cylindrical; available in various lengths and diameters
Low-voltage lamp	25 to 75	Tungsten-halogen lamp that incorporates transformers to reduce the voltage to the source; usually with built-in reflectors; especially good for display lighting, downlighting, and spotlighting; often used in recessed or track fixtures

Halogen lamps have halogen gas around the tungsten filament. As the tungsten burns off, the halogen reacts with the tungsten to create a bright light. Tungsten-halogen lamps usually cost more than standard incandescent lamps but last longer. They are now available as bulbs that can screw into any incandescent socket. Advantages of tungsten halogen lamps over standard incandescent lamps are as follows: they last three times longer, they burn up to 20 percent brighter, and they resemble natural sunlight more.

Torchiere-style halogen lamps are freestanding lamps with open-bowl tops that provide up-lighting. They have tubular-halogen bulbs that operate at temperatures much hotter than standard incandescent bulbs and can cause fire if clothing, curtains, or other flammable materials contact the bulb. Consumers must read and follow all manufacturer's instructions regarding safe use of these lamps.

Halogen-PAR lamps and low-voltage halogen lamps are also available. Halogen-PAR lamps are used for well-defined beams in spotlights or flood lights. Low-voltage halogen lamps usually have a reflector to focus a small beam. Their light is very white, and they produce very little heat.

Gaseous–Discharge Lamps

Gaseous-discharge lamps are also called **electric-discharge lamps.** They produce light when an electric current or arc passes through a gas vapor sealed in a glass tube. Because the light is not produced by heat it is called luminescent or cold light. Ballast, which is usually installed between the power line and the lamp, is required to regulate the amount of current and provide the proper starting voltage. **Ballast** is a device used to establish the circuit conditions necessary to start and operate the lamp. The electric-discharge lamps most commonly used in interiors are fluorescent. **High-intensity discharge (HID) lamps,** a second type of gaseous-discharge lamp, are used primarily in nonresidential settings, both indoors and outdoors.

Fluorescent lamps, the most popular low-pressure electric-discharge lamps, were developed in the 1930s. A fluorescent lamp produces light when an arc passes between two electrodes inside a glass tube filled with very low-pressure mercury vapor. There is a phosphorus coating on the inside of the tube. The arc produces ultraviolet radiation that activates the coating, causing the phosphorus to glow. See Figure 14.11 for a diagram of a fluorescent lamp.

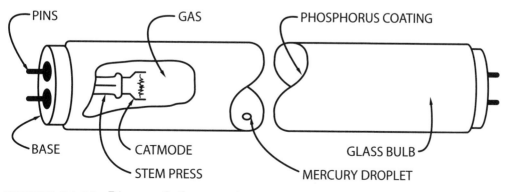

FIGURE 14.11 *Diagram of a fluorescent lamp.*

Fluorescent light is excellent for general lighting because it is even and relatively shadowless. It provides clear light for tasks where task lighting is not practical. Fluorescent light is commonly used in commercial settings. In the home it is primarily used in offices, hobby rooms, under-the-cabinet lighting in the kitchen, and in bathrooms. It is also often used in luminous ceiling panels in a drop ceiling.

Generally, fluorescent lamps are more expensive than incandescent lamps, but they require less energy to run and last longer. Thus, they are very economical. Fluorescent lamps may hum or flicker prior to burning out and lose lumens as they age. Rapid-start fluorescent lamps are available. They do not flicker when the lights are turned on, and they have the additional advantage of being able to be dimmed or flashed.

Fluorescent lamps are available in both warm- and cool-color spectrums. In general, the less expensive lamps distort many colors. They also cost more to run than the more expensive lamps. To overcome the color distortion, fluorescent lamps are available in many colors, including cool white, cool white deluxe, warm white, warm white deluxe, white, and daylight. Cool white, warm white, white, and daylight generally appear bluish-green. The deluxe lamps are less efficient, but they have better red tones. Fluorescent lamps with a triphosphorous coating provide excellent color rendition and are efficient.

When selecting colors for a room with fluorescent lighting it is essential to view the colors under the exact lighting conditions. Cool lamps or triphosphorous lamps should be used with cool color (greens and blues) schemes. They are available in a wide variety of styles and wattage (see Figure 14.12). Table 14.3 summarizes the characteristics of selected types of fluorescent lamps.

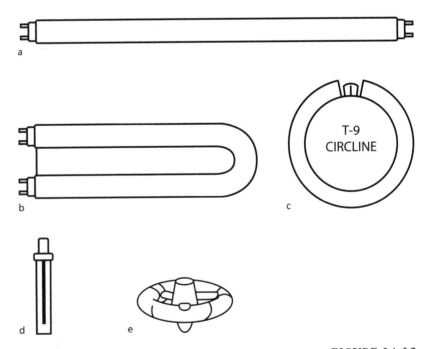

FIGURE 14.12
*Selected fluorescent lamps: a. standard fluorescent, b. U-shaped, c. circline (circular tube),
d. compact fluorescent lamps, e. low-wattage compact lamps.*

TABLE 14.3

Characteristics of Selected Types of Fluorescent Lamps

Type of Lamp	Length	Wattage	Characteristics
Standard fluorescent (see Figure 14.12a)	4′ to 8′	40	Low brightness, long life, low cost, high efficiency, available in a variety of colors; the most widely used fluorescent lamp
Energy-efficient fluorescent	2′ to 8′	25 to 34	More efficient than the standard fluorescent lamp; may give off less light than the standard fluorescent because of reduced wattage
U-shaped (see Figure 14.12b)	2′	35 to 40	Provides more light, lasts longer, and is more efficient than the standard fluorescent; available with 3″ or 6″ leg spacings
Circline—circular tube (see Figure 14.12c)	6 1/2″ to 16″ diameter	20 to 40	Used with circular or square luminaires; sold with a screw-in adapter ballast for use in place of incandescent lamps
Trimline	2′ to 5′	17 to 40	Has diameter of 1″; more efficient than the standard fluorescent lamp
Compact fluorescent (see Figure 14.12d)	16 1/2″ to 22 1/2″	40	Initially more expensive but consumes only 1/5 of the power and lasts up to 13 times as long as incandescent lamps
Low-wattage compact (see Figure 14.12e)	4 5/32″ to 9″	5 to 26	Usually used in task lights, downlights, or wall sconces; can be adapted for use in incandescent luminaires

When compared to incandescent lamps the advantages of fluorescent lamps are that they:

- Last 10 to 15 times as long.
- Produce about 4 times as much light per watt, so they are more energy efficient.
- Produce almost no heat.
- Give off diffuse shadowless light that promotes good vision.
- Produce less glare.

One disadvantage is that fluorescent lamps create a flat, monotonous lighting effect. Some of the colors of fluorescent lamps are not complementary to skin tones. Fluorescent lamps can be annoying if they hum and/or flicker. This can be overcome with the proper ballast, but that can cause heat.

High-intensity discharge lamps include metal-halide, high-pressure, and sodium-mercury HID lamps. They are very efficient, but they generally lack a well-balanced distribution of color, creating conditions for poor color perception. They are also noisy. Therefore, HID lamps are not usually used in residential settings.

Metal-halide lamps usually produce icy-blue light, but color-corrected versions are available. In lower wattage, they are suitable for use in homes. They are inexpensive to operate.

Other Types of Artificial Lighting

Other types of artificial lighting include cold cathode, fiber optic, laser, and neon.

- *Cold Cathode* Can be shaped like a neon lamp but operates like a rapid-start fluorescent. They have a very long life.
- *Fiber Optics* Thin glass or plastic fibers that produce intense pinpoints of light. They are used to produce special effects, such as a starlight pattern on a ceiling. The light travels only a short distance after it leaves the fiber, so fiber optics are only used for decorative effects.
- *Laser* (light amplification by stimulated emission or radiation) Used in special interior or theatrical settings. The beams can be dangerous, causing skin burns and damage to the retina of a person who looks directly into the beam.
- *Neon* A type of electrical-discharge lamp usually used for decorative or display purposes. The characteristics of neon lighting are a very long life, a low amount of light, available in many colors, can be bent to any shape, and can be dimmed or flashed. They can also be noisy and fragile.

LUMINAIRES

A luminaire, or a fixture, is the housing for the lamp. The shape and size of the luminaire can determine the shape and direction of the light beam. It is important that the luminaire be appropriate for the intended activity or purpose. Selected brands of luminaires are listed in Table 14.4. Luminaires are either structural or portable.

Structural Luminaires

Structural luminaires are sometimes referred to as **architectural lighting.** This type of lighting is permanently installed and includes wall and ceiling fixtures that are affixed to permanent wiring. There are six types of structural luminaires.

TABLE 14.4
Selected Brands of Luminaires

Alsy Lighting	J. Hunt	Stiffel
Catalina Lighting	Lightolier	Tensor
Cheyenne Lamps	Maxim Lighting	Thomas Lighting
Emess Lighting	Pacific Rim	
Holmes Lighting	Sea Gull Lighting	

Recessed Luminaires

Recessed luminaires are mounted above the ceiling line and are usually flush with the ceiling. They provide direct light. They are good for general lighting, wall washing, and accent lighting. See Figure 14.13 for an example of a recessed downlight.

Surface-Mounted Luminaires

Surface-mounted luminaires can be attached to either the wall or the ceiling. Ceiling-mounted luminaires can direct the beam of light in pattern or focus it in one direction (see Figure 14.14). A disadvantage of ceiling-mounted luminaires is that they effectively lower the height of the ceiling.

Wall-mounted luminaires are often called **sconces** (see Figure 14.15). They provide direct, indirect, or diffuse light. They are mainly used for decorative purposes. Sometimes a reflector plate is used to reflect light away from the wall.

Suspended Luminaires

Suspended luminaires are sometimes called **pendant luminaires.** They are suspended below the ceiling and produce direct, indirect, or diffuse light. They can be entirely functional, like a suspended fluorescent lamp in a workshop, or they can be very decorative like an elaborate **chandelier** in a dining room (see Figure 14.16). When suspended luminaires are used in conversation areas, they should be hung about 40 inches above the floor or 20 inches above the seating.

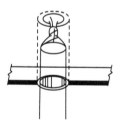

FIGURE 14.13
Recessed luminaire.

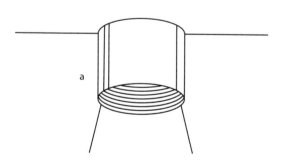
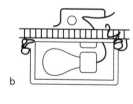

FIGURE 14.14
a. *Surfaced-mounted downlight,* b. *ceiling-mounted luminaire.*

FIGURE 14.15 *Sconce.*
Courtesy of Fairchild Publications, Inc.

FIGURE 14.16 *Chandelier.*
Courtesy of Fairchild Publications, Inc.

Luminous Panels

Luminous panels are strips of lights with glass or plastic translucent panels placed over them. They can be inset into floors ceilings, or walls. Usually the lights are fluorescent. The panel produces a soft white light or colored light if the panel is tinted. Sometimes the panel is textured. They are frequently used in kitchen ceilings.

Track-Mounted Luminaires

Track lighting is very flexible, and it can be used in a wide variety of locations. It has two parts—the track, which is an electrified holder that can be cut to any size, and the fixtures, which are available in many sizes, shapes, and finishes. The track supplies the electrical power and holds the luminaires. It can be recessed in the ceiling or attached to the ceiling or wall. The luminaires can be mounted anywhere on the track, and the light can be directed as desired (see Figure 14.17).

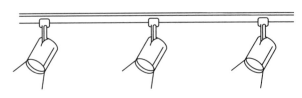

FIGURE 14.17
Track lighting.

Built-In Luminaires

Built-in luminaires, or **spatially-integrated lighting,** is lighting that is integral to the construction of the building. An important advantage of built-in luminaires is that the brightness can be controlled without creating glare. Seven varieties of built-in luminaires are described below:

- *Cornice Lighting* A board or other opaque shield is attached to the ceiling near the wall. The light is mounted to the ceiling behind the board so that the light washes down onto the wall (see Figure 14.18a).

- *Cove Lighting* A trough is mounted on the wall close to the ceiling. The light fixture is mounted on the wall within the trough. The light washes up and deflects off the ceiling. Cove lighting increases the apparent height of the wall. It provides soft uniform lighting with no glare but should be supplemented with other light (see Figure 14.18b).

- *Valance Lighting* The light fixture and opaque shield are mounted at the top of a window above drapes or other window treatments. The top of the valance may be covered with a shield. The light washes the window treatment and the ceiling if the valance is not covered. The light will emphasize the texture of the window treatment (see Figure 14.18c).

- *Bracket Lighting* Bracket lighting is similar to valance lighting except that it is not mounted over a window treatment. It can be placed low or high on a wall. The light can be directed up or down depending on the placement of a deflector board. The light can also go up and down if no deflector board is attached. It can be used for ambient light, task lighting, or a combination of both. It can be installed over work areas or beds, or it can be used decoratively over display shelves or wall art (see Figure 14.18d and e).

- *Soffit Lighting* Soffit lighting is generally placed over work areas, as in a kitchen or bathroom. It can provide a high level of direct light. A diffuser or louver is used to even the light. The light is directed downward, frequently from an overhead cabinet (see Figure 14.18f).

- *Toe-Mold Lighting* Toe-mold lighting is sometimes called base lighting. A strip of lights is placed against or very near the floor where a deflector directs the light. If the light is directed down, it gives the effect of usher lights in a theater (see Figure 14.18g).

- *Specialty Built-in Lighting* Specialty built-in lighting has the important benefit of increased safety and easy access in the dark. Three examples of specialty built-in lighting are:

  1. *Riser lighting* The light fixture is mounted under a stair tread (see Figure 14.18h).
  2. *Toe-kick lighting* The light fixture is mounted under cabinets in the toe-kick area.
  3. *Handrail lighting* The light fixture is mounted under handrails (see Figure 14.18i).

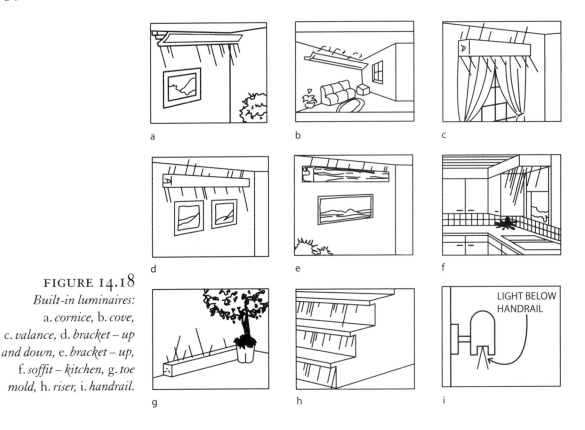

FIGURE 14.18
Built-in luminaires:
a. *cornice,* b. *cove,*
c. *valance,* d. *bracket – up*
and down, e. *bracket – up,*
f. *soffit – kitchen,* g. *toe*
mold, h. *riser,* i. *handrail.*

Portable Luminaires

Portable luminaires are sometimes called **nonarchitectural lighting.** They include lighting that is plugged into an electrical outlet, such as floor and table lamps. Floor and table lamps are limited by the length of their cords, and they must be used on or near furniture. Aesthetics are important in selecting a lamp, but it is critical to select the correct lamp for the task. The height of the lamp and the width of the shade determine the usefulness of the lamp. Lamps with opaque shade confine light. Lamps with white silk shades spread light. The wider the bottom of the shade, the wider the light will spread. Selected floor and table lamps are illustrated in Figures 14.19 and 14.20.

SELECTION OF LAMPS AND LUMINAIRES

Selection of lamps and luminaires requires careful attention to both aesthetics and function. Some general recommendations for selection of lighting include the following:

- If a room is used for an activity, select the correct lighting for the activity first and then select the light for the rest of the room.
- Areas for relaxation should be softly lit.
- Areas used for vigorous activity should be brightly lit.
- Outlets must be placed every 6 to 12 feet along a wall for portable luminaires.

FIGURE 14.19
Selected floor lamps: a. *swing-arm lamp,* b. *torchiere lamp,* c. *table/floor lamp,*
d. *Akari lanterns (handcrafted of paper and bamboo),* e. *pharmacy lamp.*

FIGURE 14.20
Table lamps: a. *canister lamp,* b. *column-base lamp,* c. *candlestick lamp,*
d. *apothecary jar lamps,* e. *ginger jar lamp.*

Suggestions for using lighting to create specific effects are:

- An **ambient bank,** or **plane of light,** is a large well-lit area. It can be used to designate a smaller space within a large space.
- A soft plane of light from spotlights or track lights is called an **even wash.** It can be used to highlight a painting or other artwork.
- Texture is best emphasized with a light that is very close to the object or by a light that shines at a steep angle.
- Use spotlighting from more than one direction to balance the light and eliminate shadows. It will emphasize details. The circle of light from a spotlight is called a **pool of light.**
- Use perimeter lighting to visually expand a space. Perimeter lighting goes around the outside of a room or space.
- Use point or pinpoint lighting to spotlight a small area. It can create shiny accents if light hits a reflective surface.
- Lights that shine directly down cause shadows beneath and around objects below the lights. Downward light is particularly unflattering to people because it creates shadows.
- Silhouette lighting creates a shadow of the object by shining a light directly on the object.
- Lights that shine upward behind objects, such as plants, will create interesting patterns on walls and/or ceilings.

Lighting Recommendations for Specific Rooms

Lighting recommendations for specific rooms are presented in Table 14.5.

TABLE 14.5
Lighting Recommendations for Specific Rooms

Room or Area	Lighting Recommendation
Entrance areas	Diffused lighting from the ceiling or wall sconces to create a warm, inviting atmosphere.
Living rooms and family rooms	A combination of both direct and indirect light; a dimmer can be used to control the brightness as activities change.
Dining rooms	Should be lit so the table and surrounding area are emphasized and to enhance the sparkle of the silver, china, and crystal. Diffused light is more flattering and lessens glare.
Kitchens	Work areas should be very well lit; the rest of the room should be fairly bright.
Bathrooms	Good ambient lighting from a ceiling fixture and strip lighting on the sides of mirrors. In very small bathrooms, luminaires by the mirrors may be enough light for the room. Bare bulbs around the mirror give clear, shadowless light. In general, there should be no portable fixtures in a bathroom.
Bedrooms	Ambient lighting with dimmers; nightstands with reading lights.
Hallways	Ambient lighting from glare-free ceiling or wall fixtures.
Stairways	Should be well lit for safety with ceiling or wall fixtures that direct the light downward.

Selection of Chandeliers

Chandeliers are often expensive focal points of a dining room. The size of the chandelier should be in proportion to the table and the room. Other guidelines for selecting a chandelier are:

- The diameter of the chandelier should be in inches what the diagonal of the room is in feet. For example a chandelier with a 20-inch diameter would be appropriate for a dining room that has a diagonal of 20 feet.
- A chandelier should be small enough so people do not hit their head when getting up—about 12 inches smaller than the table.
- For a rectangular table, the diameter of the chandelier should not be more than 2/3 the length of the table.
- Most dining room chandeliers are hung about 30 inches above the table.

Color–Rendering Properties of Lamps

The color-rendering properties of a lamp are an important component of overall lighting. Table 14.6 summarizes the characteristics of common lamps and their effects on color.

CARE OF LAMPS AND LUMINAIRES

All luminaires and lamps should be cleaned regularly. Dust and dirt obscure the light. Lamp-shades attract dust and need regularly dusting. Always turn the light off before cleaning. All wiring should be checked periodically, and any frayed or damaged wires should be immediately replaced.

TABLE 14.6
Characteristics of Common Lamps and Their Effects on Color

Types of Lamp	Characteristics of the Light	Effect on Color
Standard incandescent	Most commonly used lamp, relatively inefficient, warm and inviting light	Brightens yellows, oranges, and reds Darkens greens and blues
Tungsten halogen	Brighter and whiter light than standard incandescent, more efficient than standard incandescent	Brightens yellows, oranges, and reds Darkens greens and blues
Fluorescent	Wide selection of colors, generally high efficiency, much longer life	Can be selected in warm to cool colors that complement an interior
High-intensity discharge (metal halide, high-pressure sodium, mercury)	High efficiency, very long life	Provides excellent color rendering; high-pressure sodium and mercury are seldom used in residential interiors because of their poor color rendering

ENVIRONMENTAL ISSUES

The most important environmental issue related to lighting is the consumption of energy. Increasing cost of electricity and its drain on natural resources are major factors in the need to reduce the amount of energy used. There are two main ways to reduce the amount of energy—1.) purchase more efficient lamps and fixtures and 2.) use less electricity.

Energy-Efficient Lighting

Use fluorescent lighting in place of incandescent lighting when possible. Warm white deluxe fluorescent lamps are aesthetically pleasing replacements for incandescent lamps. Fluorescent lamps use approximately one-third to one-fifth the energy of standard incandescent bulbs.

In portable luminaires, replace incandescent lamps with circular-fluorescent (CF) lamps that can be screwed in. They do not hum and do not interfere with radio or television reception. A CF lamp can last as long as ten average incandescent lamps and an 18-watt fluorescent lamp gives light equal to a 75-watt incandescent lamp (see Industry Statement 14.2).

Lighting Energy-Conservation Practices

The following energy-conservation practices must be followed routinely in reducing energy consumption and, consequently, the consumer's utility bill.

- Turn out all lights when not in use.
- Put light where it is needed. Use portable luminaires with fewer lamps and lower wattage instead of ambient light. It is important to remember that high contrast between the task and the surrounding area (for example, a pool of light in a dark room) is not recommended. It can cause discomfort and fatigue.
- Use dimmers to control and reduce wattage.
- Supplement natural light with artificial light only when necessary. Open or remove window treatments to allow natural light in.
- Select light-colored surfaces and textures that do not absorb light. They will reflect light and increase the light in the room.
- Use a single higher-wattage lamp instead of several lower-wattage lamps.
- Replace existing bulbs with lower-wattage bulbs.

INDUSTRY STATEMENT 14.2

Saving Energy in Style

As consumers feel the pinch of higher gasoline prices and utility bills, they're seeking ways to save money and electricity in their homes. But many energy-efficient lighting fixtures still don't address style and prices that will incite consumers to buy.

The market has a long way to go, said Good Earth Lighting President Marvin Feig. "To some degree, we can overcome being slightly higher priced than an incandescent fixture because of the great energy savings that more than pays for the fixture. But it is impossible to overcome ugly."

Retailers have begun to demand better-looking lamps and fixtures at affordable prices, and suppliers are beginning to respond. They are putting more effort into new designs that accommodate compact fluorescent bulbs, use electronic ballasts and incorporate dimmer switches and automatic controls. For their part, Lowe's and Menard have been leaders in supporting the Energy Star program, which now encompasses more than 50 lighting suppliers and 2,000 SKUs.

Source: HFN, June 18, 2001, p. 25. Courtesy of Fairchild Publications, Inc.

SUMMARY

Careful selection, placement, and control of light create a visual environment that is functional, aesthetically pleasing, and cost effective. Thus, light illuminates tasks and activities and makes interiors more pleasant.

Lamp is the technical term for what is commonly called a light bulb. A *luminaire* is the technical term for what is commonly called a lamp or a light fixture. The overall goals of residential lighting are to provide ambient lighting, task lighting, and decorative lighting.

Direct light is when nearly all (90 to 100 percent) of the light is directed toward the surface to be lit. Indirect light is when 90 to 100 percent of the light is re-directed toward the surface to be lit. There are two main categories of light—natural and artificial. Sunlight and combustion light are two main forms of natural light. Incandescent lamps, fluorescent lamps, and high-intensity discharge lamps are the main types of artificial light. Incandescent light is aesthetically pleasing. Fluorescent light is very economical. High-intensity discharge (HID) lamps are not usually used in residential settings.

It is important that the luminaire be appropriate for intended activity or purpose. Luminaires are either structural or portable. Structural luminaires are permanently installed. Portable luminaires are those that are plugged into an electrical outlet.

Selection of lamps and luminaires requires careful attention to both aesthetics and function. All luminaires and lamps should be cleaned and inspected regularly. The most important environmental issue related to lighting is the consumption of energy. There are two main ways to reduce the amount of energy used in lighting—purchase more efficient lamps and fixtures, and use less electricity.

INDUSTRY PROFILE

Focus on Mass Key to Longevity for Cheyenne

Cheyenne Industries has built an enviable position for itself as the leader in value-priced lighting for volume retailers.

In the 20 years since owner Frank Fletcher founded Cheyenne, its image has evolved. But its focus remains on limited distribution to international, national and regional mass merchants, warehouse clubs and home centers.

Cheyenne's laser-beam focus on driving volume in key lamp styles for these volume accounts is the reason for its success and longevity in a market that has seen many suppliers and retailers drop out, and channels shift.

Cheyenne built its business on making higher-end looks affordable for the mass-market consumer. From brass table and floor lamps and crystal, wood and iron to Tiffany-style and other higher-end styles, Cheyenne found ways to design products for under $50 retail and, often, well under $30. With its understanding of the value-conscious retailer and consumer, Cheyenne still designs lamps to target certain retail prices, whether a $29 floor lamp, $14.99 table lamp, or $9.99 accent lamp or accessory. The focus is on driving volume at key prices and offering differentiated products to each retailer. Cheyenne has extended this concept to accessories and ready-to-assemble furniture.

Cheyenne updates styles, colors and finishes, replacing items once volume drops off. To do this, it closely monitors inventory and works with buyers on forecasting and replenishment.

"Where we're allowed, we love to get involved with the replenishment process and have input into how inventory is maintained," said Alan Long, president. "That helps us understand that particular retailer and what their needs are."

Cheyenne was one of the first lamp companies to source components, then import fully assembled lamps from Taiwan, and then China in the mid-'80s, giving the company even quicker turnaround and sharper prices.

"We built an extremely strong organization overseas. To this day, we have one of the largest overseas operations, and that's a big part of our success," Long said. Cheyenne currently has one joint-venture factory in China and buys from five other lighting factories.

Most buyers visit the factory in China for tailored full-day presentations in the company's larger showroom, or they stop by Cheyenne's showrooms in Hong Kong or Taipei.

"We can go from design sketch to actual sample within two weeks, which is very hard to do," Long said.

Cheyenne is one of the largest lamp suppliers to Wal-Mart and, due to its quality and service, last month received a Supplier of the Year award at a banquet in Hong Kong. Cheyenne has also scored top vendor awards from ShopKo and other retailers where it remains a key resource.

"Our image has evolved in the last couple of years from a follower to more of a leader in our class of trade…as the leader in value-priced goods, with a fashion flair," he continued. Cheyenne was the first lamp company to set up an office in Bentonville two years ago, even though its own headquarters are just a three-hour drive from Wal-Mart. "I wish we'd done it five years ago," Long said. "It makes it work more smoothly, to have several people there interacting with their people daily to help manage both of our businesses."

Source: HFN Image Makers, May 29, 2000, p. 66. Special supplement to *HFN*.

TERMS FOR REVIEW

accent lighting
ambient bank (plane of light)
ambient (general) lighting
architectural lighting
baffle
ballast
brackets
built-in luminaires (spatially-integrated lighting)
chandelier
decorative lighting
dimmer
direct glare
direct light
downlights
even wash
fixture
fluorescent lamps
gaseous-discharge lamps (electric-discharge lamps)
glare
halogen lamps
high-intensity discharge (HID) lamps
incandescent light
indirect light
lamp

lumens

luminaire

luminous panels

metameric shift

mood lighting

nonarchitectural lighting

pool of light

portable luminaires

reflecting glare

sconces

special emphasis lighting

structural luminaires

suspended luminaires
  (pendant luminaires)

task lighting

uplight

veiling glare

wall washers

wattage

REVIEW QUESTIONS

1. What is the purpose of each of the following—ambient lighting, task lighting, and decorative lighting?
2. Compare the overall cost of incandescent lamps and fluorescent lamps.
3. Why are high-intensity discharge lamps not used in residential settings?
4. List three ways you could reduce the cost of lighting in your home.
5. Why is it important to keep lamps and luminaires clean?
6. List three types of structural luminaires. Sketch an example of each.

LEARNING ACTIVITIES

1. Visit a lighting show room. Talk with the salesperson about the advantages and disadvantages of the various types of lighting displayed in the store.
2. Evaluate the lighting in your home. Classify the lighting in each room as ambient, task, and/or decorative. Is it adequate? How could you improve it?

CHAPTER 15

TABLEWARE

Tabletop is, by its very nature, luxurious.

After all, one does not need sterling silver, crystal, or bone china in order to survive.
But the tabletop industry continues to thrive and grow because it appeals to more than
mere necessity—there is a strong emotional component to the business.

—Raising the bar, *HFN,* May 14, 2001, p. 34

TABLEWARE INCLUDES A BROAD RANGE OF PRODUCTS USED FOR DECORATING THE TABLE, SERVING food, and dining. Categories of tableware include dinnerware, glassware, flatware, and hollowware. These products are primarily made from glass, ceramics, plastics, and metals (see Chapters 4–7). Consumers have the luxury of selecting from a wide variety of products designed to suit every budget, lifestyle, season, and social occasion. Tableware is often purchased as a gift. A bride frequently selects tableware for listing in her gift registry. The recent trend in tableware has been toward the casual setting, but more formal settings are gaining renewed popularity (see Industry Statement 15.1). Formal settings usually are more costly than casual and require more pieces. In addition to formal and informal tableware, ethnic and seasonal pieces are popular.

Lifestyle, budget, and aesthetic preference must be carefully considered in selecting tableware. The concept of matching all pieces of tableware may result in a visually uninteresting table (see Figure 15.1). Accent pieces such as salad plates, flatware serving pieces, contrasting hollowware, etc., offer the opportunity to add visual excitement and interest to the table.

Many manufacturers have branched out to offer a wider variety of glassware, dinnerware, and flatware to the consumer. Oneida, traditionally associated with flatware, also offers crystal and dinnerware. High-end manufacturers of formal dinnerware, such as Lenox, have started to make less formal, and less expensive, dinnerware. Table 15.1 lists some brand names of tableware. Industry Statement 15.2 describes two companies that have successfully used the Internet to sell tableware.

INDUSTRY STATEMENT 15.1

Raising the Bar

Tabletop is, by its very nature, luxurious.

After all, one does not need sterling silver, crystal or bone china in order to survive. But the tabletop industry continues to thrive and grow because it appeals to more than mere necessity—there is a strong emotional component to the business.

Brides will agonize for hours over choosing just the right dinnerware or crystal pattern for their gift registries, and their guests will or will not adhere to the choices if they themselves do not respond in a positive, emotional way to it. You just don't get that with sheets.

Tabletop today is all about lifestyle. It's about how consumers really live—how, when and where they eat, how often they entertain, how much they're willing to spend on a wedding gift.

Tabletop is also all about design. It always has been.

Lifestyle and design are the keys to success in the business. And as virtually every level of manufacturer and every retail channel of distribution has adopted this way of merchandising (think Martha Stewart at Kmart and Michael Graves at Target), premium tabletop manufacturers—the most luxurious of the luxurious, if judging by price point—have gotten into the act.

Most top-tier tabletop manufacturers have moved away from highly decorative, ornamental products and are now presenting sleek, functional designs that appeal to a wider range of consumers and fit into any style of decor. As Anita Brady, Waterford's vice president of marketing put it, luxury is about timeless design and quality.

At the most recent tabletop market, Hoya introduced a martini set and barware in response to the growing cocktail trend. Waterford unveiled its W collection of crystal giftware, an uncut, highly polished assortment of vases, bowls, candlesticks and clocks that are meant to link the artistry of the past with contemporary design and state-of-the-art technology. And Bernardaud showcased a porcelain line of dinnerware that "makes both a refined and elegant statement for a modern interior."

Premium tabletop companies have further distinguished themselves by building lifestyle brands, either through the acquisition of luxury categories outside the tabletop industry, such as jewelry or luggage, or through licensing agreements that extend the brand, such as Rosenthal's partnerships with Versace and Bulgari.

Others have moved beyond their core business in an effort to become total tabletop companies. Christofle, for example, now has complete lines of dinnerware, crystal and table linens to accompany its flatware collections. Christofle also sets itself apart with its boutiques that are flourishing in high-end neighborhoods across the country. It's another way to establish itself as a lifestyle company while maintaining a reputation as a luxury brand.

Source: HFN, May 14, 2002. Courtesy of Fairchild Publications, Inc.

FIGURE 15.1 *Eclectic mixing of contemporary and classic patterns.*
Courtesy of Fairchild Publications, Inc.

TABLE 15.1
Selected Tableware Brand Names

Category	Brands	Category	Brands
Formal dinnerware	Franciscan	Fine glassware (continued)	Miller Rogaska
	Haviland		Noritake
	Lenox		Orrefors
	Nikko		Royal Doulton
	Noritake		Waterford Crystal
	Rosenthal	Casual glassware	Anchor Hocking
	Royal Doulton		Artland
	Royal Worcester		Block
	Spode		Colony
	Villeroy & Boch		Crisa
	Waterford		J.G. Durand
Casual dinnerware	American Atelier		Libbey
	Caleca		Owens Corning
	Dansk	Sterling silver and silverplate	Carrs
	Denby		Continental
	Fiestaware		Collection
	Fitz and Floyd		Elkington
	Gibson		Georgian House
	Lenox		Gorham
	Libbey		International Silver
	Lindt-Stymeist		Company
	Lotus		James Dixon & Sons
	Mikasa		Kirk Stieff
	Nautica		Lenox
	Nikko		Lunt Silversmiths
	Noritake		Oneida
	Pagnossin		Reed & Barton
	Pfaltzgraff		Towle Silversmiths
	Royal Stafford		Wallace Silver
	Sakura		Yamazaki
	Sango	Stainless steel	Couzon
	Spode		Dansk
	Tabletops Unlimited		Georgian House
	Villeroy & Boch		Gorham
	Waechtersbach		Lenox
	Wedgwood		Mikasa
Fine glassware	Block		Oneida
	Cristal d'Arques		Portugal
	Cristal J. G. Durand		Reed & Barton
	Da Vinci		Towle
	Fostoria		Tuttle
	Galway		Wallace
	Gorham		Waterford
	John Rocha		Yamazaki
	Lenox		
	Marquis		
	Mikasa		

INDUSTRY STATEMENT 15.2

Two Tabletop Retailers Touted for Online Success

CHICAGO–An Internet retailing magazine has ranked Replacements and Williams-Sonoma among the top 25 retailing Web sites in a survey published Dec. 31, 2001.

The two tabletop retailers shared space with names like Amazon, Lands' End and IBM, and beat out companies such as Disney, Dell and REI.

This is the third year that Chicago-based Internet Retailer, a monthly trade publication, has put out its list of the top-performing retail Web sites. Its criteria are subjective, according to editor-in-chief Kurt Peters. Rather than simply study the biggest sites or those with the most sales, recommendations—which come from consultants, Internet Retailer's editorial staff and others—are based on retailers "that do interesting, innovative things that fit in with their strategies and from which other retailers can learn," Peters said.

Replacements caught Internet Retailer's eye as a home-grown site that has achieved nationwide reach because it has made its massive inventory readily available to its online shoppers.

The Hillsboro, N.C.-based company, which specializes in discontinued china, silver, and crystal, fills a specific need for its customers, Peters said. "People go to that Web site because they need a particular item. It's a testament to Replacements, that has such [large] inventory, that they meet customers' needs as well as stimulate customers to buy."

In a profile of the company, Internet Retailer wrote: "…The Web is emerging as the critical driver of [Replacements'] increasing phone orders, driving $11.1 million, or 15 percent of sales, double the rate of a year earlier. A key element: Web shoppers can browse much of an 8 million-piece inventory online."

Replacements generates roughly $70 million in annual sales, according to spokesman Liam Sullivan, and he attributed some of the company's growth in recent years to the Internet. "We would never be where we are today without the Web site," he said. "And it just keeps growing."

Replacements' Web site, which attracts roughly 500,000 visitors monthly, was created by founder Bob Page and his staff in 1998 and redesigned last April. Sullivan said that Page "was jumping up and down" over the news that his company made Internet Retailer's list. "For us to come above [Disney and Dell] is amazing," Sullivan said.

Disney and Dell did not make the top 25, but were cited as companies to watch in terms of their Web retailing.

Internet Retailer commended Williams-Sonoma for successfully recreating its in-store and catalog atmosphere online. "We like [Williams-Sonoma] because of the excellent job they do merchandising on the Web," said Peters. "The have a nicely presented assortment of merchandise, done in a way that entices people to buy."

Shelley Nandkyeolar, then vice president of e-commerce at Williams-Sonoma, was quoted by Internet Retailer as saying, "Customers buy brand, whatever the channel, so it's important for us to have one brand persona across channels."

Source: HFN, Jan. 14, 2002. Courtesy of Fairchild Publications, Inc.

Disposable tableware, suitable for picnics, children's parties, and other informal social occasions, is usually sold in stationery and gift shops or departments rather than with other tableware. The variety of pieces in disposable dinnerware is typically more limited than the variety of reusable tableware products.

DINNERWARE

The industry term ***dinnerware*** refers to all items used to serve and present food to the diner. This includes oven-to-table bakeware that matches a dinnerware pattern (see Figure 15.2).

FIGURE I5.2
Oven-to-table bakeware.
Courtesy of Fairchild Publications, Inc.

Categories of Dinnerware

Dinnerware is categorized by shape, size and type.

Shape of Dinnerware

Rim and **coupe** are the two basic shapes for flat dishes, such as plates and saucers. Rim dishes have a flat edge that can be used to hold when serving. Coupe dishes have no rim or flat edge (see Figure 15.3a and b). Traditional dinnerware is round, but other interesting shapes, such as square, hexagonal, and octagonal, are being produced by modern designers. Dinnerware may also have fluted rims, metallic trim, and a wide variety of other decorative accents.

Size of Dinnerware

There are two methods to measure the size of flat dishes such as plates and saucers. The **overall measurement** is the diameter from one edge to the other (see Figure 15.4a). The size of a coupe dish is determined by the overall measurement. The **well-to-edge measurement** is used for rim dishes. The distance is taken from one side of the well, across the well to the other side of the dish (see Figure 15.4b). Older manufacturers often use the well-to-edge measurement. It is also called the *trade measurement.*

Oval platters and gravy boats are measured by their length. Round bowls are measured by the diameter of the opening; oval bowls are measured by the length of the opening.

Types of Dinnerware

There are many types of dishes available. Table 15.2 lists and briefly describes the various types of dinnerware according to their end use. Figure 15.5 shows the shapes of selected dishes. Mugs of various sizes (see Figure 15.6) are frequently used for informal or casual service of coffee, tea, soup, or other liquid.

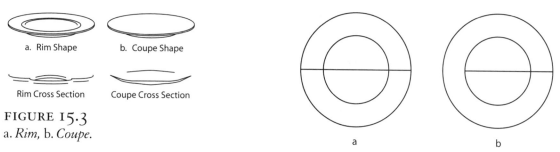

a. Rim Shape   b. Coupe Shape

Rim Cross Section   Coupe Cross Section

FIGURE 15.3
a. *Rim,* b. *Coupe.*

a   b

FIGURE 15.4 *Methods of determining dish size:*
a. *overall,* b. *well to edge.*

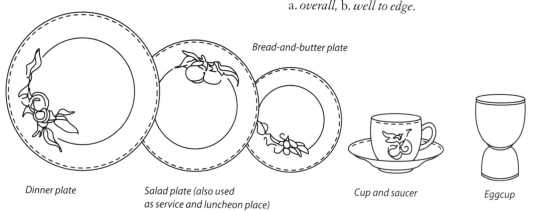

Bread-and-butter plate

Dinner plate   Salad plate (also used   Cup and saucer   Eggcup
                as service and luncheon place)

Consommé cup and saucer

FIGURE 15.5 *Shapes of selected dishes.*

FIGURE 15.6
Mug used in a table setting.
Courtesy of Fairchild Publications, Inc.

Purchasing Dinnerware

Dinnerware may be purchased as individual pieces, in place settings, and in sets.

Individual Pieces

Purchasing individual pieces is usually the most expensive way to purchase dinnerware. The desired piece is special-ordered through the manufacturer.

TABLE 15.2

Types of Dinnerware

Item	Size and Description
Plates	
Dinner	Usually 10 inch, but can vary in size. A European dinner plate is smaller than an American one.
Salad, luncheon, or service	Usually 9 inch and placed on top of the dinner plate for service of the first course.
Dessert	8 inch.
Bread and butter	6 inch.
Saucer	5 1/2 to 6 1/2 inches, used under a cup.
Soup Bowls	
Cream soup	Wide shallow bowl without handles.
Soup, cereal, or all-purpose	Deep bowl without handles.
Bouillon or consommé cup	Deep bowl with two side handles.
Coupe	Large bowl with no rim.
Rimmed	Large bowl with a rim.
Cups	
Teacup	Cup used for tea or coffee.
After-dinner cup or demitasse (used with a small saucer)	A small cup used for after-dinner coffee.
Egg cup	Hourglass cup used to hold an egg to be eaten from the shell.
Mug	Various sizes; used for tea, coffee, and other beverages.
Miscellaneous Individual Pieces	
Ramekin or individual casserole dish	Small rounded (sometimes oval), covered or uncovered vegetable dish, sometimes used to serve individual portions.
Salt and pepper shakers	Can be large for use in the center of the table or small and individual; large are more common.
Fruit bowl	Small individual bowls used for serving fruit, vegetables, and puddings at the side of the dinner plate.
Serving Pieces	
Coffeepot with cover	Used to serve coffee.
Teapot with cover	Used to serve tea.
Cream pitcher	Used to serve cream for tea or coffee.
Sugar with cover	Used to serve sugar for tea or coffee.
Gravy or sauce boat	Oblong or rounded bowl with attached or separate saucer; may have handle and/or spout.
Platter	Flat serving plate that can be any size; shaped round, oval, or square; used to serve food.
Vegetable dish with cover	Covered dish used to serve food.
Round vegetable dish (sometimes called a *nappy*)	Open dish used to serve food; available in various sizes.
Oval vegetable dish (sometimes called a *baker*)	Open dish used to serve food; available in various sizes.
Tureen	Large serving bowl with two side handles and a cover; used to serve soup, stew, or beans.

TABLE 15.3
Place Settings

Number of Pieces	Pieces
Three piece	Dinner plate, cup, and saucer
Four piece	Dinner plate, dessert/salad plate, cup, and saucer
Five piece	Dinner plate, dessert/salad plate, bread and butter plate, cup, and saucer (sometimes a soup/cereal bowl is substituted for the bread and butter plate)
Six piece	Dinner plate, dessert/salad plate, bread and butter plate, soup/cereal bowl, cup, and saucer

Place Settings

A **place setting** is a service for one person. It may include three, four, five, or six pieces (see Table 15.3). Higher-priced dinnerware is usually purchased by the place setting (see Figure 15.7).

Sets

Sets include place settings to serve four or more people and are usually offered at a considerable price advantage when compared to individual pieces or place settings. The most common sets include service for four, six, eight, or twelve people. Sets are described by the number of pieces they contain. Common sizes of sets are:

- 12-piece set for 4
- 16-piece set for 4
- 20-piece set for 4
- 32-piece set for 6
- 40-piece set for 6
- 47-piece set for 6
- 60-piece set for 12
- 67-piece set for 12
- 105-piece set for 12

FIGURE 15.7
A place setting of china.
Courtesy of Fairchild Publications, Inc.

The twenty-piece set, often called the **starter set** or **basic service,** includes:

- 4 dinner plates
- 4 salad plates (also used as a luncheon plate and a service plate)
- 4 soup/cereal bowls, sometimes called all-purpose bowls (or 4 bread and butter plates)
- 4 teacups
- 4 saucers

A five-piece **completer set** includes the following serving pieces:

- Platter
- Vegetable bowl
- Creamer
- Sugar bowl with top, which counts as two pieces

Completer sets come with different numbers and assortments of pieces. A nine-piece completer set might include teapot with lid, creamer, sugar bowl with lid, salt and pepper shakers, platter, and serving bowl.

A 47-piece set for eight might include:

- 8 dinner plates
- 8 salad plates
- 8 bread and butter plates (or soup/cereal bowls)
- 8 cups
- 8 saucers
- 1 platter
- 1 round vegetable dish
- 1 oval vegetable dish
- 1 gravy boat
- 1 sugar bowl with top (two pieces)
- 1 creamer

Open and Closed Stock

Open-stock dinnerware may be purchased in any quantity or combination of items for as long as the manufacturer continues to make the design. Open stock may be discontinued when popularity wanes. **Closed-stock** dinnerware is available only in predetermined sets that have been packaged by the manufacturer. Extra pieces are not available for purchase.

Raw Materials and Selection of Dinnerware

Many different raw materials can be used to make dinnerware—pottery, glass, plastic, paper, and sometimes metal.

The occasion and budget determine the consumer's choice of dinnerware. A formal dinner, child's birthday party, summer picnic, camping trip, and patio breakfast are some of the events requiring specialized dinnerware.

Pottery

Dinnerware is commonly made from pottery, which is baked clay. The most common types of pottery used for dinnerware are china, bone china, stoneware, and earthenware.

China China is the most expensive and durable ceramic used for dishes. Many people reserve their china for special occasions requiring formal or semiformal service. China is porcelain that has been fired at approximately 1,300 degrees Centigrade. Bone china is similar to china except that it is about 50-percent animal bone.

High-quality china and bone china are translucent, quite thin, and when tapped by a pencil or pen, emit a clear ringing sound. Decoration may be applied to china underglaze or overglaze. Underglaze design is added before the final firing process. Overglaze decoration is applied after the final fire. This decoration is less durable, and this china should not be washed in a dishwasher. Gold and silver trims are overglaze because they cannot withstand the firing process.

Stoneware and Earthenware Stoneware and earthenware are used for less formal service and are commonly called **kitchen dishes** or **everyday dishes.** As with china, decoration may be added underglaze or overglaze. Stoneware resembles china, but it is thicker, less dense, and more fragile than china. It can be used in the oven and is dishwasher and microwave safe. Earthenware is fired at a relatively low temperature that allows for more vibrant colors. It is quite thick, the most crude, and least durable form of ceramics. Pottery is a type of earthenware. Hand washing is recommended for earthenware.

Glass

Glass may be used for dinnerware plates, saucers, bowls, and other pieces that can be shaped from glass. Corelle®, a trade name produced by Corning Ware, is a glass product made from two types of glass—a core glass of dense opal and a thin clear glass used to cover the surface of the opal. It resembles china but is heat resistant and very durable.

Plastic

A wide variety of plastic dishes are available. They are commonly used for informal occasions (see Figure 15.8). Plastic dinnerware is especially appropriate for small children. Some plastic dishes are disposable and are intended to be thrown away after each use. Some lightweight

FIGURE 15.8
Plastic dinnerware for informal occasions, such as this set which is used for outdoor barbecues and picnics.
Courtesy of Fairchild Publications, Inc.

plastic dishes may be used multiple times or thrown away as the consumer chooses; and some, such as melamine, are very durable and are sold as unbreakable.

Paper and Metal

Paper products and plastic-coated products are available for casual entertaining, such as children's birthday parties, picnics, or other events requiring easy cleanup. Decorative motifs, color, and style may be selected for a theme and to complement or accent any décor. Designs and colors of paper dinnerware and paper tablecloths and napkins are often coordinated. Metals, such as stainless steel or aluminum, are often used for mess kits for dining while camping or for other casual dining, such as picnics.

Care of Dinnerware

Durable plastics can be washed by hand or on the top rack of a dishwasher. The most durable plastic dinnerware, such as melamine, can be washed in the dishwasher, but it is subject to staining from tea and coffee. Baking soda and hot water can be used to remove stains. Melamine is also subject to scratching from harsh abrasive cleaners, and sharp knives will mark the surface.

While stoneware can be washed in a dishwasher, earthenware may not. The instructions on the care label should be followed. If decoration has been added on top of the glaze, dishwashing may remove it. Fine china with gold or silver decoration should be hand washed because the dishwasher will damage the metal. Abrasive cleaners and steel wool should not be used on any ceramic product because they can cause scratching. Mild porcelain cleaners can be used to remove the gray metal marks that sometimes appear on dinnerware. Baked-on foods should be soaked and then scrubbed with a plastic or nylon pad.

The manufacturer's directions for heating dinnerware in a conventional or microwave oven must be carefully followed. Fine china cannot be used in a microwave oven. Durable plastic dishes may char; the glaze on pottery may craze (form tiny cracks). Products with metal trim should not be used in a microwave. Even products that are heat resistant as well as those labeled for use in freezers and ovens must be precooled or preheated to avoid cracking.

Storage of Dinnerware

Pottery dinnerware must be stored carefully to prevent chips and cracks. Soft plastic cases are available to store formal dinnerware safely and keep it clean. Durable plastic dinnerware is easy to store because it resists breakage. Earthenware, stoneware, and china require more careful storage. To avoid chipping, cups should not be stacked, and plates should not be slid over one another.

GLASSWARE

Glassware may be chosen to match or to complement the dinnerware. It can be very informal, such as plastic or Styrofoam cups for a picnic, to very formal and elegant glassware for a wedding. As with dinnerware, glassware is available at many price points and in many designs and colors to meet consumer demands.

Styles of Glassware

Glassware can be categorized into four main styles—stemware, tumblers and footed tumblers, barware, and glass accessories.

Stemware

Stemware refers to drinking glasses that have a bowl, stem, and foot (see Figure 15.9). They are usually used for formal and semiformal occasions. See Figure 15.10 for illustrations and names of styles of stemware.

Tumblers

Tumblers are drinking glasses that have no foot or stem. They are usually used for semiformal and informal occasions (see Figure 15.11) Footed tumblers are drinking glasses that have a foot but no stem (see Figure 15.12).

Barware

Barware refers to drinking glasses for serving alcoholic drinks (see Figure 15.13). Many of the stemware and tumbler glasses are also considered barware. Highball and old-fashioned glasses have many uses. The **highball glass** is used for bourbon or scotch and water, vodka and tonic, beer, and soft drinks. The **old-fashioned glass** is used for martinis, manhattans, scotch or bourbon on

FIGURE 15.9
Parts of a piece of stemware.

FIGURE 15.10
Selected styles of stemware.

a. *Water goblet*, b. *Hock or Rhine wine-often decorated or made of colored glass*, c. *Red wine-Bordeaux, 6-9 oz*, d. *Red wine-Burgundy, 6-9 oz*, e. *White wine-Alsace, 4-6 oz*, f. *White wine-German, 4-6 oz, may also be used as an all-purpose wine glass*, g. *Table wine-4-6 oz. can be used for white wine, port, red table wines, Irish coffee, may also be used as an all-purpose wine glass*, h. *Sherry-traditional, approximately 4 oz.*, i. *Sherry-alternate, approximately 4 oz.*, j. *Brandy-Large—8—12 oz.*, k. *Brandy-Small—2 oz.*, l. *Champagne (solid stem preferred) also used for daiquiris and champagne cocktails*, m. *Tulip-shaped champagne glass*, n. *Cocktail (shape optional) -1 oz or more*, o. *Crème de menthe, frappe, stingers-about 4 oz.*, p. *Sweet liqueur or cordial glass-1-2 oz.*, q. *Whisky sour or parfait*

FIGURE 15.11 *Selected styles of tumblers.*
a. *Water tumbler*, b. *Old-fashioned, "rocks" or "on the rocks"— 10-14 oz.*, c. *Juice-3-4 oz.*, d. *Delmonico or whisky sour*, e. *Highball*

COCKTAIL GLASS   WATER GLASS   PILSNER

SHOT GLASS   MARTINI GLASS   PUNCH GLASS   IRISH COFFEE MUG

FIGURE 15.12 *Footed tumblers.*

FIGURE 15.13 *Barware.*

ice, aperitifs with or without ice, and wine served as a cocktail. The wine glass may also be used to serve wine or aperitifs at cocktail parties.

Glassware Accessories

Glassware accessories are the many types of glass products available for the table. Included in this category are fruit/dessert sets, punch bowl sets, candlesticks, vases, decanters, ice buckets, pitchers, and serving dishes (see Figure 15.14).

Purchasing Glassware

Glassware may be purchased in open stock or in sets. Sets usually consist of eight matching pieces. For example, one could purchase eight water goblets. Sometimes less expensive glassware is available in larger sets of 24 or 32 tumblers and may include:

- 8 10-oz. old-fashioned glasses
- 8 9-oz. water glasses
- 8 12-oz. water or iced tea glasses
- and sometimes, 8 9-oz. juice glasses

Raw Materials and Selection of Glassware

As the term suggests, glass is the primary material used to make glassware, but plastic and paper drinking vessels are also considered part of the glassware category. The occasion determines which material is appropriate for use.

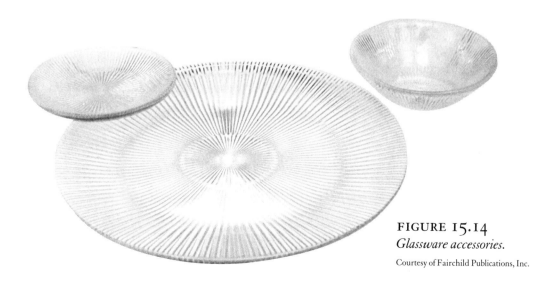

FIGURE 15.14
Glassware accessories.
Courtesy of Fairchild Publications, Inc.

Glass

Glass is the most common material used to make glassware. Lime-soda and lead glass are the two types of glass typically used. The commonly accepted definition of tableware crystal is clear, transparent glassware made from one of these two types of glass. It may be colored or colorless.

Decorative elements in the dinnerware can be highlighted in the choice of glassware. For example, gold trim on the china can be repeated in gold trim on the crystal.

Lime-Soda Glass Lime-soda glass is cheaper than lead glass and therefore usually used for less formal occasions. Frequently it is used with kitchen dishes. It may be colored or colorless.

Lead Glass Lead glass is also called flint glass or lead crystal and contains high levels of lead oxide. The lead increases the brilliance, weight, clarity, and durability of the glass. Because it is expensive, it is usually reserved for semiformal or formal use. Lead glass that has been decorated by cutting is very costly. To conform to international standards, glass labeled as lead crystal must contain no less than 24 percent lead.

Plastic

Plastic glassware is available for casual occasions. It may be appropriate for only one use and labeled as disposable. Some plastic glassware is very durable and labeled as unbreakable. Plastic glassware is available in basic stemware, tumbler, and footed tumbler shapes.

Paper

Paper glassware is traditionally reserved for children's birthday parties and other very informal occasions that require easy cleanup. In some cases, paper cups are used when sanitary issues are important, such as in a bathroom or medical facility.

Care of Glassware

Most glassware can be washed in a dishwasher. Fine lead glass should be carefully washed by hand using a mild detergent and warm water. Crystal with silver or gold trim should not be put in the dishwasher. Sudden temperature changes can cause glass to shatter. Usually durable plastic glassware can be washed on the top rack of a dishwasher. The manufacturer's instructions should be carefully followed.

Storage of Glassware

Glasses should never be stacked but should stand individually on a shelf with space between the glasses so rims do not chip. Never store fine glassware upside down since the rim of the glass can chip.

FLATWARE AND HOLLOWWARE

Forks, spoons, knives, and other small utensils used to eat and serve food are called **flatware.** **Hollowware** refers to metal tableware that is deep and hollow, such as bowls, coffee pots, pitchers, gravy boats, sugar bowls, and vases (see Figure 15.15). To create an aesthetically pleasing table, flatware and hollowware are often selected to complement dinnerware and glassware. They are available at all price points and in many different designs.

Styles of Flatware

Each piece of flatware serves a different purpose. The more formal the occasion the more different pieces of flatware are required. Figures 15.16, 15.17, and 15.18 show shapes and uses of different forks, knives, and spoons. The salad fork can also be used as a dessert fork or a luncheon fork. The teaspoon has replaced the dinner spoon in most modern flatware sets.

Flatware can be categorized into four basic groups—basic place settings, other place pieces, carving pieces, and serving pieces. Figures 15.19 and Figure 15.20 show the carving pieces and serving pieces that are available.

Purchasing Flatware

Flatware is sold in sets or open stock. Sets of flatware usually contain a variety of pieces and various numbers of place settings (see Figure 15.21). Sometimes flatware is sold in sets of 4, 6, 8, or 12 place settings. The basic five-piece place setting contains:

- 1 place fork
- 1 place knife
- 1 dessert/salad fork
- 1 soup spoon or place spoon
- 1 teaspoon

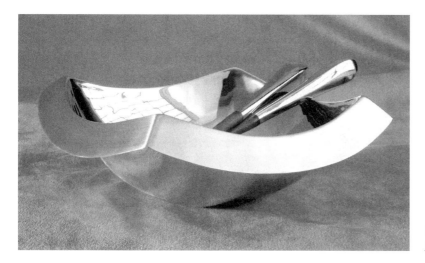

FIGURE 15.15
Hollowware.

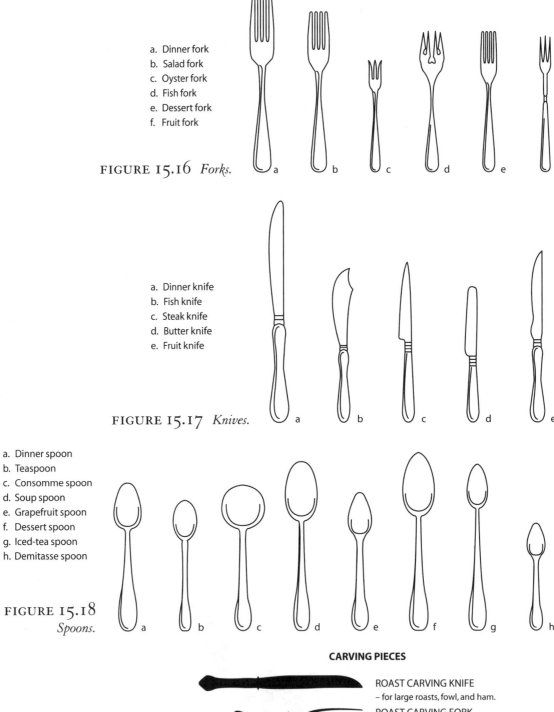

a. Dinner fork
b. Salad fork
c. Oyster fork
d. Fish fork
e. Dessert fork
f. Fruit fork

FIGURE 15.16 *Forks.* a b c d e f

a. Dinner knife
b. Fish knife
c. Steak knife
d. Butter knife
e. Fruit knife

FIGURE 15.17 *Knives.* a b c d e

a. Dinner spoon
b. Teaspoon
c. Consomme spoon
d. Soup spoon
e. Grapefruit spoon
f. Dessert spoon
g. Iced-tea spoon
h. Demitasse spoon

FIGURE 15.18
Spoons. a b c d e f g h

CARVING PIECES

ROAST CARVING KNIFE
– for large roasts, fowl, and ham.

ROAST CARVING FORK
– to hold roasts and fowl for carving or slicing.

SLICER
– sharp and slim and long, essential for
   thin-slicing roasts.

STEAK CARVING KNIFE
– for steaks and small roasts, fowl, and other
   meats, such as sliced ham.

STEAK CARVING FORK
– for use with either carving knife as a server
   when roasts or fowl have been sliced or carved.

FIGURE 15.19
Carving pieces.

SERVING PIECES

TABLE OR SERVING SPOON
– serves salads, vegetables, berries, fruits, and desserts.

PIERCED TABLE OR SERVING SPOON
– for vegetables or fruits served in their juices.

GRAVY LADLE
– serves sauces, gravies, or dressings from either boat-shaped dishes or round bowls.

COLD MEAT OR BUFFET FORK
– serves cold meats, chops, and food served on toast, or a variety of platter salads.

TOMATO OR FLAT SERVER
– can be used for tomatoes, cucumbers, eggs, asparagus on toast, or for platter salads.

SALAD OR SERVING SPOON
– for fruits, berries, desserts, salads, vegetables. It can be used as a spare serving spoon.

BUTTER SERVING KNIFE
– for use on the butter plate in informal dining and on the cheese tray for serving certain jams.

SUGAR SPOON
– for the sugar bowl and for small bowls of mayonnaise or sauce.

CREAM OR SAUCE LADLE
– ladles gravy, stews, liquid dishes, dressings, or cream sauces.

JELLY SERVER
– serves cream cheese, preserves, jam, relishes, jellies, or marmalades.

LEMON FORK
– serves lemon slices.

BON BON OR NUT SPOON
– for nuts, candies, and some canapés.

OLIVE OR PICKLE FORK
– in addition to serving olives and pickles, it doubles as a lemon fork and butter pick.

SALAD BOWL SERVERS
– for graceful efficient service of tossed salads. (Note: the Cold Meat Fork and the Salad Spoon make a small salad set.)

CHEESE SERVING KNIFE
– serves brick cheese and cheese or similar spreads, and can be used for molded jellies.

PIE OR CAKE SERVING KNIFE
– essential for cutting and serving pies and cakes, and for aspics and frozen desserts.

RELISH OR JAM SPOON
– for relishes, jams, jellies, and preserves, and useful for serving mayonnaise.

SUGAR TONGS
– for use in the sugar bowl or on the candy dish.

FIGURE 15.20 *Serving pieces.*

FIGURE 15.21
A place setting of flatware.
Courtesy of Fairchild Publications, Inc.

The salad, dessert, or luncheon and place fork and knife are slightly smaller than the traditional dinner fork and knife. They are commonly used instead of the dinner fork and knife for all meals except on very formal occasions. The dinner size is also called the *continental size*. For a six-piece place setting, the butter spreader is added. See Figure 15.22 for placement of basic flatware and dinnerware on the table. The pattern for the serving pieces may match the place setting pattern or complement it.

Hollowware

Hollowware is available in many different styles, qualities, and prices. Table 15.4 summarizes some of the most common pieces of hollowware. Hollowware is usually purchased by the individual piece, but some sets, such as console sets and coffee and tea services, are available.

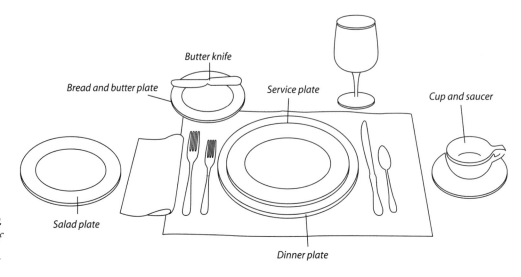

Butter knife

Bread and butter plate

Service plate

Cup and saucer

FIGURE 15.22
Placement of basic flatware.

Salad plate

Dinner plate

TABLE 15.4
Selected Hollowware Pieces

Candelabra	Candlesticks with two or more branches.
Candlesticks	10–15 inches high, to hold candles.
Centerpieces	Large deep bowls to hold flowers or fruit.
Coffee and tea service	Includes coffeepot, teapot, sugar bowl, creamer, and sometimes a tray for serving.
Compote	Short- or long-stemmed candy and nut bowls.
Console sticks	Short candlesticks; when a pair is used with a centerpiece, it forms a console set.
Creamer and sugar bowl	Used to serve cream and sugar, may have a matching tray; most sugar bowls have a matching lid.
Gravy boat	Oblong or rounded bowl with attached or separate saucer; may have a handle and/or spout.
Salt and pepper shakers	Small matching sets for individual use or larger for table use. (Note: Silver is adversely affected by salt so sometimes open cellars with small spoons are used.)
Sherbet dishes	Stemmed bowls for serving fruit, ice cream sherbet, or seafood cocktails; may have a glass liner.
Vase	Container used to hold flowers.
Vegetable dishes	Open or covered dish used to serve food, available in various sizes; some have a removable glass insert.
Water pitcher	Tall vessel for serving water, milk, or iced drinks.

Raw Materials and Selection of Flatware and Hollowware

Metals are commonly used to make flatware and hollowware. Plastic flatware is available for casual dining. The most common metals used are stainless steel, sterling silver, silverplate, and pewter. Sterling-silver and silver-plated flatware knives have stainless-steel blades.

Stainless Steel

Stainless-steel flatware and hollowware are usually used for informal service and are often used with kitchen dishes. Some stainless-steel flatware patterns resemble silver patterns. Stainless steel is available at many price points and in many different patterns and styles.

The quality of stainless steel is determined by its weight and alloy mixture. Heavier pieces are usually considered to be of higher quality. The higher quality and more durable stainless flatware is 18:8 or 18:10 ratio of chrome to nickel steel. It is available in shiny or matte finish. It is very hard and resistant to stains, heat, and corrosion. Higher-quality stainless flatware is graded or shaped so that it is thicker where strength is needed and thinner where it needs to be graceful. Less-expensive stainless flatware is the same thickness from one end of the piece to the other.

Pewter

Pewter, an alloy of tin and other metals, is also a popular material for informal hollowware. It is very soft and dents easily. Also, it has a low melting point and should be kept away from heat. It is usually used for decorative purposes or to serve cold beverages. Gold-colored alloys are also available in flatware and hollowware.

Sterling Silver and Silverplate

Sterling-silver and silver-plated flatware is used for more formal occasions. Sterling silver must by law contain 92.5 percent silver and 7.5 percent alloy, such as copper. In the United States, the term *sterling* refers to the fineness of the silver, not the thickness of the item. In England, the hallmark is the official stamp to indicate purity.

Sterling silver is available is two finishes—bright or matte. With use, silver acquires a **patina** or network of fine scratches. This is considered desirable since it gives the metal a soft glow. The price of silver is determined by its weight and the amount of decoration. Silver items of greater weight and more ornate patterns will cost more.

Silver-plated flatware is less expensive because it is made from a base metal, usually an alloy of nickel, copper, brass, or stainless steel that is electroplated with silver. Higher-quality silver-plated flatware has numerous platings and extra thick coats on wear areas, such as the backs of forks and spoons where they rest on the table.

Silver-plated flatware does not have the wear life of sterling silver, and the coatings will eventually wear off. They can be restored by replating. A wide variety of patterns and levels of quality is available.

Vermeil

Vermeil is sterling silver that has been electroplated with 24-karat gold. It is very expensive but has an extremely hard surface that gives years of service. It does not tarnish.

Gold-Plated Flatware

Gold-plated flatware is also available. The base metal is electroplated with a layer of 24-karat gold.

Care and Storage of Flatware and Hollowware

Stainless steel is durable, easy-to-care-for, and very resistant to scratches. It does not tarnish, rust, or stain. Washing and drying by hand, hand drying after dishwashing, and use of a stainless-steel polish will prevent discoloration. Knife blades do require special care, because they can be made from a special grade of stainless steel. They may "pit" or form small holes if left in contact with chloride-containing foods, or if allowed to soak in water overnight. Stainless steel does not require special storage.

The main disadvantage of silver is that it tarnishes or oxidizes. It must be polished or stored in specially treated silver chests or chamois bags. Silver should not be washed in a dishwasher. It should be washed promptly in hot soapy water and dried thoroughly before storage to help prevent water spotting and tarnishing. A high-quality silver polish should be used to remove tarnish.

To prevent deep scratches, silver should not be stored loose in a drawer but carefully stacked. Silver-plated flatware must be cared for in the same manner as sterling silver. The knife blades of sterling silver and silver-plated flatware are stainless steel and require the same care as stainless steel knives.

TABLEWARE AND THE ENVIRONMENT

Glass, metal, plastic, and pottery are used as tableware. Environmental issues related to each of these raw materials are covered in an earlier chapter (Chapter 4 "Glass", Chapter 5 "Pottery," Chapter 6 "Plastics," and Chapter 7 "Metal"). Issues related to lead contamination are especially important in pottery and glass.

SUMMARY

Tableware includes a broad range of products used for decorating the table, serving food, and dining. Categories of tableware include dinnerware, glassware, flatware, and hollowware. These products are primarily made from glass, ceramics, plastics, and metals.

Dinnerware refers to all items used to serve and present food to the diner. Rim and coupe are the two basic shapes for flat dishes, such as plates and saucers. Overall measurement and well-to-edge measurement are the two methods to measure the size of flat dishes, such as plates and saucers. Dinnerware may be purchased as individual pieces, in place settings, and in sets. Open-stock dinnerware may be purchased in any quantity or combination of items for as long as the manufacturer continues to make the design. Closed-stock dinnerware is available only in sets predetermined and packaged by the manufacturer.

Glassware can be categorized into four main styles—stemware, tumblers and footed tumblers, barware, and glass accessories. Glass is the primary material used to make glassware, but plastic and paper drinking vessels are also considered part of the glassware category. The occasion determines which material is appropriate.

Forks, spoons, knives, and other small utensils used to eat and serve food are called flatware. Hollowware refers to metal tableware that is deep and hollow, such as a bowls, coffee pots, pitchers, gravy boats, sugar bowls, and vases. Flatware is sold in sets or open stock. Metals are commonly used to make flatware and hollowware. Plastic flatware is available for casual dining. The most common metals used are stainless steel, sterling silver, silverplate, and pewter. Sterling-silver and silver-plated flatware knives have stainless-steel blades.

Silver and silver-plated flatware and hollowware demand careful storage and cannot be washed in a dishwasher. Fine-lead glassware and fine dinnerware with overglaze decoration should be hand washed. The consumer should be fully aware of the product-care requirements before purchasing tableware.

INDUSTRY PROFILE

Corelle Dinnerware

In the late 1960s, Corning scientists discovered a way to laminate glass, strengthening the fragile material in much the same way lamination strengthens wood. The result was a plate far stronger than anything on the market, yet one that looked like china, with the hard feel of glass.

When this new product, called Corelle Livingware, debuted in 1970, it brought a distinct brand identity to an everyday dinnerware field dominated by plastic and earthenware. Corelle tapped into a niche: Plastic at that time was durable, but looked like plastic. Earthenware chipped easily.

Corelle gave consumers dinnerware that was dishwasher- and oven-safe, durable, affordable and attractive.

Within 18 months after Corelle hit the market, more than 40 million pieces had been sold.

Today, Corelle, now owned by World Kitchen, is the most recognized brand of dinnerware on the globe. Corelle dinnerware can be found in almost half of the households in America, is sold in 40 countries and has been released in 250 patterns and over 100 shapes.

In 1996, the two-billionth piece of Corelle was produced. In celebration of this event, a newspaper columnist wrote that it would be customary to wish for future good luck by breaking a Corelle coffee cup on the floor instead of a wine glass. It didn't work. Corelle was too durable.

Source: HFN, May 27, 2002, p. 64. Courtesy of Fairchild Publications, Inc.

TERMS FOR REVIEW

barware	hollowware	sets
closed stock	kitchen (everyday) dishes	starter set (basic service)
completer set	old-fashioned glass	stemware
coupe	open stock	tableware
dinnerware	overall measurement	tumblers
flatware	patina	vermeil
glassware accessories	place setting	well-to-edge measurement
highball glass	rim	(trade measurement)

REVIEW QUESTIONS

1. List and describe the two basic shapes of dinnerware.
2. List the basic pieces included in a "starter set" of dishes.
3. Why might open-stock merchandise be favored over closed stock?
4. List the main styles of glassware and give examples of each.
5. List the items in a five-piece place setting of flatware.
6. Compare the cost and durability of sterling silver and silver-plated flatware.

LEARNING ACTIVITIES

1. Compare and contrast the tableware offerings of a large department store and a discount store. What are the differences in presentation, quality, and price?
2. Clip advertisements from catalogs, magazines, Internet sites, etc., of tableware. Mount the clippings, list the price points, and describe the potential ultimate consumer. Justify why you think the consumer would be interested in purchasing the items.

GLOSSARY

above grade Above ground level.

abrasion resistance Ability to withstand the effects of rubbing or friction.

accent lighting Highlights an area of a space, such as a piece of art or an accessory and gives it greater importance in the room. Sometimes called *special emphasis lighting*.

acrylic paint Synthetic resin water-based paint.

acrylonitrile-butadiene-styrene (ABS) An important rubber blend.

adjustable beds Beds with specially designed frames that allow the head and foot of the bed to be raised and lowered, much like a hospital bed.

advertising The vehicle a company uses to communicate information about the company and its products. It is the presentation of facts and benefits of a product to a group of potential consumers. It is always paid for and it is nonpersonal.

aesthetic finish Finish that improves the appearance or hand of the fabric.

afghan A small blanket.

air-drying Wood is simply allowed to dry naturally in the open air.

air-filled mattress A heavy-duty vinyl bladder that is encased in a foam shell.

alkyd resins A subcategory of polyester. They are thermoset and are used extensively in paints.

alloy A metallic substance that is formed by blending two or more elements, one of which must be a metal.

amalgamation The process of recovering metal by passing a solution of finely ground particles of ore over a plate covered with mercury. The mercury attracts the metal and forms an amalgam, or compound, with the metal.

amalgams Alloys that contain mercury.

ambient bank A large well-lit area. It can be used to designate a smaller space within a large space. Sometimes called a *plane of light*.

ambient lighting Provides uniform light for general use. This lighting is pleasant but does not usually provide enough light for specific tasks. Also called *general lighting*.

American Oriental rugs See MACHINE-MADE ORIENTAL DESIGN RUGS.

anchor Major mall tenant, typically located on a corner or end of the mall.

animal fiber Fiber derived from animal sources. Also called *protein fibers*.

annealing (1) Process of improving the durability of glass by heating it and allowing it to cool slowly. (2) Process of heating a metal to just below its melting point, allowing it to stay at that temperature for a while, and then slowly cooling it, creating a metal that is less brittle.

annual ring The layer of wood produced by one year's growth.

anodizing A form of electroplating that is used on aluminum. The process works in reverse to deposit an oxide film on aluminum.

architectural lighting See STRUCTURAL LUMINAIRES.

Axminster carpet Carpet woven on an Axminster loom. The carpet has a one-level cut pile and is identified by heavy ridges across the back of the carpet. Each tuft is inserted individually.

back Technically, the "wrong" side of the fabric.

baffle A screening device.

bagasse The residue after sugar cane has been crushed.

bagging A paint-texturizing technique that creates a marbled effect by using a plastic bag to remove wet glaze to reveal a base color.

balanced weave Fabric having a thread count with the same number of threads in the warp and in filling.

ballast A device used to establish the circuit conditions necessary to start and operate a lamp.

ball clay Sedimentary clay that has been carried in a stream and deposited on the bottom of a body of water, very fine in grain, nearly white. Also called *blue clay.*

bamboo Large tropical grass.

band springs Mattress support system in which flat strips of metal that run lengthwise are held on the ends by helical coil springs.

bark The protective covering of the tree.

barware Drinking glasses for serving alcoholic drinks.

basalt Hard black unglazed stoneware developed by Wedgwood in the 1700s.

basic service See STARTER SET.

bast fibers Fibers derived from the stems of plants.

batch Raw ingredients for glass, including the coloring agents.

bating Removal of the lime from the skins by washing them with cold water and a lime neutralizing agent. Bating softens the skin and gives it a silky feel.

Battenberg lace Lace that has a design outlined with tape.

bedboard A hard panel that provides extra firmness in a bed.

bedding Refers to furniture that is used to sleep on at night.

bed-in-a-bag Entire ensembles for the bed, typically includes sheets, pillow case(s), quilt or comforter, dust ruffle, and sham(s).

bedrest A pillow that has a back and arms. Sometimes called a *husband.*

bedspread Bedding that covers the top of the bed and traditionally extends to the floor on three sides.

below grade Below ground level.

bend The center back section of an animal.

beveled glass Made by grinding and polishing the edges of a piece of glass at an angle, used for mirrors, doors, leaded-glass windows, and in other decorative applications.

bird's eye Veneer pattern with tiny markings in the wood thought to be caused by undeveloped buds.

biscuit firing See BISQUE FIRING.

bishop's sleeve treatments See POUFED CURTAINS.

bisque firing Initial firing to make the ware more durable and improve its appearance.

blanket binding Satin or taffeta nylon binding used to finish the top and bottom of a blanket.

blank stock The material used as a base under wallpaper to provide a smooth or slightly textured surface so that the wall will look smooth and even. Also called *lining paper.*

bleed Lose color in water, causing color loss and staining.

blending The use of more than one fiber in a textile product.

blisters See BUBBLES.

blow molding A hollow tube of molten thermoplastic is placed in a mold and expanded with air pressure.

blowpipe A hollow steel pipe four to six feet long used to make glassware.

blue clay See BALL CLAY.

boarding Creates a creased, bumpy texture on the surface of the leather. The leather is folded over itself, and the two surfaces are rubbed together.

boards Solid wood lumber less than two inches thick and two or more inches wide.

body The prepared ingredients used to make pottery.

bonded leather Waste leather fibers are mixed with a plastic binder and then formed into sheets. The sheets are cut into patterns that resemble leather. Also called *reconstituted leather.*

bonding The process of using heat and pressure to join two or more layers of metal.

bone ash Made from cattle bones imported from South America.

bone china First produced in England in 1800. Originally oxen bone ashes were pulverized and added to the kaolin.

Bonnell-type innerspring mattress Mattress in which rows of hourglass-shaped coil springs are joined together by a continuous small spiral spring. Also called *open-coil mattress* or *traditionally sprung mattress.*

border A band of wall covering paper that is used as a

trim and/or accent on ceiling lines, chair rails, door windows, and other architectural features.

borosilicate glass Heat-resistant glassware that contains boric oxide.

box spring Foundation for an innerspring mattress.

bracket A length of board or other opaque screen placed in front of the light.

braided carpet Carpet in which three groups of yarns are braided, and the braided strands are then assembled side by side in a round or oval shape and stitched together.

brazing Solder that is usually 60 percent zinc and 40 percent copper. It melts at about 850 degrees Centigrade and is referred to as *hard solder.*

broadleaf trees Most broadleaf trees are deciduous. These trees, except the southern oak, shed their flat, broad leaves in the fall. Broadleaved trees are sometimes referred to as *hardwoods.*

broadloom Seamless carpeting that is constructed on a wide loom.

Brussels carpet Carpet with an uncut pile, made on a jacquard loom with three sets of warp yarns.

bubbles Result from gases created during the melting of the batch. Also known as *seeds* or *blisters.*

built-in luminaires Lighting that is integral to the construction of the building. Also called *spatially integrated lighting.*

bunk bed One bed stacked on top of another.

burl Veneer patterns with small round or oval markings, caused by unusual growths on a tree.

butler finish A distinctive surface luster produced on silver by mechanical buffing with abrasives. The traditional butler finish was originally achieved by hand rubbing.

cabinet woods Woods used for veneers.

café curtains Double- or triple-tiered curtains, usually windowsill length.

cambium layer A sticky substance found between the bark and the sapwood. It is composed of living cells and creates the new wood, usually late in summer.

canopy Refers to both the frame that is attached to a four-poster bed with six- to seven-foot posts and to the fabric that is draped over the frame. Frames may be flat or arched.

carded yarns Yarns that have not been combed.

carpet Soft floor covering that is sold by the square yard. It is usually installed as wall-to-wall carpeting.

carpet cushion The structure that is placed between the floor and the rug or carpet. Alternate terms include *cushion, foundation, lining, padding,* and *underlayment.*

carpet modules 12, 18, or 36 inches squares of carpeting. Also called *carpet squares* or *carpet tiles.*

carpet squares See CARPET MODULES.

carpet tiles See CARPET MODULES.

carpincho A water rodent from South and Central America.

carved glass Glassware that is deeply cut by sandblasting. The results are similar to engraving but take much less time.

cascades Soft window treatments in which falls of fabric hang in graduated lengths on either side of the window.

case glass Very expensive decorative glassware. Layers of colored glass are superimposed over a layer of transparent or opal glass and then decorated by cutting.

case goods Box-like furniture such as desks, chests of drawers, buffets, bookcases, and china closets. Since chairs, tables, and beds are commonly sold with case goods, the term generally refers to dining room and bedroom furniture as a whole.

casements Medium-weight fabrics made from novelty yarns. They have some transparency. They may be lined and hung as drapes or left unlined and hung as curtains.

casework Cabinets, cases, storage units, and other fixtures that are built in or attached to the building.

casting (1) Shaping plastic by pouring liquid polymer into lead-covered molds and baking in ovens until the plastic hardens. (2) An inexpensive method of shaping metal. The metal is melted and poured into molds.

cast iron Iron that contains between five and ten percent other elements. Usually four to six percent will be carbon. The other elements may include silicon, manganese, phosphorus, and sulfur. It is one of the cheapest metals.

Caucasian rugs Handmade Oriental rugs originally made in central Asia. Their patterns are crowded with strong geometric designs and usually combinations of red, blue, and yellow.

ceiling paper Wall covering used specifically on ceilings when blank stock is too thin to hide the defects.

cellulosic fiber Fiber derived from the seed, stem, or leaves of plants.

cellulosic plastic Thermoplastic using cellulose, in the form of cotton or wood fibers, as part of the resin.

central business districts Usually located in downtown areas, where there is a wide assortment of stores with variety in prices, products, and services.

ceramic mosaic tiles Small (no larger than six square inches) porcelain or natural clay tiles, glazed or unglazed. The most common sizes are one inch square and two inches square.

ceramics Refers to articles made from clay; another term for *pottery.*

ceramic tiles Commonly made from natural clay, they can also be made from porcelain or mixtures of clay and ceramic materials.

cervical roll foam pillow A collar pillow designed to prevent neck pain caused by arthritis or muscle spasms.

chandelier A large pendant fixture.

chasing The process of ornamenting metal by tapping indented lines that outline a design in the surface of the metal.

checking The formation of small checks on the surface of the wood.

chemical finish Finish that involves the application of chemicals. Also called *wet finishes.*

chemical wood pulp Pulp produced by cooking wood chips in a chemical solution.

chenille carpet Carpet made with chenille filling yarns.

china Originally made from fine, white clay called kaolin (silicate of alumina) and china stone, completely vitrified.

china stone Component of china, contains feldspar.

Chinese rugs Handmade Oriental rugs characterized by motifs such as trees, animals, dragons, and clouds. The colors are usually soft and muted. Chinese rugs are often sculpted.

classic A product that never becomes completely obsolete. There is demand for the product for an extended period of time.

clay Decomposed granite. It consists of aluminum oxide, silica dioxide, and water.

closed stock Dinnerware that is only available in sets predetermined and packaged by the manufacturer. Extra pieces are not available for purchase.

coasters Small squares used under glasses to protect tabletops from moisture.

coating A very thin protective layer applied to a material.

coiling Method of coiling ropes of clay around a disk to create pottery.

coil-on-coil A smaller, finer coil rests on top of the innerspring to provide more cushion.

coin silver The silver used to make American dimes, quarters, and half dollars prior to 1965. It is an alloy of 90 percent silver and 10 percent copper.

color washing A paint-texturizing technique in which a coat of thinned or translucent paint is applied over a white or colored background. If the surface is rough, the effect is a rugged texture. If the surface is smooth, the effect is shimmering translucence.

coloration Adding color to a textile product by using dyes or pigments.

colorfast Colors that are permanent.

COM (customer's own material) The customer supplies the fabric to be installed on an upholstered piece of furniture.

combing (1) Process to remove short fibers and further parallel the fibers, creating a smoother, finer, more uniform yarn. (2) A paint-texturizing technique that produces fine lines and may be used in wood graining; a hard, comb-like tool is dragged over a wet glaze to reveal a base coat. Cross-hatching can produce a fabric-like texture.

comforter Usually throw-type bedding that covers the top of the bed and falls partially down the sides of the bed but not completely to the floor. Composed of three layers—a backing fabric, filling, and top fabric.

commode An enclosed end table that is round, hexagonal, or octagonal and has doors that open.

common clay The material used to make bricks, usually dark red or brown; hardens at low temperatures.

completer set Serving pieces to match the starter set.

compression molding Plastic pellets, powder, or pre-formed discs are preheated and poured into steel molds. The mold is closed, and heat and pressure are applied.

coniferous trees These trees do not shed their long, needle-like leaves. Conifers are sometimes referred to as *softwoods*.

contemporary furniture Furniture that originated in the late 19th century. It was the result of advances in technology and uses a variety of materials such as wood, plastic, glass, chrome, and steel.

continuous springing Supple steel wire is used to make an interwoven spring web that is similar to an old iron frame bed.

contoured pillows Foam pillows that are lower in the middle and higher on the sides to support the neck.

contour sheet See FITTED SHEET.

contract furniture Furniture designed to be used by institutions, businesses, or in public buildings.

copperplate decoration See TRANSFER PRINTING.

copper-wheel engraving Engraving glass with a small copper disk that is covered with oil and emery.

cords Almost invisible variations in the density of the glass, that appear as streaks.

cord yarn Created when two or more ply yarns are twisted together.

correlated groupings The groupings of furniture designed to go together to create living environments.

cotton linters The short fibers that remain on the cotton seed after ginning.

country furniture See PROVINCIAL FURNITURE.

coupe Basic shape for flat dishes; the dishes have no rim or flat edge.

courses Rows that appear on the back of a weft knit.

cover Ability of a fabric to hide what is beneath it.

coverage rate See SPREADING RATE.

crackle glaze The ware is cooled very quickly after firing to create a fine web of lines on the surface. The cracks are often accentuated with coloring.

crimp Waves or bumps of a fiber.

crock Transfer of color by abrasion.

cross section The appearance of the fiber when viewed across its diameter.

crotch Veneer with a V-shaped pattern caused by branches extending from a tree.

crystal Fine glassware, which may or may not be lead crystal.

cullet Old scrap glass.

curing See SEASONING.

curtains Lightweight window coverings that do not have linings.

cushion See CARPET CUSHION.

cutting Use of a carborundum wheel to create faceted designs in lead glass.

cut size The dimensions of tablecloths after hemming and/or trimming.

dado joint A piece of wood fits into a groove that has been cut into another piece of wood.

damasks The traditional fabric for a formal tablecloth. It is an intricate weave with long floats that create the pattern. A float may be as long as 20 threads.

daybed A twin or single sized mattress on a frame, used for sitting or sleeping.

decalcomania A decal is stenciled on the glass and then the glass is fired. This process imitates hand painting and is permanent. Sometimes a printed tissue is rubbed to transfer a design. Also called *lithography*.

deciduous Trees that lose their leaves in the fall.

deckle edge A rough or uneven edge on paper.

decorative drapes Drapes that do not move. They are hung so they open in the center and are held back on the sides.

delftware See FAIENCE.

demographics Important statistics about the characteristics of a group of people. It includes information about size, age distribution, ethnic mix, sex, education, distribution, occupation, and income.

derivative cellulosic Fiber manufactured from cellulose but chemically changed during production; its properties are different from those of cellulose.

dhurrie (durrie, dhurry, durry) rugs Rugs handmade in India. They usually have striped designs and are made entirely from cotton. The filling yarns are hand spun.

dhurry Alternate spelling for *dhurrie*.

diameter Width of the cross section.

dimension All lumber of any width with thickness from two inches up to but not including five inches.

dimensional stability Ability of a fiber to maintain its original shape, neither shrinking nor stretching.

dimmer A switch that is pushed to turn a light on and rotated to increase or decrease the brightness of a light.

dinnerware All items used to serve and present food to the diner.

dip casting A heated mold is dipped into a liquid dispersion of the polymer. The plastic adheres to the hot mold. After curing, the plastic is peeled off the mold.

dipping A mold is dipped in liquid latex. A thin layer of rubber adheres to the mold.

direct glare A bright or inadequately shielded light in the field of view.

directional pile lay See PILE SWEEP.

direct light The lighting that occurs when nearly all (90 to 100 percent) of the light is directed toward the surface to be lit.

doilies Small decorative coverings, frequently lace.

domestics Department store classification that traditionally includes sheets and pillowcases, blankets, comforters and quilts, bedspreads, mattress covers and pads.

double roll Length of wall covering that is twice as long as a single roll and contains about 72 square feet. Also called a *double roll bolt*.

double roll bolt See DOUBLE ROLL.

dovetail joint The ends of the wood are cut so the pieces will interlock.

dowel joint Holes are drilled into the pieces of wood to be joined. Pegs, or pieces, of kiln-dried hardwood are fitted into the holes with glue.

down The undercoat of waterfowl.

downlights Fixtures installed on the ceiling or wall to cast pools of light below.

dragging A paint-texturizing technique in which subtle stripes are created by dragging a dry brush over a wet glaze to reveal a base color. Dragging can imitate fabric.

drape Ability of a fabric to hang in graceful folds.

drapes Heavy opaque window coverings that are usually lined.

draw curtains Sheer or opaque curtains hung on traverse rods.

draw draperies Draperies that can be opened and closed. There are two basic styles of draw drapes—two-way draw and one-way draw. A two-way draw will open at the center and pull back to both sides. A one-way draw will draw to one side only.

drawing Shaping metal by pulling it through increasingly smaller and smaller holes in a die (or mold) until it reaches the required size. Wires and rods are made by drawing.

Dresden china May refer to Meissen porcelain, other ware made in the city of Meissen, or any figurine made in the Meissen style.

drop The length of fabric that falls from the top of the bed to the floor.

drop match Wall covering pattern in which the second strip has to be lowered to match the first strip.

dry print Fabric that has been printed with pigments. Also called *heat-transfer print* or *paper print*.

ductile The substance can be hammered into thin sheets or it can be drawn into thin strands or wires.

durable finish Finish that usually lasts for the life of the product, but its effectiveness will diminish as the product ages.

durrie Alternate spelling for *dhurrie*.

durry Alternate spelling for *dhurrie*.

dust bottom Thin layer of wood that separates drawers to prevent dust from settling on the contents of the lower drawer.

dust ruffles Lengths of fabric that hide the space between the edge of the quilt or comforter and the floor.

duvet French term that refers to a down comforter with a removable cover.

duvet cover Envelope-style cover for a duvet that minimizes the need for cleaning. Sometimes called *sheet casings*.

dye Coloring agent that chemically bonds with fibers.

earthenware Pottery or semi-vitreous ware.

edge guards Prebuilt borders along the edges of the mattress.

efflorescence A white powder caused by an alkaline chemical reaction with water. Masonry may require an alkaline-resistant primer to prevent efflorescence.

egg-crate foam mattress pads Latex or urethane mattress covers made of open-celled foamed plastics, either latex or urethane.

elastic recovery Ability of a fiber to return to its original length after being stretched.

electric discharge lamps See GASEOUS DISCHARGE LAMPS.

electrodeposition An electric current is run through a bath of latex. Negatively charged rubber particles adhere to metal molds.

electrolysis The process of collecting metals from the leaching solution by placing the solution in an electrolytic cell where electric current flows from a positive pole through the solution to a negative pole.

electroplating (1) Used to apply silver to glassware. (2) The decomposition of a chemical compound by an electric current.

elongation Lengthening or stretching of a fiber.

embossing Pressing designs into glass before it cools completely.

encrusting The application of gold or platinum over an etched surface.

epoxy Widely used thermoset plastic that is especially good for bonding under difficult conditions.

esparto A desert grass found in northern Africa and southern Spain.

étagère A cabinet used to display items.

etching The process of decorating glass or pottery by treating it with hydrofluoric acid.

even wash Soft plane of light from spotlights of track lights.

everyday dishes See KITCHEN DISHES.

extended decisions Occur when the customer goes through all steps of the decision-making process.

extenders Fillers that are used to reduce cost.

external market research Research that occurs outside the company, it includes collecting data on the competition, tracking overall sales in the industry, following economic trends, and learning about the customer.

extractive metallurgy The taking of metals from their ores and refining them.

fabric Cohesive structure made from yarns or directly from fibers.

face Technically, the "right" side of the fabric.

face fibers Fibers used in the surface, or pile, of the carpet, rug, or broadloom.

face weight The weight of the fabric on the face of the carpet.

fad A style or product that is popular for a relatively short period of time.

fade General loss of color.

faience Earthenware with a glaze that has been made opaque with tin oxide. Also called *majolica, maiolica,* or *delftware.*

famille Chinese porcelain decorated with enamel; famille jaune—yellow decoration, famille noire—black decoration, famille rose—pink decoration, famille verte—green decoration.

fat liquoring The process replacing the natural oil that the tanning process has removed from leather. Animal, mineral, or vegetable oils are rubbed into the surface of the leather.

faux finishes Paint-texturizing techniques; some techniques make the surface look old and imitate the patina found in antiques, while other techniques create the look of marble or granite.

feather bed A thick mattress pad filled with feathers.

feathers Plumage of fowl.

federbett German term that refers to a down comforter with a removable cover.

feldspar A crystalline mineral that melts at a rather low temperature.

ferrous metals Iron and its alloys.

fettling Use of small scalpels called fettling tools to trim excess material, remove bumps from the surface, and smooth the joints of the ware.

fiber Fine, hair-like strand used to make yarn or fabric. It may be natural or manufactured.

fiberfill Staple polyester suitable for use as filling or stuffing.

fiddleback Veneer pattern of fine wavy lines that run crosswise at right angles to the regular grain; seen in mahogany and maple.

filament yarn Yarn made from long or filament fibers.

fill leakage The penetration of the filling through the fabric.

fillers Materials that are added to plastics to improve or to extend the product.

filling knit Knit fabric in which the yarns run horizontally across the fabric. Also called *weft knit.*

filling yarn The crosswise yarn in woven fabric.

fine earthenware Earthenware that is fired at higher temperatures than pottery and is more durable. The clay underneath the glaze is less porous and more sanitary.

finish Process that modifies the properties of a textile product.

fire clay Rough textured refractory (resistant to high temperatures) clay.

firing The process of baking clay in a kiln to make it more durable.

fitted sheet Sheet with fitted elasticized corners or edges, used as a bottom sheet. Also called a *contour sheet*.

fixture See LUMINAIRE.

flagged bristles Paintbrush bristles that have split ends. They help the brush hold more paint and allow the paint to flow more smoothly.

flat package furniture See READY-TO-ASSEMBLE FURNITURE.

flat sheet Used as a top sheet, may be used as a bottom sheet.

flat-sliced veneers Veneers made from logs that have been cut in half. The blade moves across the cut edge of the log.

flatware Forks, spoons, knives, and other small utensils used to eat and serve food.

fleshing Removal of the flesh from the inner side of the skin to leave a clean surface.

flesh side The inner side of the skin.

flexibility Ability to be bent or folded easily.

flint A hard stone that is ground and mixed with the clay.

flint glass See LEAD GLASS.

float glass Flat glass shaped by layering molten glass over tin. The most widely used method to make flat glass.

floating construction Solid wood furniture is built so it can expand and contract without damage by placing the screws that hold the sides and top together in slotted screw holes.

floats Long strands of yarn on the surface of the fabric.

Floccati Alternate spelling of *Flokati*.

flocked carpet Large quantities of straight non-textured high-denier fibers of uniform length are embedded in an adhesive coating on a substrate. The substrate is frequently heavy-gauge vinyl sheeting.

flocked wall covering A wall covering with a decorative effect that imitates velvet.

Flokati (Floccati) rugs Hand-woven rugs made in Greece. They are made of wool and have a very long pile.

fluorescent lamps The most popular low-pressure electric discharge lamp.

fluorescent paint Paint that glows under ultraviolet light.

fluting A special type of carving in which perpendicular grooves are carved into posts or legs. They may be parallel or funnel shaped.

foam casting or molding The molding of plastics that have been expanded or foamed.

foam glass Used for thermal insulation batts.

foam rubber Rubber that has air mechanically incorporated into the rubber mixture.

foil/Mylar® wall coverings Highly reflective wall coverings; may be patterned or flocked.

follow-the-leader pricing Pricing policy in which the company sets prices that are consistent with other companies.

forge welding The hammering of metal parts together. The metal may be heated before hammering.

forging The hammering of heated metal.

foundation (1) The framework that supports the mattress. (2) See CARPET CUSHION.

free-blown glass See HAND-BLOWN GLASS.

free match See RANDOM MATCH.

freestanding stores Stores that are located on a highway or smaller street that is away from the traditional commercial area.

freestanding systems Office furniture that is independent of wall or panels. They function much like a freestanding desk and may be surrounded by panels or traditional walls.

fringe trading area Encompasses all of the potential customers outside the primary and secondary trading areas.

frit A fused mixture of glass and enamel that has been ground into a fine powder.

frost Loss of color due to localized abrasion.

frosting A slightly pitted surface in glassware.

full-body pillows Pillows that are about five feet long and are often filled with down or feathers.

full-grain leather The top layer of skin. The surface is not embossed or altered. Also called *full-top-grain leather*.

full-lead crystal Lead crystal that is at least 24 percent lead.

full-top-grain leather The top layer of skin. The surface is not embossed or altered. Also called *full-grain leather.*

fully tempered glass Three to five times more resistant to breakage than annealed glass. The glass is heated almost to the softening point and then quickly cooled with air or in a liquid bath. Fully tempered glass qualifies as safety glass.

fume fading Loss or change of color due to exposure to atmospheric gases in homes heated with gas; seen in acetates.

functional finish Finish that improves the performance of the fabric.

fusion-bonded carpet The pile yarns are imbedded in a vinyl adhesive compound that is spread on a backing.

fusion welding Welding with heat.

futon A traditional Japanese futon is a mattress stuffed with a natural fiber; now refers to sofa bed with a removable mattress.

galvanized steel Steel that has been dipped into molten zinc.

gaseous discharge lamps Lamps that produce light when an electric current or arc passes through a gas vapor sealed in a glass tube. Also called *electric discharge lamps.*

gather A small amount of molten glass.

general lighting See AMBIENT LIGHTING.

generic name Name for manufactured fiber that has been established by the Federal Trade Commission.

genuine leather Only full-grain leather and top-grain leather may be labeled and sold as genuine leather.

Ghiordes knot Oriental rug knot in which the tufting yarn wraps around adjoining warp yarns and extends from between them. Also called a *Turkish knot.*

gilding Powdered gold suspended in oil and painted with a brush onto china.

glare Excessive light that can cause irritation or fatigue.

glass Hard, nonporous amorphous material that results from the fusing of silica from sand and alkali at high temperatures.

glass blocks Solid or hollow blocks of glass for use in homes.

glass-ceramic Heat-resistant glassware that is a combination of glass and ceramic.

glass curtains See STATIONARY CURTAINS.

glass cutting The glass is faceted by grinding on a carborundum wheel. The cutter holds the glass above the wheel and looks through the glass to cut it.

glass fibers Glass fibers are made by drawing out strands of molten glass. Glass fibers are strong, chemically stable, and resistant to water and fire.

glassware accessories The many types of glass products available for the table. Included in this category are fruit/dessert sets, punch bowl sets, candlesticks, vases, decanters, ice buckets, pitchers, etc.

glaze Finish that is added to some pottery. The word glaze is derived from the word "glass." It refers to the process of covering the ware with a glass-like coating after firing.

glazing (1) Undesirable shine caused by high heat; also a calendering process that produces a polished surface. (2) A paint-texturizing technique in which transparent colors are overlayed in sequence to produce gradations of color.

glory hole Small furnace for reheating glass.

glost firing After the ware is glazed, it is exposed to high temperatures to fuse the glaze to the surface of the body of the ware.

gold bonding See GOLD FILLED and ROLLED GOLD PLATING.

gold filled A thin layer of gold is fused to a base metal. The base metal may be copper, brass, or nickel silver. The gold layer must weigh at least 1/20 of the weight of the entire piece.

graffito The technique of stacking two layers of differently colored clays and then scratching through the top layer to reveal the underlayer. Also called *sgraffito.*

grain (1) The relationship between the warp and filling yarns. (2) The pattern made by the annual rings in sawed wood. (3) The natural markings that are used to identify the animal from which the leather came.

grain side The hair or scale side of the leather.

graining A paint-texturizing technique in which a glaze is brushed on to create the effect of wood grain and lines.

greenware Clay that has not been fired.

greige fabric Fabric that has no finish or color.

groundwood pulp See MECHANICAL PULP.

gusseted pillow Pillow with side wall construction.

gypsum board Thin piece of plaster covered with heavyweight paper.

half-round sliced veneers Veneers that are cut from a log that has been cut in half and then revolved against the cutting blade.

halogen lamps Lamps with halogen gas around the tungsten filament.

hand Texture or how the fiber feels.

hand-blown glass Handmade glassware using a blowpipe. Also known as *free-blown glass*.

hardanger A drawn thread technique used to embellish fabric; a traditional handicraft.

hardboard Wood fibers are bonded with lignin, the natural bonding substance found in wood.

hard-paste porcelain Similar to the original Chinese china. It is made from kaolin and feldspar.

hard rubber Rubber that has been vulcanized with as much as 32 percent sulfur.

hardwoods See BROADLEAF TREES.

heading The arrangement of fabric at the top of curtains or drapes.

heartwood The center part of the tree. It is inactive and darker in color.

heat-resistant glass Glass that is resistant to breakage when exposed to temperature extremes.

heat-strengthened glass Twice as resistant to breakage as annealed glass. It is only partially tempered.

Hevea brasiliensis Rubber tree.

hide A skin that weighs more than 25 pounds.

highball glass A glass used for bourbon or scotch and water, vodka and tonic, beer, soft drinks, etc.

high carbon steel Steel that is about 1–1.5 percent carbon. It has increased hardness but decreased strength.

high-fired ware See STONEWARE.

high-intensity discharge (HID) lamps Metal halide, high pressure, and sodium mercury are HID lamps. Not usually used in residential settings.

high-pressure laminates Laminates created using high heat and high pressure.

hollowware Tableware that is deep and hollow, such as bowls, coffee pots, pitchers, gravy boats, sugar bowls, and vases.

home textiles Textile products used in the home; traditionally includes products used on the bed, in the bathroom, and on the table.

hybrid flotation system Water bed with a water-filled bladder surrounded by a foam shell.

hydrophilic fibers Fibers that can absorb moisture.

hydrophobic fibers Fibers that do not readily absorb moisture.

Imari A type of Japanese pottery with blue and iron-red enamel and gold.

incandescent light Light produced by heating a metal with an electric current until it glows. The metal is usually a tungsten filament and it is sealed in a glass bulb.

Indian rugs Oriental rugs handmade in India, usually of Persian design. They frequently have floral, vine-like designs, or "tree of life" designs.

indirect light The lighting that occurs when 90 to 100 percent of the light is redirected toward the surface to be lit.

injection molding Thermoplastic pellets of powder are melted and forced from a cylinder into a cool mold.

inlaid vinyl sheeting Vinyl sheeting in which the pattern runs through the entire thickness of the sheet.

inlay Refers to all the techniques used to combine different woods, metals, ivory, and other materials so the patterns are relatively smooth.

innerspring mattress Mattress that contains springs.

inorganic fiber Fiber from inorganic sources.

insulating glass Window glass that has been double or triple glazed.

intaglio cutting Intaglio cutting is softer and uses more curves than glass cutting. The cutter uses a small sandstone wheel and holds the glass under the wheel.

intarsia A special type of inlay in which the pieces are inlaid in solid wood.

internal market research Research that occurs within the company. It includes accurately tracking sales by region and by store, conducting interviews with sales associates and department managers for feedback on consumer preferences, and conducting postpurchase surveys with customers.

in-the-clay decorations Decorations that are added while the piece is still wet.

in-the-glaze decorations Colored glazes.

intumescent paints Paints that create a foam-like material when exposed to high heat. The foam protects the substrate from the fire.

ironstone A type of semi-vitreous ware.

jabots Soft window treatments that are pleated on the sides.

jasperware Unglazed intrinsically colored stoneware embellished with a slip decoration that was formed in a mold. Originally made by Josiah Wedgewood.

jersey knit Weft knit with no distinct rib. Sometimes called *single knits.*

jiggering The shaping of flat pieces of pottery such as plates, saucer, and platters.

joining The process of attaching one piece of wood to another.

jollying The shaping of hollowware such as cups, bowls, teapots, and vases.

Kakiemon Japanese or Japanese-style porcelain enameled in green, blue, red, and yellow, frequently with gold decoration.

kaolin Fine white clay.

karat gold Used to refer to gold that has been alloyed and indicates the proportion of pure gold in the metal. It is measured in twenty-fourths.

kelim (khilim or **kilim) rugs** Tapestry woven rugs made in eastern European countries.

khilim Alternate spelling for *kelim.*

kilim Alternate spelling for *kelim.*

kiln A specially designed oven that can be heated to very high temperatures.

kiln-drying The lumber is placed in large ovens for one to two days. The temperature and humidity are controlled.

kip A skin that weighs between 15 and 25 pounds. These usually come from oversized calves.

kitchen dishes Stoneware and earthenware used for less formal service. Also called *everyday dishes.*

knits Fabrics created by knitting.

knitted carpet Pile and backing yarns are integrated in one operation. Needles interlace yarns in a series of connecting loops.

knitting The interlooping of yarns to create fabric.

knock-down furniture See READY-TO-ASSEMBLE FURNITURE.

kraft process Production of pulp using sodium hydroxide and sodium sulfide. Also called the *sulfate process.*

laid paper Paper with a watermark design of heavy vertical lines and finer horizontal lines.

laminate flooring A high-pressure melamine laminate bonded to a wood-base core.

laminated glass Heat-resistant glassware made of two glasses: a dense core glass covered with a thin coating of clear glass; or transparent plastic is laminated between two or more layers of glass.

laminated wood Similar to plywood except that the grains of the laminated wood panels do not run at right angles to each other.

laminating The process of bonding two or more layers of any material together.

lamp The correct term for what is commonly called a light bulb.

lap joints Equal amounts are cut away from two pieces of wood so they can be fitted together.

latex A white liquid collected from the bark of the *Hevea brasiliensis* tree.

latex-coated fabric Wall covering fabric with a latex compound applied to the wrong side.

leaching Separating the metal from the ore by dissolving the metal in a chemical solvent. The metal is recovered by precipitation.

lead crystal See LEAD GLASS.

lead glass Glass that contains high levels of lead oxide. Also called *flint glass* or *lead crystal.*

leaded glass Lead crystal that is at least five percent lead oxide.

leather The treated hides and skins of animals.

leather hardness A general term to refer to ware that has dried to a stage where most of the moisture is gone but the ware can still be carved or joined.

leaves Matching panels that can be attached to the table so the table can be easily expanded.

lehr Tunnel-like oven for glassware where the heat is gradually lowered to room temperature.

library table A long narrow table.

lignin Natural bonding substance found in wood.

lime-soda glass The most common type of glass; made from sand and alkali.

limited decisions Occur when the customer goes through the five steps of the decision-making process very quickly.

linen Fabric made from flax.

linens Department store classification that traditionally includes towels, shower curtains, bathroom rugs and mats.

lining See CARPET CUSHION.

lining paper See BLANK STOCK.

link springs Mattress support system that has interlacing wires in a checkerboard pattern.

linoleum Biodegradable resilient floor covering made of ground cork, wood, flour, linseed oil, and resins. The mixture is pressed on to a jute or burlap backing.

lithography See DECALCOMANIA.

low-pressure laminates Laminates created using low heat and low pressure. Sometimes called *thermoset laminates.*

low-profile foundation Mattress support system that has metal grids or torsion bars bent in a square zigzag-shaped torsion bar design using steel leaf springs.

lubricants Materials added to plastics to reduce friction, aid in internal lubrications, or add a non-adhering surface.

lumber Wood which has been sawn into boards.

lumens The amount of light produced by a lamp or light source.

luminaire The correct term for what is commonly called a lamp. It includes the lampholder, power connection, and any internal devices such as reflectors. It is sometimes called a *fixture.*

luminous paints Paints that glow in the dark or under ultraviolet light.

luminous panels Strips of lights with glass or plastic translucent panels placed over them.

luster Amount of light that is reflected from a fiber.

lusterware Created by adding metallic powder to the glaze so the ware is covered with a thin layer with a mirror-like sheen.

machine-made Oriental design rugs Oriental design rugs woven on an Axminster loom. Sometimes called *American Oriental rugs.*

maiolica See FAIENCE.

majolica See FAIENCE.

mall Planned grouping of stores with controlled climate. Frequently the terms *shopping center* and *mall* are used interchangeably.

malleable Ability of a substance to be shaped by hammering or by pressure from rollers.

manufactured cellulosic Man-made fiber reformed from cellulose.

manufactured fiber Fibers created by man.

marbling A paint-texturizing technique that imitates polished marble.

marketing All the activities required to direct the flow of goods to consumers. It includes everything that takes place from the inception of the design idea through to the sale to the final consumer.

market research The systematic gathering of current information that can be used to make decisions about any component of marketing.

market segmentation A company tailors all the components of marketing (product, price, promotion, place, and people) to meet the expectations of its target market(s).

marquetry Inlaid design, especially in furniture.

Marshall-type innerspring mattress Mattress in which each spring is individually sewn into a pocket of muslin. Also called *pocket-coil mattresses* or *pocket-spring mattresses.*

marver A metal plate used to cool and shape the exterior of the gather.

mattress cover A cover used to protect mattresses from dust, dead skin cells, and dirt.

mattress pads A pad used to protect mattresses from dust, dead skin cells, and dirt.

mechanical finish Finish that involves manipulation of the fabric. Also called *dry finish.*

mechanical pulp Pulp produced by grinding wood into very fine fibers. Also called *groundwood pulp.*

medullary rays Thin cellular lines that extend from the pith to the outside of the wood.

melamine formaldehyde Thermoset plastic used extensively in dishware.

metallic paints Paints containing tiny flakes of metal.

metallurgy The science of extracting and processing metals.

metals Chemical elements that are usually found in ores. There are two major categories of metals—ferrous and non-ferrous.

metameric shift Color shift that occurs when one color appears different under different lighting conditions.

Mexican tiles Handmade, dried in open fields, and fired in ovens. They are about one inch thick, porous, and are uneven. They must be sealed after installation. Commercially made Mexican tiles are available. They are more uniform, stronger, and less porous.

mildew-proof paints Paints with a mildew-resistant additive.

mineral dressing Removal of waste materials from the ore. Usually done by grinding the ore and washing away the waste.

mineral fiber Fiber derived from mineral sources.

miter joint A relatively weak joint that is commonly used in picture frames. Two pieces of wood are joined together at the ends to hide the ends.

modern furniture Usually refers to furniture produced during the late 1800s.

modular groupings Groupings or pieces of furniture that are designed to be used separately or together in a variety of ways.

moil Excess glass found around the tip of the glass where it was attached to the blowpipe.

moiré Wall covering embossed to look like watered silk.

mold-blowing Molten glass is collected on the blowpipe, a bubble of air is blown into the glass, and it is then placed in a cast iron mold.

molding The process of pressing a lump of clay into a mold to form a desired shape.

momie weave Special class of weaves that have a grainy surface. The fabric frequently used for tablecloths in institutional settings.

monofilament yarn Yarn made of one filament.

mood lighting Creates not only visual interest but also an air of comfort. It is usually soft and mellow.

mortise-and-tenon joint One piece of wood has a projection (tenon) that is inserted into a rectangular hole (mortise) in another piece of wood.

mottle Veneer patterns with a blurred figure created by the grain.

multifilament yarn Filament yarns with more than one fiber, multifilament yarns usually contain 20 to 140 filaments.

muslin Sheeting made with carded yarns. The thread count of muslin sheets will be from 112 to 140; 128 is common.

nap See PILE SWEEP.

napery An industry term sometimes used to refer to tablecloths and napkins.

Native American rugs Tapestry rugs woven by the Navajo, Cheyenne, or Hopi tribes. The ends of the filling yarns are woven in so the rugs are reversible Sometimes they are referred to as *Navajo rugs.*

natural fiber Fibers that come from plant, animal, and mineral resources.

natural rubber Rubber that is harvested from the *Hevea brasiliensis* tree.

Navajo rugs See NATIVE AMERICAN RUGS.

needlepunched carpet Barbed needles are repeatedly inserted into a fiber web to tangle the fibers; a scrim may be added for strength and stability. Commonly used as indoor-outdoor carpeting.

niche marketing Marketing to a very small market within a larger market.

nickel silver An alloy composed of nickel, zinc, and copper.

non-architectural lighting See PORTABLE LUMINARIES.

nonferrous metals Non-iron bearing metals.

nonwoven Fabric made directly from fibers.

nostalgia or **revival product** A previously successful product that is brought back to the marketplace.

Nottingham lace Lace that usually has a large design and fairly rough texture.

novelty yarn Decorative yarn that adds textural interest to fabrics. Sometimes called *fancy yarn.*

nylon blanket binding Satin or taffeta binding on the top and bottom of blankets.

occasional furniture A wide variety of small pieces of furniture that can be considered as accessories.

off-gassing The dissipation of toxic fumes from floor textiles; unpleasant and potentially harmful.

old-fashioned glass A glass used for martinis, manhattans, scotch or bourbon on ice, aperitifs with or without ice, and wine served as a cocktail.

on grade At ground level.

on-grain The warp and filling yarns are perpendicular to each other.

opacity The hiding power of the paint.

open-coil mattresses See BONNELL-TYPE INNERSPRING MATTRESS.

open-coil springs Foundation springs that are open on top.

open stock Dinnerware that may be purchased in any quantity or combination of items for as long as the manufacturer continues to make the design. Open stock dinnerware may be discontinued when popularity wanes.

ore Metal-bearing rock.

Oriental rugs Rugs in which pile tufts are tied in as the ground. They are characterized by traditional designs that reflect the culture and history of the original weavers.

orthopedic bed A bed designed for people with disabilities or back pain.

ottoman An upholstered seat or stool that is placed in front of an upholstered chair to be used as a footrest.

overall measurement The diameter from one edge of a dish to the other edge. The size of a coupe dish is determined by the overall measurement.

overdrape A drape that is combined with a sheer curtain.

overglaze decorations Decorations that are applied after glazing.

padding See CARPET CUSHION.

paint A thin, protective, liquid film that, when applied to a surface, dries to a hard finish. It may be white, black, colored, or clear. It is the most commonly used finish for walls.

pallet base See SOLID BASE.

panel-supported systems Office furniture that is attached to dividers or panels.

paper-backed fabric Paper is laminated to the back of the fabric for use as a wall covering.

Parian ware Unglazed china, resembles marble.

parquet flooring Small pieces of wood laid in a pattern.

parquetry A mosaic of wood used for flooring.

particleboard Adhesives are used to bond the wood chips of any size and from any type of wood.

pâte-sur-pâte Decorative technique perfected by Minton; carved slip design.

patina Network of fine scratches seen in polished silver. This is considered desirable since it gives the metal a soft glow.

pavers Unglazed porcelain or natural clay tiles. They are six square inches or more in size.

pavilions Draperies that are tied back much like the flaps of a tent.

peccary Wild hog from South America and Mexico.

peelable wall covering Wall covering in which the top layer of the wallpaper will peel off and leave a substrate material that can be papered over.

pendant luminaires Luminaires suspended below the ceiling. Sometimes called *suspended luminaires.*

penetration pricing Pricing policy in which the company offers its products at prices that are consistently lower than competitors' prices.

percale Sheeting made with combed yarns. The thread counts start at 168 and go up from there.

permanent finish Finish that lasts the full life of the product.

Persian knot See SEHNA KNOT.

Persian rugs Handmade Oriental rugs with elegant all-over designs, soft colors, and high density of knots. Frequently the designs are floral patterns or may have animal or human figures represented.

phenolics Thermoset plastic considered to be the first synthetic plastic and the forerunner of plastics production.

phosphorescent paints Paints that glow in the dark.

physical metallurgy Any process that converts a refined metal into a finished product.

piece dyeing Adding color at the fabric stage.

pierced decoration Latticework or lace effect created by cutting small holes in the clay before bisque firing.

pig-grained pig Excessively scarred pigskin that has been embossed.

pig iron Crude iron produced from the blast furnace. It contains impurities such as four percent carbon and small amounts of manganese, silicon, phosphorus, and sulfur.

pigments Coloring substances.

pigment volume concentration (PVC) The volume of pigment relative to the volume of resin in a paint. Higher amounts of pigment produce a more textured, flatter appearance.

pile The yarns that project from the backing of a tufted fabric.

pile sweep The angle at which the pile yarns are oriented; determines the quantity of light that is reflected. Also called *directional pile lay* or *nap*.

pillow ticking The interior case that covers the filling of a pillow.

pillow top Mattresses with an extra layer of padding on top of the cover.

pinching Shaping a lump of clay with the hands.

pinpoint percale Basket or rib weave sheeting with thread count of 220 to 250.

pinsonic melding This process involves the use of heat and sound waves to meld the three layers of a comforter, quilt, or mattress pad together. Only fabrics of at least 50 percent thermoplastic fibers may be used. It simulates the appearance of stitching. Sometimes called *electronic welding*.

pith Core of the tree trunk.

place setting A service for one person.

plain butt joint One piece of wood is held against another piece of wood using glue, nails, or screws. It is a poor-quality joint.

plain sawing One of the two principle methods for making lumber from trees. After each cut the log is rotated so additional cuts can be made on each side of the log. The annual rings are at a slight angle to the surface of the lumber.

plain weave Weave in which a filling yarn alternately goes over and under filling yarns across the width of the fabric. The next filling yarn will go under warp yarns that had been on the bottom.

plane of light See AMBIENT BANK.

plank flooring Wood flooring made of planks that are three to eight inches wide.

plant fiber Fiber derived from plant sources.

plastic A synthetic material that is composed of long chains of atoms called polymers.

plasticizers Materials that make the plastic softer and more pliable at increased temperatures by reducing the intermolecular bonds that make some resins too viscous for use.

plate glass Flat glass formed by using rows of rollers to flatten the molten glass; no longer made in the United States.

platform-top springs Foundation springs that are covered with a crossed bar of flat metal that aids in supporting the mattress and prevents the spring from penetrating the mattress.

plating Coating one metal over another metal.

plumage Bird feathers.

plywood A veneer construction of thin layers of wood that are bonded together so that the grains run at right angles to each other.

ply yarn A yarn that has two or more single yarns twisted together.

pocket-coil mattresses See MARSHALL-TYPE INNERSPRING.

pocket-spring mattresses See MARSHALL-TYPE INNER-SPRING.

polyamides Thermoplastics, commonly known as nylon.

polycarbonate Expensive thermoplastics that are used mainly as molding compounds.

polyester Thermoset plastic, but some polyesters are thermoplastic. Dacron®, a well-known textile fiber, is a thermoplastic polyester resin.

polyethylene (PE) Form of polyolefin.

polymerization The chemical process that creates large molecules from small molecules.

polymers Giant molecules that are comprised of many simple molecules.

polymethyl methacrylate Thermoplastic, commonly known as acrylic.

polyolefins Thermoplastic plastics.

polypropylene (PP) Form of polyolefin.

polystyrene plastic Thermoplastic plastic.

polytetrafluroethylene (PTFE) Thermoplastic commonly known by the trade name Teflon®.

polyurethane Thermoset plastic that is well known as a constituent of foam.

polyvinyl butyral (PVB) Important vinyl plastic.

polyvinyl chloride (PVC) Important vinyl plastic.

pontil Solid iron rod used in finishing the glassware.

pontil mark Mark left in the glassware after the pontil is removed.

pool of light Circle of light from a spotlight.

porcelain European term for china.

porcelaine noire Black china (or porcelain) that results from metal oxides in the clay and firing in a special kiln.

porphyry A paint-texturizing technique that simulates porphyry, a family of rock types. The painting technique produces a granite-like texture.

portable luminaries Lights that are plugged into an electrical outlet. Examples of portable luminaries are floor and table lamps. Sometimes called *non-architectural lighting.*

potash crystal Is not lead crystal and is much less expensive.

potter The person who operates the potter's wheel.

potter's wheel A horizontal wheel on which the clay is shaped.

pottery Refers to all articles made from clay, including earthenware, stoneware, china, and bone china; also refers to a type of earthenware made from crude porous clay and fired at low temperatures; another term for *ceramics.*

poufed curtains The fabric of the curtain panels is gathered horizontally to create puffs that are held in place with cords, tiebacks, or stitching. Also called *bishop's sleeve treatments.*

precious metals Platinum and rest of the platinum group, gold, and silver.

preparatory finish Finish that prepares the fabric for additional treatment.

prepasted wall covering A wall covering that has an adhesive coating. The paper is soaked in water or wet with a damp sponge before hanging. Most of the more expensive papers are not pre-pasted.

pressing Hot glass is shaped by pressing it into molds with a metal plunger.

prestige pricing Policy of charging a higher price to suggest quality and distinction. If the product is priced too low, the consumer may not feel it is of high enough quality.

pretrimmed wall covering The selvages have been cut off the wall covering.

primary trading area The area closest to the store. Approximately 55 to 70 percent of a store's potential customers will come from the primary trading area.

primers Liquid sealers that are applied to the substrate, or the surface to be painted, prior to painting. Primers may be solvent based or water based. They make the surface smoother and help the paint become more durable.

product development The process of creating products that are appealing to the consumer and conform to the image of the company.

product/garment dyeing Adding color after the end product has been produced.

product life cycle The five stages of consumer acceptance—introduction, rise, maturity, decline, and obsolescence.

promotion The communication about a company and its products. The purpose of promotion is to create an atmosphere that is favorable for the sale of the company's products. It includes advertising and public relations.

protein fibers Fibers from animal sources.

provincial furniture Furniture that reflected the lives of people who lived in the more rural areas of the country; first made during the 16th to 18th centuries in France. Also called *country furniture.*

psychographics Descriptions about lifestyles. It segments people into categories based on the way they live, how they spend their money, and their personality characteristics.

public relations The conscious effort to create a positive image for the company. It involves news about the company or its products, but it is not paid for by that organization.

puff New England term that refers to a down comforter that has a removable cover.

pulp A moist, cohesive mass of fibers. Wood, recycled paper, and rags are the primary sources for pulp.

pugging The process of shredding and kneading the clay mixture in a pug mill to create a smooth mixture.

punty See PONTIL.

quarry tiles Very heavy porous tiles made from shale and fine clays, usually square or rectangular in various sizes, and available in buff, yellow, various reds, browns, dark blue, and black.

quarter sawing One of the two principle methods for making lumber from trees. In this method, after debarking, the log is cut into lengthwise quarters, called flitches. Each quarter is then sawed at right angles to the annual ring.

quarter-sliced veneers Veneers that are cut from a log that has been cut into quarters. The log is sliced at right angles to the annual rings of the wood.

quilt Throw-type bedding that covers the top of the bed and falls partially down the sides of the bed but not completely to the floor. It is composed of three layers—a backing fabric, filling, and top fabric. A quilt usually has less filling and is thinner than a comforter.

rabbet joint The end of a piece of wood is trimmed to accept the width of another piece of wood.

ragging or rag rolling A paint-texturizing technique in which wet paint or glaze is partially removed by dabbing with rag or rolling the paint off with a rolled rag.

rag pulp Cotton and linen rags are cut into small pieces and then boiled in a solution of lime and caustic soda.

Raku Low-fired, lead-glazed Japanese earthenware associated with the tea ceremony. It was frequently molded by hand.

random match Wall covering pattern with designs that are not split at the seam. Also called *free match*.

raschel Type of warp knit.

rattan A climbing plant found in the Southeast Asia. Cane is the stem of large rattans.

rawhide The untanned animal skin or hide.

ready-to-assemble (RTA) furniture Furniture that is designed to be assembled by the consumer. It is also called *flat package furniture* or *knock-down furniture*.

ream A package of 500 sheets of paper.

ream weight Refers to the weight of one ream of writing paper 17 × 22 inches.

reclaimed wood Particleboard and hardboard, made from sawdust and wood chips, are examples of reclaimed wood being processed into useable products.

reconstituted leather See BONDED LEATHER.

reed The cores of the rattan vine. More commonly it refers to items made by weaving swamp grasses. Early American wicker chairs are made from reed.

reeding A special type of carving that creates raised lines with rounded edges, used to decorate posts or legs.

reflecting glare Something shiny reflecting in the area of the task.

reflective glass A thin film of transparent metal or metal oxides is bonded to the glass surface and reflects the rays of the sun.

regenerated cellulosic Fiber manufactured from cellulose; retains the chemical properties of cellulose.

regenerated fibers Classification of fibers that are made from chemically processed materials that cannot be used as fibers in their original form.

reinforcements Fillers that increase the tensile strength (resistance to pulling forces) and impact strength (resistance to forceful blows) of the plastic.

relief decorations Raised designs.

repeat pattern An identical shape or image that occurs in a set sequence on a wall covering.

repoussé Small hammers and other tools are used to create a bas-relief design on the surface of metal.

repoussé chasing Repoussé is combined with chasing.

residential furniture Furniture purchased by the individual consumer for use in a home.

resiliency Ability of a fiber to return to its original shape following bending or folding.

resin (1) Compound often used for durable press finishes. (2) An organic substance made by the polymerization of simple molecules. The term *resin* is sometimes used in place of the word plastic.

resist designs Sizing is applied to the ware to protect certain areas from color or glazing.

resistance welding Two metal parts are placed in separate current-carrying clamps and butted together while an electric current passes across the joint. Also called *resistance butt-welding*.

reused denim Denim that is 50 percent reclaimed cotton and 50 percent virgin cotton.

rice patterns Small holes are cut in the clay and covered with glaze to form transparent spots.

rift-cut veneer Veneer produced in oak with a comb grain effect made by cutting perpendicular to the medullary rays.

rim Basic shape for flat dishes such as plates and saucers. Rim dishes have a flat edge that provides a convenient place to hold when serving.

rivet A thick pin or bolt.

riveting A mechanical method of joining metal.

roasting Heating the ore to remove impurities such as sulfur.

rolled gold plating Similar to gold filled, but the layer of gold is much thinner. It is only 1/30 to 1/40 of the total weight of the base metal.

rolling Shaping metals by passing it between power-driven steel or cast iron rolls.

rose window A circular window with bars that radiate from the center, frequently made with stained glass.

rotary cut veneers Veneers that are sliced off a rolling log and create bold variegated grain markings.

rotational casting Polymer is placed in hollow metal molds and rotated. The mold is heated and the plastic melts on the wall of the mold. As the mold is rotated, the plastic flows over the entire surface of the mold.

rotogravure vinyl sheeting Vinyl sheeting in which the pattern and/or color is printed or embossed on the surface of the sheet and protected by a coating of vinyl resin or urethane. Also called *rotovinyl*.

rotovinyl See ROTOGRAVURE VINYL SHEETING.

routine decisions Occur when the consumer is purchasing the same products on a regular basis. The customer simply purchases what has been purchased before.

ruffled curtains Curtains that have ruffles sewn onto the hem, sides, and sometimes the middle. Usually they have a ruffled valance and are tied back. Sometimes called *ruffled tiebacks*.

ruffled tiebacks See RUFFLED CURTAINS.

rug A soft floor covering that has finished edges. The edges may be finished with serging or binding with tape. Often a decorative fringe is added to the edge of a rug. Usually a rug covers only a portion of the floor. Rugs are not attached to the floor.

rya rugs Handmade rugs from Scandinavian countries. Weavers use the Ghiordes knot to create a pile that is one to three inches long. The pile yarns are usually wool. The traditional designs for a rya rug are gently curving patterns of related colors.

salt-glazed pottery Pottery that has been glazed by throwing salt into the glost oven, forming a glass-like skin over the ware.

sandblasting The process of directing a jet of sand onto the surface of a glass; achieves a frosted appearance.

sapwood Newly formed outer wood that is lighter in color and contains more moisture than the heartwood.

sash curtains See STRETCHED CURTAINS.

sateen Satin weave fabric made from spun yarns.

satin Satin weave fabric made from filament yarns.

satin weave Weave in which the warp yarns float over four or more filling yarns. The interlacings are regularly spaced so the fabric appears to be smooth.

scarves Pieces of fabric used on the tops of dressers and cabinets; may be any shape but are frequently sized to fit.

scavenge colors Pick up colors from other fabrics during cleaning.

sconces Wall-mounted luminaires.

sealers Products that prevent absorption on porous surfaces such as gypsum board and some woods. They also reduce the damage when a wall covering is removed.

seasonal product Product that lasts one season and then is reintroduced one year later.

seasoning The process of removing moisture from the lumber.

secondary trading area The area just outside the primary trading area. Approximately 15 to 25 percent of the store's potential customers will come from the secondary trading area.

seeds See BUBBLES.

Sehna (Senna) knot Oriental rug knot made by wrapping the tufting yarn around one warp yarn and under the adjacent warp yarn. Also called a *Persian knot*.

self-cushioned carpet Carpeting with a layer of latex cushion bonded to the underside.

selvage Lengthwise edge of the fabric.

semi-lead crystal Lead crystal that contains 10 to 12 percent lead.

semi-trimmed wall covering One side of the selvage has been trimmed off the wall covering. The other side must be left on as an overlap or is trimmed off at the site.

semi-vitreous Used to describe ware that is somewhat like glass. See FINE EARTHENWARE.

senna knot Alternate spelling of *Sehna knot*.

set Make the color permanent.

sets Sufficient dishes to serve four or more people; usually offered at a considerable price advantage when compared to individual pieces or place settings.

sgraffito See GRAFFITO.

shading Paint-texturizing technique in which color values from light to dark are blended across a wall or ceiling.

shams Pillow covers that match quilts or comforters.

shear marks Slight puckering of the glass where the glassblower snipped off excess molten glass during shaping.

sheers Curtains made of very lightweight fabric.

sheet casings Envelope-style cover for a duvet that minimizes the need for cleaning. Sometimes called a *duvet cover.*

sheet glass Flat glass produced by pulling the molten glass. It has optical distortions and is no longer made in the United States.

shirred curtains Curtains that have the fabric gathered directly on rods and hang straight down. They are not put on traverse rods.

shopping center Planned grouping of stores, usually found in suburban areas. They are not necessarily covered with a central roof. Frequently the terms *shopping center* and *mall* are used interchangeably.

sick building syndrome (SBS) Poor indoor air quality that impairs worker well-being, comfort, and productivity.

sidens Lopsided glassware.

silencer A thick, flannel-like, heavily napped fabric used under a tablecloth.

silicone Thermoset plastic; some varieties are thermoplastic, often combined with rubber.

silver depositware Glassware that has been decorated by electroplating silver onto the glass.

silver plate Silver plated over a base metal or alloy.

single damasks Damasks that have shorter floats, up to four threads. Sometimes called *utility damasks.*

single glazing A single layer of glass.

single knit Weft knit fabric with no distinct rib. Sometimes called *jersey knits.*

single roll Length of wall covering that is usually 27 inches wide and 28 feet long.

single yarn A yarn that will separate into individual fibers when untwisted.

sintering Roasting the ore at very high temperatures to partially melt fine particles of ore into coarse lumps.

skin The skin of a young animal. The skin of the animal must weigh 15 pounds or less when it is shipped to the tannery.

slab method Slabs of clay are cut and assembled to make pottery.

slatted wood A foundation that does not have any springs. It is made entirely of wood slats.

sleeper sofa A sofa that looks much like a traditional sofa. It has a concealed spring mechanism and mattress that pulls out to form a bed.

slip decorations Raised decorations painted on the clay with slip.

slip Liquid clay that has the texture of thick cream, formed by adding water to clay.

slipcovers Temporary fabric covers for upholstered furniture.

smelting Melting the ore to remove impurities.

smooshing Paint-texturizing technique that creates a slightly marbled effect. A thin piece of plastic is applied to a wall of wet paint, rubbed with the hands, and peeled off.

soda process Production of pulp using caustic acid.

sofa beds Beds that can be used for sitting during the day and for sleeping when necessary.

sofa table A long narrow table used behind a sofa.

soft-paste porcelain Also known as *artificial porcelain.* It is made by mixing clay and glass frit instead of kaolin and feldspar.

soft rubber Rubber that has been vulcanized with one to three percent sulfur.

softwoods See CONIFEROUS TREES.

solder An alloy used to join metallic components. Most solders are tin and lead. They melt at a low temperature (200 degrees to 250 degrees Centigrade) and are called *soft solders.*

soldering Method of joining metallic components.

solid base Solid wood foundation. Sometimes called *pallet base.*

solid vinyl tiles Flooring tiles made of vinyl chloride with a small amount of additive. The color is throughout the depth of the tiles.

solution dyeing Addition of color to manufactured fibers before extrusion.

solvents Materials that make the resins more manageable so they can be processed more efficiently. The solvent will evaporate during processing and leave only the resin.

spatially integrated lighting See BUILT-IN LUMINAIRES.

spattering Paint-texturizing technique in which uneven spots or spatters are achieved by filling a brush with paint and flipping the paint onto the base color.

special emphasis lighting See ACCENT LIGHTING.

specific gravity (density) Compares the fiber mass to an equal volume of water.

spinneret Device through which chemical solutions are forced in order to create fibers.

splines Thin pieces of metal or wood.

splits Layers of skin under the top grain; may be napped or have artificial grains embossed on them.

sponging A paint-texturizing technique using sponges to create a broken, splotchy effect.

sponging Use of damp sponges to smooth the surface of the pottery before firing.

spreading rate The number of square feet of a specific surface (rough surfaces require more paint) that can be covered by a specific quantity of paint. Also called *coverage rate.*

sprigging Molding is used to crate relief ornaments that are to be applied to a clay surface.

sprung bed Foundation made of an iron frame with a dense web of wires stretched over the springs.

spun yarn Yarn made from short or staple fibers.

stablilizers Chemical additives that give the plastic product protection from degradation by the environment.

stained glass Glass that has been colored, set in lead or strips of copper foil. It is used for decorative purposes such as windows, lampshades, and interior and exterior doors.

stainless steel A minimum of 11.5 percent chromium is added to the steel to make it corrosion resistant. It may contain up to 18 percent chromium. Nickel is sometimes added to stainless steel to make it finer and whiter.

stains Pigments applied to bare or sealed wood. They may be transparent or opaque.

stamping (1) Use of a stamp to create designs in pottery. (2) Dies press and pound metal into its desired shape.

starter set A 20-piece set of dishes. Often called the *basic service.*

stationary curtains Sheer curtains used under draperies. Also called *under curtains* or *glass curtains.*

steel Alloy of iron and about 1.5 to 3 percent carbon.

stemware Drinking glasses that have a bowl, stem, and foot.

stenciling A decorative technique using a cut-out pattern to reproduce a painted design; frequently seen around windows and doorways.

sterling Indicates the purity of the silver in the product. In order to be labeled sterling the item must be 92.5 percent pure. It is weighted in troy ounces.

sticking up The joining of the parts using thick slip.

stippling Paint-texturizing technique in which a stipple brush, or other brush, is used to dab on a colored glaze or paint; creates a mottled, orange peel texture.

stitch-through fabric Fabric created when a group of crosswise yarns are laid over a group of lengthwise yarns and stitched together with thread. Also called *mali fabrics.*

stock (fiber) dyeing Adding color at the fiber stage.

stoneware Made from clay mixed with a fusible stone that has been vitrified at a high temperature.

straight match Wall covering pattern in which the left side of the strip will match with the right side of the previous strip.

stretched curtains The top and bottom of the curtain are gathered on rods and stretched from top to bottom; used on French doors and windows. Also called *sash curtains.*

string streets Secondary shopping areas that are on the side streets of the central business district.

stripe Veneer pattern with straight line effects in shadings of dark and light, seen in walnut and mahogany.

strip flooring Flooring with strips or boards that are usually two inches wide and 25/32 inches thick. Strips may be as narrow as one inch.

strippable wall covering A wall covering that can be pulled off the wall in strips without scraping or the use of a steamer. Many, but not all, fabric-backed vinyl wall coverings are strippable.

strips Solid wood lumber less than two inches thick and less than six inches wide.

structural luminaries Lighting that is permanently installed. It includes wall and ceiling fixtures that are installed to permanent wiring. Sometimes called *architectural lighting.*

studio couch A sofa with two sets of springs. One set is under the regular sofa spring unit. The bottom set is pulled out, and detachable seat cushions are placed on it to form a double bed.

stump Veneer with swirled grain pattern from the stump of the tree.

style A particular set of design characteristics.

styrene-butadiene rubber One of the most common types of rubber encountered by the consumer.

subflooring The floor to which the finish floor is attached.

suede A napped surface effect on leather.

suite A grouping of furniture pieces for use in a specific room.

sulfate process See KRAFT PROCESS.

sulfite process Production of pulp using a solution of bisulfite and sulfuric acid or its normal salt.

surface contour Longitudinal appearance.

suspended luminaires See PENDANT LUMINAIRES.

swags Lengths of fabric that are draped.

synthetic fiber Fiber synthesized by man.

synthetic leather Imitation leather made from plastics such as vinyl or polyurethane.

synthetic rubber A synthetic polymer that has properties similar to those of natural rubber.

systems furniture Modular pieces that can be arranged in different configurations to provide flexible use of office space. Vertical panels, work surfaces, and storage units are combined to create what are commonly called workstations.

tableware A broad range of products used for the decoration of the table, serving food, and dining.

tanning The conversion of rawhide into leather.

target market A group of consumers that a company wants to reach.

target return pricing Pricing policy by which the company sets a price that meets its profit goal.

task lighting Directs a pool of light where it is needed in order to complete a task.

temporary finishes Finishes that are removed or considerably reduced during washing and dry cleaning.

tenacity Fiber strength.

terra-cotta Unglazed earthenware.

terry towels Towels that have an uncut or looped pile. Also called *Turkish towels.*

textured filament yarns Filament yarns made from manufactured fibers that have been treated to change the shape of the yarn by adding curl, crimp, or loop.

texture paint A water-based paint with a silica sand additive that creates a stucco-like texture on the wall.

thermal blankets Blankets characterized by a distinctive waffle-like effect.

thermoforming Large sheets of plastic are softened and made to conform to a molded surface using air, mechanical, or vacuum pressure.

thermoplastic Melts or softens when exposed to heat.

thermoplastics Plastics that become soft and pliable when exposed to heat and harden when the heat is removed. They may be shaped and reshaped numerous times.

thermoset laminates See LOW-PRESSURE LAMINATES.

thermoset plastics Plastics that are set into their permanent shape by heat. They cannot be remelted and reshaped.

thread count The number of threads in one square inch of fabric.

throwing The process of shaping a piece of clay free-hand on a potter's wheel.

throw pillows Another term for *decorative pillows.*

throws Small blankets.

throw-style bedspread An unfitted bedspread.

ticking Any fabric used to cover pillows, mattresses, or box springs.

tieback Fabric or other item (chain, ring, ribbon, tape, sash, etc.) used to hold curtains back on the sides.

timbers Any lumber measuring at least five inches in the smallest dimension.

tongue-and-groove joint Edges on wood that provide interlocking joining.

top-grain leather The top layer, but the original surface pattern, including scars, is removed by abrasion. This surface is embossed with a pattern, usually similar to the grain of the skin that was removed.

towing Using a small mop to take the seams off plates and to round off sharp edges.

trade measurement See WELL-TO-EDGE MEASUREMENT.

trade name Name established by companies in order to identify their products.

trading area Refers to the area from which a store attracts potential customers.

traditional furniture Formal furniture style adapted from cabinet makers and artisans of the 17th, 18th, and 19th centuries.

traditionally sprung mattresses See BONNELL-TYPE INNERSPRING MATTRESS.

transfer printing A design is engraved into a copper plate, filled with the oil-based oxide color, and transferred to a piece of tissue paper. The tissue paper is placed on the dish and rubbed until the design is transferred to the ware. Also called *copperplate decoration*.

tricot Type of warp knit.

triple roll Length of wall covering that is three times the length of a single roll; contains about 108 square feet. Also called a *triple roll bolt*.

triple roll bolt See TRIPLE ROLL.

trundle bed A bed with storage space underneath the mattress. Can be used for storage or to hold an extra bed.

tufted fabric Fabric that has a pile, or yarns, projecting from a backing.

tufting Yarns stitched into finished fabric to form a looped pile.

tumblers Drinking glasses that have no foot or stem.

Turkish knot See GHIORDES KNOT.

Turkish rugs Handmade Oriental rugs with designs similar to those used in Caucasian and Turkoman rugs, usually have a longer pile and a coarser construction. Geometric designs are common.

Turkish towels Towels that have an uncut or looped pile. Also called *terry towels*.

Turkmen Alternate spelling for *Turkoman*.

Turkoman (Turkmen) rugs Handmade Oriental rugs from central Asia. They are usually red or red/brown with green and white and have bold geometric designs or medallion-like designs.

turning The process of making round pieces of wood to be used as bedposts, stair railings, and legs of furniture.

twill weave Weave in which the warp yarns go over as many as three yarns and then under one. Each subsequent warp yarn starts the sequence one warp yarn further in.

under curtains See STATIONARY CURTAINS.

underglaze decorations Decorations that are added before glazing.

underlayment See CARPET CUSHION.

unhairing Removal of the hair from the skin.

untrimmed wall covering The selvages must be cut off the wall covering at the site.

unvulcanized rubber Rubber that has not been vulcanized.

uplight Lighting that casts light onto the ceiling where it is reflected back into the room.

urea formaldehyde Thermoset plastic similar to melamine formaldehyde.

urethane foam Commonly used to refer to all types of foam, even those made from other materials such as polyesters.

utility damasks Damasks that have shorter floats, up to four threads. Sometimes called *single damasks*.

veiling glare Light that reflects off a surface and causes a blind spot.

velour towels Towels that have traditional terry towel loops on one side but with the loops sheared, or cut, on the other side of the towel.

velvet carpet Cut pile carpet with an extra warp or filling yarns that produce the pile.

veneer Wood that has been cut into very thin strips.

veneering The method of gluing thin slices of wood over less expensive woods or other core products.

Venetian lace Needlepoint lace. The pattern is embroidered over base threads.

vermeil Sterling silver or silver plate that has been electroplated with 24-karat gold.

vertical pattern The distance between one point and the next repeated same point.

vinyl A very large group of thermoplastics.

vinyl composition tiles (VCT) Flooring tiles made of vinyl, resins, plasticizers, fillers, and coloring agents.

vinyl laminate Fabric or wallpaper custom laminated and made into flooring.

vinyl tiles Sheet vinyl cut into tiles, usually 9 inches square or 12 inches square.

Visa® A well-known soil-release finish.

vitreous Having the qualities of glass.

volatile organic compounds (VOCs) Hazardous compounds released into the air while solvent-based paints dry.

vulcanization Curing rubber by mixing it with sulfur, molding, and heating it.

wale Diagonal line created by the interlacings in a twill weave; vertical column of loops in a weft knit.

wall system Furniture that is composed of a number of wall units placed together. These units can be rearranged to meet the needs of the customer.

wall upholstery Fabric and foam or polyester padding are adhered to the wall.

wall washers Downlights that are directed toward the wall. They bathe the wall in light.

wall-to-wall carpet Carpeting that covers the floor completely. It is secured to the floor with stripping that hooks the carpet into place.

warp knit Knit fabric in which the yarns loop vertically.

warp yarn The lengthwise yarn in woven fabric.

warping The bending or twisting out of shape of a flat surface.

washing A paint-texturizing technique in which a sponge dipped in glaze is washed over the wall in a circular motion.

water-filled mattresses Water beds.

watermarking A special kind of embossing that presses a design into the paper. The design area is thinner than the rest of the paper.

wattage The unit for measuring electricity consumed by a lamp.

weaving Process to create fabric by interlacing yarns.

weft knit Knit fabric in which the yarns run horizontally across the fabric. Also called *filling knit.*

welding The process of joining metal by heat or hammering with or without heat.

well-to-edge measurement Measuring system for rim dishes. The distance is taken from one side of the well, across the well to the other side of the dish. The well-to-edge measurement is often used by older manufacturers. It is also called the *trade measurement.*

wet print Fabric that has been printed with dye.

wholesale markets Regularly scheduled exhibits of products not normally purchased from photographs.

wholesalers Distribution liaisons between manufacturers and retailers. They act as middlemen between the manufacturers and retailers. They buy products that are to be resold.

wicker Refers to a classification of furniture that is woven from a variety of materials such as rattan, bamboo, reed, and willow.

willow pattern Widely used decorative transfer-printed pattern for china in the 1800s; Chinese scenes in cobalt blue ink.

Wilton carpet Cut pile carpet made on a modified Jacquard loom with three sets of warp yarns. Most Wilton carpets are plain with a smooth velvety surface.

wired glass Plate glass reinforced with wire mesh.

wob foot Foot set at an angle in glassware.

wool underblanket A wool mattress pad.

woolen yarns Wool and wool-like yarns that have not had the shorter fibers removed.

worsted yarns Wool and wool-like yarn that have had the shorter fibers removed.

wovens Fabrics created by weaving.

wrap groupings Groupings of furniture that are designed to be used beside or on top of each other.

wrinkle recovery See RESILENCY.

wrought iron Refined pig iron. It is almost pure iron but does contain about one percent impurities.

yarn Assemblage of fibers into a continuous strand that can be used to make fabric. Both natural and manufactured fibers may be made into yarns.

yarn dyeing Adding color at the yarn stage.

INDEX

Abaca, 39
Accent lighting, 376–377
Acetate, 44
Acid bath, 108
Acrilan®, 42
Acrylic, 42, 45
Acrylic paint, 354
Acrylonitrile-butadiene-styrene (ABS),
    152
Additives, paint, 350
Adjustable beds, 259
Advertising
    in home furnishing magazines by
        category, 12
    manufacturer's flow of, 12
    objectives of, 11
Aesthetic finishes, 60
Agave, 39
Air-drying lumber, 76–77
Air-filled mattresses, 258–259
Alkalis, 94–95
Alkyd paints, 351
Alkyd resins, 149
All-Clad, 162, 181
Alloys, 162, 167–168
    see also Metals
Alpaca, 41
Aluminum furniture, 242
Amalgamation, 167
Amalgams, 167–168
Ambient bank, 394
Ambient lighting, 375
American Drew, 222
American Oriental rugs, 323
American Textile Co., 268
American Textile Manufacturers Insti-
    tute (ATMI), 63
Ancell, Nathan "Nat," 219, 248
Anchor, 16
Annealed glass, 105, 110
Annual rings, 69
Anode, 173
Anodizing, 173
Antimicrobial finishes, 61
Antique satin, 51
Antistatic finishes, 61
Antron®, 42
Applique, 230

Aramid, 45
Architectural cabinetry, defined, 223
Architectural lighting. *See* Structural
    luminaires
Armoire, 225
Artificial light, 382–388
Artificial porcelain, 124
Asbestos, 343
ATMI. *See* American Textile Manufac-
    turers Institute
Aubusson rugs, 322
Avon, 16
Axminster, 318

Bachelor's chair, 225
Back
    fabric, 50
    furniture, 229
Baekeland, Leo, 142
Bagasse, 197
Bagging, 357
Bakelite®, 142–143
Balanced weave, 52
Ball clay, 125
Bamboo, 86, 197
Bamboo furniture, 242
Band springs, 262
Bard, Maurice, 274
Bark, 69
Barware, 411–413
Basic service, 408
Basket weave, 50
Bast fibers, 33, 39
Batch, 100
Bathroom rugs and mats, 298–299
Bating, 206
Battenberg lace, 301
Baumritter, Theodore, 248
Bed Bath & Beyond, 306
Bed linens. *See* Linens
Bed rest (husband), 294
Bed-in-a-bag, 281
Bedding, 251–278
    history of, 252
    manufacturers, 276–277
    mattress care, 262–263, 265
    mattress pads and covers, 266–
        267

alternatives to, 266–267
    construction, 266
    styles, 266
mattress selection, 262–263
mattress sizes, 252–253
mattress support systems, 260–262
    bank springs, 262
    box springs, 260–261
    foam, 262
    link springs, 262
    low-profile foundations, 261
    open-coil springs, 261
    platform-top springs, 261
    slatted wood, 262
    solid (or pallet) base, 262
    sprung bed, 262
mattresses, 251–259
    adjustable beds, 259
    air-filled, 258–259
    crib mattresses, 259
    foam, 257–258
    innerspring, 253–256
    orthopedic beds, 259
    water-filled, 258
pillows, 268–273
    care of, 273
    cervical-roll foam, 273
    contour, 273
    down, 269–270
    down terminology, 270
    down/feather blends, 270, 272
    feather terminology, 272
    feathers, 270–272
    foam, 272
    full-body, 273
    gusseted, 272
    polyester fiberfills, 271
    sizes, 268
    synthetic/down blends, 271
    ticking, 272
sofa beds, 274–275
space-saving, 276
Bedroom furniture, 225
Bedspread drops, 291
Bedspreads, 289
Beveled glass, 113–114
Biagio Cisotti by Alessi's Diabolix bottle
    opener, 19

Biederlack of America, 295
Binary alloy, 168
Binder yarn, 49
Bird feathers (plumage), 40, 42
Bird's eye, 80
Biscuit-firing (bisque firing), 132
Bishop's sleeve treatments, 310
Bisque firing (biscuit-firing), 132
Bladder-type water-filled mattresses, 258
Blank stock, 364
Blankets, 286–289
Blast furnace, 166
Bleaching, 60
Bleeding, 56
Blending, 47
Blisters (seeds or bubbles), 109
Bloomingdale's, retro look, 21
Blotch printing, 58
Blowpipe, 100–101
Blue clay, 125
Boarding leather, 207
Boards, 77
Body, 126
Bokhara rugs, 323
Bomb spreads, 130
Bonded leathers, 213
Bonding, metals, 173
Bone ash, 123, 125
Bone china, 123–124
Bonini, Daniel L., 370
Bonnell-type innersprings, 254–255
Borders, 364
Boric oxide, 94
Borosilicate glass, 98, 100
Boston and Sandwich Glass Company, 94, 104
Böttger, Johann Friedrich, 123
Bottle-making machine, 104
Boucle yarn, 49
Bowed filling yarn, 50–51
Box springs, 260–261
Box-like furniture, 232
Bracket lighting, 391–392
Brady, Anita, 401
Braided rugs, 319
Bran, 145
Brass, 168
Brazing, 170
Brentwood, 295
Bright light, 378
Broadcloth, 50
Broadleaf trees (hardwoods), 70–72, 197
Broadloom, 317
Brocade, 52
Bronze, 168
Brush dyeing, 208
Brussels, 318
Bubbles, 102, 109
Built-in luminaires, 391–392
Bulk continuous filament, 330
Bunk beds, 276
Burl, 80

Burlap, 39
Burlington Industries, 64
Burn-out printing, 58

C&F Enterprises, 295
Cabinet woods, 78
Café curtains, 310
Calendering, 59, 194
    simple, 60
Calf skins, 204, 209–210
Calico, 50
Cambium layer, 69
Candleholders, 6
Cannon, 306
Canopies, 293–294
Carbon paper, 202
Carbonless paper, 202
Carded yarns, 48
Carpet cushioning, 326, 328–329
Carpets. *See* Soft floor coverings
Carpincho, 210
Carved glass, 107
Carving, 230
Carving pieces, 415–416
Cascades, 311
Case glass, 108
Case goods. *See* Furniture
Cast iron, 178
Casting, 168–169
Casual furniture. *See* Furniture
Catalogs, 16
Cathode, 173
Caucasian rugs, 322
Ceiling paper, 364
Celluloid, 142
Cellulosics, 150
Central business districts, 15–16
Centura®, 99
Ceramic tile, 338–339
Ceramics, 119
Cereal straw, 197
Ceramic mosaic tile, 338
Cervical-roll foam pillows, 273
Chairs, 231
    tufted, 240
    upholstered, 233–235
        motion, 233–235
        shapes of, 234
Chandeliers, 389–390
    selection of, 395
Chasing, 184
Chatham Manufacturing Company, 287
Chemical finishes, 60
Chemical properties, of metals, 163
Chenille, 318
China, 123–124, 409
China grass. *See* Ramie
China stone, 123
Chinese rugs, 322
Chino, 51
Chippendale, 221
Christofle, 401
Classic products, 19–20

Clay, 119
    types of, 125
Cleaning, furniture, 246, 248
Clerestory windows, 381
Closed-stock, 408
Coaster, 299
Coating (paper), 202
Cocooning, 9
Coil-on-coil mattresses, 254
Coiling, 127
Coin silver, 176
Coir, 39
Cold cathode lighting, 388
Cole, Alan, 220
Color, furniture, 229
Color washing, 357
Colorants, 144–145
    special-effect, 145–146
Coloration. *See* Textiles
Colored lighting, 377
Colorfast, 56
Coloring leather, 207–208
Combing, 48, 357
Comforters, 289
Commodes, 241
Common clay, 125
Community shopping center, 16
Completer set, 408
Compression strength, 68
Computers, 9
Conductivity, 162
Conifers (softwoods), 70, 73–74, 197
Consumer Product Safety Commission, 252
Contemporary furniture, 221
Continuous springing, 254
Contour sheet, 282
Contract furniture, 219
Contoured pillows, 273
Copper-wheel engraving, 106
Copperplate decoration, 136
Cord yarn, 48–49
Cords, 109
Corduroy, 52
Corium, 205
Cork floor covering, 334
Cork wall covering, 369
Corkscrew yarn, 49
Cornice lighting, 391–392
Corning Glass, 150
Correlated groupings, 222
Cotton, 32–34, 36–38
    cotton boll, 37
    properties of, 36
    varieties of, 37
Cotton batting, 291
Cotton linters, 197
Country furniture. *See* Provincial furniture
Coupe shape, 404
Courses, 53
Cove lighting, 391–392
Cow hair, 41
Cowhides, 204, 209–210

Crackle glaze, 136
Crease-resistant finishes, 61
Credit manager, 5
Crib mattresses, 259
Crinkled paper shade, 196
Crocking, 56
Crotch, 80
Crown process, 109
Crude rubber, 190
Crystal. *See* Lead glass
Crystal structure, 162
Cullet, 100, 117
Cultivated silk, 40
Cuprammonium rayon, 43–44
Curtains, 309–310
Cushioning, 238–239
   carpets, 326, 328–329
Customer purchase behavior. *See* Purchase behavior
Customer's own materials (COM), 239
Cut pile, 56
Cylinder method, 109

Dacron®, 149
Dado joint, 227–228
Damask, 52, 299, 301, 302
Danish oil, 360
Daybeds, 274
de la Renta, Oscar, 22
Debarking, 73
Decalcomania, 107, 135, 230
Deciduous trees, 197
Decisions, types, 17–18
Decorating, furniture, 230
Decorative drapes, 311
Decorative firings, 132
Decorative lighting, 376–378
Decorative pillows, 293–295
Deer skins, 212
Demographics, 6–8
Denim, 51
Derivative cellulosics, 44
   see also Textiles
Dhurrie rugs, 324
Digester, 198
Dimension, 77
Dimmers, 379, 383
Dining room furniture, 226
   selected sizes, 226
Dining-room chairs, 224
Dining tables, 224, 232
Dinnerware. *See* Tableware
Dip dyeing, 208
Dipping, 195
   metals, 172
Direct light, 375
Direct selling, 16
Director of marketing, 5
Dobby weaves, 52
Doilies, 299
Domestics. *See* Linens
Double glazing, 113
Double knits, 53
Dovetail joint, 227–228

Dowel joint, 227–228
Down, 42
Down pillows, 269–270
Down/feather pillows, 270
Downlights, 375
Downward light, 394
Dragging, 357–358
Drapes, 309, 311
Draw curtains, 310
Draw draperies, 311
Drawers, furniture, 229
Drawing, metals, 168–169
Dressers, 224
Drop, 290–291
Dry-cleaning, 39, 41
Dry finishes, 60
Dry prints, 59
Duck batiste, 50
Ductile iron, 178
Duncan Phyfe, 221
Duoppioni silk, 40
DuPont, 42, 143, 150
Durable finishes, 59–60
Durable press (permanent press), 61
Dust bottoms, 229
Dust ruffles, 293
Duvet covers, 292
Dyes, 57

Eames, 209
Early American, 221
Earthenware, 120–122
Eason, Terry, 378
Economic trends, 7
Edge guards, 256
Edging (paper), 202
Edison, Thomas, 382
Egg-crate-foam mattress pads, 267
Elder duck down, 42
Electric-discharge lamps. *See* Gaseous-discharge lamps; Fluorescent lamps
Electrodeposition, 195
Electrolysis, 167
Electroplating, metals, 173
Electroplating glass, 109
Electrostatic bonding, 288
Elk skins, 212
Embossing, 60, 107, 184, 200
Embossing leather, 208
Embroidery, 55
Embroidery stitches, 284–285
Enamel dots, 133
Encrusting glass, 108
End tables, 241
Energy-conservation practices, 396–397
Energy-efficient lighting, 396
English Country, 221
Engraving, 184
Environment
   and floor coverings, 342–343
   and glass, 116–117
   and leather, 213

   and lighting, 396–397
   and paint, 371
   and paper, 203
   and plastics, 159
   and pottery, 138
   and rubber, 196
   and tableware, 421
   and textiles, 63–65
   and wood, 87–90
Environmental Excellence, 63
Epidermis, 205
Epoxies, 147
Epoxy paints, 352
Ermini, Savitri, 274
Esparto, 197
étagère, 241
Etching, 107, 137, 184
Ethan Allan, 223
Ethnic diversity, 6–7
Everyday dishes, 409
Ex-Cell, 295
Extended decisions, 17–18
Extenders, 145
External market research, 5
Extractive metallurgy. *See* Metals
Extrusion, 168, 170, 194
Extrusion machines, 143

Fabrics. *See* Textiles
Face, 50
Face fibers, 330
Fading, 56
Fads, 19–20
Fancy yarns, 49
Fat liquoring, 208
Faux finishes, 357
Feather beds, 267
Feather pillows, 270–272
Federal Trade Commission (FTC), 42
Federal Trade Commission on the Weighting of Silk, 62
Feldspar, 123, 124, 125
Felling trees, 73
Felt cushioning, 328
Ferrous metals. See Metals
Festival marketplace, 16
Fettling, 131
Fiber optics, 388
Fiberfill, 45
Fiberglass furniture, 243
Fibers
   defined, 32
   floor coverings, 330
   and paper, 197
   see also Textiles
Fiberwoven Process®, 288
Fiddleback, 80
Fieldcrest, 306
Fiesta Ware, 138
Filament fibers, 32, 34
Filament yarns, 47–48
Fill leakage, 291
Fillers, plastics, 145
Filling knits, 53

Filling yarns, 50
Films, 55
Fine earthenware (semi-vitreous), 120, 122
Finishes. *See* Textiles
Fire clay, 125
Firing, 119–120, 131–132
Firing glass, 100
Fitted sheet, 282
Fixtures, light, 374
Flame-resistant finishes, 61
Flammability, and plastics, 159
Flammable Fabrics Act, 62, 252
Flannel sheets, 284
Flash, 173
Flat-bed screen printing, 58
Flat glass, 109–115
    see also Glass
Flat sheet, 282
Flat-sliced veneers, 79
Flatware. *See* Tableware
Flax, 33, 38–39
Flesh side, 205
Flesh tissue, 205
Fleshing, 206
Flint, 125
Flint glass. *See* Lead glass
Flitches, 76
Float glass, 110
Floating construction, 229
Floats, 51
Flock printing, 58
Flocked carpet, 319
Flocked wall covering, 364
Floco rugs, 322
Flokati rugs, 320, 322
Flooring. *See* Resilient flooring; Hard flooring
Fluorescent lamps, 385–387
    characteristics of, 387
    types of, 386
Fluoropolymer, 46
Fluting, 230
Flying Geese quilt, 290
Foam block beds, 276
Foam foundation, 262
Foam glass, 115
Foam mattresses. *See* Bedding
Foam pillows, 271
Foam rubber, 194
Foam rubber cushioning, 328
Foamex Carpet Cushion Group, 329
Foamex Performance®, 329
Foams, 55
Foil/Mylar® wall coverings, 364
Fold-up beds, 276
Folk art, 321
Follow-the-leader pricing, 11
Footboards, 230
Forests, sustainable, 88–89
Forge welding, 171
Forging, 168
Forks, 415–416
FORTEL ECOSPUN®, 64

Fourdrinier paper machine, 199
Fox, 41
Frame, upholstered furniture, 236
Free-blown glass. *See* Glass
Freestanding stores, 15
Freestanding systems, 245
French Provincial, 221
Fringe trading area, 14
Frit, 124
Frosting, 56, 107
FTC. *See* Federal Trade Commission
Full top-grain leather, 207
Full-body pillows, 273
Full-grain leather, 207
Full-lead crystal, 96
Fume fading, 44
Functional finishes, 61–62
Fur fibers, 41
Fur Products Labeling Act, 62
Furniture, 219–250
    care of, 246–247, 249
    case goods, 223–232
        bedroom furniture, 225
        chairs, 231
        construction details, 229
        decorating, 230
        defined, 223
        dining room furniture, 226
        dining tables, 232
        external construction, 227
        finishing, 231
        joining, 227–229
        parts of, 223–224
        reinforcing joints, 229
        type of wood, 227
    casual and summer, 241–243
        aluminum, wrought iron, and steel, 242
        plastic and fiberglass—reinforced plastic, 243
        redwood, 242–243
        selecting, 243
        wicker, rattan, and bamboo, 242
    contemporary, 221
    correlated groupings, 222
    modulated groupings, 223
    occasional, 241
    provincial (country), 221
    ready-to-assemble (RTA), 243–244
    selected brand names, 247
    systems furniture, 244–246
        classifications of, 245–246
        configurations of, 244–245
    traditional, 220–221
    upholstered, 233–241
        chairs, 233–235
        inner construction, 236–239
        outer construction, 239–240
        sectionals, 236
        selection of, 240–241
        sofa beds, 236
        sofas and loveseats, 235
    wall systems, 243
    wrap groupings, 223

Fusion-bonded carpet, 319
Fusion welding, 171
Futons, 275

Gaffer, 100
Galvanized steel, 172
Garnetted, 255
Gaseous-discharge lamps, 385–387
Gas-filled polyester fiber cushioning, 328
Gather, 101–102
General Electric, 150
General lighting. *See* Ambient lighting
Generic name, 42
Genuine leather, 207–208
Geographic trends, 7
Ghiordes knots, 320
Glare, controlling, 379–380
Glass, 93–118, 119
    coloring glass, 108–109
    colorless glass decorations, 106–108
        copper-wheel engraving, 106
        frosting, 107–108
        glass cutting, 106–107
        intaglio cutting, 107
    for dinnerware, 409
    environment impact and recycling, 116–117
    flat glass, 109–115
        annealed, 110
        beveled, 113–114
        heat-treated, 111–112
        insulating, 113
        laminated, 110–111
        reflective, 113
        stained, 114–115
        wired, 112–113
    foam glass, 115
    glass blocks, 115
    glass fibers, 115
    hand-blowing, 100–104
    heat-resistant, 98–99
    history of, 94
    improving durability, 105
    inspecting and finishing, 105–106
    inspection of, 109
    lead glass, 96–98
    lime-soda glass, 95–96
    mixing and firing, 100
    mold-blowing, 104
    pressing, 104–105
    properties of, 94–95
    for stemware, 414
    uses for, 93–94
Glassbake®, 98
Glass blocks, 115
Glass blower's chair, 100–101
Glass blowing. *See* Glass
Glass-ceramic, 99
Glass curtains, 310
Glass cutting, 106–107
Glass fibers, 46, 115
Glassware. *See* Tableware

Glazing, 44, 60, 113, 119, 131–133, 357
Globalization, 24
    manufactured fibers, 43
Glory hole, 102
Glost firing, 132
Goatskins, 210–211
Gold, 168, 174–175
Gold alloys, 174
Gold bonding, 174
Gold-plated flatware, 420
Gold plating, 174
Goose down, 42
Grading, 73
Grading lumber, 77
Graffito, 134
Grain, 75, 205
Graining, 357
Graves, Michael, 401
Grease-resistant paper, 202
Greenware, 132
Greige fabric, 50
Guilding, 137

Hald, Edvard, 101
Half-round sliced veneers, 79
Halogen lamps, 385
Hamadan rugs, 322
Hammering, 184
Hand-blowing glass. *See* Glass
Hand-crocheted tablecloth, 302
Handrail lighting, 391–392
Hand woven flat rugs, 324
Hardanger, 303
Hardboard. *See* Wood
Hard fibers, 39
Hard flooring, 335–342
    care of, 342
    ceramic tile, 338–339
        Mexican tiles, 339
        mosaic tiles, 338
        pavers, 338
        quarry tiles, 339
    and the environment, 342–343
    selected hard floors, 339–341
    selection of, 341–342
    wood, 336–338
        laminate, 338
        prefinished and unfinished, 337–338
        styles of, 336–337
        types of wood, 336
Hard-paste porcelain, 124
Hard rubber, 194
Hardwoods (broadleafs), 70–72
Headboards, 224, 230
Heading, 308
Heartwood, 69
Heat-reflectant finishes, 62
Heat-resistant glass, 98–99
Heat-transfer printing, 59
Heat-treated glass, 111–112
Heavy metal, 185
Hemp, 39, 63, 197

Henequen, 39
Hepplewhite, 221
Heriz rugs, 322
Herringbone, 51
Hevea brasiliensis (rubber tree), 188–189
Hide, 205
Highball glass, 411
High-carbon steel, 179
High-fired ware, 122
High-intensity discharge (HID) lamps, 385, 387
High wet modulus (HWM) rayon, 43–44
Hollowware. *See* Tableware
Home Shopping Network, 16
Home textiles. *See* Linens
Horizontal windows, 381
Horsehair, 41
Hoya, 401
Hyatt, John, 142
Hybrid flotation system, 258

IKEA, 3, 25
    plastic opener, 19
Imitation leather, 213
Incandescent lamps, 383–385
Indian rugs, 322
Indirect light, 375
Injection mold equipment, 143
Inlaid vinyl sheeting, 333
Inlay, 82–87, 230
Innerspring mattresses. *See* Bedding
Inorganic pigments, 144
Insulating glass, 113
Intaglio cutting, 107
Interiors, 67
Interlock knits, 53
Internal market research, 5
International marketing, 25–27
    advantages of, 26–27
    disadvantages, 27
Internet shopping, 16
In-the-clay decorations, 134–135
In-the-glaze decorations, 136
Intumescent paint, 352–353
Iron, 162, 177–178
Ironstone, 122
Isfahan rugs, 322
Italian Provincial, 221

Jabots, 311
Jacknife bed, 236
Jacquard weaves, 52
Jarves, Deming, 94, 104
Jasperware, 122
Jersey knits, 53
Jet printing, 58
Jewelry, 173
Jiggering, 129–130
Joining, case goods, 227–229
Jollying, 129–130
Jute, 39, 197

Kabistan rugs, 322

Kalkin, Eugene, 283
Kall, Terry, 329
Kaolin, 123, 124, 125
Kapok, 39
Karaja rugs, 322
Karat weight, 174
Kashan rugs, 322
Kazak rugs, 322
Kelim rugs, 324
Kelly, Jean, 274
Kenaf, 39, 65
Kidskins, 210–211
Kiln, 119
Kiln-drying lumber, 76–77
King Koil, 264
Kip, 204
Kirman rugs, 322–323
Kitchen dishes, 409
Kmart, 401
Knaf, 197
Knit blankets, 287
Knits, 32
Knitted carpet, 319
Knitted fabric, 53–54
    warp knits, 53–54
        raschel knits, 54
        tricot knits, 54
    weft knit, 53
        jersey knits, 53
        purl knits, 53
        rib knits, 53
Knitted jersey sheets, 284
Knitted-pile fabrics, 53
Knives, 415–416
Kraft process (paper), 198
Krgyzstan, 321
Kurdistan rugs, 322

Lace, 55
Lacquer, 360
Laid paper, 200
Lalique, René, 101
Lambskins, 210–211
Laminate flooring, 338
Laminated glass, 99, 110–111
Laminated wood. *See* Wood
Lamps, 374
    selection, 382
Lap joints, 228
Laser light, 388
Lasky, Julie, 67
Lastrile, 46
Latex, 189
    see also Rubber
Latex backing, 195
Latex-coated fabric, 367
Latex foam mattresses, 257, 267
Laughlin, Homer, 138
Laws, affecting textiles, 62–63
Leaching, 167
Leaded glass, 96
Lead glass (flint glass or lead crystal), 96–98, 100
    for stemware, 414

Lead oxide, 96
Leaf fibers, 33, 39
Leather, 203–213
  boarding, 207
  bonded, 213
  coloring, 207–208
  cowhides and calf skins, 209–210
  deer and elk skins, 212
  embossing, 208
  environmental impact of, 213
  fat liquoring, 208
  finishing, 206
  goatskins and kidskins, 210–211
  grain, 205
  imitation, 213
  metallic finishes, 208
  napping, 208
  other sources of, 212
  patent finish, 208
  pigskins, 210
  preparation, 206
  sheepskins and lambskins, 210–211
  skin quality, 203–204
  skin sizes, 204–205
  splitting, 207
  synthetic, 213
  tanning, 206–207
  wall covering, 370
  waterproofing, 209
Leather hardness, 130
Lehr, 105
Leno weaves, 52, 287
Lenox, 94, 124, 400
Library tables, 241
Lifestyle Furnishings International, 220
Light-stabilizing finishes, 62
Lighting, 374–399
  ambient, 375
  as an art form, 378
  artificial light, 382–388
    cold cathode, 388
    fiber optics, 388
    fluorescent lamps, 385–387
    gaseous-discharge lamps, 385
    incandescent lamps, 383–385
    laser, 388
    neon, 388
  built-in luminaires, 391–392
  care of lamps and luminaires, 395
  chandelier selection, 395
  color-rendering properties of lamps, 395
  controlling glare, 379–380
  decorative, 376–378
  environmental issues, 396–397
    energy efficiency, 396
    energy-conservation practices, 396
  luminous panels, 390
  natural light, 380–382
    combustion light, 382
    sunlight, 380–382
  portable luminaires, 392–393

  recessed luminaires, 389
  selection of lamps and luminaires, 392, 394–395
  for special needs, 378–379
  for specific rooms, 394
  surface-mounted luminaires, 389–390
  suspended luminaires, 389–390
  task, 376
  to create specific effects, 394
  track-mounted luminaires, 390
Lignin, 84
Lime, 94–95
Lime-soda glass, 95–96, 100, 414
Limited decisions, 18
Linen fabric, 38
Linens, 279–315
  bathroom rugs and mats, 298–299
    care, 298
    construction, 298
    selection, 298
    styles, 298
  blankets and throws, 286–289
    bedspreads, 289
    care, 292
    comforters and quilts, 289–290
    construction, 286, 291–292
    knit blankets, 287
    nonwoven blankets, 287–288
    selection, 292
    styles, 286
    woven blankets, 286–287
  canopies, 293–294
  commercial *vs.* residential interior textiles, 280
  coordinated, 280
  decorative pillows, 293–295
  dust ruffles, 293
  place mats, 304–305
    construction, 304
    selection and care, 305
    styles, 304
  regulation of, 280
  selected brands, 281
  sheets and pillowcases, 281–286
    care, 285–286
    construction, 284–285
    pillowcase sizes, 284
    selection, 285
    styles, 282, 284
  shower curtains, 297–298
    selection and care, 298
    styles and construction, 297
  slipcovers, 305–307
    care, 307
    construction, 305, 307
    selection, 307
    styles, 305
  soft window treatments, 307–313
    care, 313
    construction, 312
    curtain styles, 310
    drapery styles, 311
    hardware for, 308

    headings for curtains and draperies, 309
    selection, 312–313
    styles, 308–311
    styles of valances, 309
    uses for, 307–308
  tablecloths and napkins, 299–304
    care, 304
    construction, 301–303
    napkin sizes, 301
    selection, 303–304
    styles, 300–301
  towels, 294, 296–297
    care, 297
    construction, 296–297
    names and sizes, 296
    selection, 296–297
    styles, 296
    uses, 279–280
Linens'n Things, 283
Lining paper, 364
Link springs, 262
Linoleum, 334–335
Liquid latex, 195
Litharge, 96
Lithography, 135
Louis XVI, 221
Louisville Bedding, 295
Loveseats, 235
Low lighting, 377
Low-profile foundations, 261
Lubricants, plastics, 145–146
Lumber. *See* Wood
Lumens, 383
Luminaires. *See* Lighting
Luminous paint, 354
Luminous panels, 390
Lusterware, 136

McClintock, Jessica, 222
McDonough, William, 67
Machine-made Oriental rugs, 323
Mackintosh, Charles Rennie, 221
Magazines, home furnishing and advertising, 12
Magnetic properties, of metals, 163
Mail order, 16
Mali fabrics, 54–55
Malleable metals, 162–163
Malls, 16
Manila fiber, 39
Manila hemp, 39
Manufactured fibers. *See* Textiles
Manufacturers, market perspective, 23
Marbling, 357
Marco Polo, 123
Marinot, Maurice, 101
Market research, 5
  external, 5
  internal, 5
Market segmentation, 5–8
  demographics, 6–8
  psychographics, 8–9

Marketing
  advertising, 11–12
  defined, 4
  international, 25–27
  niche, 6
  place (trading area), 13–16
  pricing, 9–11
  product development, 9
  promotion, 11–13
  public relations, 12–13
Marketing channel, 4
Marketing department
  heads and responsibilities of, 5
  organization chart, 4
Markets
  manufacturer's perspective, 23
  retailer's and wholesaler's perspec-
    tives, 23
Marquiesette, 52
Marshall-type innersprings, 254
Marver, 101–102
Mason, William, 84
Masonite®, 84
Masticating, 191
Matching, wall coverings, 366
Mats, 299
Mattress covers. *See* Bedding
Mattresses. *See* Bedding
Mattress pads. *See* Bedding
Mattress support systems. *See* Bedding
Mechanical finishes, 60
Medullary rays, 69
Mega-mall, 16
Melamine formaldehydes, 147
Melting, 44
Mercerization, 60
Merchandise manager, 5
Merino sheep, 40–41
Metallic arc welding, 171
Metallic fiber, 46
Metallic finish, leather, 208
Metallic oxides, 136
Metallic paint, 354
Metallurgy. *See* Metals
Metals, 145, 162–187
  decorating metals, 180, 184–185
    applied borders, 184
    chasing, 184
    embossing, 184
    engraving, 184
    etching, 184
    hammering, 184
    piercing, 184
    polishing, 185
    repoussé, 185
  for dinnerware, 410–411
  discoveries, 164
  and the environment, 185–186
  ferrous metals, 162, 176–180
    cast iron, 178
    iron, 177–178
    stainless steel, 179–181
    steel, 179
  history of, 163–165

metallurgy, 165–171
  alloys and amalgams, 167–168
  extractive, 166–167
  joining metals, 169–171
  physical, 167–171
  riveting, 169, 171
  shaping metals, 168–169
  soldering, 170
  welding, 170–171
  nonferrous metals and alloys, 162,
    180, 182–183
    plating metals, 172–173
      bonding, 173
      dipping, 172
      electroplating, 173
    precious metals, 173–176
      gold, 174–175
      silver, 175–176
  properties of, 162–163
Metameric shift, 382
Mexican tile, 339
Mildew-proof paint, 354
Mineral dressing, 166
Mink, 41
Minor cellulosic fibers, 39
  see also Textiles
Mirrors, 225
  wall covering, 369
Miter joint, 228
Mixing rubber, 191, 194
Modacrylic, 45
Modern furniture, 221
Modular casework, defined, 223
Modular groupings, 223
Mohair, 41
Moil, 106
Moiré, 60–61, 364
Mold-blowing, 104
Molding, 194, 230
Monk's cloth, 50
Monofilament yarn, 47
Mood lighting, 377
Morgan, Don, 370
Mortise-and-tenon joint, 228
Moth-proofing finishes, 61
Motion chairs, 233–235
Mottle, 80
Multifilament yarn, 47
Muslin sheets, 48, 50, 52, 285

Nambé, 164
Nandkyeolar, Shelley, 403
Nap, 330
Napery, 299
Napkins, 299–304
Napping, 60, 208
Native American rugs, 324
Natural cellulosic fibers, 33–39
  see also Textiles
Natural Cotton Colours, Inc., 65
Natural fibers. *See* Textiles
Natural light, 380–382
Natural protein fibers. *See* Textiles
Natural rubber. *See* Rubber

Navajo rugs, 324–325
Needle-punched blankets, 287–288
Needle-punched carpet, 319
Neighborhood shopping center, 16
Neon, 388
New wool, 62
New Zealand flax or hemp, 39
Niche marketing, 6
No-flip mattresses, 255
Nodular cast iron, 178
Nonferrous metals and alloys. *See*
  Metals
Nonstore retailing, 16
Nonwoven blankets, 287–288
Nonwovens, 32, 54
Noritake, 121
North Carolina State University, 64
Nostalgia products, 21
Nottingham lace, 301
Novelty yarns, 49
Novoloid, 46
Nub yarn, 49
Nylon, 32, 42, 45
Nylon blanket binding, 288

Obsidian, 94
Occasional furniture. *See* Furniture
Off-gassing, 343
Oil-based paints, 351
Old-fashioned glass, 411
Olefin, 45
Oneida, 400
On-grain the warp, 50
Opacity, 349
Open-coil mattresses, 254
Open-coil springs, 261
Open-stock, 408
Optical brightening, 60
Optical properties, of metals, 163
Organic pigments, 145
Oriental rugs, 320, 322–323
Orthopedic beds, 259
O'Sullivan entertainment center, 244
Ottmans, 236
Overall measurement of dinnerware,
  404–405
Overglaze decorations, 134, 136–137
Owens, Michael J., 94, 104

Padding, 255
Pads, 299
Page, Bob, 403
Paint, 348–361
  acrylic, 354
  additives, 350–351
  application, 355–356
  Danish oil, 360
  decorative techniques, 357–358
  environmental issues, 371
  epoxies, 352
  finishes, 349–350, 361
  lacquer, 360
  luminous, 354
  metallic, 354

mildew-proof, 354
pigment, 349
primers, 354
resin, 350
selected brands, 349
selection of, 360–361
shellac, 360
solvent-based, 351
stains, 359
surface preparation, 354–355
texture, 354
thinner, 354
varnishes, 359
water-based, 352
Painting glass, 108
Pale crepe, 190
Paneling, 369
Panel-supported systems, 245
Paper, 196–203
decorative finishes, 200, 202
for dinnerware, 410
environmental impact, 203
functional finishes, 202
for glassware, 414
grades and standardizations, 200–202
manufacture of, 198–200
pulp production, 198–199
sources of, 196–197
wallpaper, 202–203
Paper-backed fabric, 368
Paper printing, 59
Paper wall coverings, 362
Parkes, Alexander, 142
Parkesine, 142
Parquet, 82–84
Parquet flooring, 336–337
Particleboard. *See* Wood
Patent leather, 208
Patina, 420
Pavers, 339
Pavilions, 311
Peau-de-soie, 51
Peccary, 210
Peelable wall covering, 364
Pendant luminaires, 389
Penetration pricing, 11
Percale sheets, 48, 50, 52, 285
Performance®, 329
Perimeter lighting, 394
Permanent Care Labeling Ruling of the Federal Trade Commission, 62
Permanent press (durable press), 61
Persian knots, 320
Persian rugs, 322
Peters, Kurt, 403
Pewter, flatware and hollowware, 420
Phenolics, 147–149
Phillip Jeffries wall covering, 362
Physical metallurgy. See Metals
Piano-type hinges, 229
Pierced decoration, 134
Piercing, 184
Pig iron, 166

Pigments, 57
paint, 349
plastics, 144–145
Pigment volume concentration (PVC), 349
Pigskins, 210
Pile, 330, 332
Pile sweep, 330
Pile weaves, 52
Pilkington, Alistair, 110
Pilling, 44, 45
Pillowcases, 281–286
see also Linens
Pillows. *See* Bedding
Pillow top mattresses, 255–256
Piña, 39
Pinching, 127
Pinpoint lighting, 394
Pinpoint percale, 285
Pith, 69
Place mats, 304–305
Place settings, 407
Plain butt joint, 228
Plain sawing, 75–76
Plain weave, 50–51
Plane of light, 394
Plank flooring, 336–337
Plank wall covering, 369
Plant fibers (cellulosic fibers), 33
see also Textiles
Plaster-of-paris, 130
Plasticator, 191
Plastic furniture, 243
Plasticizers, 146
Plastics, 141–161
colorants, 144–145
for dinnerware, 409–410
and the environment, 159
fillers, 145
finishing, 159
flammability, 159
for glassware, 414
history of, 142–143
lubricants, 145–146
plasticizers, 146
recycling, 159
resins, 143–144
shaping, 153–158
casting, 154–155
coating, 155
extrusion, 155
foam casting, 157–158
laminating, 155–157
molding, 156–158
thermoforming, 158
solvents, 146
stabilizers, 146
thermoplastics, 150–153
cellulosics, 150
polyamides, 150
polycarbonates, 152
polymethyl methacrylate, 152
polypropylene (PP), 152
polystyrenes, 152

polytetrafluoroethylene (PTFE), 153
polyethylene (PE), 152
vinyl, 153
thermoset plastics, 147–150
epoxies, 147
melamine formaldehydes, 147
phenolics, 147–149
polyesters, 149
polyurethanes, 149–150
silicones, 150
urea formaldehydes, 150
Plate glass, 110
Platform-top springs, 261
Plating metals. *See* Metals
Plumage, 40, 42
Ply yarn, 48–49
Plywood. *See* Wood
Pocket-coil mattresses, 254
Pocket-spring mattresses, 254
Polarscopic test, 105
Polishing, 107, 185
Polyamides, 150
Polybenzimidazole (PBI), 46
Polycarbonates, 152
Polyester, 42, 45
Polyester fiberfill, 291
Polyester fiberfill pillows, 271
Polyesters, 149
Polyethylene (PE), 45, 152
Polymerization, 141
Polymers, 141
Polymethyl methacrylate, 152
Polyamide, 45
Polypropylene (PP), 45, 152
Polystyrenes, 152
Polytetrafluororethylene (PTFE), 153
Polyurethane-foam mattresses, 257, 267
Polyurethanes, 149–150
Polyvinyl butyral (PVB), 153
Polyvinyl chloride (PVC), 153
Pontil mark, 103
Pontil (punty), 102–103
Pool of light, 394
Population trends, 7–8
Porcelain, 123–124
Porphyry, 357
Portable luminaires, 392–393
Potash, 94–96
Potash crystal, 96
Potter, 128
Potter's wheel, 128
Pottery, 119–140
assembling, 130
china, 123–124
decorating, 133–137
in-the-clay, 134–135
in-the-glaze, 134, 136
overglaze, 134, 136–137
underglaze, 134–136
defined, 119
for dinnerware, 409
earthenware, 120–122, 409
environment and, 138
finishing, 131

firing, 119–120, 131–132
glazing, 131–133
materials used in making, 125
preparing and mixing, 126
shaping, 126–130
stoneware, 122–123, 409
types of, 137–138
Poufed curtains, 310
Powdered grains of glass, 108
Preparatory finishes, 60
Prepasted wall coverings, 364
Pressing, 104–105
Prestige pricing, 11
Price, 8–9
Primary trading area, 13–14
Primers, 354
Printing, 58–59, 230
Processing wood. *See* Wood
Product design manager, 5
Product development, 8–9
process, 11
Product life cycle, 18–21
classic, 19–20
fad, 19–20
nostalgia or revival products, 21
seasonal products, 20
Production of plastics. *See* Plastics
Promotion, 11–13
Protein fibers. *See* Textiles
Provincial furniture, 221
Psychographics, 8–9
Public relations, 12–13
objectives of, 13
Puckered seams, 285
Pugging, 126
Punty (pontil), 102–103
Purchasing behavior, 17–18
decision-making model, 17
extended decision, 17–18
limited decisions, 18
routine decisions, 18
Purl knits, 53
Pyrex®, 98
Pyroceram®, 99

Quarry tile, 339
Quarter sawing, 75–76
Quarter-sliced veneers, 79
Queen Anne, 221
Quilting patterns, 290
Quilts, 289–290

Rabbet joint, 228
Rabbit, 41
Raffia, 39
Rag paper, 197
Rag pulp, 199
Ragging, 357–358
Railroaded upholstery fabric, 240
Rain forest woods, 89
Ralph Lauren, 26
Ramie (China grass), 33, 38–39
Raschel, 53–54
Raschel-knit thermal blankets, 287

Rattan, 86–87
Rattan furniture, 242
Rawhide, 203
Rayon, 43–44
properties of, 43
see also Regenerated cellulosics
RBI International Carpet Consultants, 326
Ready-to-assemble furniture. *See* Furniture
Ream weight, 200
Recessed luminaires, 389
Recker, Keith, 321
Recliners, 233–234
Recurring cycle, 21
Recycling, 343
paper, 197, 199
plastics, 159
Recycling glass, 116–117
Redwood furniture, 242–243
Reeding, 230
Reflected light, 375
Reflective glass, 113
Regenerated collulosics, 42–44
see also Rayon; Textiles
Regional mall, 16
Reinforcements, plastics, 145
Relief decoration, 134
Replacements, 403
Repousse, 185
Research manager, 5
Residential Carpet Analysis, 326
Residential furniture, 219
Resilient flooring, 332–335
care of, 342
cork, 334
and the environment, 342–343
linoleum, 334–335
rubber, 335
selection of, 341–342
vinyl, 333–334
Resins, 60, 143–144, 350
Resist designs, 135
Resistance to wear, of metals, 163
Resistance welding, 171
Retailers, market perspective, 23
Retailing formats, 13–16
see also Trading areas
Reused denim, 64
Revival products, 21
Rhead, Frederick Hurton, 138
Rib knits, 53
Rib weave, 50
Rice paper, 202
Rice patterns, 135
Rift-cut veneers, 79
Rim shape, 404–405
Riser lighting, 391–392
Riveting, 169, 171
Roasting, 166
Rocking chairs, 234–235
Roll estimator for wall coverings, 365
Rolled gold plating, 174
Roller printing, 58–59

Rolling, metals, 169–170
Roselle, 39
Rotary-cut veneers, 79
Rotary-screen printing, 58
Rotogravure vinyl sheeting, 333
Roughing out, 107
Routine decisions, 18
Rubber, 188–196
environmental impact of, 196
history of, 188–189
liquid rubber, 195
masticating, 191
mixing, 191, 194
natural rubber
characteristics and end uses of, 190
harvesting of, 189–190
production of, 189
shaping, 194
synthetic rubber, 190–195
types of, 191–193
vulcanizing, 194–195
Rubber floor covering, 335
Ruffled curtains, 310
Ruffled tiebacks, 310
Ruggiero, Joe, 248
Rugs. *See* Soft floor coverings
Ruttenberg, Reid, 268
Rya rugs, 323

Sales manager, 5
Salton, 380
Sandblasting, 107
Sandpaper, 202
Sapwood, 69
Sarabend rugs, 322
Saran, 46
Sarouk rugs, 322–323
Sash curtains, 310
Sateens, 51, 284
Satins, 51
Satin sheets, 284
Savonnerie rugs, 322
Sawing, 73, 75–76
Scarves, 299
Scavenge colors, 45
Schneiderman, Larry, 265
Schreinering, 60
Sconce, 390
Sealy Posturpedic, 265
Seasonal products, 20
Seasoning, 73, 76–77
Secondary trading area, 14
Sectionals, 236
Seed fibers, 33, 39
Seeds (bubbles or blisters), 109
Seed yarn, 49
Sehna (senna) knots, 320
Self-cushioned carpet, 328
Selvages, 50
Semi-lead crystal, 96
Semi-vitreous earthenware (fine earthenware), 120, 122
Service manager, 5

Serving pieces, 415, 417
Sets of place settings, 407–408
Sgraffito, 134
Shading, 358
Shaping rubber, 194
Sheepskins, 210–211
Sheers, 310
Sheet casings, 292
Sheet glass, 110
Sheets, 281–286
   see also Linens
Shellac, 360
Shirred curtains, 310
Shirvan rugs, 322
Shlensky, Bert, 306
Shopping centers and malls, 16
Shower curtains, 297–298
Shrinkage control treatments, 61
Shyrdaks, 321
Sick building syndrome, 343
Silicones, 150
Silencer, 300
Silhouette lighting, 394
Silica sand, 94–96, 145
Silk, 40
Silk noil, 40
Silver, 168, 175–176
Silver depositware, 109
Silverplate, flatware and hollowware, 420
Simmons, 251
Simple calendering, 60
Singeing, 60
Single damask, 301
Single glazing, 113
Single knits, 53
Single yarn, 48–49
Sintering, 166
Sisal, 39
Sisal hemp, 39
Sizing, 77
Sizing wood, 73
Skewed filling yarn, 50–51
Skylights, 381
Slab method, 128
Slack-tension weaving, 297
Slag, 166
Slatted wood foundation, 262
Sleeper sofas, 275
Slide off, 136
Slip, 126
Slip casting, 131
Slipcovers. *See* Linens
Slip decorations, 135
Slub yarn, 49
Smelting, 163, 166
Smith, Jaclyn, 22
Smoke sheet, 190
Smooshing, 358
Smoothing, 107
Social responsibility, and floor coverings, 344
Social trends, 8
Soda ash, 94–96
Soda process (paper), 198

Sofa beds, 236, 273–274
Sofas, 235
   shapes of, 235
Sofa tables, 241
Soffit lighting, 291–292
Soft floor coverings, 316–332
   broadloom, 317
   care of, 332
   carpet, 317
   carpet characteristics, 327, 331
   carpet cushioning, 326, 328–329
   carpet modules, 317
   and the environment, 342–343
   hand woven flat rugs, 324
      dhurrie rugs, 324
      kelim, 324
      Native American rugs, 324–325
   hand woven pile rugs, 320, 322–323
      flokati rugs, 320
      oriental rugs, 320, 322–323
      rya rugs, 323
   installation, 329
   machine methods, 319
   rugs, 317
   selection of, 329–332
      fibers, 330
      pile, 330, 332
      yarns, 330
   tufting, 317–318, 324–325
   weaving, 318
Soft rubber, 194
Soft window treatments. *See* Linens
Soft-paste porcelain, 124
Softwoods (conifers), 70, 73–74
Soil-release finishes, 61
Soil-resistant finishes, 61
Soldering, 169–170
Solid (pallet) base foundation, 262
Solid vinyl tiles, 334
Solid wood. *See* Wood
Solutia, Inc., 42
Solvent-based paints, 351
Solvents, 146
Spandex, 46
Spattering, 358
Special emphasis lighting. *See* Accent lighting
Special-effect colorants, 145–146
Specialty built-in lighting, 391–392
Specialty hair fibers, 41
Spicer, Rick, 380
Spinneret, 42
Spiral yarn, 49
Splines, 228
Splitting leather, 207
Spode, Josiah, 123
Sponge rubber cushioning, 328
Sponging, 358
Spoons, 415–416
Spotlighting, 375, 394
Spot welding, 171
Spray dyeing, 208
Sprigging, 130

Springs, 237–238
   types of, 238
Sprung bed, 262
Spun yarns, 47–48
Stabilizers, plastics, 146
Stained glass, 114–115
Stainless steel, 179–181
   flatware and hollowware, 419–420
Stain-resistant finishes, 61
Stains, 359
Stamping, 136
Standinger, Hermann, 143
Staple fibers, 32, 34
Starter set, 408
Static load for furniture, 343
Stationary curtains, 310
Steel, 168, 179
Stem fibers, 33
Stemware, 411–412
Stenciling, 358
Sterling silver, 176
   flatware and hollowware, 420
Stretched curtains, 310
Stewart, Martha, 401
Sticking up, 130
Stiegel, Henry William, 94
Stippling, 358
Stitch-through fabrics, 54
Stoneware, 122–123
Street peddlers, 16
String streets, 16
Stripe, 80
Strip flooring, 336
Strippable wall coverings, 364
Strips, 77
Structural luminaires, 388–392
Studio couches, 236, 275
Stump, 80
Suede, 203
   see also Leather
Suites, 220, 222–223
Sulfite process (paper), 199
Summer furniture. *See* Furniture
Sunn, 39
Sunn hemp, 39
Super regional mall, 16
Surface-mounted luminaires, 389–390
Surfacing, 77
Surfacing wood, 73
Sure Fit, 295, 306
Suspended luminaires, 389–390
Sustainable forests, 88–89
Swags, 311
Swirl, 80
Swivel chairs, 233, 235
Synthetic/down pillows, 271
Synthetic leathers, 213
Synthetic rubber. *See* Rubber
Systems furniture. *See* Furniture

Tablecloths, 299–304
Table linens. *See* Linens
Tableware, 400–422
   dinnerware, 403–411

care of, 410–411
china, 409
earthenware, 409
glass, 409
open and closed stock, 408
paper and metal, 410
place settings, 407
plastic, 409–410
pottery, 409
purchasing, 405
sets, 407–408
shapes of, 404–405
size of, 404–405
stoneware, 409
storage of, 411
types of, 404–406
and the environment, 421
flatware, 415–418
care and storage, 420–421
carving pieces, 415–416
forks, 415–416
gold-plated, 420
knives, 415–416
pewter, 420
purchasing, 415, 418
serving pieces, 415, 417
spoons, 415–416
stainless steel, 419
vermeil, 420
glassware, 411–414
accessories, 413
barware, 411–413
care of, 414
glass materials, 414
paper materials, 414
plastic materials, 414
purchasing, 413
stemware, 411–412
storage of, 414
tumblers, 411–412
hollowware, 418–419
care and storage, 420–421
gold-plated, 420
pewter, 420
selected pieces, 419
stainless steel, 419
sterling silver and silverplate, 420
vermeil, 420
selected brand names, 402
Tabriz rugs, 322
Taffeta, 50
Tanning, 203, 206–207
Tapestry, 52
Target, 401
Target market, 6
Target return pricing, 11
Task light, 376
Tatami, 275
Teflon®, 153
Tempering, 105, 111–112
Temporary finishes, 59
Tensile strength, 67
Tentering, 60
Ternary alloy, 168

Terra-cotta, 121
Terry cloth, 52
Terry towels, 296
Textile binder, 57
Textile Fiber Products Identification
Act, 62, 280
Textiles, 31–66
coloration, 32, 56–59
color permanence, 56
dyeing, 57–58
dyes and pigments, 57
printing, 58–57
and the environment, 63–65
fabrics, 50–56
creating, 50
knitted, 53–54
nonwoven and other, 54–56
woven, 50–52
finishes, 32, 59–62
aesthetic finishes, 60–61
functional finishes, 61–62
preparatory finishes, 60
laws affecting, 62–63
manufactured fibers
acrylic, 45
aramid, 45
blending, 47
classification of, 34
cross sections and contour, 37
derivative cellulosics, 44
glass, 46
metallic, 46
modacrylic, 45
nylon, 45
olefin, 45
polyester, 45
properties and definitions, 35–36
regenerated cellulosics, 42–44
spandex, 46
natural fibers, 33–42
bast fibers, 38–39
cellulosic fibers, 33–39
cotton, 33–34, 36–38
cross sections and contour, 37
filament and staple comparison,
32, 34
minor cellulosic fibers, 39
properties and definitions, 35–36
summary of types, 34
natural protein fibers, 39–42
fur fibers, 41
silk, 40
specialty hair fibers, 41
wool, 40–41
production and distribution pipeline,
32
regenerated protein fibers, 34
as wall coverings, 367–368
wood used to make fibers, 69
yarn, 47–48
conventional yarn, 48
cord yarn, 48–49
filament yarns, 47–48
novelty yarns, 49

ply yarn, 48–49
single yarn, 48–49
spun yarn, 47–48
Texture paint, 354
Textured filament yarn, 47–48
Theme mall, 16
Thermoplastics. *See* Plastics
Thermoset plastics. *See* Plastics
Thinner, 354
Thonet, Michael, 221
Throw-style bedspread, 290–291
Throwing, 128
Throws, 286–289
Ticking, 256, 272
Tiffany lamps, 114
Tiffany, Louis C., 114
Tiles, wall covering, 369
Timbers, 77
Time, 9
Tin, 168
Toe-kick lighting, 391–392
Toe-mold lighting, 391–392
Tongue-and-groove edges, 336
Tongue-and-groove joint, 228
Top-grain leather, 207
Torchiere-style halogen lamp, 385
Towels, 294, 296–297
Track lighting, 390
Trade names, 42
Trading areas, 13–16
central business districts, 15–16
diagram of, 14
freestanding stores, 15
nonstore retailing, 16
site selection for store-based
retailing, 14–16
types of shopping centers and
malls, 16
Traditional furniture, 220–221
Traditionally sprung mattresses, 254
Transfer printing, 136
Trees. *See* Wood
Triacetate, 44
Tricot, 53–54
Tricot sheets, 284
Triple glazing, 113
Trundle beds, 276
Tufting, 55–56, 317–318, 324–326
Tumblers, 411–412
Tupperware Home Parties, 16
Turkish knots, 320
Turkish rugs, 323
Turkish towels, 296
Turkoman rugs, 323
Turning, 67–68
Twill weave, 50–51
TYVEK®, 45

Ultra-Fresh, 329
Uncut pile, 56
Under curtains, 310
Underglaze decorations, 135
Unhairing, 206
Unvulcanized rubber, 191

Upholstered furniture. *See* Furniture
Uplight, 375
Upward lighting, 394
Urea formaldehydes, 150
Urena, 39
Urethane foam, 149
Urethane foam cushioning, 328

Valance lighting, 391–392
Valances, 308–309
van der Rohe, Ludwig Mies, 221
Varnishes, 359
Vellum, 200
Velour towels, 296
Velvet, 318
Velvet terry cloth, 52
Veneer. *See* Wood
Venetian lace, 301
Vermeil, flatware and hollowware, 420
Vertical mall, 16
Vertical upholstery fabric, 240
Vertical windows, 381
Victorian, 221
Vinyl, 153
Vinyl composition tiles, 334
Vinyl floor covering, 333–334
Vinyl laminate, 333
Vinyl tiles, 334
Vinyl wall coverings, 363–364
Virgin hemp, 65
Virgin wool, 62
Viscose rayon, 43–44
Volatile organic compounds (VOCs), 351, 353
Volcanic gasses, 94
von Tschirnhaus, Ehrenfried Walther, 123
Vulcanization, 189, 194–195

Wales, 50
Wallace Silversmith, 20
Wall beds, 276
Wall coverings, 361–371
    choosing color, 363
    cork, 369
    installation, 366
    latex-coated fabric, 367
    leather, 370
    mirrors, 369
    panels, 369
    paper, 362
    paper-backed fabric, 368
    planks, 369
    roll estimator for, 365
    selected brands, 363
    selection of, 364–366
    tiles, 369

types of, 364
    vinyl, 363–364
    wall upholstery, 368
Wallpaper, 202–203
Wall systems. *See* Furniture
Wall upholstery, 368
Walther, Ehrenfried, 123
Warping, 68
Warp knits, 53–54
Warp printing, 58
Warp warns, 50
Wash, 173
Washing, 358
Waste paper, 197
Waste silk, 40
Water-based paints, 352
Water-filled mattresses, 258
Waterford, 401
Watermarking, 200
Waterproofing leather, 209
Water-resistant finishes, 61
Wattage, 383
Waugh, Sidney, 101
Waverly, 363, 370
Waxed paper, 202
Wax, 145
Weaving, 50
    floor coverings, 318
    see also Woven fabrics
Webbing, furniture, 236–237
Weber grill, 20
Weft knits, 53
Weighted silk, 40
Welding, 169–171
Wellman, Inc., 42, 64
Well-to-edge measurement of dinner-ware, 404–405
WestWane, Inc., 370
Wet block, 102–103
Wet finishes, 60
Wet prints, 58
Whetting, 102–103
Wholesale markets, 22–24
Wholesalers, 21, 24
    market perspective, 23
Wicker, 87
Wicker furniture, 242
Wild silk, 40
Williams-Sonoma, 403
Wilton, 318
Windows, and light, 381
Wired glass, 112–113
Wistar, Casper, 94
Wood, 67–92
    advantages of, 67–68
    bamboo, 86
    and case goods, 227

disadvantages of, 68
    and the environment, 87–90
        rain forest woods, 89
        sustainable forests, 88–89
    hardboard, 84
    lumber, 73, 75–77
        grading, 77
        sawing, 75–76
        seasoning, 76–77
        sizing and surfacing, 77
    ornamenting and finishing, 82–84
        inlay, 82–84
        wood finishes, 83–85
    particleboard, 84–86
    processing, 73
    rattan, 86–87
    solid wood, 77–78
    trees, 69–73
        broadleaf trees (hardwoods), 70–72
        coniferous trees (softwoods), 70, 73–74
        parts of a tree trunk, 69
    veneer, 78–82
        construction of, 79–81
        laminated wood, 81–82
        plywood, 80–82
    wicker, 87
Wood flooring, 336–338
Wood flour, 145
Wool, 40–41, 62
Woolen yarns, 48
Wool Products Labeling Act, 62
Wool underblankets, 267
Worsted yarns, 48
Woven blankets, 286–287
Woven fabrics, 50–52
    dobby weaves, 52
    fabric weight, 52
    jacquard weaves, 52
    leno weaves, 52
    pile weaves, 52
    plain weave, 50–51
    satin weave, 51–52
    thread count, 52
    see also Textiles
Wovens, 32
Wrap groupings, 223
Wrinkle-resistant, 61
Wrinkles, 44
Wrought iron, 167
Wrought iron furniture, 242

Yarns, 32
    floor coverings, 330
Young, Candace, 135
Yucca, 39